The influence of the Passover on the ritual and thought of Judaism and Christianity has probably been more profound than that of any other festival. There are few facets of social and religious practice among the Hebrews upon which a study of this festival must not in some measure touch. Nevertheless, no full-scale study of the Hebrew Passover has appeared for the last fifty years. During that period, the expansion of our horizons in the field of comparative Semitic religion has been rapid; and it appears opportune to re-examine the early history of the festival within the framework of this new knowledge.

In the first part of this volume the author analyses closely the Biblical and extra-Biblical documents on the Passover and the principal modern theories concerning its origins. In the second part he expounds the thesis that the primitive Passover was a New Year festival of the springtime, with rites analogous to those of neighbouring countries of the Near East. He traces the development of the festival in Canaan, where the centralization of the cult at the Temple brought about some dissociation between the Pesaḥ of the pilgrims at Jerusalem and the Maṣṣoth week of Israelites elsewhere. Of particular interest is his discussion of the *ḥaggim* and his analysis of the treatment of the Passover by the Book of Jubilees, in the New Testament and by Jewish sectarians, including those of Qumran. The volume concludes with details of the Passover rites during the last decades of the Temple at Jerusalem.

Dr. J. B. Segal, Professor of Semitic Languages in the University of London, was educated at St. Catharine's College, Cambridge and St. John's College, Oxford, and has been on the staff of the School of Oriental and African Studies since 1946. He is author of *The Diacritical Point and the Accents in Syriac*, 1953 (in this Series), and of articles on Syriac and cognate subjects. He is at present engaged on a study of the history of Edessa.

SCHOOL OF
ORIENTAL AND AFRICAN STUDIES
UNIVERSITY OF LONDON

London Oriental Series
Volume 12

LONDON ORIENTAL SERIES · VOLUME 12

THE HEBREW PASSOVER

FROM THE EARLIEST TIMES TO A.D. 70

BY

J. B. SEGAL

Professor of Semitic Languages in the University of London

LONDON
OXFORD UNIVERSITY PRESS
NEW YORK TORONTO
1963

Oxford University Press, Amen House, London E.C.4
GLASGOW NEW YORK TORONTO MELBOURNE WELLINGTON
BOMBAY CALCUTTA MADRAS KARACHI LAHORE DACCA
CAPE TOWN SALISBURY IBADAN NAIROBI ACCRA
KUALA LUMPUR HONG KONG

PRINTED IN GREAT BRITAIN

TO

PROFESSOR SIDNEY SMITH

Teacher, Mentor, Friend

PREFACE

THE subject of the present inquiry scarcely calls for an introduction. The influence of the Passover on the ritual and thought of Judaism and Christianity has probably been more profound than that of any other festival. There are few facets of social and religious practice among the Hebrews upon which a study of this festival must not in some measure touch. Nevertheless, no full-scale study of the Hebrew Passover—which, by definition, we shall regard here as extending to the destruction of the Temple of Jerusalem in A.D. 70—has appeared since G. Beer's introduction to his edition of the Mishnah tractate *Pesaḥim* nearly fifty years ago. During that period the expansion of our horizons in the field of Semitic religion has been rapid, and it may be not inopportune to re-examine the early history of the festival within the framework of this new knowledge.

In the first two chapters of this work I have considered it necessary to present in full all the relevant texts, with the exception only of passages from the New Testament and Josephus. An exposition of modern theories on the origins and development of the festival follows in the third chapter. Only thus will the reader, in possession of the facts contained in the written sources, be himself in a position to assess the plausibility of those theories and to arrive at conclusions of his own. He will the more readily reject or accept the views of the present writer which are set out in the remainder of this work.

This method of presentation imposes, however, a heavy burden on the reader who is less interested in an analysis of the primary sources than in the conclusions to be drawn and the bearing of these conclusions upon the broad evolution of Hebrew religion. I have therefore set out my own hypotheses concerning the festival, its origins, and development, separately, as a second part of the book. I have sought, moreover, to reduce citations from earlier authors to a minimum. To have given references to all the innumerable works which treat of some aspect of the Passover would have swollen the footnotes—without, I believe, corresponding profit to the reader. I have endeavoured rather to cite only the author by whom an opinion was expressed first or most clearly, and to return, wherever possible, to the primary source.

I have derived assistance at certain points of the book from my colleagues Dr. H. W. F. Saggs of the University of London and Mr. M. A. Ghul of the University of St. Andrews; the former also read the volume in typescript and made helpful criticisms—although he has no responsibility for the opinions expressed in it. To my wife I owe much for her encouragement and guidance. The School of Oriental and African Studies have defrayed the expenses of publication, and they have made their generosity the more marked by including this book in the London Oriental Series. And, finally, I would like to express to the staff of the Oxford University Press my gratitude—and my admiration—for the care which they have lavished on this book. The author whose work is entrusted to their hands is indeed fortunate.

Of the imperfections of this little book I am well aware. It may well hold immature inferences derived from faulty analysis and incomplete knowledge. I would only add, in the words of Sir Thomas Browne: 'all that is contained therein is in submission unto maturer discernments; and I . . . shall no further father them than the best and learned judgments shall authorize them'.

J. B. S.

London
Passover Eve, A.M. 5722–A.D. 1962

CONTENTS

PRINCIPAL ABBREVIATIONS

Ab.	*Abhoth*
ʿAb. Zarah	*ʿAbhodah Zarah*
AJSL	*American Journal of Semitic Languages and Literature*
AJT	*American Journal of Theology*
Akk.	Akkadian
ANET	*Ancient Near Eastern Texts relating to the Old Testament*, ed. J. B. Pritchard, 1955
Ant.	*Antiquitates Judaicae*
Aq.	Aquila
ʿAr.	*ʿArakhin*
Arab.	Arabic
Aram.	Aramaic
BASOR	*Bulletin of the American Schools of Oriental Research*
B. Bathra	*Babha Bathra*
Bek.	*Bekhoroth*
Ber.	*Berakhoth*
BJ	*De Bello Judaico*
BJRL	*Bulletin of the John Rylands Library*
B. Qamma	*Babha Qamma*
BSOAS	*Bulletin of the School of Oriental and African Studies*
BT	*Babylonian Talmud*
CBQ	*Catholic Biblical Quarterly*
Chr.	Chronicles
CIS	*Corpus Inscriptionum Semiticarum*
Col.	Colossians
Cor.	Corinthians
Dan.	Daniel
DB	*Dictionary of the Bible*, ed. J. Hastings, &c., 1900–4
Deut.	Deuteronomy
Dict. Bib. Suppl.	Pirot, &c., *Dictionnaire de la Bible, Supplément*, ed. L. Pirot, A. Robert, and H. Cazelles, 1928–
Doc. Comm.	*Document of the Community* (Qumran, 1QS)
Doc. Cong.	*Document of the Congregation* (Qumran, 1QSa)
EB	*Encyclopaedia Biblica*, ed. T. K. Cheyne and J. S. Black, 1899–1903
Eccl.	Ecclesiastes
Ecclus.	Ecclesiasticus
ʿEd.	*ʿEduyyoth*
Enc. Br.	*Encyclopaedia Britannica*
ERE	*Encyclopaedia of Religion and Ethics*, ed. J. Hastings, 1908–26

ʿErub.	*ʿErubhin*
Esdr.	Esdras
Est.	Esther
Eth.	Ethiopic
E.V.	English Versions
Ex.	Exodus
Ezek.	Ezekiel
Gal.	Galatians
Gen.	Genesis
Gr.	Greek
Hab. Comm.	*Habakkuk Commentary* (Qumran)
Hag.	Haggai
Ḥag.	*Ḥagigah*
Ḥal.	*Ḥallah*
Heb.	Hebrew
Hebr.	Hebrews
Hor.	*Horayoth*
Hos.	Hosea
HTR	*Harvard Theological Review*
HUCA	*Hebrew Union College Annual*
Ḥul.	*Ḥullin*
I.C.C.	The International Critical Commentary
Is.	Isaiah
JAOS	*Journal of the American Oriental Society*
JBL	*Journal of Biblical Literature*
JCS	*Journal of Cuneiform Studies*
JE	*Jewish Encyclopaedia*
Jer.	Jeremiah
JJS	*Journal of Jewish Studies*
JNES	*Journal of Near Eastern Studies*
Jos.	Joshua
JPOS	*Journal of the Palestine Oriental Society*
JQR	*Jewish Quarterly Review*
JSS	*Journal of Semitic Studies*
JT	*Jerusalem Talmud*
JTS	*Journal of Theological Studies*
Jub.	Jubilees
Jud.	Judges
Ker.	*Kerithoth*
Ket.	*Kethuboth*
Lam.	Lamentations
Lat.	Latin
Lev.	Leviticus
LXX	Septuagint
Maʿas. Sh.	*Maʿaśer Sheni*

Macc.	Maccabees
Mak.	*Makkoth*
Mal.	Malachi
Matt.	Matthew
Meg.	*Megillah*
Meg. Taʿan.	*Megillath Taʿanith*
Men.	*Menaḥoth*
Mic.	Micah
Mid.	*Middoth*
Mish.	*Mishnah*
M.T.	Massoretic Text
Ned.	*Nedarim*
Neg.	*Negaʿim*
Neh.	Nehemiah
Nid.	*Niddah*
N.T.	New Testament
Num.	Numbers
Ohol.	*Oholoth*
OLZ	*Orientalistische Literaturzeitung*
Onq.	Onqelos
Or.	*Orientalia*
PAAJR	*Proceedings of the American Academy for Jewish Research*
Par.	*Parah*
PEFQS	*Palestine Exploration Fund Quarterly Statement*
PEQ	*Palestine Exploration Quarterly*
Pes.	*Pesaḥim*
Pesh.	Peshiṭta
P.G.	*Patrologia Graeca*
Prov.	Proverbs
Ps.	Psalms
PSBA	*Proceedings of the Society of Biblical Archaeology*
Qid.	*Qiddushin*
Qur.	Qur'an
RB	*Revue biblique*
REJ	*Revue des études juives*
RES	*Répertoire d'épigraphie sémitique*
Rev.	Revelations
R.H.	*Rosh haShanah*
RHR	*Revue de l'histoire des religions*
R.V.	Revised Version
Sam.	Samaritan
Sanh.	*Sanhedrin*
Shab.	*Shabbath*
Sheb.	*Shebhuʿoth*
Sheq.	*Sheqalim*

Soṭ.	*Soṭah*
Suk.	*Sukkah*
Sym.	Symmachos
Taᶜan.	*Taᶜanith*
Targ.	Targum
Targ. Jer.	Jerusalem Targum
Targ. Jon.	Targum ascribed to Jonathan ben ᶜUzziel
Targ. Onq.	Onqelos Targum
Tem.	*Temurah*
Ter.	*Terumoth*
Theod.	Theodotion
ThLZ	*Theologische Literaturzeitung*
Tos.	*Tosephta*
Ugar.	Ugaritic
VT	*Vetus Testamentum*
Vulg.	Vulgate
War	*War of the Sons of Light against the Sons of Darkness* (Qumran)
ZA	*Zeitschrift für Assyriologie und verwandte Gebiete*
Zad. Doc.	*Zadokite Documents*
ZAW	*Zeitschrift für die alttestamentliche Wissenschaft*
ZDMG	*Zeitschrift der Deutschen morgenländischen Gesellschaft*
ZDPV	*Zeitschrift des deutschen Palästina-Vereins*
Zeb.	*Zebhaḥim*
Zech.	Zechariah
Zeph.	Zephaniah
ZNW	*Zeitschrift für die neutestamentliche Wissenschaft und die Kunde der älteren Kirche*

SCHEME OF TRANSLITERATION

b	בּ (*dageš lene*)	q	ק
bh	ב	r	ר
d	ד & דּ (*dageš lene*)	s	ס
ḍ	ض	ṣ	צ
g	ג & גּ (*dageš lene*)	ś	שׂ
gh	غ	š, sh	שׁ
h	ה	t	תּ (*dageš lene*)
ḥ	ח ح	ṭ	ט
ḫ	خ	th	ת
k	כּ (*dageš lene*)	w	ו
kh	כ	y	י
l	ל	z	ז
m	מ	ʿ	ע
n	נ	ʾ	א (frequently omitted, especially at the beginning of a word)
p	פּ (*dageš lene*)		
ph, f	פ		

Dageš forte is usually shown by the doubling of the consonant; it is omitted after the definite article. *Mappiq* is not shown.

Šewa mobile is usually shown by *e*; compound *šewa* is treated as a full vowel. The length of vowels is usually not indicated.

Proper names and nouns in common use are shown in the conventional manner.

NOTE

In the following pages the term 'Pesaḥ' is used to denote the ceremonies at the end of the fourteenth and the beginning of the fifteenth day of the spring month; the term 'Passover' is used to denote the ceremonies of the whole Passover week, including the Pesaḥ.

Citations from the English Version of the Bible are from the Revised Version, unless otherwise stated.

PART I

1

THE SOURCES AND THE TRADITION: THE HISTORICAL DOCUMENTS

He that takes up conclusions on the trust of authors and doth not fetch them from the first items in every reckoning . . . loses his labour.
Hobbes, *Leviathan*

THE primary sources for a study of the origins and history of the Hebrew Passover are those documents which received their extant form before the destruction of the Temple at Jerusalem in A.D. 70. They are to be found in the Bible, in the pseudepigraphical books of Jubilees and the Wisdom of Solomon, in two ostraca and one papyrus from Elephantine, in the fragments of Ezekielos and the brief 'calendar' discovered at Qumran, in *Megillath Ta'anith*, and, finally, in the works of Philo and Josephus. Valuable information on Passover ritual during the last decades of the Temple is to be obtained from the Mishnah—notably from the tractate *Pesaḥim*—but this was not codified before the end of the second century A.D. We may seek secondary evidence elsewhere—in the records of those countries that border on Palestine, in other Jewish writings and practices, both orthodox and sectarian, and in analogous ritual in the modern Near East. This evidence, however, remains secondary and of relatively minor importance. It can only confirm the rejection or acceptance of arguments based upon the primary sources.

Of the primary sources, the large majority were certainly or probably written inside Palestine.[1] With few exceptions, moreover, the primary sources reflect the traditions and practices of orthodox Hebrew religion.[2] At first sight, then, we may expect our sources to present a uniform picture of the festival in its various aspects. But they are far from homogeneous. Each source is the product of its own age; and collectively the sources range over a period of seven centuries—if we take as our extreme limits the celebration of the Passover by King Josiah in 621 B.C. and the

[1] Documents that were certainly written outside Palestine are the ostraca and the papyrus from Elephantine and the work of Philo; those that may have been written outside are Ezek. 45, the fragment from Ezekielos, and the Wisdom of Solomon.

[2] The exceptions are Ezek. 45, and probably also Jubilees, the Ezekielos fragment, and the Qumran text.

destruction of the Temple in A.D. 70. During this long period momentous events took place in Palestine. The empires of Assyria, Babylonia, Persia, Greece, and Rome in turn embraced that country within their orbit. The Hebrews experienced many and varied stresses—war and conquest, Exile and Return, and constant foreign pressure and domination. Not only in the political and economic spheres were these centuries eventful. The expansion and interaction of thought and ideas throughout the Near East could not but have far-reaching effect on the social and religious practices of the Hebrews. Our sources reflect this process of change and development in the ritual of the Passover festival.

The primary sources on the Passover may be conveniently classified into two well-defined groups of documents. The first I have termed the Historical Documents—those documents, that is, that purport to describe actual occurrences of the festival to which a date can be ascribed with approximate certainty and those documents whose authors may be regarded as historical personages. In this category we may include, on the one hand, the description of the celebration of the Passover by Joshua upon the entry of the Israelites into Canaan, although (as we shall see) the narrative probably belongs to the realm of legend rather than of history. We may also include in it, on the other hand, the idealized scheme of religious practice ascribed to Ezekiel, although this was probably never carried out, and the Chronicler's description of Hezekiah's celebration of the Passover, although in its details it has little foundation in history. The entry into Canaan, on the one hand, and the authors of Ezek. 45 and 2 Chr. 30, on the other, can each be reasonably assigned to a definite epoch of Israelite history.

The Historical Documents all belong to the period of Israelite settlement in Canaan. The other group of primary sources, however, contains material that may be older, in its content if not in its extant form. They are to be found in the Pentateuch—in Exodus, Leviticus, Numbers, and Deuteronomy. Unlike the Historical Documents, they have no certain contact with a definite point in history. Yet they cannot be dismissed as unhistorical, for each reflects an aspect or phase of the social and religious development of Israel; and the words of these passages have been hallowed by tradition. I have termed them, somewhat loosely, the Traditional Documents. They recount the celebration of the Passover at the Exodus, and prescribe detailed legislation for that occasion and for subsequent Passovers in the Wilderness and in Canaan. It is upon these documents that we must lean most heavily in any attempt to reconstruct, or indeed to analyse at all, the origins of the festival.

There are obvious difficulties in arranging the Traditional Documents in order of composition and redaction. It is prudent, therefore, to set out first the Historical Documents; they fall into a chronological pattern with comparative ease.

I

The first allusion to the Passover in the Historical Documents is at the very outset of Israelite settlement in Canaan. The children of Israel are said to have performed ceremonies of ritual purification[1] and to have crossed the Jordan, by means of a miracle, on the tenth day of the first month.[2] This was the time of the spring harvest.[3] The menfolk were then circumcised, for, it is alleged, the first time since the Exodus from Egypt.[4] The Passover ceremonies followed, Jos. 5:10–12:

> And the children of Israel encamped in Gilgal; and they kept the passover[5] on the fourteenth day of the month at even[6] in the plains of Jericho.[7] (11) And they did eat of the old corn of the land[8] on the morrow after the passover,[9] unleavened cakes[10] and parched corn,[11] in the selfsame day. (12) And the manna ceased[12] on the morrow,[13] after they had eaten of the old corn of the land;[8] neither had the children of Israel manna any more; but they did eat of the fruit of the land of Canaan that year.

According to most scholars Jos. 3:1 to 5:9 is to be attributed in parts to JE, D, and P. The inconsistencies and repetitiveness of that section of the text certainly indicate composite authorship or redaction; there are, for example, two separate accounts of the crossing of the Jordan.[14] But the passage on the Passover shows neither repetitiveness nor contradictions. It is commonly assigned to a P editor.[15]

Three features of this passage are of interest. We are given the date of the Passover—it is held on the evening (at the end) of the fourteenth day of the first month.[16] It is preceded by circumcision; and, finally, this rite of circumcision takes place on the tenth day of the month. Both the role of circumcision as a prerequisite for the Passover and the significance of the tenth day will recur in the Passover documents.[17]

Beyond this the passage tells us little. The eating of unleavened cakes, *maṣṣoth*, on the 'morrow after the passover', is unlikely to be an oblique

[1] Jos. 3:5. [2] Jos. 4:19. [3] Jos. 3:15, cf. 4:18. [4] Jos. 5:2, 5 ff.

[5] Heb. *'śh pesaḥ*. [6] Heb. *ba'erebh*: LXX ἀπὸ ἑσπέρας (or ἀφ' ἑσπέρας).

[7] LXX has a conflate rendering which reflects a Heb. doublet; but see p. 238 n. 1 below.

[8] Better 'of the produce of the land'. [9] LXX omits; see p. 238 below.

[10] Heb. *maṣṣoth*. [11] LXX has νέα; see p. 4 below.

[12] LXX omits 'and', and joins this to the preceding clause. [13] LXX omits.

[14] See, for example, J. Dus, 'Analyse zweier Ladeerzählungen des Josuabuches', *ZAW* lxxii, 1960, 107, on a particular aspect.

[15] See the usual Commentaries, and the works discussed by N. H. Snaith, 'Historical Books', in H. H. Rowley, *The Old Testament and Modern Study*, 1951, 84 ff. An analysis is given by P. Auvray, art. 'Josué', *Dict. Bib. Suppl.* M. Noth, *Buch Josua*, in loc., regards only the date in Jos. 5:10 and בעצם היום הזה in 5:11 as certainly to be ascribed to P; the rest of the Passover narrative is, he maintains, early. [16] See p. 131 below.

[17] See pp. 135 and 142 below.

allusion to the *maṣṣoth* of the Passover week, since we are not informed that the festival lasts a week and the length of the festival is prescribed in other relevant documents on the Passover.[1] But it may be argued that 'passover' here refers to the Passover week, rather than to the Pesaḥ. The (new) 'produce of the land'—the E.V. 'old corn of the land' is wholly misleading—was never eaten on the fifteenth day of the Passover month, which would be the natural interpretation of the words 'morrow after the passover' if 'passover' refers to the Pesaḥ only; and there are grounds for supposing that at one time the initial ceremony of Sheaf-waving which preceded the eating of the new corn was performed on the day after the complete Passover week.[2]

We must beware, however, of reading too much into this passage. The writer is not concerned with the details of Passover ritual. He is concerned with the inauguration of the new life in Canaan and more particularly with the eating of the new crops.[3] He assumes that the time of the Passover is the proper season for the auspicious opening of this new epoch in the history of the nation, and that there is some connexion in time between the Passover and the new harvest. It is to be noted that the setting of this spring harvest is the Jordan valley near Jericho.[4]

II

Our next allusion to the Passover refers to the practice in the tenth century. Among miscellaneous information about the administrative activity of Solomon's reign occurs the following passage, 1 Kings 9:25:

> And three times in a year did Solomon offer burnt offerings[5] and peace offerings[6] upon the altar which he built unto the Lord, burning incense[7] therewith,[8] (upon the altar) that was before the Lord.[9]

This passage may be regarded as an authentic 'archival element'.[10] It alludes unmistakably to the three annual *ḥaggim*, and one of these must be the

[1] See further pp. 176 f. below.

[2] For a discussion of the Sheaf-waving, see p. 194 below. There may, however, be a reminiscence of a seven-day festival in the seven-day siege of Jericho; p. 238 below.

[3] On the eating of new cereals in the form of parched corn, see Lev. 23:14 and, particularly, 2:14; they are not normally eaten in the form of *maṣṣoth*. See further p. 195 below.

[4] See p. 250 below.

[5] Heb. *'oloth*.

[6] Heb. *šelamim*. Targ. Jon. has נכסת דקודשין, 'sacrifices of holy (offerings)'; on *qodašim*, see pp. 202 and 227 below.

[7] We should probably point וְהִקְטִיר for M.T. וְהַקְטֵיר.

[8] M.T. אִתּוֹ is incomprehensible; some Heb. manuscripts have אתּוֹ or אוֹתוֹ. Klostermann's suggestion of אִשּׁוֹ is improbable; see J. A. Montgomery and H. S. Gehman, *Books of Kings* (I.C.C.), in loc. LXX Alex. has αὐτός; Targ. and Pesh. have 'upon it'. Perhaps omit, with LXX Vat.

[9] See C. F. Burney, *Notes on the Hebrew Text of the Books of Kings*, 1903, and the usual Commentaries, especially A. Šanda, *Bücher der Könige*, ii, 1912, and Montgomery and Gehman, op. cit. See further the analysis in Snaith, op. cit. 102.

[10] Montgomery and Gehman, op. cit., in loc.

Passover. This was certainly the view of the Chronicler, who expands the description, 2 Chr. 8:12–13:

Then Solomon offered burnt offerings[1] unto the Lord on the altar of the Lord, which he had built before the porch, even as the duty of every day required, offering according to the commandment of Moses, on the sabbaths, and on the new moons, and on set feasts,[2] three times in the year, (13) (even) in the feast of unleavened bread,[3] and in the feast of weeks,[4] and in the feast of tabernacles.

In both these passages the stress is upon the royal sacrifices. In 1 Kings 9 they fall into the two categories of burnt offerings and peace offerings, and to these are added the greater luxury of incense. In 2 Chr. 8 only burnt offerings are mentioned.[5]

III

We come now to the first specific celebration of the Passover to which an historical date can be assigned with some certainty. The annalist of 2 Kings relates the discovery of the 'Book of the Law' in the Temple in the eighteenth year of King Josiah—in, that is, 622–621 B.C.[6] The king ordered the book to be read in public.[7] He then decreed the removal of heathen priests and cult objects, the cleansing of the Temple at Jerusalem, and the destruction of pagan high-places throughout Judah.[8] The reforms were (if we may trust our text)[9] extended to Bethel and elsewhere in the province of Samaria.[10] The climax of the campaign was reached with the celebration of the Passover, 2 Kings 23:21–23:

And the king commanded all the people, saying, Keep the passover[11] unto the Lord your God, as it is written in this book of the covenant. (22) Surely there was not kept such a passover[11, 12] from the days of the judges that judged Israel, nor in all the days of the kings of Israel, nor of the kings of Judah; (23) but in the eighteenth year of king Josiah was this passover kept to the Lord in Jerusalem.[13]

[1] Heb. *'oloth.* [2] Heb. *mo'adoth.* [3] Heb. *ḥag haMaṣṣoth.*

[4] Pesh. has 'feast of the fast (of the Day of Atonement)' for 'feast of weeks'.

[5] See p. 201 n. 17 below. Pesh. adds 'and peace offerings' in 2 Chr. 8:12, presumably under the influence of 1 Kings 9:25.

[6] 2 Kings 22:8 ff. On the question whether the 'Book of the Law' is to be identified with Deuteronomy, see briefly p. 219 below.

[7] 2 Kings 23:1 ff. It is possible that this took place at the feast of Tabernacles, when it was customary to read the Law; see Deut. 31:11 and p. 149 below. On the date of Josiah's Passover, see p. 216 below.

[8] 2 Kings 23:4 ff. The numeration of the verses of this passage may be in disorder, but the stages in the reforms may be clearly discerned. The Temple at Jerusalem was first cleansed, and pagan priests removed; the environs of the Temple were then cleansed, and the cleansing was extended successively to the area outside the walls of the city, to the rest of Judah, and finally to the province of Samaria. See p. 217 below.

[9] Montgomery and Gehman, op. cit., in loc., regard this section of the text as a 'Midrash', on grounds that are scarcely convincing.

[10] On 2 Kings 23:9, see p. 216 n. 8 below. [11] Heb. *'śh pesaḥ.*

[12] M.T. 'like this passover', but LXX 'this passover'; M.T. is to be preferred.

[13] For Commentaries, see p. 4 n. 9 above.

The text is in good condition, and there is little doubt as to its authenticity. Many scholars are agreed that it is likely to have been written not later than *c.* 550 B.C., and some maintain that the *terminus ante quem* is 586 B.C. or even the year of Josiah's death. The passage is commonly held to be the product of a double Deuteronomistic redaction.

This passage provides important evidence as to the antiquity of the Passover—it is likely that the word פסח refers to the Passover week rather than only to the Pesaḥ[1]—and its widespread observance. It was, we are told, celebrated in the pre-Monarchy period of Israel and subsequently by the rulers of both the northern and southern kingdoms. In the present state of the text[2] we can do little more than surmise that the special quality of Josiah's Passover may lie in one of three features—the fact that this Passover was held by royal edict, or that it was held (though the text does not explicitly state this) only at Jerusalem, or, finally, that it was celebrated with particular pomp.

IV

Regulations for the observance of the Passover are included in the scheme for a theocratic State in a New Jerusalem which is attributed by tradition to the prophet Ezekiel. There is no general agreement among scholars as to the authorship of Ezek. 40–48 or the date of its composition. But it is either Exilic or early post-Exilic, and whether it belongs to the sixth or the fifth century, these verses on the Passover stand, on chronological grounds, in this place in the present study.[3]

The legislator divides the (non-embolismic) 'year' of twelve months into two equal halves of six months each. The first day of both the first and seventh months[4] is to be marked by a ceremony of 'de-sinning' the sanctuary; the blood of a sin offering is to be smeared by the priest on the doorposts, the four corners of the altar ledge,[5] and the posts of the gate of the

[1] See p. 4 above on Jos. 5:10–12.

[2] H. Guthe, 'Passahfest nach Dtn 16', in W. Frankenberg and F. Küchler, *Abhandlungen zur semitischen Religionskunde . . . von Baudissin . . . überreicht*, 1918, 217, and K. Budde, 'Deuteronomium und die Reform Josias. Ein Vortragsentwurf', *ZAW* xliv, 1926, 190 ff., suggest that the original text here gave details of Josiah's Passover that were omitted by a later editor; but see p. 219 below.

[3] An admirable summing-up of recent studies of Ezekiel, with an exhaustive bibliography, may be found in Rowley, 'Book of Ezekiel in Modern Study', *BJRL* xxxvi, 1953–4, 146. See also J. A. Bewer, 'Notes on the Book of Ezekiel', *JBL* lxxii, 1953, 158, and W. A. Irwin, 'Ezekiel Research since 1943', *VT* iii, 1953, 54. Among other studies on Ezekiel that have appeared in recent years may be noted G. Fohrer, *Hauptprobleme des Buches Ezechiel* (Beihefte zur *ZAW*, 72), 1952, and particularly H. Gese, *Verfassungsentwurf des Ezechiel* (*Kap. 40–48*), 1957.

[4] Following LXX 'in the seventh month, on the first (day) of the month', rather than M.T. 'on the seventh (day) of the month'; see the Commentaries, in loc. On Ezek. 45:20, see A. B. Ehrlich, *Randglossen zur hebräischen Bibel*, v, 1912, 154.

[5] See G. R. Driver, 'Ezekiel: Linguistic and Textual Problems', *Biblica*, xxxv, 1954, 307.

inner court.[1] There follows the passage, probably by a different hand,[2] Ezek. 45:21–24:

In the first (month),[3] in the fourteenth day of the month, ye shall have the passover, a feast[4] of seven days;[5] unleavened bread[6] shall be eaten. (22) And upon that day shall the prince[7] prepare for himself and for all the people of the land[8] a bullock for a sin offering. (23) And the seven days of the feast[4] he shall prepare a burnt offering[9] to the Lord, seven bullocks, and seven rams without blemish daily the seven days;[10] and a he-goat daily for a sin offering.[11] (24) And he shall prepare[12] a meal offering, an ephah for a bullock, and an ephah for a ram, and an hin of oil to an ephah.[13]

The text contains serious difficulties of wording which are indicated here in the footnotes. Stylistically these verses are not attached to the previous verses on the 'de-sinning' ceremonies; on the other hand, they form a single unit with the following verse on the feast of Tabernacles.

The term פסח here denotes the Passover; there is no reference to the Pesaḥ. It should be observed that the passage attaches great importance to the date of the festival since this contradicts the symmetry between the spring and autumn which is a remarkable feature of Ezekiel's scheme of festivals; the Passover begins on the fourteenth day of the first month,[14] but Tabernacles on the fifteenth day of the seventh month.[15] The central role of the king in earlier Passover documents[16] is here taken by the Naśi', but the main interest of the writer is in sacrifice—the communal burnt offerings of the Passover week, the he-goat as a sin offering, and the bullock

[1] Ezek. 45:18–20.

[2] See Gese, op. cit. 75, who divides vv. 18–20 from 21 ff. He attributes vv. 18–20 to the same hand as 43:18 ff.; 45:20b he regards as a gloss.

[3] Targ. 'in Nisan'.

[4] Heb. *ḥag*. Pesh. 'the passover and the feast'.

[5] R.V. here follows two Hebrew manuscripts and all the Versions, including LXX. M.T., with a different pointing of שבעת, has 'ye shall have the passover, a feast of weeks of days'. The M.T. may have adopted this reading in order to remedy the omission of the feast of Weeks in this passage; but the reading is improbable. 'Feast of Weeks of days' is not the title of the feast of Weeks, and if that festival were mentioned here it would scarcely be followed by a reference to *maṣṣoth*. Some scholars suggest that the original text was חג הפסח שבעת וכו'; but if this were so, a later transposition of the words חג and פסח would be hardly explicable. Perhaps the wording of the original text of v. 21b contained a date and read ובחמשה עשר יום לחדש הזה חג שבעת ימים מצות יאכל as in Num. 28:17. This would give a satisfactory significance to ביום ההוא in Ezek. 45:22. See P. Grelot, 'Papyrus pascal d'Éléphantine et le problème du Pentateuque', *VT* v, 1955, 251 n. 1.

[6] Heb. *maṣṣoth*.

[7] Heb. *naśi'*.

[8] See p. 218 below on this phrase.

[9] Heb. *'olah*.

[10] 'Daily the seven days' is omitted in Pesh.—correctly, according to O. Procksch, 'Fürst und Priester bei Hesekiel', *ZAW* lviii, 1940–1, 127.

[11] LXX adds *καὶ θυσίαν*.

[12] LXX 'thou shalt make'.

[13] See p. 6 n. 3 above and the usual Commentaries.

[14] To read 'fifteenth' for 'fourteenth' in v. 21a (as H. G. May, 'The Relation of the Passover to the Festival of Unleavened Cakes', *JBL* lv, 1936, 76, and other scholars) would be, in the judicious words of G. A. Cooke, *Book of Ezekiel* (I.C.C.), 1936, 503, 'to remove a feature of interest'; so Gese, op. cit. 81. The difference is in fact a minor one—between the (evening at the end of the) fourteenth day and the (evening at the beginning of the) fifteenth day.

[15] Ezek. 45:25.

[16] pp. 4 and 5 above.

offered by the Naśi' as a sin offering. This last offering is made apparently at the spring, but not at the autumn, festival; it is not, however, the Pesaḥ sacrifice.[1]

V

To the fifth century belong our earliest extra-Biblical texts on the Passover. They are two ostraca and one papyrus from Elephantine; all are in Aramaic.

A. The first ostracon has been assigned, on not wholly satisfactory grounds,[2] to the earlier half of the fifth century. The reference to the Passover reads:

(concave side) 5. . . . on the Passover[3] and arise
6. . . . that[4] I may install you[5] with
7. . . . and his vessels[6] do thou examine.[7]

B. The second ostracon is ascribed to *c.* 500 B.C. on the basis of the script.[8] The reference to the Passover here reads:

(convex side) 3. . . . send thou
4. to me when[9] ye will make the Passov-
5. er . . . .[10]

The two ostraca show only that the Passover was observed by the Jews of Elephantine. This bare fact is, of course, important, but we are given no details of the ritual. It has been suggested that l. 7 in the first text alludes to the examination of vessels for ritual impurity before the Passover week; the hypothesis is, however, open to grave doubt.[11]

[1] See p. 220 below.

[2] A. Dupont-Sommer, 'Sur la fête de la Pâque dans les documents araméens d'Éléphantine', *REJ*, N.S. vii (= cvii), 1946–7, 43 ff., regards the texts on both the convex and concave sides of this ostracon as forming a single inscription. He dates it to the beginning of the fifth century on account of the mention of the pr. name RWK on the convex side; cf. A. E. Cowley, *Aramaic Papyri of the Fifth Century B.C.*, 1923, No. 1. But it is doubtful whether the texts on both sides are in fact by the same hand; see *RES*, No. 1792.

[3] M. Lidzbarski, *Ephemeris für semitische Epigraphik*, ii, 1903–7, 232; iii, 1909–15, 257 n. 1, translates, less satisfactorily, as 'ford'; he appears to have changed his view later, cf. ibid. ii, Wortregister A. 2, s.v.

[4] Or 'which'.

[5] So Dupont-Sommer, op. cit. 45; Lidzbarski, op. cit. ii. 232, suggests 'I bring you together'.

[6] Or 'garments'; Aram. *mana*'.

[7] A photograph of this ostracon is given by Lidzbarski, op. cit. See the discussion there and in *RES*, No. 1792, and Dupont-Sommer, op. cit.; the last-named gives a full bibliography.

[8] E. L. Sukenik and E. Y. Kutscher, 'Passover Ostracon from Elephantine' (in Heb.), *Kedem*, i, 1942, 53 f. In its comparison of the script of this ostracon with that of papyri, that article makes, however, no allowance for the difference of the material on which they are written.

[9] Aram. *'mt*. This had been incorrectly rendered as 'handmaid(s)', until Sukenik and Kutscher, op. cit. 55 f., and Dupont-Sommer, op. cit. 47 f., arrived, apparently independently, at the rendering given here.

[10] *'bd psḥ*', cf. Heb. *'śh pesaḥ*. A photograph of this ostracon is given by A. H. Sayce, 'Aramaic Ostracon from Elephantine', *PSBA* xxxiii, 1911, facing 184. On the text, see Sukenik and Kutscher, op. cit., and *RES*, No. 1793, and Dupont-Sommer, op. cit. 46 ff., who gives a bibliography.

[11] See p. 224 n. 2 below.

C. The papyrus, on the other hand, provides valuable information on the ritual of the Passover. It is dated in the fifth year of Darius (II), 419 B.C.:

(Recto)

1. . . . my [brethren]
2. Yado]niah[1] and his colleagues the [J]ewish s[oldiers], your brother Ḥanan[iah]. The peace of my brethren may the gods . . .
3. And now this year, the year 5 of Darius the king, from the king there was sent[2] to Arsh[am
4. . . . . Jew]ish. Now, as for you, thus shall ye count: fo[urteen . . .
5. . . . . ma]ke and from the 15th day to the 21st day of . . .
6. . . . . be ye clean and take heed. Work n[ot . . .
7. . . . . ye shall n[ot] drink, and anything at all of leaven[3] [do] n[ot[4] . . .

(Verso)

8. . . . . f]rom the setting of the sun to the 21st day of Nisa[n . . .
9. . . . . ye shall not br]ing[5] into your chambers and ye shall seal[6] during[7] the day[s
10. . . . . the ki]ng(?)
11. . . . . . my brethren Yadoniah and his colleagues the Jewish soldiers, your brother Ḥananiah.[8]

The defective state of this text poses problems concerning its writer and the general circumstances in which it was written that we shall consider later.[9] Here we may observe that the document in its present form does not contain any reference to the Pesaḥ, although (as we have seen from the ostraca) the name of the festival was known at Elephantine. The restoration of the word פסחא in the text[10] is attractive and likely. But if the word was in the text, the mention of the Pesaḥ ceremonies must have been brief; there

[1] Or Yadeniah, with Grelot, 'Études sur le "Papyrus Pascal" d'Éléphantine', *VT* iv, 1954, 351.

[2] Perhaps, with Grelot, op. cit. 355, '(order) was sent'.

[3] Or 'leavened food'.

[4] i.e. '[do] n[ot eat]', rather than 'let there] n[ot be found]', but the latter is equally possible in the present state of the text.

[5] The photograph in C. E. Sachau, *Aramäische Papyrus und Ostraka aus einer jüdischen Militär-Kolonie zu Elephantine*, 1911, Tafel 6, seems to support the reconstruction of תה]נעלו of Cowley, op. cit. 63, 65, against ועלו by A. Ungnad, *Aramäische Papyrus aus Elephantine*, 1911; Sachau, op. cit., in loc.; and A. Vincent, *Religion des Judéo-Araméens d'Éléphantine*, 1937, 247, &c.

[6] Reading *ḥtmw;* Grelot, op. cit. 374, 383, prefers *stmw*, 'keep hidden'.

[7] Grelot, op. cit. 366.

[8] For the text, see the photograph in Sachau, op. cit., Tafel 6. A selection of the large bibliography on this papyrus is given by E. G. Kraeling, *Brooklyn Museum Aramaic Papyri*, 1953, 92 ff.; see also the treatment of the text by Cowley, op. cit. No. 21, and Grelot, op. cit. 349.

[9] p. 221 below.

[10] With Cowley, op. cit. 64; l. 4, 'let there be a Passover for the Jew]ish [soldiers'; l. 5, 'ma]ke [the Passover] and from the fifteenth . . .'.

is no space for any detailed regulations in the place where one would logically expect to find this—that is, in ll. 4–5, before the rules about the Passover week.[1] On the other hand, the papyrus provides much information about the Passover week:[2] indeed, this is the first of the Historical Documents to prescribe rules other than those concerning sacrifice.[3]

VI

The chronicler of the Return of the Jews from Exile relates that Zerubbabel and his comrades completed the rebuilding of the Temple at Jerusalem on 3rd Adar in the sixth year of the reign of Darius.[4] The ceremony was, we are told, accompanied by lavish sacrifices, and the priests and Levites were installed in their ministrations at the sanctuary. Then, continues the annalist, Ezra 6:19–22:

The children of the captivity[5] kept the passover[6] upon the fourteenth (day) of the first month. (20) For the priests and the Levites had purified themselves[7] together; all of them were pure:[7] and they[8] killed the passover[9] for all the children of the captivity, and for their brethren the priests, and for themselves. (21) And the children of Israel, which were come again out of the captivity, and all such as had separated themselves unto them from the filthiness of the heathen of the land, to seek the Lord, the God of Israel, did eat,[10] (22) and kept the feast of unleavened bread[11] seven days with joy: for the Lord had made them joyful,[12] and

[1] An excellent analysis of the width of the papyrus and the extent to which it is justifiable to 'restore' words in the space to the side of the extant text is found in Grelot, op. cit. 369.

[2] The dates of the festival, ritual cleanness, the prohibition of work, the prohibition of certain drink, and of leaven.

[3] Vincent, loc. cit., following Ungnad, op. cit. (see p. 9 n. 5 above), suggests the rendering of l. 9, 'Go into your houses and seal (the houses) between the two days'. He compares Ex. 12:22, cf. 12:46. The suggestion must be rejected. It is not supported by the photographs; 'seal' is a peculiar term for closing the houses; no parallel can be drawn between 'between the two days' of Vincent's rendering and 'between the two evenings' of the Pesaḥ texts—the former is unknown, the latter is a well-known technical phrase, see p. 131 below. In the context of the papyrus, moreover, it is not likely that regulations about the Passover week would be followed, rather than preceded, by regulations about the Pesaḥ.

[4] Ezra 6:15; but on this date, see p. 225 below and n. 6 there.

[5] The parallel text of Esdr. 7:10 reads: 'The sons of Israel that came out of the captivity'; see J. A. Bewer, *Text des Buches Ezra*, 1922, in loc.

[6] Heb. *'śh psḥ.*

[7] Heb. *ṭhr.*

[8] 'They' evidently refers to the Levites. Esdr. 7:10–11 has: 'when the priests and the Levites were sanctified together, and all they that were of the captivity; for they were sanctified. For the Levites were all sanctified together, and they offered . . .'. The texts of both Ezra 6:20 and Esdr. 7:10–11 are probably corrupt; see Bewer, op. cit., in loc. L. W. Batten, *Books of Ezra and Nehemiah* (I.C.C.), 1913, in loc., restores: 'Now the priests and the sons of the captivity were not cleansed, but the Levites to a man were all of them clean, and they (the Levites) sacrificed . . . .' Bewer simply omits 'the priests and' from the M.T., with some Versions.

[9] Heb. *šḥṭ pesaḥ.*

[10] The text is in disorder. Batten, on the basis of Esdr. 7:13, reads: 'And the sons of Israel, all that had separated themselves from the uncleanness of the nations of the earth, and those who had returned unto them from the captivity to seek Yahweh ate the passover.'

[11] Heb. *'śh ḥag haMaṣṣoth.*

[12] Esdr. 7:14, 'making merry before the Lord'.

had turned the heart of the king of Assyria unto them, to strengthen their hands in the work of the house of God, the God of Israel.[1]

This rededication of the Temple took place, according to the narrator, in 515 B.C. There is nothing improbable in the formal celebration of the Passover immediately after such an occasion,[2] and the account may well have some basis in fact. It is to be observed that the account of the rededication of the Temple is in Aramaic, while that of Zerubbabel's Passover is in Hebrew; they come, then, from different sources.[3] But the very fact that the description of the Passover has been inserted at this point—and deliberately inserted, as the difference in languages shows—indicates that the editor believed the narrative to be plausible. There are, however, strong similarities in style and—more important—in content[4] between this passage of Ezra and the work of the Chronicler. It is likely, therefore, to be by a member of the same school. The books of Chronicles, Ezra, and Nehemiah are generally held to have received their present form between 400 B.C. and 250 B.C.[5] The ritual of the Passover described in Ezra 6 reflects the practice at that period or, rather, the manner in which the Jews of that period conceived that the Passover would have been celebrated two or three centuries earlier.[6] The text of Ezra 6:19 ff. appears to have undergone some mutilation.[7]

In the account of Ezra 6 the Pesaḥ is held, as in Ezek. 45, on the (evening at the end of the) fourteenth day of the first month and in the Temple. פסח is used here, for the first time in the Historical Documents, to indicate also the Pesaḥ victim. There is a specific allusion to the Pesaḥ meal. On the other hand, there is no mention of sacrifices during the Passover week; but we may assume that they took place—they would have been a natural expression of the 'joy' with which the festival was, according to the annalist, celebrated.

[1] See the usual Commentaries, in addition to those already mentioned above, and the works cited by Snaith, op. cit. 107 ff. For a discussion of the date of this text, see Rowley, *Servant of the Lord*, 1952, 131, and H. Cazelles, 'Mission d'Esdras', *VT* iv, 1954, 113. On Esdras, see W. J. Moulton, 'Über die Überlieferung und den textkritischen Werth des dritten Esrabuchs', *ZAW* xix, 1899, 209, xx, 1900, 1; S. A. Cook, '1 Esdras', in R. H. Charles, *Apocrypha and Pseudepigrapha of the Old Testament*, 1913, i. 1; E. Bayer, *Das dritte Buch Esdras und sein Verhältnis zu den Büchern Esra-Nehemia*, 1911; and B. Walde, *Esdrasbücher der Septuaginta*, 1913.

[2] So in Ezra 3:4 Zerubbabel celebrates the autumn festival when the altar is set up at Jerusalem; cf. p. 216 below on the autumn festival celebrated by Solomon and pp. 5 f. above on the Passover celebrated by Josiah.

[3] Batten, op. cit., in loc., holds that Ezra 6:19–22 is early and should stand before the passage in Aramaic, after 4:3 or even in the first part of ch. 3.

[4] See pp. 225 ff. below.

[5] See the summary of views in Snaith, loc. cit., and W. Rudolph, 'Problems of the Books of Chronicles', *VT* iv, 1954, 401, and id., *Chronikbücher*, 1955, x. M. Noth, *Überlieferungsgeschichtliche Studien*, i, 1943, 146, maintains, however, that Chronicles is to be dated between 300 and 200 B.C.

[6] For Commentaries, see n. 1 above.

[7] This is shown by a comparison of this passage with Esdr. 7:10 ff. (although the latter is not always to be preferred).

Two features receive special prominence. The Levites have a privileged role—this has survived the clumsy redaction of the text[1]—in contrast to the disparagement of the general body of the Levites in Ezekiel.[2] More important, there is great emphasis on ritual cleanness. The laymen[3] had 'separated themselves . . . from the filthiness of the heathen'—that is, abstained from pagan practices and from intermarriage;[4] but perhaps, unlike the priests and the Levites, they had not purified themselves,[5] and for this reason the Levites[6] slew the Pesaḥ victim on their behalf. However this may be, the implication is that normally the laymen would have performed the slaughtering themselves. Certainly they were not debarred by lack of ritual cleanness from participating in the Pesaḥ meal and from celebrating the ceremonies of the 'Maṣṣoth festival' during the following days.

VII

The summary account in 2 Kings 23 of the Passover held by Josiah in 621 B.C., as the climax of his religious reforms,[7] is expanded by the Chronicler in 2 Chr. 35:1–19:

And Josiah kept a passover[8] unto the Lord in Jerusalem: and they killed the passover[9] on the fourteenth (day) of the first month. (2) And he set the priests in their charges,[10] and encouraged them to the service of the house of the Lord. (3) And he said unto the Levites that taught[11] all Israel, which were holy unto the Lord,[12] Put the holy ark[13] in the house which Solomon the son of David king of Israel did build; there shall no more be a burden upon your shoulders: now serve the Lord your God, and his people Israel. (4) And prepare yourselves[14] after your fathers' houses by your courses,[15] according to the writing[16] of David king of

[1] See p. 10 n. 8 above on Ezra 6:20. A convenient summary of the Chronicler's preference for Levites may be found in R. H. Pfeiffer, *Introduction to the Old Testament*, 1952, 796; see also R. de Vaux, *Institutions de l'Ancien Testament*, ii, 1960, 257.

[2] Ezek. 44:10 ff., but see 'the priests the Levites, the sons of Zadok', vv. 15 ff., cf. 40:46, 43:19. Instead of 'the priests the Levites' of M.T. and LXX in 44:15, Pesh. and Vulg. have 'the priests and the Levites'; cf. the quotation from Ezekiel in *Zad. Doc.* iii. 21 (C. Rabin, *Zadokite Documents*, 1958, 13), see *Doc. Comm.* i. 18 f., ii. 11, cf. ii. 19 f. (M. Burrows, *Dead Sea Scrolls of St. Mark's Monastery*, ii, 1951).

[3] 'Children of the captivity'; Ezekiel, in a different context, calls them 'people of the land'; p. 7 above.

[4] Cf. Neh. 9:2, 10:29 ff. (E.V. 10:28 ff.).

[5] Ezra 6:20; cf. Neh. 12:30, 45. On the degree of ritual cleanness denoted by Heb. *ṭhr*, see p. 226 n. 8 below.

[6] Adopting the reading of Esdr.; see p. 10 n. 8 above.

[7] p. 5 above.

[8] Heb. *'śh pesaḥ*. In v. 1 Pesh. renders M.T. 'passover' by 'festival'.

[9] Heb. *šḥṭ pesaḥ*.

[10] משמרות.

[11] Esdr. 1:3 has 'the temple-servants', i.e. Heb. נתינים, a misreading of M.T. LXX has δυνατοί.

[12] Better translate the M.T. 'who explain to all Israel (the things that are) holy to the Lord'; cf. Neh. 8:7, 9 and 2 Chr. 17:8 f., &c. Pesh. has 'make yourselves holy . . .'; Greek, Latin, Esdr. 1:3 have 'that they should make themselves holy'.

[13] Better, with LXX, Esdr., 'when the Ark was placed'; or 'leave the Ark'.

[14] So *Kethibh* (*niph.*); *Qere* has 'prepare' (*hiph.*).

[15] מחלקות; LXX ἐφημερίαι.

[16] בכתב for ככתב; a few Heb. manuscripts have ככתב, and so LXX and other Versions.

Israel, and according to the writing[1] of Solomon[2] his son. (5) And stand in the holy place according to the divisions[3] of the fathers' houses[4] of your brethren the children of the people, and (let there be for each) a portion[5] of a fathers' house[4] of the Levites.[6] (6) And kill the passover,[7] and sanctify yourselves,[8] and prepare for your brethren,[9] to do according to the word of the Lord by the hand of Moses.

(7) And Josiah gave to the children of the people, of the flock, lambs and kids, all of them for the passover offerings,[10] unto all that were present, to the number of thirty thousand, and three thousand bullocks: these were of the king's substance. (8) And his princes gave for a freewill offering unto the people, to the priests, and to the Levites. [11]Hilkiah and Zechariah and Jehiel, the rulers of the house of God, gave unto the priests for the passover offerings two thousand and six hundred (small cattle), and three hundred oxen. (9) Conaniah also, and Shemaiah and Nethanel, his brethren, and Hashabiah and Jeiel and Jozabad, the chiefs of the Levites, gave unto the Levites for the passover offerings[10] five thousand (small cattle), and five hundred oxen.

(10) So the service was prepared, and the priests stood in their place, and the Levites by their courses,[12] according to the king's commandment. (11) And they killed the passover,[7] and the priests sprinkled[13] (the blood,[14] which they received) of their hand, and the Levites flayed them. (12) And they removed[15] the burnt offerings,[16] that they might give them according to the divisions[17] of the fathers' houses[4] of the children of the people, to offer unto the Lord, as it is written in the book of Moses. And so did they with the oxen.[18] (13) And they roasted the passover with fire[19] according to the ordinance: and the holy offerings[20] sod they[21] in pots, and in cauldrons, and in pans, and carried them quickly to all the children of the people. (14) And afterward they prepared for themselves, and for the priests;[22] because the priests the sons of Aaron (were busied) in offering the burnt offerings[23] and the fat until night: therefore the Levites prepared for themselves, and for the priests the sons of Aaron. (15) And the singers the sons of Asaph were in their place, according to the commandment of David, and Asaph, and Heman, and

[1] M.T. ובמכתב; one Heb. manuscript and Versions have וכמכתב. Esdr. has 'magnificence'.

[2] LXX has *διὰ χειρὸς (βασιλέως) Σαλαμών*.

[3] פלגות; LXX *διαιρέσεις*.

[4] בית האבות.

[5] חלקה; LXX *μερίς*.

[6] The insertion of the R.V. is not represented in the M.T. Rudolph suggests that there is a haplography and restores ולכל בית אב לבני העם at the beginning of v. 5b.

[7] Heb. *šḥṭ pesaḥ*.

[8] התקדשו. This comes belatedly after 'kill the passover'. Esdr. 1:6 and some Greek Versions have 'and prepare the holy offerings (*qodašim*) for your brethren', i.e. Heb. והקדשים הכינו. I. Benzinger, *Bücher der Chronik*, 1901, in loc., omits התקדשו, with LXX.

[9] i.e. the laymen, cf. v. 5.

[10] Heb. *pesaḥim*.

[11] Probably insert 'And' before 'Hilkiah', with some Versions and Esdr. 1:6.

[12] מחלקות; LXX *ἐφημερίαι*.

[13] Better 'poured, threw'.

[14] R.V. follows LXX; M.T. has omitted מהדם or את הדם (as 2 Chr. 30:16) before מידם, by haplography. Pesh. has 'sprinkled of the blood', omitting 'of their hand'.

[15] LXX, however, has *ἡτοίμασαν*, i.e. Heb. ויכינו; this is followed by N. M. Nicolsky, 'Pascha im Kulte des jerusalemischen Tempels', *ZAW* xlv, 1927, 245 n. 2. On the text of the Versions and Esdras here, see J. Hänel, 'Recht des Opferschlachtens in der chronistischen Literatur', *ZAW* lv, 1937, 50.

[16] Heb. *'olah*.

[17] מפלגות.

[18] R.V. 'did they' is not in the Heb. Some Heb. manuscripts, LXX, Pesh., and Vulg. read לַבֹּקֶר for לַבָּקָר. The pointing of M.T. should be retained; see pp. 56 and 204 below.

[19] בשל הפסח באש; LXX *ὤπτησαν ἐν πυρί*.

[20] קדשים.

[21] בשל; LXX *ἥψησαν*. Pesh. repeats the phrase used of the cooking of the Pesaḥ victims (n. 19 above), obviously incorrectly.

[22] Pesh. 'the priests prepared their own for themselves'; M.T. is to be preferred.

[23] Heb. *'oloth*.

Jeduthun the king's seer;[1] and the porters[2] were at every gate: they needed not to depart from their service, for their brethren the Levites prepared for them. (16) So all the service of the Lord was prepared the same day, to keep the passover,[3] and to offer burnt offerings[4] upon the altar of the Lord, according to the commandment of king Josiah.

(17) And the children of Israel that were present kept the passover[3] at that time, and the feast of unleavened bread[5] seven days. (18) And there was no passover like to that kept[3] in Israel from the days of Samuel the prophet; neither did any of the kings of Israel keep such a passover as Josiah kept,[3] and the priests, and the Levites, and all Judah and Israel that were present, and the inhabitants of Jerusalem. (19) In the eighteenth year of the reign of Josiah was this passover kept.[3]

The Hebrew text is confused and in places inconsistent, and minor amendments may be introduced from the Versions and the parallel text of Esdr. 1:1–22. They do not, however, affect the main lines of the description of the Passover ceremonies.[6]

A comparison of the description of Josiah's reforms in 2 Kings 22–23 and that of 2 Chr. 34 shows wide divergencies.[7] It is, on the other hand, difficult to compare the two accounts of Josiah's Passover in 2 Kings 23:21–23 and 2 Chr. 35:1–19, since the former is extremely brief and the latter is unclear at certain points. The two accounts have two features in common—in both the festival is celebrated by order of the king and in both it is held at Jerusalem. At other points they diverge—in 2 Kings 23 the celebration of the Passover is said to go back to the time of the Judges, in 2 Chr. 35, more explicitly, to the time of Samuel; in the former, this Passover is the outcome of the discovery of the 'Book of the Law', in the latter it is not said to have direct connexion with that event. The historicity of 2 Kings 23 is fairly certain; that of 2 Chr. 35 is open to grave doubt.

The narrative of 2 Chr. 35 is suspect because it bears close resemblance in points of detail to the account of the Passover in Ezra 6, rather than to the account in 2 Kings 23. In both 2 Chr. 35 and Ezra 6 the Pesaḥ is essentially a Temple ceremony; it requires ritual cleanness,[8] and must be carried out with punctilious care. The following seven days, the Passover

[1] One Heb. manuscript, Versions, and Esdr. 1:5 have pl., 'seers'.

[2] LXX inserts 'and the princes', Heb. והשרים, before 'and the porters', והשערים.

[3] Heb. *'śh pesaḥ.* [4] Heb. *'oloth.* [5] Heb. *ḥag haMaṣṣoth.*

[6] See the usual Commentaries and the bibliography in Snaith, op. cit. 107 ff.; of special relevance are A. C. Welch, *Work of the Chronicler*, 1939, 135, 139 ff., and Hänel, op. cit. 46. For studies on Esdras, see p. 11 n. 1 above.

[7] The account of the reforms in 2 Chr. 34:3–7 (which is much briefer than the corresponding 2 Kings 23:4–20) is followed by the finding of the 'Book of the Law' only six years later (2 Chr. 34:8, 14 ff.), by the covenant (34:29 ff.), and by the removal of 'all the abominations out of all the countries that pertained to the children of Israel' (34:33). In 2 Kings 22–23, on the other hand, it is the finding of the 'Book of the Law' (22:8 ff.) that leads to the covenant (23:3) and the religious reforms (23:4–20) and is finally confirmed by the Passover (23:21 ff.). The references to North Israel are broader in 2 Chr. 34:6–7, 9, 33 and 35:17a, 18b than in 2 Kings 23:4 f., 15–20.

[8] But in Ezra 6:20 the verb is *ṭhr*, in 2 Chr. 35:6 it is *qdš*; see p. 226 and n. 8 below.

week, are, however, merely accorded a cursory remark.[1] Like Ezra 6, 2 Chr. 35 shows a preference for Levites.[2] Here too it is the Levites who kill and flay all the Pesaḥ victims[3]—but the reason does not, according to our extant M.T., lie in the uncleanness of the laymen; it is regarded rather as normal Temple procedure. It is nevertheless implicitly acknowledged that the Levites are acting formally as representatives of the laity. The Levites are instructed to prepare themselves after their fathers' houses by their courses, and they officiate 'according to the divisions of the fathers' houses of . . . the children of the people'.[4] The meal which followed is also to be consumed according to the same unit.[5]

2 Chr. 35 presents us with an insight into Pesaḥ ceremonial at, presumably, the time of the Chronicler. The victims are from the lambs and kids,[6] they are roasted, and they are consumed by all classes of the people—priest, Levite, and layman—according to household units. The sacrifices take place apparently in the evening, the meal at night. The priests are busied in receiving and pouring out the sacrificial blood and burning the fat parts of the victims. The Levites perform the killing and flaying of the victims, and prepare the meals for themselves and the priests; groups of Levites act as musicians[7] and others as gate-keepers.[8] The laity do no more than consume the Pesaḥ meal and keep the festal week that followed.

Side by side with the Pesaḥ victims are two other categories of sacrificial animals. The 'holy offerings' are prepared by the Levites—from the cattle, not from the small animals,[9] and they are boiled, not roasted like the Pesaḥ victims. They are eaten by all the people. These additional sacrifices will be discussed briefly later.[10] Here we may note that the allusions to the 'holy offerings' provide the writer of 2 Chr. 35 with a means of reconciling discrepancies between the text of Deut. 16 and that of Ex. 12. The latter restricts the Pesaḥ victims to the lambs and kids, the former admits also cattle; the latter limits the treatment of the Pesaḥ victim to roasting, the former uses the term *bšl* which, at any rate at the time of 2 Chr. 35, had come to imply boiling.[11] In these and other respects the writer of 2 Chr. 35 adheres strictly to the Pesaḥ procedure of Ex. 12—his adoption of the

[1] 2 Chr. 35:17.

[2] The priests have to be 'encouraged' to take part in the Pesaḥ, 35:2; the Levites, however, are the 'teachers', 35:3 (but see, on this verse, p. 12 n. 12 above).

[3] The Levites are probably the subject of 'they killed', 35:11, cf. 35:6.

[4] 35:4–5.

[5] 35:12–13.

[6] This emerges more clearly from the M.T. of 35:7–9 than from the R.V.

[7] Cf. 1 Chr. 6:16, 16:4, 41, 23:25 ff., 2 Chr. 29:26, &c.

[8] On the opening of the Temple gates at the Pesaḥ, see p. 256 below.

[9] By implication, 2 Chr. 35:7–9; see p. 227 below. In 29:33 they are taken from both categories of animals, and are distinguished from the *'olah*; but this passage belongs to the same hand as 2 Chr. 30, which is not that of 2 Chr. 34–35. See pp. 19 and 228 ff. below.

[10] p. 227 below.

[11] The full term was *bšl bamayim*. On the apparent discrepancies between Ex. 12 and Deut. 16, see p. 204 below.

peculiar phrase *bšl ba'eš* makes this particularly clear—and he regards the regulations of Deut. 16 as applicable to the complementary 'holy offerings', not to the Pesaḥ victim.

More obscure are burnt offerings at the Passover of 2 Chr. 35.[1] They are, as we shall see, probably no more than the product of the Chronicler's imagination.[2]

VIII

According to the Chronicler, Hezekiah not only carried out religious reforms in Judah;[3] he also, like Josiah three generations later,[4] extended his reforms to North Israel. The Chronicler credits him further with having made partially successful overtures to the northern population to join in a formal celebration of the Passover at Jerusalem, 2 Chr. 30:1–27:

And Hezekiah sent to all Israel and Judah, and wrote letters also to Ephraim and Manasseh, that they should come to the house of the Lord at Jerusalem, to keep the passover[5] unto the Lord, the God of Israel. (2) For the king had taken counsel, and his princes, and all the congregation[6] in Jerusalem, to keep the passover[5] in the second month.[7] (3) For they could not keep it[5, 8] at that time,[9] because the priests had not sanctified themselves[10] in sufficient number, neither had the people gathered themselves together to Jerusalem. (4) And the thing was right in the eyes of the king and of all the congregation. (5) So they established a decree to make proclamation throughout all Israel, from Beer-sheba even to Dan,[11] that they should come to keep the passover[5] unto the Lord, the God of Israel, at Jerusalem: for they had not kept it in great numbers[12] in such sort as it is written.

(6) So the posts went with the letters from the king and his princes throughout all Israel and Judah, and[13] according to the commandment of the king, saying, Ye children of Israel, turn again unto the Lord, the God of Abraham, Isaac, and Israel, that he may return to the remnant that are escaped of you out of the hand of the kings of Assyria. (7) And be not like your fathers, and like your brethren, which trespassed against the Lord, the God of their fathers, so that he gave them up to desolation, as ye see. (8) Now be ye not stiffnecked, as your fathers were; but yield yourselves unto the Lord, and enter into his sanctuary, which he hath sanctified[10] for ever, and serve the Lord your God, that his fierce anger may turn away from you. (9) For if ye turn again unto the Lord, your brethren and your

[1] 2 Chr. 35:12, 14, 16; the priests received them from the Levites; cf. Hänel, op. cit. 51.

[2] See p. 227 below.

[3] Cf. 2 Kings 18:3–7, where Hezekiah's reforms are described very briefly.

[4] pp. 5 and 12 above. The parallel between the two kings is already suggested in 2 Kings. Hezekiah mourns and sends to the prophet Isaiah (2 Kings 19:1 ff.), Josiah sends to the prophetess Huldah (2 Kings 22:11 ff.), although the cause is not the same in both cases. Both Hezekiah and Josiah are compared to David, 2 Kings 18:3b, 22:2b.

[5] Heb. *'śh pesaḥ*.

[6] Heb. *qahal*.

[7] Targ. 'in the month of Iyyar, that is the second month'.

[8] Rudolph inserts בְּעִתּוֹ or לְעִתּוֹ, which may have been omitted through haplography.

[9] Targ. 'to make the Pesaḥ in Nisan'.

[10] Heb. *qdš*.

[11] Targ. 'and even to Apamea'!

[12] The Heb. could also be rendered 'for a long time'; the R.V. is to be preferred.

[13] Omit, with some manuscripts, Greek and Latin Versions.

children shall find compassion before them that led them captive, and shall come again into this land: for the Lord your God is gracious and merciful, and will not turn away his face[1] from you, if ye return unto him. (10) So the posts passed from city to city through the country of Ephraim and Manasseh, even unto Zebulun: but they laughed them to scorn, and mocked them. (11) Nevertheless divers of Asher[2] and Manasseh and of Zebulun humbled themselves, and came to Jerusalem. (12) Also in Judah[3] was the hand of God to give them one heart, to do the commandment of the king and of the princes by the word of the Lord.

(13) And there assembled at Jerusalem much people to keep the feast of unleavened bread[4] in the second month, a very great congregation.[5] (14) And they arose and took away the altars that were in Jerusalem, and all the altars for incense took they away, and cast them into the brook Kidron. (15) Then they killed the passover[6] on the fourteenth (day) of the second month: and the priests and the Levites[7] were ashamed, and sanctified themselves,[8] and brought burnt offerings[9] into the house of the Lord. (16) And they stood in their place after their order,[10] according to the law of Moses the man of God: the priests sprinkled[11] the blood, (which they received) of the hand of the Levites.[12] (17) For there were many in the congregation[5] that had not sanctified themselves:[8] therefore the Levites had the charge of killing the passovers[6] for every one that was not clean,[13] to sanctify them[8] unto the Lord. (18) For a multitude of the people, even many[14] of Ephraim and Manasseh, Issachar and Zebulun, had not cleansed themselves,[13] yet did they eat the passover[15] otherwise than it is written. For Hezekiah had prayed for them, saying, The good Lord[16] pardon[17] every one[18] (19) that setteth his heart to seek God, the Lord, the God of his fathers, though (he be) not (cleansed) according to the purification of the sanctuary.[19] (20) And the Lord hearkened to Hezekiah, and healed the people.

(21) And the children of Israel that were present at Jerusalem kept the feast of unleavened bread[20] seven days with great gladness: and the Levites and the priests praised[21] the Lord day by day, (singing) with loud instruments[22] unto the Lord. (22) And Hezekiah spake comfortably unto all the Levites that were well skilled (in the service) of the Lord. So they did eat throughout the feast[23]

[1] Heb. lit. 'turn a face'; Rudolph reads פניו for M.T. פנים.
[2] But 'Issachar' in 2 Chr. 30:18.
[3] LXX attaches these words to the previous verse.
[4] Heb. *ḥag haMaṣṣoth.*
[5] Heb. *qahal.*
[6] Heb. *šḥṭ pesaḥ.*
[7] Rudolph omits 'and' before 'the Levites'; cf. p. 12 n. 2 above.
[8] Heb. *qdš.*
[9] Heb. *'oloth.*
[10] ויעמדו על־עמדם כמשפטם.
[11] Better 'poured, threw'.
[12] LXX and Pesh. 'the priests received the blood from the hands of the Levites'.
[13] Heb. *ṭhr.*
[14] M.T. רבת; Curtis omits as a dittograph of מרבי״ת.
[15] Heb. *'kl . . . pesaḥ.*
[16] The Heb. phrase occurs nowhere else and is dubious.
[17] Heb. *kpr.*
[18] R.V., following LXX and Vulg., joins to the next verse, and so most commentators.
[19] ולא כטהרת הקדש.
[20] Heb. *'śh ḥag haMaṣṣoth.*
[21] Heb. *hll.*
[22] בכלי עז; Targ. has 'with instruments of praise', Pesh. 'with praises of their mouth'. Perhaps read, with most commentators, בכל עז, 'with all their might', as 1 Chr. 13:8.
[23] R.V. 'throughout' is not in the M.T. ויאכלו את המועד; perhaps render 'so they did eat (the offerings of) the appointed time', after Targ. which has 'and they did eat the sacrifices of the holy offerings (*qudšayya*) of the appointed times'. Greek Versions have 'and they completed', Heb. וַיְכַלּוּ; and this reading is adopted by Rudolph and others.

for the seven days, offering sacrifices of peace offerings, and making confession[1] to the Lord, the God of their fathers. (23) And the whole congregation[2] took counsel to keep other seven days: and they kept (other) seven days with gladness. (24) For Hezekiah king of Judah did give to the congregation[2] for offerings a thousand bullocks and seven thousand sheep; and the princes gave to the congregation[2] a thousand bullocks and ten thousand sheep: and a great number of priests sanctified themselves.[3] (25) And all the congregation[2] of Judah, with the priests and the Levites, and all the congregation[2] that came out of Israel, and that dwelt in Judah, rejoiced. (26) So there was great joy in Jerusalem: for since the time of Solomon the son of David king of Israel there was not the like in Jerusalem. (27) Then the priests the Levites[4] arose and blessed the people: and their voice was heard, and their prayer came up to his holy habitation, even unto heaven.[5]

The wording of 2 Chr. 30 is confused; since an original text cannot be restored with certainty, our discussion must be confined to the extant text. The style is similar to that of 2 Chr. 35, but the writer (as we shall see later) is probably not the same. Like 2 Chr. 35, 2 Chr. 30 lays stress on the celebration of the Passover by royal decree at Jerusalem and on the maintenance of ritual cleanness.[6] In 2 Chr. 30, however, the Passover is the climax of the cleansing and rededication of the Temple,[7] rather than the cleansing of the whole country.[8] Jerusalem and its shrine are, it is held, the centre of Israelite religion in northern, as well as southern, Palestine.

It is certainly possible—even likely—that Hezekiah observed the Passover, but no special celebration of the festival is alluded to in the account of Hezekiah's reign in 2 Kings 18–20. Indeed, it is excluded by the words not only of 2 Kings 23:22, but also of the parallel passage in 2 Chr. 35:18.[9] It is unlikely (though not impossible) that Hezekiah made overtures to the people of Samaria in the first year of his reign,[10] since Samaria had fallen probably only a few years previously, and he would have drawn upon himself the wrath of its conqueror.[11] This account of a special observance of the

[1] This may also be rendered 'giving thanks'. Cf. Neh. 9:3.

[2] Heb. *qahal*.

[3] Heb. *qdš*.

[4] Several manuscripts and Versions insert 'and' before 'the Levites'; see p. 12 n. 2 above on Ezekiel. Here it is better to retain the M.T., since only the priests had the right to bless the people.

[5] For Commentaries, see p. 14 n. 6 above.

[6] See pp. 228 ff. below. In 2 Chr. 30:15 the act of ritual purification by the priests is confirmed by the sacrifice of burnt offerings.

[7] After the acts of Ahaz, 2 Chr. 28:1–4, 22–25, cf. 2 Kings 16:2–4, 10–18. The Chronicler here refuses to admit that the Temple had been polluted; it was only, he maintains, shut up (2 Chr. 29:6 f.). The sanctification of the Temple began on the first day of the first month, and was carried out in time-units of eight days (29:17); the offerings were *'olah* and *ḥaṭṭa'th* (29:20 ff.), and then the people brought *todoth* (29:31, 35), *šelamim* (29:33, 35), and *'oloth* (29:31 f., 34 f.).

[8] Compare 2 Chr. 29 before the Passover of Hezekiah and 2 Chr. 31 after it, with 2 Chr. 34 before the Passover of Josiah.

[9] Rudolph, op. cit., in loc., suggests that 2 Chr. 30:26 does not contradict 2 Chr. 35:18 because the former alludes only to the joy of the occasion. The suggestion has little to commend it.

[10] 2 Chr. 29:3, 17, 30:1–11, 18.

[11] See p. 228 below.

Passover by Hezekiah can scarcely, then, be historical. It may have been inspired by the tradition of his piety, for his trust in the Lord surpassed, we are told, that of all the kings of Judah after him as before him.[1] And, indeed, history may have been held to have proved his merit as greater than the merit of Josiah; Josiah was slain in battle, but Hezekiah died a natural death. But it is probable that the attribution of a special Passover to Hezekiah was derived from political and religious considerations; it was desired to show that the central shrine of Jerusalem was revered by the northern as well as the southern tribes even in the first years after the destruction of Samaria.

There are grounds for believing that 2 Chr. 30 was written after 2 Chr. 35. 2 Chr. 30 appears to attempt deliberately to outdo the Passover of 2 Chr. 35 by adding a further seven days of festival.[2] In other details of procedure, 2 Chr. 30 conforms more closely than 2 Chr. 35 to the practice of later times. Both passages show preference for Levites over priests.[3] But in 2 Chr. 30 it is the laymen who take the initiative in celebrating the Passover. It is the laymen, too, who slaughter the Pesaḥ victims;[4] the Levites slay the victims only for those persons who are not ritually clean—as in Ezra 6 where all the laymen were perhaps unclean.[5] All the blood is carried by the Levites, and poured away at the altar by the priests, as in 2 Chr. 35. Other features of 2 Chr. 30, however, appear for the first time in the Historical Documents. The term *ḥag haMaṣṣoth* is used interchangeably with 'Pesaḥ' as the title of the festival. The term *hillel* is employed of the ceremonial singing by Levites during the Passover week;[6] and we are told that during the seven days peace offerings were sacrificed. We have, too, an apparent allusion to the public blessing of the congregation by the priests. All this was the accepted practice in later times.

IX

The Book of Jubilees is generally held to have been composed shortly

[1] 2 Kings 18:5.

[2] This is probably based on 1 Kings 8:56; cf. 2 Chr. 30:26. The Chronicler has, however, misinterpreted the passage in 1 Kings. See p. 229 below.

[3] See p. 15 above. See also 1 Chr. 23:24 ff. Cf. 2 Chr. 29:34, and note the perfunctory self-purification of the priests in 30:15. The categories of priests and Levites are apparently combined in 30:27, cf. the suggested reading in 30:15, p. 17 above. In 2 Chr. 29, on the other hand, the role of the Levites is confined to making music (vv. 25 ff.). In 29:31 ff. the disposal of the blood and the burning of the fat were the concern of the priests; the Levites assisted in the flaying. The text may, however, be at fault.

[4] So in 2 Chr. 29:22 Hezekiah and the princes slay all the sacrificial victims except the goats for the sin offerings; in the case of the latter they perform a symbolic laying-on of hands, while the actual slaughter is carried out by the priests (29:23–24). In 29:31 ff. the sacrificers are evidently laymen. On the text of 2 Chr. 29:20 ff. and on the relation between priests and Levites, see Hänel, op. cit. 46 ff.

[5] Cf. p. 12 above. In 2 Chr. 30, as in Ezra 6 and 2 Chr. 35, all those present, whether ritually clean or not, are permitted to partake of the Pesaḥ meal.

[6] 2 Chr. 30:21.

before 105 B.C.[1] The central formula around which the book is woven, and from which it receives its name, is the era of the jubilee of years; and each year is itself a multiple of seven—364 days or fifty-two weeks. The author sets the history of Israel, from the Creation to the Exodus, within this pattern. His use of a schematic 'solar' year shows him to have been a member of a heterodox sect.[2]

The Book of Jubilees has, curiously, not one, but two accounts of the Exodus from Egypt. The first, ch. 48, is inserted in the framework of the Jubilees chronology—but it contains no allusion to the Passover. The second, ch. 49, which alone concerns us here, seems to be independent of the preceding chapter. It is not related to the Jubilees era.[3] It gives a detailed description of the Passover traditions and practices in, we may presume, the latter half of the second century B.C.

(1) Remember the commandment which the Lord commanded thee concerning the passover, that thou shouldst celebrate it in its season on the fourteenth of the first month, that thou shouldst kill it before it is evening, and that they should eat it by night on the evening of the fifteenth from the time of the setting of the sun. (2) For on this night—the beginning of the festival and the beginning of the joy—ye were eating the passover in Egypt, when all the powers of Masṭema had been let loose to slay all the firstborn in the land of Egypt, from the firstborn of Pharaoh to the firstborn of the captive maid-servant in the mill, and to the cattle. (3) And this is the sign which the Lord gave them: Into every house on the lintels of which they saw the blood of a lamb[4] of the first year, into (that) house they should not enter to slay, but should pass by (it), that all those should be saved that were in the house because the sign of the blood was on its lintels.

[1] Except ch. 23. On the date of Jubilees, see R. H. Charles, op. cit. ii. 6; S. Klein, 'Palästinisches im Jubiläenbuch', *ZDPV* lvii, 1934, 16; L. Finkelstein, 'Pre-Maccabean Documents in the Passover Haggadah', iii, Appendix, *HTR* xxxvi, 1943, 19; Rowley, *Relevance of Apocalyptic*, 1944, 81; Rowley and S. Zeitlin, 'Criteria for the Dating of Jubilees', *JQR* xxxvi, 1945–6, 183, 187; Zeitlin, 'Apocrypha', ibid. xxxvii, 1946–7, 226; O. Eissfeldt, *Einleitung in das Alte Testament*, 1956, 749 ff.; and A. Jaubert, *Date de la Cène*, 1957, 139. The Ethiopic text is edited in Charles, *Ethiopic Version of the Hebrew Book of Jubilees*, 1895, and trans. E. Littmann, 'Buch der Jubiläen', in E. Kautzsch, *Apokryphen und Pseudepigraphen des Alten Testaments*, 1900, ii. 31; the Latin text is edited in H. Rönsch, *Buch der Jubiläen*, 1874. Fragments in Hebrew discovered near Qumran are listed by C. Burchard, *Bibliographie zu den Handschriften vom Toten Meer*, 1957, while Syriac fragments are published by E. Tisserant, 'Fragments syriaques du Livre des Jubilés', *RB* xxx, 1921, 55, 206. Chapters 48 and 49 have not so far been found in languages other than Latin and Ethiopic.

[2] For studies in the Jubilees calendar, see in particular Jaubert, op. cit., and id., 'Calendrier des Jubilés . . .', *VT* iii, 1953, 250, and 'Calendrier des Jubilés et les jours liturgiques de la semaine', *VT* vii, 1957, 35; see also J. Morgenstern, 'Calendar of the Book of Jubilees, its Origin and its Character', *VT* v, 1955, 34, and E. Kutsch, 'Kalender des Jubiläenbuches und das Alte und das Neue Testament', *VT* xi, 1961, 39. The suggestion of E. R. Leach, 'A possible method of intercalation for the calendar of the Book of Jubilees', *VT* vii, 1957, 392, that an intercalary period of seven days was inserted in the Jubilees calendar, and that sometimes this was extended to seventeen days, cannot be accepted. After the insertion of the longer period the days of the festivals would no longer fall uniformly on the same day of the week—a feature that scholars have rightly recognized as fundamental to the Jubilees calendar.

[3] See pp. 234 ff. below, where I discuss the relationship between Jub. 48 and 49.

[4] Better 'small animal', Eth. *bg'*, i.e. Heb. *śeh*.

(4) And the powers of the Lord did everything according as the Lord commanded them, and they passed by all the children of Israel, and the plague came not upon them to destroy from amongst them any soul either of cattle, or man, or dog. (5) And the plague was very grievous in Egypt, and there was no house in Egypt where there was not one dead, and weeping and lamentation. (6) And all Israel was eating the flesh of the paschal lamb,[1] and drinking the wine, and was lauding and blessing, and giving thanks to the Lord God of their fathers, and was ready to go forth from under the yoke of Egypt, and from the evil bondage.

(7) And remember thou this day all the days of thy life, and observe it from year to year all the days of thy life, once a year, on its day, according to all the law thereof, and do not adjourn[2] (it) from day to day, or from month to month. (8) For it is an eternal ordinance, and engraven on the heavenly tablets regarding all[3] the children of Israel that they should observe[4] it every year on its day once a year, throughout all their generations; and there is no limit of days, for this is ordained for ever. (9) And the man who is free from uncleanness, and does not come to observe[4] it on the occasion of its day, so as to bring an acceptable offering before the Lord, and to eat and to drink before the Lord on the day of its festival, that man who is clean and close at hand shall be cut off: because he offered not the oblation of the Lord in its appointed season, he shall take the guilt upon himself. (10) Let the children of Israel come and observe the passover[4] on the day of its fixed time, on the fourteenth day of the first month, between the evenings,[5] from the third part of the day to the third part of the night, for two portions of the day are given to the light, and a third part to the evening. (11) This is that which the Lord commanded thee that thou shouldst observe it between the evenings. (12) And it is not permissible to slay it during any period of the light, but during the period bordering on the evening, and let them eat it at the time of the evening until the third part of the night, and whatever is left over of all its flesh from the third part of the night and onwards, let them burn it with fire. (13) And they shall not cook it with water, nor shall they eat it raw, but roast with fire: they shall eat it[6] with diligence,[7] its head with the inwards thereof and its feet they shall roast with fire, and not break any bone thereof; for of the children of Israel no bone shall be crushed.[8] (14) For this reason the Lord commanded the children of Israel to observe the passover[4] on the day of its fixed time, and they shall not break a bone thereof; for it is a festival day, and a day commanded, and there may be no passing over from day to day, and month to month, but on the day of its festival let it be observed. (15) And do thou command the children of Israel to observe the passover[4] throughout their days, every year, once a year on the day of its fixed time, and it shall come for a memorial[9] well pleasing before the Lord, and no plague shall come upon them to slay or to smite in that year in which they celebrate the passover[4] in its season in every respect according to His command.

(16) And they shall not eat it outside the sanctuary of the Lord, but before the sanctuary of the Lord, and all the people of the congregation of Israel shall celebrate it in its appointed season. (17) And every man who has come upon[10] its

[1] Better 'passover offerings'. [2] Eth. *ḫlf*. [3] See Charles, op. cit., in loc.
[4] Lit. 'make (the passover)'. [5] Lat. 'towards evening'; Eth. 'between the evenings'.
[6] So Charles, op. cit., in loc.
[7] Eth. *ba'astaḥamәmo*, which implies mingled care and passion; the meaning is close to that of 'haste' in v. 23.
[8] Lat. 'there will be no disaster among the children of Israel on this day'.
[9] Lat. 'for a testimony'. [10] Lat. *omnis homo in visitatione*.

day shall eat it in the sanctuary of your God before the Lord from twenty years old and upward; for thus is it written and ordained that they should eat it in the sanctuary of the Lord. (18) And when the children of Israel come into the land which they are to possess, into the land of Canaan, and set up the tabernacle of the Lord in the midst of the land in one of their tribes until the sanctuary of the Lord has been built in the land, let them come and celebrate the passover[1] in the midst of the tabernacle of the Lord, and let them slay it before the Lord from year to year. (19) And in the days when the house has been built in the name of the Lord in the land of their inheritance, they shall go there and slay the passover in the evening, at sunset, at the third part of the day. (20) And they shall offer its blood on the threshold of the altar, and shall place its fat on the fire which is upon the altar, and they shall eat its flesh roasted with fire in the court of the house which has been sanctified in the name of the Lord. (21) And they may not celebrate the passover[1] in their cities, nor in any place save before the tabernacle of the Lord, or before His house where His name hath dwelt; and they shall not go astray from the Lord.

(22) And do thou, Moses, command the children of Israel to observe the ordinances of the passover, as it was commanded unto thee; declare thou unto them every year and the day of its days, and[2] the festival of unleavened bread, that they should eat unleavened bread seven days, (and) that they should observe its festival, and that they bring an oblation every day during those seven days of joy before the Lord on the altar of your God. (23) For ye celebrated this festival with haste[3] when ye went forth from Egypt till ye entered into the wilderness of Shur; for on the shore of the sea ye completed it.[4]

Although this account is found in the work of a heterodox sect, it shows greater dependence on the Traditional Documents than any previous Historical Document.[5] The chapter falls into two parts, the second part having three sections. In the first part[6] the legend of the Exodus is briefly recounted in accordance with the story of Ex. 12. Certain features are omitted, notably the special dress of the celebrants, and the eating of bitter herbs and *maṣṣoth* at the Pesaḥ. On the other hand, wine appears for the first time as an accompaniment of the meal,[7] and there may be an oblique reference to the psalmody already mentioned by the Chronicler.[8] Care is taken to avoid anthropomorphism.[9]

The second part of Jub. 49 consists of instructions for the observance of the Passover after the Exodus.[10] Here two regulations distinguish the scheme of Jubilees from that of earlier documents. One is the sharper definition of the time of the Pesaḥ sacrifice and the meal which follows.[11] The second is

[1] Lit. 'make the passover'.
[2] Lat. 'during its days' for 'and the day of its days, and'.
[3] Eth. *bawəlwale,* as in Eth. at Ex. 12:11.
[4] The translation follows that of Charles, op. cit.
[5] But see p. 15 above on 2 Chr. 35.
[6] Jub. 49:2–6.
[7] 49:6, cf. 'eat and drink', v. 9. See pp. 231 f. and 233 below.
[8] 49:6.
[9] 49:2, 'the powers of Masṭema' are controlled by the Lord; cf. the 'destroyer' in Ex. 12:13, 23, 'Satan', 1 Chr. 21:1 opp. 2 Sam. 24:1. See also 'powers of the Lord', Jub. 49:4.
[10] 49:1, 7–15.
[11] 49:11 shows that vv. 10–13 are introduced as a deliberate explanation of 'between the

the appearance of an apotropaic element—not only must the victim's bones not be broken, but the whole ceremony must be properly performed, if the ensuing year is to be free from misfortune.[1] As in Ezra with its emphasis on the joy of the Passover, so in Jubilees the festival seems to have become a less solemn affair.[2] The meal is to be eaten in haste.[3]

The second section of this part of Jub. 49[4] stresses the injunction that the Pesaḥ is to be carried out at a shrine—in early times at the Tabernacle, subsequently at the Temple when that had been built and dedicated. Every male Israelite of twenty years and over must perform this obligation.[5] The treatment of the blood and fat of the Pesaḥ victim is the same as that of normal sacrifices at the Temple;[6] the meal is to be eaten in the Temple court.[7]

The last section mentions briefly the daily offerings during the Passover week.[8] The brevity with which these sacrifices are prescribed is perhaps an indication that the chapter is addressed to laymen. We observe that there is no regulation in Jubilees about subsidiary offerings at the Pesaḥ itself—a remarkable contrast to the accounts of 2 Chr. 35 and 30. Jub. 49 cites directly from Num. 9,[9] and was presumably familiar with that text, yet it contains no allusion to the 'Second Pesaḥ'.[10]

X

Contemporary, or nearly contemporary, with the writer of Jubilees was Ezekielos, a Jewish dramatist who composed a tragedy in Greek on the theme of the Exodus.[11] Fragments have been preserved by Christian writers by whom they were derived through Alexander Polyhistor; and among them are some verses on the Passover:[12]

And thou[13] shalt say to all the Hebrews together, This month is the first of the year for you: it is in this (month) that I shall lead the people to another land which I have promised to the ancestors of the Hebrew race. And thou shalt say to all the people, At the full moon[14] of the month of which I speak, having sacrificed the Pesaḥ[15] to God on the preceding night, they will touch the doors with blood, so that the terrible angel will pass by[16] the sign. You on the night will consume the

(two) evenings', Ex. 12:6, &c.; see p. 131 below. Jubilees divides the day and night into three watches each; see below, p. 233.

1 Jub. 49:13–15.

2 'Joy', 49:2, 22, 'eat and drink', v. 9.

3 49:23, cf. v. 13 and p. 21 n. 7 above. The regulations on the special dress are omitted. As in the Chronicler, the Pesaḥ victims are called *pesaḥim*.

4 49:16–21.

5 49:17.

6 The ritual smearing of the sacrificial blood is discontinued, as in the Chronicler—a contrast not only to the Exodus legend of Ex. 12 but also to the legend of the first part of Jub. 49 itself (see 49:3). Instead the second part of Jub. 49, like the Chronicler, prescribes that the blood must be poured away at the altar, and the fat burned.

7 49:20.

8 49:22–23.

9 49:7 ff.

10 See pp. 59 and 199 below.

11 I. Trencsényi-Waldapfel, 'Tragédie grecque à sujet biblique', *Acta Orientalia Academiae Scientiarum Hungaricae*, ii, 1952, 148, suggests that Ezekielos flourished about 90 B.C.

12 Trencsényi-Waldapfel, op. cit., points out, however, that the parts of Ezekielos's tragedy which must have described the actual preparations for the Exodus Passover and the observance of that Passover are missing.

13 God is addressing Moses.

14 K. Kuiper, 'Poète juif Ezéchiel', *REJ* xlvi, 1903, 65, translates incorrectly 'new moon'.

15 τὸ Πάσχα.

16 παρέλθῃ.

roasted flesh. But the king will expel the people together in haste. And when you will be on the point of fleeing, I shall give favour to the people, and one woman will receive from (another) woman vessels and all the ornaments that a person bears, gold and silver and garments, so that they pay recompense to mortals for that which they have done. . . .

But when you enter (your) own country . . .[1] from the day that you fled from Egypt . . ., journeying on the way for seven days, so many days in each year shall you eat unleavened bread, and shall serve God, sacrificing to God the firstborn[2] of animals, all the male offspring that young females bear for the first time, that open the mother's womb. . . . On the tenth day of that month take thou from each family of Hebrew men small animals and the calves of cattle,[3] unblemished. And let them be kept until the fourteenth day is bright; then sacrificing them towards evening (you will eat them) all roast, together with (their) entrails. Thus shall you eat them—girt about, with boots[4] bound on (your) feet, and holding a staff in (your) hands. For in haste will the king give order to expel (you) all from the country, and each man will be called. And when you sacrifice you must take in (your) hands a bunch of hyssop leaves, and dip (it) into the blood, and lightly touch[5] the two (door)posts, that death may pass over[6] the Hebrews. This festival shall you observe to the Lord, seven days unleavened bread, and no leaven shall be eaten. For it is the release[7] of those evils, and in that month God grants the going-forth, and this is the beginning of months and of times.[8]

These verses for the most part follow slavishly—though with some omissions[9]—the texts of the Traditional Documents on the Passover which Ezekielos evidently knew through the LXX. Like the passage in Jubilees, the verses of Ezekielos on the Passover fall broadly into two parts; the first part gives the events of the Exodus Pesaḥ, the second gives the regulations for subsequent celebrations of the festival. Allowance must be made for the licence of the poetaster, and one must not press too closely those points in which Ezekielos differs from other Historical Documents. His audience or readers probably included non-Jews who were not greatly interested in the accuracy of these details; he was not instructing Jews in the laws of the Passover. Two features should be noted. First, Ezekielos follows the text of

[1] The text (Gr. ὅπως) seems to be corrupt.

[2] The text has πρωτότευκτα; the variant πρωτότοκα is to be preferred.

[3] πρόβατα καὶ μόσχους βοῶν.

[4] κοῖλα, lit. 'hollow', boots reaching half-way up the leg; see Kuiper, op. cit., in loc. (on v. 181).

[5] This corresponds exactly to Heb. הגיע, Ex. 12:22, see pp. 53 and 159 below.

[6] παρέλθῃ.

[7] ἀπαλλαγή, but see Kuiper, op. cit., in loc. (on v. 190), on this word.

[8] For the text, see Eusebius, *Praeparatio evang.* ix, ch. 29 (Migne, *Patrologia Graeca*, xxi, col. 744); Kuiper, op. cit. 64; and id., 'Ad Ezechielem Poetam Judaeum curae secundae', *Rivista di Storia antica*, viii, 1904, 62. See also Clemens Alexandrinus, *Strom.* i, ch. 23 (Migne, *P.G.* viii, col. 901), and the discussion in Dieterich, art. 'Ezekielos', Pauly–Wissowa, *Realenc.*; A. Kappelmacher, 'Zur Tragödie der hellenistischen Zeit', *Wiener Studien. Zeitschrift für klassische Philologie*, xliv, 1924–5, 69; and Trencsényi-Waldapfel, op. cit. The other literature cited by the last-named has not been available to me.

[9] Notably the eating of bitter herbs at the Pesaḥ meal, the law on circumcision as a prerequisite for the Pesaḥ, and the celebration of the rites according to family units.

Deut. 16 in permitting the Pesaḥ victims to be taken from the herds as well as the flocks.[1] In the second place, the sacrifice of firstlings is, according to Ezekielos, to be performed during the Passover week. The firstlings are, however, not identified with the Pesaḥ victims.

It is generally held that Ezekielos was a resident of Alexandria.[2] Kuiper, however, maintains, on grounds not connected with these extracts on the Passover, that he was a native of Samaria.[3] In support of this view it may be observed that Ezekielos appears to regard the ordinances on the selection of the Pesaḥ victim on the tenth day, the ceremony of the smearing of the blood of the Pesaḥ victim, and the special dress as binding not only at the Exodus but also on later generations. This was also the opinion and the practice of the Samaritans in later times but not of the Jews. Nevertheless, for reasons which are given later, it may be doubted whether the practices of the modern Samaritans are admissible as evidence for Samaritan practices in the first century B.C.[4]

XI

Belonging to the same period as the work of Ezekielos—but perhaps somewhat later—are two possible allusions to the Passover in the Wisdom of Solomon:[5]

A. 10:18–20. (Wisdom) brought them over the Red Sea, and led them through much water; (19) but their enemies she drowned, and out of the bottom of the deep she cast them up. (20) Therefore the righteous spoiled the ungodly; and they sang praise to thy holy name, O Lord, and extolled with one accord thy hand that fought for them. . . .

B. 18:8–9. For as thou didst take vengeance on the adversaries, by the same act thou didst glorify us, and call us unto thyself. (9) For holy children of good men offered sacrifice in secret,[6] and with one consent took upon themselves the covenant of the divine law, that the saints would partake alike in the same blessings and perils; singing the while the fathers' songs of praise.[7]

The writer may have been an Alexandrian Jew. The two passages belong

[1] He does not (like the writer of 2 Chr. 35) modify the rule to make it conform to what is likely to have been the practice in his own time. That Ezekielos knew the Bible through the text of LXX was long ago maintained by L. M. Philippson, *Ezechielos des jüdischen Trauerspieldichters Auszug aus Ägypten . . .*, 1830, 40.

[2] So Trencsényi-Waldapfel, op. cit. 160.

[3] Kuiper, *REJ* xlvi, 1903, 174 ff.; M. Gaster, *The Samaritans*, 1925, 143.

[4] See pp. 251 ff. below.

[5] S. Holmes, 'Wisdom of Solomon', in Charles, op. cit. i. 520, ascribes the work to a date between 50 B.C. and the first decade of the first century A.D.; C. C. Torrey, *Apocryphal Literature*, 1945, 102, prefers the last quarter of the second century B.C. as the date of the completed work.

[6] Gr. κρυφῇ. Has this notion of secrecy arisen from the description of the unleavened bread in Ex. 12:39 as ἐγκρυφίας ἀζύμους in LXX? See p. 28 n. 1 below on Philo.

[7] For Commentary, see Holmes, op. cit., and the brief analysis in Torrey, op. cit. See the bibliography in Eissfeldt, op. cit. 742 ff.; to the works mentioned there, should be added the edition of the Pesh. text (which contains several variants, none of importance) by J. A. Emerton, *Peshitta of the Wisdom of Solomon*, 1959.

to independent sections of the Wisdom of Solomon. The only Passover ritual to which they refer—the singing of hymns at the Pesaḥ—has already been observed in previous Historical Documents.[1]

XII

The works of Philo contain scattered references to the Passover. The central allusions are the following passages in his *De specialibus legibus*, ii. 144–75:

After the New Moon comes the fourth feast called the Crossing-feast,[2] which the Hebrews in their native tongue call Pascha. In this festival many myriads of victims from noon till eventide are offered by the whole people, old and young alike, raised for that particular day to the dignity of priesthood. For at other times the priests according to ordinances of the law carry out both the public sacrifices and those offered by private individuals. But on this occasion the whole nation performs the sacred rites and acts as priest with pure hands and complete immunity.[3] The reason for this is as follows: the festival is a reminder and thank offering for that migration from Egypt. . . .[4]

But to those who are accustomed to turn literal facts into allegory, the Crossing-feast[2] suggests the purification of the soul. They say that the lover of wisdom is occupied solely in crossing[5] from the body and the passions, each of which overwhelms him like a torrent, unless the rushing current be dammed and held back by the principles of virtue.[6] On this day every dwelling-house is invested with the outward semblance and dignity of a temple. The victim is then slaughtered and dressed for the festal meal which befits the occasion. The guests assembled for the banquet have been cleansed by purificatory lustrations, and are there not as in other festive gatherings, to indulge the belly with wine and viands, but to fulfil with prayers and hymns the custom handed down by their fathers. The day on which this national festivity occurs may very properly be noted. It is the fourteenth of the month,[7] a number formed of the sum of two sevens, thus bringing out the fact that seven never fails to appear in anything worthy of honour but everywhere takes the lead in conferring prestige and dignity.

With the Crossing-feast is combined one in which the food consumed is of a different and unfamiliar kind, namely, unleavened bread, which also gives its name to the feast. This may be regarded from two points of view, one peculiar to the nation, referring to the migration just mentioned, the other universal, following the lead of nature, and in agreement with the general cosmic order. . . . This month comes seventh in order and number as judged by the cycle of the sun, but in importance it is first, and therefore is described as first in the sacred books. The reason for this I believe to be as follows. In the spring equinox[8] we have a

[1] See pp. 15, 19, and 22 above.

[2] διαβατήρια, so also *De Vita Mosis*, ii. 224, &c., opp. διάβασις, 'the (abstract) act of passing over', *De migr. Abrah.* 25, &c.

[3] Cf. *De Vita Mosis*, loc. cit., *De Decalogo*, 159.

[4] Cf. *De Vita Mosis*, ii. 222 ff.

[5] διάβασις.

[6] Cf. *De Vita Mosis*, ii. 224, *De Congressu quaerendae eruditionis gratia*, 106.

[7] Cf. *De Vita Mosis*, loc. cit., '(a festival) about the fourteenth day when the disc of the moon is becoming full'.

[8] In *De Vita Mosis*, ii. 222, it is the Pesaḥ which is said to coincide with the spring equinox.

kind of likeness and portraiture of that first epoch in which this world was created. The elements were then separated and placed in harmonious order with reference to themselves and each other. The heaven was adorned with sun and moon and the rhythmical movements and circlings of the other stars, both fixed and planetary. So too the earth was adorned with every manner of plants, and the uplands and lowlands, wherever the soil had depth and goodness, became luxuriant and verdant. So every year God reminds us of the creation of the world by setting before our eyes the spring when everything blooms and flowers. And therefore there is good reason for describing it in the laws as the first month because in a sense it is an image of the primal origin reproduced from it like the imprint from an archetypal seal. . . .[1]

The feast begins at the middle of the month, on the fifteenth day, when the moon is full, a day purposely chosen because then there is no darkness, but everything is continuously lighted up as the sun shines from morning to evening and the moon from evening to morning, and while the stars give place to each other no shadow is cast upon their brightness.[2] Again, the feast is held for seven days to mark the precedence and honour which the number holds in the universe. . . .[3] Two days out of the seven, the first and the last, are declared holy. In this way (Moses) gave a natural precedence to the beginning and the end; but he also wished to create a harmony as in a musical instrument between the intermediates and the extremes. Perhaps too he wished to harmonize the feast with a past which adjoins the first day and a future which adjoins the last. These two, the first and the last, have each the other's properties in addition to their own. The first is the beginning of the feast and the end of the preceding past, the seventh is the end of the feast and the beginning of the coming future. . . .

The bread is unleavened either because our forefathers, when under divine guidance they were starting on their migration, were so intensely hurried that they brought the lumps of dough unleavened, or else because at that season, namely, the springtime, when the feast is held, the fruit of the corn has not reached its perfection, for the fields are in the ear stage and not yet mature for harvest. It was the imperfection of this fruit which belonged to the future, though it was to reach its perfection very shortly, that he considered to be paralleled by the unleavened food, which is also imperfect. . . . Another suggestion made by the interpreters of the holy scriptures is that food, when unleavened, is a gift of nature, when leavened is a work of art. . . . Since, then, the springtime feast, as I have laid down, is a reminder of the creation of the world, and its earliest inhabitants, children of earth in its first or second generation, must have used the gifts of the universe in their unperverted state before pleasure had got the mastery, he ordained for use on this occasion the food most fully in accordance with the season. He wished every year to rekindle the embers of the serious and ascetic mode of faring, and to employ the leisure of a festal assembly to confer admiration and honour on the old-time life of frugality and economy, and as far as possible to assimilate our present-day life to that of the distant past. These statements are

[1] See also *Quaestiones et Solutiones in Genesin et in Exodum*, i. 1 (cf. p. 30 below).

[2] F. H. Colson and G. H. Whitaker, *Philo* (Loeb Classical Library), 1929–41, in loc., maintain that the text is faulty here. Perhaps, however, we should regard the 'stars', with Heinemann, as including also the sun and the moon; cf. 'lights', Gen. 1:14 ff.

[3] Cf. *De Decalogo*, 161: 'To seven he gives the chief feasts prolonged for many days, two feasts, that is, for the two equinoxes, each lasting for seven days, the first in the spring to celebrate the ripeness (better, 'ripening') of the sown crops, the second in the autumn . . .'.

especially guaranteed by the exposure of the twelve loaves corresponding in number to the tribes, on the holy table. They are all unleavened, the clearest possible example of food free from admixture, in the preparation of which art for the sake of pleasure has no place, but only nature, providing nothing save what is indispensable for its use. . . .[1]

But within the feast there is another feast following directly after the first day. This is called the Sheaf,[2] a name given to it from the ceremony which consists in bringing to the altar a sheaf as a firstfruit, both of the land which has been given to the nation to dwell in and of the whole earth, so that it serves that purpose both to the nation in particular and for the whole human race in general. The reason of this is that the Jewish nation is to the whole inhabited world what the priest is to the State. . . .

We have shown, then, that the Sheaf was an offering both of the nation's own land and of the whole earth, given in thanks for the fertility and abundance which the nation and the whole human race desired to enjoy. . . . The sheaf thus offered is of barley, shewing that the use of the inferior grains is not open to censure. It would be irreverent to give firstfruits of them all, as most of them are made to give pleasure rather than to be used as necessaries, and equally unlawful to enjoy and partake of any form of food for which thanks had not been offered in the proper and rightful manner. And therefore the law ordained that the first-fruit offerings should be made of barley, a species of grain regarded as holding the second place in value as food. For wheat holds the first place, and as the firstfruit of this has greater distinction, the law postponed it to a more suitable season in the future. It does not anticipate matters, but puts it in storage for the time being, so that the various thank offerings may be adjusted to their appointed dates at they recur.

In another place Philo gives the regulations for the observance of the 'second Pesaḥ':

. . . While (mourning for the dead) is still running its appointed course, it should be banished from the sacred precincts which must be kept pure from all pollution, not only that which is voluntary but also that which is unintentionally incurred. But when its term is finished let not the mourners be denied an equal share in the sacred services (of the Pesaḥ). . . . Let them form a second set to come on the second month and also on the fourteenth day, and sacrifice just as the first set, and observe a similar rule and method in dealing with the victims. The same permission also must be given to those who are prevented from joining the whole nation in worship not by mourning but by absence in a distant country. For settlers abroad and inhabitants of other regions are not wrongdoers who deserve to be deprived of equal privileges, particularly if the nation has grown so populous that a single country cannot contain it and has sent out colonies in all directions.[3]

[1] Cf. *De sacrificiis Abelis et Caini*, 62: 'They . . . baked this dough . . . into buried unleavened cakes (ἐγκρυφίας ἀζύμους; see LXX at Ex. 12:39, p. 50 n. 5 below), that is, they kneaded the savage untamed passion with the aid of reason that softened it as though it were food'; Philo plays on the double sense of πέσσω, 'bake, soften'. See also *De congressu quaer. erud. gratia*, 161, and *De Vita contemplativa*, 81.

[2] δράγμα; cf. *De Decalogo*, 160.

[3] *De Vita Mosis*, ii. 231 f. The excerpts given here follow the translation of Colson and Whitaker, op. cit. The paragraphs are numbered in accordance with the numeration in that edition.

In an analysis of Philo's description of the Passover, allowance must be made for the fact that he spent most of his life at Alexandria,[1] that he was greatly under the influence of Greek philosophy, and that his talent for allegorization led him to stress moral elements in Jewish religious practice that may have been—at any rate, at the early period—of lesser importance. We should not look to Philo for full or precise details of ritual. Philo, for example, tells us that laymen act as priests in slaughtering the Pesaḥ victim. But he writes nothing about the manipulation of the blood, and it should not be assumed that also in this respect the laymen acted in the place of the priests.[2] Nevertheless, we do obtain from his writings a picture of the salient features of the festival as it was celebrated during the last decades of the Temple at Jerusalem—a picture that is corroborated by other sources. Philo's account follows closely the Traditional Documents, in particular, Ex. 12 and Num. 9; his views on *halakhah* are those of an orthodox Jew, however greatly he was attracted to Hellenistic culture.[3]

In these passages Philo is the first among writers of the Historical Documents on the Passover to comment upon the etymology of the name Pesaḥ.[4] His translation of Pesaḥ by the Greek διαβατήρια, the ceremonies performed before crossing a frontier, provides him with allegoric material which is, however, somewhat misleading since it belongs to a Greek rather than a Jewish milieu.[5] In Philo, as elsewhere, the date of the Pesaḥ is the fourteenth day of the first month. Again he is first among writers of the Historical Documents—and indeed of all the Passover documents, since the Traditional Documents do not mention the point—to remark on the association of that date with the spring equinox.[6] The further association of the spring equinox with the Creation, on which he enlarges, was (as we shall see) familiar to the Rabbis.[7] Philo's astronomical knowledge is shown by his statement that on that date the moon is visible from sunset to sunrise.[8]

In other respects Philo does little more than recapitulate the narrative

[1] *De Providentia*, ii. 64, implies that its author visited Palestine. But it is doubtful if this work should be attributed to Philo; see H. Graetz, 'Das Korbfest der Erstlinge bei Philo', *Monatsschrift für Geschichte und Wissenschaft des Judenthums*, xxvi, 1877, 441 f. Graetz, however, finds other grounds for holding that Philo visited Palestine.

[2] See, in particular, S. Belkin, *Philo and the Oral Law*, 1940, 63.

[3] On Philo and the Passover, see B. Ritter, *Philo und die Halacha*, 1879, 110 ff.; E. Stein, *Allegorische Exegese des Philo aus Alexandria*, 1929, 31; I. Heinemann, *Philons griechische und jüdische Bildung*, 1932, 33 f.; and E. R. Goodenough, *Introduction to Philo Judaeus*, 1940, 208. For a general study of Philo's treatment of *halakhah* see, in addition to the works mentioned, J. Z. Lauterbach, art. 'Philo', *JE*, and Goodenough, 'Philo's Exposition of the Law', *HTR* xxvi, 1933, 109.

[4] He usually renders by Gr. πάσχα; but see p. 97 n. 6 below.

[5] See Pauly–Wissowa, *Realenc.*, s.v., and p. 185 below.

[6] So also Aristobulus of Paneas, an Alexandrian Jew of probably the second century A.D. (see P. Wendland, art. 'Aristobulus of Paneas', *JE*), cited in Eusebius, *Hist. Eccles.* vii. 32 (Migne, *P.G.* xx, col. 728).

[7] See p. 149 below.

[8] p. 27 n. 2 above.

and the regulations of the Traditional Documents. He describes the Passover as it was observed at Jerusalem, not as he himself may have observed it in the Diaspora. He stresses the condition of ritual cleanness to be maintained by officiants at the Pesaḥ, and the fact that this was the one formal occasion in the year on which laymen performed the priestly function of slaying an animal victim. The time of the sacrifice is given approximately as between noon and evening—less precisely than in Jubilees—perhaps because Philo was concerned with broad principle rather than with detail.[1] The meal was eaten apparently in private houses, and apparently in haste;[2] its accompaniment by 'prayers and hymns' may refer to the Hallel psalms. The 'second Pesaḥ' is known to Philo.

Philo is the first among writers of the Historical Documents to mention the special observances on the first and seventh days. The offering of the Sheaf of barley on the second day of the Passover week is also mentioned here for the first time in the Historical Documents. Philo explains the ceremony as a thanksgiving offering of firstfruits, and from his text it seems certain—even allowing for the lack of detail in his description of ritual—that a sheaf was deposited on the altar in its simple state. It is clear from Philo's words that the barley was normally not ready for harvesting at the time of the spring equinox.

In the passages cited here Philo gives, then, the general lines of Passover procedure among orthodox circles at Jerusalem. There is, however, a treatise, the *Quaestiones et Solutiones in Genesin et in Exodum*[3] (extant in complete form only in Armenian), ascribed to Philo, which provides a somewhat more detailed account of the festival. Whether Philo was in fact the author of this treatise cannot be decided on the evidence that we are considering here. The treatise in no way contradicts the statements of Philo on the Passover. In one respect, indeed, it defines one of his statements more exactly—the time of the Pesaḥ is said to be after 3 p.m. This was probably the usage in the time of Jesus and certainly at the time of Josephus;[4] in Jubilees the time is less exact,[5] in the Mishnah it is more exact.[6] We may, therefore, reasonably assign this treatise to the period of Philo or slightly later, but we cannot maintain that it is from his pen.[7]

[1] According to *Quaestiones . . . in Exodum*, i. 11, however, the Pesaḥ sacrifice was not to be offered before 3 p.m.; see below.

[2] See *De sacrificiis Abelis et Caini*, 63; *Quis rerum divinarum heres sit*, 255; and *De migr. Abrah.* 25.

[3] See R. Marcus, *Philo. Supplement, i, ii: Quaestiones et Solutiones in Genesin et in Exodum* (Loeb Classical Library), 1953, and Introd. ix. The Greek and Latin fragments of this work are of little importance; see L. Früchtel, 'Griechische Fragmente zu Philons Quaestiones in Genesin et in Exodum', *ZAW* lv, 1937, 108, and Marcus, op. cit. ii. 179 ff. (Appendixes).

[4] pp. 34 and 39 below.

[5] p. 21 above.

[6] See p. 262 below.

[7] See the brief comment of Goodenough, *JBL* lxxiii, 1954, 169. In one regulation, however, the practice prescribed in the treatise appears to differ from what was probably the ancient usage and also that of the LXX and the Mishnah—the age of the Pesaḥ victim. See pp. 32 n. 1 and 140 ff. below.

The treatise is of some importance in the analysis of Passover ritual because it appears to indicate which rites were still performed at the time of its composition. It enumerates the individual ceremonies of the Passover and gives the author's explanation—largely allegorical—of the motive underlying each ordinance. Certain ordinances are introduced with the formula '(Why) does he command (or, "say") that . . .?' The ordinances that are introduced in this way are precisely those that prescribe practices that appear in the Bible but were subsequently, as we shall see later, abandoned or modified by Rabbinic usage. The divergence between the regulations of the treatise and those of the Mishnah to which I have just referred—the ruling on the time of the Pesaḥ sacrifice—shows that these amendments are likely to have been introduced earlier than the time of the Mishnah.

It may be assumed, then, that the following practices, which are not prefixed by the formula in the treatise, were fully observed at the Passover at the time of the writer. The Pesaḥ was performed in the first month, at the spring equinox, and the offering of the barley Sheaf was made on the second day of the Passover week. The Pesaḥ was regarded as the festival of 'passing over',[1] the victims were small male animals,[2] offered whole[3] by all the people[4] at, but not before, 3 p.m.;[5] the flesh was not to be eaten raw,[6] but to be consumed together with unleavened bread and bitter herbs;[7] the celebrants did not go out of the house on that night.[8] The regulations, on the other hand, that, I have suggested, had been abandoned—they are introduced by the special formula—comprise the selection of the victim on the tenth day and its custody until the fourteenth day,[9] the smearing of the blood of the victim on the doorposts and lintel,[10] the wearing by the participants of a girdle and shoes and their carrying a staff in their hands,[11] and the burning of the remains of the victim at dawn.[12] Other regulations—also accompanied by the formula—were modified but not abandoned in later Rabbinic practice; these are the provision of the Pesaḥ victims 'in accordance with the houses of the clans',[13] the addition of neighbours to the family group if the 'house of the clan' is too small to consume the victim,[14] the rule that everyone 'should number sufficient for himself for the sacrifice',[15] and

[1] Cf., on Philo, p. 29 above.

[2] *Quaestiones . . . in Exodum*, i. 8.

[3] i. 17.

[4] i. 10.

[5] i. 11: 'not before the ninth hour'. This means that the time of sacrifice began with the ninth hour; see pp. 34 and 39 below.

[6] i. 16.

[7] i. 15. See also *De congressu quaer. erud. gratia*, 162.

[8] *Quaestiones . . . in Exodum*, i. 22.

[9] i. 2, 9. See also *De congressu quaer. erud. gratia*, 106.

[10] *Quaestiones . . . in Exodum*, i. 12.

[11] i. 19; cf. *De sacrificiis Abelis et Caini*, 63.

[12] *Quaestiones . . . in Exodum*, i. 18.

[13] i. 3. Probably 'houses of clans' is the equivalent of *οἶκοι πατριῶν*, בית אבות; cf. Marcus's note, in loc.

[14] i. 5.

[15] i. 6.

rules on the condition and age of the victim.[1] The regulation that the victim was to be roasted seems also to have been regarded as having been modified,[2] perhaps because not only the blood but also the fat parts were treated separately, as we have already observed.[3] If we may judge from the use of the formula in the treatise at this point, the rule that the meal was to be eaten only at night had also been modified—perhaps on account of the great numbers of pilgrims who now participated at the Pesaḥ.[4]

XIII

The Aramaic text of *Megillath Ta'anith* prescribes days which are to be observed with joy and on which, in consequence, no mourning or fasting is to take place. The passages which concern us here are:

> From the eighth (day) therein [Nisan] and until the end of the appointed season[5] was restored the festival:[6] for no mourning and for no fasting. . . .[7] On the fourteenth (day) therein [Iyyar], the minor Pesaḥ:[8] for[9] no mourning and for no fasting. . . .[7] On the eighth and on the ninth (day) of Adar is the day of blowing (the trumpet)[10] for rain. . . . On the fourteenth (day) therein and on the fifteenth (day) therein are the days of Purim: for no mourning.[11]

This Aramaic text received its extant form before A.D. 66. The extracts given here may have been composed earlier.[12]

The observance of 8th Nisan which is prescribed in *Megillath Ta'anith* has been the subject of dispute among scholars. In the view of the (evidently late) Scholion on this passage, the date is celebrated in commemoration of the victory of the Pharisees over the Sadducees in the well-known controversy over the date of the Sheaf-waving.[13] The 'restoration of the festival' refers, it is held, to the restoration of the orthodox date of the feast of Weeks.[14] This, however, provides no obvious reason for assigning the commemoration to 8th Nisan.[15]

Another view explains this date as the beginning of the ritual seven-day purification ceremony observed by Jewish soldiers before they were

[1] *Quaestiones . . . in Exodum*, i. 7. The treatise is of the opinion that the regulation of Ex. 12:5 prescribes that the victim should be a year old, not in its first year; the latter was probably the ancient usage. See the discussion on pp. 140 ff. below.

[2] i. 14.

[3] p. 15 above.

[4] i. 13; see pp. 39 and 240 below.

[5] מועדא.

[6] אתותב חגא.

[7] התענאה.

[8] Cf. *BT Ḥul.* 129b. A variant reads, 'the slaughtering of the minor Pesaḥ'.

[9] Variant 'and for . . .'.

[10] תרועה.

[11] For the text, see H. Lichtenstein, 'Fastenrolle. Eine Untersuchung zur jüdisch-hellenistischen Geschichte', *HUCA* viii–ix, 1931–2, 257, and the bibliography there.

[12] See Lichtenstein, op. cit.; cf. *BT Shab.* 13b.

[13] See S. Zeitlin, *Megillat Taanit as a source for Jewish chronology . . .*, 1922, 75.

[14] So *BT Men.* 65a reads, אתותב חגא דשבועייא; cf. *BT Ta'an.* 17b.

[15] Zeitlin, loc. cit., suggests that the first week of Nisan was observed as a public holiday to commemorate the rededication of the Temple by the returning Exiles (Ezra 6:14–22; cf. Ex. 40:2, 17), and that the present text reflects the practice of observing a further week's holiday from 8th Nisan so that 'as the time was close to Passover the people could be induced to remain in Jerusalem'. But we have no real evidence of a holiday from 1st to 7th Nisan, nor does *Meg. Ta'an* here restrict the observance of 8th Nisan to Jerusalem.

permitted to perform the Passover rites at the time of the early Hasmonean campaigns.[1] We may accept the general argument underlying this hypothesis, while rejecting its restriction to the Hasmoneans. 8th Nisan falls exactly seven days before the Pesaḥ; it was the last day on which those who had contracted ritual uncleanness (including soldiers—but the category of persons affected by the rule was much wider) could, by ceremonies of purification, restore their right to participate in the festival.[2] This interpretation involves, however, a slight change in the order of the words. We should probably read: 'On the eighth (day)[3] therein is restored the (right to participate in the) festival and until the end of the appointed season'[4]—that is, the ceremonies of the Passover week.

The blowing of trumpets for rain which is enjoined by *Megillath Taʿanith* for 8th–9th Adar is a well-attested practice.[5] Scholars have found difficulty in explaining why not one but two days in Adar should be prescribed.[6] The reason probably lies in the following words that prescribe two days for the celebration of Purim, as in Est. 9:17f., 21f. Each of the two days of Purim occurs on the seventh day after the blowing of the trumpets—a perfect parallel to the observance of 8th Nisan followed by the celebration of the Pesaḥ on 14th Nisan, seven days later.[7]

The 'second Pesaḥ' referred to briefly in this passage in *Megillath Taʿanith* has already been recorded in the Historical Documents.[8]

XIV

The allusions to the Passover in the New Testament may be regarded, with certain reservations,[9] as reflecting the practice of the Palestinian Jews a generation after Philo. The festival is referred to variously as 'the Pesaḥ'[10] or 'the feast of unleavened bread',[11] once as 'the Pesaḥ and unleavened bread',[12] and several times as 'the feast' where the context makes it clear that the passage alludes to the Passover.[13] In the New Testament, as in

[1] L. Ginzberg in Zeitlin, op. cit., n. 209. [2] See pp. 139 f. below.

[3] Reading בתמניה; all the following entries in *Meg. Taʿan.* are introduced by the preposition ב. This ב may have been emended to the מן of the extant text under the influence of the preceding entry and of the ועד which follows.

[4] i.e. בתמניה ביה אתותב חגא ועד סוף וכו׳. There is no justification for omitting סוף with Lichtenstein, op. cit. 277, since he offers no explanation as to how the word came to be interpolated. [5] See *Mish. Taʿan.* i. 6; iii. 1 ff. [6] See Lichtenstein, op. cit., in loc.

[7] pp. 153 f. and 239 below. [8] Above, p. 28, cf. p. 23.

[9] See pp. 241 and 242 ff. below.

[10] Gr. *πάσχα*, John 12:1, 13:1, 18:39, Acts 12:4; *πάσχα ἡ ἑορτή*, John 2:23, cf. 6:4; *πάσχα τῶν Ἰουδαίων*, John 2:13, 11:55; *ἑορτὴ τοῦ πάσχα*, Luke 2: 41. In John 19:14, Matt. 26:18 *πάσχα* probably refers to the Pesaḥ, not to the Passover week.

[11] Matt. 26:17, Mark 14:12, Luke 22:7, Acts 12:3, 20:6, cf. 'feast of unleavened bread which is called the Passover', Luke 22:1. The term '(feast of) unleavened bread' is not found in John.

[12] Mark 14:1. Note the interchange of the two terms in Acts 12:3–4.

[13] Matt. 27:15, Mark 14:2, 15:6, Luke 23:17 (margin), John 12:12, 20, 13:29, 1 Cor. 5:8.

other Historical Documents, the term 'Pesaḥ' also denotes both the animal victim of the Pesaḥ night and the meal at which it is consumed;[1] the celebrants are said to 'make the Pesaḥ'.[2]

The pilgrims who came to celebrate the Pesaḥ at Jerusalem, both from country districts and from abroad, were many.[3] Among them were boys of twelve years;[4] the age at which participation was compulsory for male adults was presumably now thirteen as in later Rabbinic practice. Some pilgrims stayed at Jerusalem throughout the days of the festival,[5] but it was evidently permissible to leave immediately after the first day (unless the next day was a Sabbath).[6] On the eve of the festival it was apparently customary for the administrative authorities to release a prisoner under sentence of death.[7] Individual Jews used to donate alms before the Passover,[8] presumably to enable the poor to purchase the minimum requirements for the celebration of the festival.[9]

When we turn to the preparations for the festival and the details of its observance, we must treat separately the Synoptic Gospels, on the one hand, and the Fourth Gospel, on the other, in view of the apparent discrepancies between them. In the Synoptic Gospels the preliminaries on the eve of the festival were of such importance that the eve of the festival (13th–14th Nisan) was called the 'first day of the festival'.[10] They involved—in addition, of course, to the removal of leaven—the choice of a venue for the meal, and the purchase of the Pesaḥ victim and of the subsidiary sacrifices.[11] Some details tally exactly with those of Philo or the treatise attributed to him. Thus the Pesaḥ victim was probably slain at 3 p.m.[12] The meal, by an extension of earlier practice, was not held in the precincts of the Temple itself, but in houses within the boundaries of Jerusalem.[13] On the eating of unleavened bread with the Pesaḥ victim, it is explained that leaven represents impurity, and seems to work unseen. Its removal at the Passover, the festival which opens a new period of time, is symbolic of the desire to remove evil which may have corrupted the year that was coming to an end.[14]

[1] Matt. 26:17–19, Mark 14:12, 14, 16, Luke 22:7, 8, 11, 13, 15, John 18:28, 1 Cor. 5:7 (verb).

[2] Cf. Heb. *'śh pesaḥ*.

[3] Luke 2:41, John 2:13, 11:55; John 2:14 (note the reference to the changing of money, perhaps into small coin), 12:20. Cf. the pilgrims for the feast of Tabernacles, John 7:2 ff.

[4] Luke 2:42.

[5] Luke 2:43.

[6] Luke 24:13, cf. v. 21.

[7] Matt. 27:15, Mark 15:6, Luke 23:17 (margin), John 18:39; cf. p. 242 below.

[8] Matt. 26:8 ff., Mark 14:3 ff., John 12:4 ff., cf. 13:29.

[9] p. 243, cf. p. 259 below.

[10] Matt. 26:17, Mark 14:12 (which adds 'when they sacrificed the passover'), Luke 22:7 (which adds 'in which the passover must be sacrificed'); see p. 245 below.

[11] See the references in n. 10 above.

[12] See p. 262 below; Jesus dies at the ninth hour, that is, 3 p.m., Matt. 27:45 ff., Mark 15:33 ff., Luke 23:44 ff., cf. 1 Cor. 5:7. On Jubilees, pp. 21 f. above; see also p. 30 above on *Quaestiones . . . in Exodum*.

[13] Matt. 26:18, Mark 14:13, 16, Luke 22:10 ff.

[14] 1 Cor. 5:6–8, cf. Matt. 16:5 ff., Mark 8:14 f., Gal. 5:9. On this view of leaven, see pp. 168 f. below.

Other features of the Passover are not mentioned in the Historical Documents before the Synoptic Gospels. At the Pesaḥ meal the participants, all male adults, could be persons united by bonds of friendship rather than of kinship.[1] Women were, nevertheless, also present at Jerusalem.[2] Night had fallen when the celebrants assembled for the Pesaḥ;[3] they reclined, as at other meals.[4] The meal appears to have opened with food other than bread, the 'sop' was dipped in the common bowl,[5] and then the bread was broken and the wine drunk; this was not the order of the service on Sabbath and on the other festivals.[6] The wine is likely to have been red,[7] and perhaps new.[8] The service ended in hymns[9]—we have found this to have been the case already in 2 Chr. and in Philo.[10] It was perhaps customary to go out after the Pesaḥ service, but not beyond the boundaries of Jerusalem.[11]

It is evident that the Synoptic Gospels regard the Last Supper as having been a Pesaḥ meal.[12] In that year it occurred on the night of Thursday/Friday.[13] Here, however, we are confronted with certain difficulties. The meeting of the Sanhedrin and the trial of Jesus, his crucifixion, and the preparations for his interment would then have taken place on a festival day; this is wholly contrary to accepted Jewish practice, in so far as we know it from later regulations.[14]

[1] See p. 241 below.

[2] Luke 2:41; Matt. 27:55, Mark 15:40 f., Luke 23:49, 55.

[3] Matt. 26:20, Mark 14:17, 1 Cor. 11:23.

[4] Matt. 26:20, Mark 14:18, Luke 22:14.

[5] Matt. 26:23, Mark 14:20; cf. Luke 22:21. See the discussion in J. Jeremias, *Eucharistic Words of Jesus*, 1955, 26, 44.

[6] Matt. 26:26 ff., Mark 14:22 f., 1 Cor. 11:24 ff. But in Luke 22:17 ff. the wine is blessed before the bread, cf. 1 Cor. 10:16 opp. 11:25 f. This was the usual order at other festivals and at Sabbaths, and it may have arisen as a 'correction'. A. Wünsche, *Neue Beiträge zur Erläuterung der Evangelien aus Talmud und Midrasch*, 1878, 333 n., maintains, however, that the present text of Luke is original. See, on this passage, Jeremias, op. cit. 23.

[7] Cf. the comparison with blood in the references in n. 6 above. See also Gen. 49:11, Deut. 32:14, Is. 63:3, 6, Ecclus. 39:26, 50:15, 1 Macc. 6:34; cf. also Rev. 14:20, *BT Sanh*. 70a, *Men*. 87a.

[8] Matt. 26:29, perhaps cf. Prov. 23:21, Is. 63:1 f.

[9] Matt. 26:30, Mark 14:26.

[10] See pp. 19 and 30 above; cf. the references in Jubilees and the Wisdom of Solomon, pp. 21 and 25 above.

[11] Jesus did not go to Bethany on that night.

[12] Matt. 26:17–19, Mark 14:12–16, Luke 22:7–15.

[13] Mark 15:42, Luke 23:54 (see p. 36 n. 4 below), cf. Matt. 27:62.

[14] Cf. *Mish. Sanh*. iv. 1, *BT Sanh*. 35a, where it is stated that no trial on a capital charge may be held on a Sabbath or festival or on the preceding day. It was forbidden to write records on a festival day, *Mish. Shab*. xii. 3 ff., *Beṣah* v. 2, but this was obligatory at a trial on a capital charge, *Sanh*. iv. 3. It is true that the elder who rebels against the Court was to be 'kept in guard until one of the *ḥaggim*, and was put to death on one of the *ḥaggim*', *Mish. Sanh*. xi. 4; but in this case the formal trial would have been held previously. On the Sanhedrin, see A. Büchler, *Synedrion in Jerusalem*, 1902, especially p. 42 on the move of the Court in about A.D. 30 according to *JT Sanh*. i. 18 (fol. 19c); but see now S. B. Hoenig, *The Great Sanhedrin*, 1953, 109, 211, and H. Mantel, *Studies in the History of the Sanhedrin*, 1961, passim. On the competence of the Sanhedrin, see J. Juster, *Juifs dans l'empire romain*, 1914, ii. 127 ff.; H. Strack and P. Billerbeck, *Kommentar zum Neuen*

In the Fourth Gospel, on the other hand, the festival is always called Pesaḥ, never 'the feast of unleavened bread'; the use of the latter term in the Sinaitic Syriac version is either an idiosyncrasy of the translator or an attempt to bring John into harmony with the Synoptic Gospels. This emphasis on the solemn ritual at the beginning of the Passover week is in keeping with the general character of this Gospel. It alone refers to rites of purification to be observed by persons who wished to attend the pilgrimage. They came to Jerusalem at least six days before the festival opened.[1] The priests, moreover, would not enter the praetorium for fear of being defiled, and of being unable, in consequence, to eat the Pesaḥ victim.[2] John alone mentions the types of animals purchased at the approach of the Passover; of these, the doves were associated with ceremonies of ritual cleanness.[3]

John appears to agree with the Synoptic Gospels that the Last Supper was on Thursday night.[4] But he does not identify the Last Supper with

Testament . . ., 1922–8, i. 1026; M. Goguel, *Vie de Jésus*, 1932; Zeitlin, 'Crucifixion of Jesus', *JQR* xxxi, 1940–1, 334 ff., xxxii, 1941–2, 175, 279, 'Political Synedrion', ibid. xxxvi, 1945–6, 109; H. A. Wolfson and Zeitlin, ibid. 303, 307; and Hoenig and Zeitlin, ibid. xxxvii, 1946–7, 179, 189; but especially H. Lietzmann, *Prozess Jesu*, Sitzungsberichte der preussischen Akademie der Wissenschaften, Phil.-hist. Kl., 1931, 313 ff., and O. Cullmann, *State in the New Testament*, 1957, 41 n. 4 and the references there; against Lietzmann see G. D. Kilpatrick, *Trial of Jesus*, 1953. See further J. Blinzler, *Prozess Jesu*, 1957, and T. A. Burkill, 'Competence of the Sanhedrin', *Vigiliae Christianae*, x, 1956, 80; P. Winter, 'Marginal Notes on the Trial of Jesus', *ZNW* l, 1959, 14 ff., 221 ff., id., *On the Trial of Jesus*, 1961, 75 ff.; and Mantel, op. cit., ch. 6. John 19:31 is scarcely correct in stating that it was on account of the Sabbath or the festival—the meaning of the verse is obscure—that the body of Jesus was taken down; it was a general practice in Jewish law that the body of an executed man must not be left overnight, Deut. 21:23, *Mish. Sanh.* vi. 4, Josephus, *BJ* IV. v. 2; on the subsequent disposal of the remains, see *Mish. Sanh.* vi. 5; Büchler, 'Enterrement des criminels . . .', *REJ* xlvi, 1903, 74 f.; and S. Krauss, 'Double inhumation chez les Juifs', *REJ* xcvii, 1934, 1. The passage in John may be explained, however, as indicating that in the view of the writer the execution was purely an affair of Roman jurisdiction.

[1] John 11:55, cf. 12:1. See pp. 32 f. above on *Meg. Ta'an.*, and on the preliminal week of purification pp. 139 f. below.

[2] John 18:28. In the Synoptic Gospels, on the other hand, the priests did in fact enter the Governor's Court, Matt. 27:11 f., Mark 15:2 f., Luke 23:1 f. We do not know how the laws of ritual cleanness were interpreted at the time of Jesus. On these laws in the Mishnah, see the summary in H. Danby, *Mishnah*, 1933, 800 ff.

[3] John 2:14, 16, cf. Lev. 14:4–6, 22, 30, 49, 53, 12:6–8, 15:29 f., 5:7, &c.

[4] John 19:14. 'The preparation of the passover' is to be interpreted as the preparation (or eve) of the Sabbath which occurred in the Passover week, cf. 19:31, 42, Mark 15:42, Luke 23:54. See Torrey, 'Date of the Crucifixion According to the Fourth Gospel', *JBL* l, 1931, 227, and id., 'In the Fourth Gospel the Last Supper was the Paschal Meal', *JQR* xlii, 1951–2, 237, in particular p. 241 on the Greek misrendering of Matt. 27:62; here, suggests Torrey, 'preparation' is to be taken in the sense of 'sunset', not 'Friday'—against this, Zeitlin, 'Date of the Crucifixion according to the Fourth Gospel', *JBL* li, 1932, 268. (John, it has been remarked on this page, uses the term 'Pesaḥ' for the Passover week, where other Gospels use the term 'unleavened bread'.) The Aramaic word *'rwbh*, which underlies 'preparation' here, already has the meaning 'eve of the Sabbath' in an ostracon from Elephantine, edited by Dupont-Sommer, 'Sabbat et Parascève à Éléphantine d'après des ostraca araméens inédits', *Mémoires présentés par divers savants à l'Académie des Inscriptions et Belles-Lettres*, 1950. So in later Aramaic texts the term *'rwbt* means always 'eve of the Sabbath', not 'eve of a festival', unless it is explicitly defined otherwise; see, for example, *JT Ta'an.* ii. 13 (fol. 66a), *Ter.* viii. 5 (fol. 45c), *Ned.* viii. 1 (fol. 40d).

the Pesaḥ meal.[1] The Last Supper would derive symbolical significance from the circumstance that it coincides with the Passover season, but John does not give it a precise date in relation to the Pesaḥ.[2] In spite of his obvious knowledge of complex details of ritual, he makes no mention of the preparations for the Passover or of the peculiar food eaten at the Passover or the order of service or the special prayers that distinguished the Pesaḥ meal.[3] The one detail that he does give—the washing of feet[4]—is not in fact a feature of the Pesaḥ meal, according to later Jewish practice; the other details of the Last Supper in John—reclining and dipping into a common bowl[5]—would have occurred at any communal meal. On the other hand, alms are said by John to have been donated at the Last Supper;[6] this might have taken place at any time before the Passover—but it could not have taken place at the Pesaḥ meal itself, when money could no longer be employed for the festival requirements.[7]

XV

Josephus was born in A.D. 37–38, and died after A.D. 100. By birth and training he was well qualified to appreciate the traditions and practices of Pharisees, Sadducees, and Essenes. The *De Bello Judaico* appeared probably between A.D. 75 and 79, and the *Antiquities* in A.D. 93–94.

Josephus calls the festival 'Pascha' when he is writing of the Pesaḥ ritual,[8]

1 Torrey, loc. cit. 243, maintains that 'eat the passover', John 18:28, refers to the meals of the Passover week after the Pesaḥ night. But ritual cleanness was required for the Pesaḥ itself rather than for the offering of the *re'iyyah* of 15th Nisan; see Zeitlin, 'Last Supper', *JQR* xlii, 1951–2, 256 (where substitute *re'iyyah* for *ḥagigah*), and p. 138 below.

2 John 13:1 opp. Matt. 26:17, Mark 14:2, Luke 22:7.

3 The Last Supper took place in the evening and extended into the night; John 13:30, as well as Mark 14:17, 30 ff., 1 Cor. 11:23, &c. It has been maintained that supper among the Jews at this time usually took place in the late afternoon or early evening, cf. the practice of Agrippa, *BT Pes.* 107b. The evidence given by Jeremias, op. cit. 17 f., alludes, however, to general usage. But this was not a rule, cf. Judith 9:1; and the fact that Jesus and his contemporaries may have been accustomed to partake of a second meal of the day in the afternoon is no argument that the Last Supper—which (whether the Pesaḥ meal or not) was a special farewell meal—did not continue into the night.

4 John 13:4 ff. See on this W. L. Knox, 'John 13:1–30', *HTR* xliii, 1950, 161.

5 John 13:12, 23, 25, 28; 13:26 f., 30. There is no need to assume, with Wünsche, op. cit. 241 n., that the writer of the Fourth Gospel has confused the Passover with Tabernacles. This might, it is true, provide an easy explanation for the insertion of the Hosanna incident in the context of the Passover (John 12:12 f.), but palm branches were carried at a triumphal celebration in the second month of the year, 1 Macc. 13:51, and at the festival of Ḥanukkah near the winter solstice, 2 Macc. 10:7. They were a symbol of victory, cf. Judith 15:12. We may recall, too, that both the Passover and Tabernacles were New Year festivals, and some overlapping of ritual may be expected; see pp. 127 ff. below. For the Hosanna incident, see F. C. Burkitt, *JTS* xvii, 1916, 139, and E. Werner, '"Hosanna" in the Gospels', *JBL* lxv, 1946, 97.

6 John 13:29, cf. 12:4 ff.; see Jeremias, op. cit. 30.

7 On the giving of alms at the Passover, see Josephus, *BJ* II. i. 3.

8 *Ant.* II. xiv. 6, III. x. 5, IX. xiii. 3, XI. iv. 8; *BJ* VI. ix. 3. On the spelling of Pascha in texts of Josephus, see the references on p. 97 n. 6 below. The text of Josephus followed here is that of the edition by H. St. J. Thackeray and R. Marcus, *Josephus* (Loeb Classical Library), 1926–43.

and 'the feast of unleavened bread' when he writes of the Passover week.[1] On the other hand, he refers to the whole Passover, inclusive of the Pesaḥ, as either 'the feast of unleavened bread'[2] or 'the feast of unleavened bread which is called the Pascha'.[3] It takes place at the association of a lunar with a solar phase.[4] The name Pascha is explained by 'passing over'.[5] Josephus also follows traditional lines in his account of the institution of the festival, in Egypt.[6] At the Exodus it was celebrated by *φρατρίαι*, subdivisions of the *φυλή*, tribe,[7] because these were the appropriate units for the march from Egypt. In the same way, Josephus explains the eating of unleavened bread as arising from the needs of the journey through the Wilderness, not (as in the Bible) from the Exodus.[8] This form of bread was eaten for thirty days, until its place was taken by the manna;[9] and the incident was commemorated—adds Josephus illogically—by the annual festival of unleavened bread lasting eight days.[10] Beyond a brief reference to the sacrifices,[11] Josephus has little to record about the ritual during the festal week.

His description of the Sheaf-offering represents, on the other hand, a remarkable advance upon the rite described by Philo. Philo, it may reasonably be assumed, maintains that the whole Sheaf was to be laid in its natural state on the altar.[12] According to Josephus, however,

> on the second day of unleavened bread, that is to say, the sixteenth, our people partake of the crops which they have reaped and which have not been touched till then. . . . They offer the firstfruits of the barley, in the following wise. After parching and crushing the little sheaf of ears and purifying the barley for grinding, they bring to the altar an *assaron* for God, and, having flung a handful thereof on the altar, they leave the rest for the use of the priests. Thereafter all are permitted, publicly or individually, to begin harvest.[13]

The feast of Weeks, the fiftieth day after the Sheaf-offering, is called, Josephus informs us, Asarta.[14]

Of special interest is the account by Josephus of individual celebrations of the Passover near his own time—although we cannot regard their details as necessarily of general application. The people, he tells us, assembled

[1] *Ant.* II. xv. 1, III. x. 5. The fact that Josephus in *Ant.* III. x. 5 declares that the Pesaḥ is followed by the festival of unleavened bread does not, of course, mean that he therefore regarded the two as separate in origin (as P. J. Heawood, 'Time of the Last Supper', *JQR* xlii, 1951–2, 37); he is simply reproducing literally the Bible text.

[2] *Ant.* V. iii. 1, VI. v. 3, ix. 3, xiv. 3, IX. xiii. 2–3; *BJ* II. xii. 6.

[3] *Ant.* X. iv. 5, XIV. ii. 1, cf. XVII. ix. 3, XVIII. ii. 2; *BJ* II. i. 3.

[4] *Ant.* III. x. 5, cf. II. xv. 2. Note the Greek phrase *κατὰ σελήνην*. Josephus uses the Roman calendar; but where the interest is purely Jewish he makes clear that the date he gives is lunar. See B. Niese, 'Zur Chronologie des Josephus', *Hermes*, xxviii, 1893, 197 ff., and Zeitlin, *Megillat Taanit* . . ., 48 ff.

[5] *ὑπερβασία*, *Ant.* II. xiv. 6; see p. 186 below.

[6] *Ant.* II. xiv. 6.

[7] See Liddell and Scott, *Lexicon*, s.v.

[8] *Ant.* II. xv. 1.

[9] Cf. Ex. 16:1, where the manna is said to have come one month after the Exodus.

[10] *Ant.* II. xv. 1; elsewhere Josephus regards the Passover as lasting seven days. For an explanation of this period of eight days, see p. 256 below.

[11] *Ant.* III. x. 5.

[12] p. 30 above.

[13] *Ant.* III. x. 5; see p. 194 below.

[14] *Ant.* III. x. 6; see p. 212 below.

for the festival at Jerusalem on 8th Nisan.[1] Both foreigners and the impure—persons afflicted with leprosy or gonorrhoea, women in menstruation, and 'persons otherwise defiled'—were excluded in principle;[2] but it could not have been difficult for them to gain access to the Temple rites.[3] Prior to, at any rate, A.D. 6, sectarians were not dissuaded from participating.[4] The crowds of pilgrims, from all Palestine and from abroad, were immense.[5] Josephus estimates those who performed the sacrifice in A.D. 65 at 'not less than three millions',[6] and at a not much lower number those who performed it in the year of the fall of Jerusalem.[7] But these figures are a palpable exaggeration.[8] Some of the pilgrims seem to have stayed outside the Temple area.[9] The great concourse was often unmanageable, and easily roused to demonstrations of fervour or anger.[10]

The units of the Pesaḥ celebrants, φρατρίαι, consisted normally of between ten and twenty persons.[11] The sacrifices were performed between 3 p.m. and 5 p.m.;[12] the celebrants then left the Temple to eat the meal in houses within the city, and just after midnight the priests reopened the Temple gates.[13]

XVI

Among the Historical Documents examined so far, only one—Jubilees—presents the Passover ritual from the standpoint of a heterodox sect; and I have suggested that Jub. 49 is not composed by the author of the main part of the Book of Jubilees. The Passover is not mentioned in Enoch or the Zadokite Documents, and its name has not so far been found among the festivals celebrated annually by the Qumran sect.[14] The following text was, however, discovered in Cave 4 at Qumran:

> The first year: its appointed times.[15]
> On 3 [in] Maʿuzziyah the Pesaḥ.

[1] *BJ* VI. v. 3; see pp. 32 f. and 36 above.

[2] *BJ* VI. ix. 3.

[3] *BJ* V. iii. 1, on the seizure of the Temple by the followers of John of Gischala; cf. *BT Pes.* 3b and the non-Jew denounced by R. Judah b. Bathyra.

[4] *Ant.* XVIII. ii. 2.

[5] In 4 B.C., *Ant.* XVII. ix. 3, *BJ* II. i. 3; between A.D. 48 and 52, *Ant.* XX. v. 3, *BJ* II. xii. 1; in A.D. 70, *BJ* V. iii. 1, VI. ix. 3–4. Cf. IV. vii. 2, where we are told that in A.D. 68 the bulk of the population of Ein Gedi had gone to Jerusalem for the Passover.

[6] *BJ* II. xiv. 3.

[7] Ibid. VI. ix. 3.

[8] See C. C. McCown, 'Density of Population in Ancient Palestine', *JBL* lxvi, 1947, 425. Tacitus, *Hist.* V. xiii, gives the total population of Jerusalem when it was besieged by the Romans as 600,000; the same figure is given in *Lamentations Rabba*, i. 2. The figure may not be original, cf. Ex. 12:37, and LXX at 1 Sam. 11:8 (600,000 for the 300,000 of the M.T.). It is curious to note that both here and in his explanation for the eating of unleavened bread by the Jews, *Hist.* V. iv, Tacitus appears to echo a single passage of the Bible, Ex. 12:37–39.

[9] *Ant.* XVII. ix. 3.

[10] *Ant.*, loc. cit., *BJ* II. i. 3; *Ant.* XX. v. 3, *BJ* II. xii. 1, V. iii. 1.

[11] *BJ* VI. ix. 3 (the manuscripts have φατρία); cf. *Ant.* III. x. 5.

[12] Loc. cit.

[13] *Ant.* XVIII. ii. 2 (about A.D. 6).

[14] See p. 247 below.

[15] *mwʿdyh.*

[On 1] in Yedaʿ[yah] waving of the [Sheaf].
On 5 in Śeʿorim the [second] Pesaḥ.
On 1 in Yeshuʿ the festival[1] of Weeks.[2]
[On] 4 in Maʿuzziyah the Day of Remembrance.[3]
[On] 6 in Yoyaribh the Day of Atonement.[4]
[On 4 in Yedaʿ]yah the festival[1] of Tabernacles.[5]

On archaeological grounds this text is to be dated probably before A.D. 68.[6] It establishes the correspondence between certain units of time and the principal Hebrew festivals.[7] The latter, it should be noted, follow the order of the normative Jewish calendar, and begin with the Passover. The units of time are the twenty-four priestly courses, *mišmaroth*, prescribed in 1 Chr. 24:7–18;[8] here they open with the 24th, instead of the 1st, course of that list.[9] Members of these courses worked in the Temple by rotation. Each course entered on its duties at noon on the Sabbath,[10] but its effective work commenced with the offering of the *Tamid* in the evening.[11]

Each priestly course lasted one week.[12] On the basis of the list in 1 Chr. 24, it is evident that the figures in the Qumran text represent the day of the week, from Sunday to the Sabbath.[13] There appear to be twenty-six courses and one day, that is, 183 days, between the Pesaḥ and Tabernacles, but this is not in fact the case. The writer of the text assigns

[1] *ḥg.* [2] *šbwʿym.* [3] *ywm hzkrwn.*

[4] *ywm hkpwrym.*

[5] J. T. Milik, 'Édition des manuscrits du désert de Juda', *Volume du Congrès Strasbourg 1956* (Supplements to *VT*, iv), 1957, 24; Milik's restoration of letters in the lacunae has been accepted here. The following articles should be consulted: S. Talmon, 'Calendar Reckoning of the Sect from the Judaean Desert', *Scripta Hierosolymitana*, iv, 1958, 162, and E. Vogt, 'Kalenderfragmente aus Qumran', *Biblica*, xxxix, 1958, 72 ff.; cf. id., 'Antiquum kalendarium sacerdotale', *Biblica*, xxxvi, 1955, 403, and see Milik, *Ten Years*, 1959, 107.

[6] R. de Vaux, 'Fouilles de Kh. Qumrân', *RB* lxiii, 1956.

[7] Cf. the other fragments quoted by Milik, op. cit.: 'On the 6th of yḥzq'l (corresponding) to the 29th, on the 22nd belonging to (?) the 11th month' and 'On the 22nd therein is the appointed time of oil (*mwʿd hšmn*).'

[8] W. Rudolph, *Chronikbücher*, in loc., regards 1 Chr. 24 as the latest elements in the work of the Chronicler, belonging to the period of the Hasmoneans or thereabouts.

[9] Individual names of these courses are found in 1 Macc. 2:1; *BT Taʿan.* 29a; *Mish. B. Qamma*, ix. 12; Luke 1:5; *Mish. Suk.* v. 8. Cf. Neh. 10:3–9, 12:1–7, 21–27; 1 Chr. 9:10, Ezra 2:36 ff.; Neh. 7:39 ff., Ezra 2:61, Neh. 7:63, Josephus, *Ant.* XII. vi. 1, &c.

[10] So already in 2 Kings 11:5, 9, cf. Josephus, *Ant.* VII. xiv. 7, '(David) found that there were twenty-four families of priests...; he further arranged that one family should minister to God each week from Sabbath to Sabbath'; cf. *Vita*, i. In *Contra Ap.* ii. 8, Josephus writes: 'Although there are four (*sic*) priestly tribes . . . these officiate by rotation for a fixed period of days; when the term of one party ends, others come to offer the sacrifices in their place, and assembling at midday in the temple, take over from the outgoing ministers the keys of the building and all its vessels, duly numbered.' See further *Mish. Suk.* v. 6–8, *Taʿan.* iv. 2, *Tam.* v. 1, and cf. *Taʿan.* ii. 6–7, *B. Qamma* ix. 12, *Yeb.* xi. 7, *Tos. Taʿan.* iv. 2, 9, *Suk.* iv, *Numbers Rabba*, iii. 9, &c.

[11] See especially *Tos. Suk.* iv. 24–25.

[12] See the interval between 1st and 10th Tishri, ll. 6–7, of the Qumran text.

[13] It is possible that at the time of the Qumran texts the officers of the Temple regarded the day as opening with dawn and ending with night, like the service of the Temple; see pp. 131 n. 3, 172, and 250 f. below.

the Pesaḥ sacrifice to the eve of the festival (14th Nisan)—that is, the evening at the end of Tuesday—and it therefore belongs to Tuesday. Tabernacles, on the other hand, is not introduced by a sacrifice on the day preceding the festival. Its ritual does not begin until Wednesday, 15th Tishri—that is, the evening at the beginning of Wednesday. The true interval between the Passover and Tabernacles is therefore 182 days, according to the writer of the Qumran text—half, that is, of a year of 364 days. We observe, too, that the waving of the Sheaf takes place in the Qumran 'calendar' on the first Sunday after the Passover week, and presumably in daytime.[1] The interval between the Pesaḥ and the 'second Pesaḥ' is thirty days.

The twenty-four courses revolve through the period of twenty-six weeks that is the subject of this Qumran text, the place of each course changing in its relation to festivals with each revolution; it may be assumed, therefore, that these courses rotated through the fifty-two weeks of the 364-day year, exactly as the priestly courses of the Temple rotated through the lunisolar year of normative Judaism.[2] Here, then, we have the explanation of the term 'first' in line 1 of the text. It makes no difference whether we interpret it as the first year of a schematic calendar series, or as the first year of an ideal age.[3] In both cases the implication is that in the second and the following years a different course will coincide with each festival until the twenty-four courses have performed the full cycle. Only the days of the week remain constant.[4]

This 'calendar' is clearly not that of normative Judaism. I shall suggest in a later chapter that it is likely to be in conformity with what we know of Sadducean practice.[5]

[1] See pp. 247–51 below.

[2] The reason—or the result—is to be found in the equitable distribution of Temple dues among the priests, *Mish. Suk.* v. 7–8, cf. *B. Qamma* ix. 12, *Parah* iii. 11. Talmon, op. cit. 172, can scarcely be correct in making up the annual total of priestly courses to fifty-two and exactly equal to the year of fifty-two weeks ($24\times 2+4$). It probably was, on the contrary, necessary that the courses should not equal the weeks of the year, and that they should rotate through successive years so that control of particular festivals or annual occasions should not seem to be the perquisite of any single course.

[3] As Talmon, op. cit. 173.

[4] Cf. the Jubilees calendar; see p. 20 above.

[5] p. 248 below.

2

THE SOURCES AND THE TRADITION: THE PENTATEUCH

THE second group of texts on the Passover—those that I have called the Traditional Documents—are found in the Pentateuchal books of Exodus, Leviticus, Numbers, and Deuteronomy. We are confronted here with a problem that was absent in our treatment of the Historical Documents. As regards the latter, knowledge of their historical background enabled us to place them, with comparative ease, in chronological order, and to assess in some degree the gradual evolution of Passover ritual. This background is lacking in the case of the Traditional Documents. I therefore set out these texts according to the conventional scheme of literary sources as propounded by S. R. Driver[1] and representatives of the moderate school of 'Higher Critics'. Where other scholars differ radically from this classification of individual texts, their opinion is indicated in footnotes.[2] I have subdivided the documents further, where it appears that literary units of smaller size may be isolated with some certainty. This treatment does not mean that I accept the premisses of the 'literary-critical' school; I adopt the method largely to test the validity of these premisses in the present context.

The Traditional Documents are arranged also according to their contents. They fall under the following headings:

1. Possible references to the Passover before the Exodus;
2. The Exodus Passover
   (*a*) The legend
   (*b*) The ritual of the Exodus Pesaḥ
   (*c*) The ritual of the Exodus Passover week (Maṣṣoth festival);
3. The post-Exodus Passover
   (*a*) The post-Exodus Pesaḥ
   (*b*) The post-Exodus Passover week (Maṣṣoth festival).

Texts on the post-Exodus Passover are distributed in the following documents:

(i) documents incorporated in the Exodus narrative: Ex. 12:14–20, 24–27, 42, 13:3–10

[1] *Introduction to the Literature of the Old Testament*, 1913.

[2] Among the general works consulted may be particularly noted A. Weiser, *Einleitung in das Alte Testament*, 1939; R. H. Pfeiffer, *Introduction to the Old Testament*, 1952; A. Bentzen, *Introduction to the Old Testament*, 1952; M. H. Segal, *Mebho' haMiqra'* (in Hebrew), 1955; and O. Eissfeldt, *Einleitung in das Alte Testament*, 1956.

(ii) summary code A: Ex. 23:14 ff.
(iii) summary code B: Ex. 34:18 ff.
(iv) festal calendar: Lev. 23:4 ff.
(v) regulations on the 'second Pesaḥ': Num. 9:1 ff.
(vi) sacrificial tariff: Num. 28:16 ff.
(vii) Deuteronomic code: Deut. 16:1 ff.

Passages dealing with the dedication of firstborn and firstlings and with the Sheaf-waving ceremony—which appear to have close association with the Passover—are set out on the subsequent pages.

1. POSSIBLE REFERENCES TO THE PASSOVER BEFORE THE EXODUS

The events that culminate in the Exodus are already forecast at the beginning of the mission of Moses. The Israelites, Moses is told, will demand freedom to perform a *zebhaḥ* at a distance of three days in the Wilderness. Pharaoh will grant them permission only after Egypt has been smitten with 'wonders', and, as they leave, the Israelite women will be given gifts of gold and silver and raiment:

J

(Ex. 3:18) And they shall hearken to thy voice: and thou shalt come, thou and the elders of Israel, unto the king of Egypt, and ye shall say unto him, The Lord, the God of the Hebrews, hath met with us:[1] and now let us go, we pray thee, three days' journey into the wilderness, that we may sacrifice[2] to the Lord our God.

E

(3:19–22) And I know that the king of Egypt will not give you leave to go, no, not[3] by a mighty hand. (20) And I will put forth my hand, and smite Egypt with all my wonders, which I will do in the midst thereof: and after that he will let you go. (21) And I will give this people favour in the sight of the Egyptians: and it shall come to pass, that, when ye go, ye shall not go empty: (22) but every woman shall ask of her neighbour, and of her that sojourneth in her house, jewels of silver, and jewels of gold, and raiment: and ye shall put them upon your sons, and upon your daughters; and ye shall spoil the Egyptians.[4]

[1] נקרה עלינו, cf. 5:3 (with the cognate קרא), Num. 23:3 f., 15 f., &c. Targ. 'has been called over us (by name)' is to be rejected since this presupposes the word שם in the Hebrew text.

[2] Heb. *zbḥ*.

[3] M.T. ולא is difficult; perhaps read אם לא, with LXX, as A. Dillmann, *Bücher Exodus und Leviticus*, 1880, in loc.

[4] On this, see further p. 146 below.

This sacrifice (*zebhaḥ*) is the ceremony peculiar to the pilgrimage festival (*ḥag*); if it is omitted the Israelites may be punished by pestilence or the sword:

E

(Ex. 5:1–2) And afterwards Moses and Aaron came, and said unto Pharaoh, Thus saith the Lord, the God of Israel, Let my people go, that they may hold a feast[1] unto me in the wilderness. (2) And Pharaoh said . . . I know not the Lord, and moreover I will not let Israel go.

J

(5:3) And they said, The God of the Hebrews hath met with us:[2] let us go, we pray thee, three days' journey into the wilderness, and sacrifice[3] unto the Lord our God; lest he fall upon us with pestilence, or with the sword.

The festival is a religious service, and, it is repeated, this service can be performed only in the Wilderness:

J

(7:16) And thou shalt say unto him, The Lord, the God of the Hebrews, hath sent me unto thee, saying, Let my people go, that they may serve[4] me in the wilderness . . . .[5]

In one passage the reason for holding the festival, with its sacrifices, in the Wilderness is said to be fear of the Egyptians:

J

(8:21–24; E.V. 25–28) And Pharaoh . . . said, Go ye, sacrifice[3] to your God in the land. (22) And Moses said, It is not meet so to do; for we shall sacrifice[3] the abomination of the Egyptians to the Lord our God: lo, shall we sacrifice[3] the abomination of the Egyptians before their eyes, and will they not stone us? (23) We will go three days' journey into the wilderness, and sacrifice[3] to the Lord our God, as he shall command[6] us. (24) And Pharaoh said, I will let you go, that ye may sacrifice[3] to the Lord your God in the wilderness; only ye shall not go very far away . . . .

[1] Heb. *ḥgg*.

[2] נקרא עלינו, cf. p. 43 above.

[3] Heb. *zbḥ*, cf. Ex. 8:4 (E.V. 8:8; J), 8:25 (E.V. 8:29; J).

[4] Heb. *'bd*.

[5] See also 7:26 (E.V. 8:1), 8:16 (E.V. 8:20), 9:1, 13, 10:3, 7; all these passages are assigned to J. See, too, the important passage 4:22 f. (also J): 'And thou shalt say unto Pharaoh, Thus saith the Lord, Israel is my son, my firstborn: and I have said unto thee, Let my son (LXX 'my people') go, that he may serve (*'bd*) me; and thou hast refused to let him go: behold, I will slay thy son, thy firstborn.' There is a play on the other sense of *'bd* in 5:17–18 (J): 'But he said, Ye are idle, ye are idle: therefore ye say, Let us go and sacrifice (*zbḥ*) to the Lord. Go therefore now, and work (*'bd*) . . .'

[6] LXX 'hath commanded', less satisfactorily.

But the full requirements of the festival must, insists Moses, be fulfilled. They are prescribed in a subsequent passage:

J

(Ex. 10:8–11)... And (Pharaoh) said unto them, Go, serve[1] the Lord your God: but who are they that shall go? (9) And Moses said, We will go with our young and with our old, with our sons and with our daughters, with our flocks and with our herds will we go; for we must hold a feast[2] unto the Lord. (10) And he said unto them, So be the Lord with you, as I will let you go, and your little ones: look to it; for evil is before you. (11) Not so: go now ye that are men, and serve[1] the Lord; for that is what ye desire....

The sacrifices are now stated to include burnt offerings as well as *zebhaḥim*:

J

(10:24–26) And Pharaoh ... said, Go ye, serve[1] the Lord; only let your flocks and your herds be stayed: let your little ones also go with you. (25) And Moses said, Thou must also give into our hand sacrifices and burnt offerings,[3] that we may sacrifice[4] unto the Lord our God. (26) Our cattle also shall go with us; there shall not a hoof be left behind; for thereof must we take to serve[1] the Lord our God; and we know not with what we must serve[1] the Lord, until we come thither.

We observe that throughout this narrative and the exchange of speeches, it is a pilgrimage festival (*ḥag*) that is described; there is no mention of the Pesaḥ by name. And even when the Pesaḥ had been performed, Pharaoh, according to the narrator, believed that the sacrifices for the festival were still to come:

E

(12:31–32)[5] And he called for Moses and Aaron by night, and said, Rise up, get you forth from among my people, both ye and the children of Israel; and go, serve[1] the Lord, as ye have said. (32) Take both your flocks and your herds, as ye have said, and be gone; and bless me also.

What are the characteristic features of the pilgrimage festival (*ḥag*) in this context? The text should probably not be pressed too closely; this is a vigorous narrative, told with obvious relish. The outcome of the struggle between Pharaoh and the God of Israel is certain, and the writer taunts Pharaoh as he is impelled towards his fate. As Pharaoh's concessions grow, so the demands of Moses increase until the prophecy of the Exodus is fulfilled.

[1] Heb. *ʿbd*. [2] Heb. *ḥag*. [3] Heb. *zebhaḥim* and *ʿoloth*. [4] Heb. *ʿśh*.
[5] Eissfeldt, op. cit. 237 ff., assigns Ex. 12:31 to E and 12:32 to J.

But some features are reiterated, and these, we may assume, were regarded by the writer as essential for the proper celebration of a *ḥag*. It was to be performed in the Wilderness, apparently not at a fixed shrine in the circumstances of the Exodus, but at a place at the end of a journey of three days. Most important, it was performed in honour of the God of the Hebrews. Other details are less clear. The *ḥag* may have been an occasion for the wearing of gold and silver jewels and of choice garments by women and children,[1] Israelites of both sexes and of all ages may have participated, and the sacrifices may have been both *zebhaḥim* and burnt offerings. The *ḥag* may have had some apotropaic significance, to ward off divine punishment.

2. THE EXODUS PASSOVER

(*a*) *The legend*

The association of the Passover with the Exodus, as seen through the Traditional Documents, is intimate and constant.[2] Indeed, the festival is said to be derived from the historical event. As our narrative approaches the actual Exodus we find that there has been an almost imperceptible change of atmosphere. In the previous section we have examined allusions to the *ḥag* and its ceremonial as this might (according to the writer) have been regarded by the Egyptians; and I have pointed out that it has no obvious connexion with the Pesaḥ. But as we draw near to the climax of the Exodus, the claims (or pretexts) of Moses are ignored.[3] The Israelites did not go on a three days' journey into the wilderness in order to carry out the festival and its sacrifices; they celebrated the Pesaḥ in Egypt. The Exodus did not take place in order to celebrate the festival; but the festival was celebrated, and the Exodus followed.

The Passover legend, as it is presented in the Bible text, may be summarized briefly. God announced to Moses the tenth plague in which the divine chastisement of the Egyptians and their gods was to culminate. Moses warned Pharaoh of the impending slaughter of the Egyptian first-born and firstlings and the departure of the Israelites from Egypt—in the knowledge that Pharaoh would remain unmoved. The Passover regulations were prescribed to Moses and transmitted to the elders of Israel.[4] The Pesaḥ victims were slain and eaten at night in haste; their blood was

[1] See p. 146 below.

[2] The exceptions are three of the Traditional Documents which prescribe special features of the Passover and are not concerned with its origins—the festal calendar (Lev. 23:4 ff.), the regulations on the 'second Pesaḥ' (Num. 9:1 ff.), and the sacrificial tariff (Num. 28:16 ff.). See p. 190 below.

[3] See the notable treatment of the Exodus narrative by J. Pedersen, *Israel. Its Life and Culture*, iii–iv, 1959, 393 ff., 728 ff.

[4] But see p. 70 below.

smeared outside the dwelling-places and the deity (or his agent) performed some action[1] over the dwelling-places. From this action the Pesaḥ apparently took its name. The Egyptian firstborn and firstlings were slain, and the Israelites spared. Pharaoh and his people then begged the Israelites to leave quickly, and bestowed on them silver and gold and raiment. As they went the Israelites took unleavened bread, either because they had bound up their kneading-troughs in expectation of the journey or because they had not enough time to allow the dough to ferment. The Exodus is said to have taken place on the fifteenth day of the first month:

E

(Ex. 11:1–3) And the Lord said unto Moses, Yet one plague more will I bring upon Pharaoh, and upon Egypt; afterwards he will let you go hence: when he shall let you go, he shall surely thrust you out hence altogether.[2] (2) Speak now in the ears of the people, and let them ask every man of his neighbour,[3] and every woman of her neighbour, jewels of silver, and jewels of gold.[4] (3) And the Lord gave[5] the people favour in the sight of the Egyptians. Moreover the man Moses was very great in the land of Egypt, in the sight of Pharaoh's servants, and in the sight of the people.[6]

J

(11:4–8) And Moses said, Thus saith the Lord, About midnight will I go out into the midst of Egypt: (5) and all the firstborn in the land of Egypt shall die, from the firstborn of Pharaoh that sitteth upon his throne, even unto the firstborn of the maidservant that is behind the mill; and all the firstborn of cattle.

[1] Heb. *psḥ*.

[2] J. Coppens, *Bulletin d'Histoire et d'Exégèse de l'Ancien Testament*, 1947, 178, regards verses 1aαbβ, 4 ff. as the primary stratum and 1aβbα, 2–3 as a secondary stratum. See Morgenstern, 'Despoiling of the Egyptians', *JBL* lxviii, 1949, 1.

[3] Morgenstern, loc. cit., omits as a gloss.

[4] LXX, Sam., and a Heb. manuscript add 'and raiment'; cf. Ex. 3:22, 12:15.

[5] Vulg. 'will give'.

[6] Morgenstern, op. cit., inserts Ex. 4:22 at this point.

J

(6) And there shall be a great cry throughout all the land of Egypt, such as there hath been none like it, nor shall be like it any more. (7) But against any of the children of Israel shall not a dog move his tongue, against man or beast: that ye may know how that the Lord doth put a difference[1] between the Egyptians and Israel. (8) And all these thy servants shall come down unto me, and bow down themselves unto me, saying, Get thee out, and all the people that follow thee: and after that I will go out. And he went out from Pharaoh in hot anger.

P

(Ex. 11:9–10)[2] And the Lord said unto Moses, Pharaoh will not hearken unto you: that my wonders may be multiplied in the land of Egypt. (10) And Moses and Aaron did all these wonders before Pharaoh: and the Lord hardened Pharaoh's heart, and he did not let the children of Israel go out of his land.

(12:1, 11b–13) And the Lord spake unto Moses and Aaron in the land of Egypt, saying.... (11b) Ye shall eat it in haste:[3] it is the Lord's passover.[6a] (12) For I will go through[4] the land of Egypt in that night, and will smite all the firstborn[5] in the land of Egypt, both man and beast; and against all the gods of Egypt I will execute judgements: I am the Lord. (13) And the blood shall be to you for a token upon the houses where ye are: and when I see the blood I will pass[6] over you, and

[1] LXX *παραδοξάζει*. [2] A. H. McNeile, *Book of Exodus*, 1917, in loc., assigns to Rje.
[3] Heb. *ḥippazon.* [4] Heb. *'br.* [5] Heb. *bekhor.*
[6] Heb. *psḥ.* LXX has 'shelter'; Targ. Jer., Onq. חוס, 'spare'. See the discussion on pp. 97 f. and 185 f. below.
[6a] Heb. *pesaḥ*; Targ. Jer. חייסא, 'sparing'; Aq. *ὑπέρβασις*, 'passing-by'.

P

there shall no plague be upon you to destroy[1b] you, when I smite the land of Egypt.

JE

(Ex. 12:21, 23)[2] Then Moses called for all the elders of Israel, and said unto them . . . . (23) The Lord will pass through[3] to smite the Egyptians; and when he seeth the blood upon the lintel, and on the two side posts, the Lord will pass[4] over the door, and will not suffer the destroyer[1a] to come in unto your houses to smite you.

(12:28)[5] And the children of Israel went and did so; as the Lord had commanded Moses and Aaron, so did they.

J

(12:29–30)[6] And it came to pass at midnight, that the Lord smote all the firstborn[7] in the land of Egypt, from the firstborn[7] of Pharaoh that sat on his throne unto the firstborn[7] of the captive that was in the dungeon; and all the firstborn[7] of cattle. (30) And Pharaoh rose up in the night, he, and all his servants, and all the Egyptians; and there was a great cry in Egypt; for there was not a house where there was not one dead.

1a המשחית; LXX *ὀλεθρεύοντα*, 'destroyer'.

1b למשחית; LXX *τοῦ ἐκτριβῆναι*, 'for destruction'. R.V. margin 'Or, for a destroyer'.

2 May, op. cit. 71, assigns Ex. 12:21–28 to P, like 12:1 ff.; so also H. Gressmann, *Die Schriften des Alten Testaments*, i/2, 1922, 51, and Pfeiffer, op. cit. 189. Eissfeldt, op. cit. 231, attributes 12:21–27 to the 'Lay Code'. Dillmann, op. cit., in loc., regards vv. 21 ff. as early. Weiser, op. cit., holds that 12:21–27 is J, 12:40–51 is P, and the rest of the chapter generally as E mixed with J and P.

3 Heb. *'br*.

4 Heb. *psḥ*; LXX *παρελεύσεται*, 'pass by'; Targ. Jer. 'defend'; Targ. Onq. 'spare'. See pp. 97 f. below.

5 For the reasons for attributing this verse to P, see H. L. Strack, *Bücher Genesis, Exodus, Leviticus und Numeri*, 1894, in loc., and Dillmann, op. cit., in loc.

6 May, loc. cit., regards these verses as the work of JE and the 'natural sequel' to Ex. 11.

7 Heb. *bekhor*.

E

(Ex. 12:31–36)[1] And he called for Moses and Aaron by night, and said, Rise up, get you forth from among my people, both ye and the children of Israel; and go, serve[2] the Lord, as ye have said. (32) Take both your flocks and your herds, as ye have said, and be gone; and bless me also. (33) And the Egyptians were urgent upon the people, to send them out of the land in haste; for they said, We be all dead men. (34) And the people took their dough before it was leavened,[3] their kneading-troughs[4] being bound up in their clothes upon their shoulders. (35) And the children of Israel did according to the word of Moses; and they asked of the Egyptians jewels of silver, and jewels of gold, and raiment: (36) and the Lord gave the people favour in the sight of the Egyptians, so that they let them have what they asked. And they spoiled the Egyptians.

P

(12:37a)[1] And the children of Israel journeyed from Rameses to Succoth,

(12:37b–39)[1] about six hundred thousand on foot that were men, beside children. (38) And a mixed multitude went up also with them; and flocks, and herds, even very much cattle. (39) And they baked unleavened cakes[5] of the dough which they brought forth out of Egypt, for it was not leavened;[3] because they

[1] Eissfeldt, op. cit. 231, 237, 239, assigns Ex. 12:31 to E, 12:32 to J, and 12:33–39 to the 'Lay Code'.

[2] Heb. *'bd*.

[3] Heb. *ḥmṣ*.

[4] Heb. מִשְׁאֲרֹת, cf. שְׂאֹר. Pesh. has ܦܝܪܝܗܘܢ here and for Heb. משמרת in Ex. 16:23, where also the context refers to baking; see R. Payne Smith, *Thesaurus*, s. ܦܪ. Targ. Jer. renders ומן דמשתייר לכון מן פטירי וכו׳, i.e. 'what is left over'; cf. *š'r*, remain.

[5] Heb. *'ugoth maṣṣoth*; LXX *ἐγκρυφίας ἀζύμους*, Vulg. *subcinericios panes azymos*, cakes covered with hot ashes.

E

were thrust out of Egypt, and could not tarry, neither had they prepared for themselves any victual.

P

(Ex. 12:41b) Even the selfsame day it came to pass, that all the hosts[1] of the Lord went out from the land of Egypt.

(12:51) And it came to pass the selfsame day, that the Lord did bring the children of Israel out of the land of Egypt by their hosts.[1]

(Num. 33:3–4) And they journeyed from Rameses in the first month, on the fifteenth day of the first month; on the morrow after the passover[2] the children of Israel went out with an high hand in the sight of all the Egyptians, (4) while the Egyptians were burying all their firstborn, which the Lord had smitten among them: upon their gods also the Lord executed judgements.

(*b*) *The ritual of the Exodus Pesaḥ*

The Exodus Pesaḥ was held in the first month:

P

(Ex. 12:1–2) And the Lord spake unto Moses and Aaron . . ., saying, (2) This month shall be unto you the beginning of months: it shall be the first month of the year to you.

The instructions that follow were given to 'all the congregation' or to 'all the elders' of Israel:

JE	P
(12:21a)[3] Then Moses called for all the elders of Israel	(12:3a) Speak ye unto all the congregation[4] of Israel . . . .

The Pesaḥ victim was, we are told in one document, to be chosen on the tenth day of the month and by each unit of a 'fathers' house'; another document calls the unit the 'family', and omits reference to the tenth day:

JE	P
(12:21b) Draw out, and take you lambs according to your families[5]	(12:3b) In the tenth (day) of this month they shall take to them every man a lamb, according to their fathers' houses,[6a] a lamb for an household:[6]

[1] Heb. *ṣabha'*.

[2] ממחרת הפסח.

[3] See p. 49 n. 2 above.

[4] Heb. *'edah*.

[5] Heb. *mišpaḥah*.

[6] Heb. *bayith*.

[6a] Heb. *beth 'abhoth*.

In certain circumstances it might be necessary to extend the units:

P

(Ex. 12:4) and if the household[1] be too little for a lamb, then shall he and his neighbour next unto his house take one according to the number[2b] of the souls; according to every man's eating ye shall make your count[2a] for the lamb.

The victim was to be a male sheep or goat without blemish and 'of the first year':

JE

(12:21) . . . take you lambs . . . .[3]

P

(12:3, 5) . . . they shall take to them every man a lamb[4] . . . a lamb[4] for an household: . . . (5) Your lamb[4] shall be without blemish, a male of the first year:[5] ye shall take it from the sheep, or from the goats:

and it was to be kept until the fourteenth day:

P

(12:6) and ye shall keep it up[6] until the fourteenth day of the same month:

when it was to be killed in public in the evening (at the end) of that day. One document uses the term 'passover' of the Pesaḥ victim:

JE

(12:21) . . . and kill[7] the passover.[8]

P

(12:6) and the whole assembly of the congregation of Israel[9] shall kill[7] it at even.[10]

Some of the blood was to be drawn off into a basin, and applied to the en-

[1] Heb. *bayith*. [2a] Heb. *kss*.

[2b] Heb. *mikhsah*. Targ. Jer. has ואין זעירין אינשי ביתא ממנין עשרא כמיסת למיכול אימרא ויסב הוא ושיבביה דקריב לביתיה בסכום נפשתא גבר לפום מיסת מיכליה תיכסון ית אמרא במנין נפשתא; cf. *Mekhilta* in loc. אין מכסת אלא מנין. On מיסה, cf. pp. 72 n. 6 and 213 below on Deut. 16:10.

[3] Heb. *ṣon*, collective of *śeh*.

[4] Heb. *śeh*, a small animal, whether sheep or goat; E.V. 'lamb' is misleading. See p. 140 n. 9 below.

[5] Heb. *ben-šanah*, LXX *ἐνιαύσιον*. See pp. 141 f. below.

[6] והיה לכם למשמרת. [7] Heb. *šḥṭ*.

[8] Heb. *pesaḥ*.

[9] Heb. *kol qehal 'adath Yisra'el*.

[10] Heb. lit. 'between the two evenings'; the E.V. is misleading. LXX *πρὸς ἑσπέραν*; Targ. Jer. ביני שמשתא; Targ. Onq. בין שמשיא; Pesh. ܒܝܢܝ ܪ̈ܡܫܐ. See p. 131 below.

trance of the dwelling-place. We are not told what was to be done with the remainder of the blood:

JE	P
(Ex. 12:22) And ye shall take a bunch of hyssop, and dip it in the blood that is in the bason,[1] and strike[2] the lintel and the two side posts with the blood that is in the bason;[1]	(12:7) And they shall take of the blood, and put it on the two side posts and on the lintel, upon the houses wherein they shall eat it.

There follows the preparation of the victim for the repast:

P

(12:8–9) And they shall eat the flesh in that night, roast with fire . . . . (9) Eat not of it raw, nor sodden at all with water,[3] but roast with fire; its head with[4] its legs and with[4] the inwards thereof.

It may be inferred that the ceremonies up to this point were to be carried out by the heads of families (or households). What comes now was clearly obligatory upon a wider circle, both Israelites and those identified with them by rights of residence; the condition of circumcision shows that the eating of the Pesaḥ victim was restricted to males. These regulations appear in a 'supplementary' document attached in a curiously loose way to the account of the Exodus Passover:

P

(12:43–45, 47–49) . . . This is the ordinance of the passover: there shall no alien[5] eat thereof: (44) but every man's servant that is bought for money, when thou hast circumcised him, then shall he eat thereof. (45) A sojourner[6] and an hired servant shall not eat thereof. . . . (47) All the congregation of Israel[7] shall keep it.[8b] (48) And when a stranger[9a] shall sojourn[9] with thee, and will keep the passover[8a] to the Lord, let all his males be circumcised, and then let him come near and keep[8b] it; and he shall be as one that is born in the land:[10a] but no uncircumcised person shall eat thereof. (49) One law shall be to him that is homeborn,[10] and unto the stranger[9a] that sojourneth[9] among you.

[1] Heb. *saph*; Targ., Pesh. *man*, *mana*. Heb. *saph* may also be interpreted as 'threshold', and so LXX, *τοῦ παρὰ τὴν θύραν*. See p. 158 n. 1 below.

[2] The Heb. verb means lit. 'cause to touch'. See p. 159 below.

[3] בשל מבשל במים; see pp. 166 f. and 205 below. Targ. Jer., Onq. 'roast'.

[4] Heb. *'al*, LXX *σύν*, 'together with', as Ex. 12:8 (p. 54 n. 4 below), 35:22, Gen. 32:12. The preposition has this sense in accounts of sacrificial ritual, Lev. 2:2, 16, 3:4, 10, 15, 4:9, 11, 7:4, 23:20aβ, cf. Ex. 23:18, 34:25; so also על־הדם, Lev. 19:26, 1 Sam. 14:32, Ezek. 33:25 (though some prefer to read הרים for הדם in this passage, as 18:6)—a similar phrase is found in Egyptian, according to B. Couroyer, *RB* lxv, 1958, 114.

[5] Heb. *ben-nekhar*; Targ. Jer. בר ישראל דאיסתלק; Targ. Onq. בר ישראל דאשתמד.

[6] Heb. *tošabh*. [7] Heb. *kol 'adath Yisra'el*. [8a] Heb. *'śh pesaḥ*. [8b] Heb. *'śh*.

[9] Heb. *gwr*. [9a] Heb. *ger*. [10] Heb. *'ezraḥ*. [10a] Heb. *'ezraḥ ha'areṣ*.

Those who participated were to wear special dress:

P

(Ex. 12:11) And thus shall ye eat it; with your loins girded, your shoes on your feet, and your staff in your hand:

with an extension of this motif of the special dress, the passage declares that

P

(12:11) . . . ye shall eat it in haste:[1] it is the Lord's passover.[2]

The flesh was to have certain accompaniments:

P

(12:8) And they shall eat the flesh in that night . . . and unleavened bread;[3] with[4] bitter herbs[5] they shall eat it.

Certain precautions were to be taken at the meal. The participants were forbidden to leave their dwelling-places:

JE

(12:22) . . . none of you shall go out of the door of his house until the morning.

So, too, the victim's flesh was not to be taken out of the dwelling-places:

P

(12:46) In one house[6] shall it be eaten; thou shalt not carry aught of the flesh abroad out of the house;

and its bones were not to be broken:

P

(12:46) neither shall ye break a bone thereof.[7]

The remains of the meal were to be destroyed before the following morning:

P

(12:10) And ye shall let nothing of it remain until the morning; but that which remaineth of it until the morning ye shall burn with fire.

[1] Heb. *ḥippazon*. [2] Heb. *pesaḥ*.

[3] Heb. *maṣṣoth*. [4] Heb. *'al;* cf. p. 53 n. 4 above.

[5] Heb. *merorim*; LXX πικρίδων; Vulg. *lactucis agrestibus*. Targ. Jer. תמכא ועולשין. See pp. 169 f. below.

[6] Targ. Jer., Onq. 'in one *ḥabhurah*'. See p. 256 and n. 8 below.

[7] LXX inserts this regulation also in Ex. 12:10.

(*c*) *The ritual of the Exodus Passover week* (*Maṣṣoth festival*)

In the Passover legend two divergent reasons are given for associating the eating of unleavened bread with the Exodus.[1] We have seen, too, that unleavened bread is to be an accompaniment of the flesh of the victim at the meal on the Exodus night.[2] But there is nothing in the Exodus narrative to suggest that at the Exodus the Pesaḥ was followed by a seven-day festival.[3]

3. THE POST-EXODUS PASSOVER

(*a*) *The post-Exodus Pesaḥ*

The perpetuation of the Pesaḥ ceremonies is prescribed already in the Exodus narrative:

JE	E
(Ex. 12:24–27)[4] And ye shall observe[5] this thing for an ordinance to thee and to thy sons for ever. (25) And it shall come to pass, when ye be come to the land which the Lord will give you, according as he hath promised, that ye shall keep[5] this service.[6] (26) And it shall come to pass, when your children shall say unto you, What mean ye by this service?[6] (27) that ye shall say, It is the sacrifice[7] of the Lord's passover,[8a] who passed[8] over the houses of the children of Israel in Egypt, when he smote the Egyptians, and delivered our houses.	(Ex. 12:42) It is a night to be much observed[5a] unto the Lord for bringing them out from the land of Egypt: this is that night of the Lord, to be much observed[5a] of all the children of Israel throughout their generations.[9]

Other documents declare that the ritual is to be observed annually on the date of the Exodus Pesaḥ, the fourteenth day of the first month. The Deuteronomist, however, prescribes the month only and calls it Abib:

D	P		
	Festal calendar	*Second Pesaḥ*	*Sacrificial tariff*
(Deut. 16:1, 6) Observe[5] the month	(Lev. 23:5)[10] In the first month,[11] on	(Num. 9:1–3, 5) And the Lord	(Num. 28:16) And in the first

[1] Ex. 12:34, 39. See p. 50 above.

[2] Ex. 12:8. See p. 54 above.

[3] Indeed, in Num. 33:3 the Israelites are said to have travelled from Egypt on the day following the Pesaḥ.

[4] See p. 49 n. 2 above.

[5] Heb. *šmr*.

[5a] Heb. *šimmurim*.

[6] Heb. *'abhodah*.

[7] Heb. *zebhaḥ*.

[8] Heb. *psḥ*; LXX ἐσκέπασεν, 'shelter'; Targ. Jer., Onq. 'spare'.

[8a] Heb. *pesaḥ*; Targ. Jer., Onq. 'sparing'.

[9] The second part of this verse is regarded by Driver, op. cit., in loc., and most critics as a gloss. On the significance of this verse, see pp. 131 f. below.

[10] Eissfeldt, op. cit. 246, 278 ff., maintains that Lev. 23:4–6 is the work of P; he holds further that 23:9–12, 15 ff. belongs to the Holiness Code but has been greatly redacted.

[11] Targ. Jer. 'in the month of Nisan'.

D	P		
	Festal calendar	*Second Pesaḥ*	*Sacrificial tariff*
of Abib, and keep the passover[2a] unto the Lord thy God: for in the month of Abib the Lord thy God brought thee forth out of Egypt . . . . (6) Thou shalt sacrifice the passover[2c] . . . at the season that thou camest forth out of Egypt.	the fourteenth day[1] of the month . . . is the Lord's passover.[2]	spake unto Moses . . . saying, (2) Moreover let the children of Israel keep the passover[2a] in its appointed season.[3] (3) In the fourteenth day of this month . . . ye shall keep it[2b] in its appointed season:[3] according to all the statutes of it, and according to all the ordinances thereof, shall ye keep it.[2b] . . . (5) And they kept the passover[2a] in the first (month),[4] on the fourteenth day of the month	month, on the fourteenth day of the month, is the Lord's passover.[2]

There is no instruction about the selection of the Pesaḥ victim on the tenth day. Only the Deuteronomist prescribes the species of the victim and appears to state that it may be chosen from the herds as well as from the flocks. Deuteronomy, however, makes no mention of its sex, age, or ritual cleanness:

D

(Deut. 16:2) And thou shalt sacrifice the passover[2c] unto the Lord thy God, of the flock and the herd[5] . . .

In none of the documents is there mention of the size of the units by which the post-Exodus Pesaḥ is to be sacrificed; but Deuteronomy stresses the place of the ceremony:

D

(Deut. 16:2, 5–6) . . . in the place which the Lord shall choose to cause his name to dwell there. . . . (5) Thou mayest not sacrifice the passover[2c] within any of thy gates,[6] which the Lord thy God giveth thee: (6) but at the place which the Lord thy God shall choose to cause his name to dwell in, there thou shalt sacrifice the passover.[2c]

[1] E.V. 'day' is not in the Heb. [2] Heb. *pesaḥ*. [2a] Heb. *'śh pesaḥ*.
[2b] Heb. *'śh* (*pesaḥ*). [2c] Heb. *zbḥ pesaḥ*. [3] Heb. *mo'ed*. [4] Targ. Onq. 'in Nisan'.
[5] Targ. Onq. 'passover (offering) of the flock and sacrifices of holy offerings (*qudšayya*) of the oxen'; cf. *Siphre*, in loc., and *Mekhilta* on Ex. 12:5.
[6] LXX, Targ. Onq., Pesh. 'cities'.

In the P documents the time of the Pesaḥ sacrifice is defined exactly as 'between the two evenings' (inadequately rendered by E.V. 'at even'); the Deuteronomist is less precise:

D	P	
	Festal calendar	*Second Pesaḥ*
(Deut. 16:4, 6) ... the flesh, which thou sacrificest[1] ... at even[2a] ... (6) thou shalt sacrifice the passover[1a] at even,[2a] at the going down of the sun, at the season that thou camest forth out of Egypt.	(Lev. 23:5) ... at even[2b]	(Num. 9:3, 5, 11) ... at even[2c] ....

None of the documents on the post-Exodus Pesaḥ makes reference to the smearing of blood on the lintel and doorposts, and they give no description of the method in which the blood was manipulated. There is no allusion to special dress at the meal.

At the Exodus Pesaḥ stress was laid on the roasting of the victim whole; Deuteronomy is less precise:

D
(Deut. 16:7) And thou shalt roast[3] and eat it ....

The regulations on ritual cleanness for the participants at the Pesaḥ are prescribed in a passage composed for that purpose; it also prescribes a 'second Pesaḥ' for those unable to keep the ceremony at the proper time:

P
Second Pesaḥ
(Num. 9:6, 7, 9–11) There were certain men, who were unclean by the dead body of a man, so that they could not keep the passover[4] on that day: ... (7) and those men said ..., We are unclean by the dead body of a man: wherefore are we kept back, that we may not offer the oblation[5] of the Lord in its appointed season[6] among the children of Israel? ... (9) And the Lord

[1] Heb. *zbḥ*. [1a] Heb. *zbḥ pesaḥ*.

[2a] Heb. *ba'erebh*. LXX *ἑσπέρας*; Targ. Jer., Onq. ברמשא, so Pesh.

[2b] Heb. *ben ha'arbayim*; see p. 52 n. 10 above. LXX *ἀνὰ μέσον τῶν ἑσπερινῶν*; Targ. Jer. ביני שימשתא; Targ. Onq. בין שמשיא; Pesh. ܒܝܬ ܪ̈ܡܫܐ.

[2c] Heb., Targ. Jer., Onq., Pesh. as n. 2b above. LXX has *πρὸς ἑσπέραν* in Num. 9:3, 11; it omits in v. 5, but has *ἐναρχομένου τῇ τεσσαρεσκαιδεκάτῃ ἡμέρᾳ τοῦ μηνός*.

[3] Heb. *bšl*, R.V. margin 'seethe'; see pp. 205 f. below. LXX has the conflate *ἑψήσεις καὶ ὀπτήσεις*; Targ. Onq. *bšl*; Targ. Jer. *ṭwy*, 'roast'.

[4] Heb. *'śh pesaḥ*. [5] Heb. *haqribh qorban*.

[6] Heb. *mo'ed*.

P

Second Pesaḥ

spake unto Moses, saying, (10) Speak unto the children of Israel, saying, If any man of you or of your generations shall be unclean by reason of a dead body, or be in a journey afar off,[1] yet he shall keep the passover[2a] unto the Lord: (11) in the second month on the fourteenth day . . . they shall keep[2b] it . . . .

There is no direct allusion in the documents on the post-Exodus Pesaḥ to the condition of circumcision; but it may be inferred from the following provision:

P

Second Pesaḥ

(Num. 9:14) If a stranger[3a] shall sojourn[3] among you, and will keep the passover[2a] unto the Lord; according to the statute of the passover,[4] and according to the ordinance thereof, so shall he do: ye shall have one statute, both for the stranger,[3a] and for him that is born in the land.[5]

The penalty for omission to observe the Pesaḥ in the first month by those who are not debarred by ritual uncleanness is excommunication; this had not been stated in the regulations on the Exodus Pesaḥ:

P

Second Pesaḥ

(Num. 9:13) . . . The man that is clean, and is not in a journey, and forbeareth to keep the passover,[2a] that soul shall be cut off from his people: because he offered not the oblation[6] of his[7] Lord in its appointed season,[8] that man shall bear his sin.

As at the Exodus Pesaḥ, so also at subsequent celebrations the flesh of the victim is to be accompanied by unleavened bread and bitter herbs; this is prescribed for the 'second Pesaḥ', and must therefore have been required for the Pesaḥ at its proper date in the first month also. The Deuteronomist associates the unleavened bread with the haste and misery of the Exodus, but he does not mention the bitter herbs:

[1] M.T. has a point over the last letter of רחקה; cf. *Mish. Pes.* ix. 2. LXX here has ἐν ὁδῷ μακρὰν (for μακρᾷ), Vulg. *in via procul*, referring the adjective to the subject of the sentence, not to the journey.

[2a] Heb. *'śh pesaḥ*. [2b] Heb. *'śh (pesaḥ)*. [3] Heb. *gwr*.

[3a] Heb. *ger*. [4] Heb. *pesaḥ*. [5] Heb. *'ezraḥ ha'areṣ*.

[6] Heb. *haqribh qorban*. [7] Not in the Heb. [8] Heb. *mo'ed*.

D

(Deut. 16:3) Thou shalt eat no leavened bread[1] with[2] it; seven days shalt thou eat unleavened bread[3] therewith,[4] even the bread of affliction; for thou camest forth out of the land of Egypt in haste:[5]

P

Second Pesaḥ

(Num. 9:11) . . . they shall eat it with[2] unleavened bread[3] and bitter herbs:

The Deuteronomist prescribes that the post-Exodus Pesaḥ is to be held at a shrine, and he does not declare expressly that the participants are not to leave their dwelling-places during the night or to take the flesh out of doors:

D

(Deut. 16:7) And thou shalt . . . eat it in the place which the Lord thy God shall choose . . . .

The regulation against breaking the bones of the Pesaḥ victim is prescribed for the 'second Pesaḥ', and therefore must have obtained also at the Pesaḥ proper; the rule against leaving any of the remains until morning was observed after, as at, the Exodus celebration of the Pesaḥ:

JE

(Ex. 34:25) Thou shalt not offer[6] the blood of my sacrifice[7a] with[2] leavened bread;[1] neither shall the sacrifice[7a] of the feast of the passover[8b] be left unto the morning.[9]

D

(Deut. 16:4) . . . neither shall any of the flesh, which thou sacrificest[7] the first day at even, remain all night until the morning.

P

Second Pesaḥ

(Num. 9:12) they shall leave none of it unto the morning, nor break a bone thereof: according to all the statute of the passover[8a] they shall keep it.[8c]

[1] Heb. *ḥameṣ*. [2] Heb. *'al*. See p. 53 n. 4 above. LXX ἐπί. [3] Heb. *maṣṣoth*.

[4] Most critics omit as a dittography; see, for example, G. B. Gray, 'Passover and Unleavened Bread: the Laws of J, E, and D', *JTS* xxxvii, 1936, 252.

[5] Heb. *ḥippazon*. [6] Heb. *šḥṭ*. [7] Heb. *zbḥ*.

[7a] Heb. *zebhaḥ*. LXX has 'my sacrifices' (pl.).

[8a] Heb. *pesaḥ*. [8b] Heb. *ḥag haPesaḥ*. [8c] Heb. *'śh* (*pesaḥ*).

[9] Cf. 23:18, 'Thou shalt not offer (Heb. *zbḥ*) the blood of my sacrifice (Heb. *zebhaḥ*) with (Heb. *'al*; cf. p. 53 n. 4 above) leavened bread (Heb. *ḥameṣ*); neither shall the fat of my feast (Heb. *ḥag*) remain all night until the morning.' Targ. Jer. has here לא תכסון קדם עד לא תבטלון חמיע נכסת פסחי ולא יביתון לצפרא בר ממדבחא תרבי נכסת פיסחא, and in 23:18 לא תכסון עד חמיע בבתיכון אדם נכסת פיסחי ולא יבית בר מן מידבחא תרבי נכסת פסחי עד צפרא. Targ. Onq. has here לא תיכוס על חמיע דם פסחי ולא יביתון לצפרא בר ממדבחא תרבי נכסת חגא דפסחא, and in 23:18 לא תכוס על חמיע דם פסחי ולא יביתון בר מן מדבחא תרבי נכסת חגא עד צפרא. Pesh. has here ܠܐ ܢܒܘܬ ܠܨܦܪܐ ܕܒܚܐ ܕܥܐܕܐ ܕܦܨܚܐ, and in 23:18 ܠܐ ܢܒܘܬ ܬܪܒܐ ܕܥܐܕܐ ܥܕܡܐ ܠܨܦܪܐ.

The celebrants might leave the shrine, according to the Deuteronomist, on the morning after the Pesaḥ:

D

(Deut. 16:7) . . . thou shalt turn[1] in the morning, and go unto thy tents.[2]

The documents are agreed that the Pesaḥ ceremonies, like those of other Hebrew festivals, are to be carried out in perpetuity:

D	P	
	Festal calendar	*Second Pesaḥ*
(Deut. 16:1, 3) . . . keep the passover[4a] unto the Lord thy God . . . (3) . . . that thou mayest remember the day when thou camest forth out of the land of Egypt all the days of thy life.	(Lev. 23:4, 5) These are the set feasts[3] of the Lord, even holy convocations, which ye shall proclaim in their appointed seasons.[3] (5) . . . the Lord's passover.[4]	(Num. 9:2, 3) . . . let the children of Israel keep the passover[4a] in its appointed season[3] . . . (3) according to all the statutes of it, and according to all the ordinances thereof, shall ye keep[4b] it.

(*b*) *The post-Exodus Passover week* (*Maṣṣoth festival*)

We have observed that, although the Passover legend traces the practice of eating unleavened bread for seven days to the circumstances of the Exodus, yet there is no evidence from the Exodus narrative that the Passover week was in fact celebrated at the Exodus.[5] Nevertheless, tradition continues to ascribe its beginnings to that event:

JE	D	P	
		Exodus narrative A	*Exodus narrative B*
(Ex. 13:3–4)[6] . . . Remember[7] this day, in which ye came out from Egypt, out of the house of bondage; for by strength of hand the Lord brought you out from this place: . . . (4) This day ye go forth in the month Abib.	(Deut. 16:3) . . . unleavened bread[8] . . . even[9] the bread of affliction; for thou camest forth out of the land of Egypt . . . : that thou mayest remember[7] the day when thou camest forth out of the land of Egypt all the days of thy life.	(Ex. 12:14) And this day shall be unto you for a memorial,[7a] . . . throughout your generations . . . by an ordinance for ever.	(Ex. 12:17) And ye shall observe[10] the (feast of) unleavened bread;[8] for in this selfsame day have I brought your hosts out of the land of Egypt:

[1] Heb. *panah*. [2] LXX *οἴκους*. [3] Heb. *mo'ed*. [4] Heb. *pesaḥ*.
[4a] Heb. *'śh pesaḥ*. On וְיַעֲשׂוּ in Num. 9:2, see Gray, *Book of Numbers* (I.C.C.), in loc.
[4b] Heb. *'śh* (*pesaḥ*). [5] p. 55 above.
[6] Eissfeldt, op. cit. 231, assigns Ex. 13:3–16 to the 'Lay Code'; McNeile, op. cit., in loc., regards 13:3 as the product of a Deuteronomistic redactor; Morgenstern, op. cit. 22 n. 35, attributes 13:3–11, 14–16 to D². [7] Heb. *zkr*. [7a] Heb. *zikkaron*.
[8] Heb. *maṣṣoth*. In Ex. 12:17 LXX has *τὴν ἐντολὴν ταύτην*, i.e. מִצְוֹת or מִצְוָה for מַצּוֹת; so Sam. [9] Not in the Heb. [10] *Heb. šmr*.

JE	E
(Ex. 34:18)[1] . . . unleavened bread[2] . . . for in the month Abib thou camest out from Egypt.	(Ex. 23:15) . . . unleavened bread[2] . . . in the month Abib (for in it thou camest out from Egypt);

The festival is a pilgrimage festival (*ḥag*):

JE	E	D	P: *Exodus narrative A*	P: *Festal calendar*	P: *Sacrificial tariff*
(Ex. 34:18)[1] The feast of unleavened bread[3a] shalt thou keep.[4]	(Ex. 23:14, 15) . . . thou shalt keep a feast[3] unto me . . . (15) the feast of unleavened bread[3a] shalt thou keep;[4]	(Deut. 16:16) . . . shall all thy males appear before the Lord thy God . . . in the feast of unleavened bread[3a] . . .	(Ex. 12:14) . . . and ye shall keep it a feast[3b] to the Lord	(Lev. 23:6) . . . the feast of unleavened bread[3a] . . . unto the Lord:	(Num. 28:17) . . . shall be a feast[3c] . . .

It takes place, according to some documents, in the first month on the fifteenth day—according to others, simply at the time fixed in the month Abib:

JE	E	P: *Festal calendar*	P: *Sacrificial tariff*
(Ex. 13:4, 5)[5] . . . in the month[6] Abib. (5) And . . . thou shalt keep this service[7] in this month.		(Lev. 23:5, 6) In the first month[6] . . . (6) on the fifteenth day of the same month[6]	(Num. 28:16, 17) And in the first month[6] . . . (17) on the fifteenth day of this month[6] . . . .
(Ex. 34:18)[1] . . . at the time appointed[8] in the month[6] Abib	(Ex. 23:15) . . . at the time appointed[8] in the month[6] Abib		

Two documents, however, integrate the Pesaḥ and the Maṣṣoth week closely in date. One, in the Exodus narrative, gives the latter the date and time of the Pesaḥ, the other, Deut. 16, treats the Pesaḥ as the opening ceremony of the Maṣṣoth week:

D	P: *Exodus narrative B*
(Deut. 16:3, 4) . . . shalt thou eat unleavened bread[9] therewith . . . (4) . . . any of the flesh, which thou sacrificest[10] the first day at even.[11a] . . .	(Ex. 12:18) In the first (month),[12] on the fourteenth day of the month at even,[11b] ye shall eat unleavened bread[9] . . . .

[1] Driver, op. cit., in loc., suggests that this may belong to J, cf. Rudolph, 'Aufbau von Ex. 19–34', in P. Volz, F. Stummer, and J. Hempel, *Werden und Wesen des Alten Testaments*, 1936, 46 ff. [2] Heb. *maṣṣoth.* [3] Heb. *ḥgg.* [3a] Heb. *ḥag haMaṣṣoth.* [3b] Heb. *ḥgg ḥag.* [3c] Heb. *ḥag.* [4] Heb. *šmr.* [5] See p. 60 n. 6 above. [6] Heb. *ḥodeš.* [7] Heb. *'bd 'abhodah.* [8] Heb. *mo'ed.* [9] Heb. *maṣṣoth.* [10] Heb. *zbḥ.*
[11a] Heb. *ba'erebh*; LXX τὸ ἑσπέρας, i.e. in the evening of the fifteenth day.
[11b] Heb. *ba'erebh*; LXX ἀφ' ἑσπέρας, i.e. from the evening (at the end) of the fourteenth day. [12] Targ. Jer., Onq. 'In Nisan'.

At the post-Exodus Passover leaven must be removed for seven days; only unleavened bread may be eaten:

JE	E	D	P: *Exodus narrative A*	P: *Exodus narrative B*	P: *Festal calendar*	P: *Sacrificial tariff*
(Ex. 13:3,[1] 6, 7) . . . there shall no leavened bread[2a] be eaten. . . . (6) Seven days[3] thou shalt eat unleavened bread[4] . . . . (7) Unleavened bread[4] shall be eaten throughout the seven days; and there shall no leavened bread[2a] be seen with thee, neither shall there be leaven[5] seen with thee . . . . (Ex. 34: 18)[7] Seven days thou shalt eat unleavened bread,[4] as I commanded thee	(Ex. 23: 15) . . . seven days thou shalt eat unleavened bread,[4] as I commanded thee	(Deut. 16:3, 4, 8) Thou shalt eat no leavened bread[2a] with it; seven days thou shalt eat unleavened bread[4] therewith . . . . (4) And there shall be no leaven[5] seen with thee . . . seven days . . . . (8) Six days thou shalt eat unleavened bread:[4] and on the seventh day	(Ex. 12: 15) Seven days shall ye eat unleavened bread;[4] even the first day ye shall put away leaven[5] out of your houses: . . . from the first day until the seventh day. . . .	(Ex. 12: 18–20) . . . on the fourteenth day of the month at even, ye shall eat unleavened bread,[4] until the one and twentieth day of the month at even.[6] (19) Seven days shall there be no leaven[5] . . . (20) Ye shall eat nothing leavened[2b] . . . shall ye eat unleavened bread.[4]	(Lev. 23: 6) . . . seven days ye shall eat unleavened bread.[4]	(Num. 28: 17) . . . seven days shall unleavened bread[4] be eaten.

The prohibition against leaven is to be applied throughout Israelite territory:

JE	D	P: *Exodus narrative A*	P: *Exodus narrative B*
(Ex. 13:7)[1] . . . there shall no leavened bread[2a] be seen with thee, neither shall there be leaven[5] seen with thee, in all thy borders.	(Deut 16:4) . . . there shall be no leaven[5] seen with thee in all thy borders	(Ex. 12:15) . . . ye shall put away leaven[5] out of your houses:	(Ex. 12:19, 20) . . . shall there be no leaven[5] found in your houses . . . . (20) Ye shall eat nothing leavened;[2b] in all your habitations shall ye eat unleavened bread.[4]

The threat of excommunication as the penalty for those who eat leavened bread (not, it should be noted, for those who abstain from un-

[1] See p. 60 n. 6 above. [2a] Heb. *ḥameṣ.* [2b] Heb. *maḥmeṣeth.*

[3] LXX Vat., Luc., and Sam. have 'six days', perhaps under the influence of Deut. 16:8. [4] Heb. *maṣṣoth.* [5] Heb. *śe'or.*

[6] Heb. *ba'erebh*; LXX ἕως ἑσπέρας, i.e. until the evening at the end of the twenty-first day.

[7] See p. 61 n. 1 above.

leavened bread) at the post-Exodus Passover is directed alike to all Israelites and to the *gerim* attached to the Israelite community:

P	
Exodus narrative A	*Exodus narrative B*
(Ex. 12:15) . . . whosoever eateth leavened bread[1a] from the first day until the seventh day, that soul shall be cut off from Israel.	(Ex. 12:19) . . . whosoever eateth that which is leavened,[1b] that soul shall be cut off from the congregation[2] of Israel, whether he be a sojourner[3] or one that is born in the land.[4]

Like other *ḥaggim*, the Maṣṣoth festival is celebrated by males and at shrines:

JE	E	D
(Ex. 34:23–24) Three times in the year shall all thy males appear before the Lord God, the God of Israel. . . . (24) when thou goest up to appear before the Lord thy God three times in the year.	(Ex. 23:17) Three times in the year all thy males shall appear before the Lord God.	(Deut. 16:16) Three times in a year shall all thy males appear before the Lord thy God in the place which he shall choose; in the feast of unleavened bread[5] . . . .

The seventh day of the festival is marked by special observances—called variously pilgrimage festival (*ḥag*), solemn assembly (*ʿaṣereth*), or holy convocation (*miqraʾ qodeš*):

JE	D	P		
		Exodus narrative A	*Festal calendar*	*Sacrificial tariff*
(Ex. 13:6)[6]. . . in the seventh day shall be a feast[7] to the Lord.	(Deut. 16:8) . . . and on the seventh day shall be a solemn assembly[8] to the Lord thy God:[9]	(Ex. 12:16). . . in the seventh day an holy convocation:[10]	(Lev. 23:8) . . . in the seventh day is an holy convocation;[10]	(Num. 28:25) And on the seventh day ye shall have an holy convocation;[10]

On that day work is forbidden; the definition of this regulation varies in the different documents:

[1a] Heb. *ḥameṣ*. [1b] Heb. *maḥmeṣeth*.
[2] Heb. *ʿedah*. [3] Heb. *ger*. [4] Heb. *ʾezraḥ haʾareṣ*.
[5] Heb. *ḥag haMaṣṣoth*. [6] See p. 60 n. 6 above. [7] Heb. *ḥag*.
[8] Heb. *ʿaṣereth*; Sam. has *ḥag* and LXX ἐξόδιον ἑορτή, representing a conflate Heb. *ʿaṣereth ḥag*.
[9] Targ. Jer. adds here: 'On the first day (of the festival week) ye shall offer the Sheaf and ye shall eat unleavened bread of the new produce.' [10] Heb. *miqraʾ qodeš*.

D	P		
	Exodus narrative A	*Festal calendar*	*Sacrificial tariff*
(Deut. 16:8) . . . thou shalt do no work (therein).[1]	(Ex. 12:16) . . . no manner of work[1a] shall be done . . ., save that which every man must eat, that only may be done of you.	(Lev. 23:8) . . . ye shall do no servile work[1b]	(Num. 28:25) . . . ye shall do no servile work.[1b]

The Deuteronomist permits the celebrants to leave on the morning after the Pesaḥ meal—evidently the first day of the Maṣṣoth week. Other documents, however, call this day a 'holy convocation' (*miqra' qodeš*), and prescribe abstention from work as on the seventh day:

D	P		
(Deut. 16:4, 7) . . . the flesh, which thou sacrificest the first day at even . . . (7) thou shalt turn[2] in the morning, and go unto thy tents.	(Ex. 12:16) And in the first day there shall be to you an holy convocation[3] . . . no manner of work[1a] shall be done in them, save that which every man must eat, that only may be done of you.	(Lev. 23:7) In the first day ye shall have an holy convocation:[3] ye shall do no servile work.[1b]	(Num. 28:18) In the first day shall be an holy convocation;[3] ye shall do no servile work.[1b]

During the Passover week, as at other *ḥaggim*, worshippers offer sacrifices at the shrine; the documents differ as to the details:

E	D	P	
		Festal calendar	*Sacrificial tariff*
(Ex. 23:15) The feast of unleavened bread[4] shalt thou keep: . . . and none shall appear before me empty:[5]	(Deut. 16:16, 17) . . . the feast of unleavened bread[4] . . . and they shall not appear before the Lord empty:[5] (17) every man shall give as he is able, according to the blessing of the Lord thy God which he hath given thee.	(Lev. 23:8) But ye shall offer[6] an offering made by fire[7] unto the Lord seven days:	(Num. 28:19–24) but ye shall offer[6] an offering made by fire,[7] a burnt offering[8] unto the Lord; two young bullocks, and one ram, and seven he-lambs of the first year: they shall be unto you without blemish: (20) and their meal offering, fine flour mingled with oil: three tenth parts shall ye offer[9] for a bullock, and two tenth parts for the ram; (21) a several tenth

[1] Heb. *mela'khah*. But Sam. is based on Heb. *kol mele'kheth 'abhodah* and LXX has πᾶν ἔργον πλὴν ὅσα ποιηθήσεται ψυχῇ; cf. nn. 1a and 1b below.

[1a] Heb. *kol mela'khah*; LXX has πᾶν ἔργον λατρευτὸν . . . πλὴν ὅσα ποιηθήσεται πάσῃ ψυχῇ, and so Sam. [1b] Heb. *kol mele'kheth 'abhodah*. [2] Heb. *pnh*.

[3] Heb. *miqra' qodeš*.

[4] Heb. *ḥag haMaṣṣoth*. [5] Heb. *reqam*; cf. Ex. 34:20bβ. [6] Heb. *hiqribh*.

[7] Heb. *'iššeh*. [8] Heb. *'olah*. [9] Heb. *'śh*.

P

Sacrificial tariff

part shalt thou offer[1] for every lamb of the seven lambs; (22) and one he-goat for a sin-offering, to make atonement[2] for you. (23) Ye shall offer[1] these beside the burnt offering[3] of the morning, which is for a continual burnt offering.[3] (24) After this manner ye shall offer[1] daily, for seven days, the food of the offering made by fire,[4] of a sweet savour unto the Lord: it shall be offered[1] beside the continual burnt offering,[3] and the drink offering thereof.

The festival is to be celebrated in perpetuity:

JE

(Ex. 13:5, 8–10)[5] And it shall be when the Lord shall bring thee into the land of the Canaanite, and the Hittite, and the Amorite, and the Hivite, and the Jebusite, which he sware unto thy fathers to give thee, a land flowing with milk and honey, that thou shalt keep[6] this service[6a] in this month. . . . (8) And thou shalt tell thy son in that day, saying, It is because of that which the Lord did for me when I came forth out of Egypt. (9) And it shall be a sign unto thee upon thine hand, and for a memorial[7] between thine eyes, that the law of the Lord may be in thy mouth: for with a strong hand hath the Lord brought thee out of Egypt. (10) Thou shalt therefore keep[8] this ordinance[9] in its season from year to year.

P

Exodus narrative A

(12:14) And this day shall be unto you for a memorial,[7] and ye shall keep it a feast[10a] to the Lord: throughout your generations ye shall keep it a feast[10] by an ordinance[9] for ever.

Exodus narrative B

(12:17) . . . therefore shall ye observe[8] this day throughout your generations by an ordinance[9] for ever.

[1] Heb. *ʿśh.* [2] Heb. *kpr.* [3] Heb. *ʿolah.* [4] Heb. *ʾiššeh.*

[5] See p. 60 n. 6 above. F. V. Winnett, *Mosaic Tradition*, 1949, 160, maintains that Ex. 12:25–27a, 13:8a, 14–16 should be assigned to the reign of Hezekiah. See p. 85 below. [6] Heb. *ʿbd.* [6a] Heb. *ʿabhodah.* [7] Heb. *zikkaron.*

[8] Heb. *šmr.* [9] Heb. *ḥuqqah.* [10] Heb. *ḥgg.* [10a] Heb. *ḥgg ḥag.*

(*c*) *Other ritual*

(i) In juxtaposition to the legislation on the Maṣṣoth festival in the Exodus narrative are passages prescribing the dedication of firstborn and firstlings:

JE

(Ex. 13:11–16)[1] And it shall be when the Lord shall bring thee into the land of the Canaanite, as he sware unto thee and to thy fathers, and shall give it thee, (12) that thou shalt set apart[2] unto the Lord all that openeth the womb,[3a] and every firstling[3c] which thou hast that cometh of a beast; the males shall be the Lord's. (13) And every firstling[3] of an ass thou shalt redeem[4] with a lamb; and if thou wilt not redeem[4] it, then thou shalt break its neck:[8] and all the firstborn[5] of man among thy sons shalt thou redeem.[4] (14) And it shall be when thy son asketh thee in time to come, saying, What is this? that thou shalt say unto him, By strength of hand the Lord brought us out from Egypt, from the house of bondage: (15) and it came to pass, when Pharaoh would hardly let us go, that the Lord slew all the firstborn[5] in the land of Egypt, both the firstborn[5] of man, and the firstborn[5] of beast: therefore I sacrifice[6] to the Lord all that openeth the womb,[3a] being males; but all the firstborn[5] of my sons I redeem.[4] (16) And it shall be for a sign upon thine hand, and for frontlets[9] between thine eyes: for by strength of hand the Lord brought us forth out of Egypt.

P

(13:1–2) And the Lord spake unto Moses, saying, (2) Sanctify[7] unto me all the firstborn,[5] whatsoever openeth the womb[3b] among the children of Israel, both of man and of beast: it is mine.

Two other passages describing the treatment of firstborn and firstlings stand in juxtaposition to regulations on the post-Exodus Passover; the Deuteronomist states that firstlings are to be eaten at a communal meal (*zebhaḥ*), at a central shrine if they are clean:

JE

(Ex. 34:19–20) All that openeth the womb[3a] is mine; and all thy cattle that

D

(Deut. 15:19–23) All the firstling[5] males that are born of thy herd and of

[1] See p. 60 n. 6 above. [2] Heb. *he'ebhir*. [3] Heb. *peṭer*.
[3a] Heb. *peṭer reḥem*. [3b] Heb. *peṭer kol reḥem*. [3c] Heb. *peṭer šeger*.
[4] Heb. *pdh*. In some passages LXX has 'exchange (for a small animal)'.
[5] Heb. *bekhor*. [6] Heb. *zbḥ*. [7] Heb. *qdš*.
[8] וערפתו. LXX has *λυτρώσῃ αὐτό*, 'redeem it', perhaps by error.
[9] Targ. Jer., Onq. 'phylacteries'; Pesh. 'memorial'.

JE

is male, the firstlings[1] of ox and sheep. (20) And the firstling[1] of an ass thou shalt redeem[2] with a lamb: and if thou wilt not redeem[2] it, then thou shalt break its neck.[6] All the firstborn[3] of thy sons thou shalt redeem.[2]

D

thy flock thou shalt sanctify[7] unto the Lord thy God: thou shalt do no work with the firstling[3] of thine ox, nor shear the firstling[3] of thy flock. (20) Thou shalt eat it before the Lord thy God year by year in the place which the Lord shall choose, thou and thy household. (21) And if it have any blemish, (as if it be) lame or blind, any ill blemish whatsoever, thou shalt not sacrifice[4] it unto the Lord thy God. (22) Thou shalt eat it within thy gates:[5] the unclean and the clean (shall eat it) alike, as the gazelle, and as the hart. (23) Only thou shalt not eat the blood thereof; thou shalt pour it out upon the ground as water.

In another passage near to, but not in juxtaposition to, regulations on the Maṣṣoth festival, we read:

E

(Ex. 22:28b, 29; E.V. 22:29b, 30) The firstborn[3] of thy sons shalt thou give unto me. (29) Likewise shalt thou do with thine oxen, (and) with thy sheep:[8] seven days it shall be with its dam; on the eighth day thou shalt give it me.

In the following passage the law on clean firstlings is repeated; and the ransom of unclean animals is to be given a monetary value assessed by the priests, apparently according to their own judgement:

P

(Lev. 27:26–27) Only the firstling[3] among beasts, which is made a firstling[3a] to the Lord, no man shall sanctify[7] it; whether it be ox or sheep, it is the Lord's. (27) And if it be of an unclean beast, then he shall ransom[2] it according to thine estimation, and shall add unto it the fifth part thereof: or if it be not redeemed,[9] then it shall be sold according to thine estimation.

The communal meal which followed the firstlings sacrifice in Deut. 15 may not necessarily imply that *all* the flesh of the victim was consumed by the celebrant and his family; the following instructions to the priests

[1] Heb. *peṭer*. [2] Heb. *pdh*. [3] Heb. *bekhor*. [3a] Heb. *bkr*.
[4] Heb. *zbḥ*. [5] LXX, Targ. Jer., Onq., Pesh. 'cities'.
[6] וערפתו. LXX has τιμὴν δώσεις, 'estimate', corresponding to וערכתו.
[7] Heb. *hiqdiš*. [8] LXX adds καὶ τὸ ὑποζύγιόν σου, beast of burden, i.e. ass.
[9] Heb. *g'l*.

indicate that portions were, at some period, the perquisite of the priests. The ransom money is here fixed not by the priest but by the code itself:

P

(Num. 18:15–18) (And the Lord spake unto Aaron,) Everything that openeth the womb,[1] of all flesh which they offer[2] unto the Lord, both of man and beast, shall be thine: nevertheless the firstborn[3] of man shalt thou surely redeem,[4] and the firstling[3] of unclean beasts shalt thou redeem.[4] (16) And those that are to be redeemed[4a] of them from a month old shalt thou redeem,[4] according to thine estimation, for the money of five shekels, after the shekel of the sanctuary (the same is twenty gerahs). (17) But the firstling[3] of an ox, or the firstling[3] of a sheep, or the firstling[3] of a goat, thou shalt not redeem;[4] they are holy:[5] thou shalt sprinkle their blood upon the altar, and shalt burn their fat for an offering made by fire,[6] for a sweet savour unto the Lord. (18) And the flesh of them shall be thine, as the wave breast and as the right thigh, it shall be thine.[7]

Elsewhere the Levites and their cattle are said to replace the persons of the human firstborn and the firstlings that should properly belong to the deity; and this is further stated to commemorate the tenth plague before the Exodus from Egypt. The redemption price for male firstborn is the same as in Num. 18; the redemption price for cattle is ignored:

P

(Num. 3:11–13, 40–42, 44–48) And the Lord spake unto Moses, saying, (12) And I, behold, I have taken the Levites from among the children of Israel instead of all the firstborn that openeth the womb[3a] among the children of Israel: and the Levites shall be mine; (13) for all the firstborn[3] are mine; on the day that I smote all the firstborn[3] in the land of Egypt I hallowed[5a] unto me all the firstborn[3] in Israel, both man and beast: mine they shall be; I am the Lord. . . . (40) And the Lord said unto Moses, Number[8] all the firstborn[3] males of the children of Israel from a month old and upward, and take the number of their names. (41) And thou shalt take the Levites for me (I am the Lord) instead of all the firstborn[3] among the children of Israel; and the cattle of the Levites instead of all the firstlings[3] among the cattle of the children of Israel. (42) And Moses numbered[8] . . . all the firstborn[3]

[1] Heb. *peṭer reḥem.* [2] Heb. *hiqribh.* [3] Heb. *bekhor.*
[3a] Heb. *bekhor peṭer reḥem.* [4] Heb. *pdh.* [4a] Heb. *peduyim.*
[5] Heb. *qodeš.* [5a] Heb. *hiqdiš.* [6] Heb. *'iššeh.*
[7] But see p. 181 n. 11 below on the rendering of this passage. [8] Heb. *pqd.*

P

among the children of Israel. . . . (44) And the Lord spake unto Moses, saying, (45) Take the Levites instead of all the firstborn[1] among the children of Israel, and the cattle of the Levites instead of their cattle: and the Levites shall be mine; I am the Lord. (46) And for the redemption[2] of the . . . firstborn[1] of the children of Israel, which are over and above (the number of) the Levites, (47) thou shalt take five shekels apiece by the poll; after the shekel of the sanctuary shalt thou take them (the shekel is twenty gerahs): (48) and thou shalt give the money wherewith the odd number of them is redeemed[2] unto Aaron and to his sons.

(ii) A second practice, the ceremonial waving of the Sheaf (*ʿomer*), is associated with the Passover, but it is not mentioned in the context of the Exodus. It is, however, prescribed in passages directly following regulations on the post-Exodus Maṣṣoth festival in both Deuteronomy and the 'Holiness Code'.

D

(Deut. 16:9–10) Seven weeks shalt thou number[3] unto thee: from the time thou beginnest to put the sickle to the standing corn[4a] shalt thou begin to number[4b] seven weeks. (10) And thou shalt keep the feast[5] of weeks unto the Lord thy God with a tribute of a freewill offering of thine hand,[6] which thou shalt give . . . .

H

(Lev. 23:9–17)[7] And the Lord spake unto Moses, saying, (10) Speak unto the children of Israel, and say unto them, When ye be come into the land which I give unto you, and shall reap the harvest thereof, then ye shall bring the sheaf of the firstfruits of your harvest[8a] unto the priest: (11) and he shall wave the sheaf[8b] before the Lord, to be accepted for you: on the morrow after the sabbath[9] the priest shall wave it. [8c] (12) And in the day when ye wave the sheaf,[8b] ye shall offer a he-lamb without blemish of the first year for a burnt

[1] Heb. *bekhor*. [2] Heb. *peduyim*. [3] Heb. *spr*.

[4a] Heb. *mehaḥel ḥermeš baqamah*. LXX has ἀμητόν, 'harvest, harvesting', for Heb. *qamah*.

[4b] Heb. *taḥel lispor*.

[5] Heb. *ʿśh ḥag*.

[6] Heb. *missath nidebhath yadekha*. LXX renders freely καθότι ἡ χείρ σου ἰσχύει; Targ. Onq., Pesh. reproduce the words of the Heb. text.

[7] According to Eissfeldt, op. cit. 246, largely revised under the influence of the P code.

[8a] Heb. *ʿomer re'šith qaṣir*. For *ʿomer* LXX has δράγμα.

[8b] Heb. *heniph haʿomer*.

[8c] Heb. *heniph* (*haʿomer*).

[9] ממחרת השבת. LXX has τῇ ἐπαύριον τῆς πρώτης; Targ. Jer. 'on the morrow of the first festival day of the Passover'; Targ. Onq. 'on the morrow of the festival day'; Pesh. 'on the morrow of the other day'. Cf. further Targ. Jer. at Deut. 16:8: 'on the first day ye shall offer the Sheaf, and ye shall eat unleavened bread of the old produce, and on the six days that remain ye shall be permitted to eat unleavened bread of the new produce, and on that seventh day . . . .'

H

offering unto the Lord. (13) And the meal offering thereof shall be two tenth parts (of an ephah) of fine flour mingled with oil, an offering made by fire unto the Lord for a sweet savour: and the drink offering thereof shall be of wine, the fourth part of an hin. (14) And ye shall eat neither bread, nor parched corn, nor fresh ears,[1] until this selfsame day, until ye have brought the oblation[2b] of your God: it is a statute for ever throughout your generations in all your dwellings. (15) And ye shall count unto you from the morrow after the sabbath,[3a] from the day that ye brought the sheaf of the wave offering;[4a] seven sabbaths shall there be complete:[3c] (16) even unto the morrow after the seventh sabbath[3b] shall ye number fifty days; and ye shall offer[2a] a new meal offering unto the Lord. (17) Ye shall bring out of your habitations two wave loaves[4b] of two tenth parts (of an ephah): they shall be of fine flour, they shall be baken with leaven,[5] for firstfruits[6] unto the Lord.

In the preceding pages I have arranged the Passover texts in accordance with the classification commonly accepted by exponents of the 'Source hypothesis' of Higher Criticism. We may now seek to assess the plausibility of this hypothesis within the limits of the Passover documents. That a number of these documents can be identified and isolated is evident. The arrangement of the Massoretic Text in itself implies the existence of several individual documents. Some are separated one from another by verses on wholly unrelated topics. Others are shown to be independent by the incongruity of their present position in the Pentateuch. Ex. 12:21 ff., for example, cannot be the original sequel to Ex. 12:1 ff., because it does 'not describe the execution of the commands received by Moses in

[1] Heb. *leḥem . . . qali . . . karmel.*

[2a] Heb. *hiqribh.* [2b] Heb. *qorban.*

[3a] ממחרת השבת. LXX renders *ἀπὸ τῆς ἐπαύριον τῶν σαββάτων*; Targ. Jer. 'on the morrow of the first festival day of the Passover'; Targ. Onq. 'on the morrow of the festival day'; Pesh. 'on the morrow of the day'.

[3b] ממחרת השבת השביעת. LXX renders *ἕως τῆς ἐπαύριον τῆς ἐσχάτης ἑβδομάδος*; Targ. Jer., Onq. 'until after the seventh week'; so Pesh.

[3c] שבע שבתות תמימת. LXX renders *ἑπτὰ ἑβδομάδας ὁλοκλήρους.*

[4a] Heb. *'omer hatenuphah.* [4b] Heb. *leḥem tenuphah.*

[5] Heb. *ḥameṣ.* [6] Heb. *bikkurim.*

vv. 1–13'.[1] So, too, Ex. 12:43 ff. stands awkwardly in its present place; it contains supplementary regulations, appended without any attempt to incorporate them into the general context of the chapter. Some of the Passover texts, moreover, appear to treat only of the Pesaḥ ritual, others only of the 'Maṣṣoth festival'.[2] Even so, there is considerable overlapping. Laws are repeated—though at varying length and with varying degree of detail. Ceremonial described fully in one passage is described perfunctorily or even ignored in a 'parallel' passage.[3] More striking are the apparent discrepancies and contradictions between one document and another. They are found in the Pesaḥ legend[4] and the Maṣṣoth legend;[5] they are found in the Pesaḥ ritual[6] and the ritual of the Maṣṣoth week.[7] Whether these discrepancies can be explained away—with some straining of hypotheses—is not the point here; the fact that they have been allowed to appear at all

[1] Driver, op. cit. 29.

[2] On Pesaḥ only: Ex. 12:3 ff., 21 ff., 43 ff., Num. 9; on the Maṣṣoth festival only: Ex. 12:14 ff., 13:3 ff. In Ex. 12:24 ff. it is the Pesaḥ that is to be perpetuated, in 12:14 ff. and 13:3 ff. it is the Maṣṣoth festival. The haste of the ceremony is associated with the Pesaḥ meal in Ex. 12:11, but with the eating of *maṣṣoth* in Deut. 16:3. Excommunication is the penalty for omitting to observe the Pesaḥ in Num. 9:13, it is the penalty for eating leavened food during the festival week in Ex. 12:15, 19.

[3] The condition of circumcision is prescribed only in Ex. 12:43–45, 48 f., and probably alluded to in Num. 9:14; the rules of ritual cleanness appear in Num. 9:14, and nowhere else. The qualifications of the victim are given only in Ex. 12:5, not in the 'parallel' passage 12:21 ff.; that the victim's bones must not be broken is prescribed only in Ex. 12:46 and Num. 9:12 (LXX has the rule also in Ex. 12:10); that the flesh must not remain until the morning is prescribed in Ex. 12:10, Num. 9:12, and Deut. 16:4—but not in Ex. 12:21 ff. On the other hand, the use of the hyssop is described in Ex. 12:22, but not in Ex. 12:3 ff.; participants are forbidden to leave the dwelling-place on Pesaḥ night in Ex. 12:22 (cf. 12:46), but not in 12:3 ff. The victim is chosen on the tenth day only in Ex. 12:3. The special dress is prescribed only in Ex. 12:11, and the eating of *maṣṣoth* at the Pesaḥ meal in Ex. 12:8, Num. 9:11, and Deut. 16:3—but not in Ex. 12:21 f. Bitter herbs are mentioned in neither Deut. 16 nor Ex. 12:21 f.

[4] In Ex. 12:13 God himself acts as destroyer, in 12:23 it is his agent; on the relation between the two passages, see p. 74 and n. 3 below. In Ex. 12:22 the Israelites are forbidden to leave their homes during the Pesaḥ night (cf. 12:46); in Ex. 12:30 ff. and Deut. 16:1 they do in fact leave Egypt during the night; in Num. 33:3 they leave in the morning.

[5] Different reasons are given for the inability of the Israelites to allow their bread to rise in Ex. 12:34, 39; cf. p. 72 below.

[6] The Pesaḥ is held in 'the first month', Ex. 12:2, 3, Lev. 23:5, Num. 9:1–5, 28:16, 33:3; in Abib, Deut. 16:1. The victim is to be from the sheep or goats in Ex. 12:3 ff., 12:21; also from the cattle, Deut. 16:2. The Pesaḥ is celebrated by households, Ex. 12:3 ff., by families, Ex. 12:21 f.; by all the congregation, Ex. 12:47, by the assembly of the congregation, Ex. 12:6. It is held 'in the evening', Deut. 16:6 (cf. Jos. 5:10), but 'between the two evenings', Ex. 12:6, Lev. 23:5. The Pesaḥ sacrifice is a *zebhaḥ*, Ex. 12:27, 34:25, cf. Deut. 16:2, 4–6, a *ḥag*, Ex. 34:25 (but cf. 23:18), a *qorban*, Num. 9:7, 13; the flesh is roasted, Ex. 12:8–9, but 'cooked', Deut. 16:7.

[7] The Maṣṣoth festival takes place in 'the first month', Ex. 12:17–18, in Abib, Ex. 23:15, 34:18, 13:4, cf. Deut. 16:1, 3, 8; on the evening of the fourteenth day, Ex. 12:17–18, on (the beginning of) the fifteenth day, Lev. 23:6, Num. 28:17. The seventh day of the festival is a *ḥag*, Ex. 13:6, an *'aṣereth*, Deut. 16:8, a *miqra' qodeš*, Ex. 12:16, Lev. 23:8, Num. 28:25. The definition of the work prohibited on this day varies, Deut. 16:8 opp. Lev. 23:8, Num. 28:25 opp. Ex. 12:16. The Israelites return home on the first day, Deut. 16:8 (cf. Num. 33:3), other documents prescribe the observance of the first day in the same way as the seventh day, Ex. 12:16, Lev. 23:7, Num. 28:25.

proves the independence from each other of the documents in which they occur.

But while it is evident that there are several documents, their identification is not helped by using the Source hypothesis, based upon literary criteria. The dissection of the text into J, E, JE, D, H, and P does not provide us with several complete, coherent narratives or even a single complete narrative in place of our present composite narrative. More surprising is the dexterity of the Compiler, if the Source hypothesis be accepted, in forming this composite narrative. An excellent illustration is to be found in the Passover legend. In Ex. 11:1–3 Moses is informed of the tenth plague which will be followed by the Exodus; the Israelites are instructed to borrow from their Egyptian neighbours. According to the Source hypothesis this text is the work of E. In Ex. 12:31 ff. Moses (with, this time, Aaron also) is urged by Pharaoh to leave Egypt, and the Israelites do in fact borrow from the Egyptians; this passage, too, is assigned to E. But for the link between the two passages, the violence and terror of the tenth plague—which alone makes the second passage intelligible—the Compiler turns, if we follow the Source hypothesis, to a J document. There we are told of the interview of Moses with Pharaoh (Ex. 11:4–8) and of the slaughter of the Egyptians (Ex. 12:29–30). And for details of this plague, necessary for our narrative because they provide the aetiological explanation of the name Pesaḥ, the Compiler uses another document, Ex. 12:21–23, assigned, somewhat uncertainly, to JE.[1]

On the other hand, where a discrepancy appears even in our present composite text, this is not resolved by an appeal to the Source hypothesis. In Ex. 12:34 it is maintained that leaven could not be introduced into the dough because the kneading troughs had been packed, but Ex. 12:39 holds simply that there was no time to allow the dough to ferment. And both statements—inconsistent with each other—are assigned by the Source hypothesis to a single Source, E.[2]

These inconsistencies, it may be objected, arise in the narrative of the Exodus legend; it would be unreasonable to expect to be able to reconstruct the original form of a legend which may have been the product of a centuries-old oral tradition before it was committed to writing. This objection, however, can scarcely be advanced where matters of terminology are concerned—and least of all where the terms are used of ritual practices, for there vocabulary should be used with precision and should leave little room for doubt or misunderstanding. Technical terms, proponents of the Source hypothesis maintain, are frequently the hall-mark of certain documents. So, in the Passover texts, the term *beth 'abhoth* is used only in the P Source,[3] while the term *mišpaḥah* is found in the parallel JE text.[4]

[1] See pp. 47 ff. above. [2] p. 50 above. [3] Ex. 12:3 f. [4] Ex. 12:21.

In P, it is pointed out, the Passover month is called 'the first month',[1] in JE and D it is called Abib.[2] In P the time of the Pesaḥ sacrifice is 'between the two evenings',[3] in D it is 'in the evening'.[4] The word *zbḥ*, both noun and verb, is said to be restricted to the Deuteronomic account of the Pesaḥ and to passages that have been redacted by D;[5] *qorban*, on the other hand, is peculiar to P.[6]

Here lies perhaps the strongest argument of those who accept the Source hypothesis. It can, however, scarcely carry conviction. *Beth 'abhoth* and *mišpaḥah* are evidently synonyms; the text that uses *mišpaḥah* has also *bayith* in the following verse as the dwelling-place of the *mišpaḥah*.[7] The other inconsistencies in terminology are equally capable of explanation, though the explanation is of a different nature. The reason for the use of Abib as the name of the Passover month rather than the more exact term 'the first month' is to be sought in the popular character of the documents.[8] That is the reason also for the use of *ba'erebh* in Deut. 16 rather than the precise phrase *ben ha'arbayim*;[9] indeed, the former term is found in the equally popular narrative of Jos. 5, though this is usually ascribed to P.[10] The employment of *zbḥ*, either as noun or verb, is to be accounted for by the significance of the word—the slaying and preparation and consumption of a sacrificial victim in a communal meal.[11] It sums up a series of actions in a single term, and it is well suited to the popular work of the Deuteronomist. *Qorban*, on the other hand, like the related verb *qarabh*, *hiqribh*, is found in contexts where the formal regulations for sacrifice and the preliminaries for sacrifice are prescribed. Where it occurs in the Passover texts, cleanness regulations as a preliminary to sacrifice are discussed;[12] it is not found in Deut. 16, whose regulations are not formal since they are directed to a public that consisted chiefly of laymen. In short, these terms are not a guide to the age of the various documents. Documents are, of course, distinguished by idiosyncrasies of style;[13] but their choice of technical terms is dictated primarily by the function and purpose of the individual passage.

There is evidence of the interdependence of the Passover documents, irrespective of their alleged Sources. The unusual word *ḥippazon* is employed in the Bible only in the context of the Exodus story or the Exodus ritual. But it is found in passages ascribed to both D and P—in the former in connexion with the eating of *maṣṣoth*, in the latter in connexion with the

[1] Ex. 12:2, 3, Lev. 23:5, Num. 9:1, 2, 5, 28:16, 33:3.
[2] Ex. 13:4, 5, Deut. 16:1.
[3] Ex. 12:6, Lev. 23:5, Num. 9:3, 5, 11.
[4] Deut. 16:4, 6.
[5] Deut. 16:2, 4–6, Ex. 12:27, 34:25 (cf. 23:18).
[6] Num. 9:7, 13.
[7] Ex. 12:22.
[8] See pp. 193 and 207 below.
[9] pp. 131 n. 4 and 207 below.
[10] Jos. 5:10. See p. 3 above.
[11] Cf. Ex. 13:15, Deut. 15:21 on firstlings.
[12] Ex. 12:43, Num. 9:7, 13, cf. 28:19; see further 18:15 (firstlings), Lev. 23:15 (feast of Weeks), and cf. p. 138 below.
[13] See pp. 204 ff. below.

Exodus Pesaḥ itself.[1] Furthermore, in one important feature of the Pesaḥ legend a passage ascribed to P agrees with another ascribed to J, but is opposed to a passage ascribed to JE. In P we are told that it is the deity himself who spares the Israelites and brings death to the Egyptians; in JE the deity works through the agency of a 'destroyer'.[2] Both documents use the term *mašḥith*. And here, it seems, the Compiler had before him the two texts of JE and P side by side since the two crucial words *hamašḥith* and *lamašḥith* appear to have been interchanged.[3] Surprisingly, too, the Source hypothesis assigns the more anthropomorphic conception to the late Source, P—precisely where one would least have expected to find it.

The Source hypothesis leads to other results equally unexpected when we examine the Passover documents. Ex. 12:1 ff., which is attributed to the Priestly writer or redactor, appears to describe the slaughter of the Pesaḥ victims at the Exodus as having been performed near the dwelling-places in which the meal was later eaten.[4] Yet this is contrary to the practice of post-Exilic times, to which that Source is said to belong. At that period it was imperative that the Pesaḥ sacrifice should be performed only at the Temple at Jerusalem; and this is the procedure described in the Mishnah.[5] Another feature is even more remarkable—if we accept the arrangement of texts according to the Source hypothesis. In Ex. 12:3 ff. (P)—as well as in Ex. 12:21 ff. (JE)—it is the heads of households or families who handle the blood of the Pesaḥ victim and apply it to the doorposts and lintels. The majority of these persons must, in the nature of things, have been laymen. The handling of the blood of sacrificial victims was, however, a jealously guarded prerogative of the priests at Jerusalem in post-Exilic times, and it was one that was not waived even in the case of the Pesaḥ.[6] Why, then, should the P author or redactor—single-minded as most critics would have us believe him to be—have hesitated to suppress a tradition that can have had little meaning for his own age—a tradition, indeed, that ran counter to the practice of his contemporaries? Why did he not, too, expunge the verses Ex. 12:24–27 (commonly ascribed to JE) which appear to demand the perpetuation of all the rites of the Exodus Pesaḥ, including the smearing of blood?[7] It is true that the smearing of the victim's blood had been

[1] Ex. 12:11 (P), Deut. 16:3; see further p. 173 below on Is. 52:12.

[2] Ex. 12:12 f. (P), cf. 11:4 (J), against 12:23 (JE).

[3] Ex. 12:13 reads ולא־יהיה בכם נגף למשחית בהכתי וכו׳; 12:23 reads: ולא יתן המשחית לבא אל־בתיכם לנגף. The syntax of both passages would be improved by the interchange of the words למשחית and המשחית; we would then have the phrases נגף המשחית and ולא יתן למשחית. This transfer would at the same time remove a strange anomaly of the existing text, for Versions and commentators are obliged to render the same word, in these two parallel accounts, as 'destroyer' in one passage and 'destruction' in the other.

[4] Ex. 12:6 f.

[5] See pp. 211 and 260 below.

[6] See the discussion on pp. 226 f. below.

[7] F. V. Winnett, op. cit. 155 f., maintains that the P editor did in fact suppress regula-

abandoned in the course of time. But the very preservation of this text was likely to give a wrong impression. Such 'carelessness' on the part of the P redactor might well play into the hands of sectarians. The Samaritans observed punctiliously the ceremonies of the Exodus Pesaḥ, and they could claim that in this respect they were acting as the rightful guardians of tradition and the Bible text.[1]

There is only one conclusion to be drawn. The *contents* of Ex. 12 must be early. The Passover and its traditions stood, in certain respects, in a class by themselves. The age and sanctity of the festival and the popular esteem in which it was held placed these early documents beyond the reach of the would-be reformer—even though the practices which they enjoined had been amended with the passage of time. Whether these or other Passover texts passed through the hands of later redactors is therefore of little importance. They contain material considerably older than the date at which—according to the Source hypothesis—they were redacted. If this is so—and it can scarcely be gainsaid—it follows that to attribute portions of the text to schools of redactors on the grounds of their literary composition is lacking in both force and value.

Bentzen has argued[2] that strata should be recognized in the Pentateuch not simply according to stylistic or linguistic criteria, but rather in accordance with the theological content of individual documents. We have, however, seen already that the ritual of blood-smearing in one document ascribed by him to P[3]—and it is a document of central importance in the description of the Exodus Pesaḥ—does not conform to the tenets of the Priestly School. The results are no happier if we apply logically a main criterion used by Bentzen in his theory of the stratification of the Pentateuch text. In JE, he maintains, there is no suggestion of the centralization of the Israelite cult, in D centralization is fighting for recognition, in P it is presupposed.[4] But Welch has shown[5] how improbable is the sequence of events which this theory postulates, when it is applied to the texts of the Passover. Ex. 12:21 ff., assigned by most critics to JE, appears to prescribe the Pesaḥ (according to Bentzen) as a family ritual; by Deut. 16 (D) the ritual is transferred to a central shrine or shrines—and subsequently, by a complete volte-face, Ex. 12:1 ff., ascribed to P, regards the ritual as again a family celebration. This scarcely seems credible; as Welch points out,

tions concerning the Pesaḥ meal that stood originally after Ex. 12:27. He did this, suggests Winnett, 'in favour of his own regulations. These he introduced in a very awkward manner at the beginning of the chapter, before the institution of the rite has been narrated.' It may be argued against this hypothesis that an editor would hardly carry out his task so inefficiently.

[1] pp. 251 ff. below.

[2] A. Bentzen, *Introduction to the O.T.*, 1952, ii. 60 ff. See also his 'Bemerkungen über neuere Entwicklungen in der Pentateuchfrage', *Archiv Orientální*, xix, 1951, 226.

[3] Implicitly, *Introduction*, 44, 215. Bentzen, however, prefers the title 'Aaronitic' to 'P', op. cit. 33.

[4] Op. cit. 64, following Wellhausen.

[5] A. C. Welch, 'On the Method of celebrating Passover', *ZAW* xlv, 1927, 26.

we cannot believe that the priests in P would have given up the victory they had won in D.[1]

If we reject the methods of classifying the Passover texts postulated by the 'Source hypothesis', what can we put in their place? That there are a number of individual documents has already been shown. The documents on the legend of the Passover we may set aside as of less immediate importance and as presenting, in any case, a fairly cohesive, if composite, account. When we examine the 'legal' texts on the Passover we find that certain fragments appear in the context of the Exodus narrative—although in part they prescribe the post-Exodus Passover—Ex. 12:1–11, 12:14–16, 12:17–20, 12:21–23, 12:24–27, 12:42, 12:43–49, 13:3–10. Outside the Exodus narrative are Lev. 23:5–8, Num. 9:1–14, Num. 28:16–25, Deut. 16:1–8, 16–17. Each may at one time have been more complete than it appears today; this is shown by the overlapping between the documents, and perhaps by clauses that are preserved in the LXX but are omitted in the M.T.[2] The crucial point, however, is that each document stresses some particular aspect of the ritual; they supplement each other. It is precisely for this special approach of each document to the ritual that it has been preserved for us in its present state. Thus Ex. 12:1 ff. gives a fairly full account of the preparations for the Pesaḥ, but Ex. 12:21 ff. expands in greater detail the ceremony of the smearing of the blood. Ex. 12:43 ff. lays down (among various regulations) the condition of circumcision and other qualifications for attending the Pesaḥ. Ex. 12:14 ff., 17 ff., and 13:3 ff. are concerned with different facets of the seven-day Passover. The two brief parallel passages in Ex. 23 and 34 deal only with the character of the Passover as one of the *ḥaggim*. Lev. 23 prescribes the festal calendar, Num. 9 the 'second Pesaḥ', and Num. 28 the sacrificial tariff, while Deut. 16—perhaps the most interesting of all the Passover documents—is a popular review of the whole festival.

These documents will be treated severally and in detail later in the present study. But it is, I suggest, unprofitable to seek to set them out in chronological order of their composition at periods of time of which we know little. Instead we should visualize the situation that faced the Compiler of the Hebrew Pentateuch—if we may assume such a personality as representing a School and a tradition. He had before him documents of varying length, of various ages, and doubtless from various sources or regions. Each writer, too, had written in the idiom of his own time or in an idiom derived

[1] I am summarizing here the arguments propounded by other scholars, not my own views. For these, see ch. 6 below.

[2] In Ex. 12:10 LXX inserts the rule against breaking the bones of the Pesaḥ victim (cf. Ex. 12:46, Num. 9:12). In Ex. 12:16 LXX has 'servile work' for M.T. 'work'. On the reading of LXX in Deut. 16:8 (corresponding to Heb. *'aṣereth ḥag*, for M.T. *'aṣereth*), see p. 213 below.

from his own idiosyncrasies. From each the Compiler selected and incorporated those passages that suited best his general narrative or that described best some particular aspect of the ritual. It was, it may be repeated, the differences between one text and another that secured their preservation; they would not have survived had they been the duplication or reduplication of a passage already chosen for incorporation by the Compiler.

The Compiler arranged the passages into a broad pattern, the pattern in which they appear in our Hebrew texts and Versions. Where passages were independent of the general context,[1] what impelled the Compiler to place them in their present order? Why do some appear in the Exodus narrative, some later? To this there seems to be only one satisfactory answer. It was this order that appeared to the Compiler to fit most exactly the evolution of the festival. A process of evolution is self-evident in any religion. That there was evolution in the history of the Passover was recognized by the Rabbis, who enumerate the usages of the 'Pesaḥ of Egypt' that had been abandoned in the 'Pesaḥ of (later) generations'.[2] The main course of this evolution is admitted by most Old Testament scholars. In the process of time religious practices appear to conform—whether consciously or not—to a norm. Those that cannot be adapted are gradually discarded, unless the written text in which they are prescribed has acquired such sanctity that it becomes preferable to explain away incongruities rather than to set aside or tamper with the text itself.

The Compiler was well aware of this general process of evolution. Some laws appeared to him to be older than others. Some, in his view, went back to the patriarchal age of Israel,[3] some belonged to a later stage in the history of his people. In the case of the Passover some laws were so old that, in his opinion, they were observed at the Exodus, and these he assigns to the primitive Passover in Egypt. Others arose later. In their present order, the Passover documents of the Pentateuch reflect the picture of the evolution of the Passover as it was seen by the Compiler.[4]

There is a strong presumption that the Compiler was right and that this was in fact the course of evolution of the festival. He lived closer to the events described in these texts than do we. He is likely to have completed his work by the time of the Chronicler.[5] The order of the documents that is adopted in the Hebrew Pentateuch is the order that will be followed in the present study.

[1] And not embedded in codes of a general nature, like Ex. 23 and 34. The most striking example of an independent text on the Pesaḥ is Num. 9:1 ff.; see p. 192 below.

[2] p. 257 below.

[3] So, for example, the Sabbath (Gen. 1–2:3), sacrifice (4:2 ff., 8:20 f., 15:9 ff., &c.), circumcision (17, 21:4), rights of inheritance (25, 27).

[4] The method of conveying a picture of the historical evolution of Israelite religion employed by the writer of the Book of Jubilees is somewhat different and has different results. See p. 234 below.

[5] p. 227 below.

3

MODERN THEORIES ON THE ORIGINS AND EARLY DEVELOPMENT OF THE PASSOVER

. . . The acquisition of fresh knowledge . . . must itself be preceded by a love of inquiry, and therefore by a spirit of doubt; because without doubt there will be no inquiry, and without inquiry there will be no knowledge.
Henry Thomas Buckle

THE preceding chapters demonstrate the difficulties that beset an attempt to reconstruct the evolution of the Passover. The earliest Historical Document to describe the festival in some detail belongs to the Exilic or post-Exilic period.[1] Yet it is generally agreed that the Passover ritual contains elements that may go back to the time of the Exodus—if not earlier. This view rests on the Traditional Documents. But the Traditional Documents themselves appear to be seriously at variance with each other at more than one point.[2] The first text that seeks to reconcile these apparent discrepancies belongs to the late epoch of the Chronicler.[3]

The most exhaustive analysis of the Passover in recent times is by Beer.[4] Beer maintains that the Israelites in Canaan celebrated, simultaneously but independently, three springtime festivals. One was the Pesaḥ, a nocturnal firstlings sacrifice, held at the full moon; this had been known to the Israelites already when they were still nomads in Egypt.[5] After their settlement in Canaan, only the people of Judah continued to observe this practice, at local shrines, as a preliminal ritual at the opening of the harvesting season. The J documents show that the blood of the Pesaḥ victim was poured, in an atonement ceremony, at the base of the altar; its flesh was consumed whole with unleavened cakes. The victim had divine qualities. Leaven was avoided because of its ritual impurity.[6] Subsequently the innovation[7] was introduced of smearing the victim's blood upon the doorposts in commemoration of the slaughter of the Egyptian, and the sparing of the Israelite, firstborn. The ritual was now held at individual houses, not at shrines, and it was not followed by a meal. It is likely, however, that

[1] Ezek. 45:21 ff.
[2] p. 71 above.
[3] 2 Chr. 35:12–13. See p. 15 above.
[4] G. Beer, *Pesachim (Ostern). Text, Übersetzung und Erklärung*, 1912, 9 ff.
[5] Beer, loc. cit., finds references to this in the earlier chapters of Exodus; pp. 43 ff. above.
[6] Ex. 34:25, ascribed by Beer, op. cit. 23, to J. He maintains that the reference to *ḥag haMaṣṣoth* in 34:18 is a later insertion from Ex. 23 (E).
[7] It is not prescribed in Ex. 3:18, 5:3, which, according to Beer, op. cit. 9, allude to the Pesaḥ.

this ritual was of little importance, and was carried out only sporadically before the Exile.[1]

While the Pesaḥ was observed in Judah, the people of the northern kingdom are shown by the documents of the E Source to have observed the Maṣṣoth festival at the full moon before the spring harvest.[2] Like the ceremony of blood-smearing at the Pesaḥ, this festival had an historical motif, for it recalled the haste of the Exodus;[3] but it was not, like the Pesaḥ, a sacrament. It is uncertain whether it lasted one day or seven days.[4]

The third spring festival is described in the H Source. It was not celebrated on a fixed date. It was the offering of a sheaf of barley at local shrines; and it was held whenever the crops were sufficiently advanced.[5]

In the reign of Josiah, continues Beer, the Pesaḥ was raised to the status of a national ceremony, a status that it retained throughout its subsequent history. It was to be held only at the central shrine at Jerusalem,[6] and in commemoration of the Exodus from Egypt, not of the tenth plague.[7] The victim was no longer to be a firstling,[8] since the distance from the farms to Jerusalem made this condition impossible; and the victim might now be from the herds as well as from the flocks,[9] perhaps because the groups of sacrificers were now larger. The rite of smearing the victim's blood was omitted. The flesh was now to be boiled, instead of being roasted.[10] These features were prescribed in the primary text of Deut. 16.[11]

A decisive turning-point in the history of the Passover came, according to Beer, with the religious reforms of Ezekiel. The religious calendar was to be divided into two symmetrical halves, beginning with spring and autumn respectively.[12] The Pesaḥ and the Maṣṣoth festival were to be merged to form a single festival, with the name of the former and the duration and ritual of the latter. It was to commence on the fifteenth day of the month.[13] The Pesaḥ ritual had no parallel in the autumn, and was to be omitted, although it is recalled in some degree by the 'de-sinning' ritual of blood on the first day of the month.[14] The eating of *maṣṣoth* during seven days,[15] which is prescribed in Ezekiel, was in some way a fast and in striking

[1] Ex. 12:21–24, regarded by Beer, op. cit. 26, as a secondary J document.

[2] Ex. 23:14 f., ascribed by Beer to E.

[3] Ex. 12:34, 39.

[4] Ex. 12:8, 17, 13:5 opp. 12:15, 16, 18, 19, 13:6, 7.

[5] Lev. 23:9–12, ascribed by Beer, op. cit. 28, to H.

[6] Cf. 2 Kings 23:21–23.

[7] Deut. 16:1.

[8] Beer, op. cit. 31, considers Deut. 15:19 ff. to have no connexion with 16:1 ff.

[9] Deut. 16:2.

[10] Deut. 16:7.

[11] Deut. 16:1–17 has, in Beer's view, op. cit. 29, undergone drastic revision. The original text is Deut. 16:1–3aα, 4b (excluding ביום הראשון), 6–7. H. J. Elhorst, 'Die deuteronomischen Jahresfeste', *ZAW* xlii, 1924, 136, on the other hand, regards the original text as Deut. 16:1–2, 5–7. For an outline of other views, see pp. 81 ff. below and the discussion on p. 203.

[12] Ezek. 45:18 ff. See p. 219 below.

[13] Beer, op. cit. 33 f., regards 'fourteenth' in Ezek. 45:21 as a textual emendation for an original 'fifteenth'; but see p. 7 n. 14 above.

[14] Ezek. 45:18.

[15] Beer, op. cit. 34, adopts the reading of LXX in Ezek. 45:21. See p. 7 n. 5 above.

contrast to the lavish offerings that were made to the deity during the same period.

Ezekiel's scheme of reform was never carried out. But it had, maintains Beer, a far-reaching impact on the Passover legislation of the Pentateuch. The documents of the J and D Sources (Ex. 34 and Deut. 16) that originally contained no reference to the Maṣṣoth festival were now amended and given their present form; the document of the E Source (Ex. 23) that had taken no account of the Pesaḥ now had an (oblique) allusion to it; the document of the H Source (Lev. 23) on the Sheaf-waving that originally had made no mention of either the Pesaḥ or the Maṣṣoth festival now had regulations about both. The Pesaḥ and the Maṣṣoth festival were henceforth fused into a single whole.

This is clear, asserts Beer, from the two groups of later documents which he classifies as P_1 and P_2 and in which the association of the Pesaḥ and the Maṣṣoth festival is taken for granted. P_1 describes the 'Pesaḥ of Egypt', with all details of the ritual.[1] The date of the ceremony is in practice, though not by definition, the same as in Ezekiel.[2] Regulations on circumcision are the sign of a later epoch.[3] In P_1 the Passover lasts for only one day.[4] In P_2, however, which describes the 'Pesaḥ of (later) generations', it lasts for seven days, as in Ezekiel.[5] An innovation that was introduced after the time of Ezekiel is the special observance of the first and seventh days of the festival week. There appears to be a contradiction between the celebration of these days at, presumably, a central shrine and the instructions to 'eat *maṣṣoth* in your dwellings';[6] and this may reflect a compromise between the new laws on the Pesaḥ as a house-festival and the earlier laws which insisted that it should be held only at a shrine, whether this was a local or a central shrine. Among the group of laws which Beer calls P_2 are Lev. 23 in its redacted form which relates the Passover to the barley harvest, and the sacrificial tariff of Num. 28 which prescribes offerings in excess of those prescribed by Ezekiel. Beer finds a date for the extension of P_1 to P_2. The Elephantine papyrus on the Passover tallies with P_2 since it lays down a festival of seven days with special attention to both the first and the seventh days; and the papyrus is dated 419 B.C.[7]

McNeile[8] modifies Beer's thesis at certain points. The mention of the Pesaḥ in Ex. 34:25 (J) is probably not, maintains McNeile, the primary

[1] Ex. 12:1 ff. It prescribes, among other particulars, the dress of the celebrants and the age of the victim.

[2] Ex. 12 assigns it to the evening (at the end) of the fourteenth day; Ezek. 45:21a (Beer reads 'fifteenth' for 'fourteenth') assigns the ceremony to the evening at (the beginning of) the fifteenth day.

[3] Beer, op. cit. 40. But see p. 135 below.

[4] Ex. 12:14 (which Beer regards as alluding to the Pesaḥ; most scholars regard it as alluding to the Maṣṣoth festival), 12:17.

[5] Ex. 12:15–16, 18–20.

[6] Ex. 12:16 opp. 12:20.

[7] See p. 9 above.

[8] A. H. McNeile, *Book of Exodus*, 1917, 62.

text but an interpolation from Ex. 23 (E). He regards the whole of the present text of Deut. 16 as original, not as the product of a late redactor under the influence of Ezekiel; already in the reign of Josiah, he asserts, the Pesaḥ and the Maṣṣoth festival had been blended into a single festival held at the central shrine on a fixed date.

Steuernagel[1] also agrees broadly with Beer that the Maṣṣoth festival was celebrated only in North Israel, and that references to it in the 'Judean' laws (Ex. 34 and Deut. 16) are the work of redactors who introduced North Israelite practices. But he holds that it was only with the introduction of a late P code—not with the religious programme of Ezekiel—that the Maṣṣoth festival was first introduced to Judah. This he regards as having taken place shortly before the composition of the 'Passover papyrus' from Elephantine in 419. The papyrus applied the regulations of the Maṣṣoth festival, themselves an innovation at Jerusalem, to the Jews of the Diaspora.

Arnold,[2] like Steuernagel, makes the 'Passover papyrus' the central feature of his argument, but he proposes a very different thesis. The Pesaḥ, he holds, was probably not celebrated before the Exodus, and it was unknown to the J as well as to the E Source;[3] only in the primary text of Deut. 16 is it considered of sufficient importance to be regarded as a national occasion celebrated at the national shrine.[4] The Maṣṣoth festival, on the other hand, was, Arnold maintains, celebrated in both Judah and North Israel, since it is prescribed in both J and E[5] and in the redacted version of Deut. 16.[6] Unlike the Pesaḥ, which may always have been a full-moon ceremony, the Maṣṣoth festival was not primarily bound to a fixed date; it was held on any seven days in the month of Abib, when the state of the crops warranted it. The date of the Maṣṣoth festival is fixed for the first time in Lev. 23:5–8, which Arnold attributes, with the following verses, to H. This was the situation at the promulgation of the 'Passover papyrus' in 419. Subsequently the Pesaḥ and the Maṣṣoth festival—which were still separate in H[7]—were merged to form a single festival in the P laws of Ex. 12:3–14[8] and 12:15–20.[9]

[1] D. C. Steuernagel, 'Zum Passa-Maṣṣothfest', *ZAW* xxxi, 1911, 310.

[2] W. R. Arnold, 'Passover Papyrus from Elephantine', *JBL* xxxi, 1912, 1.

[3] Arnold, op. cit. 9, regards פסח in Ex. 34:25 as a gloss.

[4] Deut. 16:5–6, cf. 2 Kings 23:21–23.

[5] Ex. 34:18, 23:15.

[6] This redacted version of Deut. 16, Arnold maintains, goes farther than J and E in that it appoints special observances for the seventh day in v. 8. Arnold, op. cit. 10, holds that Ezek. 45:21 deals only with the Maṣṣoth festival; he omits פסח in v. 21 as a gloss.

[7] The Pesaḥ on the fourteenth day, the Maṣṣoth festival beginning on the fifteenth day.

[8] Arnold, op. cit. 12, interprets *ḥag* in Ex. 12:14 as referring to the Pesaḥ, not to the Maṣṣoth festival.

[9] *Maṣṣoth* are already part of the Pesaḥ meal in Ex. 12:8, while Ex. 12:18 declares that the combined festival extends from the (end of the) fourteenth to the end of the twenty-first day. Arnold, op. cit. 14, suggests that P, but not H, prescribes the rule of removing leaven from the houses of the Israelites, as in the Elephantine papyrus: this, he explains, is likely to be a custom older than the P code.

Guthe[1] confines his discussion to the treatment of the Passover in Deut. 16. The Maṣṣoth festival was, he maintains, connected with agriculture, and it was celebrated by all the Hebrews in Judah as well as in North Israel. The Pesaḥ, on the other hand, was an ancient firstlings sacrifice which was also offered throughout the country—in, that is, North Israel and Judah—but only by herdsmen. It took place on the eighth day after the birth of the animal.[2] Deut. 16 extended the Pesaḥ to the whole community[3] and gave it, for the first time, an approximate date—the month of Abib, the month in which most firstlings were born. It was no longer possible to restrict Pesaḥ victims to firstlings, but the proximity of the firstlings regulations in Deut. 15:19–23 to the Pesaḥ laws in Deut. 16:1 ff. shows that they continued to be the most desirable form of offering. The victims might now be chosen from the herds as well as the flocks, and since large animals could not be roasted whole, it was also permitted to boil the victim. A redactor then added the regulations of the Maṣṣoth festival to those of the Pesaḥ in Deut. 16.[4]

Gray[5] treats of the Passover passages in Ex. 23 and 34 and Deut. 16. He holds that there has been considerable interchange between Ex. 23 and 34. He is unwilling to assent to the view that the reference to the Pesaḥ in Ex. 34:25 is original;[6] indeed, he maintains that if Ex. 34 mentioned the spring festival, it would be the Maṣṣoth festival, not the Pesaḥ.[7] The reference to the Maṣṣoth festival in 23:15, on the other hand, belongs to the original text. Gray agrees that the primary text of Deut. 16 set out regulations for a single-night Pesaḥ, and that this has been expanded into the seven-day Maṣṣoth festival.[8] But, he adds cautiously, we cannot on this

[1] H. Guthe, 'Passahfest nach Dtn 16', *Abhandlungen zur semitischen Religionskunde und Sprachwissenschaft Wolf Wilhelm Grafen von Baudissin . . . überreicht . . .* (Beihefte zur *ZAW*, No. 33), ed. W. Frankenberg and F. Küchler, 1918, 217.

[2] Cf. Ex. 22:29, Lev. 22:27.

[3] Guthe agrees that Deut. 16 is to be ascribed to the reign of Josiah, but suggests that a detailed account of Josiah's Passover once appeared in the text of 2 Kings 23 and was then omitted by a later editor. (But see p. 219 below.) He points out that there are important discrepancies between 2 Chr. 35 and Deut. 16.

[4] So Beer, pp. 79 f. above. *Maṣṣoth* were already a feature peculiar to the Pesaḥ meal; Guthe, op. cit. 228 f., maintains that מַצּוֹת in 2 Kings 23:8a, 9 refers to the Passover celebration of Josiah. But see p. 216 n. 8 below.

[5] G. B. Gray, 'Passover and Unleavened Bread: the Laws of J, E, and D', *JTS* xxxvii, 1936, 241.

[6] It rests, he holds, 'on an uncertain text', since it does not occur in Ex. 23:18 and since the verb is not, as one might expect, in 2nd m.s. Gray discusses in some detail the reconstructions of Ex. 34 by Wellhausen, S. R. Driver, and Beer, and declares that they involve changes 'too numerous for . . . use . . . as the basis of an argument'; the same view is advanced by Rudolph, op. cit. 47.

[7] Although Gray holds that, in its present form, the specific description of the Maṣṣoth festival in 34:18 is a late interpolation.

[8] If the description of the Maṣṣoth ritual is removed from Deut. 16, there remains a 'perfectly clear and complete law of Pesaḥ only'. Inconsistencies are removed—e.g. the reference to the Passover as the Pesaḥ in 16:1 but as the Maṣṣoth festival in 16:16.

evidence assume that the Pesaḥ was unknown to E and the northern kingdom down to the time of the redaction of Deuteronomy, or that the Maṣṣoth festival was unknown to J and D and the southern kingdom down to the seventh century B.C. 'We do', Gray concludes, 'obtain . . . a strong impression of the original independence of (Pesaḥ) from (the Maṣṣoth festival). . . . Both observances may have prevailed alike in the northern and southern kingdoms before the 8th or 7th centuries, but their union was at most one that still bore obvious traces of previous separation.'

May[1] maintains, like Gray, that the Maṣṣoth festival was observed as an annual celebration before, as after, the time of Deuteronomy. It was held at the new moon.[2] Like Gray, May, too, regards the allusion to the Pesaḥ in Ex. 34:25 as an interpolation. The Exodus, he holds (here following Guthe), was commemorated by the sacrifice of firstlings and the redemption of the firstborn of sons and asses, on the eighth day after birth.[3] Deuteronomy converted this into an annual ceremony,[4] but—and here May differs from other scholars—in the text of Deut. 16 it has remained subordinate to the Maṣṣoth festival; it consisted of the sacrifice of an ox and a sheep on the first day of the Maṣṣoth festival. The day following the festal week was an *'aṣereth*.[5] Ezek. 45:21 also regards the Pesaḥ[6] and the Maṣṣoth festival as a single festival, now held at the full moon.[7] The Pesaḥ attains its highest development with its appearance in the official festal calendar of Lev. 23:4 ff.[8] Finally, in P—May ascribes Ex. 12:21–28 to P, as well as 12:1–20[9]—the Pesaḥ has become a 'simple celebration with the sacrificial animal a sheep', performed by laymen. The blood rites make it a sacrament and more important than the Maṣṣoth festival.[10] The P code,

[1] H. G. May, 'The Relation of the Passover to the Festival of Unleavened Cakes', *JBL* lv, 1936, 65.

[2] Interpreting *ḥodeš*, Deut. 16:1, as 'new moon', May, op. cit. 65, 74. See, however, p. 132 n. 4 below.

[3] Ex. 13:11 ff.; cf. the 'interpolation' in Ex. 34:19–20, May, op. cit. 66.

[4] The allusion to the Pesaḥ in Deut. 16 is not, May holds, op. cit. 67 f., to be dated before Josiah, since the Pesaḥ is not mentioned among Solomon's annual sacrifices in 2 Chr. 8:12–13.

[5] May therefore regards the festival as lasting eight days in all. He finds a similar duration of time prescribed in Lev. 23:5 and Num. 28:16 ff., where the Pesaḥ is held, he maintains, op. cit. 77, on the fourteenth day and is followed by the seven days of the Maṣṣoth festival.

[6] The blood rites of Ezek. 45:18–20 resemble those of the Pesaḥ, but they are for a different purpose and have a different significance.

[7] May, like Beer, amends 'fourteenth' in Ezek. 45:21 to 'fifteenth', op. cit. 76.

[8] Ascribed by May, op. cit. 69, to H, like the following verses, not (as many scholars) to P.

[9] Op. cit. 70 ff. Most scholars assign Ex. 12:21–28 to JE. May points out, op. cit. 81, that the phraseology of H is echoed in the 'Passover papyrus' of Elephantine, and suggests that the latter was promulgated to show that the Pesaḥ was henceforth to be held at the full, not the new, moon.

[10] In the same way a prerequisite for the Pesaḥ was circumcision and ritual cleanness. Failure to observe the Pesaḥ entailed expulsion from the community.

'promulgated first when the Temple was destroyed or soon after it had been restored . . . soon became obsolete', and was replaced by the conventional treatment of sacrificial blood. In P the boiling of the Pesaḥ victim, which had been usual in pre-Exilic times,[1] was forbidden, perhaps to emphasize that the Pesaḥ was held at home, not in the Temple.

Pfeiffer[2] holds that the law of the Maṣṣoth festival in Ex. 23:15 goes back, in part, to a period before 1200 B.C.; it was edited before 650 B.C.[3] The festival took place at local shrines. Before Deuteronomy (which was composed shortly before 621) the festival was connected with the Exodus and was to last seven days. Deut. 16 restricts the Maṣṣoth festival, with the other annual feasts, to the Temple at Jerusalem; at the same time the Pesaḥ was introduced and attached to the Maṣṣoth festival. Ex. 34 in its present form is the work of a Deuteronomistic redactor,[4] and appeared at about 550 B.C. The author of H, with its regulations on the Sheaf-waving,[5] is also dependent on Deuteronomy in some respects and is post-Exilic;[6] the document was composed after Ezekiel, but both used common sources.[7] Subsequently H was incorporated into the P code—certainly before 444 B.C.—with the addition of the Pesaḥ–Maṣṣoth festival regulations and the sacrifices at the ceremony of the dedication of the Sheaf.[8] P was written in the first half of the fifth century B.C.;[9] the festivals now had no association with agriculture or shepherding, but were purely commemorative. The Pesaḥ had become a family celebration; precise details are given in P of the sacrifices by which it was marked.[10]

Winnett[11] suggests that the Pesaḥ 'may have been a Canaanite (festival) which was gradually adopted and merged into the specifically Israelite festival of Unleavened Bread'. The Pesaḥ may have been celebrated for the first time as a national festival by Hezekiah (cf. 2 Chr. 30); previously it had been observed at many of the local sanctuaries. It was 'firmly established in official Yahwism' by the time of Josiah (cf. Deut. 16:1 ff.). The priests of the post-Exilic period inserted a reference to the Pesaḥ in Ex. 34:25b;[12]

[1] Deut. 16:7. May, op. cit. 79, compares 1 Sam. 2:13, Ezek. 46:24.

[2] R. H. Pfeiffer, *Introduction to the O.T.*, 1952, 221 ff.

[3] So also the 'Feast of the harvest', Ex. 23:16a, and the 'Feast of the ingathering' at the exit of the year, Ex. 23:16b; so also 23:17, 18 a, b, &c. Pfeiffer renders *ḥaggi*, 23:18, as 'my feast'.

[4] Pfeiffer, op. cit. 224. He regards the mention of Pesaḥ as among signs of the dependence of this passage upon Deuteronomy. He maintains further that *šḥṭ* in Ex. 34 is a later term than *zbḥ* in Ex. 23:18, Deut. 16:2. The term *tequphath hašanah*, Ex. 34:22, was, he holds, adopted by the Jews in Babylon at about 600 B.C., while the term *ṣe'th hašanah*, 23:16, is early.

[5] Lev. 23:9–12, 15–17.

[6] Pfeiffer suggests that the H code may have been composed in Babylonia.

[7] A recent study of the relation between H and Ezekiel will be found in L. E. Elliott-Binns, 'Some Problems of the Holiness Code', *ZAW* lxvii, 1955, 26.

[8] Lev. 23:4–8, 13–14. Pfeiffer, op. cit. 239 ff.

[9] It may, holds Pfeiffer, op. cit. 257, be reflected in the 'Passover papyrus' from Elephantine.

[10] Especially in Num. 28:19 ff. Pfeiffer, op. cit. 250 ff.

[11] F. V. Winnett, *The Mosaic Tradition*, 1949, 155 ff.

[12] But see p. 172 n. 10 below.

there were also added the regulations in Ex. 12:43–49, which 'are quite foreign to anything in the earlier Deuteronomic version of the law in Deut. 16'.

Winnett regards the development of the Maṣṣoth festival as reflected in these texts: Ex. 23:15 and 12:33 f. were followed by 13:3–10, then came Deut. 16:1–8 with the centralization of the cult at Jerusalem, and the final position is given in the P law of Ex. 12:15–20. Firstlings laws are found in their earliest form in Ex. 22:28b–29 (E.V. 29b–30), which presupposes the sacrifice of firstborn sons; in the later 13:11–16 firstborn sons are redeemed, and the phrases *peṭer reḥem* and *he'ebhir* appear for the first time in this context. Centralization is then reflected in Deut. 15:19–23, which uses the terms *bekhor* and *hiqdiš*. Finally P introduced a law on firstlings in Ex. 34:19 f. and 13:2, although, Winnett admits, 'it may seem odd that P should take the trouble to mention the law of firstlings at all at this point'. Winnett suggests further that the law of the redemption of firstborn sons, Ex. 13:11–16, was promulgated after Ahaz (cf. 2 Kings 16:3, 2 Chr. 28:3), while the Pesaḥ law of Ex. 12:21–27 was enacted by Hezekiah (cf. 2 Chr. 30). Hezekiah, he holds, laid special emphasis on the Passover, and to his reign should be attributed the verses of Ex. 12:25–27a, 13:8 f., 14–16, which are commonly assigned to a Deuteronomistic redactor of a slightly later period.

The theories on the evolution of the Passover that have been summarized so far rest primarily upon the literary-critical analysis of the Bible text. Before we subject them to examination, it will be well to set out views representative of another group of scholars; these lay greater stress upon the development of Hebrew religion against the general background of religions of the Near East, and upon the influence of historical events within that area.

Mowinckel[1] maintains that it was the festival of Tabernacles, not the Passover, that was originally associated with the story of the Exodus. Tabernacles was the New Year festival on which the king formally ascended his throne or renewed annually his royal dignity. It was the season of Creation; and Creation myths, widespread throughout the Near East, are echoed in the history of Israel. Just as the world was created from water, so the nation of Israel had been created from the sea through which they passed on their release from Egypt.[2] The Pesaḥ, on the other hand, was a family ritual, at which a victim was slain, its blood smeared, and its flesh eaten. In pre-historic times the victim represented the deity, and those who ate of its flesh absorbed some of its divine qualities. For this reason they ate it in haste; and care was taken that none of its bones should

[1] S. Mowinckel, *Psalmenstudien*, ii, 'Das Thronbesteigungsfest Jahwäs und der Ursprung der Eschatologie (Skrifter utgit av Videnskapsselskapet i Kristiana, 1921. Historisk-filosofisk Klasse, 2. Bind), 1922.

[2] Ibid. 54.

be broken so that it might arise whole at the resurrection. In the recital of the Pesaḥ story each year, Mowinckel finds trace of an annual re-enactment of a cultic drama.[1]

In post-Exilic Israel, Mowinckel holds, the festival of Tabernacles, which was the occasion for the formal enthronement of the king, had little meaning. This is reflected in the Passover documents. In the early narratives of J and E[2] the Pesaḥ had been the festival of the tenth plague. With Deuteronomy it gained greater importance; the Pesaḥ, instead of Tabernacles, was regarded now as the commemoration of the Exodus,[3] although it still was not the principal festival of Israel. The growing preference for the spring, rather than the autumn, festival may have been due to the influence of the Assyrian calendar that opened in the spring. The promulgation of the P code[4] weakened yet further the association of the autumn festival with the Exodus; indeed, the connexion survived now only in the ceremony of dwelling in booths[5] and in oblique allusions in the Psalms.[6] The Exodus story had become the cult saga of the Pesaḥ. Now the religious year commenced in the spring. The importance of the Pesaḥ was increased by its artificial amalgamation with the Maṣṣoth festival, an agricultural ceremony adopted by the Israelites after their settlement in Canaan.[7]

Nicolsky[8] regards the Pesaḥ as a relic of the nomadic age of the Israelites which they had preserved in Canaan. The victim was not a firstling, but (following Mowinckel) it had divine qualities. The smearing of its blood[9] was a prophylactic against misfortune during the ensuing year. Of special significance is the consumption of the victim by families in the nomadic epoch of the Israelites,[10] but by households in the agricultural setting of Canaan.[11]

By Josiah the Pesaḥ was transferred to the Temple at Jerusalem. Nicolsky maintains that the primary text of Deut. 16 prescribed not legislation on the Pesaḥ, but legislation on the Maṣṣoth festival and the festivals of Weeks and Tabernacles.[12] The primary text underwent a double process of redaction. The ordinances of the Pesaḥ were first introduced with the status of a national ceremony, and then the rites were restricted to the central shrine at Jerusalem.[13] These were separate stages of development,

[1] Mowinckel, op. cit. 37.
[2] Ex. 12:11 f., 27.
[3] Deut. 16:1; so Ex. 34:18, 23:15 under the influence of Deuteronomy.
[4] Ex. 13, according to Mowinckel, op. cit. 205.
[5] Lev. 23:42 f.
[6] As, for example, Ps. 81.
[7] Mowinckel, op. cit. 204–6.
[8] N. M. Nicolsky, 'Pascha im Kulte des jerusalemischen Tempels', *ZAW* xlv, 1927, 171, 241.
[9] Ex. 12:21–23 (assigned by Nicolsky to eighth–seventh century B.C.), supplemented by the later Ex. 12:1–13.
[10] Ex. 12:21.
[11] Ex. 12:3.
[12] So Nicolsky maintains that the original text on the feast of Weeks is Deut. 16:9–11a, and on Tabernacles Deut. 16:13–14. The addition of vv. 11b and 15 contradicts the preceding clauses.
[13] According to Nicolsky, the original text of Deut. 16:1–8 was v. 1 (where חג המצות

for, Nicolsky points out, the introduction of the Pesaḥ brought no advantage to the Temple personnel since the victims were wholly consumed by the celebrants and were not donated to the priests. The reason for both processes Nicolsky finds in the contemporary political scene during the reign of Josiah. Assyria had been expelled from Palestine and Syria; Egypt was extending its dominion. King Amon of Judah who had supported Assyria had been removed and Josiah was installed in his place with the help of the 'people of the land'.[1] The policies of Judah stood at the cross-roads—would Josiah throw in his lot with Egypt as advocated by the aristocrats of Jerusalem, or would he adopt an independent line as recommended by the priests, the prophets, and the 'people of the land'? The reforms set on foot by the priests and prophets were intended to encourage an independent policy; they were accompanied by threats against the Judean aristocracy, by opposition to an Egyptian alliance—and by pointed allusions to the Exodus at which Israel had been freed from subjection to Egypt. The Pesaḥ, the festival of the Exodus, was observed with great ceremony. Nicolsky finds an echo of these arguments in the prophecies of Zephaniah, the contemporary of Josiah. The *zebhaḥ* of Zeph. 1:7–8 is, he maintains, the Pesaḥ, and it was performed at night;[2] 'those that are settled on their lees'[3] are those who had not removed leaven on the approach of the spring festival.

Josiah's struggle for independence ended in disaster, but the transfer of the Pesaḥ to Jerusalem that was a major feature of his reform had opened a new phase in the history of the festival. The nomadic family ritual was adapted gradually to normal Temple procedure; this is shown by the final form of the text of Deut. 16, where cattle may be offered in addition to small animals, where the victim is to be boiled and the smearing of its blood is omitted, and where the sacrifice is called a *zebhaḥ*.[4] The same process is reflected in Ex. 34:25b and 12:27, which Nicolsky ascribes to a Deuteronomistic redactor.[5] But the Pesaḥ was too popular to allow it to become a preserve of the priests. Later documents, in particular 2 Chr. 35,[6] represent a compromise, and the final form of the ceremonial in the Mishnah demonstrates both resemblances and differences between the Pesaḥ sacrifice and the *zebhaḥ*.

stood in place of the present פסח לה׳), and vv. 3, 4a, and 8; at a later stage vv. 2 and 4b were inserted (though not the whole of our present text) and פסח לה׳ replaced חג המצות in v. 1; finally, צאן ובקר (v. 2a) and ביום הראשון (v. 4b) and vv. 5–7 were introduced, with the emphasis on centralization.

[1] 2 Kings 21:20 ff.

[2] Zeph. 1:12. Nicolsky also suggests that 'those that leap over the threshold', Zeph. 1:9, refers to the Pesaḥ ceremony, and that the term *psḥ* has the primary meaning of 'dance, leap'; against this, see p. 214 n. 11 below.

[3] Zeph. 1:12.

[4] See above, pp. 56 f.

[5] Nicolsky compares Deut. 12:3 with Ex. 34:13; Ex. 34:24 implies centralization.

[6] In 2 Chr. 35:13 the Pesaḥ offerings are roasted, the *qodašim* are boiled; all sacrifices are offered by households. On the other hand, there is no mention of the smearing of blood in this passage.

Pedersen[1] rejects literary criteria as a basis for the reconstruction of the evolution of the Passover. Written documents in their extant form[2] cannot, he maintains, be shown to be earlier than the Exilic and post-Exilic periods.

The Pesaḥ is considered by Pedersen to have been a firstling sacrifice[3] with apotropaic significance which was performed by Israelite nomads[4] already before the Exodus. The Maṣṣoth festival, on the other hand, was probably a harvest ceremony at which the new crops of Canaan were eaten without the contamination of leaven.[5] The amalgamation of the two rituals was 'simply due to the fact that the two feasts coincided' in time. They are already joined in Ex. 23 and 34.[6]

By Deuteronomy the festival was restricted to the royal central shrine,[7] and the Pesaḥ took place on the first day of the Maṣṣoth week. The week was now celebrated by lavish sacrifices of boiled victims from both flocks and herds—and not only of firstlings.[8] The celebrants probably stayed in tents within the Temple area, a practice that was later discontinued.[9] The festival was held in Abib, the month of the Exodus. In Lev. 23 and Num. 28 there is a division between the Pesaḥ and the following seven days of the Maṣṣoth week. In 2 Chr. 30, 35—where the festival is a royal ceremony as this was conceived at a time when the Monarchy had long disappeared—the festival has become largely a Temple institution.[10] But the writer vacillates between regarding the Pesaḥ as a family offering, as in early times, or as sacrifices donated by the king and his nobles and slaughtered by the Temple staff.

From this course of development Pedersen concludes that the Passover had become a festival commemorative of the Exodus. The legend of Ex. 1–15[11] was composed in Canaan, and it reflects the social order of the settled Israelite community.[12] The ritual of the Pesaḥ recalls the actual Exodus in

[1] J. Pedersen, *Israel. Its Life and Culture*, iii–iv, 1959, 383 ff., 728 ff.

[2] Including Ex. 23 and 34.

[3] This is shown, in Pedersen's view, by the emphasis on firstborn and firstlings in the Exodus narrative.

[4] The roasting of a small animal, Pedersen points out, conforms to the practice of Beduins.

[5] Cf. Jos. 5:10 ff.

[6] Where we have an allusion to the avoidance of leaven at the Pesaḥ and the prohibition against leaving the flesh until the morning, Ex. 34:25, cf. 23:18. The absence of a definite date for the Passover in these laws is due, Pedersen holds, to their brevity.

[7] Cf. 2 Kings 23:21–23. Deuteronomy refers to the festival as either the Pesaḥ or the Maṣṣoth festival.

[8] Pedersen maintains that Deut. 16 does not mention the actual Pesaḥ sacrifice; צאן ובקר, Deut. 16:2, refers, in his opinion, to the sacrifices during the Maṣṣoth week.

[9] Cf. Hos. 12:10 (E.V. 12:9).

[10] See also Ezek. 44:11 and 45:21 ff., Ezra 6:19–22.

[11] Pedersen regards Ex. 1–15 as a single unit and a central complex of the Moses story.

[12] By the use of the terms *tošabh*, *śakhir*, *'ezraḥ*, and *ger*, Ex. 12:43 ff., and cf. 12:25, 26 f., Pedersen, op. cit. 397. Pedersen, op. cit. 706, suggests, however, that Ex. 8:22 displays a knowledge of Egyptian customs that may indicate that the story received its form in Egypt.

the haste of the meal, the special costume, and perhaps the running and jumping of Canaanite cults.[1] The events of the Exodus were, Pedersen holds, re-enacted each year on the night of the Pesaḥ; it was a ritual drama, culminating in the paean of victory of Ex. 15 and the dances of the women. Some features of the legend reflect the conditions of the monarchical period. Moses has the traits of an idealized king, but gradually Aaron is brought to the foreground—as in the post-Exilic period of Israelite history the priesthood usurped the authority that had once been exercised by the kings. The Exodus was the 'starting-point of a new era', and its month was the first of the year.[2] But it was more than that—it was set in the pattern of Near Eastern myth, it was the celebration of an event of cosmic proportions, fitting to a New Year. The victory over Pharaoh was the victory of order over the dragon of chaos.

Within this framework the original functions of the Pesaḥ as a firstling sacrifice and of the Maṣṣoth festival as the offering of harvest firstfruits had largely disappeared. They survived only in the emphasis on firstborn in the Exodus legend and the prohibition against leaven at the Pesaḥ sacrifice. The sacrifice of firstlings and the dedication of the new Sheaf are independent of the ritual of the Passover. On the other hand, the family unit continued to be a feature of the Passover even when it had become part of normative Temple ritual; there was an uneasy combination of private and public ceremonial. This persistence of the family unit may be due to local conditions in Jerusalem after the Exile or in Jewish colonies outside Jerusalem.

On the relationship between the spring and autumn festivals Pedersen holds an opinion contrary to that of Mowinckel.[3] 'From the beginning', Pedersen maintains, the spring festival was the main festival of the Israelites; the autumn festival, which was preferred by Solomon, was of Canaanite origin. Both opened with a ceremony by night,[4] and at the end of the Monarchy both were of equal standing.[5] The Exodus was always associated with the spring festival. But the influence of the Exodus became so pervasive throughout the religion of Israel that the autumn festival came to be associated with it.[6]

Engnell[7] contrasts the role of the Passover in what he calls the 'P-work' (Genesis–Numbers according to both oral and written transmission) and the 'Deuteronomic-work'. In the former it is termed variously Pesaḥ,

[1] Cf. *psḥ* in 1 Kings 18:21, 26. [2] Ex. 12:2. [3] pp. 85 f. above.

[4] Is. 30:29 may, according to Pedersen, op. cit. 447, allude to either the Passover or Tabernacles.

[5] Cf. Ezek. 45:18 ff., adopting the reading of LXX in v. 20 (see p. 6 n. 4 above); here both the Passover and Tabernacles are preceded by purificatory rites.

[6] Lev. 23:42–43.

[7] I. Engnell, '*Pæsaḥ-Maṣṣōt* and the Problem of "Patternism"', *Orientalia Suecana*, i, 1952, 39.

Maṣṣoth, and *ḥag*, and it is the Israelite festival *par excellence*; in the latter (assigned by Engnell to a largely North Israelite provenance) the festival of Tabernacles is the dominant feast, while the Passover, described as Pesaḥ or Maṣṣoth, has been 'Canaanized' and is to be held only at the central shrine. Like Pedersen, Engnell emphasizes that the history of the Passover cannot be reconstructed by the literary-critical method. Engnell rejects the theory that the Pesaḥ sacrifice was a nomadic firstlings offering 'constituted negatively with apotropaic rites and aims'. He finds in it a reflection of the 'nature festival' of Mesopotamia and Canaan. The name פסח is to be associated with 'limp, dance' of a cultic dance; perhaps the Pesaḥ victim was a substitution sacrifice and its sacrificers danced as they mourned. The motif of resurrection at the Passover is reflected in the prayers for dew at the modern Jewish Pesaḥ, and the motif of the sacred marriage may be reflected in the Song of Songs, which Jews recite on the eighth day of the festival. The judgements against Pharaoh recall the judgement theme of the *akitu* festivals. In the titles and function of Moses in the Bible and in Rabbinic tradition Engnell sees the reflection of a Messianic royal figure, while Pharaoh (according to Jewish tradition, not slain but bound alive in the Red Sea) is to be compared to Kingu, the Akkadian personification of the *šar puḫi*.

This widespread Near Eastern ritual was historicized and given a specifically Israelite character. It was a *ḥag* or procession festival; it included a cultic exodus into the open field, בשדה.[1] Ex. 1–15 is (with Pedersen) the ritual text of the Pesaḥ cult-drama. In the course of time the cult myth was revised and recast. In particular, Aaron the High Priest is played off against Moses the King. But it is impossible to reconstruct a 'primary edition' of the text, 'and least of all by means of the literary-critical method'.

The Pesaḥ of the 'P-work' represents, according to Engnell, 'a southern form of the Canaanite vernal New Year festival . . . probably brought to Egypt by the "Jacobite" emigrants'. After the entry of the Mosaic tribes into Canaan, it was fused with the parallel north Canaanite annual feast of Maṣṣoth. This was not only because they coincided in time, but also because Pesaḥ and Maṣṣoth 'must have been two variants of one and the same annual feast . . . in the centre of which stood the maintaining of fertility and "blessing", of cosmos against chaos', but with the accent 'a little different' owing to the varying 'culture conditions'—the accent was 'on the herds and on the products of the earth respectively'. The amalgamated festival was historicized into a commemorative festival. In time it lost its 'temple-dramatic' character, the Maṣṣoth component dominated, and it became the special religious feast of the home.

[1] Cf. Akk. *ina ṣeri*.

In pre-Exilic times the autumn New Year festival (Sukkoth and Rosh haShanah) was the more important and typical form of Israelite New Year festival, in both the northern and southern kingdoms; this was due to the general victory of Canaanite ideology. It is dominant in the 'Deuteronomic-work'. It was more coherent in outward form and ideological content. Pesaḥ, on the contrary, 'is a characteristic example of the "disintegration" of this cultic pattern, its breaking up, and its adaptation'. Therefore, Engnell concludes, in Jewish times it was the Pesaḥ that won the final victory.[1]

I have set out these views on the evolution of the Passover at some length, in order to permit each scholar not merely to present adequately his theory, but to indicate the stress which he lays on some particular feature of the theory. How far may we accept these varied hypotheses? The first group—Beer, McNeile, Steuernagel, Arnold, Guthe, Gray, May, and Pfeiffer—base their theses squarely upon the Source hypothesis. Their criteria are largely literary criteria, and among these the greatest weight is given to the use of special terminology, words, and phrases peculiar to one or more Sources. I have suggested in the previous chapter that this is unlikely to be a reliable method for ascertaining the identity of individual documents among our Passover texts.[2] Technical terms are not the special stock-in-trade of individual Sources; they are employed as the context requires.[3]

Nevertheless, although the use of terminology cannot be accepted as a yardstick to determine the stratification of the Passover texts, we are not entitled on that ground alone to reject theses based upon the Source hypothesis. These theses do not, in fact, rest primarily on textual analysis; the variations of language revealed by textual analysis and ascribed to individual Sources are regarded rather as the outward reflection of a deeper process. The succession of Sources corresponds to the broad lines of evolution in Israelite beliefs and modes of thought, and the expression of that evolution in religious practice. Two factors are held to have governed or modified this process. Different social and economic conditions are said to have obtained in northern and southern Palestine; and, secondly, it is maintained that in the course of time ritual was made to conform to the rigid conventions of a central shrine and of a growing formalism in religious ceremonial.

I shall return to the first point later.[4] The second I have already broadly accepted[5]—and we shall find sufficient evidence for it in the course of this study. But it may be seriously doubted whether the case is sensibly advanced by the arguments of the proponents of the Source hypothesis on the grounds of literary criticism. Our analysis has exposed the great

[1] T. H. Gaster's *Passover. Its History and Traditions*, 1958, follows the same general line of approach, but it is too brief to be more than cursory in its analysis of the Passover ritual.

[2] pp. 72 f. above. [3] See also pp. 201 f. and 203 f. below on *zebhaḥ*, *'olah*, and *qorban*.

[4] p. 94 below. [5] See p. 77 above.

measure of disunity among those scholars who use the literary-critical method. The tools employed are the same; the results of their work are different—sometimes widely different.[1] Perhaps, it may be argued, it is not the general method that is at fault, but details in the manner of its application; one of these scholars may be right, and the remainder wrong. But all these scholars are at one in maintaining that Ex. 12:3 ff. is the product of P, a late redactor of the Priestly school. Yet the ritual that it describes is undoubtedly archaic. Perhaps, it may be contended, archaic ritual was preserved by oral tradition for incorporation in a late document; this is, indeed, possible. But, as I have already pointed out, the allocation of written documents to redactors or Schools of different epochs and outlook loses force and value if they do not leave their stamp upon the contents of those documents—if, whenever a difficulty arises, we are obliged to explain it away by an appeal to oral tradition. More strange is the fact that a feature of the ritual prescribed in this document ascribed to P is in flagrant contradiction to the principles of that school and repugnant to the beliefs and practices of the period to which P is assigned. The ceremony of the smearing of the blood of the Pesaḥ victim is not a secondary feature of the passage Ex. 12:3 ff.; it is a vital and integral part of the ritual and its myth. Hypotheses which assume its insertion in a Priestly document must be viewed with grave suspicion.

The second group of theses on the evolution of the Passover—represented here by Mowinckel, Nicolsky, Pedersen, and Engnell—present a rational line of approach to the problem. It is axiomatic that the Passover can be best analysed within the framework of contemporary Near Eastern history and religion. Mowinckel and Nicolsky, it is true, accept the Source hypothesis in a modified form; Pedersen and Engnell reject it. There seems much to recommend Engnell's division of the Pentateuch into a 'P-work' and a 'D-work', for the opposition in details of Passover ritual (as we have seen in ch. 2) appears to be strongest between Deut. 16 and the rest of the Passover texts in the Pentateuch.[2]

Nevertheless, while I accept in general terms much of the arguments presented by this second group of scholars—and particularly that of Engnell—they all suffer from a grave defect. They deny the use, wholly or partially, of literary criticism; yet they admit in some measure the conclusions of the 'textual critics', in that they regard the Passover as the artificial amalgam of an ancient Israelite New Year sacrifice (Pesaḥ) with a Canaanite agricultural festival (the Maṣṣoth festival). They accept the general deductions of the 'Documentary school' while refusing to accept their premisses and without submitting the deductions to fresh analysis. Our next step

[1] For a general analysis of modern trends in Pentateuchal criticism, see C. R. North, 'Pentateuchal Criticism', in Rowley, *Old Testament and Modern Study*, 48 ff.

[2] But see pp. 204 ff. below for an explanation of some apparent discrepancies.

must be to consider whether this view of the origin of the Passover, common to virtually all students of the festival, is in fact tenable.

The view stems from two different lines of reasoning. The first maintains that the Pesaḥ was a nomadic ritual practised by the Israelites in the period before their conquest of Canaan; the Maṣṣoth festival was, it is claimed, acquired by them from the indigenous peoples of Canaan together with the art of agriculture. This thesis is open to question. It is true that the sons of Jacob in one passage are called shepherds.[1] But the point of that passage is that this title enabled Joseph to settle them in the land of Goshen away from the main centres of Egyptian religion and civilization.[2] It does not justify the assumption that the Israelites were shepherds only and that their existence depended solely upon the care of flocks and herds. The narrator of Genesis indicates otherwise. Isaac sowed crops[3] and Joseph dreamed of the fields in which the sheaves stood bound.[4] This narrator is correct. The Hebrew patriarchs were not nomads like the cattle-breeders of the Arabian deserts, but semi-nomads.[5] They tended their flocks, but they also sowed seeds in the right season, and reaped the crops. They were acquainted with the processes of agricultural growth, as are all semi-nomads in the Near East today.[6] Indeed, Hebrew tradition is unanimous in maintaining that it was during the wanderings in the Wilderness—and only then—that the Israelites were wholly nomadic. More, they were then without resources in meat as well as grain, and dependent upon the bounty of Providence. That period was an interlude, and it stands by itself in the whole history of Israel.[7] It is contrasted not only with the period after, but also with the period before, the Israelite conquest of Canaan. Isaac is opposed to the nomad Ishmael, Jacob is opposed to the nomad Esau, and both Isaac and Jacob were semi-nomads.[8] During the wanderings through the Wilderness, on the other hand, the Israelites and their leader were intimately associated with the Kenites and came, the Bible admits, under their influence;[9] the Kenites were nomads, the Israelites were not.

It is evident, then, that the Hebrews must have been acquainted with agriculture before, as after, the settlement in Canaan. It is inconceivable that they should not have performed the ceremony of offering firstfruits from the new grain. If the Maṣṣoth festival is a firstfruits thanksgiving rite,[10] it

[1] Gen. 46:31 ff. [2] Cf. Ex. 8:22 (E.V. 8:26). [3] Gen. 26:12. [4] Gen. 37:6 ff.

[5] See the treatment of the subject in B. D. Eerdmans, *Alttestamentliche Studien*, ii, 1908, 38 f.; R. de Vaux, 'Patriarches hébreux et les découvertes modernes', *RB* lvi, 1949, 5 ff., 11 f.; and R. Dussaud, *Pénétration des arabes en Syrie avant l'Islam*, 1955, 15 f., 180.

[6] So, for example, J. A. Jaussen, *Coutumes des Arabes au pays de Moab*, 1908, 240 ff., and H. Charles, *Tribus moutonnières du Moyen-Euphrate*, 1939, 120 ff.

[7] Cf., for example, Deut. 8:2 ff., 15 f., 29:4 f., Jer. 2:2, Hos. 13:5 f.

[8] Gen. 17:19 ff., 21:8 ff.; 27:27 ff. The descendants of Ishmael live in settlements and circles of tents, Gen. 25:16. [9] Ex. 18:1 ff., cf. 2:15 ff.

[10] But see pp. 108 ff. below.

must have been familiar to them in some form from a remote period of their history.

Other scholars, while also holding that two independent elements, the Pesaḥ and the Maṣṣoth festival, have fused to form the Passover, regard the fusion somewhat differently. They maintain that after the settlement in Canaan the Maṣṣoth festival, an offering of harvest firstfruits, was celebrated only in North Israel, whose population was mainly agricultural. The Pesaḥ, a firstlings sacrifice, was, they assert, celebrated only in the southern kingdom, where pastoral occupations provided the chief source of livelihood. With the fall of Samaria the kingdom of Judah survived alone; and then, it is argued, the Pesaḥ emerged as a national festival. This is shown by the laws of Deut. 16 and the account of 2 Kings 23.[1] In the course of time the two feasts were united.

This thesis is a hazardous over-simplification. I have already suggested that the Hebrew patriarchs were semi-nomads; they must have practised both firstlings sacrifices and the dedication of firstfruits offerings in the earliest epoch of Israelite history. There are, however, more serious arguments against this thesis. In later times Palestine was divided into three regions on the ground of climate; and this reflects—but only approximately—the natural geographical division of the country.[2] But the political division of Palestine into two areas by a line running near 32° lat., as it was divided into the kingdoms of Israel and Judah, reflects differences neither of climate nor of natural vegetation. It cannot be maintained that agriculture was found only in the north and cattle-rearing only in the south. North Israel was, it is true, predominantly agricultural,[3] but the Kenites were settled there[4] and must have found grazing for their flocks. Some of the northern tribes lived, and raised flocks of small animals, on the pasture land to the east of the Jordan.[5] It is true, on the other hand, that the people of Judah were essentially a pastoral society.[6] But a section of them were employed in agriculture,[7] and there was an important commercial community[8] who

[1] Welch, op. cit. 27 ff., interprets differently. He maintains that there are two sets of documents in Exodus on the Passover and the firstlings offering. Each deals in turn with the Pesaḥ, the Maṣṣoth festival, and the firstlings offering; the first (Ex. 12:1–13, 14–20, 13:1–2) is derived from Judah, the second (12:21–28, 13:3–10, 11–16) from North Israel. None of the second group prescribes a sacrifice, because they belong to a period when the altar was not yet in existence. Josiah extended the North Israelite practices to the whole country, and introduced them to the Temple at Jerusalem. Nevertheless, Judah preserved its own differences of detail, in, for example, the species of animal from which the Pesaḥ victim was to be chosen and the method of its preparation. When the two sets of laws were united in the text of Exodus, Ex. 12:21 ff. was, Welch holds, mutilated by the Judean editor, perhaps because it diverged from Ex. 12:1–13.

[2] See p. 238 n. 1 below.

[3] Jud. 21:20, 1 Kings 21:1, 2 Kings 4:18.

[4] Jud. 4:11; so also the Rechabites, 2 Kings 10:15, Jer. 35:6 ff.

[5] See Num. 32:1 ff. and, for the Monarchy period, 2 Kings 10:33; cf. Mic. 2:12 on the Edomites and Num. 31:32 on the flocks of the Midianites. See further F.-M. Abel, *Géographie de la Palestine*, ii, 1938, 67 ff.

[6] Gen. 38:12, 1 Sam. 25:2, 1 Chr. 27:29.

[7] 1 Sam. 6:13, 23:1, Ruth 2:2, &c.

[8] 1 Kings 9:26, 10:15.

must have been concerned with the production as well as the purchase and sale of cereals. There was close intercourse between the prophets—the representatives of the ordinary folk—of both kingdoms.[1] It is, in short, impossible to assign particular occupations to the population of each kingdom, and to attribute particular religious ceremonial to the one and not the other. If we assume that the Passover was the amalgamation of a firstlings sacrifice with a harvest firstfruits offering, it should have received its shape from very early times and certainly before the occupation of Canaan; and it should have been practised throughout the whole land of Palestine.

But was the Pesaḥ in fact a nomadic rite and did the Maṣṣoth festival arise out of agriculture and the dedication of cereal firstfruits? This is a convenient point in our study at which to examine various hypotheses on the origin of these ceremonies. To some, reference has already been made in the preceding pages, in the course of the summary of theories on the evolution of the Passover. The view taken by each scholar on the evolution of the festival is dependent in no small degree upon his view concerning its origin.

The origin of the Pesaḥ has been sought in the etymology of the Heb. פסח. That is a proper approach, for Semitic names are an essential and integral element of the person or thing to which they are applied. Of particular significance would be the use of פסח in a passage where it appears to have no connexion with the Pesaḥ ritual. In Is. 31:5 פסוח is found parallel to the word גנון, 'protect', and it has been held, on this ground, that the primary meaning of the word פסח is also 'protect, save'.[2]

Others have associated the Pesaḥ with פסח, 'be lame, limp' (*qal*),[3] 'be lamed' (*niph.*),[4] 'dance with limping motions' (*piel*).[5] It is suggested that the verb means 'hop in a ritual dance',[6] and that this became the name of the festival because its ritual included dancing,[7] in the same way as *ḥag*, which is used often of the autumn festival, may be connected with a procession or circumambulation round a shrine.[8] Dancing as a sacred rite

[1] Amos 7:12, 1 Kings 13:1.

[2] F. Zorell, *Lexicon hebraicum et aramaicum Veteris Testamenti*, 1950, s.v.; see also the discussion in C. H. Toy, 'Meaning of פֶּסַח', *JBL* xvi, 1897, 178.

[3] 1 Kings 18:21, cf. the adj. פִּסֵּחַ, Lev. 21:18, Deut. 15:21, 2 Sam. 5:6, 8, 19:27, Is. 33:23, 35:6, Jer. 31:7 (E.V. 31:8), &c.

[4] 2 Sam. 4:4.

[5] 1 Kings 18:26.

[6] Thus the story of Gen. 32:24 ff. has been held to be an aetiological legend to explain a sacred limping-dance; see p. 188 n. 1 below. W. O. E. Oesterley, *Sacred Dance*, 1923, 51, points to the meaning of צלע in Gen. 32:31 f. (cf. Jer. 20:10, Mic. 4:6 f., Zeph. 3:19, Ps. 35:15, 38:18, Job 18:12), and suggests that Saul's ancestral home Zela (2 Sam. 21:14) was possibly an ancient sanctuary where this special kind of limping-dance was performed.

[7] See F. Schwally, *Idioticon des christlich palästinischen Aramaeisch*, 1893, 124; Toy, op. cit. 179; Oesterley, op. cit. 50 f.; and Pedersen, 'Passahfest und Passahlegende', *ZAW* lii, 1934, 167. G. R. Driver, *JTS* xxvii, 1925–6, 159, suggests, cautiously, that Heb. פסח is connected with Syr. ܦܣܥ, 'step'.

[8] But see pp. 129 and 151 below.

is well known in the Near East.[1] It would be particularly appropriate at a time of such mixed emotions as the spring festival; it might be a primitive ceremony of sympathetic magic to quicken and revitalize the processes of fertility and the growth of the new vegetation. The existence of the sacred dance in Palestine is demonstrated, those who maintain this theory go on to claim, by the name Baʿal Marqod,[2] and by the dance performed by David when the Ark was brought to Jerusalem.[3]

Other scholars have looked to neighbouring or cognate languages for the explanation of the name Pesaḥ. Some have found a derivation in the Akkadian *paššaḫu*, 'make soft, supple, soothe, placate'.[4] The Hebrew פסח would, in this case, be a loan-word. Others have turned to Egyptian for the source of the name as well as the scene of the inaugural celebration of the Pesaḥ. Hommel claims (though hesitantly) to identify in פסח the Egyptian masculine article followed by *sḫꜣ*, the 'commemoration'.[5] Riedel prefers the combination of the Egyptian article with *ꜣsḫ* (*poseḫ*), 'the harvest'. The Pesaḥ was, he assumes, a sacrificial meal introducing the Maṣṣoth festival of the new crops.[6] Riedel is followed by Völter, who finds a parallel for the Pesaḥ in the Egyptian festival held, according to Herodotus, on the fourteenth–fifteenth day of Pachon;[7] Epiphanius describes a ceremony of blood-smearing at the spring equinox.[8] It was, Völter declares, at the same time both a full-moon feast and a thanksgiving rite for the harvest marked by the offering of firstfruits.[9] More recently Couroyer, pointing to the repeated description of the tenth plague, in Exodus and elsewhere, as a blow inflicted directly by the deity himself, has suggested an etymology based upon the Egyptian article followed by *śḫ*, 'the blow'. He interprets the formula פסח הוא לה'[10] as meaning 'it is the blow of the Lord'. Later, Couroyer maintains, this Egyptian phrase was further naturalized in Hebrew by being artificially connected with the Heb. *psḥ ʿal*, 'limp over', and hence 'pass over, spare'.[11]

Finally, Wensinck cautiously proposes the equation of Pesaḥ with the Arab. فسخ, 'separate'.[12] On the night of 15th Shaʿban, *laylat al-tarwiḥ*,

[1] Oesterley, op. cit. 56 ff., 81 ff., 94 ff.; W. R. Smith, *Religion of the Semites*, 1927, 432.

[2] Oesterley, op. cit. 56; id., 'Early Hebrew Festival Rituals', in S. H. Hooke, *Myth and Ritual*, 1933, 117.

[3] 2 Sam. 6:14 ff.

[4] P. Haupt, 'Babylonian Elements in the Levitic Ritual', *JBL* xix, 1900, 73 n. 60, and H. Zimmern in E. Schrader, *Keilinschriften und das Alte Testament*, 1903, 610 n. 3. See also W. Riedel, 'Miscellen', *ZAW* xx, 1900, 324.

[5] F. Hommel, *Altisraelitische Überlieferung in inschriftlicher Beleuchtung*, 1897, 292 f.

[6] Riedel, op. cit. 325 ff.

[7] ii. 47.

[8] *Haeres.* xviii. 3 (Migne, *P.G.* xli, col. 260).

[9] D. Völter, *Passah und Mazzoth und ihr aegyptisches Urbild*, 1912, 10 ff.

[10] Ex. 12:11.

[11] B. Couroyer, 'Origine égyptienne du mot "Pâque"', *RB* lxii, 1955, 481.

[12] A. J. Wensinck, *Arabic New-Year and the Feast of Tabernacles* (Verhandelingen der Koninklijke Akademie van Wetenschappen te Amsterdam. Afdeeling Letterkunde, N.R., Deel xxv. no. 2), 1925, 37. Toy, loc. cit., connects مسخ with the meaning of 'striding,

the living are separated from the dead.[1] The notion of separation is cognate with that of making a decision or passing judgement. In Rabbinic tradition, Wensinck points out, the Pesaḥ was, like the New Year at Babylon, the time at which decision was made about the coming harvest.[2]

Each of these theories raises difficulties which must oblige us to reject it. The interpretation of the meaning of Pesaḥ from the passage of Is. 31:5 where פסוח apparently denotes 'protect' is not in fact independent evidence. Here there is an allusion to the Exodus. The prophet is decrying those who looked to Egypt for deliverance. God, he declares, will protect Jerusalem without the help of Egypt, just as he saved the Israelites from the Egyptians themselves at the Exodus. The verse may be rendered literally:

> . . . so will the Lord of hosts protect Jerusalem; he will protect and deliver (it); he will perform a Pesaḥ and preserve (it).

There is no evidence of פסח with the meaning of 'protect' before this passage of Is. 31:5, which is itself clearly secondary.[3] The contextual sense of פסוח in Is. 31:5 begins to exert its influence on the interpretation of the word in the Exodus narrative only (so far as we can judge from our texts) with LXX.[4] Even so, LXX is hesitant. In the Exodus narrative it renders פסח twice as 'shelter', but once as 'pass over';[5] and it simply transcribes the noun as *Πάσχα*.[6] In all these passages, then, LXX represents the sense of the context, rather than the primary significance of the

dancing, limping (which) would then be regarded as a mode of separating the legs'.

[1] Arab. تنفسخ الاحياء من الاميات.

[2] *Mish. R.H.* i. 2; see p. 148 below. The cognate languages provide no help. Syriac renders פסח in the Bible as ܦܣܚܐ, but also (in the Edessan dialect?) as ܦܨܚܐ, and even ܦܣܚܐ (see R. Payne Smith, *Thesaurus*, s.v.) and ܦܪܣܚܐ (see F. Schulthess, *Lexicon syropalaestinum*, 1903, s.v.). See Th. Nöldeke, *Neue Beiträge zur semitischen Sprachwissenschaft*, 1910, 37, and Schwally, loc. cit., who points out that ܦܨܚܐ, 'joyous (festival)', may be derived from anti-Jewish tendentiousness. Ugar. may have an obscure pr. name *psḥn*, Gordon, *Ugaritic Manual*, 1955, Glossary, s.v. On *psḥ* in Ethiopic and Berber dialects, see Toy, op. cit. 179; Nöldeke, op. cit.; R. Basset, 'Recherches sur la religion des Berbères', *RHR* lxi, 1910, 329; and H. Stumme, 'Gedanken über libysch-phönizische Anklänge', *ZA* xxvii, 1912, 128. The theory that *psḥ*, 'pass', is reflected in the place-name Thapsacus (Tiphsah, 1 Kings 5:4, E.V. 4:24) must be abandoned; Xenophon, *Anabasis* I. iv. 18, implies that there was no ford there, since before his coming the river had been crossed only by boat at that point.

[3] But the Greek versions other than LXX render פסח in Is. 31:5 as 'pass by', and so also Vulg.; Pesh. has 'help'. This is evidently under the influence of the narrative of the Exodus Pesaḥ.

[4] LXX in Is. 31:5 renders פסוח as 'save'. The influence of the context of Is. 31:5 upon the rendering of *psḥ* in the narrative of the Exodus Pesaḥ is shown in *Mekhilta* on Ex. 12:24 which cites the Isaiah passage; cf. *Exodus Rabba*, xv. 12.

[5] Ex. 12:13, 27; 12:23.

[6] Aq. has ὑπέρβασις, 'passing over', cf. p. 38 n. 5 above on Josephus. Sym. has ὑπερμάχησις, cf. n. 4 above. On the methods of transcribing Heb. פסח into Aramaic and Greek, see Riedel, op. cit. 319 ff.; Beer, op. cit. 49 f., 50 n. 10; J. Jeremias, art. '*Πάσχα*', *Theologisches Wörterbuch zum N.T.*; and H. Haag, art. 'Pâque', *Dict. Bib. Suppl.*, vi. 1122. The etymology which connects *Πάσχα* with the sufferings (*πάσχειν*) of Jesus is, of course, fanciful; see C. Bonner, *Homily on the Passion by Melito Bishop of Sardis* . . ., 1940, 115 n.

word; certainly it does not provide an etymology. So, too, the Targums, which also reflect an ancient Jewish tradition, are not based on independent testimony. They render *psḥ* in the Exodus context as 'spare',[1] and in Is. 31:5 as 'deliver'.

The suggestion that the Pesaḥ is to be associated with dancing is attractive on the grounds of philology, but not convincing on other grounds. If פסח denoted a ritual ceremony of dancing in the reign of Ahab,[2] why does not the Deuteronomist—whom most scholars ascribe to the age of Josiah—take cognizance of this in his account of the Passover ceremony?[3] The only certain allusion in the historical books of the Bible to dancing as part of a yearly ritual among the Israelites, and not in celebration of an isolated event,[4] is to be found in the dance of the 'daughters of Shiloh'.[5] But this, like the Hillulim ceremonies,[6] may well have arisen under Canaanite influence. Baʿal Marqod was a Phoenician god.[7] In the story of Elijah on Carmel it is of the priests of Baʿal that the word פסח is used.[8] The dancing and singing of Israelite women in the moment of victory[9] scarcely requires explanation—certainly it was not a recurrent ritual. And when David danced before the Ark, this was a spontaneous demonstration of emotion—and it did not, according to our narrator, win the approval of Court circles.[10] Moreover, it is not termed *psḥ*. The word Pesaḥ is not used in Hebrew of a dancing ritual. Indeed, the association of the word פִּסֵּחַ, 'lame', with a Temple limping-dance is open to considerable doubt. Lameness was a disqualification in Temple ritual, both for victims and for officiants.[11] That is not to assert that dancing was absent from the ritual of certain Israelite festivals.[12] But it is inconceivable that a dance should have been the central element of so vital a national institution as the Pesaḥ, should have given its name to the festival and even to the victims sacrificed

[1] Targ. Jer., Onq. in Ex. 12:13, Targ. Onq. in 12:23; cf. Targ. Jer. in 12:11. In 12:23 Targ. Jer. has 'defend'; see p. 48 above. On the rendering of the Targum edited by A. Díez Macho, see T. F. Glasson, '"Passover", a Misnomer: The Meaning of the Verb *Pasach*', *JTS*, N.S., x, 1959, 81.

[2] 1 Kings 18:21, 26.

[3] Deut. 16:1 ff., cf. 2 Kings 23:21–23.

[4] Cf. nn. 9–10 below.

[5] Jud. 21:21; cf. Jer. 31:3–5 (E.V. 31:4–6).

[6] Jud. 9:27.

[7] See F. Baethgen, *Beiträge zur semitischen Religionsgeschichte*, 1888; C. Clermont-Ganneau, *Recueil d'archéologie orientale*, i, 1888, 95, 103; R. du Mesnil du Buisson and R. Mouterde, *Mélanges de la Faculté Orientale de l'Université de Beyrouth*, vii, 1914–21, 387; and R. Ganszyniec, art. 'Marqod', Pauly–Wissowa, *Realenc.*, 1930.

[8] 1 Kings 18:26. For a Tyrian dance in honour of Herakles, Heliodorus, *Aethiopica* IV. xvii, cf. Herodian v. v. 9; see R. de Vaux, *Bulletin du Musée de Beyrouth*, v, 1941, 10 f., on religious dancing depicted on a Roman relief. G. Dalman, *Arbeit und Sitte in Palästina*, i, 1928, 146, and id., *Palästinischer Diwan*, 1901, 267 ff., 273, cites dancing rites in modern Palestine believed to influence the arrival of rain. For a survey of dancing as a sacred ritual, see H. H. Rowley, 'Elijah on Mount Carmel', *BJRL* xliii, 1960, 240 f.

[9] Ex. 15:20, Jud. 5:1, 11:34, 1 Sam. 18:6.

[10] 2 Sam. 6:16, cf. 6:5. Note that LXX in 2 Sam. 6:20 is derived from Heb. הרקדים in place of M.T. הרקים; H. M. Orlinsky, '*Ha-roqdim* for *ha-reqim* in II Samuel 6[20]', *JBL* lxv, 1946, 25 ff., regards the former as the original text.

[11] Deut. 15:21, Mal. 1:8, 13; Lev. 21:18, 2 Sam. 5:6, 8.

[12] See p. 150 below.

at the festival, and then have disappeared from view to remain without mention in all the many documents on the Passover.

That פסח might be a loan-word from Akkadian *pšḫ* is philologically possible. If the festival were adopted from Mesopotamia, this must have taken place very early. Our first certain historical allusion to the festival in Israel is its celebration by Josiah, but we are told in the account of that event that the festival had been held already in the days of the Judges. That it is ancient is to be expected. Its ritual differs so radically from ordinary sacrificial usages in Israel that it must have been in constant practice long before its procedure was sanctified by custom and subsequently embodied in written legislation.[1] An early borrowing from Mesopotamia may be supported by the view of the Bible that the Hebrew patriarchs came from that region. Nevertheless, the theory of an Akkadian origin for the word פסח is to be regarded with great suspicion. The corresponding Akkadian word occurs in general use in both historical and religious contexts with the meanings 'be appeased, restored (to health)',[2] but nothing is known of a festal ritual of this name in Mesopotamia.[3]

If an Akkadian prototype for the word פסח is unlikely, it is even less likely that the name would be derived from Egyptian. Philologically the association of the Egyptian article with a noun to form a single Hebrew word (as this hypothesis postulates) is improbable; it has no parallel in those Hebrew words that are claimed as loan-words from Egyptian.[4] The adoption of Arabic loan-words into European languages with the retention of the Arabic definite article *al-* cannot serve as an argument. We are dealing there with technical terms, for whose transmission, moreover, there is historical evidence; in the case of the word 'Pesaḥ', on the other hand, it is not claimed that the Egyptian words are technical terms, and there is no evidence at all of their transmission from ancient Egyptian to ancient Hebrew.[5]

Furthermore, the objection which has already been levelled against the theory of an Akkadian origin may be applied to the theory of an Egyptian origin—and with greater force. It is reasonable to maintain that the foreign

[1] See p. 184 below.

[2] For some examples see J. A. Knudtzon, *El-Amarna-Tafeln*, 1915, glossary, and C. J. Mullo Weir, *A Lexicon of Accadian Prayers in the Rituals of Expiation*, 1934, s.v., and the standard lexicons.

[3] For ceremonial in Mesopotamia that bears some resemblance to the Pesaḥ, see p. 162 below. It is not, however, called *pšḫ*.

[4] See the words analysed by T. O. Lambdin, 'Egyptian Loan Words in the Old Testament', *JAOS* lxxiii, 1953, 145.

[5] The possible derivation of proper names, e.g. Phinehas from Egyptian *pꜣ nḥsy* (cf. L. Koehler, *Supplementum ad Lexicon in Veteris Testamenti libros*, 1958, s.v.), is not a convincing argument for the derivation of the verb *psḥ*. Couroyer, op. cit. 490, cites Arab. *timsaḥ* as an example of the incorporation of the Egyptian article into a non-Egyptian word. *Timsaḥ*, however, is not found in Hebrew; and—more significant—it is found only in the Egyptian dialect of Arabic as the name of an Egyptian animal.

name of an object or even a ritual may have been adopted into Hebrew, if it had a special significance that could not be clearly expressed in the Hebrew language. So we may regard ברזל or תבה as direct borrowings. But that the Egyptian word for so neutral a term as 'commemoration' should be used in preference to the native root *zkr*—as Hommel would have us believe—is extremely unlikely. Indeed, *zkr* is actually found in the Exodus narrative.[1] The same reasoning may be used as an argument against the ingenious suggestion of Couroyer. If 'the blow' were the technical description of a ritual or of an event familiar in Egyptian religion or Egyptian history, its adoption by the Israelites would be intelligible. But Couroyer does not maintain this. We are asked to assume, in the first place, that the Pesaḥ was inaugurated at the Exodus—itself not certain—and, secondly, that the Israelites took over the phrase used by the Egyptians to describe the tenth plague as the name of the ritual which preceded the tenth plague—and in preference to one of the Hebrew terms which (as we see from the text of the Exodus Pesaḥ) would have fitted the incident equally well.[2] The Egyptian phrase was, it is further alleged in Couroyer's theory, perpetuated in Israelite religion as the name of the festival *par excellence*. The theory is improbable and must be rejected.

The hypothesis of Riedel suggests not only the incorporation of the Egyptian article into a Hebrew word—like the hypotheses of Hommel and Couroyer; it assumes also that the Pesaḥ was a harvest festival and that it coincided with the Egyptian harvest festival. That is not so. The harvesting period in Palestine begins with the late spring, in Egypt the main crops are dependent upon the phases of the Nile. Nor, again, is there a logical reason why the Israelites should have borrowed the Egyptian word for harvest; indeed, the feast of Weeks is called the '*ḥag* of harvest', and the ordinary Hebrew word is employed.[3] Neither Riedel nor Völter suggests that there was a native Egyptian ceremony similar to the Pesaḥ. The description of the blood-smearing in Epiphanius is late, and may be directly derived from the Biblical Pesaḥ with which Epiphanius was, of course, well acquainted.

I have propounded objections to these hypotheses of an Egyptian prototype of the Israelite Pesaḥ on grounds of detail. There is a general argument no less conclusive. The likelihood of a direct borrowing from Egypt is very remote. There was considerable antipathy between Egyptians on the one hand and Israelites (and other Semites) on the other, which certainly extended to the sphere of religion. And it is improbable in the extreme that the festival which was regarded as commemorating the deliverance of the Israelites from Egypt would be itself of Egyptian origin.

[1] Ex. 12:14, 13:3, 9.

[2] *nkh* (*hikkah*), Ex. 12:12, 13, 29; *ngp*, Ex. 12:13, 23, 27.

[3] Ex. 23:16. See B. Stade, 'Nachwort des Herausgebers zu . . . Riedel's 5. Miscelle: פסח', *ZAW* xx, 1900, 335.

Wensinck's theory of an Arabic parallel for the word פסח rests on too slender a foundation. We shall analyse later the association of the Passover with the fixing of fates for the ensuing year. But فسخ is not, it appears, the formal name of a ritual or a religious motif; it occurs in a phrase used apparently of 15th Shaʿban. The Arab beliefs concerning that date may themselves be borrowed from the Jews; certainly they derive from the general pattern of Near Eastern New Year festivals.[1] Wensinck's phrase can scarcely shed light on the origins or the primary significance of Pesaḥ.

Philology, then, provides no help in our search for an explanation of the origin of the Pesaḥ. We turn to those hypotheses that are based upon the ritual of the festival.

One hypothesis seeks the origin of the Pesaḥ in the tenth plague, the slaughter of the Egyptian firstborn. According to the Biblical legend, the Pesaḥ sacrifice was performed and the blood of the victim smeared upon the doorposts and lintel—and in consequence the Israelite firstborn were spared. It is pointed out that passages prescribing the redemption of human firstborn stand in close proximity to the narrative of the Exodus Pesaḥ.[2] It is suggested, then, that the Israelites had practised firstborn sacrifice,[3] but in the course of time—and, notably, it is assumed, at the Exodus Pesaḥ—an animal was substituted for the firstborn in each household. The prototype of this substitution appears in Gen. 22:13, where a ram is slain in place of Isaac. The blood-sign on the doorposts at the Pesaḥ showed that the substitute animal had been duly slaughtered; in return the deity would forgo or 'pass over' the requisite human sacrifice. Gradually the substitution rite assumed the character of a national festival.[4]

It must, however, be doubted on general grounds whether regular human sacrifice was practised among the early Israelites.[5] There is plentiful archaeological evidence of human foundation sacrifice among the Canaanites,[6] but little reliable proof of widespread human sacrifice among the Israelites

[1] See p. 148 n. 4 below.

[2] pp. 66 ff. above.

[3] On the eighth day after birth, according to A. Kuenen, *Religion of Israel*, 1875, ii. 91 ff., cf. Ex. 22:29 and (on circumcision) Gen. 17:12, Lev. 12:3.

[4] See Nöldeke, 'Baethgen's Beiträge zur semitischen Religionsgeschichte', *ZDMG* xlii, 1888, 483; H. Gressmann, *Mose und seine Zeit*, 1913, 103 f. (claiming that Yahweh was thought to be a demon who leaped each year into the house to seize the firstborn infants; but see p. 185 below); J. G. Frazer, *Golden Bough. Dying God*, 1936, 176 f.; and E. O. James, *Origins of Sacrifice*, 1933, 189.

[5] See M.-J. Lagrange, *Études sur les religions sémitiques*, 1905, 272 ff., and W. R. Smith, *Religion of the Semites*, 361; cf. A. Kamphausen, *Verhältnis des Menschenopfers zur israelitischen Religion*, 1896, 63 ff.

[6] L. H. Vincent, *Canaan d'après l'exploration récente*, 1907, and S. A. Cook, *Religion of Ancient Palestine in the Light of Archaeology*, 1930, 79, 82 ff. More evidence of the jar-burial of infants has been found in recent years at Hazor—Y. Yadin, 'Three Years of Excavation at Hazor', *Hazor in Galilee*, 1958, 6. But Yadin assigns these burials to the seventeenth century B.C., and suggests that they may have been occasioned by an epidemic.

before the late Monarchy,[1] and under the Monarchy it may have arisen as the imitation of non-Israelite customs.[2] It is suited to the sensuous and emotional religion of a mainly agricultural and commercial population living in an age of doubt and stress. Human remains that have been found under foundations on Palestinian sites are chiefly those of old women and infants. This need not reflect the gradual abandoning of an established usage; it may reflect rather the reluctant adoption of a foreign practice that had become widespread.

If general human sacrifice in early Israel is uncertain, regular human firstborn sacrifice is improbable. Indeed, among semi-nomadic peoples, who take every care to preserve the strength of the tribe in case of war, regular firstborn sacrifice is out of the question. Jaussen has shown that the modern Arabs of Transjordan usually hold celebrations not at the birth of a firstborn son but on his circumcision.[3] The supreme occasion appears to be when the boy is initiated into full tribal life. In early times this is likely to have been true of the Israelites also. There are many signs in the Bible of a great preference for eldest sons;[4] this scarcely suggests that they were slaughtered. The reverse was probably the case. Ritual was carried out at the birth of a firstborn son in order to propitiate the deity, because this event was regarded as an occasion of great good fortune and to the primitive mind it was also a moment of peril. The firstborn son was formally redeemed; we shall see later why the Pesaḥ was regarded as the appropriate occasion for this ceremony of redemption.[5] In later times child sacrifice, but not necessarily firstborn sacrifice, may, it is true, have become a common practice; but the children were burned.[6] So, too, the ram substituted for Isaac was burned.[7] The Pesaḥ, however, was essentially an eaten sacrifice. It took place at night, and it took place each year. In none of these respects can any resemblance be seen to alleged human firstborn sacrifice among the Israelites and its replacement later by an animal sacrifice.

Other scholars have maintained that the Pesaḥ victim was employed 'both as a substitute and as a symbol of the god'. The ceremonial eating of the flesh of the victim was an apotropaic rite and a means of the 'identifica-

[1] Jud. 11:30 ff. and Gen. 22:1 ff. appear to support the theory of human sacrifice among the early Israelites. But Jephthah's sacrifice may have been due to Canaanite influence; Jephthah himself was probably of mixed origin (cf. Jud. 11:1). If the sacrifice of his daughter was indeed carried out (see the commentaries), it was exceptional; cf. 11:35 ff. In Gen. 22 also, stress is laid upon the unusual nature of Abraham's action; certainly such an action was not common to every Israelite family at the time of the writer. There is no emphasis on the substitution of a ram, Gen. 22:13, and a substitution of this sort is not prescribed for the future.

[2] 1 Kings 16:34, cf. 2 Kings 3:27, Jer. 7:31, 19:5, Mic. 6:7.

[3] Jaussen, *Coutumes . . . de Moab*, 367. The omission of sacrifices at the birth of a child may, however, be due to reasons of economy, ibid. 363 ff.

[4] A. Lods, *Israel, from its Beginnings to the Middle of the Eighth Century*, tr. Hooke, 1932, 286.

[5] See pp. 183 and 187 below.

[6] Cf. Jer. 7:31, 19:5, &c.

[7] See Gen. 22:13.

tion of the interested person with the god as a means of deliverance from the attack of a hostile power'. Here, it is claimed, lies the reason for the injunction in the Pesaḥ legislation that none of the victim was to be left over; 'anything left over would at once render invalid the magical and apotropaic value of the identification by destroying its completeness'.[1] We shall discuss on a later page this detail of the Pesaḥ ceremony. But to advance a theory that the Pesaḥ victim had something of divine essence is to seek to take the origins of the ritual farther back in time than our material will in fact permit. The texts as we have them draw a clear distinction between the deity and the animal victim. Farther than that we are not justified in going.[2]

Another hypothesis assumes that the Pesaḥ sacrifice was originally a firstlings offering parallel to the offering of firstfruits. The Israelites dedicated firstfruits on three festivals—the Maṣṣoth festival, Weeks, and Tabernacles;[3] the Pesaḥ, on the other hand, was a shepherds' sacrifice of firstlings, held in the spring like the firstlings sacrifices of Arab nomads.[4] In the course of time this Israelite pastoral rite became associated with the festival of the harvest firstfruits that occurred also in the spring, the Maṣṣoth festival.[5] Later the combined ceremonial was further given an historical basis, arising from the coincidence of the spring festival with the Exodus, already accepted by the old Israelite tradition. Pharaoh, the tradition related, had withheld the firstlings which the Hebrews used to sacrifice to their God, and God punished Pharaoh by the slaughter of the Egyptian firstborn and firstlings. The Exodus, then, was not the occasion of the festival, but the festival the occasion—if only a pretended one—of the Exodus. This historical basis was strengthened by the centralization of

1 S. H. Hooke, *Origins of Early Semitic Ritual*, 1938, 49; see also pp. 78 and 85 ff. above on the theories of Beer, Mowinckel, and Nicolsky.

2 For recent expositions of this subject, see L. Moraldi, *Espiazione sacrificale e riti espiatori nell' ambiente biblico e nell' Antico Testamento*, 1956, 81 ff., and de Vaux, *Institutions de l'Ancien Testament*, ii, 1960, 291–347. It is not possible to draw inferences from the New Testament phrase 'lamb of God' (Gr. ἀμνὸς τοῦ θεοῦ). The Pesaḥ victim might be either lamb or kid, and at a time not far removed from that of Jesus there was apparently no preference for either; see p. 258 below. The conception of a divine lamb may well be an extraneous element grafted onto the Pesaḥ traditions.

3 But see pp. 108 ff. below on this hypothesis on the origin of the Maṣṣoth festival.

4 See J. Wellhausen, *Reste arabischen Heidentums*, 1897, 98, on the sacrifices in Rajab; cf. Nabih Amin Faris, *Book of Idols . . . by Hisham ibn-al-Kalbi*, 1952, 29. But it is doubtful whether these *'atair* sacrifices among the Arabs—which were perhaps tithes—are in fact to be equated with *fara'*, firstlings; see W. R. Smith, *Religion of the Semites*, 227 n. 3. Cf. further Holzinger, *Exodus*, 1900, 41, and Lods, op. cit. 292; the latter points out that modern Arabs do not eat the firstborn of each animal, but the first lamb of each flock of sheep and the first kid of each flock of goats.

5 Wellhausen, *Prolegomena to the History of Israel*, 1885, 89, compares the Pesaḥ sacrifice to the firstlings offering of Abel, and the offerings on the *ḥaggim* to the firstfruits offering of Cain, Gen. 4:3 f. Apart from this difference, he claims, 'in essence and foundation they are all precisely alike'. The contrast between nomad and farmer may now be illustrated by ancient texts not available to Wellhausen; see, for example, S. N. Kramer in *ANET* 41*a*, 159*b*.

the Israelite cult; it is not older than Deuteronomy, perhaps not older than Ezekiel. The Pesaḥ remained, nevertheless, a firstlings sacrifice *par excellence*, as is demonstrated by the proximity of the firstlings laws to the Pesaḥ laws in the Pentateuch. Later, firstlings became the perquisite of the priests; thenceforth the Pesaḥ was independent of the firstlings sacrifice. It was offered from the flocks only, not, as previously, from both flocks and herds, and it was offered on a fixed date—the night of the full moon of the spring month.[1]

This is the most widely accepted of all the theories on the origin of the Pesaḥ. It rests, in the main, on three lines of argument—the occurrence of the Pesaḥ in the spring, which is held to be the season for the yeaning of lambs and kids, the emphasis in the story of the Exodus Pesaḥ on the first-born and (to a lesser degree) the firstlings motif, and, finally, the appearance of the regulations on firstlings sacrifice in close proximity to the Pesaḥ regulations; in Ex. 13:14 ff. the firstlings sacrifice is explicitly said to derive from the tenth plague. On the other hand, the theory recognizes that the Pesaḥ became a service in commemoration of the Exodus held each year on a fixed date; when it acquired that character it was no longer identical with a firstlings sacrifice. But was it ever a firstlings sacrifice?

I hope to show later in this study that it is an essential feature of the Pesaḥ that it is to be celebrated annually on a fixed date.[2] The firstlings, on the other hand, are to be 'given' to the Lord when one week has elapsed from their birth;[3] the calendric date of the firstlings sacrifice, then, is variable. This apparent conflict of dates need not, however, disprove the identity of the Pesaḥ and the firstlings sacrifice.[4] The 'giving' of the firstlings may mean no more than their dedication. Such may be the intention of Deut. 15:19 ff., and, indeed, in later times a firstling might be kept alive as long as thirty days or fifty days or even three months after birth.[5]

Other difficulties in this firstlings theory are more serious. The firstlings are to be offered from all large and small animals that are ritually clean;[6] but in important Pesaḥ documents and according to the practice of the Chronicler and later, the Pesaḥ victim is to be chosen only from the lambs and kids.[7] The term *zbḥ* is used of the firstlings sacrifice; and this normally implies a communal meal. In Deut. 15:20 part of the flesh of firstlings is

[1] So, with only minor differences in points of detail, J. Müller, *Kritischer Versuch über den Ursprung und die geschichtliche Entwicklung des Pesach- und Mazzothfestes*, 1883, 70; Wellhausen, *Prolegomena*, 89; J. F. L. George, *Die älteren Jüdischen Feste*, 1835, 224; C. Grüneisen, *Ahnenkultus und die Urreligion Israels*, 1900, 191; K. Marti, *Geschichte der israelitischen Religion*, 1903, 109 f.; Holzinger, op. cit. 41 f.; W. R. Smith, op. cit. 464; Lods, op. cit. 292; Oesterley, *Sacrifices in Ancient Israel*, 1937, 100; and L. Rost, *ZDPV* lxvi, 1943, 205. See also the theories summarized pp. 78 ff. above.

[2] pp. 116 f. and 130 f. below.

[3] Ex. 22:29, Lev. 22:27.

[4] As argued by Nicolsky, op. cit. 174 f.

[5] *Mish. Bek.* iv. 1. See p. 181 below.

[6] Ex. 22:29, 34:19, Lev. 27:26, Num. 18:17, Deut. 15:19.

[7] See pp. 140 f. below for the explanation.

eaten by the sacrificers, in Num. 18:18 it appears to be the perquisite of the priests. This is not the place to resolve this apparent disagreement between texts.[1] The crucial point is that in none of these regulations on firstlings are we reminded of the Pesaḥ ceremonial. There are no rites of blood-smearing.[2] The firstlings are not sacrificed at night with extreme precautions against ritual uncleanness, like the victims at the Pesaḥ. If the Pesaḥ were a new institution, established when it had, for some reason, shed its original character as a firstlings offering, why did it acquire features utterly at variance with the procedure of firstlings sacrifices as well as with the norm of sacrificial practice? The Pesaḥ, too, it is agreed by all the documents, is an obligation to be performed by the head of every Israelite family—one victim to each family or group of families. This obligation is in no way dependent on the availability of suitable firstling victims.[3]

The regulations on the Pesaḥ are precise and clear, and they contain nothing that can be construed as a reference to firstlings. The firstlings laws are independent of the Pesaḥ laws. That they appear in close proximity to the Passover regulations must be explained differently.[4]

A group of scholars lay stress on the ceremony of the smearing of blood at the Pesaḥ. Ewald[5] maintains that the Pesaḥ sacrifice was an expiatory offering which was introductory to the Maṣṣoth festival; the latter he regards as a harvest festival. The motif of the Pesaḥ was purification and reconciliation. As at the Arab *fedu* sacrifices,[6] the blood was smeared on the house to make atonement for all its inmates.

Trumbull,[7] on the other hand, points out that the blood ritual had the qualities of a covenant. To confirm the covenant, the ceremony was

[1] See p. 181 n. 11 below.

[2] On the contrary, see Deut. 15:23.

[3] As Guthe, summarized on p. 82 above.

[4] So also Eerdmans, 'Passover and the Days of Unleavened Bread', *Expositor*, viii, 1909, 455. For my explanation, see pp. 181 ff. below.

[5] H. Ewald, *Antiquities of Israel*, 1876, 353; cf. Holzinger, op. cit. 41. H. Schultz, *Old Testament Theology*, 1892, i. 363 ff., regards the Pesaḥ as originally a sacrifice of atonement; later the sacred meal, with its associations of covenant, became more prominent. He declares, rightly, that the view that the Pesaḥ 'is derived from the "passing of the sun" into the sign of Aries and that the eating of the lamb has an astrological meaning of that kind, may well be regarded as an antiquated notion'. (Lods, op. cit. 291 n. 4, gives references to works that propose this view.) Lods, loc. cit., rejects the suggestion of Beer, *Pesachim*, 13 f., that the Pesaḥ was a fertility ritual 'whose principal activity consisted in leaping . . . in imitation of the ram leaping upon the ewes'; there is no evidence for Beer's hypothesis. Benzinger, *Hebräische Archäologie*, 1907, ii. 393, holds that it was believed that Mars would kill cattle on the night of the full moon of the spring equinox. But, Eerdmans objects, op. cit. 457, there is no proof that such an idea existed in the Old Testament; there is no allusion to Mars or any other star in any of the passages dealing with the Passover. Eerdmans, ibid., regards the Pesaḥ as a rite to ward off danger that might arise from the full moon. Israelites were instructed to remain awake on that night, cf. Ex. 12:42, where ליל שמורים is to be rendered 'a night of waking'.

[6] On the *fedu* sacrifices, see pp. 162 ff. below. Ewald, op. cit. 358, maintains that the Pesaḥ was held originally on the tenth day of the month, like the Day of Atonement in the autumn. On the role of the tenth day, see pp. 142 ff. below.

[7] H. C. Trumbull, *Blood Covenant*, 1885, 231 ff.

accompanied by a meal.[1] At the Exodus the blood covenant was given new significance by a threshold covenant. According to the Passover legend the deity did not, Trumbull maintains, pass over the houses of the Israelites, but he passed over the blood of the victim on the threshold[2] and entered the houses; the legend arose from the conception of a marriage between the deity and Israel.

Marti[3] holds that the Pesaḥ was neither a lunar nor a solar festival, but an annual apotropaic ritual to obtain the protection of the house-god against plague and sickness during the ensuing months of the year. Blood brought contact with the deity;[4] the sign on the doors showed that the house was under the protection of the god, and its inmates might look forward to a prosperous year.

It is doubtful whether the Pesaḥ may be explained, with Ewald, as an expiatory sacrifice. Our knowledge of Israelite expiatory offerings is based on ceremonial which had lost to some extent its natural origins, and had acquired, on the one hand, a complex and formal character and, on the other hand, higher ethical motives. More important, expiatory offerings in Israel were burned, as being too holy for human consumption.[5] But one of the most important elements of the Pesaḥ was the eating of the entire victim by the sacrificers and their household. The Pesaḥ was not merely a meal but a communion meal.

The same argument may be advanced against Marti's hypothesis. Trumbull has well stressed the importance of the blood ritual, although his theories on the threshold covenant and the theme of the sacred marriage must be viewed with considerable caution. But Marti makes no allowance for the function of the Pesaḥ meal. We shall discuss the role of the blood ceremonies in greater detail later.[6] Certainly the smearing of blood had certain prophylactic properties against plague and sickness. But the negative aspect of the blood ritual is only one aspect, and not perhaps the more important; the ritual was instinct with vital positive significance.

We turn now to the origins of the Maṣṣoth festival. In our analysis of the Traditional Documents in ch. 2 the texts dealing with the Maṣṣoth festival have been treated apart from those on the Pesaḥ. This is in accordance with the view taken by most scholars. The two groups of ceremonial are regarded as having been originally separate and having amalgamated because, at some period, they were seen to coincide in time.

[1] Trumbull, *Threshold Covenant*, 1896, 203 ff.; see also Frazer, *Folklore in the Old Testament*, 1918, iii. 1 ff.

[2] Trumbull, *Threshold Covenant*, 206, &c.

[3] Op. cit. 41. He is followed by Benzinger, art. 'Passover and Feast of Unleavened Bread', *EB*, § 10; Nicolsky, op. cit. 178; and Lods, op. cit. 292. P. Volz, *ThLZ*, xxvi, 1901, 635, maintains that the smearing of blood at the Pesaḥ was intended to keep away demons.

[4] See pp. 157 ff. below.

[5] Cf. Lagrange, op. cit. 231; G. B. Gray, *Sacrifice in the Old Testament*, 1925, 363; and, more recently, Moraldi, op. cit.

[6] pp. 157 ff. below.

As with פסח, so with מצה philology is of no help. The etymology usually advanced is that of *mṣṣ*, 'squeeze, press', derived, it is held, from the circumstance that *maṣṣoth* cakes are flat. The reasoning is dubious. In the preparation of *maṣṣoth*, the dough is not, in fact, pressed; it is simply not caused to swell by the addition of yeast. Beer's suggestion of יצא as the root of מצה is philologically unsound.[1] Nor do the cognate languages provide a suitable derivation.[2] Yahuda proposes an Egyptian derivation, *ms·t* or *msw·t*, a kind of bread or cake; the word is used also to denote food in general.[3] But it is uncertain (as Yahuda admits) whether this word should not rather be related to *mśw·t*, which is rendered 'evening meal' and in which the notion of evening rather than that of bread may be the primary significance. The improbability, too, of the linguistic formula *s* > *ṣ* or *ś* > *ṣ* and the further improbability of an Egyptian origin for the Passover[4] must lead us to reject this hypothesis.

Beer suggests the association of מצה with the Greek μάζα, which denotes barley bread, as opposed to ἄρτος, wheaten bread.[5] The μάζαι are used in springtime ritual.[6] By philologists μάζα is connected with μάσσω, 'knead'.[7] But it is the very absence of kneading-troughs that is said by the Bible narrator to have caused the fleeing Israelites to bake unleavened bread.[8] And while the *maṣṣoth* at the Passover were normally made of barley, there is, according to one source—admittedly late, but perhaps reflecting an early tradition—no reason why it should not be prepared from other grains.[9] Finally, μάζα is itself of uncertain origin. The rites in which it is used appear in a district of Arcadia where Semitic influence is probable.[10]

Holzinger[11] has regarded the laws about the eating of *maṣṣoth* at the spring festival as reflecting a symbolic return to conditions of nomadic simplicity. Unleavened bread, he points out, is the bread of the desert; it is prepared to the present day by Beduins, who simply lay flat layers of unleavened dough upon the glowing coals. The Maṣṣoth festival, according

[1] Op. cit. 21; cf. *Mish. Pes.* x. 5. It is true that a cognate significance is found in Arab. مضى, 'pass away'; and Aram. *paṭṭira*, 'unleavened bread', could be related to Syr. *pṭr*, 'depart', Jewish Aram. 'dismiss'. But it is more reasonable to connect *paṭṭira* with Arab. *fṭr*, 'split, create' (cf. Eth.), hence 'make simply, hastily'. An attractive etymology for *paṭṭira* may be found in Akk. *pṭr*, 'ransom', if the unleavened bread be closely associated with the Passover; for the prominence of the notion of ransom at the Pesaḥ, see pp. 163 ff. and 183 below.

[2] See Beer, loc. cit.; Riedel, op. cit. 325. Zorell, op. cit., s.v., compares dialectal Arab. مصّ, 'be tasteless', مزّ, 'be insipid', cf. already Dillmann, *Exodus*, on Ex. 12:20. But this scarcely provides an appropriate meaning.

[3] A. S. Yahuda, *Language of the Pentateuch in its relation to Egyptian*, 1933, 95 f.

[4] p. 100 above.

[5] Op. cit. 21 f.

[6] See p. 167 n. 4 below.

[7] See Liddell and Scott, *Lexicon*, s.v.

[8] Ex. 12:34.

[9] *Mish. Pes.* ii. 5; see p. 263 below.

[10] V. Bérard, *Les Phéniciens et l'Odyssée*, 1927, 348 ff., esp. 353.

[11] Op. cit. 42.

to this view, commemorates an historical event in the nomadic period of Israelite history. It was united to the Pesaḥ, which itself was also a nomadic ritual. By that time *maṣṣoth* had become the food of the poor man among the settled population of Israel.[1] The nomadic origin of the *maṣṣoth* eaten at the Passover is shown by the contrast in the Biblical regulations with the leavened bread of the feast of Weeks;[2] the latter is said to be a harvest firstfruits offering, the former is derived from an historical theme.

Now it is true that unleavened bread has been, and still is,[3] the food of wandering nomads. The bread of settled peoples, on the other hand, is normally leavened. Leavened bread was, indeed, already a staple diet among the early Egyptians;[4] and it has been maintained that it was an invention of the Egyptians.[5] This may well lend point to the Exodus narrative in which the Israelites carry unleavened bread at the start of their wanderings out of Egypt into the Wilderness. But at the Maṣṣoth festival the emphasis is not upon the eating of unleavened bread, but upon the removal of leaven. It is prescribed that leaven is to be wholly eliminated from the territory of the Israelites, and it is the contravention of this command that carries the severe penalty of excommunication.[6] Moreover, as we shall see, unleavened bread was always the only form of bread to be offered upon the altar;[7] this is scarcely in commemoration of the nomadic days of Israel. Nor is there an obvious reason why nomadic conditions should be recalled by a festival lasting seven days, or why this should be held in the spring. The theory of Holzinger must be rejected.

We come now to the theory on the origin of the Maṣṣoth festival that is most widely held by modern scholars. This maintains that the festival arose from an offering of harvest firstfruits—that it belonged, in other words, to the agricultural calendar of the Israelites. It is this view that lies at the bottom of the hypothesis that the Pesaḥ and the Maṣṣoth festival were originally separate groups of ceremonies, the former pastoral, the latter agricultural, and that they were fused some time after the Israelite occupation of Canaan. I have already given reasons why the theory of a pastoral origin of the Pesaḥ does not appear to be convincing.[8]

The arguments for the agricultural origin of the Maṣṣoth festival have been presented with admirable lucidity by Benzinger.[9] The Maṣṣoth festival, he declares, is associated in Ex. 23 and 34 with the agricultural festivals of Weeks and Tabernacles, and this 'establishes an antecedent

[1] Deut. 16:3a; see p. 208 below. [2] Lev. 23:17. [3] See p. 168 below.
[4] See A. Erman–H. Ranke, *Aegypten und aegyptisches Leben im Altertum*, 1923, 223 f. So also at Mari, J. Bottéro, *Archives royales de Mari*, vii, 1957, 257.
[5] A. Neuberger, *Technical Arts and Sciences of the Ancients*, 1930, 96, without, however, giving a reference to published works. [6] See p. 62 above. [7] p. 168 below.
[8] p. 104 above. [9] Op. cit., §§ 1 ff.

probability' that it was the festival of the beginning of harvest. We note further that it occurs in the month of Abib, the fresh ears of corn. In Deut. 16:9, and more clearly in Lev. 23:15, the Maṣṣoth festival fixes, in effect, the date of the feast of Weeks; in Deut. 16:16 f. it is connected with harvest festivals, and we may assume that its offerings also were harvest thanksgiving offerings.

Unleavened bread, Benzinger continues, is on the same plane as parched corn; and both were eaten at Joshua's Passover as the first of the produce of Canaan.[1] The parched corn was a favourite food at harvest time, and it is used in this way in the Near East today because it is quickly prepared. *Maṣṣoth*, Benzinger suggests, were equally suitable as a food during the harvesting period.[2] In Ex. 12:33 ff., where *maṣṣoth* are traced back to the Exodus, 'the narrative still retains the right conception of unleavened bread being the bread of haste'.

It was, however, the Sheaf-offering that was 'regarded as the characteristic and main rite of the Maṣṣoth festival, and the day of its presentation as that of the proper feast'. By this ceremony the whole crop was dedicated. It is possible, according to Benzinger, that originally the offering did not consist of a sheaf of barley but of unleavened barley cakes. We have the parallel of the leavened cakes at the feast of Weeks,[3] and the later custom of the firstfruits offering prescribed in Lev. 2:14:

> And if thou offer a meal offering of firstfruits unto the Lord, thou shalt offer for the meal offering of thy firstfruits corn in the ear parched with fire, bruised corn of the fresh ear.[4]

Moreover, in the oldest period the cereal gifts to the deity were forms of food. Since, then, *maṣṣoth* were used for human consumption, 'the sacrificial presentation of *maṣṣoth* at this festival may almost be assumed as a matter of course. In process of time a more delicate material was preferred; unleavened bread was presented instead of leavened, and in many cases the place of leaven is altogether taken by meal. The substitution of a firstfruit sheaf for the *maṣṣoth* would admit of ready explanation from this course of development.'[5]

As harvest festivals and the ritual presentation of barley firstfruits presuppose agriculture and a settled life, it may be conjectured that the Maṣṣoth festival was of Canaanite origin. A Canaanite vintage thanksgiving festival is mentioned in Jud. 9:27, and a festival of a similar nature may have occurred also at the beginning of the grain harvest. In the Bible the Pesaḥ, which was, in Benzinger's view, pre-Canaanite in origin, is not amalgamated with the Maṣṣoth festival; each retains its own separate identity.

[1] Jos. 5:11. [2] Gen. 18:6, 19:3, &c.; see further pp. 179 f. below.
[3] Lev. 23:17. [4] Heb. *'abhibh . . . gereś karmel.*
[5] Cf. O. Eissfeldt, *Erstlinge und Zehnten im A.T.*, 1917, 73.

From this we may draw the conclusion that the Maṣṣoth festival was not developed by the Israelites themselves, but taken over by them from the Canaanites. It was from the Canaanites that the Israelites learned agriculture.

The Maṣṣoth festival, being a harvest festival, was not celebrated on a fixed day each year. It was a *ḥag*, held in public, with varied ceremonies which included dancing, processions, and a joyous sacrificial meal. Every male had to appear at the 'house of the Lord'. And alongside this conception of the festival as a harvest festival, appeared another which treated it as commemorative of the Exodus. This development arose at a comparatively early date; for—even if Ex. 34:18 is to be regarded as the work of a Deuteronomistic redactor—Ex. 12:33 ff., which retains the characteristic motif of haste, is to be assigned to the J Source.[1]

So far Benzinger, with plausible and cohesive reasoning. His views still hold the field; they have, indeed, survived the radical reassessment of 'Higher Critical' theories in modern times.[2] But are they in fact valid?

Let us take, in the first place, the relation of the Sheaf-offering to the Maṣṣoth festival, which is a central argument in Benzinger's thesis. Now, orthodox Jewish practice—which was, admittedly, late—held that the Sheaf was to be presented on the second day of the Maṣṣoth festival.[3] If this was indeed the significant ceremony of the festival, there is no parallel in Hebrew religious practice for the observance of the primary ritual of a festival on its second, rather than its first, day. If it was originally performed on the first day, why was it later performed on the following day? If a feast day was so prominent that it was termed the 'Sabbath', as Jewish interpretation termed the first day of the Passover week, we may expect the first day rather than the following day to be the occasion of the principal ceremony. Nor does the situation favour Benzinger's theory if we turn to the practice of the dissident Jewish sects. They maintained that the barley Sheaf was to be offered on the day after the weekly Sabbath (Saturday) whether, with some, the Sabbath was that which fell inside the Passover week or, with others, the first to occur outside the Passover week. The Sheaf-offering in that case is related to a certain Sabbath, not to the beginning of the Maṣṣoth festival, a fact which scarcely supports Benzinger's thesis. Furthermore, there are indications that at one time the barley Sheaf was waved, not on those dates, but on the morrow of the seventh day of the Maṣṣoth festival—when the festival had come to an end. If this was indeed

[1] So Benzinger. In the scheme shown in ch. 2, p. 50 above, this passage is allotted by most critics to the E Source.

[2] So, for example, M. Noth, *Gesetze im Pentateuch*, 1940, 19. See the theories discussed in this chapter, p. 78 above; indeed, the same view that was held by Benzinger was also held by Ewald, op. cit. 359, and is held by Pedersen and Engnell and many other present-day scholars.

[3] See the discussion on pp. 238 f., 249, and 264 below.

the central rite of the festival, its exclusion from the festival has no parallel in Hebrew religion, and probably in no religion elsewhere.[1]

If we dismiss Benzinger's contention that the Sheaf ceremony formed an original—indeed, the principal—motif of the Maṣṣoth festival, can it nevertheless be maintained that the festival was a harvest thanksgiving festival?

The proximity of the regulations on the Maṣṣoth festival to those on the festivals of Weeks and Tabernacles in Ex. 23:14–16 does not prove that the former, like the latter, is a harvest festival. In the 'parallel' document of Ex. 34:18 ff. the verse on the Maṣṣoth festival is separated from that on the other two festivals by verses on different topics. And in both passages the Maṣṣoth festival—unlike other *ḥaggim*—is given an historical basis. This, it may be contended, may not have been the original motif of the festival; but it invalidates the argument that the Maṣṣoth festival, because it is mentioned in the same context as the feasts of Weeks and Tabernacles, must have arisen from a similar cause. The Maṣṣoth festival is mentioned there because, like Weeks and Tabernacles, it was an annual *ḥag*.

The contention that unleavened bread is prescribed because it is the food of harvesters and harvest time is not only based on mere analogy rather than concrete evidence—it is also illogical. Why is the eating of *maṣṣoth* enjoined for seven days, apparently at the beginning of the harvest, and not for the whole duration of the harvest? And is it likely that an agricultural people, busied in the labours of reaping, should be ordered to observe a festival lasting seven days and involving many and varied ceremonies—while, towards the end of the harvesting period, when farmers might be expected to have more time for religious ritual, a festival of only one day is prescribed?[2]

Benzinger, like other scholars, appears to have interpreted wrongly the term 'Abib'. When the barley is *'abhibh* (Abib), it is in the process of growing; it is 'in the ear', as the E.V. correctly puts it, as the flax is in the boll.[3] The implication of *'abhibh* here is not that the barley was ripe and ready for harvesting, but that it was standing above the ground and beginning to ripen. We shall return to this aspect later. But we should note here that all sects, orthodox and non-orthodox, maintain that the new crops were to be eaten only after the barley Sheaf-offering,[4] not at the beginning of the Maṣṣoth festival. It follows, then, that during at least the first day of the festival—longer, if the Sheaf was offered after the second day of the festival—it was the old corn that was eaten unleavened. So, too, of the Pesaḥ

[1] See pp. 195 ff. below.

[2] So also Holzinger, op. cit. 42; Eerdmans, 'Mazzoth-Fest', *Orientalische Studien . . . Nöldeke gewidmet . . .*, ed. C. Bezold, 1906, ii. 675.

[3] See Ex. 9:31 f.

[4] Following Lev. 23:14.

meal. It is prescribed that the flesh of the victim must be accompanied by *maṣṣoth*; this also must have been taken from the old crops.[1]

Most important, the theory that the Maṣṣoth festival is a harvest festival does not take into account the basic feature of the Bible regulations about bread offerings in the Temple. Throughout the year *maṣṣoth* are the form in which bread is placed upon the altar.[2] Ex. 34:25, which implies that no leaven should contact the Pesaḥ sacrifice, may be, as critics suggest, not the original text but an emended reading; but the fact that it appears at all indicates that the elimination of leaven was an accepted feature of the Pesaḥ.[3] This is in keeping with the avoidance of leaven at altar sacrifices—and with the absolute ban on leaven during the Maṣṣoth week. The threat of excommunication is (as we have already observed) directed not against those who do not eat *maṣṣoth* during the Passover, but against those who permit leaven to remain in their habitations. It is here that the origin of the Maṣṣoth festival must be sought, and not in any association with agricultural processes.

Eerdmans has developed the thesis that leaven was regarded by the ancients as impure and a source of corruption, particularly in an early epoch when its use was still an innovation. At the beginning of each harvest it was therefore customary to throw away the leaven of the previous year, and the new corn was eaten without leaven.[4] Eerdmans, citing analogous customs from the East Indies, derives this practice from the animistic notions of primitive man. It was believed, he suggests, that there was a spirit in the corn. As the corn was cut, the spirit was expelled. But it was necessary to preserve the spirit, for the new harvest is derived from the resowing of the crop of the previous year. In Israel this conception is borne out especially by the treatment of the last sheaf of corn; it is not cut, but left standing.[5] In the same way, Eerdmans maintains, leaven might frighten away the spirit of the barley, and it was therefore avoided throughout Israelite territory during the harvesting season. The seven days of the Maṣṣoth festival were the duration of the harvest, as in the vintage festival in the autumn. This elimination of leaven was, Eerdmans holds, an animistic idea which belongs to the 'pre-Yahwistic' epoch, and was incorporated into 'Yahwistic' practice.

I shall analyse later and in greater detail the attitude of Israelites towards leaven. But animistic ideas about the corn can scarcely explain the avoidance of leaven. Once the corn had been reaped the spirit had, according to the primitive notion, been expelled; and from this arose the usage of preserving some sheaves uncut. Yet it can scarcely have mattered whether or

[1] To regard the *maṣṣoth* of the Pesaḥ meal as an 'intrusion', with Snaith, *Jewish New Year Festival*, 1947, 23, is not only a counsel of despair; it also misses the significance of the practice. [2] See p. 168 below. [3] See the discussion, p. 172 n. 10 below.

[4] Loc. cit., and *Expositor*, viii, 1909, 459 ff. [5] Lev. 19:9, 23:22, Deut. 24:19.

not leaven was introduced into the harvested crops. It was the act of reaping that expelled the spirit, not the introduction of leaven when the corn was eaten. Nor can Eerdmans be correct in equating the duration of the Maṣṣoth festival with the duration of the harvest. A period of seven days would hardly suffice for bringing in the crops; and no community, primitive or sophisticated, would endanger its existence by enacting religious ordinances which restrict the period during which it is permissible to harvest the crops.

PART II

4

A NEW YEAR FESTIVAL

WE have now examined modern theories on the origins and early development of the Passover, and these we must, I have suggested, reject as wholly or largely untenable. But in each case it is the principal proposition that I have found unacceptable; in each case much of the subsidiary argument may be agreed to with little modification. In the following pages I endeavour to present a somewhat different approach to the problem, and my analysis owes much to the work of those scholars with whose basic hypotheses I have ventured to disagree.

Engnell correctly defined the Passover problem and the manner of its solution in the following terms:

> The Hebrew... (Passover poses) not only one of the most central problems but also one of the most debated within the realm of Old Testament research. Worked through over and over again, it has not yet found its definite solution. . . . Research in late years, especially along the 'myth and ritual' line, must however be said to have yielded important new contributions which make it possible to sketch a main line of solution.[1]

If we are effectively to pursue this line of solution, we should, I have already maintained, disregard at the outset the limitations that have been imposed upon scholars by the Source hypothesis.[2] We should consider the Pentateuch, in which the Traditional Documents on the Passover are found, as a single complex of traditions and practices—some of them of great age and all of them the product of a long process of natural evolution. We should, furthermore, look at the development of the festival through the eyes of the Compiler of the Hebrew Pentateuch. For its primitive features we should regard as our main source those documents that he considers to be the most ancient—that is, the Exodus narrative of Ex. 12–13. But we should not confine ourselves to this material. The texts that appear later within the framework of the Pentateuch nevertheless contain the relics of early practice; the minutiae of Temple ritual—for all their

[1] I. Engnell, *Orientalia Suecana*, i, 1952, 39. The appearance of the present work is evidence—however inadequate—that one need not be discouraged by Engnell's further remark (omitted from the quotation) that the problem of the Passover 'probably never will (find its solution), owing to its complicated nature given already in the sources themselves'.

[2] See pp. 70 ff. above.

formalism—were not strange rules imposed by priests from outside upon reluctant worshippers. They were in keeping with the usages and traditions of the people. And, indeed, we may go outside the Pentateuch to discover practices that appear for the first time as late as the Mishnah, yet for whose antiquity evidence is found in parallel customs in the neighbouring countries. In the Bible they have, by some quirk of Providence, been submerged—to emerge for the first time in the traditions of the Rabbis.

A striking feature of the Passover ritual is its relationship to the ritual of the festival of Tabernacles. In certain respects the two festivals differ. The Passover is held in the spring, Tabernacles in the autumn; and it is from this that the differences between them arise. Tabernacles occurs at the season in which fruit is garnered—particularly the fruit of the vine and the olive.[1] These products were of importance in the economy of ancient Palestine,[2] and the festival of Tabernacles is the occasion on which some of this fruit was offered in token of thanksgiving to the deity.[3] Tabernacles, however, is also the festival which marks the end of the summer and the beginning of a new agricultural year. The farmers of Palestine make preparations at this time for the new ploughing season;[4] this is followed by the sowing of the new corn-seed. Upon the success of the sowing depends the prosperity of the whole people—whether a farming or (like the early Israelites) a semi-nomadic community—during the ensuing year. But the ploughing and sowing require moisture. They will succeed only if the former rains are plentiful.[5] Tabernacles is the moment at which entreaty is made for sufficient but not overmuch rain, and ritual of the nature of sympathetic magic is performed in order, as it were, to put pressure upon the divine powers that control the elements of nature.[6]

The spring festival of the Passover stands, on the other hand, in a different relation to the annual revolution of nature. While Tabernacles occurs *during* the fruit harvest, the Passover takes place *before* the grain harvest. At the Passover the agricultural processes that were inaugurated at Tabernacles are approaching their climax;[7] the first crop—that of

[1] See G. Dalman, *Arbeit und Sitte in Palästina*, 1928–39, i, 6, 58, 160.

[2] For grapes, see, for example, Gen. 9:20, 27:28, 49:11 ff., Num. 13:23 f., Deut. 28:39, Jud. 9:13, 27, and cf. 20:21 f.; for olives, Gen. 3:7, Jud. 9:13. See the Gezer 'calendar', which opens with the fruit harvest (bibliography in W. F. Albright, in *ANET* 320*a*).

[3] Ex. 23:16b, 34:22b, Deut. 16:13 ff.

[4] Cf. Gen. 45:6, Ex. 34:21, 1 Sam. 8:12, Prov. 20:4.

[5] For the importance of the rains, cf. Lev. 26:4, Deut. 11:14, 17, 28:12, 23 f., 2 Sam. 1:21, Jer. 5:24, 14:2–4 (and perhaps 8:20), Ezek. 34:26, Zech. 14:16 ff., *Mish. Taʿan.* i. 1–iii. 8. On the misfortune of late rain which falls at, instead of before, harvest-time, cf. 1 Sam. 12:17, Prov. 26:1. See further on modern Palestine J. Sonnen, 'Landwirtschaftliches vom See Genesareth', *Biblica*, viii, 1927, 74, 81, and Dalman, op. cit. ii. 174.

[6] Cf. 1 Kings 18:23 ff.; *Mish. Suk.* iv. 9, v. 1 ff.; H. Klein, 'Klima Palästinas auf Grund der alten hebräischen Quellen', *ZDPV* xxxvii, 1914, 217 ff.; and Dalman, op. cit. i. 133, 147 f., 153 ff. See the discussion in S. Aalen, *Begriffe 'Licht' und 'Finsternis' im Alten Testament* . . ., 1951, 43 ff.

[7] Cf. Gen. 8:22, Ex. 23:16a.

barley—has appeared, and is standing in the green in most of the country. This is the right time to intercede for the success of the grain harvest. After the pause during the cold months of the winter, domestic animals have begun again to bear young.[1] The access of new wealth to the farmer in cereals or livestock makes this period also the beginning of the fiscal year for the tax collector and the trader.[2] And to the warrior in ancient times the spring marked the approach of a new campaigning season, when armies are mustered and kings prepare for war.[3]

The two festivals differ from each other in their relationship to the seasons of nature. But, important as they are, the differences between them are scarcely as deep-seated as the similarities. Both festivals begin on the evening of the fourteenth–fifteenth day of the month. In early Israel lunations were determined by observation, and, since the phasis follows one or two days after the conjunction, the night of the fourteenth–fifteenth day after the phasis must be the night of the full moon or the night after the full moon; certainly it cannot occur before the full moon. A further similarity between the festivals is their length—seven days; we shall discuss the significance of this period on a later page.[4] And, finally, there is a constant interval of six months between the two festivals. This indicates the dichotomy of the year;[5] but it also indicates that the date of each festival is fixed in time. We note that wherever the Passover and Tabernacles are both mentioned in a single passage of the Bible, it is the former that is mentioned first. It is said to occur in the first month, Tabernacles in the seventh month.[6] Intercalation was regularly effected in the Israelite calendar by the insertion of an extra month, and normally before the end of the year;[7]

[1] Dalman, op. cit. i. 268, 421.

[2] See p. 136 below.

[3] 2 Sam. 11:1 (reading 'kings' with *Qere* and Versions, rather than 'messengers' with *Kethibh*), 1 Kings 20:22, 1 Chr. 20:1, 2 Chr. 36:10.

[4] p. 177 below. On the addition of the eighth day of Solemn Assembly at the autumn festival, see p. 212 below.

[5] So the spring is the 'return of the (new) year', 2 Sam. 11:1, 1 Chr. 20:1, 1 Kings 20:22, 26, 2 Chr. 36:10. De Vaux, *Institutions de l'Ancien Testament*, i, 1958, 289 f., explains the phrase as meaning that the tropic year was understood to have reached the limit of its outward course at the spring equinox and to be about to return to its starting-point. This interpretation would give the Heb. term *tešubhah* the sense of '*beginning* of the return', a sense for which there seems little justification. The autumn, on the other hand, is the 'going-forth of the year', Ex. 23:16, or the 'circuit of the year', 34:22, 2 Chr. 24:23. At a later time *tequphah*, 'circuit', was commonly used for the calendric notion of a solstice or equinox; see p. 129 n. 3 below. It is far from certain that the phrase לתקפות הימים, 1 Sam. 1:20, refers to the autumn festival, as postulated by S. R. Driver, *Notes on the Hebrew Text . . . of the Books of Samuel*, 1913, in loc. 1 Sam. 1:20, as Driver makes clear, is not preserved in its original form; מימים ימימה in 1:3, 2:19 and זבח הימים, 1:21, 2:19, 20:6, are unlikely to imply a fixed annual date, cf. the indefinite ויהי היום, 1:4, and particularly חדש, 20:5. There is no factual basis for the conjecture of H. Cazelles, art. 'Nouvel An en Israël', *Dict. Bib. Suppl.*, that *zbḥ ymm* in the Karatepe inscription refers to the autumn festival.

[6] See, for example, Lev. 23:5, 34, Num. 28:16, 29:12, Ezek. 45:21, 25.

[7] Already in the early period of the Monarchy; cf. my article, *VT* vii, 1957, 257 ff., where

the interval between the first and the seventh months remained unchanged.

The Passover and Tabernacles have, we have seen, each a different relationship to the agricultural seasons; on the other hand, their relationship to the calendar is constant. The date of each is not fixed by the processes of vegetation, but by the calendar. To the Hebrews the Passover (and Tabernacles) was primarily a New Year festival.

Before we analyse the qualities of the Passover, it will be instructive to examine some features of the New Year festivals of the countries adjacent to Palestine. In ancient Egypt the calendar opened, in theory, with the heliacal rising of Sirius which normally coincided with a significant stage in the inundation of the Nile waters. Certain festivals were celebrated according to lunar reckoning.[1] The principal New Year festival began, however, on the last day of the old civil year, and continued through the five epagomenal days and the three, possibly five, opening days of the new year. The king performed the principal role, as in all Egyptian religious ceremonial. The culminating rite at Edfu—in the Ptolemaic period, but this was, it is generally agreed, the product of ancient tradition—was the solemn procession. The deities were represented by priests, a man dressed in the royal robes carried the Lance of Horus, and the king and queen followed barefoot before the portable shrine of the god. The god's statue was unveiled, anointed, and dressed in new clothes.[2] Throughout the country lights were kindled in tombs during the festival days; gifts were offered to the royal house and within individual families.[3]

This festival may be contrasted with others in Egypt. It was at the 'Festival of Reunion', held at Edfu at the new moon of the tenth–eleventh month, that the sacred marriage of Hathor and Horus was celebrated.

I suggest that the observance of the autumn festival by Jeroboam I in the eighth, instead of the seventh, month, 1 Kings 2:32 f., was due to intercalation. Talmon, op. cit. 56, holds that the date fixed by Jeroboam was due to the slower ripening of the harvest in North Israel. He compares the climate of the Shephelah with the 'mountainous settlements north of Bethel'. That is to use an arbitrary measurement; the comparison should be between Jerusalem and Bethel (only about 10 miles apart!). On the whole, the harvests in the northern kingdom must have ripened earlier than in much of the cultivable area of the southern kingdom; Dalman, op. cit. i. 41.

[1] See the discussion in S. Schott, *Altägyptische Festdaten* (Akademie der Wissenschaften und der Literatur in Mainz. Abhandlungen der geistes- und sozialwissenschaftlichen Klasse, 1950, No. 10), 1950, and the summary and bibliography in É. Drioton and J. Vandier, *Peuples de l'orient méditerranéen. II. L'Égypte*, 1952, 15. For connexions between the Sothic reckoning and Asiatic civilization, C. Autrun, 'Sothis-Sirius . . .', *Mélanges Maspero*, i, 1934–8, 529, and F. Cumont, 'Mystères de Samothrace et l'année caniculaire', *RHR* cxxvii, 1944, 55.

[2] M. Alliot, 'Cultes d'Horus à Edfou au temps des Ptolémées', *RHR* cxxxvii, 1950, 59; see the summary in H. W. Fairman, 'Worship and Festivals in an Egyptian Temple', *BJRL* xxxvii, 1954–5, 183 ff.

[3] A. Wiedemann, 'Notes on some Egyptian Monuments', *PSBA* xxxvi, 1914, 202, and Schott, 'Feasts of Thebes', *Work in Western Thebes 1931–33* (Oriental Institute Communications, No. 18), 1934, 79, 87.

Firstfruits were offered, and numerous and varied ceremonies performed. The deities went in procession outside the town, and there a complex ritual took place during a festival that continued for fourteen days; the rites included visits to sepulchral mounds, the treading of grains, the slaying of a red ox and a red goat, and the destruction of model hippopotami of wax and of sand. It was an amalgam of funerary ceremonial and of harvest ceremonial—though it was held some two or three months after the harvest had been reaped and threshed.[1] The 'day of the New Year festival of Horus' was held at the end of the period of Inundation and the beginning of the period of Sowing. Then was enacted the cult-drama of the Passion of Osiris, the search of Isis and Nephthys, the raising of the *ḏd* column, and the symbolic resurrection of the god in the person of Horus after the rout of his enemies. In this festival of vegetation, the people participated. They watered the 'beds of Osiris',[2] they kept vigil and fasted when the god had disappeared, they danced and 'fought' in the mock battle at which Horus triumphed, and they celebrated the happy denouement with feasting and merriment.[3] But here also the festival was perhaps primarily a rite of the renewal of kingship, in which the role of the victorious deity was enacted by the king; and it was the conventional date for the occasional *Sed* ceremony.[4] So, too, at the harvest festival of Min in the first month of the summer period, the king attended a procession of dead kings and sacred emblems, a white bull at his side. He dedicated a sheaf of corn to the god, and performed a ceremonial dance.[5] Egyptian festivals were accompanied by processions, sacrifices, dancing, singing, and music.[6]

The lunisolar calendar was universally accepted in Greece; the opening of the year varied between the several states, but it was invariably at the

[1] Alliot, op. cit. 81. A convenient summary may be found in Fairman, 'Kingship Rituals of Egypt', in Hooke, *Myth, Ritual, and Kingship*, 1958, 80 ff.

[2] See, for example, A. H. Gardiner and N. G. Davies, *Tomb of Amenemhēt*, 1915.

[3] On this festival at Medinet Habu, see Schott, 'Feasts of Thebes', 78 ff. See also A. Moret, *Mystères égyptiens*, 1913, passim; S. A. B. Mercer, *Études sur les origines de la religion de l'Égypte*, 1929, ch. lv; and A. Erman, *Religion der Ägypter*, 1934, 179, 182 f. For texts, see, in particular, H. Schäfer, *Mysterien des Osiris in Abydos*, 1904, and J. A. Wilson in *ANET* 329*b*. On the origin and identity of Osiris, see Erman, op. cit. 40; Mercer, op. cit. 74, 99; Moret, *Rois et dieux d'Égypte*, 1923, ch. iii; H. Gressmann, *Tod und Auferstehung des Osiris*, 1923; R. Weill, 'Notes sur l'histoire primitive des grandes religions égyptiennes', *Bulletin de l'Institut français d'Archéologie orientale*, 1948, 68; and Drioton and Vandier, op. cit.

[4] Gardiner, review, *JEA* i, 1915, 121 ff.; W. Helck, 'Herkunft des abydenischen Osirisrituals', *Archiv Orientální*, xx, 1952, 72; and 'Bemerkungen . . .', *Orientalia*, xxiii, 1954, 383. See also, on Edfu, Alliot, op. cit. 89, and Fairman, op. cit. 78 ff.

[5] H. Gauthier, *Fêtes du dieu Min*, 1931. See further H. Jacobsohn, *Dogmatische Stellung des Königs in der Theologie der alten Ägypter*, 1939, 29; A. Wiedemann, *Das alte Ägypten*, 1920, 372; and H. Kees, *Opfertanz des ägyptischen Königs*, 1912. For the absorption of Min into the Osiris cult, see Kees, *Götterglaube im alten Ägypten*, 1941.

[6] Erman, op. cit. 179, 182, 372; Moret, 'Sacrifice en Égypte', *RHR* lvii, 1908, 81. See also H. Frankfort, 'State Festivals in Egypt and Mesopotamia', *Journal of the Warburg and Courtauld Institutes*, xv, 1952, 1.

month of solstice or equinox. There is a concentration of festivals in these months and in the months immediately preceding them.[1]

The full moon of the spring equinox was marked at Athens by the sacrifice by the 'king' to Kronios, perhaps to be identified as the spirit of the New Year,[2] on the fifteenth day. A week previously there had taken place the solemn procession through the city of Dionysos with the sacred emblems (probably including phalloi); a dramatic contest followed. The previous month was a time for ritual purification. At Athens at the Anthesteria on the eleventh–thirteenth days, wine jars were opened, there was a symbolic ceremony of marriage between Dionysos and the wife of the 'king', and a merry carnival was held with dancing, the presentation of wine and cakes, and games; slaves were entertained and prisoners released. It was believed that the ghosts of the dead were abroad at this time. Houses were smeared with pitch, and buckthorn chewed as a prophylactic. A pot of seed was offered on the next day, and the ghosts departed.[3] During this month the festival of Artemis was celebrated at Ephesos with processions, dancing, and feasting; the people lived in tents or booths, and offered tithes.[4]

The lesser mysteries of Demeter were performed at Athens on the twentieth day of the month preceding the spring equinox; a truce enabled pilgrims to travel freely. But the greater (Eleusinian) mysteries were performed six months later in the month of the autumn equinox. Then, too, a truce was proclaimed; the pilgrimage rites, to which only the ritually clean were admitted, included processions, fasting, singing, and dancing. The pan-Boeotian games took place in the month of the autumn equinox, with processions, sacrifices, and a banquet. In certain states the Bouphonia was carried out in this month. The ox was slain, the slaughterer fled, and a communal meal was followed by mimic pantomime intended to restore the victim to life. At Magnesia the sacred ox had been bought months previously, and dedicated at the beginning of the season of sowing; there, the actual sacrifice of the ox at the Bouphonia took place in the spring.

At Athens, however, the year opened at the summer solstice and the

[1] On the difficulty of establishing the calendars of the various Greek states, see art. 'Kalendar', Pauly–Wissowa, *Realenc.* See also K. Pritchett, 'Months in Dorian Calendars', *American Journal of Archaeology*, l, 1946, 358.

[2] J. E. Harrison, *Themis*, 1927, 496 f.

[3] Ibid. 275 ff., and id., *Prolegomena to the Study of Greek Religion*, 1922, 32 ff. G. van Hoorn, *Choes and Anthesteria*, 1951, illustrates details of the festival; he interprets its name as 'Blossom-feast' (against Harrison, *Prolegomena*, 47 f.), perhaps cf. p. 111 above on the term *'abhibh*.

[4] In the spring month, Xanthikos, the Macedonians performed a solemn lustration of the army; the soldiers passed between the parts of the severed carcass of a dog, and the ceremony was followed by a sham battle. But N. M. P. Nilsson, *Griechische Feste von religiöser Bedeutung, mit Ausschluss der attischen*, 1906, 404 ff., maintains that this took place originally before a certain battle, and was only in the course of time adopted as an annual event.

Bouphonia was part of the solemnities of the previous month. Feasting and merriment marked the Kronia on the twelfth day of the following month; masters waited upon slaves, and prisoners were released. Upon this festival was superimposed in the course of time the pan-Athenian games, at which delegations from the colonies held a communal meal; the games were distinguished by nocturnal ceremonial with torches and music. The pan-Ionian games, on the other hand, took place six months later in the middle of the month of the winter solstice; the celebrants lived in tents and booths.[1]

When we turn to Rome we find that here too the general pattern of ritual is little different. A twelve-month calendar was introduced at Rome probably at the end of the sixth century, and presumably through Greek influence; it opened at the spring equinox. The previous month, February, was a time of solemn purification. There appears to have been a solemn assembly of the people according to *curiae*, which was of both military and religious significance, and also during this month were held the Parentalia to commemorate the dead. At the Lupercalia two youths, smeared with the blood of sacrificed goats and dressed in their hides, performed a ritual race, striking women passers-by with thongs. On 1 March the sacred fire was renewed; wives received presents from their husbands, and entertained their slaves. During March, too, the Salii, priests attired like warriors, leaped and danced through the streets. At the full moon of this month was the festival of Anna Perenna, perhaps symbolizing the circle of the year. The whole population left the city for the Tiber, and there, lying on the grass, they passed the day in revelry, drinking, and song. 'Some lay in the

[1] See, in addition to the works mentioned above, A. Mommsen, *Feste der Stadt Athen im Altertum*, 1898, and L. R. Farnell, *Cults of the Greek States*, 1896–1909. Greek festivals that fall outside the months of the equinox or solstice or the preceding months have rites not dissimilar from those already mentioned. But their primary purpose is the renewal of vegetation, and they appear to be concerned principally with phenomena of nature. At the Thesmophoria at the time of sowing the characteristic ceremony was the mixing of the seed of the new year with the remains of a pig that had been dedicated in the previous year; the women fasted, and a prisoner was released. The Skirophoria was distinguished by ritual in which symbols of fertility were carried by young girls. During the winter an offering was made to Demeter at Mykonos; later, at the time of the appearance of the new shoots, were held the lesser mysteries of Demeter at Athens. The Lenaia in winter was probably intended to rouse the sleeping vegetation. Notable among the festivals of the early summer were the Daidalia, with ritual of the sacred marriage and the solemn burning of figurines of deities, and the Thargelia at which the Eiresione was carried in procession, the *pharmakos* in special dress was driven out of the city after rites of purification, and firstfruits were offered; Nilsson regards the Thargelia as a ceremony of lustration against calamity in the fields (cf. the Roman Ambarvalia) rather than a harvest ceremonial. To the same time of the year may belong the Hyakinthia at Sparta; this was celebrated with sacrifices in which also slaves joined, a ritual meal in booths of branches, and processions; and a prominent part was taken by the women. In August were held the Karneia at Sparta, a vintage festival at which a truce was proclaimed, two runners with vine leaves raced, choirs of armed men and women danced, lustration ritual was performed, and people lived in booths; and the Megalartia, the harvest-time mysteries at Andonia, held in booths, with its sacred meal, dancing, and music. In autumn was the vintage ceremony of the Oschophoria.

open; some pitched tents and some constructed rude huts of stakes and branches. . . . As they drank they prayed for . . . years of life.' At the Liberalia in the same month old women sat in the streets selling cakes of oil and honey; then, too, boys assumed the *toga virilis*, and recruits reported for military service.

At the full moon of September, the month of the autumn equinox, was the *dies natalis* of the Capitoline temple, whose central ritual was the *epulum Jovis*, 'that most imposing of all the Roman worships'. The three deities of Rome partook of a communion feast in the company of the magistrates and senate of the city.

Something of the ritual pattern of the equinox months is found at the solstices. In the month preceding the summer solstice was a commemoration of the dead, the Lemuria. It was followed by a ceremony at which puppets were cast into the river; and this opened a period of mourning which ended with the cleansing of the temple of Vesta on 15 June.[1] At the solstice in the same month was a popular festival which was open also to slaves, and resembled in its jollity and licence the spring festival of Anna Perenna. The month preceding the winter solstice was marked by the Plebeian games, perhaps the occasion for the manumission of slaves. At the time of the winter solstice itself were celebrated the Saturnalia, a popular holiday extended by common usage to as long as seven days. A public sacrifice was followed by a public feast, private celebrations, and the exchange of gifts, particularly sweets, wax candles, and little images of paste. Slaves were treated by their masters as equals. White garments and masks were worn to impersonate the dead.

One feature of the Roman festal calendar remains to be noted. The opening of the year was moved from 1 March to 1 January, probably in 153 B.C. Among the ceremonies which marked this new year-opening were the carrying in procession of sacred twigs and the exchange of gifts.[2]

From a remote period Babylonia maintained a lunisolar calendar. The movements of the moon were observed and the heliacal risings and settings of fixed stars, especially those constellations which constituted a lunar zodiac. Measurement of the hours of daylight was a guide to the fixing of the equinoxes. At Nippur the calendar began with Nisan; elsewhere it

[1] A convenient illustration of the calendric relationship of identical ritual celebrated at different points of the calendar is provided by the sacrifice of the *rex sacrorum* on 24 May, the month preceding the summer solstice. The same ceremony was held on 24 March, the month of the spring equinox, and also a month previously, on 24 February.

[2] So the festival of Isis at Rome, which had once been held in early March, was transferred to January; see A. Alföldi, *Festival of Isis in Rome under the Christian Emperors of the IVth Century*, 1937. My summary of Roman festivals is based largely on W. Warde Fowler, *Roman Festivals*, 1899; for particular aspects, see L. Delatte, 'Recherches sur quelques fêtes mobiles du calendrier romain', *Antiquité classique*, v, 1936, 381, vi, 1937, 93; L. Gerschel, 'Saliens de Mars et Saliens de Quirinus', *RHR* cxxxviii, 1950, 145; and the relevant articles in Pauly–Wissowa, *Realenc.*, and Hastings, *ERE*.

began sometimes with the month preceding, sometimes with the month following, Nisan of Nippur.[1]

The longest text on the Mesopotamian New Year festival is a commentary on the ritual at Babylon; but it is incomplete. We learn that there the festival opened on, presumably, the first day and was completed on the twelfth day of the spring month. After certain preparatory rites the priest recited the Epic of Creation. This recounted how Bel-Marduk was imprisoned, but returned after the defeat of the forces of chaos; among them the demon Zu was conquered in a foot-race. Then man was created. The Epic ends with the construction of the temple of Bel-Marduk in heaven. On 5th Nisan the temple was purified, a sheep was sacrificed, and the shrine rubbed[2] with its body. The priestly officiant then cast the carcass into the river, and the slaughterer did likewise with the head of the animal. Neither man was permitted to re-enter the city during the festal period. On the same day the god Nabu arrived at Babylon. In a ritual of abasement the king had his symbols of royalty removed, was struck by the priest, forced to kneel and profess his devotion to Bel-Marduk; in a ritual of renewal, he was then blessed and clothed again in his royal robes. A white bull was offered in sacrifice. The order of the rites of the following days is obscure, but they included either one or two solemn processions to the *bit akitu* outside the city, the determination of the fates by Bel-Marduk attended by the other gods, possibly a second recital of the Epic of Creation, the celebration of the sacred marriage between Bel-Marduk and Ṣarpanitu, and frequent sacrifices. These sacred rites were probably enacted in the form of a cult-drama. The king took the part of Marduk; as the god's powers were renewed, so were the royal prerogatives of the king. The people had been no more than spectators of the processions, but they celebrated the outcome of the drama with rejoicing.

The text of this Babylonian New Year festival is not only incomplete, it is also late, since it belongs, in its present form, to the Seleucid epoch. Earlier fragments from other Mesopotamian cities show that the rite of the humiliation of the king was probably an accretion of later centuries; the primary motif was the revival of vegetation and fertility. We can draw a picture of the New Year festival, whose features were common to most Mesopotamian cities and to most periods of time. In each place the central deity was the national god of the locality; his part in the drama was probably enacted (as at Babylon) by the king. Indeed, the festival could not be

[1] On the Mesopotamian calendar, see, in addition to the standard works on Babylonia and Assyria, B. Landsberger, *Der kultische Kalender der Babylonier und Assyrer*, 1915, and S. Langdon, *Babylonian Menologies and the Semitic Calendars*, 1935. The Assyrian calendar presents special problems; see S. Smith, art. 'Calendar (Babylonian and Assyrian)', *Enc. Br.*, 1958. See also id., 'Practice of Kingship in Early Semitic Kingdoms', in Hooke, op. cit. 33 ff., 42 f., and R. Largement, 'Nouvel An dans la religion suméro-akkadienne', *Dict. Bib. Suppl.*

[2] Akk. *kappāru*; F. Thureau-Dangin, *Rituels accadiens*, 1921, 141.

celebrated without the presence of the king or his representative dressed, apparently, in the royal robes. It was marked by sacrifices, the sacred marriage, processions, and a banquet; and it was accompanied by popular applause. Features that are attested for individual cities, but may well have been widespread, are the presentation of gifts in kind, the relaxation of discipline and social conventions, and a military parade. A sacred tree-trunk was the object of ritual peculiar to the New Year festival of Assyria.[1]

Of some significance are the rites prescribed in the festal calendar of the pagans of Harran. In this calendar there is a concentration of festivals in the months of equinox and solstice. On the first three days of Nisan visits were paid to a temple outside the city; there sacrifices were offered and living animals burned. On 6th Nisan, ten days before the full moon, the Harranians performed a sacrifice to the moon deity. On 8th Nisan, a week before the full moon, a fast was held; according to one writer, this fast lasted thirty days—from 8th Adar to 8th Nisan—and its conclusion was followed by a great feast. The full moon of Nisan was the occasion of as olemn mystery. The full moon of Tishri was marked by a nocturnal commemoration of the dead. At the full moon of Tammuz near the summer solstice were rites of mourning for the corn-god Tammuz. The month of the winter solstice was the occasion of a festival celebrated in tents from the fourth to the tenth day; during this time animals were sacrificed by fire. It should be remarked that the poll-tax was paid four times a year, and each time at a date near the equinox or solstice.[2]

Some of the Hittite festivals were fixed by observation of the moon, others were connected with the seasons; we may assume that the Hittites followed a lunisolar calendar. The important *purulli* festival took place in the spring, and bears some resemblance to the Mesopotamian New Year festival. It was celebrated by the king in person at the various cult-centres. Its ritual included the recital of the cosmic struggle between the Dragon

[1] Among the works consulted are H. Zimmern, *Zum Babylonischen Neujahrsfest*. Zweiter Beitrag, 1918; id., *Das babylonische Neujahrsfest* (Der Alte Orient, 25, 3), 1926; F. Thureau-Dangin, op. cit.; S. A. Pallis, *Babylonian Akîtu Festival*, 1926; S. Smith, *Early History of Assyria to 1000 B.C.*, 1928; id., 'Practice of Kingship', 38 ff.; R. Labat, *Caractère religieux de la royauté assyro-babylonienne*, 1939, 160 ff.; J. van Dijk, 'Fête du nouvel an dans un texte de Šulgi', *Bibliotheca Orientalis*, xi, 1954, 83; and, for a summary, R. Largement, op. cit. Of special interest is the treatment by W. von Soden, 'Gibt es ein Zeugnis dafür, dass die Babylonier an die Wiederauferstehung Marduks geglaubt haben?', *ZA*, N.F. xvii (li), 1955, 130. On *akitu* and *bit akitu*, see Landsberger, op. cit. 4, 12, 60, 66, &c., and, recently, A. Falkenstein, 'akiti-Fest und akiti-Festhaus', *Festschrift Johannes Friedrich . . . gewidmet*, 1959, 147. The primary relation between the *akitu* festival and the New Year is obscure. The date of the former varies greatly between different localities and epochs; see Largement, op. cit.

[2] The source material is assembled in D. Chwolson, *Ssabier und der Ssabismus*, 1856, ii. 6 ff., 23 ff. The texts should be regarded with some caution, since they were transmitted at a late period by Moslems who knew little or no Syriac, the language of the pagans, and were out of sympathy with the practices they describe. On the lunisolar calendar of the Harranians, see C. E. Sachau, *Chronology of Ancient Nations . . .*, 1879, 315 ff.

and the weather-god. There was a solemn procession of the gods to a sanctuary outside the city, where the sacred marriage may have been enacted; perhaps the deities also fixed the fates there. At a festival apparently in the autumn, the image of the god was entertained by singing and feasting and a mock battle. A regular feature of festal ceremonial among the Hittites was sacrifice and libations; both gods and the king partook of banquets of meat and drink.[1]

Sources for a reconstruction of the New Year festival in ancient Syria scarcely exist. The Ugaritic texts have been regarded, and with reason, as myths in dramatic form reflecting the passage of the dry summer to the rainy autumn.[2] It has been suggested that some were recited at the New Year festival, probably in the autumn, as the Epic of Creation was recited in Mesopotamia, and that their action was re-enacted in the same way.[3] The fight between Baʿal and Mot, for example, is thought to represent a ritual combat;[4] the procreation of Baʿal before his descent to the underworld[5] and his intercourse with Anat are thought to represent an annual celebration of the sacred marriage.[6] There seems to be little concrete evidence for this view. More important, we have no account of festival practice in the texts, and it is with this that we are concerned in the present study.[7]

[1] Works on Hittite religion that have been consulted include L. Delaporte, *Hittites*, 1936; G. Furlani, *Religione degli Hittiti*, 1936; R. Dussaud, *Religions des Hittites et des Hourrites . . .*, 1945; O. R. Gurney, *Hittites*, 1952; and id., 'Hittite Kingship', in Hooke, op. cit. 106 ff. See also H. Otten, 'Text zum Neujahrsfest aus Boğazköy', *OLZ* li, 1956, 101 ff.

[2] So, for example, R. de Langhe, *Textes de Ras Shamra-Ugarit et leurs rapports avec le milieu biblique de l'Ancien Testament*, 1945, i. 363, and T. H. Gaster, *Thespis*, 1950, 122 ff., 178, &c., on the Baʿal epic. Gaster, op. cit. 227, regards the poem of Šḥr and Šlm as the description of the 'prototype of the Israelitic Feast of Weeks', but on a later page (p. 235) appears to connect it with the festival of Tabernacles. On the motif of the seasonal myth, see, however, C. H. Gordon, 'Sabbatical Cycle or Seasonal Pattern?', *Orientalia*, xxiii, 1953, 79.

[3] A. S. Kapelrud, *Baal in the Ras Shamra Texts*, 1952, 29, and J. Gray, *Legacy of Canaan*, 1957, 9 f., 19 f., 147.

[4] Kapelrud, op. cit. 130 ff.

[5] J. Pedersen, 'Canaanite and Israelite Cultus', *Acta Orientalia*, xviii, 1940, 1.

[6] Kapelrud, op. cit. 97; Gaster, op. cit. 232, finds the theme of the sacred marriage in the poem of Šḥr and Šlm.

[7] The building of the temple of Baʿal, the fire in it lasting seven days, its dedication, and the subsequent banquet are connected with the consecration of temples before the New Year, according to Gaster, op. cit. 30, 177; Kapelrud, op. cit. 116; and Gray, op. cit. 148. Kapelrud, op. cit. 123, suggests that the mourning ritual for Baʿal performed by Il and Anat reflects a cult pattern performed at the New Year. Gaster, 'Ezekiel and the Mysteries', *JBL* lx, 1941, 295 f., declares that an offering to the dead in the Aqhat poem is parallel in some way to the Israelite autumn festival, and that the seething of a goat in milk is connected with the festival of firstfruits of Weeks. Gray, op. cit. 149, holds that the winnowing of Mot by Anat recalls the offering of the Sheaf at the Passover; but we shall see that the grains of the Sheaf were not winnowed before a fairly late period of Israelite history, p. 257 below. More acceptable than these hypotheses are the contention of de Langhe, op. cit. ii. 371, that the mourning rites for Baʿal simply reflect general practice at Ugarit, and Kapelrud's view, op. cit. 19 f., that instructions for the offering of bread, mandrakes, and libations reflect general sacrificial procedure. There is no specific mention of the New Year in these texts. A recent discussion of the myth content of the Ugaritic texts may be found in de Langhe, 'Myth, Ritual, and Kingship in the Ras Shamra Tablets', in Hooke, op. cit. 122.

Phoenician records provide us with no data on ritual at the New Year.[1] Lucian's account of the ceremonies at the temple of the Mother Goddess contains a brief description of the 'pyre' or 'lamp' rite at the beginning of the spring. Sacrificial animals were tied to a tree with offerings of birds or garments or silver and gold. Images of gods were taken solemnly around the tree, and then it was set on fire.[2]

We have no certain information about New Year ritual among the pagan Arabs.[3] On the other hand, some of the practices at the equinox and solstice that are observed in modern Palestine and the neighbouring countries may well be a survival from ancient times. It is to be remarked that they are fixed by the lunisolar calendar of the Christians, not by the lunar calendar of Islam. Among them is the Palestinian ceremony of sacrificing an animal on 1 March and smearing its blood on the doorposts, on the children, and the horses.[4] The same ceremony is performed in the autumn in the Lebanon.[5] In North Africa and in Syria it is the practice to go into the fields at the time of the spring equinox.[6] At the Nebi Musa spring festival in Palestine the pilgrimage to the shrine is accompanied by sacrifices, processions, dancing, and music, new clothes are worn, and gifts exchanged; the festival lasts seven days.[7] Not dissimilar is the festival of Nebi Rubin, which lasts one month, in the summer.[8] The wearing of masks and other carnival ritual at Easter time may be old.[9] At the solstitial festival of Barbara in the winter in the Near East some people pass in procession through the streets, others blacken their faces, and gifts are exchanged.[10]

This survey of New Year festivals in the ancient Near East is necessarily brief and selective; it makes no allowance for social and economic differences between one region and another within a single area, or between one period of time and another. Nevertheless, from it we may draw some tentative conclusions. Certain features may be peculiar to one or more communities, others appear to belong to a general pattern. The New Year is fixed by the calendar. In all communities we find a ritual going-forth from

[1] Cazelles, op. cit., suggests that *zbḥ ymm* in the Karatepe inscription represents the sacrifice of the annual autumn festival. On this phrase, see, however, p. 116 n. 5 above.

[2] *De Dea syria*, 49.

[3] On the *ḥajj* among the pre-Islamic Arabs, see p. 130 below. Winnett, *Safaitic Inscriptions from Jordan*, 1957, 18 (No. 73), suggests that the writer of that inscription was awaiting the 'appearance of the new moon which marked the beginning of a new lunar year'. This seems improbable; there is nothing in the context to imply 'moon', and it is preferable to accept the interpretation already offered for the phrase in *CIS* 4251, 'he was on the watch this year'. There were ritual processions at Palmyra, R. Dussaud, *Pénétration*, 116 f.

[4] Dalman, op. cit. i. 30, 423.

[5] Ibid. i. 445.

[6] T. Canaan, 'Mohammedan Saints and Sanctuaries in Palestine', *JPOS* vi, 1926, 141, and Dalman, op. cit. i. 425, 439.

[7] Canaan, op. cit. 117, and Dalman, op. cit. i. 427.

[8] Canaan, op. cit. 140. Cf. Sozomen, *Hist. eccles.* ii. 4 (Migne, *P.G.* lxvii, cols. 941 ff.), for a similar festival at Hebron in Roman times.

[9] Dalman, op. cit. i. 423.

[10] Ibid. i. 270.

the city to the open country. In all are rites of purification, which include fasting and the wearing of new clothes, processions, the exchange of gifts, sacrifices, and feasting. In some communities there is the solemn recital of a myth of Creation, in several the sacred marriage is enacted. Most include the temporary removal of conventional social restrictions. The New Year appears to be an appropriate time for the dedication of a temple.

Before we relate these conclusions to the New Year festival of the Hebrews, certain reservations must be entered. The comparison of alleged parallels between the religious practices of Israel and those of her neighbours must not be too rigid or pressed too far. We must take into account differences of geography—particularly of climate and natural resources—between the low lands of Egypt and Mesopotamia, on the one hand, and the hill country of Palestine, on the other. There was a vast difference in temperament and in cultural attainments between Israel and the cultivated milieux of the great cities of this area. But most far-reaching in its influence on the scheme of religious practice was the social and economic structure of the various communities whose New Year festivals I have surveyed. It ranged from the absolute monarchy of the Pharaohs through the petty dynasties of Syria to the tribal society of the Arab nomads. Mowinckel and others have examined traces of divine kingship in Israel with elaborate care, but it may be doubted whether this conception extended beyond the Court and the priesthood to the Israelite farmers and peasants. The unit of society in Israel, even in the city, was the family rather than the State—and here we may find much in common with Greece and Rome and the Arabs, rather than with Egypt and Babylonia.

Nevertheless, we have found in our survey that there are phenomena common to New Year festivals throughout the Near East. The Israelites were derived from this area, and developed within it. They were heirs to the same traditions as their neighbours. Although they moulded their own cast of thought and faith—through experiences which were, in some measure, not shared by others—yet their thought and faith were that of the general commonalty of the Near East, and the idiom in which they were expressed was the idiom of the Near East. We shall observe in the course of this study how great was the conservatism of Israelite religion. Adaptation of ritual there was, but not innovations in the narrow sense. Even those heterodox minorities in Israel who disagreed on minor points of ceremonial invoked the same appeal to tradition as the majority; the divergencies between them stemmed only from divergent methods of interpretation.

On the nature of the Israelite calendar in which the Passover and Tabernacles were New Year festivals, there is little dispute. It was a lunisolar calendar in which a period of twelve lunations lasting approximately

354 days was adjusted to the tropic year of approximately 365¼ days by the insertion of an additional month every two or three years.[1] There is no need to discuss here the method by which intercalation was applied among the Israelites. It is important only to recognize that, throughout Israelite and Jewish history, the two points by which the lunar was adapted to the solar framework were the Passover and Tabernacles. It is in keeping with this that the two incidents in the Bible which probably arose from intercalation are connected with the celebration of, in the one case, Tabernacles and, in the other, the Passover.[2]

I have pointed out that these two festivals occur at an interval of six months or approximately half a year from each other. This dichotomy of the year is, of course, the dichotomy of the tropic year—a lunar 'year' is no more than a fiction. Clearly, then, it must derive from a phenomenon in the tropic year common to both spring and autumn; this can be only the equinox. That the equinox is not mentioned in the Bible—nor in Jewish documents before the time of Philo[3]—should cause no surprise. The Bible was intended for the public. It holds no secrets that the public should not know. And the secrets of the calendar—and among them the method of intercalation was most important—must have been guarded by the priesthood with jealous care.[4]

A calendar can have only one beginning. The Israelite calendar cannot have begun at both the Passover and Tabernacles in a single year. It is generally recognized by scholars that the calendar opening was moved in the course of Israelite history from the Passover to Tabernacles—or in the reverse direction. The epoch of Israelite history in which the one or the other was regarded as the calendric New Year is in dispute—but this does not concern us directly here.[5] It is sufficient to remark that both retained in varying degrees of vigour the characteristics of a New Year festival in the Near East—indeed, only thus could the change from one to the other have been effected imperceptibly and without obvious trace in the Bible or Jewish writings. There is, as it were, a 'scatter' of New Year ritual between the two, and in our description of the Passover as a New Year festival we must take into account also the ceremonial of the autumn festival. Both have features drawn from a common reservoir.

But not only are the qualities of the New Year festival shared in varying degree by the Passover and Tabernacles; in each case there has been a

[1] Hypotheses about other methods of reckoning the calendar in Israel are discussed in my article in *VT* vii, 1957, 251. To the bibliography given there should now be added A. Jaubert, *Date de la Cène*, 1957; J. van Goudoever, *Biblical Calendars*, 1959; and de Vaux, *Institutions de l'Ancien Testament*, ii, 1960.

[2] 1 Kings 12:32 f., 2 Chr. 30. See *VT* vii, 1957, 257 ff.

[3] p. 29 above.

[4] See *VT* vii, 1957, 259.

[5] See, in particular, J. Begrich, *Chronologie der Könige von Israel und Juda*, 1929; E. R. Thiele, *Mysterious Numbers of the Hebrew Kings*, 1951; and de Vaux, op. cit. i. 289–93.

'splintering' of their ritual to adjacent points of the calendar. Some of the ceremonies of the autumn New Year have become attached to Rosh ha-Shanah on the first day of the month, some to Yom haKippurim on the tenth day.[1] In the case of the spring festival, the method of 'splintering' is perhaps more logical. Some features have been attached to Purim at the middle of the previous month; and in certain circumstances part of the Pesaḥ ritual may be performed at the middle of the following month.[2] In either event, one salient characteristic of the spring festival remains—the ritual is carried out at the full moon.

Before we turn to examine the details of the New Year festival, we must touch upon a feature common not only to both the Passover and Tabernacles, but also to the feast of Weeks—the name *ḥag*. In this connexion I venture to part company from (I think) all those scholars who have treated this subject. They have regarded *ḥag* as a pilgrimage feast that is based upon the processes of the agricultural year. The *ḥaggim* were celebrated, it is maintained, when the produce of the ground was ripe; they therefore varied in date in different localities of the country and according to the vagaries of the Palestinian climate.[3] This theory stems from the circumstance that the barley Sheaf-offering, which fixed the date of the feast (*ḥag*) of Weeks, was an offering of harvest firstfruits. I believe, on the contrary, that the *ḥaggim* were held always on a fixed date, and that primarily they had nothing to do with harvests. The very notion of pilgrimage—as opposed to the visit to a shrine by an individual—loses significance as a national ceremony if it is not performed on a fixed date as well as at a fixed shrine or shrines.[4] The connexion of Tabernacles with harvest is, I hold, secondary. Indeed, the Bible does not state which is the fruit of which firstfruits are offered at this festival. I have already maintained that the origins of the Maṣṣoth festival are not to be found in the new corn-harvest; the Bible nowhere connects it directly with the harvest.[5] The feast of Weeks is, it is true, a harvest festival. But it occurs at a fixed interval of time after the Passover and it is subordinate to it; it was, indeed, always of minor importance in orthodox Hebrew festal practice.[6]

The basic meaning of the word *ḥag* is not certain. It is probably not

[1] See, for example, S. Mowinckel, *Psalmenstudien*, ii. 83, 85, and Snaith, *Jewish New Year Festival*, 1947, 150 ff. Note the move of the opening of the Jubilee Year from the tenth to the first day of the autumn month, *Mish. R.H.* i. 1, cf. *BT R.H.* 8b and *JT R.H.* i. 2 (fol. 56d).

[2] pp. 147 f. and 199 f. below.

[3] So, for example, Hooke, *Origins*, 46; Oesterley, in Hooke, *Myth and Ritual*, 112; and Snaith, op. cit. 52.

[4] Proponents of the Source hypothesis ascribe Ex. 34:24, which presupposes pilgrimage by the whole nation on a fixed date, to a late redactor; so too Pedersen, *Israel*, iii–iv. 386. E. Auerbach, 'Feste im alten Israel', *VT* viii, 1958, 15 ff., suggests that it was the Deuteronomist who introduced the practice of celebrating annual festivals on a fixed date.

[5] See p. 111 above.

[6] pp. 180 f., 194, and 235 below.

connected with the notion 'dance'.[1] It is perhaps to be distinguished from the root *ḥwg* in that the latter describes a circle in space rather than in time.[2] Nevertheless, *ḥag* probably has, like *ḥwg*, the significance of 'circuit'—not only a processional circuit by celebrants (as assumed by most scholars), but also the revolution or circuit of the tropic year.[3] The procession by the worshippers may have been in primitive times the ritual representation of the motions of the sun.[4]

The word *ḥag* is used in the Bible of the Passover, the feast of Weeks, and Tabernacles;[5] but more significant for the present study are those passages of the Bible in which the word is not directly associated with these festivals. It is always connected with the Israelite deity, either explicitly or implicitly.[6] It is a recurrent occasion held on a fixed date[7] and at a fixed shrine.[8] It is marked by sacrifice[9]—indeed, the word is used also of the sacrificial victim offered at the *ḥag*.[10] It is celebrated also with eating and drinking,[11] music[12] and rejoicing,[13] and even drunkenness,[14] to such an extent that non-Israelites at a carousal can be compared with the participants at a *ḥag*.[15] The occasion is, however, nowhere connected with firstfruits offerings or with agricultural offerings of any kind.

[1] Nöldeke, review, *ZDMG* xli, 1887, 719 n. 3. In Ex. 32:5 Targ. Jer. and Onq. have חגא, but in 32:19 they have חגגין; cf. at Jud. 11:34, 21:21 f.

[2] On חג, חוג, circle, see Wellhausen, *Reste arabischen Heidentums*, 1897, 110, 141. For *ḥwg*, see Job 26:10 (verb), Is. 40:22, Prov. 8:27, Job 22:14 (noun), cf. Is. 44:13, *meḥugah*. It is perhaps significant that in two of these passages the root *ḥwg* stands in juxtaposition to the root *ḥqq*, cf. Ps. 81:4–5. On the derivation of *ḥag*, see Morgenstern, 'Etymological History of . . . *ḤGG* . . .', *JAOS* xxxvi, 1917, 321 ff.

[3] Cf. Is. 29:1, חגים ינקפו; the verb is related to *tequphah*, 'circuit (of the year)', in later times 'solstice' or 'equinox', cf. Job 1:5, הקיפו ימי המשתה, and Ugar. *nqpt*, 'years' (C. H. Gordon, *Ugaritic Manual*, 1955, Glossary, s.v.) (? parallel to *šnt*). For a discussion of the circuit of the year, see Harrison, *Themis*, 182 ff., on ἔτος, ἐνιαυτός (cf. ἐνιαυτοῦ κύκλος, Euripides, *Orestes* 1645) and Fowler, op. cit. 52, on *annus* and the festival of Anna Perenna.

[4] Cf. F. J. Hollis, 'Sun-cult and the Temple at Jerusalem', in Hooke, *Myth and Ritual*, 87 ff., and May, 'Some Aspects of Solar Worship at Jerusalem', *ZAW* lv, 1937, 269.

[5] Of the Passover: Ex. 12:14, 23:15, 34:18, Lev. 23:6, Num. 28:17, Deut. 16:16, Ezek. 45:21, 23, Ezra 6:22, 2 Chr. 8:13, 30:13, 21, 35:17. Of the feast of Weeks: Ex. 23:16, 34:22, Deut. 16:10, 16, 2 Chr. 8:13. Of Tabernacles: Ex. 23:16, 34:22, Lev. 23:34, 39, 41, Num. 29:12, Deut. 16:13–16, 31:10, 1 Kings 8:2, 65, Ezek. 45:25, Zech. 14:16, 18, 19, Ezra 3:4, Neh. 8:14, 18, 2 Chr. 5:3, 7:8–9, 8:13, and, implicitly, Jud. 21:19, 1 Kings 12:32–33.

[6] Ex. 5:1, 10:9, 32:5–6, Ps. 81:4, cf. v. 2, 42:5, Is. 30:29, Ezek. 46:11, Hos. 9:5, Amos 5:21.

[7] Ps. 81:4, Is. 29:1, Ezek. 45:17, Hos. 2:13, cf. 9:5. There is no evidence to support Dhorme, *Évolution religieuse d'Israël*, 1937, i. 247 f., that the *ḥag* is necessarily connected with the moon. The feast of Weeks, which occurs fifty days after the Passover, cannot coincide with the full moon.

[8] Ex. 32:5, Ps. 42:5, Is. 30:29, Ezek. 45:17, 46:11.

[9] Ex. 32:5, 10:9, Ezek. 45:17, 46:11, Hos. 9:5, cf. v. 4, Nahum 2:1, Amos 5:21.

[10] Ex. 23:18, 34:25, Mal. 2:3, Ps. 118:27.

[11] Ex. 32:5 f., 1 Sam. 30:16.

[12] Is. 30:29, Ps. 81:4, 42:5.

[13] Hos. 2:13, Amos 8:10.

[14] Ps. 107:27.

[15] 1 Sam. 30:16.

Ḥag is found as the name of a festival only in Arabic among the cognate languages;[1] but the details of the Arab *ḥajj*, both pre-Islamic and Islamic, are clear enough and close enough to the Israelite *ḥag* to enable us to make a definite comparison.[2] The *ḥajj* takes place on a fixed date at a fixed shrine dedicated to a certain deity.[3] It is, at any rate in theory, attended, at least once in their lifetime, by all adult males in sound health, both physical and mental.[4] In ancient times they participated according to clans, and this usage has continued, with concessions to later circumstances, to the present day.[5] The *ḥajj* has no connexion with harvest. It has many of the characteristic qualities of the New Year festival of the Near East—ritual cleanness (including abstention from sexual relations) and fasting, a solemn sacrifice, the recital of epics of tribal ancestors ('boasting', Arab. *tafāḫur*), processions, a ritual exodus into the open country (the *'ifāḍa*), and, finally, feasting and the removal of social taboos.[6] The Passover, as we shall see in the following pages, fulfils these conditions perfectly.[7]

The Passover takes place in the first month of the year.[8] Its date and time

[1] The word *ḥag* is found also in Greek in Syria under the form Ag; cf. Ἀγγαλθαβαείθ, Epiphanius, *Haeres*. li. 24 (Migne, *P.G.* xli, col. 932), and Lagrange, op. cit. 282.

[2] The date of the *ḥajj* in the movable lunar calendar of Islam bears no relation to the dates of the Passover or Tabernacles in the lunisolar Israelite calendar. But the system of the Islamic calendar was adopted deliberately in order to remove the associations of pre-Islamic days. The *ḥajj* was by origin an autumn festival; see, for example, Wellhausen, op. cit. 99 (although Wensinck, art. 'Ḥadjdj', *Encyclopaedia of Islam*, prefers to regard the pre-Islamic *ḥajj* as a spring festival). On the other hand, it appears certain that the *'umrah* in Rajab, originally the spring month, was at one time considered the *'umrah par excellence* and as important as the *ḥajj* in autumn. Later Ramaḍān became the preferred season for performing the *'umrah*; see M. Gaudefroy-Demombynes, *Pèlerinage à la Mekke*, 1923, 192 ff., and H. Lammens, *Arabie occidentale avant l'hégire*, 1928, 132 f. On the pre-Islamic calendar, see the references in J. Henninger, 'Fêtes de printemps chez les Arabes . . .', *Revista do Museu Paulista*, N.S., iv, 1950, 402–3 nn. 54–55. On the lunisolar calendar of pre-Islamic south Arabia, see S. Smith, 'Practice of Kingship . . .', in Hooke, *Myth, Ritual, and Kingship*, 65.

[3] A visit to the Ka'aba not at the fixed time is called *'umrah*, not *ḥajj*. A pilgrimage at the fixed time but to a shrine other than the Ka'aba is a *ziyārah*; so the guide for pilgrims at Medinah is called a *muzawwir*, J. L. Burckhardt, *Travels in Arabia*, 1829, ii. 178.

[4] Moslem slaves are permitted, but not obliged, to perform the *ḥajj*, Gaudefroy-Demombynes, op. cit. 312. Women are exempt from the obligation if they have no husband or male relative to escort them, Gaudefroy-Demombynes, *Moslem Institutions*, 1950, 88, cf. Burckhardt, op. cit. i. 359. For the observance of a local pilgrimage on the fifth day of 'Arafat by men only, see C. von Landberg, *Arabica*, v, 1898, 48 f.

[5] In later times pilgrims adopted the practice of camping at 'Arafat according to their countries of origin, not their tribal affiliations, Gaudefroy-Demombynes, *Pèlerinage*, 246, Burckhardt, op. cit. ii. 43. That this modification arose from social circumstances may be shown by the parallel usage described in Lucian, *De Dea syria*, 56, where each city, rather than each tribe, has its representative at Hieropolis.

[6] See the standard works on Moslem institutions. On the pre-Islamic *ḥajj*, see G. Ryckmans, *Religions arabes préislamiques*, 1951, 8, 12, 33, and Nabih Amin Faris, *Book of Idols . . . by Hisham ibn-al-Kalbi*, 1952.

[7] For other similarities between the *ḥajj* and the Passover (special dress, the seven-day and three-day motifs, haste), see pp. 146 f., 139 n. 12, 145 n. 1, and 174 below.

[8] Ex. 12:2, 18, cf. Lev. 23:5, Num. 9:1, 5, 28:16, Jos. 5:10, cf. 4:19. On the alternative nomenclature, Abib, see pp. 193 and 207 below.

are fixed—'between the two evenings' of the fourteenth day.[1] The term 'between the two evenings' is regarded by most scholars as late;[2] but we need not suppose that the usage it prescribes is anything but early. For calendric purposes the Israelite day—in the sense of the period of twenty-four hours—begins with sunset, as in other countries where the moon provides the basis of time-reckoning.[3] The term *ba'erebh* might have referred to either the evening at the beginning, or the evening at the end, of the fourteenth day.[4] But the term *ben ha'arbayim* is used only of the evening at the end of a specified day which also begins the following day—here, then, the evening at the end of the fourteenth day.[5] In no other Hebrew festival does the festal period begin at the end of a day; the reason is probably to be found in the special precautions taken to ensure that the 'night of watching'[6] should be complete.

[1] Heb. *ben ha'arbayim*; in connexion with the Pesaḥ the term occurs only in Ex. 12:6, Num. 9:3, 5, 11. For the Versions, see pp. 52 and 57 above.

[2] The passages in which it occurs are commonly assigned to the P Source. See the references in n. 1 above.

[3] De Vaux, op. cit. i. 275 ff., maintains that early Hebrew texts show that the Israelite day began with daybreak and extended to the following daybreak; see also the discussion between Zeitlin and Heawood, *JQR* xxxvi, 1945–6, 393, 403, and Zeitlin and J. M. Baumgarten, 'Beginning of the Day in the Calendar of Jubilees', *JBL* lxxvii, 1958, 355, and lxxviii, 1959, 153, 157. It is, however, improbable that the Israelites, who, as de Vaux rightly states, regulated their calendar by the moon, should not from the earliest times have regarded the calendric day as beginning with moonrise. Side by side with this there was also a popular practice of considering the day as beginning, as did the working day, with sunrise; see *VT* vii, 1957, 254. The contrast of these two methods of reckoning persisted to a late period; so *Mish. Ta'an.* i. 4–6, *Tos. Ta'an.* ii. 4, maintain that public fasts involving strict abstention from everyday activity begin with sunset, other fasts begin with sunrise. See further pp. 171 f. and 250 f. below on the ritual of the Temple.

[4] Unless it were specifically defined. The popular code of Deut. 16 accepts the popular view that the day begins with sunrise; Deut. 16:6, therefore, employs the term *ba'erebh* rather than the formal *ben ha'arbayim*, but it proceeds to specify the evening to which it refers by adding כבוא השמש. The date of the Pesaḥ in Deut. 16 is to be understood from the word מועד in v. 6; see pp. 193 n. 5 and 207 below.

[5] From Ex. 30:8 it is evident that the time 'between the two evenings' was just before nightfall, when it was necessary to kindle the lights in the Tabernacle. The phrase is to be found in the Bible only in Ex. 16:12, 29:39, 41, 30:8, Num. 28:4, 8, apart from references to the Pesaḥ. It is used of the evening that is reckoned to the day just ending, and it is frequently opposed to an event in the morning of the same day. See further G. Schiaparelli, *Astronomy in the Old Testament*, 1905, 92 f., and also D. Chwolson, *Das letzte Passamahl Christi und der Tag seines Todes*, 1892, 38, and Driver, *Book of Exodus*, 1911, 89. '*Arbayim* has been thought to be an extended form of *'*arbam*, H. Bauer, *OLZ* xvii, 1914, 7 f.; id., *ZDMG* lxix, 1915, 566 f.; and cf. F. M. Cross and D. N. Freedman, *Early Hebrew Orthography*, 1952, 40, on *ṣohorayim*. The form is discussed in C. Brockelmann, *Grundriss der vergleichenden Grammatik der semitischen Sprachen*, 1907–13, i. 663, cf. 458 f.; F. M. Th. Böhl, *OLZ* xviii, 1915, 321; and H. Bauer and P. Leander, *Historische Grammatik der hebräischen Sprache des Alten Testaments*, 1922, 518. It seems unlikely that ערבם* should have become בין הערבים rather than בערב. The term is best explained as a dual, with Pedersen, op. cit. iii–iv. 704; cf. Arab. بين العشايين, and the references in Pedersen, ibid., and P. Joüon, *Grammaire de l'hébreu biblique*, 1923, 91g.

[6] Ex. 12:42. Note the play on the different nuances of the word *šmr* in this verse; in 42a it has the notion of 'vigil', in 42b the notion of 'observance'. For vigil at the New Year, see Wensinck, *Arabic New-Year* . . ., 32.

'Watching' here is likely to have the meaning of astronomical observation.[1] When the month is reckoned by observation of the phasis of the moon, as it was in Israel, the night of the fourteenth–fifteenth day of the month will normally coincide with the night of the full moon. In schematic calendars in Babylonia the fifteenth day of the spring month was recognized as the day of the spring equinox.[2] The Pesaḥ, then, was a nocturnal ceremony at the full moon of the spring equinox. For this there may be a twofold explanation. The ritual may have been directed towards a lunar deity at this turning-point in the tropic year; and we may observe that the moon was widely held in ancient times to have influence on fertility, a notion that may well have been uppermost at the New Year.[3] But there may also have been a practical consideration. On this night the moon would rise with sunset and set only with sunrise, and it would provide uninterrupted light in which to carry out the complex ceremonial.[4]

[1] The equivalent astronomical term in Babylonia seems to have been *maṣṣartu*; see, for example, S. Langdon, *Babylonian Menologies and the Semitic Calendars*, 1935, 108.

[2] B. L. van der Waerden, 'Babylonian Astronomy. III. The Earliest Astronomical Computations', *JNES* x, 1951, 20 ff. See also S. Smith, op. cit. 36 f.

[3] Moon-worship in the ancient Near East is too well recognized to require documentation here.

[4] Many scholars have maintained that the Pesaḥ was held at one time at the new moon and was later transferred to the full moon; so, for example, K. Kohler, 'Sabbath and Festivals in Pre-exilic and Exilic Times', *JAOS* xxxvii, 1917, 214; May, op. cit. 74; Morgenstern, *VT* v, 1955, 71 f.; and Auerbach, op. cit. 1. This theory rests partly upon the Source hypothesis; *ḥodeš*, Deut. 16:1 (cf. Ex. 13:4, 23:15, 34:18), which is assigned to an early redactor, is contrasted with the dates in Ex. 12:3, Lev. 23:5, &c., which are attributed to late redactors. It also rests upon the significance ascribed to the term *ḥodeš*. Snaith, op. cit. 96, holds that 'the true Hebrew word for month is *yeraḥ*'; *ḥodeš*, he maintains, is the first day of the month.

But the employment of the two words in the Bible seems in fact to have nothing to do with the alleged dates of the documents in which they appear. *Yeraḥ* has four nuances. It is used of the moon (like *yareaḥ*) opp. *šemeš*, Deut. 33:14; it is used of a period of time approximating to a month but not necessarily that precise length of time, Job 7:3, 29:2; it is used of a month period, that is, about thirty days, commencing from any point in the lunation, e.g. Ex. 2:2, Deut. 21:13, 2 Kings 15:13, Zech. 11:8, Job 3:6, 39:2; it is used, finally, of the name of the months of the old Israelite calendar, 1 Kings 6:37, 38, 8:2 (but never with Abib).

Ḥodeš, on the other hand, signifies a lunation. It is used where the exact date is an essential factor in the context. It may be roughly equivalent to a month period, as in Gen. 29:14, Jud. 11:37–39, 20:47, 1 Sam. 6:1, Hos. 5:7, Amos 4:7; here it is interchangeable with *yeraḥ*. But it is not interchangeable with *yeraḥ* when it implies an exact lunation, 2 Kings 25:27, 2 Chr. 7:10, and frequently, where a day is fixed by a numeral; in Ex. 23:15, 34:18, 13:4–5, 10, cf. Deut. 16:1, the day is fixed by *moʿed* in v. 6, instead of a numeral. So, too, we find *yom haḥodeš*, the day (i.e. the beginning) of the lunation, Ezek. 46:1, 6, or *ro'š haḥodeš*, Num. 10:10, 28:11, &c.; similarly, *ḥodeš* has this sense without *yom* or *ro'š* when it is governed by another noun, Num. 29:6, and frequently without another noun where a definite day of the lunation is implied, 1 Sam. 20:5, 18, 24, 27, 34, 2 Kings 4:23, Is. 1:13 f., 47:13, 66:23, Hos. 2:13, Amos 8:5, Ezra 3:5, Neh. 10:34, 2 Chr. 2:3, 8:13, 31:3, perhaps Ps. 81:4. In the following passages *ḥodeš* is numbered and stands in relation to a 'year' of twelve lunations, Gen. 8:5, Deut. 1:3, 1 Kings 8:2, 2 Kings 25:27, Jer. 52:31, Ezek. 32:1, Zech. 1:7, Ezra 10:9. In Lev. 27:6, Num. 3:15, 22, &c., *ḥodeš* stands in relation to a whole lifetime. Finally, *ḥodeš* is found of a lunation in relation to other measurements of time, Ex. 12:2, 13:4, Num. 9:22, 11:20 f., 18:16, 28:14, 1 Sam.

It is probable—although we are not explicitly told so—that the primitive Passover was performed at a shrine or shrines. This is to be expected from the fact that (as we shall observe later) all male adults were required to attend, and to observe ritual cleanness. After the settlement in Canaan all solemn communal meals took place at shrines;[1] the practice is so widespread throughout the Near East—and, indeed, so natural—that there is no reason to regard it as having been acquired by the Israelites from the Canaanites. The festival of Tabernacles was held at Shiloh, later both the Passover and Tabernacles were held at the Temple at Jerusalem, and Tabernacles was held at Bethel.[2] The restriction of the Passover to a single shrine or to certain prescribed shrines by Deut. 16 was therefore no innovation.[3] So, too, after the Return from Exile, the Pesaḥ sacrifice and meal were never celebrated outside the Temple of Jerusalem except by sectarians. Even when the immense numbers of pilgrims made it necessary to permit the meal—but not the sacrifice—to be held outside the Temple, the meal was still eaten within the bounds of Jerusalem; the Temple was,

27:7, 2 Sam. 2:11, 1 Kings 4:7, 5:7, 28, Est. 3:7, 1 Chr. 27:1, 2 Chr. 7:10, 27:1, and frequently, cf. also Job 14:5, 21:21.

In Ex. 23:15, 34:18, the day in the lunation is, I have held, fixed by the *moʿed*; in Deut. 16:1 ff. *moʿed* appears only in v. 6, but it should not be assumed that the Pesaḥ of that document took place at some different point in the lunation. Tradition is firm about the association of the Passover with the full moon. The two dates connected intimately with the Pesaḥ, the 'second Pesaḥ' in the following month, and Purim in the previous month (see pp. 199 f. and 147 below) are both at the full moon; so, too, is the cognate festival of Tabernacles six months later. But perhaps the strongest argument for regarding the full moon as the date of the Pesaḥ from the earliest times is the improbability of the transfer of a festival date from the new moon to the full moon. In Israelite ritual it is the latter that is the less familiar date; it is found, indeed, only of Tabernacles, the Passover, and Purim, all of them marked by New Year ceremonial. Our Bible texts show, on the other hand, that the new moon was widely celebrated in early Israel; see, for example, 1 Sam. 20:5 ff., 2 Kings 4:23, Is. 1:13 f., Amos 8:5, and cf. Neh. 10:34, 2 Chr. 2:3, 8:13, 31:3, Num. 10:10, 28:11. We would expect the move to be from a less familiar to a more familiar date, not the reverse—if, that is, such a move were to have taken place at all—and a parallel may be found in the growth in importance of Rosh haShanah over the festival of Tabernacles in the autumn, see p. 156 below. (The suggestion of Auerbach, op. cit. 9, that the date of the Passover was moved from the new moon to the full moon in order to avoid coinciding with the date of the Babylonian New Year has no basis in fact.)

It has been alleged that the term *ḥodeš* was employed at one phase of Israelite history to denote the day of the full moon, not the day of the new moon; Snaith, op. cit., cf. Benzinger, *Hebräische Archäologie*, 1907, 169. The theory is improbable. It is naturally the crescent that marks the opening and close of a lunation. This was certainly the case in Babylonia and elsewhere in the ancient Near East. The phasis in each month is preceded by one or more nights on which no moon is visible. On the other hand, it is extremely difficult to fix accurately the night of the full moon; and it is for this reason that the night of the full moon is defined in Israelite documents by a number in relation to the lunation.

[1] Jud. 9:27, cf. Deut. 15:20–22; the *liškah* in 1 Sam. 9:22 is part of the Temple, cf. Neh. 13:4 f.

[2] Jud. 21:19, 1 Kings 8:2, 9:25, 12:32 f.

[3] See p. 209 below on the Deuteronomic reform. We may note that the writer of 2 Chr. 35 saw no discrepancy between the Deuteronomic rule restricting the Passover to the shrine and the regulations of Ex. 12 (as he did in other details of Passover observances; see p. 227 below).

as it were, expanded to include the city around it.[1] It is in keeping with this constant association of the Passover with the Temple that, as we shall see in the course of these pages, the dedication or rededication of the Israelite shrine is performed just before the New Year festival, whether of the spring or the autumn.

The Hebrew New Year festival was directed towards the peculiar deity of Israel. The name Pesaḥ[2] and the term *ḥag*[3] are invariably associated, either explicitly or implicitly, with the Lord of Israel throughout the Bible. A notable exception is, however, the *ḥag* which was held by Jeroboam I at what our narrator regards as an improper month.[4] Here there is no reference to the deity; it was not a true *ḥag*.

The Pesaḥ, with which the Passover opened, was attended by the whole assembly or *qahal* of the congregation.[5] *Qahal* is regularly used to denote the formal reunion of the male adult members of the community—those, that is, who were born Israelites and the *gerim* who had opted for residence rights under Israelite law.[6] It was summoned for military or religious duties.[7] The performance of these duties was to be carried out according to tribes, and the subdivision of the tribe was the 'family' or 'household'.[8]

[1] See p. 240 below. Note, moreover, that the Samaritans always held their Pesaḥ at the single shrine on Gerizim, and nowhere else. J. Jeremias, *Passahfeier*, 73.

[2] פסח without a definite article is always followed by ה׳: Ex. 12:11, 27, 48, Lev. 23:5, Num. 9:10, 14, 28:16, Deut. 16:1, 2, 2 Kings 23:21, 2 Chr. 30:1, 5, 35:1. When פסח is preceded by a definite article and clearly refers to that particular occasion or to the Pesaḥ victim, it need not be followed by ה׳: Ex. 12:43, Num. 9:2, cf. v. 3, 9:4, cf. v. 5, 9:5, 6, 12–14, 33:3, Jos. 5:10, 11, 2 Kings 23:22 (but cf. v. 23), Ezek. 45:21, Ezra 6:19, 2 Chr. 30:2, 35:16–18, 19; Ex. 12:21, 34:25, Deut. 16:5, 6, Ezra 6:20, 2 Chr. 30:15, 17, 18, 35:1, 6, 7–9, 10–11.

[3] With *ḥag haMaṣṣoth*: Lev. 23:6, Deut. 16:16, 2 Chr. 30:21, cf. Ex. 13:6; by implication, Ex. 23:15 (cf. v. 14), 34:18, Num. 28:17 (cf. v. 16), Ezra 6:22 (cf. vv. 21, 22b), Ezek. 45:23 (cf. עולה לה׳), 2 Chr. 8:13, 30:13, 35:17. So usually with a *ḥag* other than the Passover: Ex. 10:9, 32:5, Lev. 23:34, 39, 41, Num. 29:12, Deut. 16:10, Jud. 21:19, Hos. 9:5, cf. Zech. 14:16.

[4] 1 Kings 12:32 f.

[5] Ex. 12:6, cf. Num. 14:5. The phrase occurs only here in the Passover laws, cf. Ex. 12:3, 47, 49, but it is not a pleonasm, and *qahal* is not a synonym of *'edah*; cf. Lev. 4:13, cf. v. 14, Prov. 5:14. On *qahal* and *'edah* in terms of the Source hypothesis, L. Rost, *Vorstufen von Kirche und Synagoge im A.T.*, 1938, especially 87 ff., and A. R. Hulst, 'Name "Israel" im Deuteronomium', *Oudtestamentische studiën*, ix, 1951, 82 ff.

[6] Ex. 12:43–45, 48 f. The alien (*ben nekhar*) and the sojourner (*tošabh*) and the hireling are not admitted, because they are outside Israelite jurisdiction, cf. A. Bertholet, *Stellung der Israeliten und der Juden zu den Fremden*, 1896, 32, 154 f., 172 f.; Pedersen, op. cit. i–ii. 40 ff.; E. Marmorstein, 'Origins of Agricultural Feudalism in the Holy Land', *PEQ*, 1953, 112 ff.; H. Cazelles, 'Mission d'Esdras', *VT* iv, 1954, 126 ff.; Grelot, 'Dernière étape de la rédaction sacerdotale', *VT* vi, 1956, 177; and the bibliography in de Vaux, op. cit. i. 327.

[7] So, for example, Gen. 49:6, Num. 22:4, Jud. 20:2, 21:5, 8, 1 Sam. 17:47, Jer. 50:9, Ezek. 16:40, 23:24, 38:7, 15; Deut. 5:19, 9:10, 10:4, 18:16, 2 Chr. 20:5, 30:25, Neh. 5:13, Joel 2:16, Ps. 107:32, Jer. 31:7, Ezra 2:64 (= Neh. 7:66). On the family as a military unit at Ugarit, see A. Alt, 'Zu *hit'ammēr*', *VT* ii, 1952, 156.

[8] The words are interchangeable in the Passover context, pp. 72 f. above; after *mišpaḥah* in Ex. 12:21 we have *bayith*, v. 22; cf. Ex. 12:3 f., 6, 47. See the discussion of these terms in Pedersen, op. cit. i–ii. 51 ff., and C. W. Wolf, 'Terminology of Israel's Tribal Organization', *JBL* lxv, 1946, 45.

It is here that lies the explanation of the statement that the Pesaḥ was to be performed by those units. The terms 'family' or 'household' do not, as has been suggested, reflect a stage in the social development of the Israelites.[1] Throughout its history the Pesaḥ was celebrated according to families or households; and this practice has continued to the present day—only sectarians, as we shall see, adopted a different practice.[2] Attendance by households[3] is the necessary corollary of the observance of formal ceremonies by the *qahal*.

'Households' or 'families' in this context implies male adults only, and a prerequisite for attendance at the Pesaḥ was circumcision. This was a sign of membership of the community. It was an initiation ceremony, a *rite de passage* into full communal life.[4] But at the Pesaḥ circumcision may have been regarded rather as evidence of virility.[5] It is probable that the age of majority, the minimum age at which male Israelites became members of the *qahal* and therefore obliged to participate at the Pesaḥ, was not, as in later times, thirteen, but twenty.[6] Twenty was the age at which Israelites were mustered for active service—in the Temple in the case of priests, in the case of others in the army.[7] It is significant, then, that the Israelites

[1] As the social development of the Israelites is reflected in the attitude towards sin. Thus in Num. 16:32 f., Jos. 7:24 f., the whole family is affected by the guilt of one of its members, cf. Lev. 20:5, Jos. 6:23, 25, Jud. 1:25; elsewhere the guilt affects only the single individual, 1 Sam. 14:44, cf. Lev. 25:10, 41 ff.

[2] See p. 246 below.

[3] *Mišpaḥah*, of warriors, Num. 2:34, 26:5 ff., Neh. 4:7; of census, Num. 1:2, 18, 3:15 ff., 1 Chr. 6:4, 45, 7:5, &c. *Beth 'abh*, of warriors, Jos. 22:14, 1 Chr. 7:2, &c.; of Temple service, Num. 3:30, 35, Ex. 6:25, 1 Kings 8:1, 1 Chr. 6:4, 23:11, Neh. 10:35; of census, Num. 1:2, 18 ff., 3:20, 24.

[4] Ex. 12:43 f., 48 f., Num. 9:14. On the general significance of circumcision, see A. van Gennep, *Rites de passage*, 1909, ch. vi; Cook, in W. R. Smith, *Religion*, 608 ff.; E. Meyer, *Geschichte des Altertums*, 1931, 156; Pedersen, op. cit. i–ii. 492; H. Granqvist, *Birth and Childhood among the Arabs*, 1947, 184 ff. (note p. 201 on the connexion between circumcision and marriage); and F. Sierksma, 'Circoncision en Israel', *Oudtestamentische studiën*, ix, 1951, 136; see further the discussion in de Vaux, op. cit. i. 78, 324. The Compiler of the Pentateuch evidently regards the ordinances on circumcision as older than the Passover, Gen. 17:10 ff., 21:4, 34:14, Jos. 5:5; and, although circumcision is closely connected with the festival, there is no need to infer (with Pedersen, op. cit. iii–iv. 736) that the story of the circumcision of Moses was meant as a preliminary to Passover. Circumcision is frequently performed in the spring at the present day; C. M. Doughty, *Travels in Arabia Deserta*, 1926, i. 430 f.; Canaan, *JPOS* vi, 1926, 117, 133 f.; and A. Musil, *Manners and Customs of the Rwala Bedouins*, 1928, 244 ff.; in either spring or autumn, S. Curtiss, *Primitive Semitic Religion Today . . .*, 1902, 178 (perhaps for reasons of economy, Jaussen, *Coutumes . . . de Moab*, 363; Granqvist, op. cit. 184); in the autumn, P. J. Baldensperger, *PEFQS*, 1893, 312, cf. E. Westermarck, *Ritual and Belief in Morocco*, ii, 1926, 420, 426; at any date, Burckhardt, *Notes on the Bedouins and Wahábys*, 1830, 50, 147, and Musil, *Arabia Petraea*, iii. 219.

[5] It was confined to males, cf. Ex. 23:17, 34:23, Deut. 16:16, 17, cf. Lev. 6:22. For the exclusion of women, see E. Crawley, *Mystic Rose*, 1932, 145 ff., cf. p. 241 below.

[6] See pp. 233 f. below, on Jubilees.

[7] Num. 1:2 f., 18 ff., 26:2, 4, 1 Chr. 23:24, 2 Chr. 25:5, 31:17, Ezra 3:8, cf. Num. 14:29 and see further, on the age of Josiah at the Pesaḥ, p. 227 n. 2 below. The rule that priests serve from the age of thirty, Num. 4:3, 23, &c., is a refinement of the rule that twenty is the age of majority for ordinary Israelites. This is demonstrated by the fact that the intermediate grade of Levites serve from the age of twenty-five.

seem to have been numbered at the Exodus Pesaḥ.[1] This was, in effect, a census, and the census was applied to men of twenty years and over.[2] In the Near East the spring is the normal season for numbering the people;[3] in Israel the practice continued until a later period.[4] It is not proved—at any rate, for an early epoch—that the Israelites disliked the numbering of the people, as scholars have maintained.[5] The census was compulsory, but it was a privilege as well as an obligation.[6]

Now, it is true that the spring is the beginning of the fiscal year in the Near East. The lambs and kids newly born after the cold weather and, to a greater extent, the cereal crops represent the first substantial access of wealth that can be made subject to annual taxation. It was customary to

[1] Ex. 12:4, *mikhsah* (elsewhere only Lev. 27:23) and *kss*, cf. the cognate phrase *epeš nikasi*, &c., in Akk. as, for example, in Landsberger, *Der kultische Kalender*, 135, 138. We may find here an attractive explanation for the obscure *keseh*, Ps. 81:4 (E.V. 81:3), and *kese'*, Prov. 7:20. It is frequently interpreted as 'full moon'; cf. the restoration in the Phoenician inscription of the third–second century B.C., Cooke, *Text-book of North-Semitic Inscriptions*, 1903, 83 (No. 29), and Job 26:9, where many scholars, like Mowinckel, *Psalmenstudien*, ii. 87, read *keseh* for M.T. *kisseh*. The word is uncertain in both etymology and meaning. The appeal by the lexicons to Akk. *kuse'u* is dubious. Syriac ܟܣܐ is both late and uncertain in significance; in the Syriac version of 1 Kings 12:32 f. it is used of the fifteenth day, in Est. 9:21 f. of 14th–15th Adar, and in 2 Chr. 7:10 of the twenty-third day of the month, see G. Bickell, *S. Ephraemi Syri Carmina Nisibena*, 1866, vi, verses 142–4 and 88 n. 24; Payne Smith, *Thesaurus*, s.v.; and Snaith, op. cit. 99. In Arabic, on the other hand, *kus' al-šahr* is used of the last decade of the month. From LXX and Jewish writers on Ps. 81:4 and Prov. 7:20 it is evident that the meaning of *keseh* or *kese'* was unknown to them; cf. *BT R.H.* 8a, 61a; *Beṣah* 16a, *Mekhilta* on Ex. 12:4. Now from the fact that the clauses of Ps. 81 are parallel, not antithetical, it may be deduced that *keseh* in v. 4b is a synonym of *ḥodeš* in v. 4a. Moreover, the verb *tq'* may be extended to *keseh* if it implies the new moon; if it indicates the *ḥag* at the full moon, one would expect *heri'*, cf. p. 154 below. Furthermore, Ps. 81 recounts the events of the Exodus, and it is reasonable to assume that the *ḥag* of v. 4 is the Passover. (Against this, however, see H. St. J. Thackeray, *JTS* xvi, 1915, 193.) The psalm is a New Year psalm according to Jewish tradition; *BT R.H.* 30b and Targ. on Ps. 81:4. *Keseh* in Ps. 81:4 is likely, then, to be the census day at the new moon of the Passover month; cf. p. 258 below. This interpretation offers a satisfactory explanation of the return home of the 'goodman' in Prov. 7:19 f. At the Passover male adult Israelites were required to be present; absence on a journey provided exemption only if it were a 'far' journey; cf. Num. 9:13, and for a possible definition of 'far', see p. 200 below.

The usual terms for 'number (for a census)' are *pqd* and *nś' r'š*; see E. A. Speiser, 'Census and Ritual Expiation in Mari and Israel', *BASOR*, No. 149, Feb. 1958, 21 ff. The former word is found with this meaning in the Qumran documents, *Doc. Cong.* i. 8 f., 27 (Barthélemy and Milik, *Qumran Cave I*, 1955, 109), *Doc. Comm.* iii. 14 f., 18, iv. 19, &c. (Burrows, *Dead Sea Scrolls of St. Mark's Monastery*, ii, 1951), *War*, ii. 4, xii. 4. The mustering at Qumran appears to have been by families; see Y. Yadin, *Scroll of the War of the Sons of Light against the Sons of Darkness*, 1962, 49 ff.

[2] Ex. 30:14, 38:26, Num. 1:26; cf. Lev. 27:3, 1 Chr. 27:23. So also at Qumran, *Doc. Cong.* i. 8–9 (Barthélemy, op. cit. i. 107).

[3] So the Babylonian army was summoned for foreign service from Ayar to Teshrit; see, for example, D. J. Wiseman, *Chronicles of Chaldaean Kings*, 1956; in an emergency the practice was waived, see ibid. on the years 626–615 B.C.

[4] p. 258 below.

[5] As A. George, 'Fautes contre Yahweh dans les livres de Samuel', *RB* liii, 1946, 177.

[6] The danger of being omitted from a military muster in Israel is vividly illustrated by the fate of Jabesh-gilead, Jud. 21:8 ff. See further p. 237 below.

assess taxation upon the corn while it was still in the green.[1] For this purpose a census was obviously of great value. After the settlement in Canaan the king levied taxes on all produce, including that of the field;[2] and like the annual census with which it may have been connected, this was carried out in the spring, down to a late period.[3]

Nevertheless, it was probably primarily in terms of military and religious obligations rather than of taxation that the Israelites held an annual census.[4] David entrusted his census to the generals.[5] The word for taxation, *mks*, is related to the word employed for the numbering of male adults at the Exodus Pesaḥ.[6] But the same word is used, in a military context, of the tribute that was taken from spoils of war.[7] In the ancient Near East, spring marked the beginning of the campaigning season. It was 'the return of the year, . . . the time when kings go forth (to battle)',[8] and it was the appropriate moment for a muster of the army.[9] In Assyria the *waraḫ ṣibi'im*, the month of (the mustering of) the host, followed, we are told, the spring equinox.[10] 'Going-forth' is a technical term in Hebrew for 'going to war'.[11] The ritual of going out, of an exodus from the inhabited regions to the open country, plays an important part in the complex of New Year motifs.[12] In the Ugaritic myth, which may be a New Year theme, the hosts go forth in rows like the array of an army.[13] So, too, in the narrative of the Exodus from Egypt, the going-forth *par excellence* of Israelite history, we observe the frequent iteration of the term *ṣabha'*, the hosts.[14]

[1] See, in particular, N. Rhodokanakis, *Katabanische Texte zur Bodenwirtschaft*, 1919, 82, 96, on south Arabia. Tribute was paid to Moslem rulers in Rajab, originally the spring month, or in Ṣafar six months later, Wellhausen, *Skizzen und Vorarbeiten*, iv, 1889, 192.

[2] 1 Sam. 8:15, cf. Deut. 14:22 ff. and 1 Kings 4:7 ff. On the poll-tax, see Ex. 30:11 ff., Num. 1–4, 26, Neh. 10:33; note that the census of military men in Num. 26:1 ff. is followed by an account of the distribution of lands. On tithes offered at the Passover, see *Mish. Ma'as. Sh.* v. 6 and p. 258 below.

[3] *BT R.H.* 7a, cf. *JT Sheq.* i. 1 (fol. 45d).

[4] See G. E. Mendenhall, 'Census Lists of Numbers 1 and 26', *JBL* lxxvii, 1958, 52. Note that the Hebrew word *ḥayil* denotes both 'wealth' and 'valour', cf. J. van der Ploeg, 'Sens de *gibbor ḥail*', *Vivre et Penser*, i, 1941, 120.

[5] 2 Sam. 24 and the parallel account in 1 Chr. 21; see S. V. McCasland, 'Soldiers on Service', *JBL* lxii, 1943, 61. We may note that the numbers 7 and 3 both recur in the passage; pp. 144 f. below. The reason for the illegality of this census is discussed on p. 215 below.

[6] p. 136 n. 1 above. *Mks* is in regular use in Semitic languages; cf., for example, Landsberger, op. cit. 135 n. 2. For the secondary formation in Heb. *mks—kss*, cf. *mgr—grr*, and perhaps *mrq—rqq*, *mkr—kry*. *Kss* may be related to *skk*, cf. Phoen. *msk* (Cooke, op. cit. 30, No. 5, ll. 3, 12–13).

[7] Num. 31:28, 37.

[8] 2 Sam. 11:1 (cf. p. 116 n. 3 above), 1 Kings 20:22, 1 Chr. 20:1. Note that Joshua's campaign is said to have begun in the spring, Jos. 3:15, cf. Jud. 6:3, 4, 11.

[9] 1 Kings 20:26, 27.

[10] J. Lewy, 'Assyrian Calendar', *Archiv Orientální*, xi, 1939, 39.

[11] See n. 8 above and Num. 31:27 f., Jud. 4:14, 1 Sam. 8:20, 17:20, 2 Sam. 5:24, Is. 40:26, 42:13, Amos 5:3, Ps. 68:8, 108:12. On Qumran, see p. 247 and n. 2 below.

[12] See pp. 118, 120, 123, 124, and 125 above.

[13] Gordon, op. cit. 185a (ll. 85 ff.), 186a (ll. 176 ff.); cf. Engnell, *Studies in Divine Kingship in the Ancient Near East*, 1943, 156 ff.

[14] Ex. 6:26, 7:4, 12:17, 41, 51, cf. also 13:17 f.; see de Vaux, *Institutions*, ii. 75, and the

At the Passover the assembly was summoned for both a military and a religious occasion, and the term *ṣabha'* is used of religious as well as military service.[1] There was, indeed, an intimate association between war and religious ceremonial; religious ritual played a frequent and integral part in the routine of military life in the ancient world. The mustering of an army, like the return of an army from war, was the moment for solemn ceremonies of purification.[2] A census of military men involved lustration.[3] The Mari texts allude to the census, presumably in connexion with enrolment into the army, and the term employed for census in these texts has the primary meaning of purification.[4] Speiser has drawn attention to the use of the term *kpr* in Hebrew documents dealing with census ceremonies in Israel.[5] This should not, however, lead us to associate the Israelite census with the autumn festival of Yom haKippurim. It was in the spring near the Passover that armies were mustered for war. We shall see that the term *kpr* is used also in the context of the Passover—though with a difference of emphasis that illustrates the underlying distinction between the Israelite spring and autumn festivals.[6]

The Pesaḥ was a solemn religious sacrament. Not only the heads of families who conducted the ceremony, but all those who participated at the meal were required to observe strict rules of ritual cleanness. That was the practice in later times. And undoubtedly it was also the practice at the primitive Pesaḥ; this, at any rate, is the view of the Compiler, for he holds that, at a later period, the laws of ritual cleanness might be adjourned in certain circumstances, but they could not be relaxed and certainly not abrogated.[7] Indeed, ritual cleanness was postulated by the very fact that the Pesaḥ was to be held at a sacred place.[8] Those who had been in contact with objects of minor uncleanness were first to be separated from the

treatment ibid. 10 ff. It should be observed that in the Exodus narrative we are given the numbers of the host, Ex. 12:37, as at the census taken by certain Israelite kings, 2 Chr. 14:7, 17:14–18, 25:5, 26:11–13.

[1] Num. 4:3, 23, 30, 35, &c., 8:24 f., 1 Sam. 2:22. See de Vaux, review, *RB* lx, 1948, 587.

[2] Deut. 23:10 ff. (E.V. 23:9 ff.), Jos. 3:5, 1 Sam. 21:6, 2 Sam. 11:11. For regulations at Qumran, see *War*, vii. 4 ff., cf. ix. 8 f., xiv. 2 f.

[3] Cf. Lat. *lustrum*, and see Pauly–Wissowa, *Realenc.*, s.v.

[4] J. R. Kupper, 'Recensement dans les textes de Mari', in A. Parrot, *Studia Mariana*, 1950, 99. The word *tebibtum*, used of 'census' (rather than 'exemption' or 'demobilization', as Gordon, 'Šamši-Adad's Military Texts from Mari', *Archiv Orientální*, xviii, 1950, 205 f.), has the primary meaning of 'purification'. See W. von Soden, *Welt des Orients*, i, 1948, 196, and, for example, J. Laessøe, *Studies in the Assyrian Ritual . . . bît rimki*, 1955, 86. The census at Mari seems to have been held at irregular intervals, Kupper, 'Recensement', passim; it was probably limited mobilization in case the need should arise, as Mendenhall, op. cit. 55 f. The list of slave-women, widows, and hierodules (?) at Mari, M. Birot, *Syria*, xxxv, 1958, 9, is scarcely a census. The seventh-century records of Harran published by C. H. W. Johns, *Assyrian Doomsday Book*, 1901, are a survey rather than a census.

[5] Op. cit. 21 ff. [6] p. 164 below. [7] See pp. 199 f. below.

[8] p. 133 above; cf. Lev. 7:19 f., 1 Sam. 16:5. Uncleanness was permitted only when animals were killed 'within the gates', Deut. 12:15, 20 ff., that is, not at a shrine. The requirement of ritual cleanness is not imposed for a casual meal, Gen. 18:7, 27:9, 1 Sam. 28:24, 2 Sam. 12:4, 1 Kings 19:21.

community until the evening and then to bathe themselves;[1] they were to change their clothes.[2] Contact with sources of major pollution was to be removed by more severe rites of purification.

The Passover was probably preceded by a preliminal period of purification lasting seven days.[3] The number seven was of great significance in Israel. It was commonly employed as a round figure.[4] It had magical properties;[5] it occurs in stories[6] and in dreams and visions;[7] it is a sign of good fortune,[8] and it is frequent in curses.[9] It is of importance in Temple ritual,[10] especially at sin offerings and related sacrifices.[11] It was a sacral period.[12] After the birth of a male child, the infant is kept for seven days before the circumcision.[13] The full period of mourning is seven days.[14] The

[1] Lev. 15:16 ff., 17:15, Deut. 23:10 ff., cf. 1 Sam. 20:26 f., 21:4–6; cf. Qur. iv. 46.

[2] Gen. 35:2, Ex. 19:10; see p. 253 below on the modern Samaritans.

[3] I discuss the post-liminal period of seven days on p. 177 below.

[4] So, for example, Gen. 29:18, 20, 31:23, Jud. 6:1, 25, 12:9, 1 Sam. 6:1, 2 Kings 3:9, Is. 4:1, Ezek. 39:12, Prov. 9:1, 26:16, Job 5:19, Matt. 22:25.

[5] Gen. 33:3, Jos. 6:14, 15, Jud. 16:7, 13, 19, 1 Kings 18:43 f., 2 Kings 4:35, 5:10, 14, Dan. 3:19, Matt. 12:45, Luke 11:26. The number 7 is frequent in the Qumran text on the order of battle, *War*, vi. 6 ff., &c.; cf. Yadin, op. cit. 261 f., 276–9, 284–99, 342 f.

[6] For example, Gen. 7:2 f. and frequently in the story of the Flood, Est. 1:5, 10, 14, 2:9.

[7] Gen. 41:3 ff., Ezek. 3:15–16, Zech. 3:9, 4:2, 10, Dan. 4:13 (E.V. 4:16), &c., Rev. 1:4, 13, 16, 20, 5:6, 8:2, and frequently.

[8] 1 Sam. 2:5, Ruth 4:15, Jer. 15:9, Job 1:2, 42:13.

[9] Gen. 4:15, 24, Lev. 26:18, 21, &c.; cf. *šbʿ*, 'swear', and see R. Gordis, 'Heptad as an Element of Biblical and Rabbinic Style', *JBL* lxii, 1943, 17.

[10] Lev. 4:6, 14:7, 16:14, &c., Num. 19:4, Ezek. 43:25 f.

[11] Num. 23:1, 29, 28:11, 19, 27, 29:32, Ezek. 45:23, Job 42:8, 1 Chr. 15:26, 2 Chr. 29:21.

[12] It was on the seventh day that Moses entered the midst of the cloud on Sinai, Ex. 24:16 ff. The Year of Release is the seventh year, Ex. 21:2, Lev. 25:1 ff., Deut. 15:1 ff., Jer. 34:8 ff. This is not the place to treat at length the importance of seven in the countries adjacent to Palestine; this feature is sufficiently clear from even a cursory examination of the documents in *ANET*. We may, however, refer to Landsberger, op. cit. 84, 87 f., 97, 98 f., and especially 119 ff., on the seventh day in Mesopotamia, cf. B. Meissner, *Babylonien und Assyrien*, 1920–5, ii. 93 f., and Benzinger, *Hebräische Archäologie*, 1907, 170. On Ugar. see Gordon, *Ugaritic Literature*, 1949, 3 ff., 57. Concerning Islam it may be observed that the formal intention to perform the *ḥajj* is declared on the first day of Dhu 'lḤijjah; the *ḥajj* begins on the seventh day of the month and continues to the thirteenth, the seventh day after its opening. Pilgrims make seven circuits around the Kaʿaba (so, too, around the grave of a *weli*, Burckhardt, *Travels in Arabia*, 1829, i. 172 f.), and throw seven stones at the stela in Mina.

[13] Gen. 17:12, Lev. 12:2 f., cf. Ex. 22:28 f. (E.V. 22:29 f.), Lev. 22:7. A female child is kept twice seven days with her mother, Lev. 12:5. For a seven-day celebration before a circumcision in modern Palestine, Granqvist, *Birth and Childhood*, 202. Gray, 'Cultic Affinities between Israel and Ras Shamra', *ZAW* lxii, 1950, 218, points to the Ugar. text which declares that the offspring of El spend their first seven years in the desert.

[14] Gen. 50:10, Num. 19:11, 6:9, Job 2:13, Judith 16:24, Ecclus. 22:12, Josephus, *BJ* II. i. 1, where the son of Herod is acclaimed in the Temple seven days after the death of his father; cf. the seven-day fast in 1 Sam. 31:13. On the other hand, mourning lasts thirty days in Deut. 34:8. We may compare Lucian, *De Dea syria*, 52–53, where a person who has touched a dead body is excluded from the community for seven days, a person who has seen a dead body is excluded for one day, while a person whose kinsman has died is excluded for thirty days. The mourning for the mother of Nabonidus lasted for seven days, C. J. Gadd, *Anatolian Studies*, viii, 1958, 53 (col. iii, ll. 25 ff.), 55. For the period of seven days as a period of ritual uncleanness in Greece, see Nilsson, *Griechische Feste*, 108, cf. 55.

period of purification for warriors returning from battle is seven days—presumably because they had contact with the dead.[1] A similar period of separation is required of a person unclean with an issue.[2] So, too, the leper and his garments undergo tests over a period of seven days or multiples of seven days before they can be pronounced clean.[3]

These rites of purification all have one feature in common with the New Year ceremonial. They are all *rites de passage* from the unclean to the clean, and the period of transition is seven days. The conception is undoubtedly primitive as well as widespread in the Semitic world. It is probable, then, that in early times the Israelite New Year festivals, also *rites de passage*, were preceded by a week of purification. This was certainly the case in later times.[4] The Chronicler declares that the feast of Tabernacles held at Jerusalem by Solomon was preceded by a seven-day feast of dedication;[5] he is giving the practice of his own age. Seven days, moreover, may be the definition of the length of the 'journey afar off' which exempts a man from participating in the Pesaḥ at the proper time.[6] A man who is far distant would not be able to spend that period of time at the shrine or in its vicinity in order to acquire the requisite degree of sanctity.

The heads of families who performed the Pesaḥ sacrifice may have been required to perform the cleanness rites of priests at the Temple,[7] although most of them must have been laymen. But these rites seem to have been little more rigorous than those that applied to laymen partaking of the sacrificial meal.[8]

Ritual cleanness at the Pesaḥ was not confined to the officiants and the human participants. The victim and the food which accompanied the victim's flesh were also to be clean. The victim was to be taken only from the sheep or goats; it was to be in its first year, male, and without blemish.[9] The restriction on the species of animals was retained throughout the history of the festival;[10] whether a sheep or a goat was chosen was, however,

[1] Num. 31:21 ff. For Hittite rites of purification among warriors, Furlani, *Religione degli Hittiti*, 238.

[2] Lev. 15:13, 19, 24, 28.

[3] Lev. 13:47 ff., Num. 12:14, cf. 5:2–4. In later times the priestly garments were handed to the priests seven days before festivals, and then given into safe custody after the festivals; Josephus, *Ant.* XVIII. iv. 3, cf. XX. i. 1.

[4] pp. 244 and 256, cf. p. 254 below.

[5] 2 Chr. 5:2 f., 7:8–10 opp. 1 Kings 8:1–2, 65–66.

[6] p. 200 below.

[7] Lev. 22:1 ff., cf. Hag. 2:11 ff.

[8] Laymen appear to perform sacrifice in Lev. 1:5, 11 (burnt offerings), 3:2, 8, 13, 7:28 ff. (peace offerings), 4:15, 23, 29, 33 (sin offerings), cf. 17:3 ff. See also Deut. 15:21–23 and 21:4, and p. 211 below.

[9] Ex. 12:3–5, 21; cf. Lev. 22:19, Deut. 15:21. See Gray, 'Misuse of the Term "Lamb" in the E.V.', *Expositor*, xxii, 1921, 241 ff. Heb. *ṣ'n* includes rams (Lev. 5:15) as well as lambs (Gen. 21:28) and kids (Gen. 27:9, cf. 38:17). At the Pesaḥ rams are excluded by the provision that the victim must be one year old; cf. Num. 28:11, 19, 27, 29:2, 13, 20 ff. In Islam the victim on the day of 'Arafat must also be ritually clean; cf., on local sacrifices at shrines, Canaan, op. cit. 33, 40; it should fast before being killed, Westermarck, *Ritual and Belief in Morocco*, ii. 116.

[10] On the apparent contradiction in Deut. 16:2, see p. 204 below.

a matter for the individual officiant.[1] The limitation to small animals has been attributed by scholars to the rule that the animal must be wholly consumed—this, it is held, would not have been possible with a large animal. Others have found the reason for the limitation in the rule that the victim must be roasted; the roasting of a large animal might have been impracticable.[2] Neither suggestion seems likely. It is prescribed in the Passover regulations that the victim shall be young, and it must therefore be small, whether lamb or calf; moreover, a family was permitted to collaborate with another family if its members were too few to eat the whole animal.[3] The reason for restricting the species of the Pesaḥ victim to sheep or goats probably lies in the regulation concerning its age. In Biblical references to the age of cattle victims, it is laid down variously that they are to be three years old[4] or seven years old[5] or simply that they should be young;[6] only of sheep and goats is it prescribed that they should be in their first year.[7]

What was the motive for this insistence on the age of the Pesaḥ victim? The view may be advanced that it was proper at the spring New Year to offer victims from among the animals that were born during the previous year in order to give some feeling of continuity. But an examination of the passages of the Bible in which it is declared that the victim must be in its first year leads to a different explanation. These passages treat of two classes of sacrifice. Some are *rites de passage* which involve an individual member of the congregation;[8] the remainder are sacrifices on behalf of the congregation—either recurrent occasions,[9] or at the dedication

[1] For a later period, cf. *BT Pes.* 57a. On the conception of a sacred lamb and the Pesaḥ, see p. 103 n. 2 above.

[2] See Guthe's explanation for the boiling of the victim in Deut. 16, p. 82 above.

[3] Ex. 12:4. The 'neighbour next unto his house' refers to nearness of relationship, rather than of dwelling-place. It is possible, however, that the families were arranged according to kinship. The Israelites were certainly disposed as a military force, and each tribe and family must have had its allotted place, cf. Num. 2:2 ff., 10:13 ff. This was the method at the Moslem *ḥajj*; see p. 130 above.

[4] Gen. 15:9, 1 Sam. 1:24 according to LXX and Pesh. followed by S. R. Driver, *Samuel*, in loc. (The LXX reading is found in a Qumran text, Cross, *BASOR*, No. 132, Dec. 1953, 19, 26.) Perhaps cf. Jer. 48:34.

[5] Jud. 6:25, and so LXX.

[6] *Ben baqar*, frequently. No age is given in Lev. 3:1, 9:4, 18.

[7] The only exceptions are Lev. 9:3 ('calf . . . of the first year') and Mic. 6:6 ('calves of a year old'). The latter is unlikely to represent normal practice, since the prophet is rebuking the people for their lavish offerings; on the former, see p. 142 n. 2 below.

[8] After childbirth, Lev. 12:6 (one male lamb); at the cleansing of a leper, Lev. 14:10 (two male lambs and one female); at the recommencement of the days of separation by a Nazarite after uncleanness, Num. 6:12 (one male lamb); at the end of the Nazarite's days of separation, 6:14 (one male lamb, one female); when an individual has sinned unwittingly, 15:27 (one female goat).

[9] The *Tamid* offerings, Ex. 29:38 f., Num. 28:3 f., Ezek. 46:13; at the Sheaf-offering, Lev. 23:12; on the Sabbath, Num. 28:9; on new moons, 28:11; at the New Year, 29:2; on the Day of Atonement, 29:8; on each day of the Passover week, 28:19 ff.; on the feast of Weeks, 28:27; on each day of Tabernacles, 29:13–32; on the day after Tabernacles, 29:36.

of the Tabernacle,[1] or at the consecration of priests.[2] The Pesaḥ belongs to the latter group; it is a congregational offering. The animals sacrificed in this group of ceremonies are always, like the Pesaḥ victim, male. But they are burned, and it is worthy of comment that the Pesaḥ is the only occasion in the Israelite sacrificial calendar on which male lambs or kids in their first year are consumed by those who make the offering.

The special sanctity of the occasion is the explanation for both the age and the sex of the Pesaḥ victim.[3] Its youthfulness was regarded as in some way a guarantee of its ritual cleanness. In Palestine male sheep do not normally mate before a year has passed.[4] The sex of the animal is restricted in certain Israelite offerings, and clearly for the same reason. Female animals might be offered as sin offerings[5] or peace offerings,[6] but they do not appear among the most sacred category of offerings—the burnt offerings and the Pesaḥ. Male animals, like male human beings, were regarded as less liable to ritual uncleanness. Physical blemish involves a taint in both man and beast, and at the solemn festival 'the sacred power resents contact with that which is not sacred'.[7] For the same reason the victim, chosen some days before the time of sacrifice, was selected and guarded with special care.[8]

Each family was directed to choose the Pesaḥ victim on the tenth day of the month; this is the first ceremony connected with the Passover that is prescribed in the Exodus narrative.[9] The regulation has been explained in different ways. It has been regarded as marking the end of a ten-day epact, the approximate excess of the days of the tropic year over the 354 days of a

[1] Num. 7:15–88.

[2] Lev. 9:3; the M.T. indicates that the calf was *ben šanah*, but this is not borne out by the LXX.

[3] Driver, op. cit., on Ex. 12:5 and Oesterley, *Sacrifices in Ancient Israel*, 104, conjecture that the preference for the male animal was due to his superior strength; this is improbable in view of the arguments advanced here. Dalman, op. cit. i. 268, suggests that male victims were offered instead of female because the latter were required for breeding.

[4] Dalman, op. cit. i. 268. It is probable, then, that *ben šanah* means 'born in that year'; this was the Jewish usage in later times, cf. LXX *'Ενιαύσιον*, at Ex. 12:5, *Mish. Parah* i. 4, *Pes.* ix. 7, Dhorme, *Évolution*, i. 211. This view is preferable to that of Gray, op. cit. 255, and id., *Sacrifice in the Old Testament*, 345 ff., and Dillmann, *Exodus*, on Ex. 12:5, who maintain that maturity rather than immaturity would be required and that the victim at the Pesaḥ was an animal which had lived through a whole year and was entering a second year. It is true that the latter usage is usual in modern Palestine, Curtiss, op. cit. 174, 215, and Dalman, op. cit. vi. 183 f., on Arab. حولى (see further the lexicons). This may, however, be under the influence of Islamic law. The Israelites certainly counted inclusively; compare Gen. 17:12 with Ex. 22:29, Lev. 12:3, 22:27. For the Samaritan usage, see p. 254 below.

[5] The female victim of Lev. 14:10 is the *ḥaṭṭa'th* of v. 19.

[6] Lev. 3:1, 6.

[7] Cook in Smith, *Religion*, 620.

[8] Ex. 12:6, *mišmereth*, cf. 16:23, 32, 34, Num. 19:9, and particularly 2 Sam. 20:3 where *mišmereth* is used of precautions against sexual intercourse; so *šmr*, 1 Sam. 21:5. Cf. the dedication of the ox for the Bouphonia at Magnesia, p. 119 above, and Harrison, *Themis*, 150 ff. Compare also the Arab practices of *taqlid* and *iš'ār*, Gaudefroy-Demombynes, *Pèlerinage*, 279, 286; for the modern practice in Palestine, Canaan, op. cit. 36.

[9] Ex. 12:3.

period of twelve lunations.[1] But if this were so, we should expect to find some formal celebration of the eleventh, not the tenth, day. Others have maintained that the month was divided into three parts of ten days each, analogous to the Egyptian decans.[2] There is, however, no evidence of such a time-division in Israel[3]—nor is there any celebration of the twentieth day of the month, as one would logically expect.[4] Finally, many scholars see this ceremony on the tenth day of the spring month as the beginning of a *tempus clausum* of eleven days at the Passover, extending from the tenth day to the end of the festival on the twenty-first day; they compare with it the duration of the New Year festival at Babylon.[5] True, the period from the tenth to the twenty-first day is not eleven but twelve days; there are, however, grounds for assigning a length of twelve days to the Babylonian festival also. But the apparent similarity between the Babylonian New Year and the Passover is not confirmed by an analysis of the Hebrew autumn festival, as is commonly assumed. The Day of Atonement on the tenth day of the month is itself, according to Jewish tradition, the end of a *tempus clausum* which begins with Rosh haShanah on 1st Tishri. It is not the beginning of a *tempus clausum*.

I have sought elsewhere to explain the function of the tenth day of the spring month differently. The Hebrews, I suggested, regarded the first nine days of the spring and autumn months as days of uncertainty. If the heliacal rising of a fixed star had not taken place before the tenth day, then it was necessary to intercalate a month. It was only on the tenth day of the spring month—and not sooner—that it was known whether it was permissible to begin preparations for the Passover.[6]

There is another explanation—which in no way detracts from the plausibility of this view, but arises out of the procedural preliminaries

[1] S. Gandz, 'Calendar of ancient Israel', *Homenaje a Millás-Vallicrosa*, 1954–6, i. 644. For a similar explanation for the duration of the New Year festival at Babylon in Nisan and at Uruk in Teshrit, see Langdon, op. cit. 107.

[2] So also in the Greek calendar. In Mesopotamia three constellations were observed in each lunation, see *Epic of Creation*, Tab. v (*ANET* 67*b*). For the belief of Moslems that the fates of the year are fixed on 10th Muḥarram, see Dalman, op. cit. i. 27, and cf. Lane, op. cit. 431.

[3] Except for an isolated example in Gen. 24:55, ימים או עשור, '(a few) days, at the least ten' (it is probably better to insert חדש before ימים, with Pesh., 'a month of days'; Pesh., however, omits או עשור), and 1 Sam. 25:38.

[4] Except Num. 10:11, 11:19. Moreover, no analogy should be drawn between the months of the schematic Egyptian civil calendar (twelve months of thirty days each, followed by an epact of five days) and the Hebrew months of 29–30 days. Little importance is attached to the tenth day in Babylonian cult; see Landsberger, op. cit. 96, and, for example, 127 f.

[5] So, for example, Hooke, *Origins*, 48. H. J. Kraus, *Gottesdienst in Israel*, 1954, 95, suggests that the celebration of 10th Tishri five days before the festival of Tabernacles is connected with the five epagomenal days of the solar year. But Tabernacles is celebrated by lunar, not solar, reckoning, and the difference should be approximately eleven, not five, days.

[6] See my article, *VT* vii, 1957, 270 ff.

for the festival. We have observed the significance of the number seven in Israel and the period of seven days as a period of transition before the Passover, as before other *rites de passage.*[1] Now, the unit of three days also marks a period of transition in Israel from one state to another—but with, on the whole, less far-reaching implications than that of seven days.[2] Tithes are offered every three years, but the more momentous Year of Release occurs in every seventh year.[3] In popular speech an epoch extended backwards three days to 'yesterday and the day before yesterday';[4] before this span of time lay an earlier and different epoch. Similarly—in this case looking forward to a new period—Moses required permission to travel a three days' journey in the Wilderness to celebrate a *ḥag.*[5]

It is in the relationship of a minor period of three days to a major period of seven days for the performance of ceremonies of ritual cleanness that we should perhaps seek the explanation of the rule that the Pesaḥ victim must be chosen on the tenth day of the month. There may have been such a minor period within a major period in the early ceremonial of the marriage week.[6] Both periods and their relation to each other appear clearly in the

[1] pp. 139 f. above.

[2] For the inferiority of 3 in relation to 7, see Job 1:2, 42:13, where Job has three daughters but seven sons.

[3] Deut. 14:28 f., against 15:1 ff. The meaning of Amos 4:4 f. seems to be that hypocrites bring tithes every three days, instead of the requisite three years. Perhaps also cf. Is. 16:14 against Ex. 21:2, Deut. 15:12.

[4] Heb. *temol šilšom.* Cf. the three days on the last of which the less holy offerings must be burned in the Temple, Lev. 7:16 ff., 19:6. There is an interval of three days before a covenant, Ex. 19:10 f., 15 f., cf. Ezra 8:32, before crossing the Jordan, Jos. 1:11, cf. Ezra 8:15, 21, before an assembly of the people, 2 Sam. 20:4, before an important decision, Est. 4:16, 1 Kings 12:5–12; cf. the stress on three in 1 Sam. 10:3. The Temple is visited by pilgrims three times a year, Ex. 23:14–17, 34:23, and prayers are offered three times a day, Ps. 55:18, Dan. 6:11, 14. See further Gen. 31:22, Jos. 2:16, Jud. 20:18 ff. (especially vv. 30 ff.), 1 Sam. 20:5, 2 Kings 20:5, 8, Hos. 6:2 (see J. J. Stamm, 'Eine Erwägung zu Hos 6:1–2', *ZAW* lvii, 1939, 266), Ezra 8:32, Neh. 2:11, 2 Chr. 20:25; cf. Ex. 2:2, 2 Sam. 13:38, and in the N.T., Matt. 12:40. See also P. Lambrechts, 'La "Résurrection" d'Adonis', *Mélanges Isidore Lévy*, 1955, 213; F. Nötscher, 'Zur Auferstehung nach drei Tagen', *Biblica*, xxxv, 1954, 313; and H. F. D. Sparks, 'Partiality of Luke for "Three"...', *JTS* xxxvii, 1936, 141. The significance of three days as an indefinite length of time is well argued by J. B. Bauer, 'Drei Tage', *Biblica*, xxxix, 1958, 354, but he overlooks the central point that the period of three days marks the transition to a new sacral period.

[5] Ex. 3:18, 5:1, 3, 8:23. Cf. the journeys of Abraham, Gen. 22:3–4, of the Israelites in the Wilderness, Num. 33:8, of Saul, 1 Sam. 9:20, 10:3, cf. Jonah 3:3. It is instructive to observe the replacement of 7 by 3 in later times, perhaps as a relaxation of severity; compare, for example, 2 Sam. 24:13 (7, 3, 3) with the parallel passage in 1 Chr. 21:12 (3, 3, 3). The opposite process is found in the tradition related in Burckhardt, *Travels in Arabia*, ii. 57 f., that the casting of seven stones at Mina was enacted by Muhammad to replace the casting of three stones enacted by Abraham; but see, on the other hand, Burckhardt, *Bedouins and Wahábys*, 151 n., 152 f., where a marriage is celebrated for three instead of the customary seven days, p. 177 below. Curtiss, op. cit. 179, reports that there must be an interval of three days before a *fedu* sacrifice may be offered after a death.

[6] Jud. 14:14, cf. p. 177 n. 7 below. For a similar practice in modern Palestine, cf. E. Pierotti, *Customs and Traditions of Palestine illustrating the Manners of the Ancient Hebrews*, 1864, 189 f., where the bride's father, we are told, sends her a gift three days after the wedding, and in the Lebanon, M. Safi, 'Mariage au Nord du Liban', *Anthropos*, xi–xii, 1917–18, 143,

regulations concerning the days of mourning. If the ritual on the third day had not been observed, the ritual on the seventh day was not valid.[1] So with the tenth day of the Passover month. The seven-day period of purification rites began on the eighth day of the month;[2] the victim was chosen on the third day of this period, on, that is, the tenth day of the month, and guarded against pollution until the hour of sacrifice arrived. The function of the tenth day arose, if this theory be correct, from rules of ritual cleanness—a constant motif at the New Year festival. Whether the practice goes back to early times is uncertain; it seems to have been abandoned by the first century—perhaps already by the epoch of the Deuteronomist.[3]

Among the rites of purification before a sacramental meal many societies include a period of fasting.[4] The autumn New Year festival in Israel, Tabernacles, is preceded by the fast of the Day of Atonement, Yom ha-Kippurim, on the tenth day of the month. On this solemn day the dominant role is taken by the High Priest—a feature that is characteristic of the general quality of the autumn, as opposed to the spring, festival; but it is the whole people who take part in the fast.[5] Fasting appears in only a

according to whom the newly married couple visit their parents on the third day after the wedding, and celebrate a feast on the seventh day after the wedding.

[1] Num. 19:12, 19. For a similar unit of three within seven, cf. the *ṭawaf* around the Ka'aba seven times, of which the first three are performed at a running pace; cf. Qur. ii. 192, according to which a penitential fast is to last three days during the pilgrimage, but seven days afterwards. For three days as a period of minor purification, cf. Ex. 19:11, 16; see also *Mish. 'Ab. Zarah* i. 1. The women taking part in the Greek Thesmophoria purified themselves for three days, Farnell, *Cults*, iii. 94 f.; we may note that at Syracuse this festival lasted ten days, ibid. 99—i.e. the combination of three days and seven days.

[2] pp. 32 f. and the references on p. 140 n. 4 above.

[3] See pp. 31 above and 207 and 211 below. If this theory is accepted, we must reject any parallel between the choosing of the Pesaḥ victim on the tenth day of the spring month and the Day of Atonement on the tenth day of the autumn month; the eighth day of the autumn month is a day of no obvious significance in historical times.

[4] Westermarck, 'Principles of Fasting', *Folklore*, xviii, 1907, 391 ff.; W. R. Smith, *Religion*, 434 f., 673; Frazer, *Golden Bough. Adonis Attis Osiris*, 1936, i. 272, 274; and see pp. 118, 119, and 123 above. Gaster, op. cit. 9 ff., argues cogently that ritual fasting is not simply the preparation of the body before a sacramental meal (as Smith, loc. cit.; Westermarck, op. cit. 392) or a precaution against demoniac forces that might enter the body (as R. Arbesmann, 'Fasting and Prophecy in Pagan and Christian Antiquity', *Traditio*, vii, 1949–51, 1), but a means of mortification. So Westermarck points out (loc. cit.) that fasting is associated with divine revelation, cf. Ex. 34:28, Deut. 9:9, Dan. 9:3. Gaster's contention is supported by the Biblical references to fasting at a time of repentance, 1 Sam. 7:6, 1 Kings 21:27, Jer. 36:9, Neh. 9:1 (on the day after the eight days of Tabernacles), Ezra 8:15, 21, 2 Chr. 20:3, Jonah 3:5, Ps. 35:13, cf. Jud. 20:26, Joel 1:14, 2:12, Est. 4:16, Judith 9:1. Four annual fasts are enumerated in Zech. 8:19—in Tammuz (cf. Ezek. 8:14), Ab, Tishri, and Tebet; Jud. 11:40 may refer to four fasts of one day each rather than one fast of the unusual length of four days. The fasts of Ab and Tishri are given an historical basis in Zech. 7:5 and 2 Kings 25:8, 25. But it is possible that they have their origin in popular ritual associated with fertility dances, Jud. 21:19 ff., cf. *Mish. Ta'an.* iv. 8. Josephus, *Ant.* v. ii. 12, states that these dances took place three times a year. For a list of Israelite and Jewish fasts, see A. W. Greenup, 'Fasts and Fasting', *Essays in Honour of the Very Rev. Dr. J. H. Hertz*, 1942, 203.

[5] Lev. 16:29, 23:27, Num. 29:7. The Moslem practice of fasting during the first ten days of Dhu 'lḤijjah may be a direct borrowing from Judaism; Wensinck, *Arabic New-Year*,

mild form at the Pesaḥ in later Jewish regulations. It lasts, appropriately, from the sacrifice of the evening *Tamid* which closed the ordinary sacrificial ritual on the fourteenth day until nightfall some hours later when the Pesaḥ formally began.[1]

All males who take part in the Pesaḥ meal—and not only heads of families—were required to wear a special costume.[2] This has been regarded by some scholars as simply the dress of nomads or as the symbolic imitation of the dress of a shepherd god; they have concluded that the regulation—and, indeed, the whole festival—belongs to what they term the nomadic phase of Israelite history.[3] This view is open to question. The wearing of a special costume is a practice common to the New Year festivals of other countries. We must, however, distinguish between forms of this practice. In Egypt and elsewhere it is only a sole representative of the nation who dons the ritual costume;[4] at the Pesaḥ every man is instructed to wear it. Nor was the Pesaḥ costume the ordinary festal attire worn by Israelites to mark the importance of a feast. The festal finery of the *ḥag* was restricted, according to the legend, to the women and children.[5] At the Pesaḥ, on

17 ff.; on the fast of the first ten days of Muḥarram, see Lane, op. cit., ch. xxiv. For a suggestion that the Moslem fast of Ramaḍan was derived from the fast of the Harranian pagans during the month of Adar, see Westermarck, op. cit. 415 f. See, however, on Moslem and Jewish fasts, G. Vajda, 'Jeûne musulman et jeûne juif', *HUCA* xii–xiii, 1937–8, 367.

[1] See Philo, *De Decalogo*, 13; *Mish. Pes.* x. 1; and p. 259 below. The fast of the firstborn on the eve of Pesaḥ is not old; see H. J. Zimmels, 'Nachtalmudische Fasttage', *Jewish Studies in Memory of George A. Kohut*, 1935, 602. There are traces of a fast of three days in Est. 4:16. The observance of 13th Adar as a fast may have been obscured by the victory over Nicanor on that day in 161 B.C.; it was thereafter treated as a day of rejoicing, 1 Macc. 7:34 ff., *Meg. Ta'an.* (see Lichtenstein, *HUCA* viii–ix, 1931–2, 279, 346), Josephus, *Ant.* XII. x. 5. Later its character as a fast returned, *BT Ta'an.* 18b, *R.H.* 18b; see, however, H. Malter, art. 'Purim', *JE*, and J. Rabbinowitz, *Mishnah Megillah*, 1931, 32 ff. The fast observed by Christians before Easter may be the echo of an Israelite fast before the Passover, see Jaubert, *Date de la Cène*, 83; it is more likely to be an independent Christian rite of commemoration. Cf. Arbesmann, op. cit. 41 ff., and S. Lowy, 'Motivation of Fasting in Talmudic Literature', *JJS* ix, 1958, 28. Some Moslems regard it as meritorious to fast on the day of 'Arafat until sunset, Westermarck, *Ritual and Belief in Morocco*, ii. 109, but against this Gaudefroy-Demombynes, *Pèlerinage*, 253. On 15th Sha'ban, on which some Moslems fast, see p. 148 n. 4 below.

[2] Ex. 12:11.

[3] So, for example, Dhorme, *Évolution*, 212. Cf. the wearing of costume in imitation of Dionysos at Attic festivals in the winter (rural Dionysia, Lenaia) and spring (greater Dionysia).

[4] Like the priest in Israel, Ex. 28:1 ff, Num. 20:26, &c. On this, see H. Riesenfeld, *Jésus transfiguré . . .*, 1947, ch. viii.

[5] Ex. 3:22, 11:2 f., 12:35, cf. 32:2 and p. 47 above. The mention of women and children in 3:22 seems to indicate a specific custom which is not contradicted by the more general wording of the other passages; see J. Morgenstern, 'Despoiling of the Egyptians', *JBL* lxviii, 1949, 1, who, however, regards the wearing of borrowed ornaments as a marriage usage and omits the reference to children in 3:22. The removal of ornaments in mourning, Ex. 33:4–6, is of interest; the verses are out of place there. See the note by C. A. Ben-Mordecai, 'Notes on Chapter 33 of Exodus', *JQR* xxxi, 1940–1, 407, who suggests, with good reason, that they belong to ch. 32. The term ויתנצלו, Ex. 33:6 (rather than ויתפרקו, 32:3), may be an indirect allusion to the manner in which the ornaments had been obtained, 3:22, 12:36.

the contrary, the men were intended all to look alike. An exact parallel—even to details of the costume—may be found in the *iḥram*, the dress worn by the Moslem on pilgrimage.[1] So, too, at the Greek spring festival of Anthesteria shrouds were worn.[2] The purpose was to disguise the individual, when he was in contact with the divine powers, and particularly at a time when the divine powers were thought to be fixing the fate of mortals during the year just beginning. It was wise for him to hide under a cloak of anonymity, perhaps to pretend that he was already dead. We may trace the same motif in the masks of the Saturnalia and in similar usages elsewhere at the turn of the year;[3] and in Jewish practice it has survived in the masks of Purim.[4] By the Compiler of the Pentateuch the Pesaḥ costume was associated with the journey out of Egypt, for it appears in juxtaposition with the regulation on haste, and the costume is that of men about to leave the cultivated regions for the desert.[5] But the following verse describes the judgements that God would inflict on the Egyptians at the Exodus. We may deduce that the costume of the Israelites, like the blood smeared upon the doorposts, would secure them against the evil that is abroad at the opening of a new year. This minimal dress is a prophylactic at the *rite de passage*.

There is another and more central feature of Purim which arises directly from Israelite conceptions of the significance of the spring New Year. The name Purim is probably derived from the 'lots'[6] which, according to the popular myth, decided the fate of men at the turn of the year. We have seen that a myth of the determination of the fates figured in the New Year rites in Mesopotamia, and was perhaps enacted in a ritual ceremony.[7] In the Book of Esther the festival of Purim is given an historical basis; it is said to have been instituted at Susa as late as the reign of Xerxes.

[1] Wensinck, *Some Semitic Rites of Mourning*, 63, who compares the dress in which Moslems are buried. In pre-Islamic times Arabs are said to have performed the rite naked; see further W. R. Smith, *Religion*, 451. According to Burckhardt, *Travels in Syria and the Holy Land*, 1822, 566, Beduins visiting the shrine of Moses at Jebel Musa on the feast day wear the *iḥram*.

[2] Harrison, *Prolegomena*, 32 ff.

[3] See A. Moret, *Mystères égyptiens*, 1913, 250. The licence given to slaves at New Year festivals which removes the distinction between master and servant (see pp. 119, 120, 121, and 123 above) may derive from the same notion; the slave acts as a 'changeling' during a period of danger for the master.

[4] For the connexion between Purim and the Passover, p. 239 below. But the masquerade at Purim may have been borrowed by Jews from their neighbours at a late period; see N. S. Doniach, *Purim*, 1933, 126 ff., 130 ff.

[5] Ex. 12:11; cf., for example, 1 Kings 18:46, 2 Kings 4:29, 9:1.

[6] Est. 3:7, 9:24, 26. See already G. Wildeboer, *Buch Esther* (K.A.T.), 1898, 173, for a summary of theories on the etymology of *pur*; and cf. J. Lewy, 'Feast of the 14th Day of Adar', *HUCA* xiv, 1939, 127; id., 'Old Assyrian *puru'um* and *pūrum*', *Revue Hittite et Asianique*, v, 1938–40, 117 ff.; F. J. Stephens, *Votive and Historical Texts from Babylonia and Assyria*, 1937, No. 73, and pl. xlv, gives an illustration of a *puru*. See further A. Bea, 'De origine vocis פור . . .', *Biblica*, xxi, 1940, 198.

[7] p. 122 above, and Hooke, *Origins*, 59.

That the festival was introduced into Palestine at a comparatively late time is certainly possible.[1] It may revolve around a myth of Ishtar and Marduk that was related at the New Year. Certainly it was a 'splintering' of the New Year festival of Nisan; and in the Mishnaic period, with increasing skill in calendar reckoning, it became customary to announce before Purim whether or not that year was embolismic.[2] The conception of the 'lots' at Purim a month before the Passover indicates that the myth of the fixing of the fates at the spring New Year was familiar also in Palestine. In later Jewish writings we are told that the destiny of man during the following year is decided at the New Year festival.[3] Not unrelated is the tradition that divine judgement is passed on mankind at the Passover through the state of the grain harvests.[4] It is customary for Jews in certain localities to play games of chance at the festivals of Rosh haShanah and Tabernacles.[5]

Another widespread New Year practice that may in early times have appeared among the Passover ceremonial but has survived in the later ceremonial of Purim is the presentation of gifts.[6] This practice, too, may have arisen from fear of the fates that were in the balance at the New Year, and a desire to forestall the envy of the divine powers. Tokens of special good fortune and happiness were distributed as the new season approached. We may perhaps find an echo of the practice—attached, and properly, to the Passover—in the presents given by the Egyptians to the Israelites

[1] See the Commentary by Wildeboer, op. cit., and the other works mentioned in Snaith, in Rowley, *Old Testament and Modern Study*, 105; a recent study is H. Ringgren, *Hohelied . . . Buch Esther übersetzt und erklärt*, 1958. A summary of theories on the origins of the Esther story is given by L. B. Paton, *Book of Esther* (I.C.C.), 1908, 77 ff.

[2] Cf. my article in *VT* vii, 1957, 297, and p. 239 below. We may note that the Peshiṭta of Est. 9:26 connects the name Purim with the Passover.

[3] *BT R.H.* 16b: 'R. Qruspedai said in the name of R. Yoḥanan, Three books are opened (in heaven) on Rosh haShanah . . .. The thoroughly righteous are inscribed forthwith and sealed for life, the thoroughly wicked for death. (But the fate of) the intermediate is held in suspense from Rosh haShanah to the Day of Atonement; if they deserve well they are (then) written for life, if they do not deserve well they are (then) written for death'; cf. *JT R.H.* i. 3 (fol. 57a), *BT B. Bathra* 10a. See also Mowinckel, *Psalmenstudien*, ii. 79. For the notion, see Dan. 7:10, *Mish. Ab.* i. 2, cf. Mal. 3:16, Is. 65:6, and Ex. 32:32 f., Neh. 13:14, &c.

[4] *Mish. R.H.* i. 2. Cf. the beliefs among Moslems about 10th Muḥarram, Dalman, op. cit. i. 27, and Lane, op. cit. 431. The same beliefs are found of 15th Sha'ban, which probably was exactly a month after (not, as Purim, a month before) the spring pilgrimage festival in pre-Islamic times; see p. 130 n. 2 above on the Moslem calendar and Wensinck, art. 'Sha'ban', *Encyclopaedia of Islam*.

[5] Dalman, op. cit. i. 442 ff. See also A. Marmorstein, 'Comparisons between Greek and Jewish Customs and Popular Usages', *Occident and Orient* (Gaster Anniversary Volume), 1936, 411 f. V. Christian, 'Zur Herkunft des Purim-Festes', *Alttestamentliche Studien F. Nötscher . . . gewidmet*, 1950, 33, sets out the reasons for regarding Purim as a New Year festival which are given also above. We need not, however, go as far as H. Schmoekel, *Heilige Hochzeit und Hoheslied*, 1956, 18 f., who seeks to trace the motif of a sacred marriage at Purim.

[6] Est. 9:19, 22. See pp. 117, 119, 120, 121, 123, and 125 above.

after the tenth plague;[1] it is in keeping with the sardonic humour of the narrator that Pharaoh should be obliged against his will to perform an act that would have normally been performed by the Israelites themselves. At a later time the practice was carried out also at the autumn festival in Israel. There, however, it was transferred, like much of the ritual that had at one time belonged to Tabernacles, to Rosh haShanah on the first day of the month.[2] For this, however, we may find another explanation. The autumn festival was, as we shall see, the celebration of the king's accession. It was customary formally to present gifts as tribute on that day, and this practice was doubtless of importance when the king was proclaimed afresh at each occasion of the autumn festival.[3]

A prominent feature of ancient New Year festivals in the Near East is the recital of epics of the Creation of the world and of human kind.[4] The account of creation or resurrection—accompanied perhaps by mimetic actions—was believed to quicken by sympathetic magic the processes of fertility at a time when the destinies of the new year were being fixed.[5] To this we may attribute the survival of several ancient epics of Creation in the Near East. The association of the New Year with Creation is reflected in the Jewish belief that the world was formed in either the spring or the autumn.[6] But the formal recital of their epics at the New Year was an old-established custom among the Israelites. The cycle of reading the Torah, which opens with the story of Creation, began with the close of the Tabernacles week; the practice derives authority from the Pentateuch itself—although there the cycle is, significantly, one of seven years.[7] Parallel to the annual cycle was a triennial cycle, and this seems to have commenced on the first Sabbath in Nisan.[8] The recital of certain psalms was, as we shall observe later, an integral part of the services of both the Passover and Tabernacles. The psalms were accompanied by music.[9]

It was a short step from the recital of epics of Creation at the New Year

[1] Ex. 12:36. See especially vv. 32 f., with the significant words, '. . . bless me also . . . for they said, We be all dead men'; ברכה has the meaning of 'gift', Gen. 33:11, Jos. 15:19, Jud. 1:15, 1 Sam. 25:27, 30:26, 2 Kings 5:15. In 1 Sam. 6:6 ff. the Ark is sent away accompanied by gifts.

[2] Neh. 8:10, 12, cf. 8:2.

[3] 1 Sam. 10:24, 27; and possibly 1 Kings 10:25. Perhaps cf. the giving of the *lulabh*, itself a symbol of growth, *Mish. Suk.* iv. 4.

[4] pp. 122, 123, and 124 above.

[5] See, for example, Hooke, *Babylonian and Assyrian Religion*, 1953, 59; R. A. Parker, *Calendars of Ancient Egypt*, 1950, 47, who points out, however, that evidence for this usage in Egypt is preserved only in late classical writers.

[6] See p. 27 above on Philo; *BT R.H.* 10b, 12a, 27a, *JT R.H.* i. 1 (fol. 56b).

[7] Deut. 31:10 ff., cf. Neh. 8:1 ff., where the recital takes place on 1st Tishri.

[8] *BT Meg.* 29b. See A. Büchler, 'The Reading of the Law . . .', *JQR* v, 1893, 420, vi, 1894, 1; J. Mann, *The Bible . . . in the Old Synagogue*, i, 1940; and, most recently, A. Guilding, *The Fourth Gospel and Jewish Worship*, 1960, 6 ff.

[9] See Is. 30:29, and pp. 215, 227, and 259 below.

festival to the recital of the story of the birth of the community that performed the ritual. At the pre-Islamic *ḥajj* a prominent feature was the boasting by poets of the heroic feats of the ancestors of their tribe.[1] A similar practice was known to the Israelites, and from ancient times. Already in the narrative of the Exodus it is ordained that each year the service of the Passover must be accompanied by the recital of the story of the Exodus.[2] The usage survived to the epoch of the Mishnah, and is maintained in the *haggadah*.[3]

That the New Year ritual in Israel as in other peoples of the Near East[4] included also dancing may be readily assumed. There are no factual grounds, however, for holding, with Pedersen,[5] that the dance of Miriam at the Red Sea was re-enacted annually after the Exodus;[6] nor is the dancing on special occasions by Israelites or non-Israelites in Canaan a conclusive argument for regarding dancing as an annual rite at the primitive Passover.[7] The annual days of fasting were, it is true, the occasion for dances, perhaps with some fertility motif.[8] The dancing in the Temple at Tabernacles which is attested in the Mishnah was evidently to induce rain,[9] and this has parallels in Canaanite practices.[10] It cannot be shown with certainty that dances were performed at the spring festival, which stood in different relationship to the seasons of nature—but this is possible.

The New Year festival may have been accompanied, in Israel as elsewhere in the Near East, by licentious behaviour.[11] There are not sufficient

[1] Wellhausen, *Reste*, 90, cf. Burckhardt, *Travels in Arabia*, i. 179. For a not dissimilar practice in Greece and its possible association with the New Year, F. M. Cornford, in Harrison, *Themis*, 257.

[2] Ex. 12:24–27, referring to the Pesaḥ, 13:5 ff., referring to the Passover week, 12:14, referring either to the Pesaḥ or the Passover—it is unnecessary to decide which, since both form, I suggest, a single festival. The same motif of commemoration recurs in the laws on the dedication of firstborn and firstlings, Ex. 13:14 ff.; for the association of this with the Exodus, p. 183 below. Note the use of Heb. *zkr* in the context of the Exodus Passover, Ex. 12:14, 13:3, 9.

[3] See p. 260 below.

[4] pp. 118, 119, and 125 above. On the function of dancing as a ritual, see Harrison, op. cit. 23 ff., 43 ff., 194, and especially 201.

[5] Op. cit. iii–iv. 408 ff. So Bentzen, *Introduction*, ii. 79, regards the recital of the Passover story as an epic, not a dramatic representation.

[6] Cf. Ex. 15:20; for similar songs and dances of triumph, Jud. 5:1, 11:34, 1 Sam. 18:6. See also Morgenstern, *JBL* lxviii, 1949, 21.

[7] p. 98 above on *psḥ* and dancing.

[8] See p. 145 n. 4 above.

[9] *Mish. Suk.* v. 4, *Tos. Suk.* iv. 2, cf. 1 Kings 18:22 ff.

[10] For a possible tradition of dancing on the Passover, see the citation in L. Ginzberg, *Legends of the Jews*, 1946, vi. 213 n. 135, where the maidens of Shiloh are said to have been seized on the Passover (cf. Jud. 21:19–23). The tradition is, however, late. For modern usages, see Dalman, *Palästinischer Diwan*, 1901, 270, R. Patai, 'Dancing of Maidens on the Day of Atonement', *Edoth*, i, 1945, 55, ii, 1946–7, 186, and I. Garbell, 'Dances of Maidens in Ramallah on Palm Sunday', *Edoth*, ii, 1946–7, 111. For dancing at a circumcision ceremony, cf. M. W. Hilton-Simpson, 'Some Notes on the Folklore of the Algerian Hills and Desert', *Folklore*, xxxiii, 1922, 184. For a general treatment of dancing and leaping to encourage the harvest to grow high, see Frazer, *Golden Bough. Magic Art*, i. 137.

[11] Ex. 32:5; see pp. 120, 121, and 123 above.

grounds for assuming that a sacred marriage was enacted. In the Jerusalem cult priestesses played no official part as in those countries where that ritual was practised. The *qedešoth* were not recognized at the Temple; the serving women of Shiloh seem to have had no more than a menial role.[1] There is no reason to connect the tents of the festival of Tabernacles with the marriage tent; indeed, this festival is associated rather with the permanent house of the deity at Jerusalem. And on the Day of Atonement, when the role of the High Priest more nearly approaches the central role of the kings of Mesopotamia and the Hittites, the ritual seems far removed from that of a sacred marriage.[2]

Whether or not dancing took place at the primitive Israelite New Year festival, it is certain that the rites included sacred processions. This is, as we have observed, one of the features of New Year festivals that are most widespread throughout the area of the Near East.[3] It may be the basic significance of the term *ḥag*;[4] it is a prominent—perhaps the most prominent—single rite of the *ḥajj*, both pre-Islamic and Islamic.[5] In Israel it survived in late historical times, and only in the autumn festival, where the procession with *lulabh* and torches and singing and music are probably to be associated with the equinox and the course of the sun through the heavens.[6] But the theme may be reflected in the story of the siege of Jericho; the Israelites, having performed the Pesaḥ, are said to have made a circuit for seven days around the city, bearing the Ark and blowing upon their horns.[7]

The sacred procession in New Year festivities of the ancient Near East culminated in the exodus from the city or the cultivated regions to the uninhabited desert.[8] This may be a reflection of the change of seasons, when nature begins to revive after the inclement weather. The forces of destruction have triumphed; wild hordes from the desert enter the city

[1] Gen. 38:21 f., Deut. 23:18, Hos. 4:14, cf. *qedešim*, 1 Kings 15:12, 2 Kings 23:7, Job 36:14, and the collective sing., 1 Kings 14:24, 22:47; 1 Sam. 2:22.

[2] Lev. 16; see p. 156 below. Against the view taken here see, however, in particular Riesenfeld, op. cit., ch. x.

[3] See pp. 117 f., 119, 122 f., 124, and 125 above.

[4] p. 129 above.

[5] Wellhausen, *Reste*, 109; Lammens, *Arabie occidentale*, 105 f. See also Nabih Amin Faris, op. cit. 4, 28, 36.

[6] *Mish. Suk.* iv. 5, v. 4–5, *Mid.* ii. 5–6, cf. Josephus, *Ant.* III. x. 4, XIII. xiii. 5. See perhaps also Neh. 12:27 ff. on the dedication of the walls of Jerusalem, and Pss. 24, 48, 68:25–27 (E.V. 68:24–26), 84:8 (E.V. 84:7). On the processions at Tabernacles, see Pedersen, op. cit. iii–iv. 424; for torch rituals at the New Year festival at Uruk and in Egypt, see Aalen, op. cit.

[7] Jos. 6:3 ff. See p. 238 below.

[8] See p. 137 above. For the uncultivated region around the city in Palestine, cf. Deut. 21:1 ff.; in Ugar. the cultivated field (*šd*) is on the edge of the desert (*mdbr*), Gordon, *Ugaritic Manual*, 1955, 145 (52, l. 68), 185 f. (ll. 104 f., 193 f.). An analysis of the contrast between desert and sown is found in P. Birot and J. Dresch, *La Méditerranée et le Moyen Orient*, ii, 1956, 304 ff.

and the Temple is sacked. Then the citizens go out to the desert to seek the powers of vegetation, just as the goddess of the myth, in its varied forms, went out with her faithful companion to seek the dead god and restore him to life.[1]

In the Bible little trace of the myth has survived,[2] though it cannot have been unknown to the Israelites. But the ritual exodus was certainly observed. Perhaps, then, we should look elsewhere for its explanation—in the desire to hasten the autumn rains by some magical process,[3] or the feeling that at the new year it was right to leave the artificial luxuries of the city for the simple existence of the desert.[4] However this may be, it was only in the autumn that the exodus was perpetuated in Israelite ritual, like the sacred processions. It appears in two forms. In the formal, complex rites of the Day of Atonement, the High Priest, on behalf of the people, makes atonement[5] and sends a substitute animal out into the desert to carry away the iniquities of all Israel.[6] At the festival of Tabernacles, on the other hand, the ceremony retains its popular basis. The people leave their houses to live in booths[7] which must, according to the ruling of the Mishnah, be open to the sky.[8] At the spring New Year festival, however, the rite has been preserved only as the theme of the Exodus legend. Moses requests Pharaoh to permit the Israelites to go into the desert to perform a *ḥag*—at a distance, it should be remarked, of three days' journey.[9] The people go forth as a military host, to live in tents in the Wilderness,[10] and with this begins a new

[1] See A. Haldar, *Notion of the Desert in Sumero-Accadian and West-Semitic Religions*, 1950. On the notion of the desert as the underworld, see M. Witzel, *Tammuz-Liturgien und Verwandtes*, 1935, x; the underworld may also be the wild, uninhabited mountain, as, for example, among the Hittites, Furlani, op. cit. 234 and n. 4. For the Egyptian attitude towards the desert, see *ANET* 9 *a*, *b*, 11*a*.

[2] In spite of the attempt by Haldar, op. cit. 43, to trace the motif in the Psalms and the Prophets. See also Pedersen, op. cit. iii–iv. 436 ff.

[3] The usage is observed in modern Palestine in time of drought, Canaan, *JPOS* vi, 1926, 143 ff., 157, and Dalman, op. cit. i. 134 ff.

[4] See E. L. Ehrlich, *Kultsymbolik im Alten Testament und im nachbiblischen Judentum*, 1959, 54.

[5] See p. 162 below on *kpr*.

[6] Lev. 16, cf. 23:27 ff., Num. 29:7 ff. Note the mention of booths in the desert at the Day of Atonement service in *Mish. Yoma* vi. 4 ff.

[7] Lev. 23:41 ff., especially v. 43, Neh. 8:17. The same motif appears in the festival of Ḥanukkah near the winter solstice, 2 Macc. 1:9, 18 ff.; see my article in *VT* vii, 1957, 298 n. 5. This may be due, however, to direct Greek influence. For tents at a winter festival in Greece, see p. 120 above.

[8] The later laws of Tabernacles are given in *Mish. Suk.* i and *Tos. Suk.* i. See also Wensinck, *Arabic New-Year*, 31. Kraus, op. cit., maintains that the feast of Tabernacles arose out of the Israelite practice of assembling at the Tent of Meeting both in the Wilderness and later in Canaan at Shiloh (Jos. 18) and Shechem (Jos. 24) and apparently once every seven years; cf. Deut. 31:10 ff., and see Alt, *Kleine Schriften zur Geschichte des Volkes Israel*, 1953, i. 329 ff., and id., 'Zelte und Hütten', in *Alttestamentliche Studien F. Nötscher . . . gewidmet*, 1950, 18. But this does not explain why the booths are always to be outside the city, or at least outside the houses—but not at the shrine—nor why the festival is traditionally celebrated by families.

[9] Ex. 5:3, &c.; see pp. 43 ff. above. On the significance of the unit of three days, see p. 144 above.

[10] Ex. 12:17, 41, 51, cf. p. 137 and n. 14 above.

chapter in the history of the nation. Why the popular practice of dwelling in booths survived only at the autumn I shall explain on a later page.[1]

On the occasion of this ceremony the people must have a leader. The New Year's day in the Near East was the day of the king's accession, and the reigning monarch was proclaimed afresh at each successive New Year. The myth–ritual complex of some communities went farther. The king was the champion of his people, even their personification. His powers of virility were to be renewed with the renewal of nature; and when the fates were to be propitiated, he was the scapegoat.[2]

In Israel the figure of a king does not appear before the settlement in Canaan. But already in the reigns of Solomon and Jeroboam I—if not under Saul and David—the king plays a leading part in the celebration of the *ḥaggim*,[3] and we may deduce that the king motif at the New Year ritual was familiar in Israel. Whether we can detect conceptions of the divinity of the king, as Mowinckel and other scholars have claimed to show in their studies on the Psalms in the New Year liturgy,[4] may be doubted. Certainly the Israelites did not believe, as did their neighbours, that the deity required annual renewal of his powers.[5] But we have remarked that the king formally ascended the throne at the New Year. Among the ceremonies that marked that occasion was perhaps a reluctance to put prisoners to death;[6] we have seen the not dissimilar practice of granting a prisoner a pardon at the New Year elsewhere in the Near East. Another ceremony that marked the accession of a king in Israel was the solemn blowing of trumpets; and this was incorporated in the ritual of Rosh haShanah and the Day of Atonement.[7] Eerdmans has interpreted the practice as intended to frighten

[1] p. 179 below.

[2] Among the numerous studies on this subject may be noted here Pedersen, op. cit. iii–iv. 429 ff.; Gadd, *Ideas of Divine Rule in the Ancient East*, 1948, ch. 2; J. de Fraine, *Aspect religieux de la royauté israélite*, 1954, 285 ff.; Widengren, *Sakrales Königtum*, 1955; A. R. Johnson, *Sacral Kingship*, 1955; Hooke, *Myth, Ritual, and Kingship*, 1958; and, most recently, K. H. Bernhardt, *Das Problem der altorientalischen Königsideologie im Alten Testament*, 1961.

[3] pp. 215 and 218 below.

[4] See the summary by Cazelles, 'Nouvel An en Israël', *Dict. Bib. Suppl.*, and Bernhardt, op. cit. Engnell regards Moses as an Israelite 'Ur-König'; see the analysis by Bentzen, 'Bemerkungen über neuere Entwicklungen in der Pentateuchfrage', *Archiv Orientální*, xix, 1951, 228.

[5] So also Pedersen, op. cit. iii–iv. 441 f., and Mowinckel, in *Regalità sacra* (VIII Congresso internazionale di storia delle Religioni), 1955, 289.

[6] 1 Sam. 11:12 f., cf. 1 Kings 1:50, but see p. 242 below. Note the interval of seven days in 1 Sam. 10:8; cf. p. 177 below.

[7] Lev. 23:24, Num. 29:1; cf. Lev. 25:9 of Yom haKippurim as the opening of the Jubilee year (when, it may be noted, slaves are released—cf., for a later period, *BT R.H.* 8b). These passages have the term *herī'*; on the other hand, Num. 10:2 ff. on the proclamation of the new moon has *tq'*. LXX in Num. 29:1 renders *teru'ah* as σημασία. Mowinckel, *Psalmenstudien*, ii. 81 f., cites Ps. 47:6 (E.V. 47:5), 98:6, and 81:4 (E.V. 81:3) as referring to the proclamation of the king; it should be noted, however, that only the first two passages have *herī'*—on the third, see already p. 136 n. 1 above. P. Humbert, *Terou'a. Analyse d'un rite biblique*, 1946, holds that the *teru'ah* is frequently the call to war

away evil spirits while the powers of good were proclaiming the destinies of the new year.[1] Such a theory would equate improbably the disciplined ceremony of trumpets on a sacred occasion with the frenzied banging of pots and pans in other societies; if the latter had ever been a motif at the Israelite New Year, it must have long been superseded by the time that the Monarchy was established in Israel.[2] We find an identical term for the ceremonial blowing of the trumpets at the proclamation of the king[3] (and at the opening of battle when the king went at the head of his army[4]), on the one hand, and the same rite at the Israelite autumn festivals, on the other. The term is used still in the Mishnah to describe the blowing of trumpets on the second day of Tabernacles;[5] it is perhaps a reminder of the times when the king ascended his throne at that festival.

The king presides over the ritual of the *ḥaggim*, but throughout Israelite history it appears to be Tabernacles at which is the royal festival *par excellence*.[6] True, there is a statement on a ceremonial blowing of trumpets in the spring; but this is in a comparatively late text, and it takes place seven days before Purim, not before the Passover—like other secondary ritual of the spring New Year festival it had moved to the full moon of the twelfth month.[7] At the Passover it is not the king but the heads of families who play the decisive part; and they represent the people. The autumn festival is the festival of formal authority; the spring festival is the festival of the people. The contrast is, as we shall see, constant throughout the history of Israel.[8]

or the acclamation of Yahweh as king. There was, according to Humbert, a 'spiritualization' of its use after the Exile. Important are the comments of Gray, *Numbers* (I.C.C.), on Num. 10:9 f.

[1] See the comment in Gray, *Sacrifice*, 304.

[2] But note the formal ceremonies connected with the sacred drum in Babylonia, *ANET* 334*b*, for use on the occasion of an eclipse. The special associations of the *teruʿah* give it, however, a different significance.

[3] 1 Sam. 10:24, cf. Num. 23:21; but in 1 Kings 1:39, 2 Kings 9:13, 11:14 we find the general term *tqʿ*. In Num. 10:3 ff. the term *tqʿ* is used both in a general sense and with a special connotation (especially v. 7). There is complete interchange between *tqʿ* and *heriʿ* in the Qumran text *War*, i. 11, iii. 1 ff., vii. 2 ff., xvi. 4 f., &c.

[4] Num. 10:9, 31:6, Amos 1:14, &c. (see the remarks of M. Bič, 'Bet'el—le sanctuaire du roi', *Archiv Orientální* (Hrozný Festschrift), xvii/1, 1949, 58); so also at the foundation of the Temple, Ezra 3:11 ff.

[5] *Mish. Suk.* v. 4. Trumpets are used also for summoning the rains, *Mish. Taʿan.* i. 6, ii. 3 ff., *BT Taʿan.* 22b; cf. Büchler, *Types of Jewish-Palestinian Piety*, 1922, 231 f.

[6] There is, however, one isolated indication that the royal accession may have been at either New Year festival. A comparison of 2 Sam. 2:11, 5:5 with 1 Kings 2:11, 1 Chr. 29:27 shows a striking discrepancy in the length of David's reign that may be explained in this way.

[7] See the extract from *Meg. Taʿan.*, pp. 32 f. above.

[8] pp. 156 f. below.

5

THE PRIMITIVE PASSOVER

THOSE aspects of the Passover that we have treated in the preceding chapter find their analogy in the general pattern of New Year festivals in the Near East. The aspects that will be treated in the present chapter do not appear to have exact parallels outside Israel. More than that, even within the framework of Israelite religion, these aspects of the Passover are peculiar to the spring festival; they are not shared with the autumn festival of Tabernacles. This does not mean that the Passover was not a New Year ceremony. On the contrary, all these minutiae of ritual conform fully to the spirit and practice of that annual turning-point in the life of the people.

The reason for the peculiarity of the ritual to be discussed here may be briefly explained. At the new year primitive man—like, indeed, his modern counterpart—is preoccupied with certain thoughts almost to the point of obsession. The events of the passing year are assessed, the coming year is awaited with mingled hopefulness and anxiety. There is a desire for continuity in the orderly benevolence of nature. It is necessary to approach and, if possible, to exert pressure upon the powers that govern the order of the universe, and to maintain friendly relations with them. Each society invokes its own deity, who is himself those powers—or, according to another notion, who can intercede with those powers. The tokens which bind the society to its deity are displayed. Ritual cleanness is scrupulously observed.

These conceptions underlie the usages that we have surveyed in the preceding chapter. The ritual is directed towards the special deity; it must be held on a fixed date and at a certain shrine or shrines. It is preceded by ceremonies of purification lasting seven days and including a fast, and all who participate, including the animal victims, are ritually clean. The climax is an assembly attended by all male adults, and this assembly is regarded as mustering for military as well as for religious purposes; the people are therefore divided into tribes and the tribes subdivided into families. The people are led by a chief, whose rank is publicly proclaimed or confirmed by festal processions and solemn blasts upon the trumpet. It is believed that at this time destinies are fixed for the coming year; men wear anonymous garb, they exchange gifts. There is a recital of the myths of Creation and the legends of the beginning of the tribe, perhaps there is also ritual dancing, and finally there is an exodus into the desert.

Those rites are common—in varying degree and form—to the whole region of the Near East. But there is a fundamental difference of approach between the Passover and the New Year festivals of Egyptians, Babylonians, and Hittites; we have seen this already in the preceding chapter and it will be yet more prominent in the present chapter. Among those peoples the whole vigour of the New Year festival was concentrated in the person and actions of an acknowledged representative of the entire community. Such was the case, I have suggested, with the Israelite autumn festival too. To Rosh haShanah and the Day of Atonement had been transferred much of the ceremonial that had earlier been performed at the autumn full moon. But in this ceremonial the people played no active part; they abstained from work on Rosh haShanah[1] and they both fasted and abstained from work on the Day of Atonement.[2] It was the priests, however, and particularly the High Priest, who performed the rites. It was the High Priest who, according to the ritual preserved in the Mishnah, entered the innermost shrine and pronounced the special name of the deity; and precautions were taken to ensure that the representative of the community at this fateful moment should be in sound health and wakeful, and wear the insignia of his office. It was the High Priest who performed the rite of substitution on the Day of Atonement, when the sins of the whole people were imposed upon an animal, and at his command the animal was thrust into the desert.[3]

At what point in the history of Israel did the autumn festival acquire this formal character? We cannot answer the question with certainty. Complex Temple ceremonial was practised, we have seen, at the New Year festivals of Mesopotamia and among the Hittites from an early date; there is therefore no reason why in Israel, too, analogous ritual should not be early—that is, pre-Exilic—rather than late.[4] Indeed, this was no more than the logical outcome of the fact that Tabernacles, rather than the Passover, was the festival of the royal accession. It had acquired that quality as early as the beginning of the reign of Jeroboam I—probably earlier, since this was already then the product of well-established tradition.[5] In the course of time the festival of Tabernacles lost much of its formal ritual to Rosh haShanah and the Day of Atonement. Most of the ritual that re-

[1] Lev. 23:24 f., Num. 29:1.

[2] Lev. 16:29, 23:27 ff., Num. 29:7.

[3] Ex. 30:10, Lev. 16, *Mish. Yoma*; see S. Landesdorfer, *Studien zum biblischen Versöhnungstag*, 1924, and cf. Riesenfeld, op. cit. 21 ff. The ritual has points of close resemblance with the New Year ritual at Babylon, notably in the special dress and the confession of the High Priest (at Babylon the king) and the removal of the substitute animal from the community. The Hittite practice of driving a ram into enemy territory when disease appeared to threaten the camp, Goetze, in *ANET* 347*b*, is similar in general character; nevertheless, it was performed only when the need arose, not annually.

[4] I here diverge from the view expressed in my article, *VT* vii, 1957, 277 ff.

[5] 1 Kings 12:32 f.; see *VT* vii, 1957, 257.

mained had popular appeal—the processions with the *lulabh*, the dancing with torches, the exodus from houses to tents, the offering of firstfruits.[1] It was a popular festival by the time of Josiah—if Deuteronomy is to be ascribed to the period of that monarch.[2] But it did not lose its association with the royal accession—until Israel abandoned all hope of national independence with the destruction of the Temple.[3]

The Passover, on the other hand, was a popular festival always. From the beginnings of its history—according to the Compiler, before the settlement in Canaan—a prominent part was taken at the Pesaḥ by the heads of families, most of whom were, of course, laymen; and they were actively supported by all the adult males of the nation.

There is a significant difference in procedure between the primitive Pesaḥ and all other sacrifices in the Israelite calendar. With other sacrifices at which the flesh of the victim was eaten, a portion was set aside under the ordinance for the priest, and the rest was eaten by the celebrants. At the Pesaḥ nothing was given to the priests, all was eaten by the celebrants. Indeed, the priests themselves slew and ate their own Pesaḥ victims. This difference between the Pesaḥ and other sacrifices is capable of ready explanation. The regulations of the Israelite Temple prescribe that the portions reserved for the officiating priest at an 'eaten' sacrifice were his due in return for manipulating the blood.[4] At the primitive Pesaḥ the blood was handled by the heads of families who slew the victims, even if they were laymen, and they and their families were therefore entitled to all the flesh.

To state the general procedure in this way is, however, to present the conclusion of the proposition without fully formulating the premisses. There were occasions on which, it appears, laymen slaughtered the sacrificial victim, but did not manipulate the blood.[5] There seem even to have been occasions on which—if we may regard the text as more precise than it may in fact be—laymen not only slaughtered the victim, but also poured out its blood.[6] None of these occasions, however, is prescribed with the precision of the ritual at the primitive Pesaḥ.

The full significance of the blood ritual at the Pesaḥ may be appreciated only from a study of its details. Some of the blood was allowed to fall into

[1] See the ritual in *Mish. Suk.*
[2] Cf. Deut. 16:13 ff.
[3] Cf. p. 215 below.
[4] For example, Lev. 7:32 f., cf. 7:8, 14.
[5] Lev. 1:5, 11 (burnt offering), 3:2, 8, 13 (peace offering), 4:15 (sin offering by an elder), 4:23 f. (sin offering by a ruler), 4:29, 33 (sin offering by one of the common people), 7:28 ff., 17:3 ff. (peace offering). In most of these passages LXX and Sam. have sing. for M.T. pl.; the implication may be that it was the priests, not the laymen, who slaughtered the victim—at the period when the Version was written.
[6] Deut. 15:21–23 (firstlings).

a basin.[1] What happened to the rest of the blood we are not told, although obviously it had the same sanctity as all sacrificial blood. It must be assumed, then, that it is the use of the blood in the basin that is vital to this part of the ceremony. Into this blood was dipped[2] a bunch of hyssop, and with it the blood was applied to the lintel and the two doorposts of the dwelling-places.[3]

Hyssop is employed in two Temple ceremonies of symbolic cleansing from ritual uncleanness.[4] The first is the cleansing of the leper and the leper's house, as soon as the disease appears to be no longer contagious. A clean bird is killed in a manner that guards against permanent contagion.[5] Another clean, living bird, cedar wood, scarlet, and hyssop are then dipped[2] into the blood, some of the blood is sprinkled seven times[6] upon the leper or his house, and the living bird is then released.[7] This ritual bears resemblance to that of the Day of Atonement[8] in the sevenfold sprinkling of the blood and the release of a substitute animal to carry away the uncleanness.[9] The hyssop is an aspergillum.[10] Its effectiveness is demonstrated by the fact that the priest is not required to perform ritual ablution after carrying out this ceremony.

[1] Heb. *saph*, Ex. 12:22, cf. Zech. 12:2, &c. The word may also be rendered 'threshold'; so LXX (p. 53 above) and Vulg., see *Mekhilta*, in loc.; Eerdmans, *Alttestamentliche Studien*, iii, 1910, 119, A. M. Honeyman, 'Hebrew סַף, "Basin, Goblet"', *JTS* xxxvii, 1936, 56 f.; and Trumbull, *Threshold Covenant*, 206 ff. It is preferable to interpret as 'basin', since it is probable that a receptacle is meant, whether it was the threshold or a vessel. In Ex. 24:6 ff., where the ritual has some resemblance to the Pesaḥ (see pp. 160 n. 7 and 165 n. 4 below), the blood is collected in pails. For the use of pails at the Pesaḥ in later times, cf. *Mish. Pes.* v. 5 f.

[2] Heb. *ṭbl*.

[3] Ex. 12:22. It is not possible to argue from the word *bayith* here that the reference is to house rather than to tent; Heb. בית may be used of 'tent', e.g. Gen. 27:15, like Arab. بيت.

[4] See also Ps. 51:9 (E.V. 51:7) and Hebr. 9:19. This plant has been identified with wild marjoram and Arab. *ṣa'tar*, cf. I. Löw, *Flora der Juden*, ii, 1924, 72; G. M. Crowfoot and L. Baldensperger, *From Cedar to Hyssop*, 1932; J. Jeremias, *Passahfeier der Samaritaner*, 1932, 89; and R. C. Thompson, *Dictionary of Assyrian Botany*, 1949, 74 ff., but the identification is disputed, S. R. Driver, *Exodus*, on Ex. 12:22; Morgenstern, 'Two Ancient Israelite Agricultural Festivals', *JQR* viii, 1917–18, 48 n. 7. Trumbull, op. cit. 214, regards the hyssop as a female symbol. It evidently is an unimpressive plant, and the 'hyssop that springeth out of the wall' is contrasted with the cedar in 1 Kings 5:13 (E.V. 4:33); the contrast may lie in the superficial roots of the former and the height and stability of the latter.

[5] An earthen vessel is used, and the bird is killed over running, not stagnant, water; for the latter, see Deut. 21:4 and cf. P. Reymond, *L'Eau . . . et sa signification dans l'A.T.*, 1958, 228.

[6] Note the significance of the number seven; p. 139 above.

[7] Lev. 14:2 ff.

[8] Lev. 16:20 ff.

[9] The motif of scarlet in the leprosy ritual is found also in the ritual of the Day of Atonement, *Mish. Yoma* iv. 2; a fillet of red wool is tied to the head of the scapegoat, and another around the neck of the goat to be slaughtered. Red is common in rites of exorcism and substitution; cf. the red heifer, p. 159 below, and the texts in *ANET* 335*b*, 349*a*, 350*b*, 352*a*, 353*a*, and for modern practices Dalman, op. cit. i. 429 f. See Thompson, *Semitic Magic: its Origins and Development*, 1908, 160, 171, and Hooke, 'Theory and Practice of Substitution', *VT* ii, 1952, 8 f.

[10] Crowfoot and Baldensperger, loc. cit. Hyssop was used in this way because it does not allow the blood to congeal; see art. 'אזוב', *Enṣiqlopediah Miqra'it* (in Heb.).

The ritual of the 'red heifer' is more complex. That animal is killed; after a sevenfold sprinkling of its blood, it is wholly reduced to ashes outside the camp, and with it cedar wood, scarlet, and hyssop. The officiants perform ritual ablution.[1] But although the hyssop has been destroyed, it continues to act as a link in the chain of contacts. If a person is unclean through touching the dead, he is sprinkled on the third and seventh days with running water mixed with the ashes. The rite is carried out by a clean person, evidently not a priest, and his medium for the sprinkling is a second bunch of hyssop, dipped[2] into the water. This hyssop presumably derives its power from the hyssop whose ashes were mixed with those of the heifer.[3] The person who sprinkles the 'waters of separation' is required to perform ritual ablution.[4]

It is clear from these ceremonies that the hyssop in Israelite ritual played the part of a 'lightning conductor', which, partially at least, protected the officiant from the danger of contact with the sacred/unholy. This was its role also at the Pesaḥ. The use of a bunch of hyssop by the lay officiant (like the priest at the leprosy rites) exempted him from the need to undergo ritual ablution after performing the blood ceremony.

An examination of the Hebrew text of the Exodus Pesaḥ indicates further that the use of hyssop was not the only precaution against contact with the sacred/unholy. In one account it is stated that some of the blood is to be taken and 'put' upon the lintel and doorposts. This term 'put'[5] is normally employed in descriptions of ritual blood-smearing. But in a more detailed account of the ceremony the officiants are instructed to 'cause some of the blood . . . to touch'[6] the lintel and doorposts. The same verb occurs in two other passages in the Bible—in the obscure narrative of the circumcision of Moses, where also blood is involved,[7] and in the vision of Isaiah in which the prophet's sin is 'purged'[8] after his lips have been touched with the burning coal from the altar.[9] The verb describes a movement of brushing lightly and swiftly over some surface; and this is a method of reducing the danger of contagion.[10]

This action of 'causing some of the blood to touch' at the primitive Pesaḥ is, nevertheless, technically a smearing, even though it has been reduced in some measure to protect the layman who performs it by the

[1] The subject of ושחט in Num. 19:3b is the priest, rather than another person; in the latter case we should have been told that he performed ritual ablution after the ceremony, like the other participants; vv. 7–8.

[2] Heb. *ṭbl*.

[3] On the link in identity, see Hooke, op. cit. 9.

[4] Num. 19:2 ff.; cf. the popular form of the regulations in Deut. 21:1 ff.

[5] Heb. *ntn*, Ex. 12:7; so, for example, Lev. 4:7, 8:15, 23, and frequently.

[6] Heb. *higgiʿ*, Ex. 12:22.

[7] Ex. 4:25.

[8] Heb. *kpr*; on this term, see pp. 162 ff. below.

[9] Is. 6:7; cf. Jer. 1:9.

[10] The smearing of the blood at the Samaritan Pesaḥ is also carried out with great swiftness; see pp. 252 f. below.

speed with which it is performed. In Israelite sacrifice there are two methods of applying blood—apart from the simple action of pouring out the blood at the base of the altar; it may be sprinkled[1] or it may be smeared. The former is used always in connexion with objects of the highest degree of sanctity, like the 'mercy seat' or the veil of the sanctuary.[2] Altars are of lesser sanctity; sometimes they are sprinkled with the blood,[3] at other times and most commonly they are smeared.[4] The difference emerges most clearly in the *ḥaṭṭa'th* rite after the commission of unwitting sin. Where the rite is on behalf of a priest or the congregation, the degree of sanctity and potential danger is greater; blood is sprinkled before the veil and smeared upon the horns of the altar of incense.[5] When the rite is on behalf of the princes and the people of the land, the first and more solemn act is omitted, and only the lesser act of smearing the altar—this time the altar of burnt offering—is performed.[6]

There is another aspect to be taken into account. Not only is the degree of sanctity of the occasion a governing factor, but also the degree of tenacity with which contact with the sacred/unholy is retained. In the ritual of the consecration of priests, the horns of the altar are smeared; so, too, are Aaron and his sons, since they can be cleansed, if necessary, by ablution.[7] But their garments are sprinkled with a mixture of oil and blood.[8] This is probably not due to the sanctity of the garments,[9] but rather to their quality of retaining the contagion of the sacred/unholy.[10] The leper is sprinkled with the blood of a bird at the preliminary ceremony of cleansing from his disease.[11] Seven days later he is regarded as less likely to transmit the disease; there is less danger of contagion, and this time he is smeared with blood and then with a mixture of blood and oil, of which some had been sprinkled seven times before the Lord.[12] But in the case of the leper's house, only one rite is performed—and it is that of sevenfold sprinkling;

[1] Heb. *hizzah*; the word may be rendered also 'spatter, splash', cf. Th. C. Vriezen, 'Term *Hizza*: Lustration and Consecration', *Oudtestamentische studiën*, vii, 1950, 201. E.V. translates *zrq*, 'pour, toss', incorrectly as 'sprinkle' in, for example, Lev. 1:5, 11, 3:2.

[2] Lev. 16:14–15, 4:6, 17, cf. Num. 19:4.

[3] See, especially, Lev. 16:19; so 5:9 (where, however, the offering is a bird), cf. 8:11, where oil, not blood, is sprinkled.

[4] Ex. 29:12, Lev. 4:7, 18, &c., 8:15, 9:9, &c.

[5] Lev. 4:6, 7, 17, 18.

[6] Lev. 4:25, 30. See also Vriezen, op. cit. 214 ff. I do not treat here of the proposals of Ezek. 43:20, 45:19 f., since they probably do not represent actual practice.

[7] Ex. 29:12–20, Lev. 8:15–24, and also on the eighth day, 9:9–18. In Ex. 24:8 Moses tosses blood upon the people—the equivalent of smearing, not sprinkling.

[8] Ex. 29:21, Lev. 8:30, cf. 6:20 (E.V. v. 27).

[9] They are kept in the holy place, Lev. 16:23.

[10] The priests therefore not only perform ablutions before putting them on, Ex. 29:4, Lev. 8:6; they also bathe after taking them off, Lev. 16:23 f. Cf. Ezek. 42:14, *Mish. Yoma* viii. 4.

[11] Lev. 14:4 ff. It is true that the blood of a bird is always sprinkled, not poured, in Israelite sacrifices; but the action is nevertheless significant.

[12] Lev. 14:14 ff.

the house, like the priests' clothes, was of material that might retain the contagion.[1]

When, now, we turn to the Pesaḥ blood rites, we observe that the outside of the dwelling-places is smeared (more precisely, brushed lightly) with blood, but not sprinkled. The degree of sanctity is not of the highest. But in other respects the Pesaḥ resembles a most holy offering.[2] It is not, therefore, the dwelling-places themselves towards which the action is directed, but the people within each dwelling-place, exactly as the priests are smeared at their consecration. This we may demonstrate formally in another way. In the Israelite cult, blood may be smeared either upon the altar of Temple buildings, or upon the priest or officiant. At the Exodus Pesaḥ the lintel and doorposts of the dwelling-place can scarcely be identified with altars or Temple precincts; they must be identified with its occupants. The entrance represents all the inmates. We recall the regulations of Deuteronomy, that the divine commandments should be affixed to the posts (*mezuzoth*) of the house and the gates of the city.[3] Those who are within are all members of a single group, and the sign on the entrance is the sign of the group.[4]

It will be observed that I have adduced the methods of treatment of sacrificial blood that appear to belong to formalized Temple procedure in order to explain the practice at the primitive Pesaḥ. It may be objected that these methods are a later development, and that the restrictions upon the handling of blood had grown more rigid with the growth of the formal cult. But even if one were to admit that the procedure outlined in regulations commonly assigned to a 'P' writer or redactor are late—and this is far from proved—it nevertheless remains certain that the procedure derives from primitive feeling and notions. The principles concerning the essence and function of blood are too deep-set and primary to admit of radical change. Even when the manipulation of blood in the Jerusalem Temple was

[1] Lev. 14:51. See the rules on the treatment of sacrificial blood in Ezek. 43–45.

[2] Cf. the regulations on the age and other qualifications of the victim, pp. 140 ff. above, and the rules on the disposal of its remains, pp. 170 ff. below.

[3] Deut. 6:6–9, 11:18–20.

[4] See Ex. 12:22, where it is forbidden to leave the dwelling-place until morning. For the identification of the dwelling-place with its inmates, cf. Ex. 21:5–6, where the slave who wishes to remain bound to the members of the household in which he is a slave has his ear affixed by 'the door or door post'. In Is. 57:8 the *mezuzah* is part of a private house; in Jud. 16:3 it is found of the posts of the doors which stood in the city gates of Gaza. Most frequently, however, it is used in connexion with the Temple; of Solomon's Temple, 1 Kings 6:31, 33, 7:5 (cf. Ezek. 41:21), with a coping, *šqp*, (cf. *mašqoph*, Ex. 12:7, 22, 23), of Shiloh, 1 Sam. 1:9, of the Temple generally, Ezek. 43:8, 46:2, Prov. 8:34. For the smearing of the *mezuzah* on the first day of the first and seventh months, Ezek. 45:19 ff., see pp. 162 n. 8 and 220 below.

For the use of blood as a mark, cf. Ex. 4:25 and the smearing of live booty taken in a foray, Doughty, *Arabia Deserta*, i. 452, and Musil, *Manners and Customs of the Rwala Bedouins*, 1928, 539; cf. Trumbull, *Blood Covenant*, 136, 192. See further W. R. Smith, *Religion*, 270 n. 1, 337, 344, 431, and Frazer, *Folklore in the O.T.*, 1918, i. 78 ff.

restricted to priests—and not permitted even to Levites[1]—the priests, with their own intrinsic sanctity, had nevertheless to observe a state of ritual cleanness.[2] For the blood was believed to contain the life;[3] and it has the qualities of a living organism.[4] It is instinct with holiness.[5] This attitude towards blood has scarcely altered in Palestine from the time of the Bible to the present day.[6] It is true that there are no priests to whom Islam can restrict the slaughter of animals; but the blood is still poured away, and the flesh is still eaten without blood. These notions and practices can have changed little between the time of the Exodus and the period of the late Monarchy or the period of the Return from Exile. The formal ritual of the Temple is the expression of popular thought and tradition.

The two ceremonies of blood-smearing which I have outlined in the previous pages—those of the 'red heifer' and the cleansing from leprosy[7]—are non-recurrent; they are performed on a specific occasion, and they need not be repeated. There is (apart from the Pesaḥ) only one blood rite of this character in the Israelite calendar that is performed at regular intervals.[8] It is that of the Day of Atonement, and this festival is a 'splintering' of the autumn New Year festival. But the autumn festival, as we have already observed, is a formal ceremonial carried out not by the people, but on behalf of the people. When we turn to neighbouring religions, we find a largely similar ritual at the Babylonian New Year.[9] And we find that here the term for the smearing of the shrine in Akkadian is *kuppuru*,[10] a term probably echoed in the Hebrew Yom haKippurim, the Day of Atonement. Like the latter, however, it is a formal ceremony.

For analogies to the popular ritual of the Pesaḥ we must turn to the present-day customs of Palestine and the neighbouring region. Arabs

[1] See, on 2 Chr. 35:11, pp. 226 f. below; cf. Ezek. 44:10 ff., against 44:15 ff.

[2] See especially Lev. 22.

[3] Gen. 9:4, Lev. 17:11, 14 (בנפשו in v. 14a is perhaps a gloss, but see H. Cazelles, *VT* viii, 1958, 315), Deut. 12:23.

[4] Gen. 4:10; Frazer, op. cit. i. 101 ff.

[5] Lev. 3:17, 7:26 f., 19:26, Deut. 12:16, 23, 15:23, cf. 1 Sam. 14:32 ff., Ezek. 33:25, and see W. R. Smith, *Religion*, 234 ff., and E. O. James, *Origins of Sacrifice*, 1933, 32 f. There is no certain evidence that at one time Semites drank blood, as maintained by W. R. Smith, op. cit. 341, 343, 368, and Couroyer, review, *RB* lxv, 1958, 114; see Lagrange, *Études*, 259, and further L. Moraldi, *Espiazione sacrificale*, 224 ff. On the incident described by Nilus in which a camel was consumed alive, see p. 166 n. 1 below. The incident in *ANET* 299*b* is exceptional.

[6] See, for example, Musil, *Arabia Petraea*, iii. 150, and cf. Doughty, op. cit. i. 492; Jaussen, *Coutumes . . . de Moab*, 338; Canaan, op. cit. 35 ff.; and *Mish. Zeb.* iv. 4.

[7] pp. 158 f. above.

[8] The periodic 'desinning' of the altar prescribed in Ezek. 45:18–20 must be regarded with caution; see p. 220 below.

[9] p. 122 above. See also Meissner, op. cit. ii. 84, and W. Schrank, *Babylonische Sühnriten*, 1908, 81 ff. For a similar rite among the Hittites, see F. Sommer and H. Ehelolf, *Das hethitische Ritual des Papanikri von Komana*, 1924, 18.

[10] G. R. Driver, 'Studies in the Vocabulary of the Old Testament. V', *JTS* xxxiv, 1933, 34. On *kpr*, see Thompson, *Semitic Magic*, 1908, 175 ff., and Moraldi, *Espiazione*, 182.

smear the blood of a slaughtered animal at the entrance to a house when the inmates are threatened with cholera,[1] and they smear the blood on their cattle to ensure that the cattle are preserved in good health; the flesh is then consumed at a communal meal.[2] This sacrifice followed by the smearing of the victim's blood is made 'before the face of Allah to deliver a man or beast from a sickness or impending destruction';[3] it is called in the Palestinian dialect *fedu*, in classical Arabic *fidyah*. It is performed not only when danger is actually at hand; it is performed on many occasions at the opening of a new epoch—on breaking new ground, on sinking a new well, on laying the foundations or completing the building of a new house.[4] It takes place, for similar reasons, at a betrothal and a marriage.[5]

The same form of sacrifice is carried out also at the fixed turning-point of the year, the New Year festival. The sacrifice at the Moslem *ḥajj* is a *fidyah*.[6] The blood of the animal victims on the day of ʿArafat is smeared on the doorposts in Palestine;[7] elsewhere it is smeared on the small children.[8] In these cases the date of the ceremony is bound to the movable lunar calendar of Islam. But the ceremony is also performed in Palestine on the first day of March[9] or a similar date at the beginning of the tropic year—that is, approximately at the time of the Pesaḥ.[10]

The remarkable parallel between the *fedu* rites and the Pesaḥ blood

[1] Jaussen, *Mission archéologique en Arabie*, 1909, i. 472, and Canaan, *JPOS* vi, 1926, 41 f. A similar ceremony is performed when a district is threatened with drought, Dalman, op. cit. i. 142.

[2] Doughty, op. cit. i. 499; cf. A. Blunt, *Pilgrimage to Nejd*, 1881, i. 203; Musil, *Arabia Petraea*, iii. 286 f.; Jaussen, *Coutumes . . . de Moab*, 339, 335, 361; and Canaan, op. cit. 42. For the *fedu* sacrifice of a firstling at a shrine in springtime in order to ensure the well-being of the whole flock, see Dalman, op. cit. vi. 185, and Canaan, op. cit. 34.

[3] Jaussen, *Coutumes . . . de Moab*, 361; cf. Canaan, op. cit. 41 ff.

[4] Doughty, op. cit. i. 136, 452, ii. 100, 198; P. J. Baldensperger, *PEFQS*, 1893, 313, 316; Curtiss, op. cit. 196 ff.; Jaussen, *Coutumes palestiniennes . . . Naplouse . . .*, 1927, 21 f.; and Canaan, op. cit. 41 ff.

[5] Jaussen, *Coutumes . . . de Moab*, 339 ff.; Musil, op. cit. iii. 195; and Burckhardt, *Notes on the Bedouins and Wahábys*, 61, 151 n. In pre-Islamic times the Arab boy was smeared with the blood of an animal victim at the ʿ*aqiqah* rite of cutting the first hair; later the blood was replaced by red ointment, cf. A. von Kremer, *Studien zur vergleichenden Culturgeschichte, vorzüglich nach arabischen Quellen* (Sitzungsberichte der philosophisch-historischen Classe der kaiserlichen Akademie der Wissenschaften, Wien, Band 120/iii, viii), 1890, 41; Wellhausen, *Reste*, 197 ff.; and Dalman, op. cit. i. 31.

[6] The same term is used of the act of atonement (fasting, alms, or sacrifice) for omission to perform the pilgrimage correctly, Qur. ii. 192, and the act of atonement (alms) for omission to keep the fast in Ramaḍan, Qur. ii. 180; cf. Qur. xxxvii. 107. For the inter-relation between sacrifice, fasting, and alms, see *BT Ber.* 6b, 17a, 32b, *Sanh.* 35a.

[7] G. R. Lees, *Village Life in Palestine*, 1905, 204.

[8] Westermarck, *Ritual and Belief in Morocco*, ii. 122.

[9] Dalman, op. cit. i. 30 ff., 423 f.; in the Lebanon the rite is observed in the autumn, ibid. 445, among Beduins in the winter, ibid. 31.

[10] At their Pesaḥ the modern Samaritans smear the victims' blood both on the doorposts and on the young children, Jeremias, *Passahfeier der Samaritaner*, 1932, 91 f., and p. 253 n. 12 below; this may be due to the influence of local custom rather than Jewish traditional practice. See pp. 251 ff. below.

ritual has been noted by scholars;[1] but little attention has been paid to the significance of the name. In the Akk. *kuppuru* and the Heb. *kippurim* we have a description of the procedure, 'smearing'; in *fdh* we have the motive that lies behind the procedure, 'redemption'.[2] At the New Year the divine powers determined the fates of the coming year. All male adults attended a solemn assembly and, as usual on such occasions, by households. They were ritually clean. Each household sacrificed a clean victim; they smeared the blood of this redemption offering outside the dwelling-place as a symbol of the occupants who consumed the flesh within.[3] It was a *pidyon* or *fidyah*, by which men sought to avert an unfavourable year.[4]

The sacrifice was not in a simple sense a *quid pro quo*; the single victim was intended to redeem the whole family.[5] In the course of time the practice was broadened in complexity of detail and reduced in depth of meaning. Side by side with the New Year offering, a different type of 'ransom' was introduced. Not each household but each adult contributed a token payment to the Temple,[6] and from this emerged the poll-tax. The practice of numbering the male adults was, I have suggested, intimately connected with the spring New Year festival; it was then that the men of the community were mustered.[7] We find the term *kpr* equally in the context of the Passover and in the laws prescribing the poll-tax; the term is used also in the regulations on firstborn, who, as we shall see, have also an intimate connexion with the Passover.[8]

[1] So, for example, Gray, *Sacrifice in the Old Testament*, 359 ff., and Ewald, p. 105 above.

[2] For the use of the word *fdh* in connexion with firstlings sacrifices, see p. 182 below. The two motifs of *fdh* and *kpr* are probably combined in the Heb. *kopher*, cf. Arab. *kaffarah*; see Ex. 21:30 and Ps. 49:8 (E.V. 49:7) (both with *fdh* also), Ex. 30:12, Num. 35:31 f., Is. 43:3, and perhaps read פדהו for פדעהו in Job 33:24. *Kopher* also acquires the meaning of a ransom wrongfully given, 'bribe', 1 Sam. 12:3, Amos 5:12, Prov. 6:35, Job 36:18. Other occurrences of the word are in Prov. 13:8, 21:18.

[3] In modern times Arabs smear blood upon shrines, Canaan, op. cit. 42; Dussaud and F. Macler, *Voyage au Safa*, 1901, 163; and E. D. Schoenfeld, *Die Halbinsel des Sinai*, 1907, 60; so also the pagan Arabs, Nabih Amin Faris, op. cit. 37. Cf. the smearing of blood on graves, Musil, *Manners and Customs of the Rwala Bedouins*, 1928, 418, 420. For the use of blood as the sign of the ratification of an oath or a covenant, see Pedersen, *Eid bei den Semiten*, 1914, 148.

[4] Heb. *pdh*, 'redeem', is found in contexts alluding to the Exodus, which followed the Pesaḥ of Egypt, in Deut. 7:8, 9:26, 13:6 (E.V. 13:5), 15:15, 24:18, 2 Sam. 7:23 (which many scholars omit) = 1 Chr. 17:21, Is. 51:10–11, Mic. 6:4, Ps. 78:42. Cf. the obscure Ex. 8:19 (E.V. 8:23): 'I will put a division (*peduth*) between my people and thy people', that is, Israel will perform the ransom ceremony which will save them from the plague with which Egypt will be afflicted. In the Talmud the word *g'l* is especially associated with the Exodus; cf. *Mish. Pes.* x. 5–6, &c. For a study on the difference of meaning between *pdh* and *g'l*, see J. J. Stamm, *Erlösen und Vergeben im Alten Testament*, 1940, and the review by J. Muilenberg, *JBL* lx, 1940, 430. On the moral aspect of the ransom offering, see Hooke, op. cit. 12.

[5] There seems no certain trace in early Israelite practice of the release of a prisoner at the New Year festival which was an accepted usage elsewhere, especially in Greece (p. 119 above); see p. 242 below.

[6] Ex. 30:12 ff.

[7] See pp. 135 ff. above.

[8] The Passover, 2 Chr. 30:18 (cf. the Day of Atonement, Lev. 16:6, 11, 17, 24); the poll-tax, Ex. 30:12 ff. (note Heb. *kopher*, v. 12, *kippurim*, v. 16); firstborn replaced by

The rite of a sacrifice of redemption was more significant at the spring than at the autumn festival—although both the name and the ceremonial of Yom haKippurim demonstrate how central a feature it was also at the latter—because the Pesaḥ, as we have observed, was not the vicarious performance of ritual by a leader of the people. The unit by which the ceremonies were carried out was the family. Here we come to our next point. In the Pesaḥ ritual there was, it will be readily appreciated, particular significance for the firstborn. Everything that was new and that stood at the opening of a new epoch was the object of special concern to the Semites.[1] So, we have remarked, a new house or a new well requires formal dedication by means of the *fedu* sacrifice. The firstborn child who was to be the head of a household had, then, to be provided for with great circumspection. That his dedication took place at the new year is to be expected. The New Year festival was the occasion on which were retold the stories of the birth of the world of nature and the birth of the society to which the celebrants belonged. It was the occasion on which a new king was proclaimed and a reigning king confirmed as leader of the community. It was the occasion on which everything that belonged to the new and unpredictable period of the future was the object of special ritual. At the spring festival each male adult was accounted for; but the firstborn was accounted for and redeemed with yet greater care. Here lies the origin of the intimate link between the firstborn and the Pesaḥ—it is derived from the character of the Pesaḥ as a New Year festival. We shall return to this topic later.[2] In the present context we may note only that the penalty is the same if any one of this group of ceremonies is omitted or observed improperly, whether it be the ritual of the New Year festival or the dedication of the firstborn or the census. Those responsible would be punished with plague or a similar disaster.[3]

The blood rites on the Pesaḥ night proclaimed the unity of each household; the eating of the victim's flesh by the members of the household together was a definite act of communion. In Israel the solemn declaration of a covenant was formally confirmed by a meal.[4]

Levites, Num. 8:19. The term *kpr* is found of the action which removes a plague, Num. 17:11 ff. (E.V. 16:46 ff.); cf. n. 3 below.

[1] Cf. החל, 'begin', lit. 'render fit for profane, everyday use'.

[2] pp. 182 f. below; note also the association of the *'Aqedah* with the New Year festival, p. 236 below.

[3] For omission to observe the Pesaḥ, Ex. 12:13, or the *ḥag*, Ex. 5:3, cf., on Tabernacles, Zech. 14:16 ff.; for carrying out the *ḥag* incorrectly, Ex. 32:35 (note *kipper*, v. 30); for omission to carry out the census, Ex. 30:12, or for carrying it out incorrectly, 2 Sam. 24:12 ff., 1 Chr. 21:10 ff. (cf. pp. 215 f. below, and Jud. 21:9 ff.); for omission to dedicate the firstborn, Num. 8:16–19 (note *kipper*, v. 19). On the apotropaic significance of the Pesaḥ, see p. 233 below on Jub. 49:15, and Hebr. 11:28; Cook, in W. R. Smith, *Religion*, 652; and Gray, *Sacrifice*, 365; this view is apparently taken by the modern Samaritans, Lees, op. cit. 209.

[4] See, for example, Gen. 14:18, 26:28–30, 31:44 ff., Ex. 24:8–11 (where the elders ate

The details of the meal, and more particularly the treatment of the flesh, conform, as we would expect, to the principle of scrupulous ritual cleanness. The animal is not to be insufficiently cooked;[1] that might perpetuate some source of pollution which, in spite of all precautions, might have been in the victim's body.[2] The animal must not be boiled, although boiling was regularly employed for cooking sacrificial victims at the established Israelite shrines.[3] It must be roasted. Roasting was the quickest and simplest method of cooking, and the motif of haste was, as we shall see, all-important at the Pesaḥ.[4] But it is likely that roasting was enjoined for another reason—it avoided the need for dissection, as in the procedure of other sacrifices.[5] The animal was roasted whole.[6] This explains the absence

as representatives of the whole people), 29:31 ff., Jos. 9:14 f., 1 Kings 1:25, 1 Chr. 29:22, perhaps Ex. 18:12, Jer. 41:1. See further W. R. Smith, *Religion*, 255, 281; Wellhausen, op. cit. 124–7, Westermarck, op. cit. i. 525, 540, 567 f.; and C. Toussaint, *Origines de la religion d'Israël*, 1931, i. 137 f., 166. For modern times, see Canaan, op. cit. 43 f.; Schoenfeld, op. cit. 60; and Burckhardt, *Travels in Syria*, 404, 430.

[1] Heb. *na'* occurs only in this passage, Ex. 12:9, in the Bible. Arab. نىء or نهىء may be rendered either 'raw' or 'insufficiently cooked'; the former is indicated in Hebrew by *ḥay*, and it is therefore reasonable to ascribe the latter significance to *na'*. Scholars, however, have interpreted *na'* here as 'raw' (following LXX and *Mekhilta*, in loc.); they have then deduced that the Pesaḥ victim originally represented or in fact was a deity, and that the prohibition against eating it raw reflects an earlier usage in which this was the accepted practice. The animal was eaten raw, it is held, in order to absorb the divine essence. So Beer, *Pesachim*, 15, cf. Mowinckel, op. cit. ii. 37; W. R. Smith, *Religion*, 313, 319; and others. The eating of raw flesh by nomads was known in ancient times, cf. S. Moscati, *Semites in Ancient History*, 1959, 53, where the Amurru are derided for this reason, and the Hittite text in *ANET* 355*b*–356*a*. The practice is not necessarily old. Smith, op. cit. 338, in a classic passage points to the account of the eating of a camel while it was still alive by 'Saracens' as reported in the text ascribed to Nilus (Migne, *P.G.* lxxix, col. 612). On the authenticity of this report, see J. Henninger, 'Ist der sogenannte Nilus-Bericht eine brauchbare religionsgeschichtliche Quelle?', *Anthropos*, l, 1955, 81; certainly the account—whether or not one accepts Henninger's strictures—has been made to support alone many weighty and far-reaching conclusions. Nevertheless, an occurrence similar to that related by Nilus is attested in Morocco in 1899 by E. Doutté, *Magie et religion dans l'Afrique du Nord*, 1909, 483 f., cf. Westermarck, op. cit. i. 278, and raw meat is not uncommon as food in the Yemen and Lebanon, Burckhardt, *Notes on the Bedouins and Wahábys*, 138. But the theory of the divinity of the Pesaḥ victim must be regarded as unproved; see pp. 102 f. above.

[2] Cf. the incident related in 1 Sam. 14:32 ff. The prohibition against eating blood was evidently not universally observed; but this incident took place in the course of a battle, and had no ritual significance like the Pesaḥ.

[3] At Shiloh, 1 Sam. 2:13 ff.; at Jerusalem, Ezek. 46:20–24, cf. Zech. 14:20. Boiled flesh is eaten by priests, Ex. 29:31, Lev. 6:21 f. (E.V. 6:28 f.), Num. 6:19 f. On the alleged boiling of the Pesaḥ victim in Deut. 16:7, see pp. 205 f. below. Wellhausen, *Prolegomena*, 68 (cf. Holzinger, *Exodus*, 37), adduces 1 Sam. 2:15 as evidence that boiling had been replaced by roasting in popular favour in Israel. But in this passage *bšl* is opposed to *ḥay*, rather than to *ṣalah*; Eli's sons preferred to have the meat raw for roasting rather than already cooked. On general grounds it may be assumed that roasting preceded boiling in the Near East rather than the reverse; the latter requires both water and utensils. See Beer, op. cit. 15 f., Dillmann, *Exodus*, 105.

[4] See the comment of Rashbam on Ex. 12:8.

[5] As in burnt offerings (Ex. 29:17 ff., Lev. 1:8 f., 12 f., 8:20 f., 9:13 f.), sin offerings (Lev. 4:8 ff., 16:25), guilt offerings (Lev. 7:3–5), peace offerings (Lev. 3:3–5, 9–11, 14–16, 9:19–20), and miscellaneous offerings (Ex. 29:13, Lev. 8:16, 25, Num. 18:17).

[6] See Ex. 12:9, p. 53 above. This does not refer to the method of cooking, or prescribe that the animal should be cooked with its head above and its legs below as maintained by

in the Pesaḥ legislation of any allusion to the disposal of the fat, as in other sacrifices;[1] at the Pesaḥ the fat simply fell into the fire as the victim was being roasted. Boiling in still water would have been liable to 'propagate the contagion'[2] of the victim. With roasting there was little risk of contamination.

At ritual meals it was customary for the meat to be accompanied by bread.[3] At the Pesaḥ meal the bread was unleavened cakes. Now, there was a tabu upon leaven in some countries, and in some it was excluded from altar offerings;[4] in the same way the Ḥums at Mekka would not drink milk when it was sour, or eat it when made into butter.[5] The details of this tabu vary from community to community and from ritual to ritual—perhaps a reflection of varying social circumstances.[6] In Israel there was a prohibition upon three forms of fermenting matter.[7] The drinking of wine

Pedersen, op. cit. iii–iv. 703 (= 393 n. 2). In that case 'with its inwards' would make little sense; and to translate Heb. *'al* as 'above' is clumsy—one would rather expect *me'al le-*. The passage directs that the head, legs, and inwards of the victim were not to be separated; *'al* here is 'together with', LXX *σύν*, cf. p. 53 n. 4 above.

[1] For the prohibition against eating the fat of sacrificial victims, Lev. 3:17, 7:24 f.; like the blood, the fat contained the 'life'. In the Qumran version of 1 Sam. 2:15, it is the priest who burns the fat, not, as may be deduced from the M.T., a layman; Cross, 'New Qumran Biblical Fragment Related to the Original Hebrew Underlying the Septuagint', *BASOR*, No. 132, Dec. 1953, 26 (col. ii, l. 1).

[2] W. R. Smith, *Religion*, 447; cf. the use of running, as opposed to stagnant, water in the rites to cleanse from leprosy and the rites of the 'red heifer', pp. 158 f. above.

[3] When the flesh was eaten by human celebrants, Lev. 7:11 ff., 8:26 ff., Num. 6:14 f.; when it was reserved for the deity, the 'bread' might with advantage appear in the form of meal, to reduce the risk of contamination, cf., for example, Num. 15:4 ff., 28:5 ff. On modern usages, see Burckhardt, op. cit. 136 f.; Musil, *Arabia Petraea*, iii. 148 f.; and Jaussen, *Coutumes . . . de Moab*, 61 ff.

[4] For Babylonia, see Zimmern, *Beiträge zur Kenntnis der babylonischen Religion*, 1896, 94 f.; leavened bread is *akal mutqi*, B. Hrozný, *Getreide im alten Babylonien. Ein Beitrag zur Kultur- und Wirtschaftsgeschichte des alten Orients* (Sitzungsberichte der kais. Akademie der Wissenschaften in Wien, Phil.-hist. Klasse, 173/i), 1913, 129, 136. For flat bread in Assyria, see A. T. Olmstead, *History of Assyria*, 1923, 19. In Greece *δαράται* were used on certain ritual occasions, Th. Homolle, *Bulletin de Correspondance hellénique*, xix, 1895, 23, and in the *rites de passage* of marriage and initiation, Homolle, op. cit. 41; cf. Nilsson, *Griechische Feste*, 134 n. 3, and Harrison, *Themis*, 178, 440, on *μάζαι*. At Rome the Flamen Dialis was not permitted to eat leaven, Aulus Gellius, *Noctes Atticae*, x. 15, and Plutarch, *Quaestiones Romanae*, 109, because it 'springs from corruption'. Persius, i. 24, uses the term *fermentum* to denote moral corruption. At circumcision ceremonies in modern Algeria adult males eat from a dish of meat, eggs, and unleavened bread, Hilton-Simpson, op. cit. 184.

[5] See Wellhausen, *Reste*, 85 f., and Wensinck, *Arabic New-Year*, 21, 25; on the Ḥums, see also A. S. Tritton, 'Notes on Religion in Early Arabia', *Muséon*, lxxii, 1959, 191 ff.

[6] So leavened as well as unleavened bread appears in sacrifices in Egypt, cf. H. Kees, *Ägypten*, 1933, 68, and among the Hittites, Sommer and Ehelolf, op. cit. 40, cf. Furlani, *Religione degli Hittiti*, 298. At Ugarit *nbt* was offered at sacrifices, Gordon, *Ugaritic Manual*, Glossary, s.v., and so also at Carthage, Cooke, *North-Semitic Inscriptions*, 125 (No. 44, l. 8); this is probably a kind of honey, cf. Heb. *nopheth*, but it need not be identical with Heb. *debhaš* that was prohibited in Israelite sacrifice, p. 168 n. 3 below. Cf. W. R. Smith, *Religion*, 220 f.

[7] Heb. *ḥameṣ*, Ex. 23:18, 34:25, Lev. 2:11, cf. Ps. 73:21, &c.; *maḥmeṣeth*, Ex. 12:19 f. The basic meaning is probably 'be sour', cf. Arab. حمض. The word is used in a derived metaphorical sense in *BT R.H.* 3b, 'become degenerate'; see A. Geiger, *Jüdische Zeitschrift*, ii,

was forbidden to priests in the performance of their duties in the Temple,[1] although it was employed in the Temple cult to a limited degree.[2] A form of honey[3] was forbidden in sacrifice. Still more stringent were the regulations against the use of leaven.[4] Bread, of which the whole or part was placed upon the altar, was not to be leavened.[5] The shewbread was unleavened,[6] and those who touched it were to be ritually clean.[7] In the sanctuary the priests might eat only unleavened bread.[8]

It has been suggested that this avoidance of leaven in the Israelite cult goes back to the time when it was a strange and mistrusted innovation.[9] But wild honey, which was equally forbidden, was no innovation. Nor was the avoidance of leaven a reminiscence of the 'nomadic' period of Israelite history.[10] Unleavened bread was carried, it is true, by nomads,[11] as it is carried today by Beduins,[12] but only because it is easily prepared and light

1863, 35. The verb *ḥmṣ* has also a secondary significance arising out of the inevitability, as well as the secrecy, of the process of fermentation, 'leave for a while, neglect', *Mekhilta* on Ex. 12:17; cf. Matt. 13:33, Luke 13:21. The notion is perhaps already reflected in Hos. 7:4 ff., where the baker leaves the dough until fermentation is complete.

[1] Lev. 10:9, Ezek. 44:21, cf. the Nazarite, Num. 6:3, and the Rechabites, Jer. 35:8 f.; see further Jud. 13:4.

[2] Ex. 29:40, Num. 15:5 ff., 28:7 f., 9, 14, &c., Deut. 32:38, Hos. 9:3, Ezra 6:9, 7:22. The offering of wine in the Temple has been regarded as a relatively late phenomenon in Israel, cf. Gray, *Sacrifice*, 374, 400; it was employed, however, at Ugarit, Gordon, op. cit., Glossary, s. *yyn*, and appears early in the Bible, Gen. 14:18. On the importance of the vine in Palestine, p. 115 above.

[3] Heb. *debhaš*, Lev. 2:11, cf. Jud. 14:8, 1 Sam. 14:25 ff., Deut. 32:13, Is. 7:18 f., Ps. 81:17 (E.V. 81:16); cf. Dalman, op. cit. vi. 107. Note the combination of honey and curds in the *Epic of Gilgamesh*, *ANET* 88*a*.

[4] Heb. *śe'or*, Lev. 2:11. Related to this word is *miš'ereth*, commonly rendered 'kneading-trough', Ex. 7:28 (E.V. 8:3), 12:34. For the Pesh. rendering, see p. 50 n. 4 above.

[5] Ex. 29:2, 23–25, Lev. 8:2, 26–28, 2:4 f., 6:7 ff. (E.V. 6:14 ff.), 10:12, Num. 6:15 ff., cf. 1 Chr. 23:29. In Lev. 7:12–14 the leavened bread is not included in the *qorban*, cf. v. 13, '*in addition to* cakes of leavened bread . . .' (cf. p. 53 n. 4 on *'al*). On the leaven at the feast of Weeks, Lev. 23:17, see p. 180 below. Amos 4:5 does not imply (as Gray, op. cit. 27, 399) that the Israelites did in fact offer leaven. On the contrary, it was incredible that the priests should offer leavened material as the *todah*, cf. Lev. 7:12 ff.; so LXX in Amos 4:5 reads Heb. *ḥuṣ* for M.T. *ḥmṣ*. The prophet is scoffing at the ostentation of the people, suggesting that they should bring *zebhaḥim* every morning and the tithes that were distributed to Levites and the needy every three days instead of every three years (Deut. 14:28, 26:12). So, he continues, Go, burn for yourselves—since the priests will not do so—leavened offerings (which were more precious than unleavened) as the *todah*, and proclaim these freewill sacrifices ostentatiously. The *todah* could be offered without limitation, Lev. 22:29; and it would be offered by the worshipper who wished to impress his friends with his liberality and devotion, since it was accompanied by music and merry-making, Is. 51:3, Jer. 30:19, 33:11.

[6] Josephus, *Ant.* III. vi. 6, x. 7; cf. 1 Chr. 23:29.

[7] 1 Sam. 21:4–7.

[8] Lev. 6:7 ff. (E.V. 6:14 ff.), 10:12, cf. 2:4. On 2 Kings 23:9, see p. 216 n. 8 below.

[9] So Pedersen, op. cit. iii–iv. 400, suggests that leaven was regarded as a 'foreign element'.

[10] As Holzinger, pp. 107 f. above.

[11] They are the ash-cakes of herdsmen, *Epic of Gilgamesh*, *ANET* 84*b*; on Arab Beduins, see G. Jacob, *Leben der vorislamischen Beduinen*, 1895, 89.

[12] Burckhardt, op. cit. 136; H. J. Van-Lennep, *Bible Lands*, 1875, i. 88 ff.; Musil, op. cit. iii. 148; and id., *Manners and Customs of the Rwala Bedouins*, 1928, 92. Cf. Jaussen, op. cit. 63.

to carry.[1] There was, rather, a twofold reason for the unleavened cakes at the Pesaḥ meal. Part of the motif of the New Year festival was the exodus from the cultivated land to the desert, and for this haste was imperative; food had to be made ready quickly and without warning.[2] But also fermentation represented the mysterious contagion of decay.[3] It was avoided at regular sacrifices—and even more so at the Pesaḥ, where failure to observe ritual cleanness might be fraught with grave consequences in the ensuing year.

Another accompaniment of the Pesaḥ meal was bitter herbs.[4] The identification of the herbs is uncertain. They may be the Akkadian *muraru*, the bitter lettuce,[5] since lettuce is one of the plants which might be employed as the bitter herbs, according to the regulations of the Mishnah.[6] However, the Hebrew term *meror* may be secondary, and adopted because of the taste of the plant; *maror* does not denote lettuce in the Mishnah, but another plant, chicory.[7] The Mishnah approves three other plants for use at the Pesaḥ meal, in addition to lettuce and chicory, but their identification is disputed.[8]

The reason for the inclusion of the bitter herbs at the Pesaḥ meal is equally uncertain. They are unlikely to be simply condiments, intended at the same time as a reminder of the bitterness of the oppression of Israel in Egypt;[9] nor are they likely to be prescribed as part of an ordinary meal.[10] They have been regarded by some scholars as an element in a spring ritual.[11] Lettuce was among the quickly sprouting herbs that were planted in the

[1] Unleavened bread was apparently carried by soldiers in ancient Egypt, although the use of leavened bread was widespread; cf. Ex. 12:34.

[2] Ex. 12:34, 39, cf. Gen. 19:3, Jud. 6:19, 1 Sam. 28:24.

[3] Cf. Matt. 16:6, Mark 8:15, Luke 12:1, 1 Cor. 5:6, Gal. 5:9, and see Geiger, loc. cit.

[4] Heb. *merorim*, Ex. 12:8, Num. 9:11. For the Versions, see p. 54 n. 5 above.

[5] Thompson, *Dictionary of Assyrian Botany*, 72, foot; note the alternative name *guzazu*, cf. Syr. *gedde*, 'absinth', *gaddida*, 'bitter'.

[6] *Mish. Pes.* ii. 6, *ḥazereth*, cf. *BT Pes.* 39a, *JT Pes.* viii. 1 (fol. 35d).

[7] Loc. cit., so M. Jastrow, *Dictionary of the Targumim* . . ., s.v. S. R. Driver, *Exodus*, on Ex. 12:8, has 'bitter coriander (?)', and H. Danby, *Mishnah*, on *Mish. Pes.*, loc. cit., has 'dandelion'. In modern Palestine *murrar* is a term used of 'thistle', Dalman, op. cit. ii. 313.

[8] They are עולשין, 'endive' (Jastrow and Driver), 'chicory' (Danby); תמכא, 'chervil, marrubium' (Rashi, Jastrow; but see I. Löw, *Flora der Juden*, ii. 74), 'garden endive (?)' (Driver), 'pepperwort' (Danby), see Targ. Jer. on Ex. 12:8, p. 54 n. 5 above; חרחבינא, 'nettles' (Driver), 'creeper (like ivy)' (Jastrow), 'snake root' (Danby). On all these plants, see Löw, *Aramäische Pflanzennamen*, Index, s.vv.

[9] Ex. 1:14. This view is held by Dillmann, *Bücher Exodus und Leviticus*, 106, following R. Gamaliel in *Mish. Pes.* x. 5, and Jewish commentators including Rashi. But note that salt would be used as a condiment in any case, Lev. 2:13, Ezek. 43:24, Ezra 6:9, 7:22, cf. 2 Chr. 13:5, Ecclus. 39:26, Mark 9:49, Col. 4:6, &c., and Josephus, *Ant.* III. ix. 1, *Mish. Zeb.* vi. 5. See W. R. Smith, *Religion*, 220, and Cook, ibid. 595.

[10] G. E. Post, art. 'Bitter Herbs', *DB*. Dhorme, *Évolution*, i. 211 f., regards the eating of bitter herbs as a nomadic practice; according to Burckhardt, *Notes on the Bedouins and Wahábys*, 136, when a lamb is cooked, herbs are added to the butter.

[11] Holzinger, op. cit. 37. He compares the use of herbs among the Arabs during the autumn; cf. Wellhausen, *Reste*, 96.

Adonis-gardens or Osiris-beds, the popular rite of sympathetic magic in the ancient Near East that was believed to promote the speedy revival of vegetation.[1] But there is no obvious stress upon the quick growth of the bitter herbs in the narrative of the Exodus Pesaḥ. Moreover, the bitter herbs were attached to the Pesaḥ ceremony rather than to the spring month, since they are prescribed also for the following month when the 'second Pesaḥ' is performed by those who had been ritually unclean.[2]

The most attractive explanation for the appearance of the bitter herbs at the Pesaḥ meal maintains that they were a prophylactic against evil spirits.[3] Certain herbs were employed for that purpose in ancient Mesopotamia;[4] in Egypt magical properties were ascribed to leeks and onions.[5] The Greeks chewed buckthorn[6] as a cathartic when the ghosts of the dead returned to the earth at the Anthesteria.[7] We need not regard the bitter herbs as purgatives, since in that case we should expect them to appear before, rather than during, the Pesaḥ meal.[8] Nevertheless, some (but not all) of the herbs approved by the Mishnah for use at the Pesaḥ have medicinal value;[9] one, nettles or ivy with a bitter smell, is closely related to the Greek buckthorn.[10]

The manner in which the Pesaḥ meal is eaten is also the subject of regulations. The bones of the victim were not to be broken.[11] This rule has been variously explained. Some scholars maintain that it is intended to ensure the reappearance of the Pesaḥ victim—whom they take to represent

[1] W. W. F. von Baudissin, *Adonis und Esmun*, 1911, 138, and Index, s. 'Adonisgärten'; Lagrange, *Études*, 302, 307 n. 3; and Frazer, *Golden Bough. Adonis*, i. 236; cf. Dalman, op. cit. i. 51, 346 ff.

[2] Num. 9:11.

[3] Beer, 'Miscellen. 2, Die Bitterkräuter beim Paschafest', *ZAW* xxxi, 1911, 152 f.; id., *Pesachim*, 18 f.; and Lods, *Israel*, 294 (who also gives a parallel from eighteenth-century Greece), Hooke, *Origins*, 49 f.

[4] So Dhorme, *Religions de Babylonie et d'Assyrie*, 1945, 270, on chicory; against this, Thompson, *Dictionary of Assyrian Botany*, 262. See also E. S. Drower, 'Phylactery for Rue', *Orientalia*, xv, 1946, 324.

[5] Kees, *Ägypten*, 32 f.

[6] Gr. ῥάμνος, cf. LXX, Vulg. (*rhamnus*), at Jud. 9:14; see Löw, *Flora der Juden*, iii. 361.

[7] See O. Crusius, 'Über das Phantastische im Mimus', *Neue Jahrbücher für das klassische Altertum*, xxv, 1910, 86; E. Rohde, *Psyche*, tr. Hillis, 1925, 168; and Harrison, *Prolegomena*, 39.

[8] On purgatives, W. R. Smith, *Religion*, 434; cf. pp. 145 f. above on the fast before the Pesaḥ.

[9] Crowfoot and Baldensperger, op. cit. 85 ff., 97 ff.; cf. 41.

[10] It may be suggested that the practice of chewing buckthorn—to which the bitter herbs of the Pesaḥ may be compared—is to be regarded not as a prophylactic to keep away the ghosts of the dead, but rather as intended to ensure the continuance of life. In the *Epic of Gilgamesh*, xi, l. 268, the plant of rejuvenation is said to resemble the buckthorn, *iṭṭittu*—how we do not know, since the end of the line is missing; perhaps the resemblance lay in its smell, cf. l. 287. In Jud. 9:14 f. the thorn (Heb. *'ṭd*) is contrasted with the trees, either because it has no roots and is of little value (cf. Ps. 58:10, E.V. 58:9), or because it grows quickly. חרחבינא, p. 169 n. 8 above, perhaps belongs to the thorn family. But it may, on the other hand, be the ivy; among the Greeks this was the primitive phytomorph, sacred to Dionysos, the spirit of the New Year, and chewed by the Bacchantes, cf. Harrison, *Themis*, 135, and Frazer, *Golden Bough. Magic Art*, ii. 251.

[11] Ex. 12:46, Num. 9:12; LXX inserts the rule also in Ex. 12:10.

a deity—in perfect form on the Day of Judgement.[1] But I have suggested that the divinity of the Pesaḥ victim is an improbable conception and remote from the period to which our Bible text belongs.[2] We know little of Israelite views on the future life, at any rate before the beginning of the Common Era. Another hypothesis sees in these precautions to preserve the animal whole something in the nature of a prophylactic. The victim represents the entire community, and only if it is kept intact will the well-being of the community be secure during the ensuing year.[3] The hypothesis is tenable, for we have already observed that the blood rites had an apotropaic significance.[4] There is, however, a simpler explanation of the regulation against breaking the bones of the Pesaḥ victim. It was designed to prevent the dispersion of the victim's limbs and the pollution which this might entail. The position of the precept in the Bible text seems to confirm this hypothesis. In one passage this regulation stands beside the rule that the flesh must not be taken outside the dwelling-place in which it is eaten,[5] in another it follows the law forbidding any of the remains of the flesh to remain overnight—whatever remained must be burned.[6]

The purpose of the first of the two rules that I have just mentioned—that the flesh must not be taken outside the dwelling-places—is self-evident; it is to avoid uncleanness.[7] The second requires some comment. Those Israelite sacrifices at which some of the flesh was to be eaten fall into two categories. At the less holy offerings the flesh may be eaten on the day of the sacrifice or on the following day; whatever is left till the third day must be burned.[8] The more holy sacrifices—those in which the danger of contagion from the sacred/unholy is more urgent—must be consumed on

[1] This is based on a belief in modern Palestine recorded by Curtiss, op. cit. 201, 242, and Canaan, op. cit. 41; cf. K. Kohler, 'Verbot des Knochenzerbrechens', *Archiv für Religionswissenschaft*, xiii, 1910, 153 f.; J. Morgenstern, 'Bones of the Paschal Lamb', *JAOS* xxxvi, 1917, 146; and Cook, in W. R. Smith, *Religion*, 652 n. 3.

[2] pp. 102 f. above. John 19:36 is based on Ps. 34:21 (E.V. 34:20), not on Ex. 12:46; see McNeile, op. cit. 77, and p. 244 n. 4 below. The evidence offered by Morgenstern, loc. cit., is late. The search for the bone (and fat) of the slain Aqhat in the Ugar. texts may be connected with the restoration of the hero to life, but unfortunately the text is imperfect at this point; see Gordon, op. cit. 180 (*I Aqhat*, ll. 111 ff.), and id., *Ugaritic Literature*, 1949, 85, 96 ff.

[3] Based on a practice in modern Palestine, Curtiss, op. cit. 178; cf. Beer, *Pesachim*, 16, and Nicolsky, *ZAW* xlv, 1927, 178 f.

[4] See also p. 233 below on Jub. 49. Theories on the regulation against breaking the bones of the Pesaḥ victim are set out with a copious bibliography by J. Henninger, 'Verbot des Knochenzerbrechens bei den Semiten', in *Studi orientalistici in onore di G. Levi della Vida*, i, 1956, 448. See also G. A. Barton, *JBL* xlix, 1930, 13, with references to ancient Egyptian literature.

[5] Ex. 12:46.

[6] Num. 9:12. For the regulation against breaking the bones of the Pesaḥ victim, see *Mish. Mak.* iii. 3, *Pes.* vii. 11, and p. 260 below.

[7] Ex. 12:10, Num. 9:12, Deut. 16:4, cf. Ex. 12:8, 'they shall eat the flesh in that night'; 12:22, 'none of you shall go out of the door of his house until the morning'.

[8] Lev. 7:16 ff. (vow or freewill offering), 19:6 f. (peace offering). The Mishnah calls them קדשים קלים.

the day of sacrifice; they cannot be allowed to remain until the morning.[1] With both categories it is in fact the evening that marks the limit of their validity. This general ruling does not mean, as has been maintained,[2] that the sacrificial flesh must not be exposed to the heat of the sun for fear of putrefaction, since even the more holy offerings had been exposed on the day of sacrifice. The evening is the limit because that was normal sacrificial procedure. In Israel, as elsewhere, sacrifice followed the pattern of the ordinary working day, beginning in the morning and ending in the evening.[3] There is no reason to suppose that this practice was of late origin.

Here, however, the Pesaḥ is different to a striking degree. We have already observed that in the regulations concerning the species, age, and sex of the victim, the Pesaḥ resembles the 'most holy offerings'.[4] But it was, furthermore, a night ritual. It commenced just before nightfall; it had to be completed and the remains to be burned before sunrise.[5] We are justified, then, in conjecturing that the reason for the regulation about the disposal of the remains of the Pesaḥ victim lies in the fear of the consequences that would follow exposure of the flesh to the sun.[6] A special sanctity attached to the Pesaḥ offering.[7]

It is in keeping with the quality of the Pesaḥ as a night ritual that we find the term *yalin* used in one passage on the disposal of the remains of the Pesaḥ victim.[8] The term means to 'pass the night'—from, that is, sunset to sunrise.[9] It is found also in the much-disputed passage of Ex. 34:25, where the phrase '*ḥag* of the Pesaḥ' is used of the Pesaḥ victim. It is found, further, with 'my *ḥag*' in Ex. 23:18, and this may indicate that the regulation against the flesh remaining overnight applies equally to the festival of Tabernacles.[10] That, too, opened with a night ritual—of which we are given details only in the late Jewish source, *Mishnah Sukkah*.

[1] Lev. 7:15, 22:29 f. (peace offering for thanksgiving), Ex. 29:33 f., Lev. 8:31 f. (offering at the consecration of priests), &c.

[2] As, for example, W. R. Smith, op. cit. 345.

[3] So with the twice-daily *Tamid* offerings, Ex. 29:39 ff., Num. 28:3 ff.; cf. *Mish. Taʿan.* iv. 1, Josephus, *BJ* VI. v. 3. See also pp. 131 n. 3 above and 250 f. below.

[4] See pp. 141 f. above.

[5] See p. 59 above; cf. Wellhausen, *Reste*, 43 n. 1, 118 f. On the concessions made in later times in respect of the time of the Pesaḥ sacrifice, pp. 233, 246, 256, and 262 below; on the disposal of the remains, p. 263 below.

[6] With Smith, op. cit. 388.

[7] Ibid. 369.

[8] Deut. 16:4. But the term does not occur in the more formal passages, Ex. 12:10, Num. 9:12.

[9] Cf. Lev. 19:13b. לין is used in a different sense in Deut. 21:23, where the exposure of the body must not be allowed to *begin* to 'pass the night'; the meaning is made clear there by the omission of the words 'until the morning', while in Deut. 16:4 we have the reference to the day of the sacrifice that preceded the night.

[10] Much labour and ingenuity have been expended on the analysis of these two verses and on their relation to each other; see, in particular, Gray, *JTS* xxxvii, 1936, 241. The wording of both verses is suspicious. The verb *zbḥ*, which implies the performance of a communal sacrifice, cannot have as its object 'blood of my *zebhaḥ*' (Ex. 23:18a), nor is the phrase improved by the use of the verb *šḥṭ* (34:25a). If *ḥag* is an allusion to the Pesaḥ

The regulations that we have discussed—the method of cooking the Pesaḥ victim, the avoidance of leaven, the prohibition against breaking the bones, the disposal of the remains, and perhaps also the eating of bitter herbs—all relate to the maintenance of ritual cleanness. We come now to one of a different nature, the rule that prescribes that the meal should be eaten in haste.[1] It has been argued that this also was intended to avoid the deterioration of the sacrificial flesh. In favour of this view the account by Nilus of the Saracens' sacrifice of a live camel to the morning star has been quoted—graphically, but hardly convincingly.[2] The Pesaḥ texts already prescribe that none of the flesh should remain until morning;[3] there seems little need for urgency, provided that the meal was finished during the night.

We should, I think, look elsewhere for the explanation of this regulation on the haste of the Pesaḥ meal. In the Pesaḥ texts it is not merely the meal that is to be completed in haste. In one passage this regulation follows that on dress, which, I have suggested, is associated with the swift exodus from the city to the desert.[4] In another the idea is expressed more pointedly—it is the whole seven-day festival that commemorates the haste of the Exodus.[5] A third text—the only other place in the Bible which has the noun *ḥippazon*, a term that appears to be used only of the haste of the Pesaḥ—is more significant to our argument. A passage in Deutero-Isaiah reads:

> Depart ye, depart ye, go ye out from thence, touch no unclean thing; go ye out of the midst of her; be ye clean, that bear the vessels of the Lord. For ye shall not go out in haste,[6] neither shall ye go by flight: for the Lord will go before you; and the God of Israel will be your rearward.[7]

Here the reference is to the exodus motif—the precautions against uncleanness and the orderly march of the Israelites in haste through the Wilderness.[8] No longer, in the days of this prophet, was there need to go forth in panic, as at the Pesaḥ of Egypt. The Lord had redeemed[9] Jerusalem—we

offering in 23:18b, the regulation about the fat is meaningless either for an early or a late period in the history of the festival; in the early passages there is no mention of the fat of the Pesaḥ offering since it was disposed of in the fire (see pp. 166 f. above), while in the later period it was treated like the fat of all Temple sacrifices (see pp. 226 f. and 232 below). Moreover, it was not the fat but the whole of the flesh that must not remain until the morning. The wording of 34:25b, '*zebhaḥ* of the *ḥag* of the Pesaḥ', is also unintelligible. In Ex. 12:27, with which this passage is usually compared, *zebhaḥ* is used of the whole Pesaḥ ceremony, not of the flesh of the victim, as here; moreover, *zebhaḥ* in 34:25b, with this unusual meaning, accords badly with *zibhḥi* in 25a, where the word has its usual meaning, 'a communal sacrifice'. Pfeiffer, *Introduction*, 224, can hardly be followed in regarding *zbḥ* in Ex. 23:18 as an 'old term' in contrast to *šḥṭ* in 34:25. It seems impossible to reconstruct the text with any confidence.

1 Ex. 12:11. The word properly implies agitation as well as hurry.

2 Wellhausen, loc. cit., and Smith, *Religion*, 338, 345, 387. But this incident (if authentic, see p. 166 n. 1 above) was a meal devoured between the rise of the morning star and its disappearance in the light of the sun; the Pesaḥ, on the other hand, was by moonlight. Smith bases his argument on the divine essence of the Pesaḥ victim, but against this, see pp. 102 f. above.

3 Ex. 12:10, Num. 9:12, Deut. 16:4.

4 Ex. 12:11; cf. p. 147 above.

5 Deut. 16:3.

6 Heb. *ḥippazon*.

7 Is. 52:11–12.

8 See Ex. 14:19.

9 Heb. *g'l*, Is. 52:9.

may note this apt allusion to redemption in an exodus context. The ritual exodus—if, indeed, it was still performed—was performed without the traditional haste; it had now acquired a spiritual meaning.[1]

The haste of the Pesaḥ is associated, then, with the exodus, and the exodus is a motif of the New Year. It is possible that we have here the reflection of a usage found among other peoples of the Near East—but in different forms. Gaster has termed it appropriately Invigoration.[2] In Greece and Rome the New Year ceremonial was marked by games which included running races; in Egypt and among the Hittites a ritual battle was enacted, while in Babylonia both a running contest and a battle, in which the forces of evil were routed, figured in the epic recited by the priests.[3] Closest in resemblance to the Pesaḥ ceremony is the *'ifaḍah* of the *ḥajj*, when the pilgrims rush headlong to Muzdalifa and Mina.[4] So, too, with the Pesaḥ ceremony.[5] The people must eat in haste before the flight or exodus, a mimetic action to speed the transition from an old to a new epoch.

So far we have analysed the details only of the Pesaḥ sacrifice and its communion meal,[6] as the Compiler of the Pentateuch conceived this ritual to have been carried out at the time of the Exodus. This was, according to tradition, the only part of the Passover ceremonies that was performed on that occasion; the Israelites left Egypt on the following day.[7] But the Compiler was of the opinion that also other practices in the complex of Passover ceremonial—the practices of the Maṣṣoth week—were no less ancient than those of the Pesaḥ. It must be for this reason that he incorporates them among the ceremonies instituted, or regulated, at the time of the Exodus.[8] Although the Maṣṣoth-week ceremonies were not performed by the Israelites at the Exodus, they were to be regarded as commemorating the Exodus.[9]

[1] Cf. p. 214 below. Is. 51:1–52:12 echoes motifs of myths and legends associated with the New Year festival of the ancient Near East—the Creation, 51:1, 13 ff.; the desert, 51:3; the drying of the sea and the return of the redeemed (*ge'ulim*) or ransomed (*peduyim*, cf. pp. 163 f. above), 51:9–11, 52:3; Rahab and the dragon, 51:9; the wearing of festive garments after mourning and the removal of ritual uncleanness, 52:1 f.; and the proclamation of God and salvation, 52:7 ff.

[2] *Thespis*, 20 ff.

[3] pp. 119 f., 118 and 124, and 112 above. On the foot races in the Greek games, see F. M. Cornford, in Harrison, *Themis*, 231 ff. (his theory on Heb. רצים on p. 242 cannot be accepted), and Harrison, ibid. 514 f.

[4] p. 130 above. The pilgrims also make three circumambulations at a hurried pace around the Ka'aba. These, however, are not an integral part of the New Year ceremonial, since they appear in the *'umrah* rites which may, at any rate in Islamic times, be carried out at any time in the year.

[5] A parallel rite was perhaps performed at one time also at the autumn festival, although—in keeping with the general character of that festival—it was performed by the priests, not by the people. *Mish. Yoma* ii. 1–2 relates that a race once took place at the Temple on the Day of Atonement, but was discontinued.

[6] For a discussion of communion meals, see J. van der Ploeg, 'Meals of the Essenes', *JSS* ii, 1957, 163, and the works cited there (notably F. Bammel, *Das heilige Mahl im Glauben der Völker*, 1950).

[7] p. 51 above.

[8] Ex. 12:14–16, 17–20, 13:3–10.

[9] See p. 60 above.

Scholars have, as we have seen, commonly assumed that the Pesaḥ and the Maṣṣoth festival were two separate festivals fused by some deliberate act of religious synthesis because they were found—at some unspecified point in Israelite history—to coincide in time.[1] Both were given an historical motive by means of a popular legend which related them to the Exodus from Egypt. But in the case of the Maṣṣoth festival this bond of the legend which attached it to the Exodus was remarkably tenuous.[2] It cannot have been more convincing to the Israelite than it is to the modern scholar. And why, it may be pertinently asked, should an historical event that took place during one night be commemorated by a festival lasting one week?[3] Indeed, one passage in the Bible narrative may imply that the eating of *maṣṣoth* by the Israelites after the Exodus continued for one month.[4]

These difficulties are removed if we regard the Pesaḥ and the Maṣṣoth festival as having always been a single festival, the Pesaḥ being the opening and principal ceremony of the Passover week. It is not that two festivals have been merged to form a single festival; but a single festival has been divided into two in the Bible narrative, because only one group of ceremonies, the Pesaḥ, appeared to have full relevance to the circumstances of the Exodus.[5] It is for this reason that the phraseology of both the Pesaḥ and the Maṣṣoth-week ordinances are so remarkably similar[6]—precisely because they do refer to what was at one time a single festival. It is for this reason that the Maṣṣoth festival—like the Pesaḥ—takes place on a fixed day, at a fixed shrine, before the peculiar deity of the people.[7] The texts on the Maṣṣoth week that are assigned by the Compiler to the context of the Exodus confirm this hypothesis.

Three documents on the Maṣṣoth festival appear in the context of the Exodus, although, as I have remarked, they have little or no direct relevance to the circumstances of the Exodus. The first, Ex. 12:14–16, follows the regulations on the Pesaḥ in Ex. 12:1–13,[8] and is closely attached both to it

[1] See the theories discussed on pp. 78 ff. above.

[2] Ex. 12:34, 39 (generally assigned by the Source hypothesis to E). But already before the tenth plague Moses is warned that the Exodus is approaching, 11:1–3 (also E). On the mutual incompatibility of Ex. 12:34 and 12:39, see p. 72 above.

[3] Ex. 12:14–16, 17–20, 13:3–4, 8, 23:15, 34:18, Deut. 16:3.

[4] Ex. 16:1 ff. The date is too precise to be fortuitous; note also *ben ha'arbayim*, v. 12, cf. 12:6. See the tradition reflected in Josephus, *Ant.* II. xv. 1, p. 38 above.

[5] There was an additional reason for differentiating between the Pesaḥ and the Maṣṣoth festival—only the latter was observed outside Jerusalem. The *terminus ante quem* for the separation of the two groups of documents is provided by the 'Passover papyrus' from Elephantine dated 419–418 B.C.; see p. 221 below.

[6] *ḥuqqath 'olam*, Ex. 12:14, 17 (cf. 13:10), and 12:24, 43; *'oth*, 13:9, 12:13, and 13:16; *ha'abhodah hazo'th*, 13:5 and 12:25 f.

[7] See pp. 176 f. below.

[8] Scholars are divided as to whether Ex. 12:14 belongs to the regulations on the Pesaḥ or to those on the Maṣṣoth festival. It is here regarded as belonging to the latter because of the appearance in it of the word *ḥag*; but in fact the issue is of little importance if the Passover is considered a single festival comprising both the Pesaḥ and the Maṣṣoth festival.

and to the additional regulations in Ex. 12:43–49. There is no precise date given for the festival in Ex. 12:14–16, because היום הזה alludes to a date prescribed in the foregoing verses.[1] The categories of persons to whom the regulations of the Maṣṣoth week apply are not prescribed in Ex. 12:14–16, and there is no threat of excommunication; to have given these rules there would have been repetitive, since they appear in the text of Ex. 12:43–49. The second document, Ex. 13:3–10, is concerned not only with the future celebration of the Maṣṣoth festival, but also with its celebration in the land of Canaan. It is a popular code, and this fact is rightly reflected in its title.[2] It is for this reason that it has given the name Abib to the Passover month, instead of 'first month'; the latter was a term for priests, not for the people.[3] For the same reason this passage omits any reference to excommunication. But it, too, clearly contains an echo of parallel regulations on the Pesaḥ ceremonies,[4] and there can be little doubt that these parallel regulations are those of the document of Ex. 12:21–27. To this document Ex. 13:3–10 bears striking resemblance.[5]

On the other hand, the third document on the Maṣṣoth festival, Ex. 12:17–20, is independent of any passage on the Pesaḥ. Its independence emerges with greater distinctness because in other respects it seems almost a doublet of Ex. 12:14–16.[6] But it sets out rules for a festival of which the opening ceremony is the Pesaḥ and which lasts seven days. It is therefore more self-contained than Ex. 12:14–16. It gives details that are absent in the latter. It prescribes the time and day and month, inclusive of the Pesaḥ at (the end of) the fourteenth day, with precision,[7] and it carefully prescribes the categories of persons to whom the rules of excommunication will, in certain circumstances, be applied.[8] In short, it does not describe the Maṣṣoth festival but the Passover, of which the component parts are the Pesaḥ and the Maṣṣoth week. It probably has been preserved, although in incomplete form, precisely because it retains the original conception of the Passover as a single festal unit.

As the Pesaḥ is fixed in date and place and celebrated in honour of the deity peculiar to the Israelites,[9] so also is the festival which it opens.[10] This

[1] The date is given in Ex. 12:2, 3, 6.

[2] Ex. 13:3, 'And Moses said unto the people'.

[3] Ex. 13:4; cf. p. 207 below on Deut. 16.

[4] 'This day', Ex. 13:3, 'this service in this month', 13:5.

[5] The reference to Canaan, Ex. 13:5, cf. 12:25; the reference to the form of worship as *'abhodah*, 13:5, cf. 12:25b; the reference to future generations, 13:8, cf. 12:26.

[6] Compare Ex. 12:14 with 12:17 ('this day', 'throughout your generations', 'an ordinance for ever'), and compare 12:15bα with 12:19bα.

[7] Ex. 12:18 opp. 12:15, which prescribes only the Maṣṣoth week without giving its position in the month or its time, since these data are given in the rules on the Pesaḥ, 12:6–8.

[8] Ex. 12:19bβ and 19bα, cf. 12:3, 6, and 47–49.

[9] pp. 130 f. and 134 above.

[10] For the date, Ex. 12:18 (which also includes the Pesaḥ and prescribes its time; see pp. 130 f. above), Lev. 23:6, Num. 28:17; cf. היום הזה, Ex. 12:14, 13:3, למועד, Ex. 23:15,

festival is to last seven days. It is this feature that makes clear the relation to each other of the two component parts of the Passover. The Pesaḥ was, as we have seen, probably preceded by a preliminal period of seven days,[1] and it is followed by a post-liminal period of the same length, the Maṣṣoth week.[2] For this there are analogies in other Israelite *rites de passage*. The priest is consecrated but is forbidden to leave the Tent of Meeting for seven days,[3] the altar is sanctified but special sacrifices are performed during the following seven days,[4] the priests are cleansed after contact with the dead but obliged to wait for seven days before ministering in the sanctuary,[5] the leper after being pronounced clean must dwell outside his tent for a further seven days,[6] the marriage ceremony is followed by a seven-day feast;[7] and so, too, it appears that seven days elapsed between the anointing of Saul and his proclamation as king.[8] This period of seven days is an essential feature of the Passover; it is recorded in almost every Passover document in the Pentateuch[9] and it is given the name of the Maṣṣoth festival.

Before we discuss the reason for the use of this name, there are other features of the festival which may be analysed briefly. Each of the seven days was marked by elaborate sacrifices in later times.[10] But already at the primitive Passover it must have been customary—indeed, obligatory—for each individual male adult to offer a sacrifice on visiting the shrine, as at every *ḥag*.[11] This is not to be confused with the exchange of gifts at the New Year.[12] It was rather the tangible recognition by the worshipper of the status of the shrine, where his deity dwelt, and of the status of its attendant priests. The consumption of the flesh of a victim offered at a solemn sacrifice made closer the bond between worshipper and shrine.[13]

34:18, cf. Lev. 23:4. Note the use of *šmr*, which has the meaning of 'observing (a fixed time)', Ex. 12:17, 23:15, 34:18, Deut. 16:1; so of the Sabbath, Lev. 19:3, 30, 26:2, Ex. 31:14, 16, Deut. 5:12, Is. 56:2, 4, 6, cf. Jer. 8:7. See also pp. 131 f. above on *lel šimmurim*. On Deut. 16:1, see p. 207 below. For the place, cf. Ex. 23:15, 17, 34:23. For the deity, see p. 134 above on the properties of the *ḥag*.

[1] See p. 139 above.

[2] May maintains that the Maṣṣoth festival lasted eight days, p. 83 n. 5 above. This hypothesis receives no confirmation from a study of the texts (cf. p. 212 below on Deut. 16:8) or from analogous practices in early Israel.

[3] Lev. 8:33, 35 (cf. 9:1), Ex. 29:35.

[4] Ex. 29:37, cf. 1 Kings 8:64 ff., Ezek. 43:25.

[5] Ezek. 44:25 f.

[6] Lev. 14:1, 8 ff.

[7] Jud. 14:10–18, Tobit 11:14, *Mish. Neg.* iii. 2, cf. Gen. 29:27 f. For modern usage in Palestine, see Jaussen, *Naplouse*, 1927, 83, Granqvist, *Marriage Conditions*, i. 145 n. 2, ii. 126 and 136 n. 1.

[8] 1 Sam. 10:8 ff.

[9] Ex. 12:15, 12:18, 19, 13:6, 7, cf. 23:15, 34:18, Lev. 23:6, Num. 28:17, Deut. 16:3, 4, 8. On the festival of Nebi Musa in modern Palestine which also lasts seven days, see Canaan, op. cit. 119.

[10] See pp. 200 ff. below on Num. 28:19 ff.

[11] Ex. 23:15, 34:20, Deut. 16:16–17; this is not mentioned in passages on the Maṣṣoth week in the context of the Exodus. On the *re'iyyah* offering, see *Mish. Ta'an.* i. 2, *Ḥag.* i. 3; it should not be confused with the *ḥagigah* and *šelamim* eaten at the Pesaḥ meal; on general regulations for the festivals, *Mish. Beṣ.*, passim, *Meg.* i. 5. The regulations of Ezekiel are different, p. 220 below.

[12] pp. 148 f. above.

[13] For a not dissimilar notion at Athens, see Nilsson, *Cults, Myths, Oracles, and Politics in Ancient Greece*, 1951, 34, 44, on the Panathenaia.

In two of the documents on the Passover week that appear in the context of the Exodus we are told of special observances on certain of these seven days. In one document the seventh day is called *ḥag*,[1] in the other both the first day and the seventh day alike are called days of 'holy convocation'.[2] It may be that we should consider the latter term, which was the norm in later times, as a sign of increasing formalism in festal ritual.[3] It is to be remembered, however, that the first day of the Passover was in fact ushered in by the Pesaḥ, itself a 'holy convocation'.[4] The use of this term for the first day may, then, simply extend the status of its opening ceremony to the whole day; if this is so, then we should regard it as early and as the equivalent of *ḥag*.[5] On the other hand, it is probable that the 'holy convocation', unlike the *ḥag*, could be held at local shrines, and need not be observed at a central shrine. Evidence may be found in the rules on the Sabbath; this was a 'holy convocation',[6] but its celebration was clearly not restricted to a central shrine. The term 'holy convocation' does not of itself imply a public rest-day, for Israelites treated the new moon as a popular holiday, although this was not a 'holy convocation'.[7] The legislation on the Passover therefore explicitly prescribed abstention from work on both the first and the last days of the Passover week—and perhaps thereby it encouraged the people to attend at the shrine. Only food might be prepared, itself a significant regulation in view of the stricter prohibition of work on the Sabbath.[8] The first and seventh days were not marked, in later times, by any increase in the scale of public sacrifices over those on the other days of the festival.

The distinctive feature of the Passover week was, however, the feature from which it received its name—the unleavened bread. The name tends to stress a positive rather than—as would be in fact more correct—a negative aspect of the festival. The documents are agreed in declaring that 'seven days shall ye eat unleavened bread'.[9] But it is not the order to eat *maṣṣoth* whose infringement carries the extreme penalty of excommunication; it is the prohibition against leaven.[10] And so firm and definite is the rule against fermenting matter that it applies not only to all Israelites, but also to *gerim*, whether circumcised or not.[11]

[1] Ex. 13:6. [2] Ex. 12:16, cf. Lev. 23:7–8, Num. 28:18, 25.

[3] See p. 191 below. [4] So Lev. 23:5, cf. v. 4.

[5] So, for the seventh day of the Passover, Ex. 13:6.

[6] Lev. 23:3. On the origin of the name 'holy convocation', see Num. 10:2–10.

[7] Amos 8:5, cf. 2 Kings 4:23, 1 Sam. 20:5 f., 28 f.

[8] Lev. 23:3, cf. Ex. 16:23, 35:3; cf. the Day of Atonement, Lev. 23:28. 'Servile work' is regarded by Dillmann, op. cit. 585, and A. T. Chapman and A. W. Streane, *Book of Leviticus*, 1914, 127, as referring to agricultural labour. On the regulations about work during the Passover week, see further p. 224 below. For a general treatment of abstention from work, see H. Webster, *Rest Days*, 1916.

[9] Ex. 12:15, 13:6, 7, cf. 12:18.

[10] Ex. 12:15, 19, cf. 13:3, 7, and Deut. 16:4. On this, see Grelot, 'Dernière étape de la rédaction sacerdotale', *VT* vi, 1956, 175.

[11] Ex. 12:19, 20, cf. 12:15, 13:7.

Now, the offering of communal sacrifices throughout the seven days and the observance of special ritual on the first and the seventh days are features common to both the spring and the autumn New Year festivals in Israel. The two festivals differ from each other precisely at those points which became the principal characteristic of each and which gave each its distinctive name. The festival of Tabernacles is distinguished by the practice of leaving the house and living during the term of the festival week in a structure that is partially exposed to the sky. The Maṣṣoth festival is distinguished by the avoidance of fermented matter.

In the Pentateuch the booths of the festival of Tabernacles are said to commemorate the sojourn of the Israelites in tents during their wanderings in the Wilderness.[1] But, it has been observed, booths bear no resemblance to the tents of the Wilderness, and the latter are referred to always as *'oholim*, not *sukkoth*.[2] The booths are temporary shelters for cattle[3] or protection for watchmen against the sun during the harvesting of the grapes.[4] This does not mean that the practice at Tabernacles goes back merely to the early days of the Israelite occupation of Canaan. On the contrary, the exodus from the city to dwellings in the desert is a feature of the New Year festival throughout the Near East,[5] and it is as likely to have been performed by the Israelites before, as after, the Exodus from Egypt. The custom survived; only the form changed. The tents had become booths. Booths were in keeping with the needs of the vintage season with which the autumn festival coincided.[6]

But the exodus from the city to the desert at the new year was once a motif of the spring festival in Israel no less than of the autumn festival. We have the reflection of this springtime exodus in the story of the departure from Egypt; a ritual exodus may have been practised during the period of the Israelite Monarchy.[7] Nevertheless, the practice was maintained in full vigour throughout Israelite history only at the autumn New Year festival—because it had been kept alive by the analogous practice of living in booths at the time of the grape harvest.

We shall not err in seeking a similar reason for the maintenance of the practice of eating *maṣṣoth* during the seven days of the spring festival. The

[1] Lev. 23:42, 43, cf. Neh. 8:14 ff.

[2] Ex. 18:7, 33:8, 10, Lev. 14:8, Num. 11:10, 16:26 f., Deut. 1:27, Jos. 3:14, 7:21, and frequently; so of the nomad neighbours of Israel, Jud. 4:11, 6:5, Jer. 49:29, Hab. 3:7, Ps. 120:5, 1 Chr. 5:10. See Pedersen, op. cit. iii–iv. 421.

[3] Gen. 33:17; so of the huts of an army during the siege of a city, 2 Sam. 11:11 (cf. v. 1aβ), 1 Kings 20:12, 16. Normally an army camped in tents, see p. 210 n. 5 below.

[4] Is. 1:8, Job 27:18; Is. 4:6, Jonah 4:5; see Ps. 31:21 (E.V. 31:20), 27:5 (where it is the equivalent of *'ohel*), 18:12 (E.V. 18:11) = 2 Sam. 22:12, cf. Job 36:29.

[5] See pp. 118, 119, 120 f., 122, 123, 124, and 125 above.

[6] Lev. 23:39, Deut. 16:13. Booths are still used during the vintage season in modern Palestine, Dalman, *Arbeit*, i. 161 ff., ii. 55 ff. See p. 120 n. 1 above for similar rites in Greece.

[7] See pp. 209 f. below.

spring festival coincided with a certain stage in the growth of the barley crops. I have stressed the fact that the period of Abib is not the time when the corn was harvested.[1] In most of Palestine at that season the corn is standing, but still in the green (*'abhibh*).[2] At this stage in the growth of the cereal crops, it is customary to observe certain precautions. Care is taken to avoid forms of uncleanness which might prejudice the hopes of a bountiful harvest and to do so before, not after, the new crop is cut and eaten.[3] It is the usage of the Near East, to the present day, to leaven each batch of newly baked bread with a lump of sour dough left over from the previous batch.[4] But before the new harvest it was necessary to break this continuity in the use of the same dough, so that 'no contamination incurred by one batch would be transmitted to all its successors'.[5] The motive here was the same as the motive for avoiding leaven at the Pesaḥ sacrifice and meal, the avoidance of impurity.[6] Furthermore, there was a close ritual bond between the Pesaḥ and the corn harvest. The Pesaḥ always preceded the harvest. The grain eaten at the Pesaḥ was always grain from the old crops—whether it was orthodox or sectarian Jews who celebrated the festival.[7] The Pesaḥ was followed by the ritual waving of the Sheaf, and only thereafter might the new crops be eaten. Usage decreed, as I have remarked, that the new corn should be eaten without leaven.[8] So it was that the practice of eating unleavened bread at the Pesaḥ meal was continued during the post-liminal week which followed the Pesaḥ.

The Sheaf-offering to which I have alluded was the opening of a seven-week period that culminated in the harvest thanksgiving festival of Weeks; the bread offered at that festival was made with leaven, in contradistinction to the Sheaf-offering. To this we shall return later.[9] Here it is sufficient to remark that it is the feast of Weeks, not the Passover, that is the springtime harvest festival. A harvest thanksgiving festival must occur when, as at Tabernacles, the harvest is in full swing, not before it had begun, as was the case at the Passover. Throughout the Bible, however, the feast of Weeks has a minor role; it is an appendage to the Passover. It appeared early—certainly it was observed in the reign of Solomon[10]—

[1] See pp. 115 f. above.

[2] On the dates of the harvests in Palestine, see pp. 237 f. below.

[3] So it is customary to perform a sacrifice, Dalman, op. cit. i. 579, or to make a prayer, ibid. i. 415, or to have a solemn meal, Jaussen, *Coutumes . . . de Moab*, 352, before reaping the crops.

[4] See A. R. S. Kennedy, art. 'Bread', *EB*, and the remarks of Thompson, *Epic of Gilgamesh*, 1930, 87 f. Thompson points out that *šibu* (*šipa* of the *Epic of Gilgamesh*, xi, l. 227) is the dough of the previous baking.

[5] Oesterley, 'Early Hebrew Festival Rituals', in Hooke, *Myth and Ritual*, 113.

[6] pp. 167 ff. above.

[7] Ex. 12:8.

[8] So in modern Palestine it is usual to eat corn of the old harvest unleavened in the fields at the beginning of the harvesting; Dalman, op. cit. i. 416. For an early illustration of the sharp division between the old and the new crops, cf. Lev. 26:10.

[9] p. 194 below.

[10] See pp. 4 f. above on 1 Kings 9:25.

but it never acquired independence from the Passover in the orthodox cult. We may reasonably assume that at one time only two *ḥaggim* were celebrated in Israel, the spring and autumn New Year festivals, and neither was directly connected with harvests. The coincidence of the fruit harvest with Tabernacles was incidental.[1]

Firstfruits, then, have no primary role at the Passover. Nor is the position greatly different when we consider firstlings. There is no fixed time for the yeaning of young lambs and kids in Palestine (though they are not normally born in the cold winter months).[2] Certainly spring is not, as in Europe, the season *par excellence* for the appearance of the young animals;[3] and, in any case, young animals born immediately before the Passover would not be fit for sacrifice at that festival.[4] Nevertheless, we have seen that the Pesaḥ victim was to be a small animal born during the previous twelve months; and in some households it may have been a firstling[5]—though to restrict the victims to firstlings was neither practicable nor necessary, nor is this prescribed. And the regulations on firstlings sacrifices appear in the Pentateuch in proximity to the regulations on the Exodus Passover.[6]

According to the Pentateuch,[7] male firstlings from animal species regarded as fit for sacrifice were to be dedicated[8]—the text does not say 'sacrificed'—on the eighth day after birth, provided that they were without blemish. When they were in fact sacrificed,[9] this was to take place at a shrine,[10] and the priest was to receive the 'wave' breast and the right thigh in return for handling the blood and the fat.[11] But, we have observed,

[1] See my article, *JSS* vi, 1961, 84, and p. 128 above.

[2] Dalman, op. cit. i. 170 f., 268, 421 ff., vi. 183.

[3] The New Year for the tithe of cattle is fixed for the autumn, *Mish. R.H.* i. 1.

[4] On the fitness of young animals for sacrifice, see *Tos. Sanh.* ii. 4, *JT Sanh.* i. 2 (fol. 18d), *BT Sanh.* 11a; cf. *JT Ma'as. Sh.* v. 6 (fol. 56c) and parallel passages.

[5] On the sacrifice of firstlings as *fedu* offerings in spring in modern Palestine, see Dalman, op. cit. i. 32, vi. 71, and especially 185.

[6] Ex. 13:2, 11 ff.

[7] Firstlings laws are found in Ex. 13:2, 11 ff., 22:29, 34:19 f., Lev. 27:26 f., Num. 18:15–18, Deut. 12:6–7, 17–18, 14:23–27, 15:19–23, cf. Neh. 10:37. See Gray, *Sacrifice*, 33 ff. J. Hempel, 'Eine Vorfrage zum Erstgeburtsopfer', *ZAW* liv, 1936, 311, discusses the terminology of firstlings sacrifices.

[8] Heb. *ntn*, Ex. 22:29 (E.V. 22:28); on *he'ebhir*, 13:12, see p. 186 n. 6 below.

[9] Heb. *zbḥ*, Ex. 13:15, cf. *'kl*, Deut. 12:6–7, 14:23, 15:20.

[10] Deut. 12:6–7, 17–18, 14:23 ff., 15:20.

[11] Num. 18:15–18. There seems to be no contradiction between this passage and other passages on firstlings where the person offering the animal is entitled to eat part of it himself. Here the priest is not to receive all the flesh—this would have been expressed by וכל בשרם rather than ובשרם, v. 18. Instead of E.V., 'the flesh of them shall be thine, as the wave breast and as the right thigh, it shall be thine', it is preferable to render '(of) their flesh shall be thine *both* the wave breast *and* the right thigh . . .'. For this use of the Heb. prepositions *k. . . k. . .*, cf. 1 Sam. 30:24, Ezek. 18:4. Num. 18:15–18, then, does not mean that the share of the priests had now become the whole of the firstling instead of the customary portions; it prescribes that the firstling is a *zebhaḥ šelamim*, not an ordinary *zebhaḥ* (as Deut. 18:3), and that the priests are to receive the breast as well as the right thigh (Lev. 7:28 ff., 10:14, cf. Ex. 29:27 f.; cf. the Qumran text of 1 Sam. 2:16, and Cross, *BASOR*, No. 132, Dec. 1953, 21, col. ii, l. 5). The disposal of the rest of the victim is not the concern of these passages, which are addressed to the priests; presumably it was

it was not possible to fix a date for this sacrifice, and, indeed, there was always the greatest latitude in this matter.[1] It was therefore also permissible, by a further extension, to sell the firstling and with the proceeds of the sale to provide a festive meal at a shrine.[2] If the animal, however, had a blemish it was to be eaten in public in the city, but not at a shrine.[3]

The principles that underlay the regulations on firstlings from clean species of animals were extended to firstlings from unclean species.[4] These could not be sacrificed; instead, they were 'redeemed'. The regulations, however, vary. According to one text, either the animal was valued by the priest and a further one-fifth added—the animal then presumably remained the property of its owner—or it was sold at the valuation of the priest and the proceeds were given to the shrine;[5] according to the other text, the animal was 'redeemed' at the price of five shekels without the option of sale.[6] The treatment of a firstling ass was different. There was no option of sale, and it was either 'redeemed' with a lamb or kid, or killed in such a manner as to shed no blood.[7]

The treatment of human firstborn[8] has certain similarities with that of the firstlings of an unclean species. In the first place, both categories were, of course, 'redeemed'. The age at which they are 'set aside'—one month—and the price at which they are to be 'redeemed'—five shekels—are also the same in the case of human firstborn as in the second regulation on

eaten by the person offering the animal, Deut. 15:20, cf. Lev. 7:15. In Neh. 10:37 the firstlings are to be brought to the priests; we are not told whether they were the perquisite of the priests. At a later time, however, this was the case, Josephus, *Ant.* IV. iv. 4, *Mish. Bek.* i. 3, &c. See, however, on the whole question, Eissfeldt, *Erstlinge und Zehnten im Alten Testament*, 1917, 29 n. 1, 49, and Pedersen, op. cit. iii–iv. 313 ff.

[1] In *Tos. B. Qamma* viii. 10 we are told that a firstling might be kept even for ten years before it is offered—clearly an extreme case, but significant.

[2] Deut. 14:24 ff. [3] Deut. 15:21 ff. [4] Lev. 27:26 f., Num. 18:15–18.

[5] Lev. 27:27. [6] Num. 18:15 f.

[7] Ex. 13:13, 34:20. The ass is an unclean animal, Lev. 11:3 ff., Deut. 14:4 ff. The reasons for the specific mention of the ass (horse and dog were also unclean and were connected with idolatrous rites, 2 Kings 23:11, Is. 66:3) and the difference in the treatment to be given it are obscure. It was in common use among various classes of the people as a beast of burden (e.g. Gen. 22:3, 42:26), for riding (Num. 22:21, Jud. 10:4, 12:14, 1 Kings 13:13, 2 Kings 4:24), and for ploughing (Deut. 22:10, Is. 30:24); its consumption as food was exceptional, 2 Kings 6:25. See the study by E. Nielsen, 'Ass and Ox in the Old Testament', *Studia Orientalia Ioanni Pedersen . . . dicata*, 1953, 263. The care to avoid shedding its blood that is recommended in the present passages may indicate that there was a practice in Canaan which Israelite legislators were seeking to counteract. In a text from Mari, C. F. Jean, *Archives royales de Mari*, ii, 1950, 82 f. (No. 37), the slaughter of 'an ass foaled by a she-ass' is a ceremony at the making of a covenant. See Mendenhall, 'Puppy and Lettuce in Northwest-Semitic Covenant Making', *BASOR*, No. 133, Feb. 1954, 26, and M. Noth, 'Das alttestamentliche Bundschliessen im Lichte eines Mari-Textes', *Mélanges Isidore Lévy*, 1955, 433. Mendenhall, op. cit. 26 n. 2, points out that in South Arabian the word *ḥmr* is used of a type of covenant; in Canaan the ancestor of Shechem was called Ḥamor, Jud. 9:28 (cf. Jos. 24:32, Gen. 33:19, 34:2, 4, 6 ff.), and the god of Shechem was Baʿal Berith, Jud. 8:33, 9:4, or El Berith, 9:46, god of covenant(-making).

[8] References are found in Ex. 13:2, 13 ff., 22:28 (E.V. 22:29), 34:20, Num. 3:11 ff., 8:15 ff., 18:15–16.

firstlings of an unclean species.[1] There is another feature common to both, and this illustrates clearly that the 'redemption' of human firstborn and of firstlings of an unclean species is little more than theoretical—in neither case is it demanded that they should be without blemish. The 'redemption' had become, in fact, a tax, without cultic significance.

We have seen that the Pesaḥ ceremony was a sacrifice of redemption.[2] It was a census at which all Israelite male adults were present and symbolically redeemed, and among them the firstborn in each family naturally had a special place.[3] The Pesaḥ commemorated, too, the destruction of the Egyptian firstborn and, as a corollary, the sparing of the Israelite firstborn. Allusions to the slaying of the Egyptian animal firstlings in the Exodus legend seem almost an afterthought.[4] Clearly, the context of the Exodus Pesaḥ was a proper place in which to prescribe the regulations on human firstborn. The regulations on firstlings—and these firstlings are (with the exception of the ass, which is in a category of its own) only firstlings of a clean species, for to mention unclean animals in the context of the Passover would have been improper—do, it is true, appear in the Exodus narrative. But they appear there only because they are associated with the human firstborn, not because they have anything to do with the Pesaḥ. This is demonstrated by an examination of the relevant texts in the Pentateuch. Regulations on human firstborn may be accompanied by a reference to the Exodus;[5] regulations on animal firstlings allude to the Exodus or appear in the Exodus story only if they also mention human firstborn.[6]

[1] Num. 18:15 f., cf. 3:11 ff., especially v. 46 f., 8:16, 18. The poll-tax for every male adult is half a shekel, Ex. 30:11 ff., cf. 38:26; later it was one-third, Neh. 10:33 (E.V. 10:32). The regulations about the payment after a vow may provide an explanation for the payment for firstborn, Lev. 27:2 ff.; they are the equivalent of a vow for a male under the age of five, v. 6. Gray, *Numbers*, on Num. 18:16, suggests that it is a late insertion in the text.

[2] p. 164 above. Cf. Kamphausen, *Verhältnis des Menschenopfers zur israelitischen Religion*, 1896, 63 ff.

[3] Cf. the census of the Levites in Num. 3:11 ff., 8:5 ff., where this special class of the people is related to the firstborn. It is reasonable to assume that at one time the firstborn discharged priestly functions in Israel, before the erection of a priestly shrine; cf. Baudissin, *Geschichte des alttestamentlichen Priesterthums*, 1889, 55. This was the view of the Rabbis, *Mish. Zeb.* xiv. 4, cf. Targ. Onq. on Ex. 24:5, which describes the 'young men' of that passage as 'the firstborn'. The objections of Gray, op. cit., on Num. 3:11–13 are hardly valid. That a special vow was made in the case of Samuel (1 Sam. 1–2), who was a firstborn son, is an unsatisfactory argument; Micah's installation of 'one of his sons', Jud. 17:5, as a priest is said in the following verse to have been irregular.

[4] Ex. 11:5b, 12:29b; see Dillmann, *Exodus*, on Ex. 12:29, Pedersen, 'Passahfest und Passahlegende', *ZAW* lii, 1934, 166. In 13:15 the destruction of the Egyptian firstlings is integrated into the general picture.

[5] Num. 3:12 f., 8:16–18, with allusions to the tenth plague.

[6] Ex. 13:2, 11 ff., 34:19 f., mention both firstborn and firstlings, and the first two passages are in the context of the Exodus, the latter follows the mention of the Exodus. There is no reference to firstborn in Lev. 27:26 f., Deut. 12:6–7, 17–18, 14:23 ff., 15:19 ff., and also no reference to the Exodus. Exceptions to the rule—but negative exceptions—are the brief passages of Ex. 22:28 f. (E.V. 22:29 f.) and Num. 18:15 f., which deal with both firstborn and firstlings but do not mention the Exodus.

The destruction of the firstborn of Egypt and the 'redemption' of the firstborn of Israel are a central feature of the Passover myth. Before we turn, however, from the ritual to the myth, it will be well to recall the argument that I have advanced in the course of these pages regarding the antiquity of the Pentateuchal documents on the Passover. I have maintained that by the time of the Chronicler—if not at an earlier epoch—they must have had approximately the form of our extant M.T.[1] There had been gradual development in the ritual of the Pesaḥ, and the traditional or official view of that process is shown by the arrangement of the various documents in the Pentateuch. The narrative (and the regulations) of the Pesaḥ of the Exodus was considered the original nucleus, that is, the earliest form of the festival.[2]

That the Pesaḥ should traditionally be associated with this remote event in the history of Israel is in itself testimony to the antiquity of the festival; and this antiquity is confirmed by other considerations. For some details of Pesaḥ ceremonial we have found analogies in the New Year festivals that were ancient, as well as widespread, in the Near East. Some analogies are found also in the *ḥag* which, according to our Pentateuch narrative, was celebrated by the Israelites even before the Exodus.[3] It is even more significant that in one important respect—the ceremonial handling of blood by laymen—the Pesaḥ is without parallel in Israelite sacrificial procedure.[4] We must conclude that this practice, so greatly at variance with the norm, was established before the codification of Israelite religious law—and the codification can have taken place only after the practices which it legalized had become firmly accepted by long-established usage. So, too, with the time of the Pesaḥ ritual. It was performed by night, and this is wholly out of keeping with the customary procedure of the Temple.

And, indeed, the Pesaḥ was a communion ceremony in a class by itself in Israelite ritual. With other Israelite sacrifices after the settlement in Canaan, it was possible for the worshippers to increase their offerings to the deity, and thereby to seek his favour with greater confidence. At the Pesaḥ, additional offerings were indeed made, but they were kept strictly apart from the Pesaḥ victims—even when the trend towards the co-ordination of ritual was strongest.[5] The Pesaḥ remained always the annual offering of a single victim on a single night by a single group of celebrants. It is never mentioned in the denunciations of sacrifice by the prophets. It was not a gift to the deity, and gave no ground for misinterpretation or reproach;[6] it was a communal sacrament of redemption.

[1] pp. 76 f. above and 189 ff. below. Cf., on the Exodus, Jud. 6:13, 1 Sam. 2:27, 4:8, 6:6, Amos 4:10, &c.

[2] With this we may contrast the arrangement of festal practices by the writer of Jubilees, p. 234 below.

[3] p. 43 above.

[4] See p. 157 above.

[5] On the Pesaḥ in the Chronicler, see pp. 226 f. below.

[6] Jer. 7:22 does not mean that a Pesaḥ sacrifice was not prescribed at the Exodus; *'olah wazebhaḥ* is used to cover sacrifice in general, and the Pesaḥ is not included among them.

This was the significance of the annual ritual. But what was the meaning of the Pesaḥ myth, and how did it come to acquire so strong a hold over Israelite thought and tradition? There seems to be no parallel in other religions of the Near East for the Exodus account of the visitation by a deity by night over the houses of the community by whom he is worshipped and the destruction of the firstborn of their enemies.[1] What was the nature of this deity? It has been suggested that the smearing of blood was a ritual against plague and demons.[2] But the deity was not a demon. He did not, according to the myth, destroy indiscriminately; he destroyed only those who did not belong to the social unit by whom he was recognized. The ceremony of blood-smearing cannot have been a ceremony directed towards a household god;[3] we are not told that the dwelling-places were new, nor was the deity a house-god. Gray finds significance in the fact that the blood was applied to the outside of the dwelling-place and that the door was closed. He deduces that it was intended to bar some power from entry.[4] Trumbull, on the other hand, regards the blood-sign as an invitation to that power to enter the dwelling-place: and he considers the ritual to be a threshold covenant.[5] Neither view seems tenable. It is not stated in the narrative of the Exodus Pesaḥ that the doors were closed; it is stated only that no Israelite was to leave his dwelling-place on that night,[6] or to take any of the flesh of the victim outside his dwelling-place.[7] The myth tells us that the deity (or his emissary) saw the blood-sign and passed over—not into—the dwelling-places, while, on the other hand, he must have slain the Egyptians by a different process—presumably by entering their dwelling-places.[8]

We are not justified in rejecting the traditional interpretation of *psḥ* in the Pesaḥ context as 'pass'.[9] On the contrary, the notion of movement is evident in words cognate to this root—*psḥ*, 'limp, be lame';[10] *pśh*, 'spread, extend';[11] *pśʿ*, 'step, march';[12] and this notion is clear in the Pesaḥ myth.

[1] Ex. 12; see ch. 2 above.

[2] A. Wendel, *Opfer in der altisraelitischen Religion*, 1927, 59, following Beer, *Pesachim*, 17; cf. P. Volz, *ThLZ*, 1901, 635 f.; Meyer, *Israeliten und ihre Nachbarstämme*, 1906, 38; and Frazer, *Golden Bough. Dying God*, 174 ff.

[3] As Benzinger, art. 'Passover', § 9, *EB*, and Lods, *Israel*, 293.

[4] Gray, op. cit. 362.

[5] Trumbull, *Blood Covenant*, 231, and *Threshold Covenant*, 203 ff. On the threshold covenant, see Frazer, *Folklore in the Old Testament*, iii. 16; and for modern Palestinian customs, Curtiss, op. cit. 233. Cf. Burckhardt, *Notes on the Bedouins and Wahábys*, 151 n., on the custom among the Copts of obliging a bride entering her bridegroom's house to 'step over the blood (of an animal) flowing upon the threshold, at the door-way'.

[6] Ex. 12:22.

[7] Ex. 12:46.

[8] It certainly seems the intention of the narrator to show that the parents of the Egyptian firstborn—and presumably also the firstborn themselves—were inside their dwelling-places on that night; see Ex. 11:5, 12:29 f.

[9] As does T. F. Glasson, *JTS*, N.S., x, 1959, 79 ff.

[10] See pp. 95 and 98 above.

[11] Lev. 13:5, 6, 7, &c.; 14:39, 44, 48.

[12] Is. 27:4, 1 Sam. 20:3, cf. 1 Chr. 19:4; see S. Adler, 'Der Versöhnungstag in der Bibel, sein Ursprung und seine Bedeutung', *ZAW* iii, 1883, 179.

It is true that another Jewish tradition renders *psḥ ʿal* as 'spare', but the tradition is late and suspect.[1] Semantics provides an uncertain guide; for the explanation of a term around which a myth has been woven, we should look rather into the beliefs of the people among whom it was current.

Fortunately, the explanation seems to be ready to hand, and in the Exodus narrative itself. The word *ʿbr* has all the meanings postulated in the Pesaḥ story for the word *psḥ*.[2] It will be recalled that I have advanced the view that the numbering of male adult Israelites at springtime was practised already at the primitive Pesaḥ. We know that this practice survived to a very late date in the history of Israel.[3] *ʿbr* is used in exactly this sense. The Israelites are said to 'pass over (intransitive) unto them that are numbered'.[4] The metaphor is derived from the counting of sheep with a rod.[5] To 'cause to pass over' in this sense comes to signify to 'set apart'.[6] And while to 'pass (intransitive) under the rod' means to be numbered, to 'pass over (transitive)' an object means to mark it out.[7] The phrase appears to be used derivatively of to 'single out (for punishment or harm)'[8] and, on the other hand, to 'single out (for forgiveness or kindness)';[9] and here *ʿbr* has exactly the significance of *psḥ* in the Exodus narrative; the phrase means at the same time both 'pass over' and 'spare'.[10]

But whether this explanation of the use of *psḥ ʿal*, 'spare', is correct or not, its employment with this meaning is confined to the story of the Exodus Passover. The significance of *psḥ ʿal* as 'pass over', on the other hand, is primary. The Pesaḥ is a *rite de passage*, as Philo saw well (although his use of the term διαβατήρια, which implies a particular Greek rite as well as a general notion, detracted from the value of his observation).[11] It marks

[1] It is largely based on Is. 31:5, which is not independent evidence; see p. 97 above.

[2] It occurs in the Exodus narrative, Ex. 12:12, 23.

[3] p. 258 below.

[4] Ex. 30:13, 14, 38:26, cf. 2 Sam. 2:15; so in Qumran texts, *Doc. Cong.* i. 8–9, 27 (Barthélemy, *Discoveries*, i. 109). Cf. the phrase 'pass over in the covenant', Deut. 29:11, at Qumran, *Doc. Comm.* i. 24 (Burrows, *Dead Sea Scrolls of St. Mark's Monastery*, ii, 1951). Should *keseph ʿobher*, Gen. 23:16, 2 Kings 12:5 (E.V. 12:4), be interpreted in this way, 'money that is counted (in payment)'? In the latter passage the text may be at fault, but the term denotes the poll-tax.

[5] See Jer. 33:13, and cf. 'whatsoever passeth under the rod', Lev. 27:32.

[6] Ex. 13:12 of the firstlings and firstborn; here probably lies the significance of *heʿebhir*, 'dedicate' to Molech, Lev. 18:21, Deut. 18:10, 2 Kings 16:3, 17:17, &c. The term can scarcely be taken literally; to 'pass through the fire' is not a natural expression for to 'burn', cf. Deut. 12:31. In later times, perhaps with the more frequent use of other terms, particularly *pqd*, the significance of *heʿebhir* was forgotten; cf. 2 Chr. 28:3 (ויבער) with 2 Kings 16:3 (העביר). The use of *heʿebhir* for passage through water, however, was well established and continued in use, cf. p. 188 n. 1 below.

[7] Cf. Deut. 24:5, 'neither shall he be charged (lit. one shall not mark him out) with any business'.

[8] See Zech. 9:8aβ, Job 13:13, cf. Nahum 2:1b (E.V. 1:15) and possibly 3:19.

[9] Amos 7:8, 8:2, followed by the preposition *l*; Prov. 19:11, Mic. 7:18, followed by *ʿal*; cf. Ezek. 20:37.

[10] Ex. 12:12 f., 23, 27; in the first two passages the verb *psḥ* describes an action that is included in the broader term *ʿbr*.

[11] p. 26 above. For *ʿbr* in the sense of performing a *rite de passage* by passing between,

the passing from the old year to the new year. According to the belief widespread in the Near East and found among the Jews also, the divine powers fix the fate of human society for the coming year at the New Year festival—who will live and who will die.[1] The myth is reflected in the ritual—or the ritual in the myth—and the Pesaḥ was performed by Israelites with punctilious reverence as a rite of redemption at a time when destiny was in the balance. In particular, the firstborn were specially exposed to the unseen workings of Providence, for by their birth they had opened a new epoch. While the people carried out the ritual, the deity (according to the myth) passed from family group to group, marking some for life and some for death; and those who had performed the ritual would be saved. And after performing the ritual, the Israelites went out in military array from the city to the desert. Perhaps they went out in order to avoid the supernatural forces in possession of the city who were determining the fates of the ensuing year. Perhaps they went in search of vegetation and the vegetation deity; for this there is little direct evidence, but the exodus occurred at night and in the middle of the month when the moon was in its vigour—and the influence of the moon on the growth of plant life is a widespread and constant motif in the Near East.[2]

The spring New Year festival cannot be assigned to a specific period or place; it is timeless, and restricted to no particular area of the Near East. It is alluded to in Near Eastern documents older than the period of the Israelite Exodus from Egypt.[3] But in the story of the Israelite spring New Year festival and its celebration at the Exodus we have more than myth; we have legend. The narrative is given a precise historical and geographical setting. The sojourn of the Israelites in Egypt reaches its end with the tenth plague.[4] This plague is not an aetiological explanation for the privileged status of firstborn among Israelites, since the Compiler has already assigned this to the patriarchal period.[5] Nor, indeed, is the sparing of the Israelite firstborn and the destruction of the firstborn of the enemy wholly the central feature of the narrative. The narrator emphasizes that it is Egyptian firstborn who are killed. It is the boundary of Egyptian

not passing over, as the sign of a covenant, see Gen. 15:9 ff. and Jer. 34:18. For a similar rite elsewhere, see O. Masson, 'A propos d'un rituel hittite pour la lustration d'une armée . . .', *RHR* cxxxvii, 1950, 5, and Henninger, 'Was bedeutet die rituelle Teilung eines Tieres in zwei Hälften?', *Biblica*, xxxiv, 1953, 344.

[1] See p. 147 above.

[2] See p. 132 above.

[3] On the date of the Exodus, see T. J. Meek, *Hebrew Origins*, 1950; Noth, *History of Israel*, 1960; and especially Rowley, *From Joseph to Joshua*, 1950, and the bibliography there. The Exodus is assigned by Rowley and by the consensus of opinion to the thirteenth century. See, however, Drioton, 'Date de l'Exode', *Revue d'histoire et de philosophie religieuses*, xxxv, 1955, 36 ff.

[4] For emphasis on the tenth plague to the exclusion of the others, see Ps. 136:10 ff.

[5] Gen. 25:29 ff., &c.

territory at the Red Sea that the Israelites cross to emerge into a new life—a *rite de passage* in national legend that was regarded as a turning-point in the history of Israel.[1] The legend is unequivocally connected with Egypt. On this, Israelite tradition is unanimous and emphatic.

What was the historical event that took place in Egypt and left this indelible mark on Israelite history? The Exodus—of at least some of the Hebrews—is placed by many scholars in the reign of Rameses II.[2] The stela of Merenptah, the son of Rameses II, shows the Israelites—or some of them—to be settled already in Canaan. Several of his brothers—at least two of them older than Merenptah—seem to have predeceased their father.[3] The death of these sons of the Pharaoh may well present the key to the story of the tenth plague[4] and the Exodus of the Israelites from Egypt that followed.[5] Perhaps one of the Egyptian princes died at the time of the Israelite spring New Year festival, perhaps later Israelite historians assigned the historical event to that annual ceremony. We cannot tell. But that Israelite tradition should have associated the New Year festival with an event which opened a new era in Israelite history[6] is a process that is amply repeated in the subsequent story of the Passover.

[1] On the crossing of water as a *rite de passage* into a new region, Gen. 32:23 ff., E.V. 32:22 ff. (cf. Deut. 2:37), Is. 47:2, Ezek. 47:5 ff. The notion is found most frequently of the passage of the Jordan, Gen. 32:11 (E.V. 32:10), Num. 32:27, 29, Deut. 2:29, Jos. 1:11, Jud. 3:28, and often; cf. Reymond, op. cit. 99. On the boundary of the 'River of Egypt', Num. 34:5, Jos. 15:4, 47, 1 Kings 8:65, 2 Kings 24:7, 2 Chr. 7:8, Is. 27:12, &c. (For a theory that the 'River of Egypt' is the Pelusiac branch of the Nile, see H. Bar-Deroma, 'River of Egypt . . .', *PEQ*, 1960, 37.)

Cook, in W. R. Smith, *Religion*, 610, 671 f., draws a parallel between the crossing of the Jabbok by Jacob and his household (Gen. 32:23 ff.), his struggle with the supernatural adversary, his being touched on the thigh and caused to limp (but cf. Hos. 12:4 f., E.V. 12:3 f.), on the one hand, and the passage of the Jordan by the Israelites before the conquest of Canaan, immediately followed by the rite of circumcision (Jos. 5), on the other. Circumcision is closely connected with the Pesaḥ (p. 135 above); one may note the similarity between *psḥ*, Pesaḥ, and *psḥ*, 'lame'. But Cook's hypothesis is hazardous. Gen. 32 may refer to an antique *rite de passage*; cf. the crossing of the Red Sea three days after the Exodus from Egypt (Ex. 14, Num. 33:5–8; cf. p. 144 above on the significance of three). But the story of Gen. 32 is largely intended to supply etymologies to Jabbok and Peniel, and to justify the prohibition against eating sinews of the thigh.

[2] Breasted, *History of Egypt*, 1950, 462.

[3] A. H. Gardiner, *Egypt of the Pharaohs*, 1961, 267. Other scholars assign the Exodus to the reign of Merenptah himself, regarding Rameses as the Pharaoh of the Oppression who had died before the Exodus, cf. Ex. 2:23. See, in addition to the works cited on p. 187 n. 3 above, de Vaux, review, *RB* lviii, 1951, 278, and M. B. Rowton, 'Problem of the Exodus', *PEQ*, 1953, 46, who gives a lower date.

[4] On the mourning for the eldest son of the Pharaoh, see Herodotus ii. 79.

[5] Compare Ex. 4:22 with 11:4 ff.

[6] References to the Exodus as opening an era are found in Ex. 16:1, Num. 1:1, 9:1, 1 Kings 6:1, cf. Deut. 1:3, Amos 2:10, 3:1, Micah 6:4, 7:15, Ps. 81:11 (E.V. 81:10), 135:8 f., 136:10 ff., &c.

6

THE PASSOVER IN CANAAN

IN the preceding chapters I have sought to present a picture of the primitive Passover as it was thought to have been celebrated at the time of the Exodus from Egypt. This, it should be stressed, is the picture conceived in the mind of the Compiler of the Pentateuch, who, I have maintained, assigned the several documents that stand in Ex. 12–13 to their present place.[1] Some of the features of this primitive Passover have analogies in the New Year practices of neighbouring peoples and are attested by ancient records. Other features of the primitive Passover are peculiar to the Israelite spring festival. They are not found in the autumn festival, nor, in their specific form, are they found in other New Year festivals of the Near East. But they are in no way at variance with the notions that underlie those New Year celebrations.[2]

In the documents on the Passover in the narrative of the Exodus from Egypt we have found few discrepancies, and they are of minor importance. The problem of discrepancies assumes larger proportions when we turn to an analysis of the documents that purport to deal with the Passover of the post-Exodus period. It is imperative, therefore, that we should view the complex of Passover documents in its entirety. We must see it as it was seen by the Hebrews who had the Pentateuch before them largely as we have it now—but who also had the inestimable advantage of being nearer than we to the date of its composition. Only they could view the picture wholly in focus. The writer of 2 Chr. 35:12–13 appears to have been in possession of texts of Ex. 12 and Deut. 16 that resembled the texts that we have today. He attempted to reconcile the apparent contradictions which he detected in them; the same contradictions are present in our extant Massoretic Text.[3] The Compiler of the Pentateuch in its extant form is therefore likely to have preceded, or to have been contemporary with, the Chronicler.

To maintain this view is not to solve the question of the relative dates of composition of each Passover document in the Pentateuch. That is a question that may never achieve satisfactory solution. The grouping of Pentateuchal documents on the basis of an analysis of their words and phrases is, I have already suggested, of little practical value in a study of the development of ritual. Technical terms are employed in accordance with the function and contents of each individual document rather than its

[1] pp. 76 f. above. [2] Chs. 4–5 above. [3] See p. 227 below.

hypothetical date. Nor is it likely that important discrepancies where they occur in our present texts should be explained away as contemporary differences of ideas and usages. The very extent and antiquity of New Year ceremonial—and the Passover, I have argued, falls within this category—would seem to disprove the restriction of particular rites or forms of rites to certain areas of Palestine, or to individual shrines. We may assume, I have already maintained, that the arrangement of the documents in the order in which they stand in the Massoretic Pentateuch is deliberate and meaningful. The Compiler conceived of certain ritual practices as so ancient that they belonged to the time of the Exodus from Egypt, a remote event in the history of Israel. Others he regarded as of later origin, and they appear in one of the later books. The chain of the Passover tradition is long and unbroken. We cannot, on our own evidence, assign each link to a particular order in the chain. But the Compiler has set them in a certain order, and we have no grounds for asserting that he is not correct.[1]

The documents on the post-Exodus Passover fall naturally into two groups, each of three passages. The first group deals only with certain aspects of the festival. Of this group two documents are embodied in a broad scheme of festal legislation in which the Passover is no more than a single item; one prescribes the festal calendar, the other gives the tariff of sacrifices in the Jerusalem Temple. The third document, Num. 9 : 1–14, also deals with particular aspects of the festival, but, unlike the other documents of this group, it is concerned solely and specifically with the Pesaḥ; and it is attached most insecurely to the framework of the book in which it appears. It is an independent document.[2]

The documents of this first group to some extent repeat the regulations of the Exodus Passover. But they also expand and develop particular aspects of those regulations. The position is very different in the case of the second group of documents. These are not concerned with certain facets of the ritual. They are general summaries of the Passover. They are, moreover, of a popular character, and we should not be surprised to find in them less formal expressions and phraseology.

The first two passages in this second group appear in the codes of Ex. 20–23 and 33–34; they are brief and succinct. The third document, Deut. 16:1–8, 16–17, on the other hand, prescribes Passover regulations in some detail. Here we have not, as in the first group, an extension of earlier ritual; we have the amendment or curtailment of certain elements of the Exodus Passover. The text of Deut. 16 appears to stand in direct opposition to the Passover passages of the rest of the Pentateuch.

[1] His arrangement of the Passover regulations into two groups—those that deal with the Exodus Passover, and those that are concerned with the celebration of the festival in Canaan—is followed by the writer of Jub. 49 and by Ezekielos; see pp. 22 and 24 above.

[2] See p. 192 below.

The details of these apparent discrepancies between Deut. 16 and other Passover regulations in the Pentateuch are discussed below in the present chapter. But the very fact that regulations which appear to stand in contradiction to each other have been preserved raises the problem that faces all students of the Pentateuch. How did the Compiler act when such discrepancies appeared in his texts? Whether these discrepancies were real or imaginary is of minor consequence, for even imaginary divergences would give rise to an attitude of doubt that it is the aim of religious codes to remove. It may be assumed that the Compiler was a representative of the official schools of teachers at Jerusalem. Did the Compiler emend the text where it was at variance with the practice of his own time? Or did he simply omit what was inconvenient? Or, on the other hand, did he pass down all those texts that had reached his day, however embarrassing they might be to the hierarchy of his time? To these questions the answer is clear—in the narrow context of the Passover. It is certain that the Compiler would not have ventured to emend the text, even where it contradicted the practices of his contemporaries. Of this the apparent opposition between our texts of Ex. 12 and Deut. 16 is proof enough. These texts are equally proof that the Compiler would not have omitted words or phrases. A small omission in the text of Deut. 16 would have removed, at one stroke, a serious embarrassment; this was not done. We may conclude that the texts are largely preserved in the form in which they reached the hands of the Compiler. Their antiquity and their sanctity were guarantees of their survival.

This general discussion is of no small importance for our study of the development of the Passover after the Exodus. Its conclusions may encourage us to rely largely upon the integrity of our Pentateuchal texts as we have them today. It induces a further consideration. The Rabbis acknowledged the thesis of gradual development in the history of the Passover; they distinguished the 'Pesaḥ of (later) generations' from the 'Pesaḥ of Egypt'. The existence of discrepancies between the texts of Ex. 12 and that of Deut. 16 enables us to take this process of evolution still farther back. We have here a tacit admission by the Compiler that there was gradual development already in the centuries before him.[1]

A reliable criterion for assessing the comparative age of the varying forms of a religious rite may be found in their similarity or dissimilarity to what is normative in the latest period. So, too, with the Passover ritual. Wherever it differs from the general pattern that had become established in later times, it can only be early. This is particularly true of

[1] The maxim of the school of R. Ishmael, אין מוקדם ומאוחר בתורה, appears at a much later time; see W. Bacher, *Älteste Terminologie der jüdischen Schriftauslegung*, 1899, 167 f. The rule was applied to Num. 9:1 opp. 1:1, see p. 192 below; it is widely employed with texts of a haggadic character.

sacrificial procedure, for the rules of public sacrifice cannot lightly admit of exceptions. Wherever, on the other hand, a rite conforms in its details to the practice of later times, it may be late—but it may also be early, since it may be the product of a long and continuous tradition.

When, now, we examine the arrangement by the Compiler of individual passages on the Passover in the Pentateuch, we observe that it agrees fully with this principle. It is the Exodus Passover, the earliest 'historical' celebration of the festival, which includes, for example, the rite of the smearing of blood that must—according to this principle—be early; it was not observed at the Temple of post-Exilic Jerusalem. Ex. 12 includes also the regulations on the special dress of the celebrants; this, too, was—for reasons which I shall advance later—omitted in later times. Ex. 12 declares, on the other hand, that the Pesaḥ is a night ritual, a feature quite out of keeping with normative sacrificial procedure. This feature has survived to the present day, yet it is none the less antique. However, the distinctive features of later Passover passages—Lev. 23, Num. 9, and Num. 28—do not appear in Ex. 12–13. But they do appear in the ritual of the later Temple. The Compiler indicates that he regards these features—the formal festal calendar, the Sheaf-offering, the amendments to the cleanness laws, and the complex sacrificial tariff[1]—in that order—as the product of later evolution.[2] He is probably right.

Perhaps most instructive in this respect is the passage in Num. 9 which lays down rules for the observance of the 'second Pesaḥ', in the second instead of the first month. Its regulations are held—according to the introductory formula of the passage—to have been prescribed at the Pesaḥ of the year after the Exodus, in, that is, the first month.[3] But there is here an inconsistency. Num. 1:1 (which prescribes the 'numbering' of Israel) has already brought us beyond the month of the Passover—to the first day of the second month; it is followed by the solemn offering each day by the twelve princes on the occasion of the dedication of the Tabernacle.[4] The day after the twelve offerings would then be, neatly enough, the fourteenth day of the second month; and it is then—in spite of the dating of the introductory words of Num. 9:1 to the first month—that we have the regulations about the 'second Pesaḥ'.[5] This arrangement is not, of course, fortuitous. It is not the cleanness laws, already given in the context of the Exodus Passover, that the Compiler regards as late, but their amendment to allow of a second Pesaḥ. This amendment was observed in late times; it does not

[1] Num. 28:19 ff. gives details of the daily 'offering by fire' mentioned briefly in Lev. 23:8.

[2] On the short Passover laws of Ex. 23 and 34, see pp. 193 f. below. They contain no material that warrants their inclusion in the discussion here.

[3] Num. 9:1.

[4] Num. 7:1 ff.

[5] *Siphre* on Num. 9:1 notes that its date is earlier than that of Num. 1:1.

appear in the account of the Exodus Pesaḥ. It is therefore, we may assume, a late development. We may detect equal deliberation on the part of the Compiler in his setting of the regulations of Num. 28. They give details of the daily offering by fire mentioned briefly in Lev. 23; and these details are inserted in regulations ascribed to the fortieth year of the wanderings in the Wilderness.[1] The details are a late development, in the view of the Compiler.

In the present chapter I shall, therefore, follow the order of the documents as they appear in the Massoretic Text. We shall find a gradual accumulation of new ritual, on the one hand, and, on the other, the amendment or adjustment of older Passover ritual to the norm of Temple procedure.

The parallel passages of Ex. 23:14–15, 17 and 34:18, 23 are set in the framework of legal codes written with great succinctness.[2] The three annual *ḥaggim* are prescribed in close proximity to each other. It is evident that they are prescribed for an agricultural community, and the brief details on the Passover are those that would concern farmers and farming.[3] This is a *ḥag*, which involves a visit to the shrine at which offerings must be made, and the absence of male adults from the farmsteads lasts seven days.[4] The period of seven days is marked on the farms, as at the shrines, by the eating of *maṣṣoth*. We note that the time of the Passover is prescribed in a way that would be readily understood by the farmer—'the time appointed in the month Abib (corn in the green)'.[5] To the farmer this was clear enough—for him there was no need for the calculations employed by priests who fixed the calendar. In this passage, too, there is no description of the Pesaḥ; the details of its ritual were the concern of those at the shrines where it was to be held, not of those on the farms.

These passages, then, provide us with little more information than that they were probably composed after the settlement in Canaan. The Passover had no direct bearing on agriculture, except that at that season of the year the corn is in the green. The autumn festival, on the other hand, stands 'at the end (lit. going-forth) of the year' or 'at the year's end (lit. circuit)'[6]—at the time, that is, when the farmer is beginning his preparations for a new

[1] Num. 27:12 f.; cf. 33:38, 48.

[2] Ex. 20:22–23:33, 34:1 ff.

[3] It is the more significant that, even in this context, the *raison d'être* of the Passover is said to be an historical event, while the other *ḥaggim* are based upon agricultural life. See p. 111 above.

[4] See also Ex. 34:24. There is no need to follow Pedersen, *Israel*, iii–iv. 386, who assigns this verse to a late writer, asserting that it is 'typical of the exilic and post-exilic way of thinking'. Bentzen, *Introduction*, ii. 57, on the other hand, finds 'Deuteronomistic elements' in the verse; cf. Alt, *Kleine Schriften*, i. 317 n. 1.

[5] Ex. 23:15, 34:18. The term למועד refers evidently to a familiar 'appointed time' in the period of Abib, while כאשר צויתך implies that there were more detailed instructions elsewhere known to the originator of this regulation.

[6] Ex. 23:16, 34:22.

farming cycle. A comparison of the two texts is of interest. I do not wish to enter here into the arguments on the relative interdependence of the codes to which they belong; this is a matter for textual criticism rather than for an analysis of ritual.[1] But the fact remains that the Compiler assigns one form of words to Ex. 23 and another to Ex. 34; the former was, according to the context, revealed at Sinai in the third month, the latter over forty days later.[2] We are justified in assuming that, in the eyes of the Compiler, developments may be observed in the latter that are absent in the former. This is indeed the case. The date of the festival of Tabernacles in the former is, as we have seen, described by the neutral phrase 'going-forth of the year', in the latter it has the more definite calendric description 'circuit of the year'.[3] So, too, with the feast of Weeks. It is true that in both Ex. 23 and Ex. 34 the Passover and Tabernacles are fixed in date, while the feast of Weeks is not dated. But while this festival is called simply the 'feast of harvest, the firstfruits of thy labours' in Ex. 23:16, in 34:22 it is the 'feast of weeks, (even) of the firstfruits of wheat harvest'. The sharper definition of calendric dating is, in the eyes of the Compiler, a later development.

It is logical, then, that the formal festal calendar of Lev. 23 also should be classed by the Compiler among the post-Exodus documents. Precision in the dates and time of the Passover had already appeared in the context of the Exodus,[4] and already there the 'appointed times' included, or actually were, special days of 'holy convocation'.[5] Lev. 23 goes farther; a sacrificial 'offering made by fire' is prescribed for each day of the festal week, and it is made on behalf of the whole community.[6] We have passed beyond the stage of the simple gift made by each visitant to the shrine;[7] this is a formal offering which foreshadows the complex sacrificial ritual of later times.[8]

But the principal contribution of Lev. 23 to the development of the Passover is a regulation which appears at first sight to have no direct bearing upon it, the waving of the Sheaf.[9] Now we observe, in the first place, that the ordinance is to be carried out 'when ye be come into the land which I give unto you';[10] it is to be observed in the land of Canaan. Secondly, the ritual has no real counterpart in Israelite practice. There were other Israelite offerings of firstfruits.[11] But these were personal offerings, and they

[1] See p. 172 n. 10 above on Ex. 23:18 and 34:25.
[2] Ex. 24:18.
[3] So also 2 Chr. 24:23; cf. p. 129 n. 3 above on the meaning of *tequphah*.
[4] pp. 130 f. above.
[5] Ex. 12:16; see p. 178 above for an analysis of this term.
[6] Lev. 23:8; cf. the similar provisions for Tabernacles, 23:36.
[7] Ex. 23:15b, 34:20b.
[8] pp. 200 f. below.
[9] Lev. 23:9 ff. On the Sheaf, see also the different views of Gray, *Sacrifice*, 323 ff., and Morgenstern, 'Origin of *Maṣṣoth* and the *Maṣṣoth*-Festival', *AJT* xxi, 1917, 278 ff. The regulation on the Sheaf is given in Deut. 16:9 f. in more popular form; cf. p. 207 below.
[10] Lev. 23:10.
[11] Of corn, wine, and oil, Num. 18:12, Deut. 18:4, 2 Chr. 31:5; of wine and oil, Neh. 10:38 (E.V. 10:37); of wool, Deut. 18:4; of firstfruits in general, Ex. 23:19, 34:26, Deut.

were accompanied by popular rejoicing; the Sheaf-offering, on the contrary, was the occasion of a solemn ritual which included sacrifices on behalf of the whole community. Other firstfruits were given to the priests; the Sheaf was apparently laid upon the altar.[1] And, perhaps most important, the feasts of Weeks and Tabernacles, the festivals of firstfruits, were held when the harvest might normally be expected to be at its height. The Sheaf-offering, on the other hand, preceded the utilization of the corn harvest; it was forbidden to eat the new crops before the Sheaf had been dedicated.[2]

Of the other firstfruit offerings in connexion with the corn crops, each represented a stage in the manufacture of bread. Offerings were made in the form of parched grain[3] and as newly made cakes of coarse flour.[4] But the beginning of the whole process—the most vital in the national economy—was celebrated by this waving of a sheaf of the crop that ripens first in Palestine, barley;[5] it was not repeated for the later crops, and it was carried out before the barley was ripe. There is no exactly similar ceremony among the other communities of the Near East. That a sheaf of corn was offered annually by the Sumerians is a matter for conjecture.[6] The rites of the Sheaf-offering to Min in Egypt were held in the summer, when (at any rate, in theory) the harvest was ripe.[7]

The solemn dedication of the Sheaf in Israel presumably took place originally at a time when the new crops were on the point of being eaten. But as soon as a rite of this character becomes attached to a fixed date in the calendar it will inevitably be divorced from its dependence upon the seasons of vegetation. It became necessary, then, to fix the Sheaf-offering, as far as might be reasonably possible, to a date on which it would normally occur before the harvest. Otherwise, the rule that it must precede the eating of the new crops would cause inconvenience which no people, primitive or sophisticated, would tolerate. In Lev. 23 the Sheaf-offering

26:2 ff., Ezek. 44:30. See Gray, *Numbers* (I.C.C.), 1903, and Eissfeldt, *Erstlinge und Zehnten im A.T.*, 1917, 11 ff., 22 ff., for a discussion of the terms *re'šith* and *bikkurim*.

[1] Compare the statement of Lev. 2:12 and see pp. 264 f. below. In 2 Kings 4:42 ff. the 'man of God' orders the firstfruits to be given to the people. Ezek. 44:30 assigns firstfruits to the priests; cf. Neh. 10:38.

[2] Lev. 23:14.

[3] Lev. 2:14–16.

[4] Num. 15:19–21, Ezek. 44:30, Neh. 10:38 (E.V. 10:37). See Pedersen, op. cit. iii–iv. 303, and, for a full analysis, Eissfeldt, *Erstlinge*, 61 ff., 151.

[5] It should be remarked that in the Bible the term *'omer* is used to denote 'sheaf' only when the allusion is to the Sheaf offered between Passover and the feast of Weeks, Lev. 23, or to the last sheaf of the grain harvest, Deut. 24:19, and rarely in a general sense, Job 24:10, Ruth 2:7, 15, cf. Ps. 129:7. Elsewhere it is used of a measure; cf. p. 265 below. On the verb *'mr*, see M. David, '*Hit'āmēr*', *VT* i, 1951, 219, and Alt, 'Zu *hit'ammēr*', *VT* ii, 1952, 153. Alt relates the word to an Ugar. term for a class of retainers with military duties, and also with agricultural duties if the noun *'omer* is connected with this verb.

[6] This is suggested by Langdon, *Babylonian Menologies*, 142, but he gives no reference to any text. See, however, E. D. van Buren, 'Ear of Corn', *Miscellanea Orientalia dedicata Antonio Deimel* . . . (Analecta Orientalia, 12), 1935, 327 ff.

[7] See p. 118 above.

is required to take place 'on the morrow of the Sabbath'. The 'Sabbath' in this celebrated crux was interpreted variously in later times. How is it likely to have been interpreted at the time of the composition of Lev. 23?

There is a presumption from the nature of this whole passage on the festal calendar that 'Sabbath' here denoted a date of some precision. The spirit of the regulations of Lev. 23 is precise. We cannot assume—as some scholars have done—that those verses that deal with the Sheaf-offering are not precise because they are early—still less that they are early because they are not precise.[1] It must be maintained, on the contrary, that the provisions of Lev. 23 concerning the date of the Sheaf-offering—'on the morrow of the Sabbath'—were regarded by its writer or redactor as sufficiently exact, since he did not add to its details. There are three principal interpretations of 'Sabbath' in this passage. The first regards it as meaning the first day of the Passover week.[2] This we must reject at the outset. The first day of the Passover, like the first day of Tabernacles, might be described as a day of שבתון, 'rest'; it certainly was not a שבת.[3] Less out of keeping with the use of the word שבת is the theory that the reference here is to the weekly Sabbath or Saturday—presumably the Saturday that occurred before the harvest, whenever that might be.[4] But this view, too, must be rejected. There is no analogy throughout the Bible for the use of the week unit to fix the date of religious ritual (except, of course, for the Sabbath itself and its institution in Gen. 2:1–3). If, as is commonly assumed, the Jubilees 'calendar' of the end of the second century B.C. does maintain such a system, it is precisely in this respect that it is at variance with ancient Hebrew practice.[5] Nor does the interpretation of שבת in this manner suit the context of Lev. 23:15.[6]

Now, שבת usually denotes the seventh day of the week unit. But it may

[1] pp. 79 ff. above.

[2] The view is neatly summed up by Sa'adya Gaon, 'Every day on which there is a rest (Heb. שביתה) is called Sabbath (שבת)'; see M. Zucker, in *PAAJR* xx, 1951, p. א׳.

[3] שבתון in Lev. 23:39 is defined by the formula of 23:7b, 8b*β*; cf. 23:24 f. on Rosh haShanah. שבתון is a derivative of the verb שבת in the notion of 'cease (from work)', e.g. Ex. 31:17, 34:21, and 23:12 (for the parallel between שבת and נוח in the last citation, cf. at Qumran, *War*, ii. 8–9, and J. Carmignac, 'Citations de l'A.T. . . .', *RB* lxiii, 1956, 242). שבתון does not in itself define the degree to which rest is observed, and this must be defined more exactly. שבת שבתון implies 'Sabbath in respect of rest', where the rest is a complete cessation from work; this phrase is employed of the weekly Sabbath, Ex. 31:15, 35:2, Lev. 23:3, cf. Ex. 16:23, but it can be used also of the Day of Atonement (which need not be on a Sabbath), Lev. 16:31, 23:32, and of the Year of Release, Lev. 25:4–6. On the morphology of שבתון, see Gesenius, *Hebrew Grammar*, § 85u. The derivation of this word should not be dependent upon the difficult problem of the derivation of the noun שַׁבָּת; see p. 197 n. 1 below.

[4] See the discussion on pp. 235, 238, and 248 ff. below.

[5] p. 235 below.

[6] 'Seven complete sabbaths.' The phrase can scarcely refer to periods of twenty-four hours from Friday evening to Saturday evening, as it must if שבת is interpreted in the usual manner. It must refer to periods of seven days, see p. 197 n. 1 below.

be used also of a period of seven days culminating in a day of rest. In later Jewish literature this period of seven days is equivalent to our modern notion of 'week', that is, a period of seven days revolving continuously without reference to months or years.[1] There is no reason why this should not have been the case also in earlier times. Indeed, the interpretation of שבת as a period of seven days ending in a day of rest—not necessarily the Sabbath, Saturday—is the only interpretation which seems to yield satisfactory sense throughout the passage Lev. 23:9–21.[2] In the present context this particular period of seven days is clearly the Passover week. Certain considerations combine to support this view. We have observed already the role of seven days as a sacral period.[3] Furthermore, the offering of the Sheaf during the Passover week—and not after its completion—would involve a sharp break in the ceremonial of the week (as, indeed, it did in later times). The *maṣṣoth* eaten at the Pesaḥ meal[4] were, according to unanimous tradition, from the old crops. It is reasonable to assume that the bread was from the old crops throughout the Passover week, and that the Sheaf ceremony, which permitted the use of the new crops, fell immediately outside the seven-day period. More striking is the fact that in the subsidiary offerings which are prescribed for the Passover week there is no mention of libations of wine;[5] this is a remarkable point of difference between these sacrifices and those of any other festal occasion in the Israelite calendar. The reason is evident. It was desired to avoid the presence of fermenting matter during the springtime festival week.[6] On the other hand, libations of wine are prescribed for the ritual at the waving of the Sheaf.[7]

These arguments lead to the conclusion that the ceremonial waving of the Sheaf took place originally on the day following the Passover week—a conclusion that is perhaps reflected in the Peshiṭta.[8] It is true that

[1] So, for example, *Mish. Ned.* viii. 1; cf. Mark 16:2, Luke 24:1, John 20:1. In Matt. 28:1 the term *σάββατον* is used in both its senses, first as 'sabbath day', then as 'week'; for the explanation of the word *ἐπιφωσκούσῃ*, see J. M. Grintz, 'Hebrew . . . in the Last Days of the Second Temple', *JBL* lxxix, 1960, 37. For שבת, 'week', cf. also Aram. שב, שבא, and see C. Levias, 'Etymology of the term Ševâ', *American Journal of Philology*, xvi, 1895, 34; Dupont-Sommer, 'Sabbat et Parascève à Éléphantine . . .', 12; and (with a different view) E. Vogt, 'Hat "šabbat" im A.T. den Sinn von "Woche"?', *Biblica*, xl, 1959, 1008.

[2] Cf. LXX at Lev. 23:15b, 16, p. 70 above. On the etymology of the noun שבת, note the suggestion of Landsberger, *Der kultische Kalender*, 134, that ʿ has been elided in Akk. *šabattu* (**šabʿantu* > *šabattu*). Other theories are summarized and analysed in M. Jastrow, 'On ממחרת השבת', *AJSL* xxx, 1913–14, 94; G. J. Botterweck, 'Sabbat im Alten Testamente', *Theologische Quartalschrift*, cxxxiv, 1954, 134, 448; R. North, 'Derivation of Sabbath', *Biblica*, xxxvi, 1955, 182; and H. Haag, art. 'Sabbat', *Bibel-Lexikon*, 1956.

[3] p. 139 above.

[4] See p. 261 below.

[5] See p. 202 below.

[6] On wine as a source of fermentation, p. 167 above. Libations of wine continued, however, to be offered with the *Tamid* sacrifice at the Passover, as at other times, Num. 28:23 f.

[7] Lev. 23:13.

[8] See pp. 69 f. above; on Jubilees and the Falashas, pp. 235 and 255 below. On a similar tradition in early Christian literature, see J. van Goudoever, *Biblical Calendars*, 1959, 177–9.

nowhere in the Bible is the Sheaf-waving explicitly tied to the Passover;[1] the reason lies probably in the circumstance that it is not properly part of the Passover ceremonial. The Pesaḥ was followed by a post-liminal period of seven days, the Maṣṣoth week. This was a period of supplication for the new year—and for the harvests, as at the autumn festival supplication was made for the rains that were required for a successful sowing.[2] On the following day there was a symbolic waving of a barley Sheaf. It was not a thanksgiving ceremony, but a rite of sympathetic magic to encourage the growth of the crops which were then in the green.[3] Only after this ceremony might the new corn be eaten—if it had already ripened. The Sheaf-waving opened a period of seven weeks—a significant period[4]—and then took place the thanksgiving offerings of the harvest festival. This was certain to occur—as a harvest thanksgiving should—when the harvesting of the crops was at its height.[5]

I have already suggested that if we identify the Israelite *ḥaggim* as New Year festivals, we must assume that at one time there were only two—one in the spring, the other in the autumn.[6] The festival of Weeks, the third *ḥag*, is properly no more than an appendage of the Passover; and so it remained throughout its history in normative Israelite religion.[7] One should not conclude that it did not come into existence early. The comparison of Ex. 23 with Ex. 34 which we have already made seems, however, to show that its insertion into the festal calendar and the use of the name of feast of Weeks took place, in the opinion of the Compiler, in Canaan.[8] Certainly the festival of Weeks was formally celebrated at the Temple at Jerusalem, possibly in the early years of the Monarchy.[9]

[1] But see p. 240 below on Philo.

[2] p. 115 above.

[3] See Frazer, *Golden Bough. Magic Art*, i. 137, and Hooke, *Siege Perilous*, 1956, 31 ff., for wave offerings elsewhere. For a list of wave offerings in Israelite ritual, Gray, *Numbers*, 224. G. R. Driver, 'Linguistic and Textual Problems: Isaiah xl–lxvi', *JTS* xxxvi, 1935, 396, and 'Three Technical Terms in the Pentateuch', *JSS* i, 1956, 100, maintains that *terumah* should be rendered 'levy' and *tenuphah* 'special contribution'.

[4] Cf. Tobit i. 21, ii. 1. See the evidence collected by R. North, *Sociology of the Biblical Jubilee*, 1954, 66, and Morgenstern, *VT* v, 1955, 45 ff. Morgenstern's rendering of *ḫamuštu* (following J. and H. Lewy, *HUCA* xvii, 1942–3, 96, and J. Lewy, 'Assyrian Calendar', *Archiv Orientální*, xi, 1939, 44) should be regarded with caution; cf. H. Winckler, *Altorientalische Forschungen*, 1901, 98, and Landsberger, op. cit. 96. See further Lane, *Modern Egyptians*, ch. xxvi, and Dalman, *Arbeit und Sitte*, i. 320, on the days of the *ḫamsin* in Egypt. For a reflection of the concern with which the Israelites viewed the weeks during the harvesting period and the notion that these follow a providential pattern, Jer. 5:24, cf. Ex. 34:21b.

[5] Dalman, op. cit. i. 462 ff., points out that in modern Palestine there is no fixed festival of harvest. He suggests that the period of seven weeks from the Passover to the feast of Weeks is not connected with the crops, but with astronomical observation; cf. the association of the harvest with the Pleiades by Hesiod.

[6] p. 180 above.

[7] Van Goudoever, op. cit. 143, points out that the Mishnah has no tractate on the feast of Weeks.

[8] pp. 193 f. above. Note also 'in all your dwellings', Lev. 23:14b, cf. v. 17a.

[9] 1 Kings 9:25; see p. 4 above. The view that the feast of Weeks is a rite of solemn covenant, as Jub. 6:17 (see p. 235 n. 2 below, cf. W. H. Brownlee, 'Light on the Manual of Discipline (DSD) from the Book of Jubilees', *BASOR*, No. 123, Oct. 1951, 32, on the annual

The development in Passover ritual which the Compiler regards as having taken place next is of a very different nature. We have seen how essential was ritual cleanness for the proper performance of the Pesaḥ. According to Num. 9:6 ff. certain men who were 'unclean by the dead body of a man' found themselves in consequence debarred from offering the Pesaḥ sacrifice.[1] Absence from this assembly of the community was, however, a serious matter; omission from the count of adult males would entail virtual excommunication.[2] It was therefore decreed that

if any man . . . shall be unclean by reason of a dead body, or be in a journey afar off, yet he shall keep the passover unto the Lord: in the second month . . . they shall keep it.[3]

I have pointed out that the insertion of this passage at this place in the Book of Numbers is clearly deliberate. It has no connexion with the following verses, and none with the preceding chapters except the date, which may be deduced from the general framework of Num. 1–8. It appears to be prescribed on the very day on which the 'second Pesaḥ' could be offered.[4]

There were causes of ritual uncleanness in addition to the two recorded here, and they too debarred men from participating even at a *zebhaḥ*, the communal meal which had none of the special solemnity of the Pesaḥ.[5] These were sexual intercourse, contact with anything unclean (whether human, animal, or inanimate), leprosy, and the flux. Why, then, it may be asked, are they not mentioned here? The reason may be advanced with confidence. The uncleanness that followed sexual intercourse and contact with the unclean lasted only until sundown.[6] It would not normally debar a man from performing the Pesaḥ. Leprosy and the flux, on the other hand, were visible; and they involved formal exclusion from the community for seven days. Moreover, control over the act of exclusion from

renewal of the covenant at Qumran), finds no support from the Bible, except possibly Ex. 19:1 ff. (v. 1, 'in the third month'). The account of Asa's covenant in the third month, 2 Chr. 15:10, is probably apocryphal, since it is not related in 1 Kings 15:9 ff. On the late period at which the giving of the Law on Sinai was first associated with the feast of Weeks, see Dalman, op. cit. i. 467.

[1] The appearance of Heb. *qorban* here is significant. The word is found in contexts where details of sacrificial procedure are given; cf. *qrb*, Ex. 12:48, on circumcision; *qorban*, Lev. 23:14 ff., on the circumstances of the Sheaf-offering; in the present context on cleanness regulations; in Num. 28:19 on the Passover week sacrifices; in Num. 18:15 on firstlings sacrifices; in Num. 17:5 (E.V. 16:40) on incense offerings; in Ex. 40:32, Lev. 21:17 f., and frequently.

[2] pp. 135 ff. above.

[3] Num. 9:1–14. It is unlikely that any importance should be attached to the fact that the single qualification of vv. 6–7 is extended to two in vv. 10, 13.

[4] p. 192 above. The 'second Pesaḥ' is performed, like the true Pesaḥ, at the full moon; there is therefore significance in this lunar phase; see p. 132 above. It should be observed, moreover, that it is only the Pesaḥ, not the whole Passover, that is carried out in the second month. A *ḥag* is properly fixed to a date in the tropic year and cannot be deferred, see p. 130 above; only the central ceremony, the Pesaḥ, is to be repeated for the reasons already given.

[5] 1 Sam. 16:5.

[6] 1 Sam. 21:4–6, Ex. 19:15, Lev. 15:16–18, cf. 22:4 ff.; Lev. 7:20, cf. 22:4 ff., Hag. 2:13, and see 1 Sam. 20:26 f.

the community on these grounds was in the hands of the priests.[1] Now, contact with the dead also involved exclusion from the community, and also for seven days.[2] But it carried no outward sign of infection, and it was therefore possible that eagerness to participate in the Pesaḥ might have led to the concealment of this cause of ritual uncleanness. The concession of Num. 9 was intended to forestall laxity in carrying out the cleanness regulations.

Contact with the dead was followed by ritual uncleanness lasting seven days. This was, I have suggested, the duration of the preliminal period before the Passover. It is probable that here too we should find the definition of the length of the 'journey afar off' which also prevented participation in the Pesaḥ.[3] An alternative explanation of the uncleanness involved by a long journey is the view of a henotheistic religion that a journey to a foreign country and the domain of foreign gods would necessarily involve impurity.[4] In later times the two sources of ritual uncleanness were neatly combined by Jewish law; contact with gentile land was, it was held, equivalent to contact with a grave area, and must be followed by the same period of exclusion from society.[5]

This amendment to the cleanness laws by the admission of a 'second Pesaḥ' is evidently considered by the Compiler to be a late development; it is formally ascribed to the wanderings in the Wilderness, but it comes after the regulations of Lev. 23. We can scarcely doubt the correctness of this view. It conforms well to what we know of ancient religion. The principles of ritual uncleanness allow of no exception. Persons who do not satisfy these ritual requirements, whether unwittingly or deliberately,[6] must be excluded from the circle of devotees. In Num. 9 the penalty of extirpation is not abolished; it is lightened by permission to perform the Pesaḥ in the second month. Whether this concession is old we cannot decide; certainly it is not as far-reaching as the comparative leniency of the last years of the Temple at Jerusalem.[7]

We have observed that the *ḥaggim* are accompanied by sacrifices, and there was a brief reference to 'offerings by fire' in Lev. 23:8; these offerings are prescribed in careful detail in Num. 28:19 ff. Israelite sacrifices fell

[1] Lev. 13–15, Num. 5:2–4.

[2] Num. 19:11 ff., 5:2–4, 6:9–11, cf. Lev. 21:11. For the regulations at Hieropolis and elsewhere, see p. 139 n. 14 above.

[3] See p. 136 n. 1 above on Prov. 7:19 f.

[4] Cf. 2 Kings 5:17; see W. R. Smith, *Religion*, 92.

[5] See the convenient summary in Danby, *Mishnah*, 800, and cf. John 18:28.

[6] Cf. the Jewish legal terms *bešogeg* opp. *bemezid*. Ex. 21:12–14, which distinguishes between the two, is concerned with actions between individuals and not with their obligations towards the community.

[7] It was possible for the unclean and for sectarians to enter the Temple at the Pesaḥ; cf. p. 237 below. For reasons which suggest that we must beware of drawing analogies between the deferred Passover attributed to Hezekiah in 2 Chr. 30 and the 'second Pesaḥ' of Num. 9, see p. 229 below.

under two main headings—*ʿolah*, which is wholly consumed by fire, and *zebhaḥ*, of which part is eaten by those who offer the sacrifice. Each group of offerings is subdivided into various categories.[1] But the opposition between the two main groups is constant throughout the Bible,[2] and, significantly, it is most striking in Deuteronomy, which is, as we shall see, a popular summary of history and legislation without pretensions to precision.[3] On those occasions where the offering is made on behalf of a small unit, *zebhaḥim* alone are offered—at a yearly sacrifice,[4] at a city sacrifice,[5] at the king's accession or the renewal of a king's accession (but not at his coronation),[6] and at a new moon family celebration.[7] The *ʿoloth*, on the other hand, are formal sacrifices, in particular sacrifices offered at the Temple; not infrequently they have a purificatory role.[8] But on the most solemn occasions both *zebhaḥim* and *ʿoloth* are offered—at a national covenant,[9] after a solemn fast following a military defeat,[10] on the assembling of the tribes,[11] on the return of the Ark,[12] at the end of a plague,[13] at the initial coronation of a king,[14] at a solemn assembly decreed by the king,[15] and in royal sacrifices, especially upon a new altar.[16] The occasions on which both types of sacrifice are offered have special religious importance, and they include occasions at which the king takes a leading part. There is significance, then, in the fact that both types of sacrifice are offered at the *ḥaggim*; there, too, the king or leader was especially prominent.[17]

The Pesaḥ offering does not fit exactly into the category of either *ʿolah* or *zebhaḥ*; it is, on the whole, more easily regarded as *zebhaḥ*, since it was eaten at a meal,[18] yet it was a special offering and it could not be increased

[1] To the group of *ʿoloth* belong *ḥaṭṭaʾth* and *ʾašam*; to the group of *zebhaḥim* and the related *šelamim* (see p. 181 n. 11 above for a difference between the two) belong *todah*, *neder*, *nedabhah*. See W. B. Stevenson, 'Hebrew 'Olah and Zebach Sacrifices', *Festschrift für Alfred Bertholet*, ed. W. Baumgartner, &c., 1950, 488; Moraldi, *Espiazione*, 164 ff., and id., 'Terminologia cultuale israelitica', *Scritti in onore di G. Furlani*, 321; L. Rost, 'Erwägungen zum israelitischen Brandopfer', in *Von Ugarit nach Qumran* (Festschrift Eissfeldt), 1958, 177; and Snaith, 'Sacrifices in the Old Testament', *VT* vii, 1957, 308.

[2] So, for example, Hos. 6:6.

[3] *zbḥ*, Deut. 12:21, 15:21, 16:2, 5, 6, 18:3, 27:7, 32:17, 38, 33:19; *ʿolah*, 12:13, 14, 27:6; *ʿolah* and *zebhaḥ*, 12:6, 11, 27.

[4] 1 Sam. 1:21, 2:19.

[5] 1 Sam. 9:12, 13, 16:5.

[6] 1 Kings 1:9, 19, 25, but cf. 1 Sam. 11:14 f.

[7] 1 Sam. 20:6, 29; cf. Amos 8:5, 2 Kings 4:23.

[8] Lev. 1:3 ff., 10 ff., 14:12 f., 16:5, 2 Chr. 1:6, 2:3 (E.V. 2:4), 8:12, 23:18, 29:24, 27 f., 30:15, 31:3, &c.; cf. Gen. 8:20, 22:13, Jud. 6:26, 11:31.

[9] Ex. 24:5, cf. 18:12; at a private pact only *zebhaḥim* are offered, Gen. 31:54.

[10] Jud. 20:26.

[11] Jud. 21:4.

[12] 1 Sam. 6:15.

[13] 2 Sam. 24:25, 1 Chr. 21:26.

[14] 1 Sam. 10:8, 1 Chr. 29:21.

[15] 2 Kings 10:24.

[16] 2 Sam. 24:25, 1 Kings 8:62–64, cf. 8:5, 2 Kings 16:13, 2 Chr. 7:7.

[17] 1 Kings 9:25, pp. 153 above and 215 below; cf. 1 Kings 12:32 f. (where, however, the text is confused), Ex. 32:6. It is probably significant that 2 Chr. 8:12, written after the end of the Monarchy, reduces the *ʿoloth* and *šelamim* of 1 Kings 9:25 to *ʿoloth*.

[18] Nicolsky, op. cit. 242, goes too far when he maintains that the use of Heb. *zebhaḥ* as the

in number. The supplementary offerings made during the Passover are therefore kept carefully apart from the Pesaḥ victims. These supplementary offerings are both *zebhaḥim* and *ʿoloth.* The former are called also by the loose term *qodašim*;[1] they are the animals offered by all visitors to shrines at the *ḥag*, and also—at any rate, at a later time—animals whose meat would add to the festivity of the Pesaḥ meal.[2] The *ʿoloth* are offered each day on behalf of the community and with solemnity, and they are prescribed with precision in Num. 28:19 ff.

One feature has already been noted. At these daily sacrifices during the Passover[3] there are no libations of wine (except at the *Tamid* with its usual accompaniment of miscellaneous subsidiary offerings). In this, the sacrifices of the Passover differ from the sacrifices at all other Israelite festivals,[4] and in this they differ too from the sacrifices at the new moon.[5] The reason must lie in the prohibition of fermenting matter.[6]

Does Num. 28 reflect an advance on Lev. 23, and does it belong to a later period? It may have been the view of the Compiler that the precision exhibited in Num. 28 was a late development, and it may have been for this reason that these detailed regulations are found in the latest of the formal Pentateuchal codes. We have little with which to compare them. The celebration of the Passover by Solomon with both *zebhaḥim* and *ʿoloth* is not described in detail; and the complex sacrifices of Egypt and Babylonia may be peculiar to countries where, unlike Israel, cultic ceremonial was from early times concentrated formally in the person of king and priest. On the other hand, the examples of Egypt and Babylonia show that complexity and precision in Temple ritual are not qualities peculiar to later ages.[7]

Within the general framework of the Pentateuch the Book of Deuteronomy stands apart from Exodus–Leviticus–Numbers. The latter belong to the period of the Wilderness, although they reach already the last year of the wanderings. Deuteronomy, likewise, is said in its superscription to have been written at the end of the wanderings,[8] and it recapitulates the story of the forty years. But it is directed entirely towards the settlement in Canaan. Individual passages in the earlier books are, it is true, also concerned with

term for the Pesaḥ sacrifice in Deut. 16 (p. 204 below) indicates that there had been modification in the Pesaḥ ritual; there had been some change (see pp. 206 ff. below), but this is not implied by the term *zebhaḥ*.

[1] For the category of *zebhaḥim*, see Num. 29:39, where the *šelamim* are prescribed, although not in detail, for all the *moʿadim*, including the Passover; cf. *qodašim*, 2 Chr. 35:13, cf. 29:33.

[2] See p. 227 below.

[3] In Num. 28:24 ונסכו refers to the *Tamid* libations, cf. v. 15.

[4] Lev. 23:18, Num. 28:31 (feast of Weeks), 29:6 (Rosh haShanah), 29:11 (Day of Atonement), 29:37 (Eighth Day of Solemn Assembly); note the plural suffix of ונסכיהם. So also the Sheaf-offering, Lev. 23:13; see p. 197 above.

[5] Num. 28:11 ff.; with the exception of the libations, the new moon sacrifices are exactly similar to those of the Passover.

[6] See pp. 167 ff. above.

[7] Gray, *Numbers*, 404, considers Num. 28–29 as possibly belonging to the fourth century B.C. and certainly later than Ezekiel.

[8] Deut. 1:1 ff.

the life in Canaan.[1] But Deuteronomy goes farther. It is a popular revision of history and law[2] within a co-ordinated scheme of thought and behaviour that is at once more general and more complete than those codes that precede it in the Pentateuch and which, by implication, were regarded by the Compiler as preceding it also in time. The scheme of thought and behaviour is that of the Israelites living as a settled community in Canaan. And—equally important for our present study—Deuteronomy is assigned by most scholars to a definite date in the history of the Israelite Monarchy.[3]

A certain unevenness of writing has been detected in the regulations of Deut. 16:1 ff., which treat of the Passover, and it has been suggested that our present text is the amalgam of two or more documents. Some scholars maintain that the original consisted of regulations on Pesaḥ only; upon this have been superimposed verses on the Maṣṣoth festival. Others have claimed to trace the reverse process, holding that it is the verses on the Pesaḥ that constitute the later addition.[4] Both theories should be treated with caution—and their plausibility is not increased by the fact that they stand in direct opposition to each other. Neither succeeds in explaining adequately the awkwardness of the text, although it was this awkwardness that was the starting-point in postulating two independent documents in this passage. In particular, the word עליו in v. 3aβ is a major difficulty in our present text. The theories of composite authorship can do no more than dismiss it as a dittography[5]—hardly convincingly, since it is precisely in a literary fusion that one would expect smoothness rather than clumsiness of writing. But in fact the view that Deut. 16 is the artificial combination of two documents stems from the view that the Passover itself is the artificial fusion of two elements, the Pesaḥ and the Maṣṣoth festival. This thesis I have found reason to dispute.[6] There is, in my view, no strangeness in the presentation of the Passover as a single festival by Deut. 16. In the Exodus narrative greater weight was given to the ceremonies of the Pesaḥ than to those of the festal week which followed; in other documents particular aspects of the festival were stressed.[7] Here in Deut. 16 we have the whole festival in its proper perspective and in its natural shape as a single unit.

It has been alleged that there is significance in the terminology peculiar to Deut. 16, and it has been suggested that it reflects a stage in the evolution of the Passover.[8] That Deut. 16 uses the term *zebhaḥ* of the Pesaḥ is

[1] For example, Ex. 13:5, Lev. 23:10. [2] Cf. *Siphre* on Deut. 16:1.

[3] It would be out of place to give here a general analysis of this complex question; summaries of theories on the provenance, authorship, redaction, and date of Deuteronomy will be found in Pedersen, op. cit. iii–iv. 750 ff., and C. R. North, in Rowley, *Old Testament and Modern Study*; cf. also Eissfeldt, *Einleitung*, 277 f. See further the views of Arnold, Welch, and Nicolsky in their studies on the Passover and outlined on pp. 79 ff. above.

[4] See pp. 79, 81, and 82; 83, 84, 85, and 86 above.

[5] See the Commentaries, and Gray, *JTS* xxxvii, 1936, 252.

[6] p. 175 above. [7] See p. 190 above. [8] Notably by Nicolsky, see p. 87 above.

certainly striking. But this does not indicate that the ritual of that sacrifice had now changed. Deuteronomy is a work intended for the general public. It has no place for details of sacrificial ritual. The writer has two terms for sacrifice, *zebhaḥ* and *'olah*. The latter would have been wholly unsuited as a description of the Pesaḥ. *Zebhaḥ*, on the other hand, covers, in the language of the Deuteronomist, the broad category of eaten sacrifices, and into this category the Pesaḥ sacrifice loosely fits.[1] Nor should we attach significance to the phrase ה׳ אלהיך, which is found only here in the Passover texts; it is a characteristic phrase of the Deuteronomist.[2] In phraseology Deut. 16 stands closer to Ex. 34 than to Ex. 23, but the points of similarity are of little consequence.[3] The resemblance of Deut. 16 to Ex. 13:3–7 is more remarkable;[4] but it may derive from the fact that both documents treat of the Passover as it is celebrated in Canaan.

When, however, we turn to an analysis of ritual, there are certain features in which Deut. 16 appears to be sharply at variance with those of the other Passover documents. Two striking discrepancies are noted by the Chronicler. In the first, Ex. 12 prescribes with great care that the Pesaḥ victim shall be chosen from the sheep and the goats;[5] Deut. 16, on the other hand, appears to permit the choice of the victim from among the cattle also.[6] Several explanations have been offered for the divergency; none of them is wholly satisfactory. That Deut. 16 prescribes a local usage[7] is improbable; there is no reason to suppose that the Pesaḥ was not performed in all Israel from early times.[8] That it gives the earlier usage—the restriction of the victim in Ex. 12 to sheep and goats being then a later development which continued to the last days of the Temple[9]—is no less unlikely. Ex. 12 contains primitive elements that must have been observed before the age of the Deuteronomist.[10] More important, the regulations on the species from which the victim was to be chosen are closely bound with the regulations on its age and sex; and these, I have sought to demonstrate, arise from the character and function of the Pesaḥ sacrifice.[11] The cattle of Deut. 16 cannot, on the other hand, be an allusion to the subsidiary offerings of the

[1] It is found also in the Exodus context, Ex. 12:27, cf. 34:25, pp. 55 and 59 above.

[2] Driver, *Deuteronomy*, 1895, lxxix–lxxx (No. 15).

[3] With Deut. 16:3aβ compare Ex. 23:15aα, 34:18aα; with Deut. 16:4b compare Ex. 34:25bα; with Deut. 16:1b compare Ex. 34:18b.

[4] With Deut. 16:3aβ compare Ex. 13:6a; with Deut. 16:4a compare Ex. 13:7bβ; with Deut. 16:3aα compare Ex. 13:3b. But we need not go so far as to detect an 'older stratum' of Deuteronomistic influence in Ex. 13:3, 5–9, 14, as Snaith, *Jewish New Year Festival*, 15, 24.

[5] Ex. 12:3–5, 21; p. 52 above.

[6] Deut. 16:2. May, *JBL* lv, 1936, 67, maintains that the Deuteronomist prescribes the offering of two victims, one from the small, the other from the large, animals. This hypothesis cannot be seriously considered; it runs contrary to the principle of the identification of the family group with a single victim, and finds no analogy either in early beliefs or late practice.

[7] As maintained by Welch, p. 94 n. 1 above.

[8] See p. 185 above.

[9] p. 258 below.

[10] See pp. 191 f. above.

[11] pp. 140 f. above.

Passover week.[1] The latter are always carefully distinguished from the *pesaḥim*;[2] and it is scarcely reasonable to assume that the phrase צאן ובקר in our present text of Deut. 16 refers to two wholly different classes of offerings. Equally improbable is the theory that Deut. 16 reflects a period of social development at which the bulk of Israelites were farmers and at which cattle had begun to assume importance in their economy.[3] Israelites always followed agricultural pursuits, certainly in Canaan; and this theory, in any case, provides no reason for the elimination of cattle as Pesaḥ victims at a later period. The correct explanation of the phrase צאן ובקר is probably simpler. It arises from an examination of the language of the Deuteronomist. Nowhere else in Deuteronomy do we find the phrase in this order; we have only בקר וצאן.[4] The word ובקר, then, is likely to be a scribal error, perhaps a dittography of the following word במקום, under the influence of 15:19. Certainly it appeared in our text early.[5]

No less simple is the probable explanation of the second crux. In Ex. 12 it is prescribed, again with emphasis and clarity, that the Pesaḥ victim must be roasted, not boiled.[6] But Deut. 16 describes the treatment of the Pesaḥ victim by the term *bšl*.[7] Some scholars maintain that this term implies boiling and that either there had been a general change in the Pesaḥ regulations or that Deut. 16 reflects local custom.[8] This is not credible. The roasting of the victim was, I have suggested, an integral and essential feature of the Pesaḥ ceremonial, and it remained so throughout the entire history of the festival.[9] It is reasonable, then, to deduce that the term *bšl* in Deut. 16 is of neutral meaning, with the significance of 'cook';[10] to express the notion 'boil' the term would be extended to בשל במים, 'cook in water'.[11] In the course of time, however, the use of water for cooking

[1] As maintained by Targ. Jer., Onq., *Mekhilta* on Ex. 12:5, *Siphre* on Deut. 16:2; see pp. 52 and 56 above.

[2] Especially in 2 Chr. 35:13, p. 227 below.

[3] For the rearing and slaughter of cattle for food in patriarchal times, see Gen. 18:7, 24:35, 26:14, &c., and during the early occupation of Canaan, 1 Sam. 11:7, 14:32, 16:2, 28:24, 2 Sam. 12:2, 17:29, 1 Kings 5:3 (E.V. 4:23), Amos 6:4, &c. On the whole question, see Benzinger, 'Viehzucht bei den Hebräern', *Realencyklopädie für protestantische Theologie und Kirche*, 1908.

[4] Deut. 14:26; 8:13, 12:17, 21b, 14:23, 15:19, cf. 32:14; 7:13, 28:4, 18, 51.

[5] p. 227 below on 2 Chr. 35:12; cf. 35:7 ff. צאן ובקר is read also by LXX at Deut. 16:2.

[6] Ex. 12:8–9.

[7] Deut. 16:7.

[8] See, for example, the views of Beer and Nicolsky, pp. 79 and 87 above, and of Welch, p. 94 n. 1 above, and the Commentaries of Bertholet and G. A. Smith on Deut. 16:7.

[9] See pp. 166 f. above, 227 and 262 below; cf. *Mish. Zeb.* v. 8, *Pes.* v. 10, vii. 1–2.

[10] So Dillmann, *Bücher Numeri, Deuteronomium und Josua*, 1886, and Driver, op. cit., in loc. *Bšl* denotes 'ripen, mature', Joel 4:13, E.V. 3:13 (*qal*), Gen. 40:10 (*hiph.*). It is used of 'cook' in a neutral sense, 1 Sam. 2:15, 1 Kings 19:21, Ex. 29:31, &c.; cf. Landsberger, *Das kultische Kalender*, 121, on a similar use of Akk. *bašlu*. In Ezek. 24:5 it clearly means 'boil', so possibly 2 Kings 4:38, Ex. 16:23. In Ex. 23:19 and Deut. 14:21 the context requires the meaning 'boil'; the word may be interpreted as 'fry' in 2 Sam. 13:8. See further the discussion in *JT Ned.* vi. 1 (fol. 39c) and especially *BT Ned.* 49a.

[11] Ex. 12:9.

became widespread, and *bšl* was used regularly in the sense of 'boil' without the addition of 'in water'. Such must have been the position at the time of the Chronicler, and he therefore saw in the text of Deut. 16 a discrepancy that did not exist when that text was written. He reconciles it with the traditional practice of roasting the Pesaḥ victim by the phrase—more ingenious than natural—ויבשלו הפסח באש.[1] The LXX, faced with the same apparent discrepancy, resorts to a conflation, 'and thou shalt boil and thou shalt roast'.[2]

But, indeed, the emphasis of the writer of Deut. 16 is not upon the species from which the victim is to be chosen or upon the method of its preparation. The Israelite of the time of the Deuteronomist can have required instruction about them as little as he required the word ואכלת (v. 7) to inform him that the victim was to be eaten. The passage is intended to make clear that all the Pesaḥ ceremonies must be held at the shrine, and the central phrase throughout the passage is 'in the place which the Lord shall choose'.[3] The victims were not to be cooked before the celebrants had come to the shrine, nor were they to be consumed at home; the whole ritual was to be held at the chosen place.

A third point of difference between Deut. 16 and other Pentateuchal passages on the Passover appears to lie in the regulations concerning abstention from work on certain days of the Passover week. In other documents the work that is forbidden is defined as מלאכת עבדה, 'servile work';[4] in Deut. 16:8 it is described simply as מלאכה.[5] Is there here a modification of the degree of labour that is prohibited? Again we should look to the language of the Deuteronomist for the explanation. עבדה occurs only once in Deuteronomy, and there it has the meaning of 'servitude', in an obvious allusion to the account in the Book of Exodus of the oppression of the Israelites in Egypt.[6] 'Work' is expressed in Deut. by מלאכה, without further definition; and in Deut. 16 this is used as the equivalent of the מלאכת עבדה of the other passages on the Passover. A more sweeping prohibition of work is indicated in Deut. by כל מלאכה.[7]

While these discrepancies between Deuteronomy and the other Passover documents are capable of comparatively easy solution, there are other features of Deut. 16 that require examination. The passage gives general and apparently complete regulations for the observance of the festival. Yet

[1] 2 Chr. 35:13.

[2] καὶ ἑψήσεις καὶ ὀπτήσεις, cf. R.V. 'roast', margin, 'seethe', and a similar uncertainty in E.V. at 1 Kings 19:21.

[3] Deut. 16:2, 6, 7.

[4] For example, Lev. 23:7, Num. 28:18, 25, cf. Ex. 12:16; see p. 178 above.

[5] The Samaritan version at Deut. 16:8 has 'servile work'; this may be under the influence of the documents mentioned in the previous note. LXX has a variant based on Ex. 12:16, 'no manner of servile work'; p. 64 above.

[6] Deut. 26:6, cf. Ex. 1:14. Note that ענה, Deut. 26:6, is found also in Ex. 1:11 f.; cf. the insertion of LXX in 1 Sam. 12:8.

[7] Deut. 5:14.

many of the details prescribed for the Passover in the context of the Exodus and in the later documents are omitted in Deuteronomy—the qualifications of the Pesaḥ victim, its selection on the tenth day and its safe keeping until the end of the fourteenth day, the definition of the household units and the qualifications of the celebrants, the cleanness regulations, the special dress, the smearing of the blood of the victim, the bitter herbs, the prohibitions against leaving the dwelling-places during the Pesaḥ night and against breaking the animal's bones, and the formal sacrifices during the Passover week.[1] The omission of these rules can scarcely mean that they were ignored by the Deuteronomist. Several of them continued in force as late as the last years of the Temple.[2] Nor can it mean that they had not yet come into being but were adopted later—that, in fact, Deut. 16 preceded the other documents in point of time. We have seen, on the contrary, that several of these rules are primitive in origin.[3] The reason for their omission lies partly in an imperfect text, but also partly in the popular approach of the Book of Deuteronomy. Some of these rules—the cleanness regulations applied to both victim and celebrant, the personal status of the participants, the sacrifices during the Passover week—were controlled by the priests rather than by the people to whom Deuteronomy addresses itself. This hypothesis is confirmed by other considerations. The month is called the month of Abib,[4] not the 'first month'. The calendar was the province of the priests, and the people were in no position to know which would be the first month; intercalation might require the insertion of an extra month before the Passover.[5] But the Passover always occurs in the month of the fresh ears of corn, and this term was familiar to the ordinary people. So, too, we find that the time of the Pesaḥ is defined in Deuteronomy not by the Temple formula 'between the two evenings', but in popular terms, 'at even, at the going down of the sun'.[6] For the same reason, the Pesaḥ is said to be held on 'the first day (of the Passover) at even'. And the need to avoid putrefaction which led to the eating of *maṣṣoth* at the Pesaḥ is prescribed alongside the rule against leaving any of the flesh of the victim overnight—both rules arose from the same cause.[7]

The words of Deut. 16:3 on the eating of *maṣṣoth* are of interest. The

[1] The offerings of the individual pilgrims at the shrines on the *ḥaggim* are, however, mentioned in general terms in Deut. 16:16 f.

[2] The qualifications of the victims and celebrants, the household units, the cleanness regulations, the bitter herbs, the prohibitions against breaking the victim's bones and taking the flesh out of the dwelling-places, the additional sacrifices during the Passover week; see pp. 232 f. and 259 ff. below on Jub. 49 and on the Mishnaic regulations.

[3] pp. 130 ff. above.

[4] Cf. pp. 193 f. above on Ex. 23, 34.

[5] So Dillmann, op. cit., on Deut. 16:1; see also M. H. Segal, 'Book of Deuteronomy', *JQR* xlviii, 1957–8, 327 f.

[6] So Deut. 23:12 (E.V. 23:11), 24:13, cf. Jos. 8:29; cf. p. 131 above.

[7] Welch, *Code of Deuteronomy*, 1924, 67.

maṣṣoth are said to be a reminder of the haste of the Exodus, a vivid indication that the Deuteronomist was familiar with the legend recounted in the Book of Exodus.[1] The same word, *ḥippazon*, is found in Ex. 12:11, although there it is used of the haste of the Pesaḥ meal.[2] The Deuteronomist also calls the *maṣṣoth* the 'bread of affliction'. The phrase is peculiar. We find לחם elsewhere in the Bible defined by an abstract noun in the same way, but everywhere else it appears to denote the general notion of food, rather than bread.[3] Perhaps 'affliction' in the Deuteronomic phrase is an oblique allusion to the sufferings of the Israelites in Egypt.[4] Possibly it refers to the eating of bitter herbs—which we might have expected to be mentioned at this point, but which are strangely omitted.[5] But the most plausible explanation of the phrase is that 'bread of affliction' is a popular epithet. It was the term used by the settled agriculturalists of Canaan when referring to the unleavened bread of the poor.

But the fact that Deuteronomy is a popular document does not explain fully the omission of all the Passover regulations that I have enumerated. Some of these were, after all, to be performed by the people, not by the priests—the choice of a victim on the tenth day and the ritual of smearing the victim's blood, for example. These were carried out at the Exodus Pesaḥ, according to tradition, yet they are not found among the precepts of Deut. 16. They were also not among the rites of what the Mishnah calls the 'Pesaḥ of (later) generations'.[6] In using this phrase the Rabbis recognized that the omission of these rites was the result of a process of evolution. It is evident that the process began already before the Exile. The Compiler himself admits the process by assigning the omission of these rites to Deuteronomy, whose regulations were prescribed, according to the superscription, at the end of the wanderings in the Wilderness and on the eve of the entry into Canaan.

The features which distinguish Deut. 16 from other Passover documents are not, however, all negative. There is no reference in Deuteronomy to distinctive ceremonies on the first day of the Passover week; but that day is recognized as opening with the Pesaḥ, and for that reason it may have been regarded by the Deuteronomist as a special day without further description. On the other hand, the seventh day is called *ʿaṣereth*[7] by

[1] Cf. p. 46 above.
[2] p. 173 above on Ex. 12:11 and on Is. 52:11–12.
[3] Hos. 9:4; Ps. 80:6 (E.V. 80:5), cf. 42:4 (E.V. 42:3); Ps. 127:2; Prov. 4:17, 9:17, 20:17, 23:3, 31:27. לחם may, however, denote 'bread' in 1 Kings 22:27, 2 Chr. 18:26, Is. 30:20, where it is opposed to water.
[4] Ex. 3:7, 17, 4:31, cf. 1:11 f.
[5] To interpret this phrase as 'food of fasting' (as the verb ענה in the *piel* and *hithp.*), with Beer, op. cit. 36, obtains a strange and self-contradictory expression.
[6] p. 260 below.
[7] 'Six days', Deut. 16:8a, does not refer to the six days that follow the first day (v. 4), since in that case 'seventh day' (v. 8b) would not be appropriate. Nor does it prescribe a Maṣṣoth festival of six days only (as Auerbach, 'Feste im alten Israel', *VT* viii, 1958, 4).

the Deuteronomist; for this there is no parallel in any other account of the Passover, nor does the term occur anywhere else in Deuteronomy. The Deuteronomist, moreover, tells us that the Israelites are to 'turn' on the morning after the Pesaḥ and to go to their tents.[1] Most important, we find, as I have remarked, a repetitive insistence throughout the passage on the restriction of the Passover to a chosen shrine or shrines.[2]

Let us analyse the circumstance that only here is the term *ʿaṣereth* found in Deuteronomy, and only here is this term used of the Passover. Elsewhere in the Pentateuch *ʿaṣereth* is applied only to the day following the week of Tabernacles.[3] Now, it is striking that in 2 Chr. 5:2 f. it is the king who assembled the Israelites at the feast of Tabernacles. The festival lasted the customary week, on the following day was an *ʿaṣereth*.[4] In Neh. 8:18 also the *ʿaṣereth* which follows the festival of Tabernacles was carried out after an official proclamation. So, too, with other historical occurrences of *ʿaṣarah* or *ʿaṣereth* in the Bible. Jehu proclaimed an *ʿaṣarah*, and it was preceded by rites of purification.[5] In Joel we read of an *ʿaṣarah* proclaimed officially, with a fast, during a plague of locusts; it was decreed, like that of Jehu, for a specific occasion.[6] Elsewhere the same prophet writes of the proclamation of an *ʿaṣarah* with a fast. It was binding upon the whole people, even old men and women and infants.[7] From these passages we may deduce either explicitly or by implication that the *ʿaṣarah* or *ʿaṣereth* is held at a shrine. It is a day specially appointed by authority; it is observed in ritual cleanness.[8]

We have observed the insistence in Deut. 16 on the restriction of the Passover to a shrine or shrines.[9] Scholars have long perceived that here lies the key to the development that is reflected in Deuteronomy—it is this that distinguishes Deut. 16 from Ex. 13:3 ff., although the latter also deals with

The phrase 'six days' refers to the first six days of the festival week; the seventh day is a day of special observance in addition to abstinence from leaven; so also S. R. Driver, *Deuteronomy*, in loc. In *Mekhilta* on Ex. 13:6 and *Siphre* on Deut. 16:8 the Rabbis give a fanciful explanation of the discrepancy between the 'six days' of Deut. and the seven of the other Passover documents. See Geiger, op. cit. 52.

[1] Deut. 16:7b. The verb may, however, be permissive, 'thou mayest turn . . .'.

[2] Deut. 16:2, 5–6, 7.

[3] Lev. 23:36, Num. 29:35; cf. Amos 5:21, where it is parallel to *ḥag*. [4] 2 Chr. 7:9.

[5] 2 Kings 10:18 ff., cf. *ʿṣr*, of royal power, 1 Sam. 9:17, and perhaps Jud. 18:7; on this, see E. Kutsch, 'Die Wurzel עצר im Hebräischen', *VT* ii, 1952, 67.

[6] Joel 1:14. [7] Joel 2:15 f., cf. Jer. 9:1 (E.V. 9:2).

[8] Is. 1:12–13. It was not a popular festival; it is not mentioned in Hos. 2:13 (E.V. 2:11). It may be reasonable to observe further that the fast proclaimed on the instructions of Jezebel and without the authority of the king, 1 Kings 21:9, 12, is not given the name *ʿaṣereth* or *ʿaṣarah*.

[9] בַּמָּקוֹם, Deut. 16:2, 6–7, need not refer to a single shrine; for this use of the definite article, see Gesenius, § 126r. For a discussion of this question, see K. Budde, 'Deuteronomium und die Reform Josias . . .', *ZAW* xliv, 1926, 189 (a single shrine), against T. Oestreicher, *Das Deuteronomische Grundgesetz*, 1923, 103 ff. (several shrines), and the bibliography on p. 203 n. 3 above. A recent treatment may be found in F. Dumermuth, 'Zur deuteronomischen Kulttheologie', *ZAW* lxx, 1958, 59.

the Passover as it is to be celebrated in Canaan.[1] Here, too, may be the explanation of the allusion in Deut. 16 to the 'tents' of the Israelites.[2] The contexts in which 'tents' is used in the Bible vary greatly. The word is rarely found of the tents of nomads in Israel after the settlement in Canaan, since Israelites normally lived in houses.[3] In some passages 'tents' is a poetic description of dwelling-places.[4] But frequently the tents are the dwelling-places of the people when they are not subject to the ordinary restraint of discipline. The discipline that is removed may be that of the army—especially when it has been defeated[5]—or that of the ruler[6] or the religious authorities.[7]

It is precisely this relaxation of normal discipline that is, as we have seen, a feature of New Year festival ritual throughout the Near East.[8] The settled communities exchange their houses and the restraints of the cities for the tents of the open country. There social conventions are removed. I have suggested that this was a motif also at the primitive Israelite New Year; the exodus from the houses of the city has continued in the *ḥag* of Tabernacles to the present day.[9] Hosea in his reproaches against Ephraim refers to the Exodus and declares that the people will be forced to return to the simple life of the Wilderness and to 'dwell in tents as in the days of the solemn feast'.[10] It is reasonable to infer that the prophet alludes to the Passover, and that the people of North Israel at the time of the prophet celebrated the festival by withdrawing from the inhabited areas and living in tents in the desert.[11]

Now, in Deut. 16:7 the injunction to go to the tents can hardly mean to

[1] pp. 60 ff. above.

[2] Deut. 16:7b.

[3] But the Rechabites live in tents, Jer. 35:7–10. Cf. 1 Kings 12:16a (= 2 Chr. 10:16a), where there is a play on the meaning of *bayith* '(royal) dynasty' and 'dwelling-place'.

[4] So Deut. 33:18, Jer. 4:20, 30:18, Zech. 12:7, Mal. 2:12, Ps. 52:7 (E.V. 52:5), Prov. 14:11, Job. 5:24, 8:22, &c.

[5] 1 Sam. 4:10, 2 Sam. 18:17, 19:9 (E.V. 19:8), 2 Kings 8:21, 14:12, 2 Chr. 25:22; Jud. 7:8, 20:8, 1 Sam. 13:2, 2 Sam. 20:22. In the field the Israelite army lived in tents (unless it was engaged in a siege; see p. 179 n. 3 above), Jud. 7:13, 1 Sam. 17:54, 2 Kings 7:7 f., Jer. 37:10, Dan. 11:45, Judith 7:18, 10:17 f. On the practice in Assyria and Egypt, see Alt, 'Zelte und Hütten', *Alttestamentliche Studien F. Nötscher . . . gewidmet*, 1950, 19 f.

[6] Jos. 22:4, 6, 7, 2 Sam. 20:1, 1 Kings 12:16 (= 2 Chr. 10:16); 1 Sam. 10:25, with *bayith*, 1 Sam. 8:22, with *'ir*. But cf. 2 Kings 13:5, where the authority is foreign.

[7] Deut. 5:27 (E.V. 5:30), 1 Kings 8:66 (= 2 Chr. 7:10).

[8] pp. 119, 120 f., and 125 above.

[9] Cf. Pedersen, op. cit. iii–iv. 388 and n. 1, 703. Wensinck, *Arabic New-Year*, 16 f., discusses the tradition that houses with a roof were tabu during 'the time of the solstice in Ramaḍan'.

[10] Heb. *mo'ed*, Hos. 12:10 (E.V. 12:9).

[11] Against this, see H. Tur-Sinai, *HaLashon wehaSepher*, iii, 1954–5, 78, who regards *mo'ed* in Hos. 12:10 as referring to any Hebrew festival. But at Tabernacles, the Israelites are said to dwell in *sukkoth*, Lev. 23:24, Neh. 8:14 ff., not in *'oholim* as in the Hosea passage. On the mention of tents at the Passover by Josephus, see p. 256 below. Pedersen, loc. cit., cites the modern Samaritan practice of living in tents on Mount Gerizim at the Passover as perhaps the survival of ancient Israelite usage; the Samaritan practice is, however, evidence of doubtful value, see pp. 251 ff. below.

return home on the first day of the festival, since the pilgrimage festival lasts seven days and the seventh day—whether it be called *ʿaṣereth* or *ḥag*—is to be celebrated at the shrine. It is improbable that the people were dismissed to their homes for the intervening days. Nor does the Heb. *panah* normally denote to 'return'; it is commonly used of turning in a different direction and particularly of motion to a new place after passing some time elsewhere.[1] The tents of Deut. 16 may be regarded, then, as the tents of the ritual exodus into the wilderness at the New Year festival. In the morning the pilgrims turn to go to their tents in the desert outside the shrine.[2] The deduction would seem to be that previously they had not waited until the morning.

We shall probably be near the truth if we regard the emphasis of the Deuteronomist on the observance of ritual at the shrine as the reason for the several changes in the Passover regulations in Deut. 16. Certainly this explains adequately the absence of any allusion to the smearing of blood. The sacrifice of the Pesaḥ victim was probably still performed by heads of households, most of whom must have been laymen.[3] But as the sacrifice was now at a permanent shrine, the priests could not have permitted laymen to handle the blood; and laymen never did so in later times. The choosing of the Pesaḥ victim on the tenth day may now have come under the supervision of the priests—it is not mentioned in Deuteronomy. So, too, the peculiar dress of adult males at the Pesaḥ may also have been abandoned at the time of Deuteronomy, and for a not dissimilar reason. The festival of Tabernacles, the autumn New Year festival, had splintered into Rosh haShanah and the Day of Atonement with their formal ritual.[4] The High Priest was dressed in the robes of his office. Had the popular custom of the common garb of the Pesaḥ been abandoned with this trend towards vicarious ceremonial? It may well be. So, too, the Deuteronomic regulation concerning the tents may also be thought to derive from the centralization of the cult. The people are instructed to pass the night of the Pesaḥ service at the shrine; only in the morning might they carry out the ritual exodus from the city. And on the seventh day of the Passover week they are recalled to an *ʿaṣereth*, a formal reunion at the shrine.

There are, nevertheless, difficulties in this argument. When the Temple was consecrated, Solomon released the people to go to their tents at the

[1] See, for example, Num. 21:33, Deut. 1:6–7, 24, Jud. 18:21, cf. v. 27. An exception is 1 Kings 10:13, and perhaps Jos. 22:4.

[2] But it should be remarked that, at the time of the Deuteronomist, tradition maintained that the Exodus from Egypt took place by night, Deut. 16:1b.

[3] Cf. 2nd m.s. וזבחת, Deut. 16:2, &c.

[4] See already p. 156 above. Wellhausen, *Prolegomena*, 125, 142, followed by Morgenstern, 'Chapter in the History of the High-Priesthood', *AJSL* lv, 1938, 1, maintains that the title of High Priest did not exist in Israel before the Exile. Nevertheless, the functions of that office, whether exercised by priest or priest-king, are likely to be ancient; see C. R. North, 'Religious Aspect of the Hebrew Kingship', *ZAW* l, 1932, 21.

end of the autumn festival.[1] The tents of that narrative can hardly, then, be those in which they lived during the festival. Moreover, a comparison of 1 Kings 8 with the parallel passage in 2 Chronicles seems to indicate that the *ʿaṣereth* of the eighth day was a late addition to the ceremonial of Tabernacles.[2] But most important is the character of the *ʿaṣereth* itself. It is, as we have observed, a day of solemnity proclaimed by authority. This was its form. But what was its purpose? Its purpose may be explained by its appearance at the end of the festival of Tabernacles. It follows a *tempus clausum* of seven days.[3] We have already discussed the sacral period of seven days. When a member of the community had been excluded from the society of his fellows on account of leprosy or some other source of uncleanness for a period of seven days or a multiple of seven days, his return to normal life was marked by a solemn sacrifice.[4] It was a formal occasion, and the leaders of the community recognized in public in this way the return of the individual to his former status. The same is true of the autumn New Year festival. The *ʿaṣereth* on the eighth day is carefully distinguished from the previous week. It marks a formal return to normal life. It may denote not restriction or tabu, but rather the removal of that restriction or tabu.[5]

How, then, are we to explain the *ʿaṣereth* of Deut. 16:8? It is a counsel of despair to regard it as an eighth day; at no time in its history did the Passover acquire an additional day as did Tabernacles. The solution may be sought in the general pattern of festal periods in Israel. The *tempus clausum* of the week of Tabernacles is terminated by an *ʿaṣereth* on the following day. In the case of the Passover the festal week was, I have suggested, followed at one time by the offering of the Sheaf on the next day.[6] That ceremony opened a *tempus clausum* of a week of weeks, and then was held the feast of Weeks;[7] this one-day festival in the middle of the harvesting season is called in later times *ʿaṣereth* or *ʿaṣarta*.[8]

[1] 1 Kings 8:66.

[2] 2 Chr. 7:8–9; cf. Deut. 16:13 ff. opp. Lev. 23:36, Num. 29:35, and Neh. 8:18. See Wellhausen, op. cit. 106.

[3] Heb. *ʿṣr* is used also of 'staying' a plague, Num. 25:8. Cf. W. R. Smith, *Religion*, 456, and see Thompson, *Demons and Evil Spirits of Babylonia*, 1904, ii. xli n. 1, and 118 f., and id., *Semitic Magic*, 126 n. 2, on Akk. *uṣurtu*. Kutsch, op. cit. 57 ff., however, concludes that the phrase עצור ועזוב denotes respectively men above and below the age of majority; it may be observed that a minimum age was probably a requisite for attendance at the Pesaḥ, see p. 135 above.

[4] p. 177 above.

[5] Cf. the Greek term *ἐξόδιον*, LXX at Deut. 16:8, Lev. 23:36, Num. 29:35, Neh. 8:18. (In Jer. 9:1, LXX has *σύνοδος*, which suits that context better.)

[6] pp. 196 f. above.

[7] So the festival of Weeks is regarded as the beginning of a year like the Passover, Rosh haShanah, and Tabernacles in *Mish. R.H.* i. 2, *BT R.H.* 4b, *Meg.* 31b.

[8] *Mish. Ḥag.* ii. 4, *Sheq.* iii. 1, &c., Josephus, *Ant.* III. x. 5, *BT Men.* 65a, *Ḥag.* 17b, cf. Arab. عنصرة in Maqrizi, Silvestre de Sacy, *Chrestomathie arabe*, 1826, 321. In a Qumran text of Is. 1:13, the form עצרתה is found for M.T. עצרת; see M. Burrows, *Dead Sea Scrolls . . .*, i, pl. 1.

The text of Deut. 16 is far from satisfactory. I have pointed out that the wording of v. 2a is likely to be suspect.[1] And vv. 9–10, although their meaning is clear,[2] contain certain textual difficulties. The phraseology of v. 9b is strange, particularly the juxtaposition of מהחל and תחל, where a single verb is used in different nuances. The phrase נדבת ידך in v. 10 is found nowhere else in the Bible; מסת of the same verse is common in Aramaic but occurs only here in Hebrew, its etymology has not been satisfactorily explained, and its exact sense was unknown to the early Versions.[3] We may, then, seek in the confusion of the text of Deut. 16 the solution of the problematic *ʿaṣereth* in v. 8. LXX here reads the equivalent of a conflate phrase *ʿaṣereth ḥag*. *Ḥag* alone would suit admirably the context of v. 8.[4] We may assume that *ʿaṣereth* has been misplaced in the M.T., and that it should belong to the section on the feast of Weeks, vv. 9–12. It would indicate (as we have seen it indicated in later times) the end of the *tempus clausum* that opened with the Passover week. Or should *ʿaṣereth* in Deut. 16 stand in the section on Tabernacles?

Whatever our explanation of *ʿaṣereth* in Deut. 16:8, it is certain that the Deuteronomic regulations require the Passover to be celebrated only at a central shrine or shrines. This was no innovation; I have argued that from very early times the Pesaḥ was restricted to a prescribed place.[5] Why, then, did the Deuteronomist find it necessary to repeat the regulation and with such emphasis? For the explanation we must turn to the writings of the prophets and the historians.[6] From Amos we learn of the extravagance of sacrifices at the *ḥaggim*,[7] and their accompaniment by songs and music.[8] He contrasts the lavish offerings of his contemporaries with the simplicity of worship of their ancestors in the Wilderness.[9] Hosea, too, speaks of the joy of the *ḥag*[10]—the allusion is to the Passover rather than to Tabernacles[11]—

[1] pp. 204 f. above.

[2] That *ḥermeš* means 'sickle' is certain; elsewhere it is found only with *qamah* and only in Deut. 23:26 (E.V. 23:25). *Qamah* is corn not yet cut opp. *gadiš*, Ex. 22:5 (E.V. 22:6), Jud. 15:5, Is. 17:5, and probably 2 Kings 19:26 (= Is. 37:27), Hos. 8:7. With the phrase of Deut. 16:9bα, Tur-Sinai, art. 'חדש', *Enṣiqlopediah Miqra'it*, compares Akk. *ina ṣibit nigali* in the texts from Kültepe, G. Eisser and J. Lewy, *Die altassyrischen Rechtsurkunden von Kültepe*, 1930, i. 62 and 69 n.(b). But the phrases are not fully equivalent in meaning—*nigalum* has its Heb. synonym in מגל—or in syntax.

[3] LXX paraphrases by *καθότι ἡ χείρ σου ἰσχύει*; see p. 69 n. 6 above.

[4] So the Samaritan version. For *ḥag* as the description of the seventh day of the Passover, p. 178 above.

[5] See p. 133 above.

[6] I refer here only to those passages where the text and the allusions are certain. I do not discuss, for example, Jer. 31:9 ff. (E.V. 31:10 ff.), where we may have a description of the New Year festival (note v. 10, E.V. v. 11, *pdh* and *g'l*, p. 163 above; v. 11, E.V. v. 12, the offerings; v. 12, E.V. v. 13, the dancing and joy). For Is. 52:11–12, see p. 173 above.

[7] Amos 5:21 f.

[8] Amos 5:23, cf. 8:10.

[9] Amos 5:25. Amos may be referring to the Passover (rather than to Tabernacles) as 'the day of the Lord' in 5:20.

[10] Hos. 2:13 (E.V. 2:11), cf. 9:5.

[11] See the reference in Hos. 2:16–17 (E.V. 2:14–15).

and the sacrifices and libations of 'the day of the Lord'.[1] To Hosea, as to Amos, the wanderings of Israel in the Wilderness were a period of simple devotion, and the Passover is a reminiscence in those early days.[2] We have already seen that in Hosea's time the Israelites of the northern kingdom probably went out to dwell in tents in the desert;[3] they may have been decked in festal attire. The prophet declares that the nettles shall possess 'their pleasant things of silver . . . thorns shall be in their tents'.[4] He goes on to allude scoffingly to the motif of mustering at the spring festival. Its days will not be days of mustering (*pqd*), but 'days of visitation (*pequddah*) . . ., the days of recompence . . . for the multitude of (the) iniquity' of Ephraim.[5]

In the southern kingdom Isaiah, the contemporary of Hosea, also inveighed against the public display of sacrifice and prayer at the 'appointed times'.[6] The *ḥaggim* come round each year at Jerusalem with the revolutions of the seasons, but there will be distress instead of festive joy.[7] But the prophet has also a message of hope. Gladness will return; and Isaiah compares it to the night when the *ḥag* is celebrated with rites of purification, with singing and gladness of heart and processions to the music of pipes to the mountain of the Lord—that is, to the Temple at Jerusalem.[8] Jewish tradition has seen in this a description of the Pesaḥ night,[9] others regard it as referring to the ceremonies of Tabernacles[10]—probably it is an allusion to features common to both festivals.[11]

From these passing references we receive an impression of the popularity and festiveness of the *ḥag* in both the northern and southern kingdoms of Israel; the Passover may have shared these qualities with the feasts of

[1] Hos. 9:4–5, cf. Hosea's rebuke on the multitude of altars, 10:1, 8.

[2] Hos. 9:10, 11:1, 13:4 f.

[3] p. 210 above.

[4] Hos. 9:5–6, cf. 2:15, and p. 146 above on the wearing of ornaments at the *ḥag*.

[5] Hos. 9:7. For the use of *pqd* with this meaning, see Num. 1:47, 2:33, 26:51, Jud. 20:15, 21:9, 1 Kings 20:27, and p. 136 n. 1 above on mustering at the Passover.

[6] Is. 1:11 ff.

[7] Is. 29:1 ff.

[8] Is. 30:29.

[9] So Rashi, Qimḥi, followed by Dillmann, *Prophet Jesaia*, in loc., and O. Procksch, *Jesaia I*, 1930, 401.

[10] G. W. Wade, *Book of the Prophet Isaiah*, 1929, 199, and J. Skinner, *Book of the Prophet Isaiah, chapters i–xxxix*, 1915, 249.

[11] On Is. 31:5, see p. 97 above, and on Is. 52:11–12, see p. 173 above. I have already discussed on p. 87 above the theory of Nicolsky that Zephaniah alludes to the Pesaḥ. Certainly that prophet refers to a nocturnal ceremony, Zeph. 1:12; but it may be doubted whether the *zebhaḥ* of the Lord (1:7), the purification of the participants, the strange clothes and the leaping over the thresholds (1:8–9) are a description of the Pesaḥ. The prophet does not mention the joy of the festival—a feature of the *ḥaggim* on which, we see here, all the other prophets who write of them are agreed. It is surprising that Zephaniah, if he is indeed alluding to the Pesaḥ, does not do so by name. The name would have been appropriate to the context in the sense of either 'pass over' (cf. *dlg*, Zeph. 1:9) or 'protect' (as Is. 31:5); and it should be remembered that Zephaniah prophesied in the days of Josiah (Zeph. 1:1) when the Passover received special prominence (p. 216 below).

Weeks and Tabernacles.[1] When we turn to the historical books, however, we find the distinction between the Passover and Tabernacles upon which I have already touched.[2] It was the autumn festival that was instituted by Jeroboam after he established his dynasty in the northern territory.[3] So Ishmael, 'of the seed royal, and the princes of the king' visited Gedaliah in the seventh month.[4] The formal proclamation of a new king and the renewal of the reign of a king already enthroned took place at the autumn New Year celebrations. The High Priest also performed the autumn *ḥag* with special pomp; in the second century it was at the festival of Tabernacles that the Hasmonean Jonathan assumed in public the 'holy garments' of the High Priest.[5]

The contrast between the solemn autumn festival and the popular spring festival may perhaps be best illustrated by earlier incidents in the history of Israel—at the end of the reign of David and the beginning of the reign of Solomon.[6] David, the annalist tells us, was punished by the deity because he had carried out a census. His fault seems to lie not in the fact that a census was made (as some scholars have maintained), but in the method which he adopted. His officers were sent out to all parts of the kingdom to number the people; the correct method was, I have suggested, to number the people on the occasion of the pilgrimage. The census was part of the complex of Passover ritual, and it was to be held at a prescribed shrine. But David's policy was the centralization of the administration,[7] and there was no central shrine. The sequel to David's census makes the point clear. The punishment for his 'fault' was plague, the punishment for a breach of the Passover regulations.[8] An altar was set up in the spot where

[1] But cf. Deut. 16:11, 14 f., where the joyous properties of the *ḥaggim* are confined to the feasts of Weeks and Tabernacles; both are festivals of harvest thanksgiving. See, however, pp. 234, 241, and 263 below, and see my art. in *JSS* vi, 1961, 85.

[2] p. 156 above.

[3] 1 Kings 12:32 f.; see my article in *VT* vii, 1957, 257. S. Smith, 'Practice of Kingship in Early Semitic Kingdoms', in Hooke, *Myth, Ritual, and Kingship*, 62 f., suggests that the assembly convened to choose Solomon's successor, 1 Kings 11:43–12:4, met at a seasonal festival.

[4] Jer. 41:1 ff.

[5] 1 Macc. 10:15–21; the practice in Roman times is discussed by Winter, *On the Trial of Jesus*, 16 ff. See also the celebration of Tabernacles by Alexander Jannaeus (Josephus, *Ant.* XIII. xiii. 5) and by the High Priest Aristobulus (id. xv. iii. 3). On the enthronement motif of Tabernacles, see Riesenfeld, op. cit., s. 'Intronisation'. Widengren, 'King and Covenant', *JSS* ii, 1957, 1, analyses the formal renewal of the Covenant of the Law by the Israelite king at the New Year festival. In all the instances he cites this ceremony takes place at the autumn New Year—with the exception only of the Covenant of Josiah related in 2 Kings 23. Here, however, it may be doubted whether Widengren's conclusion, ib. 3, can be supported. It is not the promulgation of the Covenant that precedes the Passover of Josiah, but the cleansing and rededication of the Temple.

[6] 2 Sam. 24. That this account may be an artificial appendix to the main narrative, as some scholars have maintained, adds to, rather than detracts from, the force of this argument; the account was regarded as of such relevance and significance that it was deliberately appended at this point.

[7] Mendenhall, 'Census Lists of Numbers 1 and 26', *JBL* lxxvii, 1958, 58, regards David's census as marking the transition from militia to army.

[8] See p. 165 and n. 3.

the angel stayed his hand at the end of three days' pestilence—and this spot was, according to tradition, the site of the Temple.[1] But it was not at the Passover—as one might have expected from this sequence of events—that the Ark was installed and dedicated in the new central shrine; it was at the feast of Tabernacles.[2] Solomon, we are told, celebrated all three *ḥaggim* with sacrifice,[3] but it was the autumn festival of Tabernacles that was evidently marked out as the proper occasion for the proclamation of royal and priestly authority. The Passover was a popular *ḥag*.[4]

Nevertheless, in 2 Kings 23:21–23 it is related that King Josiah gave order for the celebration of the Passover. What was the reason for this royal intervention? It lies partly in the internal affairs of the kingdom of Judah, partly in the broader pattern of events in the Near East at that time. The incident took place in 621,[5] a few years after the death of Aššur-banipal. There had been a shifting of the balance of power throughout the region. Babylonia and Egypt had re-emerged with schemes of territorial expansion, and these schemes were—as so often in the Near East—accompanied by movements of religious reform.[6] Such, we see from the text of 2 Kings 22–23, was true also, although in lesser degree, of the kingdom of Judah. Josiah aimed, according to our annalist, at extending his rule over the province of Samaria.[7] That his designs were aggressive may be shown by the different methods he is said to have employed to suppress unauthorized forms of worship in Judah and North Israel—in the former by persuasion and economic pressure,[8] in the latter

[1] 2 Chr. 3:1.

[2] 1 Kings 8:2, 65 f. = 2 Chr. 5:3, 7:8 ff.

[3] 1 Kings 9:25, cf. 2 Chr. 8:12 f., p. 153 above.

[4] p. 157 above.

[5] Rudolph, *Chronikbücher*, 329, suggests that Josiah's eighteenth year began in the spring and that the 'Book of the Law' (2 Kings 22:8; 'Book of the Covenant', 23:2, 21) was found in the eighth (variant, seventh) month, following LXX in 2 Kings 22:3; cf. F. X. Kugler, *Von Moses bis Paulus*, 1922, 139 ff. But the eighteenth year of Josiah would then have passed when Josiah celebrated the subsequent Passover. It is clear from a comparison of 2 Kings 22:3 and 23:23 that the finding of the 'Book of the Law' and the special Passover of Josiah must have occurred in the same regnal year; and since the period 1st–14th Nisan (if the year began with the new moon) would scarcely allow time for the king's far-reaching reforms, we must assume that the regnal year began in Tishri (autumn 622) and that the special Passover took place in Nisan (spring 621); see Thiele, *Mysterious Numbers*, 32, and id., *BASOR*, No. 143, Oct. 1956, 22 ff. LXX in 2 Kings 22:3 should be disregarded; but its statement that the 'Book of the Law' was discovered in the seventh month may reflect a tradition, current when the year began in Nisan, that the finding of the book took place in Tishri.

[6] See Montgomery and Gehman, op. cit., in loc.

[7] See the analysis in M. Noth, *History of Israel*, 1960, 272 ff. There is little reason to regard 2 Kings 23:15–20 as a 'Midrashic' interpolation, with Montgomery and Gehman, op. cit., in loc.

[8] 2 Kings 23:5, 8–9. Budde, op. cit. 192 ff., suggests that v. 8b should be omitted. Other scholars retain the passage, reading, however, שְׁעִרִים for שְׁעָרִים; see, for example, recently Albright, 'High Place in Ancient Palestine', *Volume du Congrès Strasbourg 1956* (Supplements to *VT*, vol. iv), 1957, 245. But this is not supported by the Versions, nor does it improve the sense. In v. 9b Kuenen, Gressmann, and others emend M.T. מַצּוֹת to מְנָיוֹת, but all Versions have מַצּוֹת with the M.T. Budde reads מְצֻוֹת, comparing Neh. 13:5 and

by violence.[1] The plans of Josiah to dominate the northern territory must have met with some success; it was at Megiddo in the north of the country that he measured his strength with Necho—and there he met his fate.[2]

Josiah's instructions to celebrate the Passover did not stem from a transfer of the opening of the civil year from the autumn to the spring[3]—so far as we may deduce from our text. Nor was it a gesture of defiance against Assyria—or of friendship towards Babylonia. The cults that were removed by Josiah were cults of Syro-Palestinian, rather than of Assyrian, character.[4] Josiah's celebration of the Passover probably arose from his desire to extend his dominion over North Israel. We observe the implication—confirmed by the brief allusions in the prophets[5]—that the Passover had been celebrated in the north as well as the south of Palestine.[6] There is significance in the claim of 2 Kings 22:2 that Josiah walked in the way of David, for it was David whose rule extended farther north than any of his successors as king of Israel[7]—and in the time of David the tribes were not yet divided. The Passover, Josiah ordered, was to be kept by all the people, of both the southern and the northern kingdoms.[8] A similar view is held by the writer of 2 Chr. 30, who tells of the Passover ascribed to Hezekiah (though his account may well be unhistorical). Hezekiah also, he declares, sought to incorporate North Israel within his kingdom.[9] But, indeed, the reason for Josiah's Passover is apparent from the order of events in the narrative of 2 Kings 23. The king returned to Jerusalem from his campaign in Samaria; then order was given for the festival to be celebrated by all the people at Jerusalem.[10] Jerusalem was to be the religious, as well as the administrative, centre of a united Israel.

connecting this with Deut. 18:3; he connects 'among their brethren' in 2 Kings 23:9 with Deut. 18:7—but he maintains that 2 Kings 23:8a*α*, 9 has nothing to do with the Passover of Deut. 16:1–8. On the other hand, Klostermann holds that 2 Kings 23:8–9 is connected with 23:21–23, and that the function of the priests is shown by 2 Chr. 35:3, 14 ff. See the discussion in Šanda, *Bücher der Könige*, ii. 345, and Montgomery and Gehman, op. cit., in loc. It is most improbable that מַצּוֹת in 2 Kings refers to the Passover. The test of ritual cleanness was not in connexion with the eating of *maṣṣoth* but the eating of the Pesaḥ victim; and it was in no way confined to the priests. Guthe, 'Passahfest nach Dtn 16', 228, points to the pluperfect tense of כי אם אכלו, 'unless they had (previously) eaten . . .'. 2 Kings 23:9 implies that only those priests who had belonged previously to the circle of the Jerusalem priesthood (for *maṣṣoth* as the food of priests, cf. Lev. 21:22 f., 6:9–11, 10:12 f., &c.) were permitted to eat among the Temple priests; the rest were excluded. Bentzen, *Introduction*, ii. 61, maintains that 2 Kings 23:9 seems to show that Deut. 18:6–8 was not obeyed.

[1] 2 Kings 23:20.

[2] 2 Kings 23:29 f., 2 Chr. 35:20 ff.

[3] Thiele, *Mysterious Numbers*, loc. cit.

[4] Gressmann, 'Josia und das Deuteronomium', *ZAW* xlii, 1924, 321 ff., and Montgomery and Gehman, op. cit., in loc. See also Noth, *Gesetze im Pentateuch*, 1940, 40 ff.

[5] pp. 213 f. above.

[6] 2 Kings 23:22b. See Welch, op. cit. 76, who, however, maintains that only in Ephraim was the Pesaḥ held at the sanctuary; p. 94 n. 1 above.

[7] 2 Sam. 8.

[8] 2 Kings 23:21a.

[9] 2 Chr. 30:1 ff.

[10] 2 Kings 23:15–20, 21. But it is possible also that the special Passover of Josiah had military significance. See E. Junge, *Wiederaufbau des Heerwesens des Reiches Juda unter*

It is a corollary of this argument that the Passover was not always celebrated at a single shrine.[1] This is, of course, evident from the statement—although it comes, it should be admitted, from a writer of the Jerusalem school—that Jeroboam endeavoured to dissuade his subjects from attending the pilgrimage at Jerusalem. But the number of shrines at which the Passover was celebrated is likely always to have been severely restricted. From its earliest beginnings the festival was, I have suggested, a national institution,[2] and there must always have been a tendency towards the centralization of its ritual. It is possible that in the reign of Solomon Jerusalem was the sole centre of pilgrimage in Israel; and we observe that even Jeroboam is said to have established a shrine for the pilgrimage only at one place, Bethel.[3] However this may be, the move to make Jerusalem the sole centre of pilgrimage throughout Palestine became feasible only after the fall of Samaria. Whether Josiah had been anticipated in this policy by Hezekiah (as claimed by 2 Chr. 30) is not of great importance.[4] There is, however, one factor which may go to show that it was Josiah who was the initiator of the policy. The Passover was a popular festival. In the account of 2 Kings 21–23 allusion is made to the popular basis of Josiah's rule. It was 'the people of the land' to whom he owed his throne.[5] It is to David, not to Solomon, that he is compared,[6] and the difference between those two early monarchs lay largely in the arbitrary rule of the latter, but not of the former.[7] I have pointed out that it was the people whom Josiah commanded to keep the Passover. His rule in the north as well as the south was to be confirmed, not by the celebration of the formal pilgrimage festival of the autumn, but by the popular pilgrimage festival of the spring.

Josia, 1937, where it is suggested that Josiah probably reorganized the Israelite army. (For a different view, see, however, Y. Yadin, 'Reorganization of the Army of Judah under Josiah' (in Hebrew), *Yedi'oth* (*Bulletin of the Jewish Palestine Exploration Society*), xv, 1949–50, 86.) I have already maintained, pp. 135 ff. above, that the Passover was the occasion of an annual census of men of military age.

[1] On shrines in Palestine, see de Vaux, *Institutions*, ii, 1960, 115 ff., and the bibliography on pp. 439 ff.

[2] pp. 133 f. above.

[3] 1 Kings 12:32 f. We are not informed that it could be celebrated also at Dan, cf. vv. 28 ff.

[4] p. 228 below.

[5] 2 Kings 21:24, 2 Chr. 33:25. See already 2 Kings 11:13 ff., where the 'people of the land' proclaim Jehoash as king and proceed to destroy the altars and images of Ba'al. E. Würthwein, *'amm ha'arez im Alten Testament*, 1936, 12 ff., followed by G. von Rad, 'Herkunft und Absicht des Deuteronomiums', *ThLZ*, 1947, 153, and others, maintains that the *'am ha'areṣ* are the landowning class. But the arguments of J. L. McKenzie, '"People of the Land"...', in *Akten des XXIV. Internationalen Orientalisten-Kongresses, München, 1957*, ed. H. Franke, 1959, 206, are more convincing. McKenzie demonstrates that the 'people of the land' were the people in general outside court circles. See also A. Malamat, 'Last Wars of the Kingdom of Judah', *JNES* ix, 1950, 218.

[6] 2 Kings 22:2.

[7] Compare Deut. 17:14–20, esp. the allusions in vv. 16–17, with the picture of Solomon in 1 Kings 9–11. 2 Chr. 30:26, on the other hand, compares Hezekiah's Passover with the festal celebrations of Solomon; cf. p. 229 below.

The question arises now whether the Passover document of Deut. 16 is to be ascribed to the period of Josiah. Guthe has maintained that the text of 2 Kings 23 has survived only in an abbreviated form, and that the original text contained a detailed account of Josiah's Passover—presumably on the lines of Deut. 16.[1] This is possible—but the assumption is not necessary. The writer of Kings recounts history; he does not prescribe religious ordinances. Nevertheless, there are obvious points of contact between Deut. 16 and 2 Kings 23. In 2 Kings 23:21 we find the phrase 'the Lord your God'; 'the Lord thy God' is found only in Deut. 16 of all the Passover documents in the Pentateuch. In Josiah's Passover stress was laid on its popular nature—and Deut. 16 is popular in character. There appears to be emphasis in 2 Kings on the venue of Josiah's Passover at Jerusalem, and this receives confirmation from Is. 30:29.[2] Here the Deuteronomic Passover provides a remarkable parallel. There was little need for the Deuteronomic regulation that the Passover was to be restricted to a prescribed place; it is probable that from the earliest times the festival was celebrated only at a prescribed place. The Deuteronomist, however, repeats again and again that the festival must not be held elsewhere, with an insistence that may be explained by the pressure of current events—similar to the events of the reign of Josiah. We cannot, on the basis of the little evidence before us, state that Deut. 16 formed part of the 'Book of the Law' of 2 Kings 22–23. But we can maintain that its provisions in no way disagree with the provisions that seem to have characterized Josiah's Passover.

The centralization of the cult at Jerusalem had, I have suggested, led to the abandonment of certain rites that had been prominent at the primitive Pesaḥ—in particular, the choosing of the victim on the tenth day, the smearing of its blood, and the special dress of the participants. They are missing in the Passover regulations of Deut. 16, and these regulations are likely to have obtained during the last years of pre-Exilic Jerusalem. The Exile brought about an upheaval in the life of the Israelites. Its effects on religious practice may not have been as radical as is commonly supposed, but it certainly caused the dislodgement of settled ideas and a temporary willingness to experiment with new ideas.[3] This period of Israelite history is represented among our Passover documents by the passage from Ezekiel, which shows a striking trend towards theocratic authoritarianism.[4] Whether there was at the same time a trend in the opposite direction cannot be proved with certainty; but this is certainly suggested by the emphasis

[1] p. 82 n. 3 above.

[2] See p. 214 above.

[3] The ritual exodus had been greatly modified—if it had not been abandoned—by the time of the author of Is. 52:11–12; pp. 173 f. above.

[4] See p. 6 above for remarks on the text and its date.

with which Ezekiel's proposals were rejected,[1] no less than by the final shape of the festival in post-Exilic Judaism.

Ezekiel's scheme for the Passover is set within the framework of his programme for a theocratic state. The (non-embolismic) year is divided into two halves.[2] On the first day of the first and seventh months[3] is held a ceremony of 'de-sinning' the Temple. Ezekiel carries this balance between the two halves of the year farther. The sacrifices on the Passover and Tabernacles are exactly similar;[4] the feast of Weeks is omitted, presumably to avoid disparity between spring and autumn.[5] Two other features distinguish Ezekiel's Passover from the conventional pattern. In conformity with his stress on purification ritual, he prescribes a 'de-sinning' ritual at the Passover also—the sacrifice of a bullock.[6] This cannot be the Pesaḥ sacrifice.[7] The Pesaḥ victim never was a bullock,[8] nor was it ever the offering of a single animal by a single celebrant, even on behalf of the whole community. The bullock of Ezekiel's regulations was, moreover, probably to be boiled;[9] and the Pesaḥ victim was never boiled.[10] The second unorthodox feature of Ezekiel's Passover is the prominence of the Naśi', evidently a layman, who represents the people.[11] It is he who is responsible for the sacrifices of the sanctuary,[12] and it is he who offers the bullock at the Passover as a sin offering. The blood, however, is handled by the priest.[13]

Yet the Passover regulations of Ezekiel[14] are not wholly at variance with tradition. As at Josiah's Passover, so in Ezekiel the festival follows closely on the dedication of the Temple.[15] We may therefore conclude that the celebration of the Passover—at least, of the Pesaḥ—was, in the view of the

[1] It was only after considerable opposition that the Book of Ezekiel was admitted into the Canon; *BT Shab.* 13b, *Men.* 45a.

[2] On the dichotomy of the year, pp. 116 and 127 above.

[3] See p. 6 above on the text.

[4] Unlike the provisions of Num. 28:19–24 (the Passover) and 29:13 ff. (Tabernacles). In Num. 28–29 the sacrifices at the Passover resemble exactly those at the new moon with the exception of libations, p. 202 above; in Ezekiel they are different, Ezek. 45:23 f. opp. 46:6 f. Note the frequency of the numeral seven among the lists of victims in the scheme of Ezekiel, and see p. 139 above on the significance of that number.

[5] p. 7 n. 5 above on the text.

[6] Ezek. 45:22.

[7] Cooke, *Ezekiel*, in loc., regards the sin offering here as a substitute for the Pesaḥ sacrifice, and compares the Day of Atonement ritual, Lev. 16.

[8] See pp. 204 f. above on Deut. 16:2.

[9] Ezek. 46:20 *bšl* opp. *'ph*, cf. vv. 23–24; see p. 205 n. 10 above on the term *bšl*.

[10] See pp. 205 f. above on Deut. 16:7. It should be remarked, furthermore, that in Ezek. 45:22 the bullock offering follows the seven-day Passover festival, not the Pesaḥ.

[11] Ezek. 45:16, 22 f. On the Naśi', see J. van der Ploeg, 'Chefs du peuple d'Israël et leurs titres', *RB* lvii, 1950, 47, and Zeitlin, 'Titles High Priest and the Nasi of the Sanhedrin', *JQR* xlviii, 1957–8, 1.

[12] Ezek. 45:16 f.

[13] Ezek. 45:19.

[14] See, however, Gese, *Verfassungsentwurf des Ezechiel* (*Kap. 40–48*), on the text of Ezekiel here.

[15] Ezek. 45:18–20. The fact that these verses may not be from the same hand as vv. 21 ff., as demonstrated by Gese, op. cit. 75, does not detract from the significance of their having been placed at this point of the text.

redactor of this text, to be restricted to Jerusalem. Furthermore, it is clear that Ezekiel, in striving to establish a balance between the Passover and Tabernacles, is most interested in the seven-day festival which provides the closest parallel. Nevertheless, he is obliged to defer to tradition. He uses the name Pesaḥ for the Passover, not 'Maṣṣoth festival'[1]—proof, if proof were needed, of the identity of the Pesaḥ and the Maṣṣoth festival, even in so unorthodox a context as Ezekiel. And the Passover opens on the fourteenth day, although this disturbs the symmetry of Ezekiel's scheme.[2] No libations of wine are included in Ezekiel's proposals for the offerings of the Passover week or of Tabernacles.[3] Finally, the popular aspect of the Passover is reflected even in Ezekiel; it is stated that the Naśi' in his sacrifice of the bullock as a sin offering is acting on behalf of himself and 'all the people of the land'.[4]

But it was not the authoritarian proposals of Ezekiel that won the day.[5] A convincing illustration of the manner in which the Passover was celebrated by Jewish communities outside Jerusalem is given by the 'Passover papyrus' from Elephantine. It is dated 419–418 B.C., and addressed by a certain Ḥananiah to the Jewish garrison there.[6] Ḥananiah communicates the terms of an edict which had been given by Darius II to Arsham, the Persian governor of Egypt, making provision for the observance of the Passover week.[7] The papyrus is severely mutilated, and poses difficult, though perhaps not insoluble, problems. We do not know who was this Ḥananiah. He has no official title.[8] He has a Hebrew name, and he was presumably from outside Egypt. He is possibly to be identified with a person of this name who came to Elephantine at this period, and whose activities seem to have caused strain between the Jews there and their Egyptian neighbours.[9]

[1] It is, however, possible that the text should be reconstituted; p. 7 n. 5 above.

[2] May and others should not be followed in reading 'fifteenth' for M.T. 'fourteenth'; see p. 7 n. 14 above.

[3] Ezek. 45:24–25; see p. 202 above.

[4] Ezek. 45:22; cf. pp. 7 f. above. No parallel procedure is prescribed for Tabernacles.

[5] The influence of Ezekiel on later Passover ritual has been greatly exaggerated by Beer, p. 79 above.

[6] For the text, see p. 9 above. Commentaries may be found in Lagrange, reviews, *RB* ix, 1912, 130, 578; Cook, 'Significance of the Elephantine Papyri for the History of Hebrew Religion', *AJT* xix, 1915, 356; Cowley, *Aramaic Papyri of the Fifth Century B.C.*, 1923, 60; A. Vincent, *Religion des Judéo-Araméens d'Éléphantine*, 1937, 234; Torrey, 'Letters prefixed to Second Maccabees', *JAOS* lx, 1940, 120; Dupont-Sommer, 'Fête de la Pâque . . .', *REJ* cvii, 1946–7, 39; and E. G. Kraeling, *Brooklyn Museum Aramaic Papyri*, 1953, 92. The numeration of the papyri used here is that of Cowley, op. cit.

[7] Arnold, *JBL* xxxi, 1912, 14, maintains that the subject of שליח in l. 3 of this papyrus is a person (that is, Ḥananiah), not a letter. But, as pointed out by Lagrange, op. cit. 578 f., שלח אגרה is found in Pap. 30, ll. 18 f., 24, 29, Pap. 31, l. 28, &c.

[8] Cowley, op. cit. 63, suggests that the absence of a title implies that Ḥananiah was a person of high rank; Arsham's name is not accompanied in the letters by a title.

[9] Cowley, op. cit. 137, on Pap. 38, ll. 7–8. There are not sufficient grounds for identifying him with Ḥanani, the brother of Nehemiah, who is mentioned in Neh. 1:2, 7:2

Various hypotheses have been advanced for the dispatch of this letter to Elephantine.[1] It has been suggested that it was intended to apply the laws of the Holiness Code to the Jews of the Diaspora, and that similar letters were sent to other communities in the Persian Empire.[2] Some scholars hold that it is the regulations of the P code that the letter sets out; the Passover was here prescribed for the first time for the wider public in its complete form and associated with a fixed date, 14th Nisan.[3] But it is improbable that a rescript of the Persian king would be used for this purpose. The Persian authorities were not accustomed to interfere in the religious practices of their subjects unless, like the official cult ceremonial at Babylon or the re-establishment of the Temple at Jerusalem, they impinged in some way on politics.[4] It is unlikely that this was the case with the affairs of this comparatively obscure community in Egypt. Moreover, the letter, so far as we can judge from its imperfect state, is not couched in the deliberate style befitting a document enacting religious regulations for the first time. There is no mention of religious sanctions, nor is the name of the deity mentioned, except in the conventional opening salutation. Other scholars have suggested that the papyrus was intended to prevent interference by Egyptian priests in the proper performance of sacrifice by the Jews of Elephantine.[5] Attempts at obstruction are reported in other papyri. But the 'Passover papyrus' makes no mention of sacrifice—a striking feature on which we shall remark later. The only conclusion that may safely be drawn from the text of this papyrus is that it is a private or semi-official letter from a Jew of Persia—rather than Palestine, since he has knowledge of an edict issued in Persia[6]—and that it gives the gist of relaxations from normal military duties granted to the Elephantine garrison during the Passover week.[7] In view of the source of the letter it is probable that these relaxations were granted after representations had been made to the Persian authorities by the Jewish community there.

We know from passing allusions in two contemporary ostraca that the Passover was known to the Jews of Elephantine.[8] In its present mutilated form the 'Passover papyrus' sets out the regulations only for the Passover week. We may reasonably assume that the words 'make the Passover' are

(in spite of Arnold, op. cit. 30, and, more recently, C. G. Tuland, 'Hanani–Hananiah', *JBL* lxxvii, 1958, 157). The name, in its different forms, was not uncommon.

[1] See the discussion in Vincent, op. cit. 265, and Grelot, 'Papyrus pascal d'Éléphantine et le problème du Pentateuque', *VT* v, 1955, 258.

[2] So Arnold; see p. 81 above. [3] So Beer and Steuernagel; see pp. 80 and 81 above.

[4] Lagrange, op. cit. 581, and Talmon, *VT* viii, 1958, 71. An opposite view is taken by Meyer, *Papyrusfund von Elephantine*, 1912, 97, and Cazelles, 'Mission d'Esdras', *VT* iv, 1954, 123 ff.

[5] So Vincent, op. cit. 307.

[6] So also Morgenstern, 'Calendars of Ancient Israel', *HUCA* x, 1935, 113.

[7] See Lidzbarski, *Ephemeris*, iii, 1909–15, 243, and Cowley, op. cit. xxiv n. 1.

[8] p. 8 above.

to be restored in ll. 4–5.[1] But 'Passover' here would refer to the Passover week, not the Pesaḥ sacrifice. There is no room in the text for a description of the procedure of the Pesaḥ sacrifice in the detail that would seem to be postulated by the general tenor of the document. The Jews of Elephantine certainly performed blood sacrifices before the destruction of their temple in 411 B.C.; these included holocausts,[2] but we cannot be certain that they included also sacrifices of the character of the Pesaḥ offering. When the Persian authorities gave permission for the rebuilding of the temple, they pointedly omitted permission to offer blood sacrifices.[3] It was politic on the part of the Persians to discourage these sacrifices in the Jewish temple in order to prevent dissension between the Jews and the Egyptians who objected to such practices. This does not mean, of course, that the Elephantine Jews did not carry out the Pesaḥ sacrifice before 411. But it is most unlikely. It would not have had the overt approval of the Jewish religious authorities at Jerusalem. The latter must have been well aware of the pantheon of deities that were worshipped at Elephantine,[4] and their omission to reply to letters from Elephantine seems to show that they regarded the Jews there with coolness. More important, there is no evidence whatever that the Pesaḥ victim was ever sacrificed outside Jerusalem after the promulgation of the Deuteronomic Code—and certainly not after the Return from Exile[5]—by any group except (and the exceptions are significant) the heretical Samaritans and possibly by the Falashas in Ethiopia.[6] And the Samaritans, with whom the Elephantine Jews were in contact, are no more likely to have countenanced the Pesaḥ sacrifice by their members outside their own settlements than the orthodox Jews outside Jerusalem.[7]

[1] See pp. 9 f. above on the text. There are no grounds for Vincent's conjectural reading, 'slay the Pesaḥ', in l. 9, op. cit. 304.

[2] עלוה, Pap 30, ll. 21, 25, Pap. 31, ll. 21, 25. We find דבח in Pap. 30, l. 28, Pap. 31, l. 27, but this seems to be a general description of sacrifice in letters to Bagoas.

[3] Pap. 32, which sanctions only meal offerings, cf. Vincent, op. cit. 144 ff., 170 ff. It is not known what answer was made to Pap. 33.

[4] Vincent, op. cit. 100, 418, &c., Kraeling, op. cit., ch. 8.

[5] See A. van Hoonacker, *Communauté Judéo-Araméenne à Éléphantine*, 1915, 17 f., and so, approximately, Meyer, op. cit. 95. *Mish. Men.* xiii. 10 does not mention the offering of the Pesaḥ at the Temple of Onias. Mlle A. Jaubert, 'Jésus et le calendrier de Qumrân', *New Testament Studies*, vii, 1960, 23, has misunderstood the allusions in *BT Pes.* 53 a, b and *JT Pes.* vii. 1. We are told there that the Sages mildly rebuked Thaddaeus because he might have conveyed to the Jews of Rome the impression that they could sacrifice the Pesaḥ there; the implication is that this would have been illegal. Josephus, *Ant.* XIV. x. 24, does not refer to the observance of the Pesaḥ sacrifice outside Palestine, as Mlle Jaubert maintains, loc. cit.; the decree in that text gives, in the most general terms, the right to the Jews to 'assemble together, according to their ancient legal custom . . .', and to offer 'prayers and sacrifices . . .'. See further J. Derenbourg, *Essai sur l'histoire et la géographie de la Palestine*, 1867, 480 ff., and E. Schürer, *Geschichte des jüdischen Volkes im Zeitalter Jesu Christi*, i, 1901, 654, cf. iii, 1898, 96. The text on the sacrifice of the Pesaḥ victim by Judaized Armenians, Migne, *P.G.* i, col. 870, should be regarded with suspicion; it is the work of a theological opponent.

[6] See pp. 251 ff. and 255 below.

[7] The Samaritan Passover was originally not restricted to Mount Gerizim; see Jeremias,

The 'Passover papyrus' sets out the observances of the Elephantine Passover in detail. The Jewish garrison were to be ritually clean[1] and to avoid leaven,[2] including a certain beverage—perhaps beer, a favourite drink in Egypt[3]—from sunset at the end of the fourteenth day until the twenty-first day of Nisan;[4] they were to abstain from work, presumably on the first and seventh days of the festival. This was the pattern of the Passover as it was observed by Jewish communities outside Jerusalem.

The fact that the Pesaḥ sacrifice was to be performed only at the Temple at Jerusalem is of central importance for the subsequent development of the Passover. It was, as I have already pointed out, no more than the logical extension of the original character of the festival—this was a communion ritual performed by the assembly of the people on a fixed date at a fixed place.[5] The provisions of Deuteronomy had already underlined the restriction of the Pesaḥ to a specified shrine or shrines. In Ezekiel the Pesaḥ is closely associated with the Temple at Jerusalem;[6] we shall ob-

Passahfeier der Samaritaner, 68 ff., and A. S. Halkin, *PAAJR* vii, 1935–6, 42 ff. On the relations between the Elephantine Jews and the Samaritans, see Cowley, op. cit., Papp. 30–32; Rowley, 'Sanballat and the Samaritan Temple', *BJRL* xxxviii, 1955–6, 166, esp. 175; and P. Antoine, art. 'Garizim', *Dict. Bib. Suppl.* Van Hoonacker, op. cit. 82, maintains that an appreciable number of Jews at Elephantine (including the Yadoniah of this papyrus) were Samaritans. H. Birkeland, *Acta Orientalia*, xii, 1934, 89, makes the suggestion that the Jews of Elephantine heard of the centralization of the cult at Jerusalem only after they had dispatched the earlier appeal to Bagoas and the High Priest referred to in Pap. 30, ll. 17–19 (Pap. 31, ll. 17–18); they made their second appeal in Pap. 30 and Pap. 31 to the sons of Sanballat because the Samaritans did not share the views of the Jerusalem Jews on the policy of centralization and to Bagoas again because he was opposed to the High Priest—the latter had ignored their first letter.

[1] Aram. *dky* is the equivalent of Heb. *ṭhr*; cf. Grelot, *VT* iv, 1954, 358. According to the Chronicler, this represents a lesser and more general grade of ritual cleanness, p. 226 n. 8 below; but we do not know what was the exact significance of the term in the late fifth century.

[2] All that contained leaven was to be 'sealed' (rather than 'hidden', as Grelot; see p. 9 n. 6 above and for *ḥtm*, 'close up, seal away', see M. Jastrow, *Dictionary*, s.v.). Dupont-Sommer, *REJ*, N.S. vii (cvii), 1946–7, 46, suggests that one of the Elephantine ostraca contains instructions that vessels should be examined in case they had leaven that should be removed before the Passover. This is improbable. In Mishnaic times vessels were not examined for leaven, but cleansed or replaced. Buildings were examined; but *Mish. Pes.* i. 1 has *bdq* for 'examine', not *bḥn* as in the ostracon. The latter word means 'test, try', rather than 'examine'. It is not certain that the Aram. term *mana'* in this ostracon should be translated 'vessel' rather than 'garment'.

[3] See Wiedemann, *Das alte Ägypten*, 1920, 298 ff.; Erman–Ranke, *Aegypten und aegyptisches Leben*, 225; and A. Lucas, *Ancient Egyptian Materials and Industries*, 1948, 16 ff.; for Mesopotamia, Hrozný, *Getreide im alten Babylonien*, 140. See *Mish. Pes.* iii. 1. Grelot, op. cit. 361 f., points out, however, that the text of the papyrus gives no clear indication of the identity of the beverage.

[4] It may be remarked that the Jews of Elephantine apparently used calculation, not observation, as their method of reckoning the calendar; J. K. Fotheringham, *Monthly Notices of the Royal Astronomical Society*, lxix, Nov. 1908, 12, and lxxi, June 1911, 661; cf. S. Gutesman, 'Calendrier en usage chez les Israélites au Ve siècle avant notre ère', *REJ* liii, 1907, 194, and D. Sidersky, 'Comput des Juifs d'Égypte au temps des Achéménides', *REJ* lxxxii, 1926, 59. See further S. H. Horn and L. H. Wood, 'Fifth-Century Jewish Calendar at Elephantine', *JNES* xiii, 1954, 6.

[5] pp. 130 f. and 133 f. above.

[6] pp. 220 f. above.

serve the same feature in all the documents that follow. And as the ceremonial was reserved to the Temple, it was inevitable that its several rites should conform to an ever-increasing degree to the general procedure of the Temple as the latter became more rigidly formal. The rites of the Passover week, on the other hand, were carried out wherever Israelites lived, in the form that they are prescribed in the Elephantine papyrus. Here lies a partial explanation of the phenomenon that has confused the treatment of the Passover by most students of the subject—the apparent separation between the Pesaḥ and the Maṣṣoth week in the Traditional Documents, in, that is, the Pentateuch.[1] It was in the period of the Chronicler or somewhat earlier that, I have suggested, the Compiler arranged the individual documents in the order in which we have them today.[2] By this artificial separation of the texts on the Pesaḥ from the texts on the Maṣṣoth week, the Compiler reflects the practice that had become established already before his time. The Pesaḥ rites were practised only by the pilgrims at Jerusalem, the rites of the Passover week—with the exception of sacrifices—were practised by Israelites everywhere.

The next group of documents, Ezra 6:19 ff., 2 Chr. 35:1 ff., and 2 Chr. 30:1 ff., all belong to the period to which the Compiler is to be assigned, the period, that is, of the Chronicler.[3] They purport to describe events that took place much earlier in Israelite history. In the present study we are not concerned with the historicity of these accounts—although on general grounds this is plausible enough—but with the details of practices which each document reflects as current at the time of its writer.

In Ezra we are told that the altar was set up at Jerusalem by Zerubbabel and the priests, and used for the first time on the first day of the seventh month, on, that is, Rosh haShanah[4]—a subsidiary festival, it will be recalled, of the autumn New Year festival of Tabernacles. The building of the Temple followed.[5] It was completed, we are informed, on 3rd Adar;[6]

[1] For another reason, see p. 175 above, where I suggest that the separation of the texts was also due to the fact that in the Exodus narrative only the Pesaḥ sections were strictly relevant.

[2] See p. 77 above.

[3] On the texts, see pp. 10 ff. above, and the works referred to there.

[4] Ezra 3:6, cf. vv. 4 f. and 7:9. It was also on the first day of the seventh month that Ezra recited from the 'Book of the Law', according to Neh. 7:73, 8:1 ff. (That this day was observed as a New Year's day is shown by the exchange of gifts, Neh. 8:10, 12; cf. p. 148 above.) There is, however, no question of Tabernacles being celebrated on 2nd–9th Tishri, as Morgenstern, op. cit. 56, followed by Widengren, op. cit. 11. Tabernacles, like the Pesaḥ, was held at the full moon. And, while Neh. 8:13 ff. does not specify the date on which the festival begins, the day of mourning of 9:1 on the twenty-fourth day of the month is certainly to be associated with the conclusion of the festival on the twenty-second day; the interval of one day after the festival and before the day of mourning is in accordance with the ruling of R. Jose in *Mish. Ta'an.* ii. 8.

[5] Ezra 3:8 ff. We may note that the Levites who perform service in the Temple are over the age of twenty; see p. 135 above.

[6] Ezra 6:15 ff. This is a date without obvious significance. Morgenstern, *VT* v, 1955, 62 n. 3, reads here 23rd Adar, with 1 Esdr. 7:5; this would be the first day of the week unit that precedes 1st Nisan.

and in the next month were celebrated the Pesaḥ and the seven-day Maṣṣoth festival.[1] Again, then, we have—in the view of the writer—a close connexion between the Temple and the Passover; the connexion is shown to be deliberate by a change of language, for the account of the Passover is in Hebrew but the preceding verses are in Aramaic. In the account of Zerubbabel's Passover there is the formal separation between the ceremonies of the Pesaḥ and those of the Maṣṣoth week which we have already explained. Two other features call for comment. There is stress upon the role of the Levites. It is they who slaughtered the Pesaḥ victims for the laymen, the priests, and themselves.[2] There is also stress upon ritual cleanness at the Pesaḥ sacrifice. Laymen (the 'sons of the captivity') were not permitted to perform the slaughter; and this prohibition was presumably based on grounds of uncleanness, since the task was delegated to the Levites,[3] who, we are informed, had purified themselves. Nevertheless, laymen were not wholly excluded. All those who had returned from Exile and all those among the residents of Palestine who 'had separated themselves unto (the returning exiles) from the filthiness of the heathen of the land, to seek the Lord, the God of Israel'—that is, those who abstained from pagan practices and intermarriage with pagans[4]—were allowed to partake of the Pesaḥ meal, evidently also at the Temple. The sacrifices of the Passover week are not specifically mentioned, but we may assume that they were offered; they would have been the natural expression of the 'joy' with which the festival was observed.[5]

In our extant text of 2 Chr. 35[6] we find the same emphasis as in Ezra 6 upon the role of the Levites and ritual cleanness at the Pesaḥ. The Levites performed the slaughter and the flaying and the cooking of all the victims, whether the actual Pesaḥ victims or the additional offerings. No explanation is given for the exclusion of laymen from this function; the Levites were, it is true, instructed to 'sanctify themselves',[7] and the term used here is the term employed by the Chronicler for the purification of priests and Levites—it is not used of laymen.[8] At this Pesaḥ the blood and

[1] Ezra 6:19–22.

[2] See on the text p. 10 n. 8 above.

[3] Adopting the reading of Esdr.; Ezra 6:20 has 'priests and Levites', but the rest of the verse shows that 'priests and' should probably be omitted. On the preference for Levites over priests, cf. Neh. 9:4 ff., 10:1 (E.V. 9:38); but the priests precede the Levites in 10:2 ff. (E.V. 10:1 ff.), 10:35 ff. (E.V. 10:34 ff.), cf. 12:1 ff., 13:4.

[4] Cf. Neh. 9:2, 10:29 ff. (E.V. 10:28 ff.).

[5] Ezra 6:22.

[6] On the text, see pp. 13 ff. above. J. Hänel, 'Recht des Opferschlachtens in der chronistischen Literatur', *ZAW* lv, 1937, 53, 63 ff., regards 2 Chr. 30, 35, as of earlier date than Ezra 6. See also the study by Guthe, 'Zum Passah der jüdischen Religionsgemeinde', *Theologische Studien und Kritiken*, xcvi–xcvii, 1925, 144, and G. von Rad, *Geschichtsbild des chronistischen Werkes*, 1930, 52 ff.

[7] If the word is to be retained in the text; see p. 13 n. 8 above.

[8] *ṭhr* is a broad term for the ritual cleanness of persons, and inclusive of *qdš*. The Chronicler uses the latter term only of priests and Levites, 2 Chr. 29:5, 15, 17, 34, 30:3,

fat were handled by the priests.[1] Again, the role of the laymen was confined to participation at the meal. Other points call for brief mention. The ritual was carried out according to households, alike among laymen, Levites, and priests.[2] But the Pesaḥ victims were provided not by individual families, but by the king and his nobles. The whole ceremony, as we might infer from allusions in the prophets which we have already cited, was accompanied by music.[3]

The writer of 2 Chr. 35 takes great pains to reconcile the apparent discrepancies between Ex. 12 and Deut. 16. We are left in no doubt what was the practice of his own time.[4] That oxen should be claimed as Pesaḥ victims was to him—and rightly—incredible;[5] so, too, it was incredible that the Pesaḥ victims could be alleged to have been boiled, as *bšl* in his day would have implied. Both these 'errors' of Deut. 16 are held by the writer to refer to the *qodašim*, the subsidiary offerings of the Pesaḥ night, which might be of oxen or sheep and goats and which might be boiled.[6] A further category of Passover offerings was, he alleges, 'burnt offerings',[7] and these were, it seems, small animals. They can scarcely be identified with the subsidiary offerings of the Pesaḥ night. They might be the *Tamid* victims that were offered daily at the Temple both morning and evening; but this, too, is unlikely.[8] Probably the 'burnt offerings' are a product of the Chronicler's imagination, like all the pomp of this colourful occasion—

15, 31:18, 35:6; in 30:17a *qdš* is used of the cleanness of the people, but in error, cf. vv. 17b and 19b. *ṭhr*, on the other hand, is of general application, 29:15b, 16a, 18a, but especially 30:17bα, 18a, 19b (here *qdš* is used of the sanctuary), 34:3, 8, Ezra 6:20. Two grades of ritual cleanness are found elsewhere in the ancient Near East; on the Hittites, for example, see Furlani, *Religione*, 237. A recent study of *qdš* is found in F. Nötscher, 'Heiligkeit in den Qumranschriften', *Revue de Qumran*, ii, 1960, 163, 315.

[1] See the discussion in Hänel, op. cit. 46.

[2] The minimum age was probably still twenty, as earlier; see p. 135 above. See 2 Chr. 34:1, 3b, where the king is said to have been twenty years old when he began to carry out his reforms, and cf. 1 Chr. 23:24.

[3] Cf. 1 Chr. 6:16 (E.V. 6:31), 16:4, 41, 23:25 ff., 2 Chr. 29:25 ff., Neh. 10:29 (E.V. 10:28), 12:27, and pp. 213 f. above; see further 1 Macc. 6:54, Josephus, *Ant.* xx. ix. 6, Gressmann, *Musik und Musikinstrumente im Alten Testament*, 1903, Büchler, *ZAW* xix, 1899, 96, 329, xx, 1900, 97, and Finesinger, *HUCA* iii, 1926, 21.

[4] The Pesaḥ victims are small animals, 2 Chr. 35:7–9; the date of the festival is the fourteenth day, 35:1; it takes place in the evening, 35:14 (by implication).

[5] 2 Chr. 35:12b, cf. 13b, *qodašim*.

[6] On the *qodašim*, see, in particular, 2 Chr. 29:33, Neh. 10:34 (E.V. 10:33), Gray, *Sacrifice*, 8, 21 ff.; see also Targ. Onq. and *Siphre* at Deut. 16:2, p. 56 n. 5 above. They are not the *re'iyyah*, *Mish. Ḥag.* i. 3 ff., which was to be wholly burned, cf. Danby, *Mishnah*, 211 n. 10. They may be the *ḥagigah*, which was a peace offering; see *Mish. Pes.* vi. 3 and Danby, op. cit., in loc. Among other uses, the term *qodašim* denotes the sacrificial meat consumed by priests, Num. 5:9, 18:19, cf. Lev. 21:22. &c.

[7] See pp. 200 f. above.

[8] Ex. 29:38 ff., Num. 28:3–8, 10, 15, 23 f., 31, 29:6, 11, &c., Dan. 8:11–13, 11:31, 12:11, Ezra 3:5. But the *Tamid* is offered before the Pesaḥ victim according to *Mish. Pes.* v. 1; cf. p. 262 below. If *'olah* refers to the *Tamid* in 2 Chr. 35, then v. 12 should probably precede v. 11. The term *'olah* cannot refer to the fat parts that were removed from the Pesaḥ victim and burned by the priests (as Rudolph, op. cit., in loc.), since 35:14 distinguishes between these fat parts and the *'olah*; Hänel, op. cit. 50, takes a similar view.

including the vast numbers of sacrificial victims and the special prominence of the king. The writer knew well that all formal ceremonies in the Temple were marked by burnt offerings;[1] and the merit of giving burnt offerings was greater than that of making offerings of which part was consumed by the participants.[2]

I have already given reasons for the view that the third of this group of documents from the School of the Chronicler, 2 Chr. 30, is no more an authentic account of the Passover held by Hezekiah than is 2 Chr. 35 of the Passover of Josiah. That Hezekiah did celebrate the Passover is probable—but this is irrelevant to our present discussion. He is certainly unlikely to have celebrated it in the manner described in 2 Chr. 30. The writer of that account reiterates the claim that the pilgrimage to Jerusalem attracted Israelites from northern as well as southern Palestine.[3] Samaria fell probably a few years before the accession of Hezekiah,[4] and our writer wished to demonstrate that little or no time passed before its population transferred their loyalties to the shrine at Jerusalem. In the details of the Passover, however, he recapitulates the usages of his own day, like the annalist of 2 Chr. 35. From internal evidence it may be assumed that it is the document of 2 Chr. 30, not that of 2 Chr. 35, that was composed later.[5]

The Passover of 2 Chr. 30 is a popular ceremony. True, it is the king who is the prime mover, but it is (at his instigation) the people who take the initiative, and who shame the priests and Levites into following suit. Laymen slaughter the Pesaḥ victims; only when they are unclean do the Levites perform the slaughtering on their behalf. But even those laymen who are unclean partake of the Pesaḥ meal, although we are told that it is the piety of Hezekiah that interceded for them. As everywhere in Chronicles, it is the priests who handle the blood. In 2 Chr. 30 we are given, and for the first time, a full picture of the rites of the Passover week[6]—the sacrifices,[7] the music in the Temple,[8] the singing of 'praises', that is, of prescribed psalms[9]—and the blessing of the priests at the end of the festival. This is a description of the familiar ceremonial of the Passover of the later days of the Temple.

[1] Cf. Ezra 3:6, where *'oloth* is the general term for sacrifice; cf. 2 Chr. 8:12 opp. 1 Kings 9:25, p. 201 n. 17 above.

[2] 2 Chr. 29:31 ff., cf. 29:24, 27 ff., 30:15, and Josephus, *Ant.* III. x. 6: 'Nor is there any of the festivals but on it they offer burnt offerings.'

[3] 2 Chr. 30:1, 5–11, 18, 25.

[4] See de Vaux, art. 'Israël', *Dict. Bib. Suppl.*; H. Tadmor, 'Campaigns of Sargon II of Assur', *Journal of Cuneiform Studies*, xii, 1958, 33; and E. Vogt, *Biblica*, xxxix, 1958, 535.

[5] p. 19 above.

[6] Note that the phrase '*ḥag* of Maṣṣoth', 2 Chr. 30:13, is interchanged with 'Pesaḥ', 30:1 ff.

[7] The word *mo'ed* as a description of the food of the *ḥag* or the sacrificial meat, 2 Chr. 30:22, is strange; see the Commentaries.

[8] See p. 227 above on music in the Temple.

[9] 2 Chr. 30:21, by priests and Levites; but 29:30, only by Levites.

Some features of 2 Chr. 30 we may attribute to the imagination of the writer. As in 2 Chr. 35, there is a vast number of sacrificial victims. There is also an extension of the Passover from seven to fourteen days. This may have arisen from a conscious desire to outdo the Passover of 2 Chr. 35, but more probably it is due to misunderstanding of the account of Solomon's celebration of Tabernacles at the time of the dedication of the Temple in 1 Kings 8. There the week of the autumn festival is preceded by the preliminal seven days of dedication; the writer of 2 Chr. 30 has misrepresented these two weeks, since they are regarded here as the week of the spring festival followed by seven days of dedication.[1] More interesting is the statement that Hezekiah's Passover had been deferred from the first to the second month. The deferment is said to be the result of ritual uncleanness, and scholars have discerned in this incident 'propaganda' for the observance of the 'second Pesaḥ' prescribed in Num. 9.[2] That is probably incorrect. We are told that the deferment was due not only to the uncleanness of the priests, but also to the absence of the people from Jerusalem—'the thing was done suddenly'.[3] Yet there was no reason for suddenness. Already in 2 Chr. 29:17 it is indicated that it was impossible to hold the Passover in that year at the proper time, because the sanctuary was not cleansed before the sixteenth day of the first month; the mention of that date is clearly deliberate—the day of the Passover had passed. Moreover, the writer claims that in the second month not only was the Pesaḥ held, but also the whole Passover week. Yet we may safely assume that it was never intended that a *ḥag* should be deferred, and in fact, according to our information, it never was deferred.[4] There is, then, only one reason for Hezekiah's postponement of the Passover—if, indeed, this was an historical event—and that reason was properly recognized by the Rabbis. That year must have been an embolismic year, and it was necessary to intercalate an extra month.[5]

[1] 2 Chr. 30:21 ff., cf. v. 26, opp. 1 Kings 8:1 f., 63 ff.; see p. 139 above. Note, however, that LXX (but not all manuscripts) omits the emphatic statement about fourteen days in 1 Kings 8:65; in the view of the translator, the seven days of Tabernacles evidently coincided with the days of the dedication of the sanctuary. On the other hand, the statements of 2 Chr. 30 do not tally with the description of Solomon's dedication of the Temple in 2 Chr. 7:8–10. The latter agrees with the account of 1 Kings 8 (except for the addition of the Eighth Day of Solemn Assembly).

[2] So, for example, Nicolsky, *ZAW* xlv, 1927, 245.

[3] 2 Chr. 29:36, 30:3.

[4] See p. 199 above on Num. 9.

[5] *BT Pes.* 56a, *Ber.* 10b, *Sanh.* 12a, *JT Pes.* ix. 1 (fol. 36c), *Ned.* vi. 13 (fol. 39d), *Sanh.* i. 2 (fol. 18d), *Tos. Pes.* viii. 5, *Sanh.* ii. 11. Talmon, *VT* viii, 1958, 60, makes the suggestion that Hezekiah held his Passover in the second, instead of the first, month as a concession to 'Ephraimite reckoning'. I have argued that 1 Kings 12:32 f. shows that details of intercalation were not uniform as between the northern and the southern kingdoms as early as the reign of Jeroboam I; see my article, *VT* vii, 1957, 257 f. But differences in climate would lead to an earlier rather than a later date for the New Year at Samaria (though the unrest which must have followed the fall of Samaria may well have led to irregularity in the calendar there); see my article, ibid. 259.

I have maintained that 2 Chr. 30 was composed later than 2 Chr. 35. Are we then justified in regarding the differences between the two as the outcome of a gradual process of development? In 2 Chr. 35 the king and his nobles are stated to have donated the Pesaḥ victims—the festival was, to all appearances, a royal occasion; in 2 Chr. 30 it is apparently the people who purchase their own victims, for the gifts of Hezekiah and the princes are provided for the celebrations of the period of seven days that follows the Passover week. It is probable that we should not press the comparison too closely. 2 Chr. 35 is a deliberate expansion of the narrative of 2 Kings 23:21 ff., where the king plays a central part; in 2 Chr. 30 there is no model for the Chronicler's story, and he follows more closely the pattern of his own times. So, too, of the status and role of laymen in 2 Chr. 35 and 30. One need not assume that there is a conflict of practice reflected in the conflicting accounts of the two chapters, or that, as a result of popular insistence, a royal festival had been transformed into a popular festival. More may be learned from the features that appear to be common to all the three narratives of Ezra 6:19 ff., 2 Chr. 35:1 ff., and 2 Chr. 30:1 ff. There is the stress on ritual cleanness which led on occasions to the performance of the rites by Levites instead of laymen, and to the restriction of the handling of the blood and the fat of the Pesaḥ victims to the priests. The Pesaḥ was assimilated as far as possible to normative Temple procedure. This accounts for the significant silence of these documents on two other features of the Pesaḥ. The time of the sacrifice is not prescribed; we are not told that it took place at the end of the fourteenth day.[1] The reason lies in the growing emphasis on the preliminaries of the fourteenth day—the ritual cleanness and the profusion of sacrifices, all to be completed, at the Temple, by daylight—that later were to give the fourteenth day the status almost of a festival. And there is no mention of the disposal of the remains of the Pesaḥ victim.[2] In this respect the Pesaḥ perhaps already resembled the ordinary festival sacrifice; the remains were disposed of at the end of the festival day, as in later times—on, that is, 16th Nisan, and on 17th Nisan if the 16th was a Sabbath.[3]

But in all three documents of the School of the Chronicler the Passover continues to have the character of a popular ceremony, in spite of its assimilation as far as possible to general Temple routine. All Israelites who had come to Jerusalem on pilgrimage, even if they were not ritually clean, were encouraged to take part in the Pesaḥ meal.

[1] Except by implication, 2 Chr. 35:14a.

[2] Unlike Deut. 16:4b.

[3] See p. 263 below.

7

THE LAST PHASE

THE description in 2 Chr. 30 of the Passover ascribed to Hezekiah bears remarkable resemblance in several respects to the form which the festival took in the last years of the Temple. But we have not yet reached the end of the story. The political fortunes of Israel were to undergo violent upheaval between the time of the Chronicler and the final catastrophe of A.D. 70; and their economic circumstances were to change radically. The effects are to be seen in the ritual of the festivals, and not least in that of the Passover.

The description of the Passover in Jubilees, ch. 49, falls into two distinct parts.[1] The first part is haggadic. It tells of the tenth plague and the Exodus from Egypt, and, naturally enough, it is based upon the narrative of Ex. 12. There is careful avoidance of anthropomorphism.[2] Strangely, there is no mention of the unleavened bread or the bitter herbs, both of which were prominent at the Pesaḥ meal.[3] There is an oblique reference to psalmody.[4] Most important, we find here the first allusion to the wine which became so prominent a feature of the Jewish Pesaḥ.[5] Was the wine a cultic substitution element, to be compared to the blood of the sacrifice? Certainly, a metaphorical analogy was drawn by Israelites between red wine and blood.[6] But this explanation for the use of wine is improbable.

[1] See the text on pp. 20 ff. above. Of special relevance to the present discussion are Büchler, 'Studies in the Book of Jubilees', *REJ* lxxxii, 1926, 253, and id., 'Traces des idées et des coutumes hellénistiques dans le livre des Jubilés', *REJ* lxxxix, 1930, 321; Ch. Albeck, *Das Buch der Jubiläen und die Halachah*, 1930; and L. Finkelstein, 'Book of Jubilees and the Rabbinic Halaka', *HTR* xvi, 1923, 39, and id., 'Some Examples of the Maccabean Halaka', *JBL* xlix, 1930, 22 ff.

[2] Cf. Ex. 12:23, 12:13. For the Masṭema of Jub. 49, cf. Jub. 10:8, 11:5, 11, 17:16, 18:9, 12, 19:28, 48:2, 12, 15, and *Zad. Doc.* xvi. 5 (Rabin, op. cit. 75). See further F.-M. Braun, 'Arrière-fond judaïque du quatrième évangile . . .', *RB* lxii, 1955, 13.

[3] R. Leszynsky, *Sadduzäer*, 1912, 206, suggests that the writer of Jub. 49 interprets the *merorim* of Ex. 12:8, Num. 9:11 as 'wine', and this, Leszynsky maintains, is in fact the correct interpretation of that word; he compares *meroroth*, Deut. 32:32, which should be rendered 'bitter (wine)'. The suggestion seems improbable; it is difficult to believe that the strange practice of the bitter herbs should be based upon a verbal misunderstanding. Moreover, if sanction were given to an incorrect interpretation, it would surely be given to replace an unfamiliar by a familiar practice rather than the reverse, as would be the case if Leszynsky's hypothesis were correct.

[4] At v. 6. In the extracts from Wisdom of Solomon, p. 25 above, this is the main feature of the allusions to the Exodus and the Passover.

[5] p. 259 below.

[6] The Pesaḥ wine was usually red in later times, *JT Pes.* x. 1 (fol. 37c), *Shab.* viii. 1 (fol. 11a), *Sheq.* iii. 1 (fol. 47b), *BT Pes.* 108b, *Men.* 87a. For the comparison between wine and blood, Gen. 49:11, Deut. 32:14, Is. 63:3, Ecclus. 39:26, 50:15, 1 Macc. 6:34, Rev. 14:20, *BT Sanh.* 70a, &c. See E. R. Goodenough, *Jewish Symbols in the Greco-Roman Period*, vi, 1956, Part viii, 'Wine', 126 ff.

There was no need for such a rite of substitution, for at the time of Jubilees the sacrifice of the Pesaḥ victims was still performed at the Temple and according to established ritual, and the blood was poured away at the base of the altar.[1] Was the introduction of wine the borrowing of Greek custom, a 'borrowing', it should be noted, that is rejected in the ritual of the modern Samaritans?[2] This is no less improbable. Wine already played a notable part in the procedure of the Jerusalem[3] Temple—the hypothesis of direct borrowing from Greece may be admitted only where the evidence is clear and inescapable. It is more likely that the introduction of wine at the Pesaḥ meal was the effect of a radical change that was now taking place in the character of the Passover. It was to be no longer a solemn annual mustering of male adults; it was to become the occasion for family festivity, in which the drinking of wine found a natural place.[4] Jubilees marks the beginning of this last phase in the history of the festival. We shall return to the point later.[5]

The second part of Jub. 49 is halakhic; it describes the festal rites as they were carried out at the time of the writer.[6] The contrast between the 'Pesaḥ of Egypt' and the 'Pesaḥ of (later) generations', which was, I have suggested, already evident in the regulations prescribed in Deut. 16,[7] was a concept familiar to the Rabbis of the Mishnaic period; it was probably known to the writer of Jub. 49. The ritual—as opposed to the legend—of Jub. 49 is largely based upon the regulations of Deut. 16 rather than upon those of Ex. 12, which they had superseded. On the other hand, those details of Deut. 16 which I have maintained were the result of textual error or misunderstanding do not appear here. The Pesaḥ animals are small animals;[8] and they are roasted. As in Deut. 16, there is no smearing of the blood of the Pesaḥ victims; instead, the blood and fat are withdrawn and handled separately, as they probably were at the time of the Deuteronomist, and as they certainly were at the period of the Chronicler.[9] There is no special dress prescribed for the participants. As in Deut. 16, so also in Jub. 49 it is stressed that the Pesaḥ must be performed at the central

[1] Jub. 49:20.

[2] Beer, *Pesachim*, 48; cf. I. Löw, *Flora der Juden*, 1928, i. 148.

[3] See p. 202 above.

[4] For wine and merriment, see Gen. 9:20 f., 19:32 ff., Jud. 9:13, 1 Sam. 25:36 f., 1 Kings 4:20, Is. 22:13, Ps. 104:15, Eccl. 10:19, Ecclus. 40:20, cf. Deut. 29:5 (E.V. 29:6), Jud. 19:19, 1 Sam. 25:18, 2 Sam. 16:1, and note the abstention from wine by Nazarites, Num. 6:2 ff., and by the Rechabites, Jer. 35:6. Cf. *Tos. Pes.* x. 4, *JT Pes.* x. 1 (fol. 37b), *BT Pes.* 109a.

[5] p. 241 below.

[6] The same division of regulations on the Passover is found in the contemporary account of Ezekielos, pp. 23 f. above. This is, however, greatly inferior to that of Jub.; it slavishly follows the text of Deut. 16 (or LXX there), and suggests that the Pesaḥ victims are to be from either small or large animals.

[7] See p. 208 above.

[8] Eth. *bg'* is the equivalent of Heb. *śeh*, Gr. *πρόβατον*.

[9] pp. 211 and 226 f. above.

shrine—at one time at the Tabernacle, later at the Temple when that was built and dedicated. The meal must be eaten in the Temple courts, as in Deuteronomy, and with haste.[1] Furthermore, Jub. 49 has no more than a brief reference to the ritual of the Passover week—exactly like Deut. 16.

There is, however, one regulation in the halakhic part of Jub. 49 that does not appear in Deut. 16, but is, nevertheless, of great antiquity. No bones of the Pesaḥ victim are to be broken. This prohibition is found in Ex. 12 and Num. 9,[2] and it was observed to the last days of the Temple;[3] it must have been observed also at the time of Deuteronomy. We can only assume that it has been inadvertently omitted from our extant text of Deut. 16. The writer of Jub. 49 goes, indeed, farther than the Bible documents by giving the prohibition an apotropaic significance. If the Pesaḥ victim's bones are not broken, no bone of the Israelites shall be broken; if, further, they carry out fully the Pesaḥ rites, no plague shall afflict them during the ensuing year. This apotropaic concept may well have been present at the primitive New Year festival.[4]

Another feature of the Passover of Jub. 49 which is not found in Deut. 16 is, on the other hand, clearly the product of changing circumstances and a sign of the growing precision in Temple procedure. The date and time at which the victims are to be slaughtered and eaten are defined with exactness—in terms of the three watches of the day and night (which, be it noted, were equal at the spring equinox). The sacrifice is to take place between 2 p.m. and 6 p.m., and the meal before 2 a.m.;[5] then the remains are to be burned. This is a deliberate clarification of the Bible text.[6] It had been made necessary by the great crowd that now flocked to the Passover pilgrimage. To an increasing extent, as we have already seen in the account of 2 Chr. 30, the Pesaḥ ritual was carried out in the daylight of 14th Nisan.

Why were the crowds now so much greater? The text of Jub. 49 is witness to a new course of development, begun but not yet fully completed. The Pesaḥ must, the writer maintains, be performed by all males of twenty

[1] Cf. Deut. 16:3, Ex. 12:11, and p. 23 n. 3 above. [2] pp. 170 f. above.

[3] See p. 260 below.

[4] Jub. 49:13–15. The Latin version of v. 13 is to be preferred, with Charles; see p. 21 above. For the apotropaic significance of the Passover, see pp. 163 ff. above, and see the remark of Ezekielos, the near-contemporary of the writer of Jubilees, p. 24 above. Cf. further Hebr. 11:28 and the practices of the modern Samaritans, p. 253 below.

[5] 'Until the third part of the night', Jub. 49:12, would normally be regarded as inclusive; in that case, the meal would continue until 6 a.m. But it is preferable to hold that the meal was to be eaten only up to, but not including, the third part of the night, until, that is, 2 a.m. In *Mish. Pes.* x. 9 the limit is given as midnight, a slight but characteristic increase in severity.

[6] Jub. 49:10–12 explains Ex. 12:6, cf. Jub. 49:11; the less precise 49:19, on the other hand, is the elucidation of Deut. 16:6.

years and upwards who are clean and not on a long journey[1]—on pain of excommunication. The regulations concerning a census at the Pesaḥ, to which I have already alluded, were, then, still enforced. Nevertheless, there is evident in Jubilees an air of informality and festiveness at the Passover,[2] which we have detected already in the ordinances on the drinking of wine. The festival had become an occasion for family rejoicing.

The provisions of Jub. 49 follow a normative pattern. Its description of the Passover stands in a direct line from the Passover of Deut. 16 to the Passover (as we shall see later) of the Mishnah. Was the writer of Jubilees, then, a Pharisee? Some scholars have held this view.[3] Others point to the calendar around which the Book of Jubilees is constructed, and which is wholly at variance with that of normative Judaism; they hold that the author must have been a member of a heterodox sect.[4] It is probable that both views are in fact correct. The author of Jub. 49 recounts the traditional Passover practices, but he makes no mention of the Jubilees calendar. The text of this chapter is evidently by a hand different from that of the bulk of the book.[5]

This becomes apparent when we compare ch. 49 with the preceding chapter. Chapter 49 is introduced with a deliberate emphasis which marks the opening of a new train of thought. Chapter 48, on the other hand, follows logically the scheme of the previous chapters. It describes the ten plagues and the Exodus. But it ignores the Passover with an absolute silence that is too pointed to be accidental. The separate authorship of ch. 49 may, however, be demonstrated more clearly. I have maintained that there is significance in the order in which the Compiler of the Pentateuch has arranged those of its documents that contain ritual legislation.[6] Those that he considers ancient he has incorporated in the earlier books, those that he considers the result of later development he has set in the later books. This method is not followed in the main part of the Book of Jubilees. The author assigns to the patriarchal period practices which the Pentateuch regards as later—the Sabbatical year (Jub. 7:35 ff.), the Second tithe (32:9), the feast of Weeks (6:17 ff., &c.), Rosh haShanah (12:16), Tabernacles (16:19 ff., &c.), the Eighth Day of Solemn Assembly (32:16 ff.), and the Day of Atonement (34:18). But most remarkable is the

[1] Jub. 49:9 follows closely the wording of Num. 9:13, although Jubilees does not prescribe the 'second Pesaḥ'.

[2] 'Eat and drink', Jub. 49:9; cf. the rejoicing in Deut. 16:11, 14f., at the feast of Weeks and at Tabernacles—but not at the Passover. See also pp. 241 and 263 below.

[3] Charles, *Apocrypha and Pseudepigrapha*, ii. 8 f.; cf. Eissfeldt, *Einleitung*, 749 ff.

[4] pp. 20 f. above. G. H. Box, in Charles, *Book of Jubilees*, 1917, viii, suggests that he was a member of the sect of Ḥasidim, Leszynsky, op. cit. 179, maintains that he was a Sadducee, Finkelstein, *HTR* xvi, 1923, 39, and Albeck, op. cit., hold that he was neither Pharisee nor Sadducee. See also the discussion in Zeitlin, 'Book of Jubilees, Its Character and Its Significance', *JQR* xxx, 1939–40, 1.

[5] On the 'textual integrity' of the Book of Jubilees, see E. Wiesenberg, 'The Jubilee of Jubilees', *Revue de Qumran*, ix, 1961, 37.

[6] p. 192 above.

difference between the treatment of the feast of Weeks in the Pentateuch and its treatment by Jubilees. In the former it has, as I have pointed out, an inferior role; it is an appendage of the Passover.[1] In Jubilees it has become the most important of the festivals in the Israelite calendar. Its observance is implied in the opening verse of the whole book. It is the first of the three pilgrimage festivals to be prescribed.[2] It is commanded again and again, and always it is connected with some important event in Israelite history.[3]

The reason for the attraction of the feast of Weeks for the writer of the main part of Jubilees is evident. It was to be celebrated on 15th Sivan.[4] The first of the preceding forty-nine days—the day of the solemn waving of the Sheaf—must then have fallen outside the Passover week. Scholars are rightly agreed that the writer of Jubilees interpreted the 'morrow after the Sabbath' of Lev. 23:9 ff. as the day after the weekly Sabbath, Sunday. This was the interpretation adopted by other sectarians—although, as we shall see, with one crucial point of difference. For the writer of Jubilees, then, the feast of Weeks always fell on Sunday. For him it was the festival of the seven-unit *par excellence*; it conformed more than any other to his scheme of recurrent weeks of days and years. But he gives no explanation for this association of the feast of Weeks with the seven-unit. He names it the feast of Weeks, as well as festival of Firstfruits,[5] but he makes no direct allusion to the waving of the Sheaf and the week of weeks which followed, although this symbolism must have been dear to his heart. The reason is not far to seek. To have alluded to the Sheaf-waving would have been to admit the dependence of the feast of Weeks upon the Passover, as this is demonstrated in the Pentateuch. But the writer of Jubilees would not admit this. No one reading the Book of Jubilees before reading the Pentateuch would regard the feast of Weeks as subsidiary to the Passover.

Wholly different is the treatment of the festival of Passover by the writer

[1] See p. 198 above.

[2] Jub. 6:17. Rosh haShanah follows in 12:16, Tabernacles in 16:19 ff. and again in 32:4, while the day before the beginning of Tabernacles is marked by the offering of tithes, 32:2, the Eighth Day of Solemn Assembly follows in 32:16 ff., and the Day of Atonement in 34:18.

[3] It is always connected with a covenant (cf. Ex. 19:1, 24:4 ff., on the covenant of Sinai in the third month and Jub. 1:1) or with an anniversary in fulfilment of a covenant: Jub. 6:15 ff. (= Gen. 9:8 ff.), 14:10 ff. (= Gen. 15:8 ff.), 15:1 f. (= Gen. 17:1 ff.), 16:13 (= Gen. 21:2, note Heb. *lamoʿed*; according to *BT R.H.* 10b, this event took place at the Pesaḥ!), 22:1 (not in Gen.), 28:15 (= Gen. 29:35), 29:7 (= Gen. 31:46), 44:4 (= Gen. 46:1–6). Whether the author of Jubilees interpreted the name of the feast of Weeks (*šabhuʿoth*) as the feast of Oaths (*šebhuʿoth*), as Zeitlin, *JQR* xl, 1949–50, 245, is open to question; the author of Jubilees associates it with covenants rather than with oaths.

[4] Jub. 15:1, 44:1 f.

[5] Jub. 6:17 ff. (esp. vv. 21 f.), 22:1. It is given the title of festival of Firstfruits without the title of feast of Weeks, 15:1 ff., 16:13, 44:4; it is never called the feast of Weeks without the addition of the term festival of Firstfruits.

of Jubilees—excluding, that is, ch. 49. The account of the Exodus in ch. 48 makes no mention of the festival. There is an allusion to a springtime festival—it could scarcely be omitted altogether—as a seven-day feast commencing on the fifteenth day of the first month;[1] but this has no connexion with the Exodus or with the Passover. It is in commemoration of the *'Aqedah*. This is indeed a pale shadow of the Israelite New Year festival. That the *'Aqedah* has any association with the new year we can deduce only from later Jewish tradition.[2] Jubilees' treatment of the festival of Tabernacles is more generous. It is mentioned, and in the framework of the Jubilees calendar; and it has retained its distinctive rites of booths and branches. But it is not regarded as a New Year festival.[3]

Here, of course, lies the reason for the disregard of the Passover by the writer of the main part of the Book of Jubilees. In ch. 49, with its detailed description of the festival ceremonies, there is, as I have already pointed out, no attempt to insert the Passover within the pattern of the Jubilees calendar. That would have been impossible, since the Passover derives from a lunisolar calendar, not from a schematic solar calendar. At the time of the composition of Jubilees, the Passover was the pivot on which the orthodox Jewish calendar turned. Tabernacles could be admitted to the scheme of Jubilees because it had largely lost its original quality as a New Year festival; that aspect of the autumn festival had been appropriated by Rosh haShanah—and we may observe that the latter is ignored in Jubilees except for an oblique allusion to the belief of Jews that it was a day of omen for the ensuing period.[4] The writer of Jubilees omits reference to the 'second Pesaḥ', although he quotes directly from Num. 9[5] and must have been well aware of its provisions; probably the 'second Pesaḥ' would fall on a day of the week which the author of Jubilees would not have considered proper for the Pesaḥ.[6]

[1] Jub. 18:18 f., cf. 17:15; the twelfth day is followed by a three days' journey, 18:3 ff. (cf. Gen. 22:3 f.). Note the mention of Masṭema to avoid anthropomorphism; cf. Jub. 49:2 and p. 22 n. 8 above.

[2] *Gen. Rabba*, lvi. 9, *BT R.H.* 16a, *Meg.* 31a; see I. Lévi, 'Le Sacrifice d'Isaac et la mort de Jésus', *REJ* lxiv, 1912, 166 ff., against Riesenfeld, op. cit. 86 ff. The account of the *'Aqedah* has a special association with the practice of the dedication of firstborn; for the connexion of this practice with the Pesaḥ, see pp. 165 and 187 above.

[3] In Jub. 16:19 ff. Tabernacles is celebrated to commemorate the promise of the birth of Isaac; in 32:2 ff. it is the festival of the tithing of produce and cattle that marks the end—not, we may note, the beginning—of the harvest year.

[4] 'Abram sat up throughout the night . . . to observe the stars from the evening to the morning, in order to see what would be the character of the year with regard to the rains', Jub. 12:16, cf. *Mish. R.H.* i. 2. The allusion of Jub. 34:12 ff. to the Day of Atonement indicates that the writer regards the origin, but not necessarily the ritual, of that festival as of minor importance. The children of Israel are to 'make atonement for themselves . . . with a young goat . . . for their sins' on the day that 'the news which made him weep for Joseph came to Jacob his father'.

[5] p. 23 above.

[6] It would occur thirty days after the Pesaḥ of the first month; see p. 248 below on the 'calendar' of Qumran.

Why, then, is the account of the Passover in Jub. 49 attached as an appendix to a book for which the festival has little meaning? Indeed, the inclusion of this chapter in Jubilees was itself a reminder that the calendrical scheme of the main part of the book is an innovation, since it cannot admit the festival which is perhaps the most important and most ancient in the religion of Israel. Was Jub. 49 a concession to potential members of the Jubilees sect who wished nevertheless to retain their attachments to orthodox ritual? This seems scarcely likely. We know that Samaritans had no difficulty in entering the Temple,[1] and a non-Jew was able to attend the Pesaḥ service at the Temple before being denounced by Ben Bathyra.[2] Evidently, the only outward obligation demanded from pilgrims by the Temple authorities was, naturally enough, observance of the proper ritual at the proper time.

The explanation for the detailed account of the Passover in Jubilees is probably to be found in the significance of the Pesaḥ as an annual census.[3] Jub. 49, as we have seen, declared that it was obligatory upon every male of twenty years and over to be present, unless circumstances made his attendance impossible. Omission to do so involved exclusion from the community—and this the members of the Jubilees sect did not venture to incur.[4] At a later period their successors were, it seems, prepared to go farther;[5] other sectarians, the Judaeo-Christians, preferred, like the author of Jubilees, to cling tenaciously to the ritual of normative Judaism.[6]

It is advisable to discuss at this point the celebration of the Passover described in Jos. 5.[7] How far can it be assigned with confidence to a particular period in the history of the festival? The narrative of Joshua may contain a conscious parallel between the crossing of the Jordan and the earlier crossing of the Red Sea.[8] To both events the Israelites came organized as a military host, after rites of purification.[9] Both opened a new era in the history of the nation. Thereafter the parallel is no longer valid. At the Exodus, circumcision and the Pesaḥ ceremonies took place, according to legend, before the crossing of the Red Sea, but in Joshua they took place after the crossing of the Jordan.[10] It is doubtful, indeed, whether the writer of Joshua lays great stress on the significance of the Passover which Joshua is said to have celebrated. It is rather the eating of *maṣṣoth* and the firstfruits of Canaan in which he is interested.[11] He shows knowledge

[1] Until A.D. 7, Josephus, *Ant.* XVIII. ii. 2.
[2] *BT Pes.* 3b. [3] pp. 135 ff. above. [4] Jub. 49:9.
[5] p. 248 below on the 'calendar' of Qumran.
[6] pp. 241 and 246 below.
[7] For the text, see p. 3 above.
[8] Jos. 4:21 ff.; Ex. 12:26 ff., 13:5 ff.
[9] Jos. 3:5, 5:4, 6; Ex. 12:17, 41, 51. [10] Ex. 12–13; Jos. 5:2 ff.
[11] מַצּוֹת וְקָלוּי, Jos. 5:11: see the interpretation of the phrase by LXX in loc., *ἄζυμα καὶ νέα*, cf. קָלוּי in the firstfruits offering of Lev. 2:14 and the cognate קלי in Lev. 23:14.

of the geography of Palestine. The corn crops are not normally ripe at the time of the Passover—but if they are, it is in the vicinity of Jericho, the scene of Joshua's Passover.[1] There is no direct reference in Jos. 5 to the duration of the Passover; an oblique allusion may, however, be provided by the fall of Jericho on the seventh day,[2] and the processions with the Ark and horns which preceded it are strongly reminiscent of traditional New Year ceremonial.[3]

All this is nevertheless so circumstantial as to make the description of Joshua's Passover virtually worthless as an historical source. The writer is concerned with the conquest of the new land; this, he maintains, took place at the Passover because that seems to him the appropriate time. It was the traditional New Year festival and an auspicious season for undertaking a new enterprise. But one detail in Jos. 5 is of interest to us in the present context. The Israelites, we are told, ate of the produce of the land 'on the morrow after the passover'.[4] The natural inference is that this took place on the fifteenth day of the month. The writer of the Hebrew text is unlikely to have had the waving of the barley Sheaf in mind, since the ceremony never took place on that date. But it is possible to draw a different conclusion from this passage of Joshua if we assume that 'passover' here is used of the Passover week, not of the Pesaḥ. It was the danger of such an interpretation that perhaps suggested itself to the LXX translator of the passage. He omitted the phrase 'morrow after the passover'.[5] We may assume that he feared that the phrase might provide support for a practice of which he disapproved—the practice of waving the Sheaf on the morrow of the Passover week.[6]

For this practice—which was, I have suggested, the original usage in Israel[7]—had been superseded some time after the date of the composition of the Book of Jubilees. The barley Sheaf was now offered on the morrow of the first day of the Passover week. This is the date indicated with somewhat self-conscious insistence by LXX and other Versions in Lev. 23.[8] The shift in date is reflected by a parallel change in the practice of the sectarians.

[1] Jos. 3:15 f., 5:11; note the conflate rendering by LXX of 5:9, *ἀφ' ἑσπέρας ἐπὶ δυσμῶν Ἱεριχὼ ἐν τῷ πέραν τοῦ Ἰορδάνου ἐν τῷ πεδίῳ*, and see further p. 250 below. For the division of Palestine into zones on the grounds of variations of climate and vegetation, see *Mish. Sheb.* ix. 2, *Ket.* xiii. 10, *B. Bathra* iii. 2, *Tos. Sanh.* ii. 3, *JT Sanh.* i. 2 (fol. 18d), *BT Sanh.* 11b, and perhaps already Jos. 10:40, Jud. 1:9. See Dalman, *Arbeit und Sitte*, i. 413, ii. 6, iii. 2, and the summary in R. O. Whyte, 'Phytogeographic Zones of Palestine', *Geographical Review*, xl, 1950, 606 ff. and pl. 2.

[2] Jos. 6:4 f., 15 ff.; cf. Josephus, *Ant.* v. i. 5; and *Seder 'Olam Rabba*, ch. xi.

[3] p. 151 above.

[4] Jos. 5:11. The writer may, however, have in mind the phrase 'morrow after the passover' in Num. 33:3.

[5] That the omission is deliberate is indicated by the further omission by LXX of 'on the morrow', Jos. 5:12.

[6] So Cooke, *Joshua*, 1918, in loc., suggests that LXX omitted the words because they appeared to disagree with the regulations of Lev. 23.

[7] pp. 197 f. above.

[8] See the texts on pp. 69 f. above.

Jubilees—by inference, not by direct statement—had interpreted the 'morrow after the Sabbath', the cryptic phrase of Lev. 23:11, 15, as the first Sunday after the Passover week. But other heterodox sects which appeared later on the scene as organized religious bodies held that it was the Sunday inside the Passover week.

The explanation for this change in date will be given on another page.[1] Here, however, it is of interest to observe that the period in which the Book of Jubilees was composed, that is, second–first century B.C., was a time of considerable activity in calendric matters in Palestine. It is to this period that we may ascribe the composition of the Book of Esther[2] and the institution of the festival of Purim on 13th–14th Adar.[3] Purim had great importance in the mechanism of the Hebrew calendar. Some of the skill of the calendar-makers among their neighbours had been acquired also by the Jews, for they were now able to calculate the calendar instead of relying on observation. The night of the full moon was known to be the thirteenth–fourteenth day (not the fourteenth–fifteenth day) after the phasis; and the announcement whether or not the year was embolismic came to be made in Adar by the public reading of the Book of Esther, not at the beginning of Nisan.[4] The Passover lost some of its New Year characteristics to the festival in Adar. The Passover retained its preliminal period of purification that lasted one week,[5] but the trumpets were sounded one week before Purim.[6] The usages that arose from the traditional licence and buffoonery at the New Year had become, in the course of time, attached to Purim, and it became customary also to exchange gifts at that festival[7]—exactly as the shift of the New Year at Rome from March to January carried with it some of the ritual that marked the springtime celebration.[8] The splintering of New Year ceremonial in Israel illustrates vividly the contrast between the solemn autumn festival of Tabernacles and the popular spring festival of the Passover. The latter ceded minor ritual to Purim, and probably not before

[1] p. 249 below.

[2] See Paton, *Book of Esther*, 60 ff. The Book of Esther was accepted into the Canon only after considerable argument; *JT Meg.* i. 7 (fol. 70d); cf. G. F. Moore, *Judaism*, 1927, i. 245.

[3] See my article in *VT* vii, 1957, 298.

[4] *Mish. 'Ed.* vii. 7, *Sheq.* i. 1, and the other passages cited in my article, op. cit. 297. The Rabbis showed their disapproval of what they regarded as intercalation in Nisan by Hezekiah, *BT Sanh.* 12a, *Ber.* 10b, *Pes.* 56a, *JT Ned.* vi. 13 (fol. 40a), and parallel passages. We may note that the date of the fifteenth day of (presumably) the twelfth month, Ezek. 32:17, cf. v. 1, is rendered in LXX by fifteenth day of the first month; this may be explained by the fact that the prophecy revealed on that day was directed against Egypt, and might appropriately be assigned to the first day of the Passover week.

[5] pp. 139 f. above; see also pp. 244 and 256 below for what may have been the practice during the period of the New Testament and of Josephus.

[6] *Meg. Ta'an.*, pp. 32 f. above; cf. pp. 153 f. above.

[7] Cf. pp. 148 f. above. Morgenstern, *VT* xi, 1961, 415, suggests that Mordecai has the 'role of substitute for king' in Est. 6:6–11; Haman, his predecessor, is hanged, 7:8–10. The story, Morgenstern adds, is relevant at a New Year celebration; cf. p. 153 above.

[8] p. 121 above.

the second century B.C.; but the former at an early date lost even its basic and characteristic rites to Rosh haShanah and the Day of Atonement.[1] The popular festival was more adaptable and able to withstand more successfully the impact of changing social and religious conditions.

The writings of Philo in the first half of the first century A.D. are not a wholly reliable source for details of Israelite ritual at Jerusalem.[2] Nevertheless, Philo corroborates the information derived from other and independent sources. He treats the waving of the Sheaf on the second day of the Passover week as an established practice. Most significant is Philo's statement that the Passover was carried out by 'the whole people, old and young alike . . . in their many myriads'. The process that we have recognized in its early stage in the Book of Jubilees had reached completion.[3] Philo makes no mention of twenty as a minimum age for participation in the Pesaḥ, as had Jubilees—and Philo would certainly have done so had this been the regulation. The festival was no longer the occasion for a military census.[4]

The reason may be sought in the political developments that had occurred between the period of Jubilees and that of Philo. Independence under the Hasmoneans had given place to vassalage to Rome, and the ancient methods of mustering the army had evidently fallen into disuse. The right to attend the Pesaḥ was extended to Israelites outside the category of men of military age. The result was a great increase in the numbers of pilgrims.[5] At the time of Jubilees the Pesaḥ meal was to be eaten in the Temple courts; Philo records that it is to be eaten in private houses. That is not, as we may be tempted to assume, a return to the primitive practice prescribed in Ex. 12, whereby each family was to consume the Pesaḥ victim within the dwelling-place on whose lintels its blood had been smeared. That practice had been abandoned, with the smearing of blood, as long ago as the reforms of the Deuteronomist.[6] On the contrary, the eating of the Pesaḥ meal in private houses at the time of Philo is an extension of the rule that it was to be eaten in the Temple precincts. With the removal of the restriction of the ceremony to adult males, the crowds could not be contained within the area of the Temple. The boundaries were enlarged, for this occasion only, to include the whole city of Jerusalem—but beyond these boundaries it was still stringently forbidden to take the flesh of the Pesaḥ victim.[7]

[1] p. 156 above.

[2] See p. 29 above.

[3] See the discussion on p. 233 above.

[4] The census held at the Passover at Jerusalem in A.D. 6 by the Roman authorities with the connivance of the High Priest, Josephus, *Ant.* XVIII. i. 1, was in accordance with the traditional usages of the springtime census. But it was for taxation records, and it was a general census of all souls, not of military men only.

[5] p. 256 below.

[6] See pp. 206 ff. above.

[7] See H. L. Strack and P. Billerbeck, *Kommentar zum Neuen Testament aus Talmud und Midrasch*, i. 839 f., 992, ii. 833 f., and J. Jeremias, *Jerusalem zur Zeit Jesu*, iiA, 1924, 16 f.; for Jerusalem at this period, L.-H. Vincent and A.-M. Steve, *Jérusalem de l'A.T.*, 1954–6,

The evidence of the New Testament concerning the Passover is of special interest. Its allusions to the Passover are largely incidental to the main narrative and to the fundamental teachings of the early Christians, and certainly they are not written from the point of view of the official administrators of the Temple. On the other hand, they are not without bias, and they may not be wholly the work, or based upon the work, of first-hand witnesses; much has undergone redaction.[1] A further caution must be entered. In analysing passages in the New Testament relevant to the Passover, scholars may have been too readily disposed to seek in them the reflection of later Jewish practice—in particular, of the Seder service.[2] It should be borne in mind that some of the rites that play so central a part in that service are intended to symbolize and commemorate the service of the Temple after its destruction. But in the lifetime of Jesus the Temple still stood, and he celebrated the Passover as a pilgrim at the Temple at Jerusalem.[3]

From the New Testament we receive further corroboration of the development of the Passover into a joyous family celebration. The right to participate had evidently been extended to boys of thirteen,[4] and thence—in accordance with halakhic usage—to boys of twelve.[5] More than that, women also took part, presumably at the meal—a practice not mentioned by Philo, perhaps because it did not obtain in his day. Whether there was an obligation upon women to attend we are not told; it is more likely to have been supererogatory, like the attendance of married Moslem women at the *ḥajj*.[6] But the discontinuance of the census motif of the Pesaḥ had a twofold result. The circle of celebrants was, as we have observed, extended to include married women and boys. On the other hand, in societies with leanings towards celibacy the Pesaḥ might be performed by groups of men united by a common fellowship rather than by kinship.[7]

258, and J. Simons, *Jerusalem in the O.T.*, 1952, 58, &c. The extension of Temple ritual to the dwellings of the city went even farther at Hieropolis. There the animal victim was presented at the altar, and dedicated by the pouring over it of a libation; the pilgrims then led it alive to their lodging, and there sacrificed it with prayer, Lucian, *De Dea syria*, § 57.

[1] See the standard Commentaries.

[2] So, for example, Beer, op. cit. 53 ff., and, more recently, D. Daube, *New Testament and Rabbinic Judaism*, 1956, 158 ff. On the date of origin which can be assigned with any certainty to the Seder service, see S. Stein, 'Symposia Literature . . .', *JJS* viii, 1957, 15, 24.

[3] For studies that refer much of the *haggadah* to pre-Maccabean times, see L. Finkelstein, 'The Oldest Midrash: Pre-Rabbinic Ideals and Teachings in the Passover Haggadah', *HTR* xxxi, 1938, 291, and id., 'Pre-Maccabean Documents in the Passover Haggadah', *HTR* xxxv, 1942, 291, xxxvi, 1943, 1. Stein's objection, op. cit. 15, that if the *haggadah* were so early we should have received an account of it from Jewish Hellenistic sources, is, however, unanswerable.

[4] Cf. p. 240 above. A relic of the observance of twenty as the age of majority is found in *Mish. Ab.* v. 21.

[5] p. 34 above. *Mish. Yoma* viii. 4.

[6] See p. 35 above on the Passover in the New Testament, and p. 130 n. 4 above on the Moslem *ḥajj*.

[7] Cf. 1 Cor. 10:17, 12:12 f., Rom. 12:5. For the attitude of the early Christians towards

At the Passover, we learn from the New Testament, it was customary to reprieve on the eve of the festival a prisoner who had been condemned to death.[1] The same practice was observed in Assyria and Babylonia at the full moons of certain months.[2] But we do not find it in Israelite history. It is true that in the early Israelite Monarchy there may have been reluctance to put men to death on the accession of a new king[3]—and the New Year festival was, we have seen, the festival of the royal accession. Nevertheless, there are insufficient grounds for assuming that this was a regular feature of the Israelite New Year, and that it lay dormant throughout the period of the later Monarchy and the Return from Exile to reappear in the Roman period. In the New Testament it is the Roman governor who frees the condemned man, not the Jewish court. This reprieve on the eve of the Passover should probably, then, be regarded as the extension to the Roman Empire of a usage found in the traditional New Year practices of Greece and Rome.[4]

When, now, we come to the description in the New Testament of the Pesaḥ night and the preparations that precede it, we encounter the problem that besets all students of the New Testament—the apparent contradictions between the Synoptic Gospels and the Fourth Gospel. Whether they can be reconciled, and how far the individual texts are dependent upon

the concept of family, see Matt. 10:35 ff., 12:48 ff., 19:29 (cf. Mic. 7:6, Deut. 33:9), Mark 10:29 f., Luke 14:26. There is no need—and indeed it is not correct—to assume that membership of a *ḥabhurah* for the express purpose of celebrating the Pesaḥ implied membership of a sacramental fellowship. In orthodox circles the *ḥabhurah* of the Pesaḥ was normally a family group who had performed those rites of cleanness that were performed by all male adult Israelites—but were not peculiar to a certain sect or society—before the Pesaḥ; the members of the *ḥabhurah* were associated for this single occasion (cf. *Mish. Pes.* viii. 3, *Tos. Pes.* vii. 3, &c.), and then withdrew from the association. For similar associations on other occasions, cf. *Mish. Sanh.* viii. 2. The *ḥabhurah* might be extended to include friends, but the basis remained family kinship; see p. 256 below. In the context of the Pesaḥ the *ḥabhurah* seems to have nothing to do with either the Greek Mysteries (as Beer, op. cit. 64 ff.) or the closed Jewish fellowship discussed by Büchler, *Der galiläische 'Am-ha'Areṣ des zweiten Jahrhunderts*, 1906, passim; S. Lieberman, 'The Discipline in the So-called Dead Sea Manual of Discipline', *JBL* lxxi, 1952, 199; C. Rabin, *Qumran Studies*, 1957, 11 ff., 16 ff.; Mantel, *Studies in the History of the Sanhedrin*, 86 f. and n. 215. In heterodox circles it was not the Pesaḥ that was the pretext for creating a *ḥabhurah*; but, on the contrary, members of a *ḥabhurah* would naturally associate together to celebrate the Pesaḥ as they associated together on other occasions. It may be significant that the members of a group to celebrate the Pesaḥ are not called *ḥabherim*, but *bene ḥabhurah*; cf. *Mish. Pes.* vii. 3, *Tos. Pes.* iii. 2, 3, 7, v. 12, vii. 12; the sing. *ḥabher* occurs, however, in ii. 12.

[1] Matt. 27:15, Mark 15:6, Luke 23:17 (margin), John 18:39.

[2] Langdon, *Babylonian Menologies*, 114 (15th Ayar), 123 (an unknown day in Tammuz), 131 (16th Araḥsamna; but also on the sixth and twenty-sixth days of this month), 142 (16th Adar). 2 Kings 25:27 gives the date of the release of the king of Judah in Babylon as 27th Adar (the same event is dated 25th Adar in Jer. 52:31); this is eleven days after the full moon of Adar, the length of the New Year's festival at Babylon. Cf. Thiele, *Mysterious Numbers*, 165.

[3] 1 Sam. 11:12 f., cf. 1 Kings 1:50 ff., cf. p. 153 above.

[4] See pp. 119 f. above. See further J. Merkel, 'Begnadigung am Passahfeste', *ZNW* vi, 1905, 293, C. B. Chavel, 'Releasing of a Prisoner on the Eve of Passover . . .', *JBL* lx, 1941, 273, and Winter, *On the Trial of Jesus*, 91 ff.

one another, is beyond the scope of the present study.[1] If, nevertheless, we approach the question from the standpoint only of the allusions to Passover ritual, one important feature emerges. Nowhere in the Gospels have we any reference to the slaughter of the Pesaḥ victim in the Temple as a preliminary to the Last Supper,[2] as should have been the case had the Last Supper been the Pesaḥ meal. If, on the contrary, the Last Supper is regarded as having occurred on the night before the Pesaḥ night, the night, that is, of 13th–14th Nisan, there would have been a fitting symbolism for Christians in the conception of Jesus, executed on the eve of the Pesaḥ, as himself a substitute for the Pesaḥ victim.[3]

This conception agrees well with the view of the writer of the Fourth Gospel. He nowhere gives the impression that the Last Supper was the Pesaḥ meal; its details in no way differ from those of an ordinary evening meal.[4] There is no reference to the complex preparations for the Passover, of which the writer certainly must have been well aware, or to the special rites of the Pesaḥ meal—the treatment of the wine and bread, the prayers and psalms. According to the Fourth Gospel, a donation was given to the poor at the Last Supper;[5] this is a statement that is easily

[1] In addition to the standard Commentaries, see H. Schürmann, *Paschamahlbericht Lk. 22 (7–14) 15–18*, 1953, and id., *Einsetzungsbericht Lk. 22 19–20*, 1955. For a discussion of the various theories, see, in particular, Strack and Billerbeck, op. cit. ii, 1924, 812–53; D. Chwolson, *Das letzte Passamahl*, Torrey, *JBL* l, 1931, 227, and id., *JQR* xlii, 1951–2, 237; G. Ogg, *Chronology of the Public Ministry of Jesus*, 1940; J. Jeremias, *Eucharistic Words*; Haag, art. 'Pâque', *Dict. Bib. Suppl.* vi. 1144; and cf. van Goudoever, op. cit. 236, and Mantel, op. cit. 254 ff. A. Jaubert, *Date de la Cène*, suggests that two calendars were in simultaneous use in Palestine. In the year of the Crucifixion, Pesaḥ eve fell according to the 'old' calendar on the night of Tuesday–Wednesday, and this was observed by Jesus; according to the other, Pesaḥ eve fell on the night of Friday–Saturday in the same week. See also E. Vogt, 'Kalenderfragmente aus Qumran', *Biblica*, xxxix, 1958, 72, and J. A. Walther, 'Chronology of Passion Week', *JBL* lxxvii, 1958, 116. This hypothesis should be regarded with great reserve. It is highly improbable that two systems of dating the Passover would have been observed side by side at this period without leaving some trace in Jewish writings—like the controversy on the date of the waving of the Sheaf, to which it would be parallel, and on which see pp. 248 ff. below. (This objection is discussed by Mlle Jaubert, *New Testament Studies*, vii, 1960, 22.) Moreover, the Book of Jubilees—which, according to Mlle Jaubert, employed the 'old', but at this period unorthodox, calendar—does not insert the Passover within the framework of the calendar; see pp. 235 f. above. See further pp. 247 f. below on the Qumran sect and the Passover.

[2] Except perhaps by implication, Luke 22:15. Haag, op. cit. 1141 ff., esp. 1146 f., suggests that the early Christians celebrated the Pesaḥ without a sacrifice. This view is based on the assumption that the same usage was followed by the Qumran sect (against this, p. 248 below); it appears to conflict with John 1:29, 36, cf. the references in the following note.

[3] 1 Cor. 5:7 f., which associates the 'sacrifice' of Jesus with the removal of leaven, cf. 1 Peter 1:19, Rev. 5:6, 8, 12. So Jesus dies at the ninth hour, that is, 3 p.m., Matt. 27:45 ff., Mark 15:33 ff., Luke 23:44 ff.; this is the time of the Pesaḥ sacrifice, p. 244 below. The 'sixth hour', John 19:14, is probably in error for the 'third hour', as Mark 15:25; cf. Torrey, op. cit. 248, but see E. Hoskyns, *Fourth Gospel*, ed. F. N. Davey, 1947, 525.

[4] pp. 36 f. above.

[5] This may be derived from the widespread practice of making gifts at the New Year, pp. 148 f. above.

explicable if this were the night before the eve of the Pesaḥ, but wholly inexplicable if this were the Pesaḥ night itself. John writes with knowledge and with more evident understanding of the intricacies of Jewish ritual than do the authors of the Synoptic Gospels. He knows the principles of the ritual cleanness that was demanded as a prerequisite for the Pesaḥ; it is in keeping with this that he refers to the Passover always as the Pesaḥ, never as the feast of unleavened bread,[1] and that he lays great stress on purification ceremonies, including a possible allusion to the preliminal week.[2] He displays, moreover, great love of symbolism—we may note in particular his epithet for Jesus of the 'Lamb of God'[3] and the striking quotations from the Psalms and from Zechariah.[4] To him the execution of Jesus on the eve of the Pesaḥ bore remarkable resemblance to the slaughter of the Pesaḥ victim.[5] Even the time of the execution tallies with the time of the Pesaḥ sacrifice—and this not only in the Gospel of John but in the Synoptic Gospels also.[6]

If we assume, then, that the narrative of John is correct—that the Last Supper was not a Pesaḥ meal, but took place on the evening of Thursday–Friday, 13th–14th Nisan[7]—then several (but not all) of the difficulties of the Synoptic Gospels also may be solved.[8] It is true that these Gospels then appear to give the day before the Passover (Friday, 14th Nisan) the name of

[1] See p. 36 above; see also Zeitlin, *JQR* xxxi, 1940–1, 348, xlii, 1951–2, 255, where it is argued that the Gospel of John was addressed to Gentiles.

[2] p. 139 above. There is contrast between 'six days before . . .', John 12:1, and 'two days before . . .', Matt. 26:2, Mark 14:1; this may well be the reflection of the opposition between sacral periods of seven days and three days; cf. p. 144 above. The period of seven days is the more important and perhaps the more likely in the present context; but cf. the 'third day' of the Resurrection, Matt. 27:62 ff., Luke 9:22, 18:33, 24:7, 21, 46, cf. Mark 15:29, John 2:19. On structural triads in Mark, see Carrington, *Primitive Christian Calendar*, 1952, esp. 90 ff., and van Goudoever, op. cit. 240 ff.

[3] John 1:29, 36, cf. 1 Peter 1:19, Rev. 5:6, 12, &c.

[4] John 19:36 (probably based on Ps. 34:21, E.V. 34:20, rather than Ex. 12:46, Num. 9:12, in view of the passive; see R. H. Lightfoot, *St. John's Gospel. A Commentary*, 1956, 327), John 19:37 (based on Zech. 12:10); cf. the similes in John 19:23 ff. (cf. Matt. 27:35, Mark 15:24, Luke 23:34, none of which has the quotation), John 2:18–22, 7:37 ff. Perhaps see also John 19:29, where 'reed' of Matt. 27:48, Mark 15:36, is replaced by 'hyssop', as in Ex. 12:22; but see Hoskyns, op. cit. 531, J. H. Bernard, *Gospel according to St. John* (I.C.C.), in loc., and other Commentaries on the text of John 19:29.

[5] See Lightfoot, op. cit. 349 ff., but, for a different view, C. H. Dodd, *Interpretation of the Fourth Gospel*, 1953, 233 ff.

[6] p. 243 n. 3 above. See R. W. Husband, *Prosecution of Jesus*, 1916, ch. III.

[7] Among the great number of books and articles on this subject in recent years, see, in addition to the works already cited, P. Gardner Smith, *Christ of the Gospels*, 1938; F. L. Cirlot, *Early Eucharist*, 1939; A. J. B. Higgins, *Lord's Supper in the New Testament*, 1952; T. A. Burkill, 'Last Supper', *Numen*, iii, 1956, 161, and id., *Vigiliae Christianae*, xii, 1958, 1.

[8] The women prepare spices and ointments, Luke 23:56, cf. John 19:39 f., against Mark 16:1; Joseph of Arimathaea buys a *σινδών* to wrap the body of Jesus, Mark 15:46 (but see Zeitlin, 'Last Supper as an Ordinary Meal in the Fourth Gospel', *JQR* xlii, 1951–2, 260); Simon of Cyrene comes from work in the fields (see Chwolson, op. cit. 9), Mark 15:21, Luke 23:26—these acts could have taken place on the eve of the Passover, but not on the first day of the festival. See, however, Higgins, op. cit. 19.

the 'first day of (the feast of) unleavened bread'.[1] But so, indeed, it was viewed; in the second–first centuries B.C. the eves of festivals were days of special observance, tantamount themselves to festivals.[2] This was particularly so in the case of the Passover, where much preparation was involved already at the period of the Chronicler, and where the major ceremony is declared in all the documents of the Bible to belong to the fourteenth, not the fifteenth, day of the month.[3] Nevertheless, one major difficulty remains. It is as impossible that the Sanhedrin should have tried a capital charge on the eve of a festival as on the day of the festival itself.[4] On the other hand, it may be contended that the trial of Jesus was conducted not by Jews but by the Roman authority.[5] Some scholars have suggested that the trial took place some days before the normative Passover, and that the events of the last days of Jesus have been telescoped by our narrators into a much shorter period than was in fact the case.[6]

Whatever the solution of this problem, it seems reasonable to assume that the Synoptic Gospels have transformed the Last Supper into a Pesaḥ meal, and have endowed it with the ritual that was characteristic of that occasion. It is more credible to maintain that the Synoptic Gospels should have changed a Last Supper which was not a Pesaḥ meal into a Pesaḥ meal—with all its well-loved and familiar associations—than that John should have denied to the Last Supper the qualities of the Pesaḥ meal which would have endowed it with special sanctity. But the transformation by the Synoptic Gospels has not been carried out thoroughly. They omit mention of the meat of the Pesaḥ victim; instead, it is the bread to which Jesus compares his body.[7] The very fact that the most important component of the Pesaḥ meal is not mentioned by the Synoptic Gospels is a clear indication that the identification of the Last Supper as a Pesaḥ meal is an artificial device.

1 Mark 14:12, cf. Matt. 26:17, Luke 22:7.

2 So Judith 8:6 (assigned to the Persian period by J. M. Grintz, *Sefer Yehudith*, 1957 (in Hebrew), but by most critics to the Hasmonean period); cf. *BT Pes.* 5a, *JT Pes.* i. 4 (fol. 27c), and see Strack and Billerbeck, op. cit. ii. 812 ff.; J. Mann, *HUCA* i, 1924, 344; and Jeremias, op. cit. 2 n. 5. See further p. 256 below on Josephus, *Ant.* II. xv. 1.

3 pp. 130 f. above.

4 p. 35 above.

5 See p. 35 n. 14 above.

6 See Jaubert, op. cit., and the review of her book by Jeremias, *JTS*, N.S., x, 1959, 131 f.; P. W. Skehan, 'Date of the Last Supper', *CBQ* xx, 1958, 192; Vogt, loc. cit.; and Walther, loc. cit., and the bibliography there. Note, however, the remarks of P. Benoit, *RB* xlv, 1958, 593, who judiciously suggests that while twelve hours is too short a period for the events preceding the crucifixion, three days may constitute too long a period. A recent treatment of the problem may be found in A. Strobel, 'Termin des Todes Jesu', *ZNW* li, 1960, 69.

7 Matt. 26:26, Mark 14:22, Luke 22:19, 1 Cor. 11:24. The saying does not, of course, appear in John. Stein, op. cit. 23 n. 42, suggests that Greek σῶμα of the New Testament 'equals (Heb.) *gufo shel pesaḥ*, especially in view of the fragmentary character of the Synoptic records'. See, however, Jeremias, *Eucharistic Words*, 140, and Dalman, *Jesus-Jeshua*, 1929, 141 ff.

A Pesaḥ meal at Jerusalem without the Pesaḥ victim was meaningless—as long as the Temple stood. This may well provide us with a valid *terminus ante quem* for the picture of the Pesaḥ meal and its preliminaries presented by the Synoptic Gospels. It must belong to a period of time no more than a generation removed from the death of Jesus. We may examine these Gospels for a description of the Pesaḥ as it was celebrated at Jerusalem at the time of the destruction of the Temple in A.D. 70.

The preparations for the Passover involved the choice of a venue for the meal, the removal of leaven, and the purchase of the Pesaḥ victim and of animals as subsidiary offerings. The Pesaḥ victim was slain in the Temple, apparently at the ninth hour,[1] the meal was eaten in private houses in the city. It was night when the group—in the case of the disciples they were all male adults—assembled; they reclined at the meal. There is some difference of opinion as to whether the bread or the wine was blessed first. The wine is likely to have been red. The participants dipped their sop into a common bowl. The service ended with hymns. That Jesus and his disciples walked in the garden of Gethsemane after the meal is not an echo of the injunction of Deut. 16 that the Israelites should (or, may) depart to their tents on the morning after the Pesaḥ—it was still night when Jesus went out.[2]

The New Testament, for all its special interest, adds little to what has been learnt from earlier sources. But one aspect of its accounts is of particular significance. We observe that Jewish sectarians spoke with two tongues with regard to the Passover. The festival was too integral a part of the history and the religious and social habits of the people to be ignored even by those who were inclined to reject orthodox practices. The writer of Jubilees substitutes for it a colourless 'historical' celebration, the *'Aqedah*, the sacrifice of Abraham's 'only son', Isaac—but in a later chapter of the same book the normative festival is prescribed in all its details as though the words had been written by an orthodox Jew.[3] So with the New Testament. The conventional pattern is reflected in the visit of Jesus to Jerusalem as a boy of twelve when his family went on pilgrimage for the Passover, and by the presence of the womenfolk at his last Passover. But the Last Supper is held by males only, linked by bonds of sacramental fellowship—not of kinship—in a manner that has little in common with the Pesaḥ. More important, the Last Supper was probably a symbolic meal that did not occur on the night when all Israel celebrated the Passover, but on the previous night. Yet the Synoptic Gospels cannot relinquish the desire to equate it and the events that preceded it with the Pesaḥ as

[1] So in the treatise *Quaestiones . . . in Exodum*, attributed to Philo; see p. 30 above.

[2] See pp. 208 ff. above; the relevant references from the New Testament are given on pp. 33 ff. above.

[3] p. 234 above.

observed by the main body of Jewry. Indeed, much time was to pass before Christians freed Easter from its archetype the Passover, both in date and in ritual.[1]

The Qumran sect appears to have followed a very different course of development. They were a small group living a life apart from the general community. They were largely organized on a military basis,[2] and among them the age of majority seems to have continued to be twenty,[3] not thirteen as among orthodox Jews. The documents of the sect in which their religious practices are described do not mention the Passover among the annual festivals.[4] But both the Pesaḥ and the 'second Pesaḥ' are mentioned prominently in the Qumran 'calendar', a table of correspondences between the list of priestly courses of 1 Chr. 24 and the Hebrew festivals.[5] On another page I have suggested that the phrase 'first year' in the title of this 'calendar' makes it probable that the correspondences would be different in subsequent years.[6] It is reasonably certain that each course was to last one week, and extended from Sabbath to Sabbath.[7]

Now, it is evident that this 'calendar' is based upon a 364-day year, not upon the lunisolar calendar of normative Judaism. We note, too, that the offering of the Sheaf occurs on the first Sunday outside the Passover week. The Day of Atonement is, furthermore, to be held on a Friday; this was carefully excluded in Jewish practice, at any rate at a late period,[8]—and the fact that the contrary is maintained in the Qumran text may indicate that this Jewish practice was in operation much earlier. These circumstances combine to make it clear that the Qumran 'calendar' is not a Pharisaic document.

[1] See in particular A. Hilgenfeld, *Paschastreit der alten Kirche*, 1860; C. C. Richardson, 'Quartodecimans and the Synoptic Chronology', *HTR* xxxiii, 1940, 177; B. Lohse, *Passafest der Quartadecimaner*, 1953; G. Ogg, *Pseudo-Cyprianic De Pascha Computus*, 1955; and van Goudoever, op. cit. 160 f.

[2] See *War*, passim, and Yadin, op. cit. 38 ff., 59 ff., *Doc. Cong.* i. 14, 26, 29, &c. Note the use of the term *ṣabha*', ibid. i. 6, 17, 21, &c.

[3] *Doc. Cong.* i. 8 f.; cf. Baumgarten, 'Testimony of Women in 1QSa', *JBL* lxxvi, 1957, 266, and P. Borgen, '"At the age of twenty" in 1QSa', *Revue de Qumran*, x, 1961, 267. But the age of conscription was twenty-five; see Yadin, *Scroll of the War*, 75 ff.

[4] The Day of Atonement, on the other hand, is mentioned in *Hab. Comm.* xi. 7, fragment in Barthélemy and Milik, *Qumran Cave I*, 153, probably in *Sayings of Moses*, iii. 10 ff., and perhaps iv. 1 ff. (Barthélemy and Milik, op. cit. 94); cf. 'fast day', J. M. Allegro, 'Newly Discovered Fragment . . .', *PEQ* lxxxvi, 1954, 71 ff. (col. i. 9 f., cf. ii. 3), *Zad. Doc.* vi. 19. There may be a reference to the feast of Weeks in a fragment of the *Sayings of Moses*, Barthélemy and Milik, op. cit. 96. The Heb. term *mo'ed* is used of the festivals of Qumran, see p. 248 n. 7 below.

[5] For the text and an analysis of the 'calendar', see pp. 39 ff. above. The fact that Jojarib appears first in the list of 1 Chr. 24:7 ff. is said to be evidence that that passage was inserted, or its order amended, after the emergence of the Hasmonean dynasty, the descendants of Jojarib; 1 Macc. 2:1. See P. R. Ackroyd, 'Criteria for the Maccabean Dating of Old Testament Literature', *VT* iii, 1953, 126.

[6] p. 41 above.

[7] So already 2 Kings 11:5 ff., not from Saturday to Friday, as Vogt, *Biblica*, xxxix, 1958, 72; see p. 250 below.

[8] See art. 'Calendar', *JE* iii. 503 b.

It has been suggested that the text is a Jubilees calendar, and there are, at first sight, grounds for holding this view. As we have seen, Jubilees also propounds a 364-day year; and it too implies that the offering of the Sheaf is to be performed on the first Sunday outside the Passover week. Furthermore, the interval in the Qumran 'calendar' between the Pesaḥ and the 'second Pesaḥ' is thirty days, the length of a month in the calendar of Jubilees.[1]

But the Passover, I have suggested, does not figure in the book of Jubilees except as an appendix, and it has no place in the Jubilees calendar; and the 'second Pesaḥ' of this Qumran 'calendar' does not appear in the Book of Jubilees at all.[2] Jubilees, too, makes no direct mention of the Sheaf.[3] In Jubilees the term 'day of remembrance' is not applied specifically to Rosh haShanah, as in the Qumran text under analysis, but to the first day of the first, fourth, seventh, and tenth months.[4] Furthermore, Jubilees ascribes the origin of the Day of Atonement to an event of so little importance that the day can hardly have been of great significance in the eyes of the writer.[5] It is unlikely, then, that the left-hand column of this 'calendar' can be connected with the Book of Jubilees. As for the right-hand column, there is no mention of priestly courses in the Book of Jubilees.[6]

Strangely enough, the Qumran 'calendar' does not conform to what we learn of the religious habits of the Qumran sect from other documents discovered on that site. I have pointed out that these do not appear to make direct mention of the Passover, a surprising omission if they in fact celebrated the festival.[7] As for the courses, the Qumran community was administered on a basis of twenty-six, not as in the Qumran 'calendar' twenty-four, courses;[8] and, indeed, a rotation of twenty-six courses would suit admirably their schematic year of 364 days or fifty-two weeks.

There is a solution which will explain satisfactorily both columns of this 'calendar'. The Sadducees offered the Sheaf on the Sunday inside the Passover week; and it may well be that at one time they offered it on the

[1] See Barthélemy, 'Notes en marge sur les manuscrits de Qumran', *RB* lix, 1952, 200.

[2] See p. 236 above.

[3] See p. 235 above.

[4] Jub. 6:23.

[5] Jub. 34:12. Riesenfeld, op. cit. 23, seems to exaggerate when he compares this passage in Jubilees with the cult of Tammuz.

[6] Although priests are mentioned in Jub. 13:25, 27, 16:18, 30:18, 31:14 ff., 32:9, 14 f., and the sanctuary is referred to frequently, 1:10, 17, &c., 3:10, 4:26, 8:19, 18:13, 25:21, 30:15, 49:16 ff., &c. It may be added that fragments found at Qumran give lists of priestly (?) families for successive Sabbaths and New Moons; J. T. Milik, *Ten Years*, 1959, 107 ff. Sometimes the Babylonian names of months are given, but this would be wholly contrary to the practice of the Book of Jubilees.

[7] Heb. *mo'ed* is used in the Qumran texts both of the normative festivals and of other set times; see *Doc. Comm.* x. 3 ff., *Hab. Comm.* xi. 6, *War*, ii. 4, 6, 7, x. 15, xii. 3, &c.; cf. Barthélemy and Milik, *Qumran Cave I*, 136 (No. 34), 152 (No. 34b).

[8] *War*, ii. 2, cf. P. Winter, *VT* vi, 1956, 215; cf. the fifty-two 'fathers of the *'edah*', ii. 1.

first Sunday outside the Passover week.[1] They observed all the festivals enumerated here. And from their service in the Temple the Sadducees were intimately acquainted with the order of the priestly courses. How this 'calendar' came to be at Qumran, if it is Sadducean, is beyond the scope of the present work to explain.[2]

Whether the Qumran 'calendar' is of Sadducean origin or not, this is a suitable point at which to discuss the attitude of the Sadducees and the related or subsidiary sect of the Boethusians[3] towards the Passover. I have suggested that the main part of the Book of Jubilees ignores the Passover.[4] The fact that it assigns the offering of the Sheaf to a Sunday and consequently the feast of Weeks to a Sunday probably arose from devotion to the Sabbath[5] and to the hebdomads of the Jubilees calendar. The Sadducees and Boethusians,[6] however, did not ignore the Passover. And, while Jubilees held that the offering of the Sheaf was celebrated on the first Sunday outside the Passover week, the Sadducees celebrated it on the Sunday inside the Passover week.[7] Here we may venture to recognize the outcome of a course of development parallel to the course of development inside orthodox Judaism. At one time, I have maintained, the Israelites performed the offering of the Sheaf on the day following the Passover week; Jubilees regards it as occurring on the first Sunday outside the Passover week.[8] At a later period the Jewish authorities brought the date of the ceremony back to the second day of the Passover week—and the Sadducees apparently followed suit by waving the Sheaf on the Sunday inside the festival week.

There are some grounds, however, for supposing that in this parallel course of development it may have been the Sadducees, rather than the Pharisees, who were the first to hold the rite a week earlier. It can scarcely be imagined that the Pharisees would have voluntarily adopted a position that led to so embarrassing an interpretation of 'Sabbath' in Lev. 23:11, 15.[9]

[1] Below on this page; on the practice of Jubilees, p. 235 above.

[2] The Qumran 'calendar' may belong to a period in the history of the sect at which they were allied to, or part of, the main body of the Sadducees; for a discussion of the relation of the sect to the Sadducees and possible affinities between them, see R. North, 'Qumran "Sadducees"', *CBQ* xvii, 1955, 164. On the other hand, this 'calendar' may have been required by members of the sect for their dealings with nearby Sadducean settlements.

[3] On the Boethusians, see in particular Josephus, *Ant.* xv. ix. 3, XIX. vi. 2, *Tos. Men.* xiii. 21, *BT Pes.* 57a; Geiger, 'Sadducäer und Pharisäer', *Jüdische Zeitschrift*, ii, 1863, 24 ff.; Derenbourg, *Essai*, 140, 155 ff., 232 ff.; Chwolson, op. cit. 64, 128; Büchler, *Studies in Jewish History*, 1956, 37; and R. Meyer, art. 'Σαδδουκαῖος', *Theologisches Wörterbuch zum Neuen Testament*, § 3.

[4] p. 234 above.

[5] Jub. 50, cf. *Zad. Doc.* x. 14 ff.

[6] In the Mishnah and Baraita the terms are freely interchanged; see H. Graetz, *Geschichte der Juden*, iii, 1905–6, 694 f.

[7] *Mish. Men.* x. 3–4, cf. *Ḥag.* ii. 4, *Tos. Men.* x. 23, *R.H.* i. 15, *Meg. Ta'an.* i, *JT R.H.* ii. 1 (fol. 57d), *BT Men.* 65a, *Siphra* on Lev. 23:15.

[8] pp. 196 ff. and 235 above.

[9] LXX, Targ., in loc. (pp. 69 f. above), Philo, *De Septen.* 20, Josephus, *Ant.* III. x. 5, *JT R.H.* i. 10 (fol. 57d); see Chwolson, loc. cit.

To explain it as the Passover week ending in a day of rest was reasonable; to explain it as equivalent to a festival day is scarcely logical. Now, the motive for moving the date was probably unwillingness to postpone the eating of an early harvest, since the offering of the Sheaf was the signal for putting the new crop to everyday use.[1] There is only one region of Palestine where the grain may sometimes ripen by the Passover—Jericho and the area of the Jordan valley.[2] The shift in the date of the ceremonial must, I suggest, have taken place after the composition of the main part of the Book of Jubilees but before the completion of the LXX translation of Lev. 23:11, 15, and probably the translation also of Jos. 5:11 f.[3] And, indeed, the insistence of the Pharisees upon their forced interpretation of the term 'Sabbath' shows that the usage was of no great antiquity. It was precisely at this period—in the second–first century B.C.—that there seems to have been intensive activity in the region of Jericho. We may deduce from our sources that the leading spirits in this enterprise were priests and possibly Sadducees.[4] At approximately the same time, there was activity also at Qumran in a nearby region of the Jordan valley;[5] and I have suggested that the Qumran 'calendar' may be Sadducean.[6] To the problems presented by the settlement at Jericho the Pharisees reacted cautiously; where the people there contravened established practice they did not condemn them outright.[7]

The change in the date of the Sheaf-offering led the Pharisees to their novel interpretation of the term 'Sabbath' in Lev. 23:11, 15, as 'festival'. This the Sadducees could not but oppose swiftly and violently. In the first place, the Sabbath had special importance for the priests. It was a day of solemn ceremony in the Temple. The conduct of the Temple was based upon the priestly courses, and the functions of each priestly course began and ended on the Sabbath.[8] In the second place, the Sadducees were probably not well disposed towards the Pesaḥ sacrifices.[9] On the occasion of these sacrifices the people flocked to the Temple and, for the only time in the year, conducted their own sacrifices—of which the priests received no portion. Moreover, the Pesaḥ was essentially a night service,

[1] Lev. 23:14; for the impatience with which it was awaited, see *Mish. Men.* x. 5.

[2] See pp. 237 f. above.

[3] p. 238 above.

[4] *JT Pes.* iv. 1 (fol. 30c), *Ta'an.* iv. 2 (fol. 67d), *BT Ta'an.* 27a, *Pes.* 57a.

[5] Cf. de Vaux, 'Manuscrits de Qumrân et l'archéologie', *RB* lxvi, 1959, 87, for the dates of settlement at Qumran. For a general treatment of the climate and vegetation of that region, see H. Klein, 'Klima Palästinas', *ZDPV* xxxvii, 1914, 217, 297 (esp. 314 f.); Whyte, loc. cit.; N. Shalem, 'Stabilité du climat en Palestine', *RB* lviii, 1951, 54; and de Vaux, *L'Archéologie et les manuscrits de la Mer Morte*, 1961, 68.

[6] p. 248 above.

[7] *Mish. Pes.* iv. 8, *Tos. Pes.* iii. 19–22, and parallel passages; cf. Büchler, *Priester*, 164 ff.

[8] Cf. p. 247 above.

[9] See also Büchler, op. cit. 172.

whereas normally the Temple service was carried out only by daylight.[1] The priests must have resented this apparent encroachment on their prerogatives—as they resented also the ritual of Tabernacles.[2] But they could not interfere. The Pharisees claimed further that the Pesaḥ sacrifice might override the Sabbath.[3] Undoubtedly the Pharisees were right. The Pesaḥ offering was a public rite, enjoined and sanctified by ancient tradition; it was to be celebrated on a fixed date, and it could not be deferred—except to the following month by reason of ritual uncleanness.[4] But the decline of the Pesaḥ from a solemn assembly to a popular festivity, to which I have alluded, had perhaps reduced its status in the eyes of the Sadducees and reinforced their assertion that it should not be permitted to overshadow the gravity of the Sabbath.

We may assume, then, that there was a twofold reason for antagonism on the part of the Sadducees when the Pharisees moved the ceremony of the waving of the Sheaf to the second day of the Passover week and justified this action by attributing to the festival day the title of Sabbath. No festival, the Sadducees must have protested, except the Day of Atonement—when, be it noted, the central role was taken by the High Priest—could assume the status of the Sabbath. The Pharisees, however, went farther, for they maintained that even the waving of the Sheaf might override the Sabbath.[5] They won the day, probably with the support of the people, to whom postponement of the Sheaf ceremony would have caused serious inconvenience. The victory of the Pharisees was made the more pointed by the celebration of the ceremony at night. There is significance in the wording, 'The Boethusians who used to say: "The *ʿomer* may not be reaped at the close of a festival day."'[6] The Boethusians objected not only to the date of the ceremony, but also to its performance by night instead of by daylight like normal Temple procedure.

What do we learn about the Passover from other heterodox Jewish sects? The Samaritans are the oldest sect of which we have information, and the

[1] Cf. in particular *Tos. Pes.* iii. 2. Chwolson, op. cit. 34 ff., maintains that the Sadducees held that the night belonged to the day just ended, while the Pharisees held that the night belonged to the following day. See S. Talmon, 'Calendar Reckoning of the Sect from the Judaean Desert', *Scripta Hierosolymitana*, iv, 1958, 187, and pp. 171 f. above.

[2] *Tos. Suk.* iii. 1, cf. iv. 2, *BT Suk.* 43b, 48b, Josephus, *Ant.* XIII. xiii. 5. The Sadducees' insistence on their rights is shown also by their claim that the *Tamid* should be offered at the expense of the High Priest, not from Temple funds, *Meg. Taʿan.* i, cf. *Mish. Sheq.* iv. 1, *BT Men.* 65a. See further *Meg. Taʿan.* viii.

[3] *JT Pes.* vi. 1 (fol. 33a)—a better text than *Tos. Pes.* iv. 1 and *BT Pes.* 66a; see Büchler, *Synedrion,* 145. It should be noted that the Pharisees did not extend the claim that the Pesaḥ sacrifice might override the Sabbath to a claim that also the *ḥagigah* on 15th Nisan might override the Sabbath, *BT Pes.* 76b, cf. 70b.

[4] Against Geiger, op. cit. 46; Derenbourg, op. cit. 180; Chwolson, op. cit. 23 ff.; and Büchler, loc. cit., all of whom maintain that the Pesaḥ sacrifice was a private offering until the time of Hillel.

[5] *Mish. Men.* x. 9.

[6] *Mish. Men.* x. 3, *Meg.* ii. 6, cf. *BT Men.* 66a.

Pesaḥ ritual that they observe in modern times contains much that is antique. There is, however, little to support the contention that this small group maintained these practices in the course of a continuous tradition, and that it is the orthodox Jewish majority who broke with tradition by their concessions to changing social and economic circumstances. The early Samaritans were the mixed population of post-Exilic Palestine. They had much to gain in their relations with the ruling powers by the avoidance of extreme religious separatism.[1] We have no reason to doubt the view of the Bible that it was those Jews who returned from Exile—and not the Samaritans—who refused to compromise on religious principles and who sought zealously to preserve the usages of pre-Exilic Israel.[2]

This analysis has, however, little bearing upon the practices of the modern Samaritans.[3] The Samaritans passed through many vicissitudes during the centuries that followed the Return from Exile of the Jews who were to constitute the great majority of the inhabitants of Palestine. From the authorities the Samaritans received treatment that ranged from passive tolerance to active persecution.[4] Not infrequently it was to their advantage to accentuate the differences between themselves and the Jewish population; and the ill-feeling which this aroused led to bitter polemics. The Samaritans sought to adopt as their own the usages which had been abandoned by normative Judaism in the process of natural evolution. They observed Pentateuchal laws with punctilious rigidity.[5] And in no ritual were they more careful than in that of the Passover. Unfortunately, however, the evidence here is not wholly satisfactory. The earliest non-Samaritan witness of their Pesaḥ was Benjamin of Tudela in the mid-twelfth century.[6] Most subsequent witnesses had difficulty in obtaining a clear view of what took place.[7]

In the following details the modern Samaritans observe what was probably the Jewish practice during the last days of the Jerusalem Temple.

[1] 2 Kings 17:24 ff., Neh. 3:33 ff. (E.V. 4:1 ff.).

[2] See in particular Neh. 10:29 ff.

[3] Against Jeremias, *Passahfeier der Samaritaner*, 1932, 66 ff., who maintains that the Samaritan Pesaḥ retains the usages of pre-Deuteronomic Israel. He holds that centralization of the ritual was resisted by the Samaritans until the sixteenth century; it remained a household ritual among them longer than among the Jews. For that reason, he continues, it survived the destruction of the Samaritan temple in the second century B.C., while the Jewish Pesaḥ in its original form could not survive the destruction of the Jerusalem Temple in A.D. 70. Jeremias is here relying on the evidence of the Samaritans themselves, although this is open to grave doubt, and his analysis of the nature and history of the Israelite Passover cannot be accepted. Cf. A. S. Halkin, 'Samaritan Polemics against the Jews', *PAAJR* vii, 1935–6, 42.

[4] J. A. Montgomery, *Samaritans*, 1907, 46 ff.; J. Créten, 'Pâque des Samaritains', *RB* xxxi, 1922, 434; and Jeremias, op. cit. 57.

[5] Cf. *BT Ḥul.* 3a–4b, *Qid.* 76a. On the relations between the Samaritans and Jews during the Talmudic period, Montgomery, op. cit. 165 ff.

[6] Apart from an uncertain reference in Justin Martyr; Jeremias, op. cit. 55.

[7] Jeremias, op. cit. 91; further Créten, loc. cit.

They wash their clothes before the festival,[1] they slay only small animals as the Pesaḥ victim,[2] the victim is roasted by laymen,[3] womenfolk participate in the meal,[4] the flesh is accompanied by unleavened bread and bitter herbs,[5] care is taken not to break the animal's bones,[6] no flesh is taken outside the circle of participants,[7] the meal is followed by a prayer,[8] the remains are burned—but not on the Sabbath.[9] In these details there was little reason for the Samaritans to deviate from the normative practice.

More illuminating are those details in which the modern Samaritans part company from orthodox Judaism. In some they follow the Pentateuchal text—the Pesaḥ victim is selected on the tenth day of the month,[10] the time of sacrifice is between sunset (more exactly, the appearance of the moon) and nightfall,[11] the victim's blood is smeared on the tents with hyssop,[12] the participants wear girdles and shoes and carry a staff,[13] and, finally, the meal is completed in haste.[14] These usages, as we have seen, had been gradually abandoned by the Israelites, for the most part with the centralization of the cult.[15] In other respects the Samaritans were obliged by circumstances to adopt customs contrary to those of the Jews—their ceremony is held on Mount Gerizim,[16] it is Levites who, with laymen, perform the act of slaughter of the Pesaḥ victim,[17] and portions of the victim

[1] Jeremias, op. cit. 74; cf. Ex. 19:10, 14.

[2] They hold that cattle may be slaughtered only at a central shrine; this is perhaps an attempt to reconcile Ex. 12:3 ff. with Deut. 16:2. See Jeremias, op. cit. 75.

[3] Ibid. 92.

[4] J. E. H. Thomson, *Samaritans*, 1919, 141; Jeremias, op. cit. 49, 97.

[5] Créten, op. cit. 439.

[6] Jeremias, op. cit. 98.

[7] Ibid.

[8] Ibid. 99.

[9] Ibid. 85, 100 ff.

[10] Thomson, op. cit. 127, and Jeremias, op. cit. 76. This is a literal observance of Ex. 12:3.

[11] Jeremias, op. cit. 80, 96, and L. Wreschner, *Samaritanische Traditionen*, 1888, ii. 25 ff.

[12] Jeremias, op. cit. 89, 91. The children are also smeared with blood, ibid. 91 f.; J. H. Petermann, *Reisen im Orient*, i. 237; Lees, *Village Life*, 208; and Crowfoot and Baldensperger, *Cedar to Hyssop*, 72 f. It is uncertain whether this is a regular practice among the modern Samaritans. Of the eleven celebrations of the Pesaḥ witnessed between 1853 and 1930, the ceremony of blood-smearing has been observed at only three, Jeremias, op. cit. 91. Its performance may have depended upon the arbitrary decision of Samaritan leaders or on political conditions; see Lees, op. cit. 209. Possibly it was not seen by non-Samaritan observers because it was done quickly or because the blood is so diluted as to leave almost no trace, Thomson, 'Samaritan Passover', *PEFQS*, 1902, 87 n. 1. A similar rite is not uncommon in modern Palestine, p. 125 above; it is thought to have apotropaic significance, Lees, op. cit. 209, cf. p. 233 above.

[13] Jeremias, op. cit. 49, 98; cf. Ex. 12:11.

[14] Créten, op. cit. 441, and Jeremias, op. cit. 98; cf. Ex. 12:11.

[15] p. 211 above.

[16] On the Samaritans and the Jerusalem Temple, see Josephus, *Ant.* XVIII. ii. 2, where it is related that the Samaritans were excluded for, it was alleged, desecrating the Temple. On Gerizim, see M. Gaster, *Samaritans*, 1925, Index, s.v., and Montgomery, op. cit. 34 ff.

[17] Jeremias, op. cit. 17, 19, 87, and Créten, op. cit. 437. The priestly family of the Samaritans having died out, their Levites have acquired priestly status.

are given to the chief Levite.[1] But it is the third group of differences between Samaritan and Jewish practice, which were in no way forced upon the Samaritans, which is of the greatest significance. The Samaritans apparently fix the Passover wholly by astronomical calculation, whereas Rabbinite Jews have never ceased to pay attention, at least in theory, to observation of both moon and crops.[2] The Samaritans, according to reports, attend at Gerizim not one week but ten days before the festival;[3] the victim must be born not merely within the twelve months before the Pesaḥ, but—to make doubly sure—between 1st Tishri and the Pesaḥ, since also 1st Tishri may be regarded as the New Year;[4] the victim is scalded and plucked before it is cooked—perhaps in an attempt to reconcile Ex. 12 with Deut. 16;[5] and infants and even lunatics are admitted to the ceremony, to extend the circle of participants as widely as possible.[6] It can scarcely be doubted that the observance of these rules arose from anxiety on the part of the Samaritans to prove that they are a devout minority who resisted concessions in religious practice, and that it is they, not the Jews, who observe the true Pesaḥ. The claim is likely to be artificial.

We may note that the Samaritans are aligned alongside the Sadducees and against the Pharisees in two respects:[7] the Samaritans maintain that the Sabbath overrides the Pesaḥ,[8] and they maintain that the offering of the Sheaf is to be performed on the Sunday within the Passover week.[9] The antagonism of the Samaritans towards the Pharisees is a reflection of their antagonism towards normative Judaism.

If we derive little useful information from an examination of the practices

[1] Créten, op. cit. 439.

[2] See E. Robertson, 'Tables and Calendar of the Samaritans', *BJRL* xxiii, 1939, 458; P. R. Weis, 'Abu'l-Hasan al-Suri's Discourse', *BJRL* xxx, 1946–7, 144; and J. Bowman, 'Is the Samaritan Calendar the Old Zadokite One?', *PEQ* xci, 1959, 23. See also my article, *VT* vii, 1957, 284 ff., 301 ff.

[3] Jeremias, op. cit. 7, 73. This may be an extension of a major sacral period of seven days by a minor sacral period of three days; see pp. 139 f. and 144 above. It is doubtful if importance should be attached to the fact that the Samaritans spend the time of the Passover and the days that precede it on Gerizim in tents, as Pedersen, *Israel*, iii–iv. 388 and note on 703. They have no houses there, Jeremias, op. cit. 6 f. On the method of hanging the Pesaḥ victim, Jeremias, op. cit. 25, 32 f., 94, and p. 166 n. 6 above.

[4] Jeremias, op. cit. 76. The Samaritans determine the calendar every six months; Robertson, op. cit. 463 f.

[5] Créten, op. cit. 439; Jeremias, op. cit. 95. On the method of cooking the Pesaḥ victim, see pp. 166 f. and 253 above. The wood for roasting is not the same among the Samaritans as that prescribed by the Mishnah, Jeremias, op. cit. 93, and *Mish. Pes.* vii. 1. According to Justin Martyr, *Dialogue*, xl. 3, the Samaritans used two spits.

[6] Thomson, *PEFQS*, 1902, 91 f., and Jeremias, op. cit. 97 f.; cf. Wreschner, op. cit. ii. 1.

[7] On the relations between Samaritans, Pharisees, and Sadducees, Gaster, op. cit. 45 ff.

[8] Jeremias, op. cit. 80 ff., 100 n. 7; Wreschner, op. cit. ii. 124; S. de Sacy, 'Correspondance des Samaritains de Naplouse', *Notices et Extraits*, xii. 120; Petermann, op. cit. i. 236; and id., Herzog, *Realenc.* xiii. 378.

[9] Wreschner, op. cit. ii. 20; Chwolson, op. cit. 60; S. Schechter, *Jewish Sectaries*, i, p. xxiii; S. Hanover, *Festgesetz der Samaritaner nach Ibrâhîm ibn Ja'ḳûb*, 1904, 26, 40, vii; and Halkin, op. cit. 44 ff.

of the ancient sect of the Samaritans, we cannot expect to learn much from the Karaites. On the method of reckoning the date of the Passover the Karaites were divided; some adjusted the calendar according to the season in which the crops ripened in Palestine, others simply adopted the Rabbinite system.[1] The Karaites insisted that the Sheaf was waved on the Sunday inside the Passover week. Earlier groups of Karaites, including Anan ben David, maintained that the Pesaḥ did not override the Sabbath; others held a contrary opinion. The views of the Karaites are, however, no more than theoretical. Nor is an analysis of the polemics between Karaites and Rabbinites of value to the present study, since the former did not appear as an organized sect before the eighth century.[2]

The Falashas,[3] the indigenous Jews of Ethiopia, regard the month of the Passover as, in some manner, the first of the year.[4] One traveller tells us that they eat a special type of bread during the three days preceding the festival.[5] It is well attested that they observe a fast on the day before the Pesaḥ. The Pesaḥ sacrifice—the only sacrifice in the Falasha calendar—is performed in public on 14th Nisan towards sunset, apparently by the priests. It is not, however, carried out if 14th Nisan falls on a Sabbath. During the Passover week the Falashas eat only unleavened bread, and drink no fermented beverages. They observe the festival as a holiday from work.[6]

The Falashas maintain that the first of the forty-nine days which connect the Passover with the feast of Weeks (called by them the feast of Harvest) is 22nd Nisan, the day, that is, following the end of the Passover week. This is the practice enjoined in the Book of Jubilees.[7] It is doubtful,

[1] On the Karaite calendar, see J. Mann, 'Tract by an Early Karaite Settler in Jerusalem', *JQR* xii, 1922, 270; Weis, 'Ibn Ezra, the Karaites and the Halakah' (in Hebrew), *Melilah*, i, 1944, 37; Zucker, *PAAJR* xx, 1951 (in Hebrew); Z. Ankori, 'Some Aspects of Karaite–Rabbanite Relations in Byzantium on the Eve of the First Crusade', *PAAJR* xxv, 1956, 157; and id., *Karaites in Byzantium*, 1959, 292 ff., 301 ff.

[2] See in particular Ankori, *Karaites in Byzantium*, passim; L. Nemoy, *Karaite Anthology*, esp. pp. 196 ff., 215 ff.; P. S. Goldberg, *Karaite Liturgy*, 1957, 105 f.; and S. Szyszman, in *Actes du XVI Congrès de l'Institut internationale de Sociologie*, Beaune, 1954. The view of Szyszman, 'A propos du Karaïsme et des Textes de la Mer Morte', *VT* ii, 1952, 343 (see also id., review, *VT* v, 1955, 329 n. 1), and others that the Karaite schism began in fact, if not in name, at the time of Alexander Jannaeus has little to support it. That Karaite doctrines have points in common with those of the Sadducees is not surprising since the Karaites replaced the Sadducees as the party of opposition to the Pharisees and Rabbinites; cf. the affinities between the Karaites and the Moslem opposition party of the Shiʿites, Nemoy, op. cit. xvii. But see B. Revel, *The Karaite Halakah*, 1913, passim.

[3] On the origins of the Falashas, see E. Ullendorff, 'Hebraic-Jewish Elements in Abyssinian (Monophysite) Christianity', *JSS*, i, 1956, 254.

[4] A. Z. Aescoly, *Sepher haFalashim* (in Hebrew), 1943, 56 ff.

[5] J. D. Perruchon and R. Gottheil, art. 'Falashas', *JE*.

[6] Aescoly, op. cit.; W. Leslau, *Falasha Anthology*, 1951, xi, xxvi, xxix, xxxi, xxxiv; id., *Coutumes et Croyances des Falachas* (Travaux et Mémoires de l'Institut d'Ethnologie, lxi), 1957, 70 f., 79; and Ullendorff, review, *BSOAS*, xv, 1953, 174.

[7] p. 235 above.

however, whether we are justified in basing firm conclusions on the usages of this remote Jewish community.

We return now to the normative method of celebrating the Passover. The last eyewitness account of the festival before the final catastrophe in A.D. 70 is that of Josephus. His own upbringing and experience make his testimony of exceptional value, but there are few points at which it adds materially to our information.[1] He confirms the preliminal period of the Passover, for the Jews, he tells us, came to Jerusalem by 8th Nisan.[2] The festival lasts—as elsewhere—one week. But in one passage Josephus states that it lasts eight days;[3] perhaps he implies here that 14th Nisan was regarded as a component part of the festival itself.[4] The people, we are informed, passed the Passover in tents outside the Temple area. It is possible that this is a reminiscence of the ancient practice of dwelling in tents at the New Year festival;[5] but it will be safer—since the custom is not attested in contemporary documents—to assume that tents were used because of shortage of space, with the vast crowds of pilgrims to be housed in the city itself. The sacrifice of the Pesaḥ was from 3 p.m. to 5 p.m. After midnight the gates of the Temple were reopened.

Of considerable importance is Josephus's definition of the unit by which the Pesaḥ was celebrated. It was, he declares, a *φρατρία* of about ten to twenty persons.[6] We have seen that the first Christians celebrated the Pesaḥ meal (according to the Synoptic Gospels) as a group of male adults associated by social rather than family ties. The *φρατρία* of Josephus is different. It is rather a subdivision of the *φυλή*.[7] It conforms to the traditional practice, for it corresponds exactly to the Mishnaic conception of the *ḥabhurah*, a family group.[8]

[1] For the summary of extracts from Josephus, see pp. 37 ff. above.

[2] On the preliminal period of one week, see pp. 139 f. above.

[3] *Ant.* II. xv. 1.

[4] See pp. 244 f. above. This is the only passage in Josephus in which he discusses the festival of Maṣṣoth as distinct from the Pesaḥ. With it we may compare *BJ* II. xvii. 7, where Josephus regards 14th Ab, not the following day, as the day of the wood offering, cf. Lichtenstein, *HUCA* viii–ix, 1931–2, 271; *Mish. Taʿan.* iv. 5; Derenbourg, op. cit. 109 n. 2; and E. Schürer, *Geschichte*, i, 1901, 757. This explanation of the eight-day Passover of Josephus is to be preferred to that of Chwolson, op. cit. 3 n. 2, who maintains that Josephus was here addressing his remarks to pagans living outside Palestine who knew that their Jewish neighbours kept a festival of eight, not seven, days. But elsewhere Josephus writes of a seven-day Passover, and his remarks there are equally addressed to non-Jews. Graetz, *Geschichte*, iii. 460, considers that the eight days in this passage of Josephus is simply an error for seven days.

[5] pp. 151 f. above.

[6] So the *ʿedah* is held to be composed of at least ten persons, *JT Ber.* vii. 3 (fol. 11c), cf. *Mish. Sanh.* i. 6. This was the usual view, but *Mish. Pes.* ix. 10 implies that a *ḥabhurah* may consist also of five persons. Bar Kappara, on the other hand, *Lamentations Rabba*, i. 2, declared that even a hundred persons could form a single group to eat the Pesaḥ victim since each was required by law to eat only an olive's bulk.

[7] Liddell and Scott, *Lexicon*, s.v. See further, on the *φρατρία*, Harrison, *Themis*, 500; Homolle, *Bulletin de Correspondance hellénique*, xix, 1895, 38, 41 ff.; and Nilsson, *Cults, Myths, Oracles, and Politics in Ancient Greece*, 1951, 150.

[8] p. 241 above. The same view was maintained by Targ. at Ex. 12:46, 'in one *ḥabhurah*', for בבית אחד, p. 54 above.

One statement of Josephus indicates a new development which we find described in greater detail in the Mishnah. Philo had alluded to the Sheaf waved on the second day of the Passover week as a simple δράγμα.[1] With Josephus it has changed in character. It is offered with the complex rites of a firstfruits offering.[2] Perhaps the shift of this ceremony from (as I have suggested) the day after the end of the Passover week to the second day of the festival had hastened this development. Foodstuffs were now imported into Palestine in appreciable quantities. We read that the ceremony of the offering of the Sheaf was the signal for the consumption of the new produce already in the markets of Jerusalem.[3] It was no longer a rite of sympathetic magic to encourage the growth of the young corn; it was rather a toll whose payment released the new produce from embargo.

Josephus, as we have remarked, is the last direct witness of the Hebrew Passover. But the final picture of the festival as it was celebrated in the closing phase of the Jerusalem Temple is preserved in Jewish writings assembled in the first centuries after its destruction. Of these writings the most important for our present purpose is the Mishnah, which set out deliberately to codify Jewish religious practice. To the study of the Passover the Mishnah makes a special contribution. It demonstrates the evolution from Biblical ordinances to Rabbinic usage. All the more striking, then, is its admission that the ceremonial of the Passover had undergone amendment in the process of time. Some of the rites of the 'Pesaḥ of Egypt' had been abandoned in the 'Pesaḥ of (later) generations';[4] in the course of the present inquiry it has been suggested that these changes had occurred centuries—in some cases several centuries—before the codification of the Mishnah.[5]

Where the Mishnah describes the ritual of the Temple it may be employed with confidence, provided that its statements are not disputed by an authority of the last decades of the Temple or of the period immediately following. It was pointless—and may rightly have been considered improper—to invent procedure for the Temple which had ceased to exist, for this procedure no longer had immediate bearing upon contemporary Jewish practice. Moreover, evidence for Temple ritual was to be found in plenty and could not be fabricated.[6] Where, however, our sources deal with practices outside the Temple, and particularly the practices of the home, the greatest

[1] p. 28 above.

[2] See Lev. 2:14, cf. Gray, *Sacrifice*, 325 ff.

[3] See p. 265 below. There is no need to follow T. Worden, 'Literary Influence of the Ugaritic Fertility Myth on the Old Testament', *VT* iii, 1953, 292, who apparently sees in the method of offering grain firstfruits in Josephus and the Mishnah a deliberate imitation of a Canaanite ritual described in the Ugaritic myth.

[4] p. 260 below.

[5] See p. 208 above.

[6] See *Mish. Ḥag.* i. 8: 'the (rules about) . . . (the Temple) service . . . have that which supports them, and it is they that are the essentials of the Law'.

caution must be exercised in attributing their observance to the period before A.D. 70. The testimony of the Mishnah and parallel writings may be corroborated at some points by independent documents (notably the works of Josephus), at others by historical accounts in which the description of rites is no more than an incidental factor of the narrative and therefore above suspicion. For our present purpose only those statements may be regarded as reliable that are accredited to Rabbis of the first generation, and even these must be viewed with caution unless they conform to the attested course of evolution.[1] For the tendency of Jewish law was twofold—on the one hand, to insist on the exact performance of practices when these were based on cardinal principles of religion or ethics, on the other, to relax the rigidity of ritual that had lost its primary significance.

We learn that fifteen days before the Passover—that is, on 1st Nisan—the *terumah* was taken out of the Sheqel chamber: this was a ceremony that took place also at the same interval before the other *ḥaggim* of Weeks and Tabernacles, and, moreover, our authorities here are comparatively late.[2] In other respects, however, 1st Nisan stood alone. It was a significant date for the determination of the calendar[3]—a feature arising directly out of its origins as a New Year festival.[4] It was also the day on which *sheqalim* were offered to the sanctuary for the new year;[5] here we have a relic of the primitive practice of numbering the people at the spring festival.[6] Furthermore, the position of the Passover in relation to the new crops made the eve of that festival an appropriate moment for the distribution of tithes in the fourth and seventh years.[7]

Before the Passover, the stones of the Temple ramp and altar were whitened.[8] The Pesaḥ victim was chosen from among the lambs and kids,[9]

[1] Note, for example, the comments of Chwolson, op. cit. 24 ff., on the historical reliability of the account in *JT Pes.* vi. 1 (fol. 33a) on the rulings of Hillel. (I have sought, however, to maintain that Hillel's arguments were in fact intended to uphold early practice, although the reasoning ascribed to him may be specious; but see p. 251 n. 4 above.)

[2] *Mish. Sheq.* iii. 1, iv. 1.

[3] *Mish. R.H.* i. 3–4: 'Because of six New Moons do messengers go forth (to proclaim the time of their appearing): because of Nisan, to determine the time of Passover . . . . Because of two New Moons may the Sabbath be profaned: (the New Moon) of Nisan and (the New Moon) of Tishri, for on them messengers used to go forth to Syria, and by them the set feasts were determined. . . .' Cf. *Mekhilta* on Ex. 12:2.

[4] The statement that '1st Nisan is the New Year for kings and feasts', *Mish. R.H.* i. 1, is to be related to the civil Seleucid calendar; but I have argued that both the Greek and the Jewish calendars may well be derived from a common Near Eastern source, pp. 125 f. above.

[5] *BT R.H.* 7a, cf. *Meg.* 29a and *JT Sheq.* i. 1 (fol. 45d). In the opinion of some it was also the New Year 'for the renting of houses', *BT R.H.* 7b, *JT R.H.* i. 1 (fol. 56d).

[6] p. 135 above. Note that, like the other *ḥaggim* (see p. 128 above), the Passover was an occasion on which appearance at Jerusalem was incumbent on all adult males, as in primitive times—but not on women and children, the sick, the aged, and certain other categories. See *Mish. Ḥag.* i. 1 and p. 241 above.

[7] *Mish. Maʿas. Sh.* v. 6; cf. *R.H.* i. 2.

[8] *Mish. Mid.* iii. 4. On the restriction of the Pesaḥ to Jerusalem, see *Meg.* i. 10–11.

[9] *Mish. Men.* vii. 6; cf. *BT Pes.* 57a.

not from among the cattle.[1] The rule of setting apart the victim on the tenth day had been waived.[2] The animal was, however, specially designated as the Pesaḥ victim, and it received thereby a certain sanctity.[3] The act of slaughter was performed at the Temple[4] by laymen; the blood was handled by the priests.[5] No leaven was permitted to come into contact with the victim;[6] and, as in earlier times, it was not accompanied by libations.[7] The celebrants, including laymen, flayed the carcasses,[8] and the prescribed portions were removed, to be burned by the priests in accordance with normal Temple procedure.[9] While these rites were performed, the Levites made music[10] and the 'Hallel' psalms were recited.[11]

The Pesaḥ ceremony had been preceded by a short fast.[12] The meal which followed the sacrifice was consumed by companies, evidently family groups;[13] but the significance of the association at the Pesaḥ began, not with the meal, but with the actual sacrifice of the victim which was the central feature of the whole Pesaḥ.[14] The Pesaḥ victim was to be eaten only by those persons by whom it had been designated,[15] and it could be consumed whole.[16] It was to be accompanied by unleavened bread and bitter herbs.[17] The order of the meal was obligatory upon all Israelites, even the poor[18] (except, of course, those who were debarred by reason of ritual uncleanness). Wine was an important constituent of the meal.[19] Everyone, even

[1] See the discussion in *JT Pes.* vi. 1 (fol. 33a), *Tos. Pes.* iv. 1, *BT Pes.* 76b.

[2] So probably already earlier; see p. 207 above on Deut. 16.

[3] *Mish. Pes.* v. 2, cf. vi. 5, viii. 2, 3, *Zeb.* i. 1–4.

[4] Cf. *BT Pes.* 53 a, b, *Beṣah* 23a, *Ber.* 19a, *JT Pes.* vii. 1 (fol. 34a). See further *Tos. Pes.* iv. 2, *JT Pes.* vi. 1 (fol. 33a), Philo, *De victimis*, 5, Josephus, *Ant.* III. ix. 1.

[5] *Mish. Pes.* v. 5–6, cf. *Men.* ix. 7, *Pes.* v. 7, *Zeb.* v. 8.

[6] *Mish. Pes.* v. 4, *Mak.* iii. 2.

[7] *Mish. Men.* ix. 6, cf. p. 202 above.

[8] *Mish. Pes.* v. 9, cf. *BT Pes.* 66a.

[9] *Mish. Pes.* v. 10. The approximation of the Pesaḥ sacrifice to the peace offering (see p. 87 above on the views of Nicolsky) may belong to a later stratum of law, *Sheq.* ii. 5, *Pes.* ix. 6–7.

[10] *Mish. Pes.* v. 5 (trumpets), *'Ar.* ii. 3 (flutes).

[11] Ps. 113–18, see *Mish. Pes.* v. 7, cf. *BT Pes.* 117a, *JT Pes.* v. 7 (fol. 32c); see Büchler, *Studies*, 57 f., and id., *ZAW* xx, 1900, 114 ff.

[12] From 'near to *minḥah* until nightfall', *Mish. Pes.* x. 1, cf. *Tos. Pes.* x. 1, *JT Pes.* x. 1 (fol. 37b), *BT Pes.* 107b. The fast of Jewish firstborn on the eve of the Pesaḥ probably arose late; see p. 146 n. 1 above.

[13] *Mish. Pes.* vii. 13–viii. 4 and *Sanh.* viii. 2, where the *ḥabhurah* of a *miṣwah* is interpreted by commentators as a group on the occasion of a wedding or circumcision, at, that is, a family celebration; cf. *BT Pes.* 88a. But women, children, and slaves alone could not form a *ḥabhurah*, *Tos. Pes.* viii. 6, *JT Pes.* viii. 7 (fol. 37a).

[14] Note the significant wording of *Mish. Pes.* viii. 3: 'Others may always be received ... within the number and withdraw from it, until such time as (the victim) is slaughtered.' A rider adds: 'R. Simeon says, Until the blood is about to be tossed on his behalf', cf. *Tos. Pes.* vii. 3, 6.

[15] *Mish. Zeb.* v. 8; cf. *Mekhilta* on Ex. 12:4, *BT Pes.* 61a.

[16] *Mish. Pes.* vii. 11.

[17] *Mish. Pes.* ix. 3, x. 3, cf. *'Erub.* ii. 6. On the definition of bitter herbs, see already p. 169 above; cf. *BT Pes.* 39a.

[18] *Mish. Pes.* x. 1; cf. pp. 243 f. above on the distribution of alms in the New Testament.

[19] *Mish. Pes.* x. 1–4.

slaves, reclined at the meal—a relaxation of ordinary social conventions that was a feature common to New Year festivals throughout the ancient Near East.[1] The benedictions, portions from the Bible (including the story of the Exodus Passover and the 'Hallel' psalms),[2] and prayers were recited;[3] among them we observe the prominence of the notion of redemption at the New Year.[4] Care was taken not to break the bones of the Pesaḥ victim,[5] and not to take it outside Jerusalem.[6] Gifts were donated to women and children, particularly spices and nuts—another widespread New Year motif.[7] During the Passover week no leavened bread was eaten.[8] On the first day of the week were offered the *re'iyyah* whole burnt offering and the *ḥagigah* peace offering;[9] work was forbidden on the first and the seventh days.[10]

All the rites that have just been enumerated are ancient or the reflection of ancient custom; we have referred to them already in the course of this study. There are other ancient rites of which the Mishnah declares (as we have observed) that they formed part of the primitive 'Pesaḥ of Egypt' and had been subsequently abandoned.[11] They are the selection of the victim on the tenth day, the ceremony of smearing the blood of the Pesaḥ victim on the lintels and doorposts, the eating of the meal in haste, and the eating of unleavened bread during one night only, not seven days.[12] The last point of difference between the 'Pesaḥ of Egypt' and the 'Pesaḥ of (later) generations' shows clearly what was the motive of the writer in drawing attention to these changes in ritual. The eating of unleavened bread during seven days was certainly primitive, for, as we have seen, these seven days were the post-liminal sacral period.[13] But according to the narrative of the Exodus Passover the Israelites left Egypt on the day after the Pesaḥ; they did not observe the festival week as it was observed at the time of the Mishnah. The author of the Mishnaic code is concerned, then, not with the 'Pesaḥ of Egypt' as such, but with the 'Pesaḥ of Egypt' as it is portrayed in the Bible text. He is seeking to forestall the objections of sectarians who based their practice directly upon appeal to the Pentateuch.

[1] *Mish. Pes.* x. 1; for the usual conventions at meals, *Tos. Ber.* iv. 8 f.
[2] *Mish. Pes.* ix. 3, x. 2, 7.
[3] *Mish. Pes.* x. 1 ff.
[4] *Mish. Pes.* x. 5–6.
[5] *Mish. Pes.* vii. 11, *Mak.* iii. 3; cf. *Tos. Pes.* vi. 8 ff.
[6] *Mish. Pes.* vii. 9, 12, *Siphre* on Num. 9; even in courtyards and on the roofs of houses, *Tos. Pes.* vi. 11.
[7] *Tos. Pes.* x. 4; cf. *JT Pes.* x. 1 (fol. 37b). Cf. p. 148 above.
[8] *Mish. Ker.* i. 1, *Ḥal.* i. 1, but cf. the assessment of the penalty, *Mak.* iii. 2.
[9] *Mish. Ḥag.* i. 3; see the convenient summary in Danby, op. cit. 211 n. 10.
[10] *Mish. Beṣah*, passim.
[11] *Mish. Pes.* ix. 5, *Tos. Pes.* viii. 11 ff.
[12] There is a lacuna in the Mishnah at this point; see *BT Pes.* 96b. The eating of *maṣṣoth* for one day in no way detracts, in the opinion of the Rabbis, from the rule that no leaven must be eaten during the whole Passover week; cf. Maimonides, *Yad*, III. v. 3.
[13] p. 177 above.

But there were other details of ritual not specifically enjoined in the Pentateuch that had been modified in the course of time and before the codification of the Mishnah. We shall detect in them the twofold tendency to which I have alluded.[1] They are designed, on the one hand, to strengthen the fence which protected the sanctity of the Pentateuchal law, and, on the other, to ease the burden of the festival ritual where this seemed unduly onerous and where some relaxation would not be out of keeping with the requirements of the written law.[2]

The eve of the Passover involved the ordinary Jew in preparations so complex as to give the eve of the festival, as we have seen, something of the character of an actual festival.[3] In particular, leaven was to be removed as early as the night of 13th–14th Nisan.[4] So, too, the by-products of grain that were to be removed were defined with great precision,[5] but the Mishnah elsewhere declares broadly that 'whatsoever is made from any kind of grain must be removed at the Passover'.[6] Of later date may be the rules that leaven is to be destroyed by burning,[7] that no new grain produce is to be used before the Passover,[8] and that grains must not be mixed.[9] The grain from which unleavened bread may be made is the grain of which the new crop must not be reaped before the offering of the Sheaf, that is, grain of the old year's crops.[10] These regulations were carried out by all Jews, whether they were on pilgrimage or not.

The age of the Pesaḥ victim was more precisely defined; the animal might be killed even on the eighth day of its life.[11] The special sanctity of the Pesaḥ victim was safeguarded by regulations. If it were lost and then found again before the time of sacrifice, it could not, of course, be offered since it might have contracted uncleanness; but it also could not be put to ordinary use. It was allowed to graze until it suffered a blemish, and then it had to be sold and a peace offering[12] donated from the proceeds.[13] Similarly, if, for

1 p. 258 above.

2 Beer, *Pesachim*, 62 ff., looks for Greek origins for these amendments to Passover practices. There seems little reason for this, if the amendments can be explained satisfactorily as the result of natural evolution.

3 Cf. p. 256 above; cf. *BT Pes.* 5a. The regulations on abstention from work in *Mish. Pes.* iv. 1, 5–8, may not be early.

4 *Mish. Pes.* i. 1 ff.; the times were later relaxed, i. 3–5. If 14th Nisan occurred on a Sabbath, the removal of leaven was carried out on the previous day, *Tos. Pes.* ii. 9.

5 *Mish. Pes.* iii. 1, but this may be late.

6 *Mish. Pes.* iii. 1; cf. ii. 7–8, iii. 2 ff. The definition may be late.

7 *Mish. Tem.* vii. 5; cf. *Pes.* ii. 1.

8 *Mish. Ḥal.* i. 1; this is already covered by the Sheaf regulations, p. 265 below.

9 *Mish. Ḥal.* i. 2; cf. i. 8 and *Ker.* i. 1.

10 *Mish. Pes.* ii. 5; cf. *Ḥal.* i. 1. The regulation is not dated. See also *Mekhilta* on Ex. 13:6 and *Siphre* on Deut. 16:8.

11 *Mish. Par.* i. 4.

12 See p. 259 n. 9 above on the relations between the Pesaḥ offering and the *zebhaḥ*. See further *Mish. Zeb.* v. 7–8, *Sheq.* ii. 5, *BT Qid.* 55b.

13 *Mish. Pes.* ix. 6. The other rules on the 'setting aside' of an animal as the Pesaḥ victim, ix. 7–11, *Sheq.* vii. 4, may be later usage.

some reason, the victim or its owners contracted uncleanness, the animal must be disposed of according to certain rules.[1] All these regulations of the Mishnah are rigid, but at this point a proviso is entered which suggests some relaxation. We are told that 'if (the Pesaḥ victim) were offered in uncleanness (unknowingly), it may also be eaten in uncleanness, since from the beginning it was offered only to be eaten'.[2] The same spirit of concession—in so far as it was consonant with the proper observance of Temple procedure—is to be found in the regulations concerning the participants; in particular, the laws of ritual cleanness were interpreted leniently.[3] If some of the participants had contracted uncleanness but the majority were clean, the sacrifice was nevertheless valid.[4]

The times of the performance of the Pesaḥ sacrifice at the Temple were carefully regulated on account of the great numbers of the participants.[5] It was not permitted, on the one hand, to interfere with the normal routine of the *Tamid*; on the other hand, the act of slaughter of the Pesaḥ victims had to be completed before nightfall.[6] The *Tamid* was usually slaughtered at 2.30 p.m., and offered at 3.30 p.m., but on the eve of the Passover it was slaughtered at 1.30 and offered at 2.30. The Pesaḥ victims were slaughtered, then, from about 3 p.m., as we have already learnt from earlier sources.[7] But when the eve of Pesaḥ coincided with the eve of the Sabbath, all these ceremonies were carried out an hour earlier.[8] The slaughter of the Pesaḥ victim and, to some extent, the disposal of its blood could be performed on the Sabbath, but not its roasting or its transportation to the Temple area.[9] It was therefore necessary to complete the roasting before sunset on Friday. If, on the other hand, the eve of the Passover coincided with the Sabbath itself, the roasting took place after nightfall.[10] The act of roasting had been modified to the extent that the flesh could be basted or

[1] *Mish. Pes.* vii. 5, 8–9; cf. *Zeb.* viii. 4.

[2] *Mish. Pes.* vii. 4.

[3] *Mish. Ker.* iii. 8; cf. viii. 5, 6, 8, ix. 4, *Ḥag.* i. 1; cf. *Tos. Pes.* vii. 11–17, *BT Pes.* 59a. On the rules for mourners, cf. *Siphre* on Num. 6:8, *JT Pes.* viii. 8 (fol. 36a); cf. *Mish. Zeb.* xii. 1, *BT Zeb.* 100b.

[4] *Mish. Pes.* vii. 6, cf. v. 3, vi. 6, ix. 4, *Tos. Pes.* vi. 1 ff.

[5] *Mish. Ab.* v. 5.

[6] *Mish. Pes.* v. 1, 3.

[7] *Mish. Pes.* v. 1; cf. pp. 233, 246, and 256 above.

[8] *Mish. Pes.* v. 1.

[9] *Mish. Pes.* v. 8–10, vi. 1; cf. vi. 2–3, 5–6, vii. 10. Cf. *JT Pes.* vi. 1 (fol. 33a) and the parallel accounts of *Tos. Pes.* and *BT Pes.* on the ruling of Hillel. The question of the antiquity of the regulation on the priority of the Pesaḥ over the Sabbath is discussed at length by Chwolson, op. cit. 20 ff.; Geiger, op. cit. 49; and Büchler, *Synedrion*, 145; see further A. Kaminka, 'Hillel's Life and Work', *JQR* xxx, 1939–40, 107. I have referred to the subject briefly on p. 251 above.

[10] *Mish. Pes.* v. 10; cf. *JT Pes.* vi. 1 (fol. 33a), *BT Pes.* 65b, and the discussion in Büchler, loc. cit. The meat which may or may not be eaten roast, *Mish. Pes.* iv. 4, is not, of course, the Pesaḥ victim, but the additional offerings; cf. p. 227 above. On the method of roasting, see *BT Pes.* 74a and *JT Pes.* vii. 1 (fol. 34a), and on the roasting ovens, see Büchler, *Priester*, 147.

dipped into liquid, but the Pentateuchal prohibition against boiling remained firm.[1]

Sacrificers passed through the Temple carrying out the rites in three groups.[2] But, as we have observed,[3] the great numbers of pilgrims made it no longer possible to roast and eat the victims inside the Temple precincts. Instead, it was permitted to hold the repast within the city boundaries of Jerusalem.[4]

The meal is prescribed in some detail.[5] It was consumed in companies,[6] numbering more than one person—sometimes five, but commonly ten.[7] The minimum amount of the meat of the Pesaḥ victim prescribed for each participant was an olive's bulk; if there was not enough meat to provide for a joyous meal,[8] it was permissible to supplement the victim with the meat of additional offerings—but only on weekdays and in cleanness.[9] These additional offerings are not to be confused with the burnt offerings of the Passover week; they are similar to the peace offerings of mid-festivals.[10] The unleavened bread eaten at the Pesaḥ meal must also be to the extent of at least an olive's bulk,[11] and the precise grains from which it is prepared are specified.[12] They include one that appears to ripen in Palestine even earlier than barley.[13] The bitter herbs are defined.[14] The Pesaḥ meal must be completed before midnight.[15] This implies greater strictness than is shown in the regulations of the Book of Jubilees.[16] On the other hand, the remains of the victim were not to be burned, as in earlier times, on the night of the Pesaḥ, but on 16th Nisan, the day after the Pesaḥ; and if the sixteenth day was a Sabbath, the disposal of the remains was deferred to the seventeenth.[17] The reason for this serious breach of the Pentateuchal regulations may be found in the need for the Temple staff themselves to carry out both the Pesaḥ sacrifices and the sacrifices of the first day of the Passover week;

[1] *Mish. Pes.* ii. 8; cf. vii. 1–3, *Zeb.* v. 8, *Tos. Pes.* v. 8–11. See p. 166 above.

[2] *Mish. Pes.* v. 5, 7.

[3] p. 240 above.

[4] *Mish. Pes.* vii. 9, 12, *Meg.* i. 11. See p. 246 above.

[5] *Mish. Pes.* x. 1–4. The order of the dishes may go back to the days of the Temple, but this is not certain from the text. See Jeremias, *Eucharistic Words*, 58, and J. J. Petuchowski, '"Do This in Remembrance of Me" (1 Cor. 11:24)', *JBL* lxxvi, 1957, 293.

[6] See p. 241 n. 7 above.

[7] *Mish. Pes.* vii. 13, viii. 1, 4, 7, ix. 10, *Zeb.* v. 8; cf. Büchler, *Der galiläische 'Am-ha'Areṣ*, 106.

[8] Cf. *Mish. Pes.* x. 6.

[9] *Mish. Pes.* vi. 3–4; cf. iv. 4, *Peah* i. 1, *BT Pes.* 69b, 76b, *Ḥag.* 7b–8a.

[10] *Mish. Ḥag.* i. 3, but cf. i. 8 on the (later) uncertainty about the festival offerings.

[11] *Mish. Ḥal.* i. 2.

[12] *Mish. Pes.* ii. 5. Details of the processes that may result in fermentation are given in ii. 7–8.

[13] Spelt, cf. Dalman, *Arbeit*, i. 402; but see Ex. 9:32. The other permissible grains are wheat, barley, goat-grass, and oats.

[14] See p. 169 above.

[15] *Mish. Pes.* x. 9, *Tos. Pes.* v. 13. This proves that the view of Heawood, *JQR* xlii, 1951–2, 41, that the Pesaḥ sacrifice could be eaten on any of the days of the Passover week is incorrect; see Zeitlin, ibid. 47.

[16] p. 233 above.

[17] *Mish. Pes.* vii. 10; cf. *BT Shab.* 24b.

and it may well have arisen early.[1] But the origin of the rule may equally well be sought in the apparent dislike of the Pesaḥ ceremonies among the Sadducees.[2]

We have observed the tendency towards relaxation in the severity of the rules of ritual cleanness. This is seen most clearly in the Mishnaic ordinances on the 'second Pesaḥ'. It may be summed up briefly in the words: 'If through error or constraint (a man) did not keep the first (Pesaḥ), let him keep the second.'[3] But if uncleanness were contracted after the intention of keeping the first Pesaḥ, it was not necessary to keep the second.[4] In the 'second Pesaḥ', moreover, the Temple service was based meticulously upon that of the first, but the ceremonies of the meal—with which the individual layman would be concerned—were as simple as possible; only those were observed that were explicitly prescribed in the text of the Pentateuch.[5] I have already pointed out that the keeping of a 'second Pesaḥ' was not extended to the keeping of a second Passover week, for the pilgrimage was to be performed on a fixed date and could not be deferred.[6] The Mishnah goes farther. In order to inconvenience as little as possible the person obliged to keep the 'second Pesaḥ', he is permitted to have both unleavened and leavened bread with him in the house.[7] The same trend is illustrated by the account of the priest Joseph who brought his sons and the members of his household to celebrate the 'second Pesaḥ' at Jerusalem; he was turned away. To permit so ostentatious a performance of this ritual would have been to create an undesirable precedent.[8]

On the morrow of the first day of the Passover week took place the offering of the barley Sheaf. It was carried out with deliberate display;[9] it was held to override the Sabbath, although the ceremonies were modified in some details if the date coincided with the Sabbath.[10] It should be noted that the Mishnah does not fix the date of the Sheaf-waving ceremony in relation to the Passover week, and we are not told explicitly that it takes place on the second day of the festival. We are informed simply that preparations for the waving are to be made 'on the eve of the festival day';[11] the ceremony itself is performed 'when it grew dark'. But there is no doubt that the ceremony was held, according to the accepted practice, on the second day of the Passover week, and there is also no doubt that the publicity with

[1] See pp. 226 ff. above on the Passover of the Chronicler. [2] p. 250 above.

[3] *Mish. Pes.* ix. 1; cf. *Tos. Pes.* viii. 1–3; for the definition of uncleanness, see *BT Pes.* 93a. [4] *Mish. Pes.* viii. 6.

[5] *Mish. Pes.* ix. 5, cf. *'Ar.* ii. 3.

[6] p. 229 above. [7] *Mish. Pes.* ix. 3.

[8] *Mish. Ḥal.* iv. 11. Büchler, *Priester*, 55, following *Tos. Pes.* viii. 10, holds that Joseph's party included females, who were exempt from keeping the 'second Pesaḥ'. In the Tosephta passage, however, Joseph is said to have brought his daughter's son, the daughter is not mentioned; the boy may also have been exempted from the 'second Pesaḥ' as a minor.

[9] *Mish. Men.* x. 3. [10] *Mish. Men.* x. 1, 3.

[11] *Mish. Men.* x. 2–3; 'festival day' (*yom ṭobh*) is a general term for any festival.

which it was held was directed against the 'Boethusians'.[1] The fact that the ceremony was held at night[2] also arose, I have suggested, as a deliberate act of defiance against the sectarians.[3] Another motive was, however, certainly no less prominent—the desire to avoid causing hardship to the people. It was imperative that the Sheaf should be offered without delay, for only after the offering of the Sheaf might the new produce be consumed.[4] It was therefore offered immediately at the close of the first festival day. The same motive is to be traced in the other modifications of this ceremony. The Sheaf was to be picked preferably from corn in the vicinity of Jerusalem—but if none was available there, it might be taken from any other place in Palestine.[5] It was to be from standing corn—but from sheaves if standing corn could not be found; it was to be from fresh corn—but from dried grain if no fresh corn were to be found (although both of these modifications seem to contravene the sense of Deut. 16:9); it was to be reaped by night—but it might be reaped by day rather than that any postponement should occur.[6] The markets of Jerusalem were full of meal and parched corn awaiting the signal of the Sheaf-offering, although the preparation of this foodstuff must have been carried out before the Sheaf had been offered and 'without the consent of the Sages'.[7] The authorities were willing to waive the rigidity of the regulations where it appeared to be in the public interest to do so.

The Sheaf was, as we have already observed,[8] no longer offered as a simple sheaf on the altar; it was treated in the same way as grain firstfruits.[9] The quantity was one-tenth of an ephah,[10] and the Rabbis seem here to have interpreted *'omer*, 'sheaf', as *'omer*, 'measure (of corn)'.[11] We have in this an instructive example of the tendency to co-ordinate Temple ritual, even though it might plainly conflict with the meaning—and even the intention—of a Pentateuchal law.[12]

[1] See the discussion p. 249 above.

[2] *Mish. Men.* x. 3, *Meg.* ii. 6.

[3] p. 251 above.

[4] Lev. 23:14.

[5] *Mish. Men.* x. 2, *Par.* ii. 1, *Kelim* i. 6. The types of corn which might not be reaped before the offering of the Sheaf are given in *Ḥal.* i. 1, &c., *Men.* x. 5, 7. On the form in which the barley was to be offered, *Soṭ.* ii. 1; cf. *BT Men.* 68b.

[6] *Mish. Men.* x. 9; cf. viii. 2. Not even uncleanness need delay the offering of the Sheaf; cf. *Pes.* vii. 4.

[7] *Mish. Men.* x. 5. Concessions were made, moreover, in the rule that the reaping of new produce must await the offering of the Sheaf, x. 7–8, cf. the less accurate *Pes.* iv. 8, and p. 250 above. The Biblical ordinance of Lev. 23:14 had, after all, prescribed that the eating, not the reaping, of the new produce must await the Sheaf-offering. Note the amendment of the text of *BT Men.* 71a, 85a, suggested by Rashi, in loc.

[8] See p. 257 above on Josephus.

[9] Lev. 2:14. The Temple ceremony is given in detail in *Mish. Men.* vi. 6–7, x. 4; see also *Soṭ.* ii. 1, *Men.* vi. 1, *Zeb.* ix. 5, *Men.* v. 3, 6, ix. 4, *Ab.* v. 5.

[10] *Mish. Men.* vi. 6.

[11] Ex. 16:36, cf. vv. 16, 18, 22, 32 f.

[12] Note *Mish. Men.* x. 5 on the effect of the destruction of the Temple upon the Sheaf ceremony and upon the use of the crops. On the Sheaf ceremony, see further *JT R.H.* i. 10 (fol. 57b), *BT Men.* 65b–68b, Maimonides, *Yad*, VIII. vi. 7.

I have set out in some detail the form of the Passover in the last years of the Temple at Jerusalem. With the destruction of the Temple, the intimate link between the New Year ritual and the shrine which had been a characteristic feature of the festival was broken. Thereafter a new phase of its story opens—but it had become the Jewish, rather than the Hebrew, Passover. What follows lies outside the scope of the present study.

We may now recapitulate briefly the argument of this work. I have submitted that we should regard as untenable those theories that assume separate origins for the Pesaḥ and the Maṣṣoth week; prominent among these theories is the view that originally the Pesaḥ was a firstlings sacrifice practised by the Israelites before their conquest of Canaan, while the Maṣṣoth week was a festival of the dedication of firstfruits of grain which the Israelites adopted from the Canaanites. I have maintained, on the contrary, that the apparent distinction between the Pesaḥ and the Maṣṣoth week in the Pentateuch stems from two causes—first, the Maṣṣoth-week regulations have no logical place in the narrative of the Exodus from Egypt, and, secondly, the distinction reflects a division in practice, since only the regulations of the Maṣṣoth week were carried out by Israelites outside Jerusalem at the time of the Compiler of the Pentateuch.

The Passover was a New Year festival. From early times it was performed by the Hebrews as a pilgrimage on a fixed calendric date—the spring equinox. It shared with the autumn feast of Tabernacles some of the features common to New Year festivals in other countries of the ancient Near East. It was carried out on the night of the full moon, at a prescribed shrine or shrines. It was directed towards the peculiar deity of the whole nation. It was attended by the assembly of all the adult males of Israel, perhaps of the age of twenty and over, who had undergone the initiation rite of circumcision. The assembly was organized according to family units; it probably had the character of a census for military, as well as religious and fiscal, purposes. It was preceded, like other Israelite *rites de passage*, by a preliminal period of seven days during which the participants acquired ritual cleanness. The rules regarding the sacrificial victim offered by each household were also based upon the need to maintain ritual cleanness. The victim was required to be a small animal, male, in its first year, and without blemish, as in other Israelite congregational sacrifices. It was chosen at the end of an 'inner' period of three days within the preliminal period of seven days, on, that is, the tenth day of the month. Other Passover practices characteristic of New Year festivals were a fast a short time before the Pesaḥ, the recital of the national epic, and perhaps solemn dancing. The participants wore a uniform costume, probably to disguise the personality of each individual. Two other New Year motifs that were probably transferred from the Passover to Purim in the course of time were the exchange of gifts and a belief that the fates of men in the ensuing year were determined by the casting of lots. The primitive Passover may also have included, like the autumn festival, a solemn procession, and a ritual exodus into the desert, where the people lived in tents.

But while the autumn New Year festival in Israel was a formal occasion at which the authority of King or High Priest was proclaimed or renewed, the Passover in the spring was a festival performed by the whole people. It was therefore marked by ceremonies which were not shared by the autumn festival or by formal New Year festivals of other nations. The victim was slain by the head of each household, in the nature of things usually a layman; its blood was smeared, with precautions against direct contact with the sacred/unholy, on the entrance to the dwelling-place of each family. It was a redemption offering on behalf of all the family on the eve of the new year; among them the firstborn were 'redeemed' with special care. The blood ceremony was followed by a communion meal on the flesh of the victim, accompanied, as usual, by bread. Here again precautions were taken against uncleanness. The victim was roasted whole, none of its bones was broken, and none of the flesh taken outside the dwelling-place; the bread was unleavened. The haste of the meal was perhaps a reminiscence of the haste of the ritual exodus which followed the meal and which may have been intended to hasten the transition into the new year.

The Pesaḥ was followed by a post-liminal period of seven days, the so-called Maṣṣoth festival, during which the people abstained from work, sacrifices were offered, and—the most characteristic feature—no leaven was eaten. The prohibition of leaven at the spring festival was maintained by the fact that it was customary in the Near East to abstain from leaven at the time of the spring harvest. The Passover has no immediate connexion with firstfruits, and its only connexion with firstlings is by analogy with the firstborn, whose redemption was a principal aim of the Pesaḥ ceremony. That the Pesaḥ ceremony was ancient is demonstrated by the uniqueness of its myth of the 'passing-over' of the Israelites by the deity, and by the uniqueness of two distinctive features—the handling of sacrificial blood by laymen and the performance of the ceremony at night; the Tabernacles festival in the autumn seems, characteristically enough, also to have been marked by a nocturnal ritual. The legend of the destruction of the Egyptian firstborn at the plague which preceded the Pesaḥ and the Exodus from Egypt may well be an echo of the deaths at an early age of the sons of Rameses II, to whose reign the Exodus is commonly ascribed.

This is the primitive Passover as it was depicted in Israelite tradition recorded in the Exodus narrative of Ex. 12–13. For the subsequent development of the festival in Canaan we must examine the Pentateuch documents in the order in which they were arranged by the Compiler of our Massoretic Text—in the period of the Chronicler or earlier. Ex. 23 and 34 give a brief description of features of the festival observed by Israelites on the farms, not at the shrine. Lev. 23 records the formal attachment of the seven-week period opening with the Sheaf ritual (originally agricultural) to the end of the Passover week; it also refers shortly to sacrifices during the Passover week. Num. 9 permits the deferment of the Pesaḥ sacrifice (but not the post-liminal week) for one month in certain cases of ritual uncleanness. Num. 28 prescribes the offerings of the Passover in detail. Deut. 16, written in an age when *maṣṣoth* were the food of the poor—possibly about the time of Josiah—restricts the Pesaḥ rigidly to a prescribed shrine or shrines, a feature that distinguishes all later accounts of the festival. It is for this reason that some elements of the primitive Pesaḥ—the smearing of the victim's blood by laymen, the wearing of a special costume, and probably the selection of the victim on the tenth day—do not figure in the Deuteronomic account. Other elements—notably the regulations on ritual cleanness and the sacrifices during the Passover week—are not mentioned in Deut. 16 because the document is addressed to the people, not to the priests. Some elements may have been omitted in Deut. 16 by error, like the eating of bitter herbs and the prohibition against breaking the bones of the Pesaḥ victim. Certain apparent discrepancies between Deut. 16 and other Pentateuchal documents on the Pesaḥ—the method of 'cooking' the victim, the selection of victims from cattle as well as from sheep and goats—are to be explained by the terminology of the Deuteronomist; in Deut. 16:8 the term *'aṣereth*, which is used to describe the seventh day of the Passover, is perhaps to be regarded as the mistake of a copyist—it would be more appropriate in a description of the feast of Weeks.

References to the *ḥaggim* in the Hebrew histories and prophetic writings show that they were joyous occasions. But the Passover, unlike Tabernacles, was also a festival at which, as we have seen, the people played the principal part. Ezekiel's proposal, then, to amend the Passover by adapting it to the framework of his authoritarian theocracy was doomed to failure. It was probably after the Exile that the ritual exodus at the Passover was abandoned. The papyrus on the Passover of the Jews at Elephantine illustrates the manner in which the Passover week was celebrated outside Jerusalem; the people rested on the first and last days, and avoided leaven throughout the seven days. The Pesaḥ, on the other hand, was observed only at the Temple at Jerusalem. A good picture of this is given in documents of the Chronicler's School, notably 2 Chr. 30. Particular attention was paid to ritual cleanness; as foreshadowed already by the centralization of ritual in Deut. 16, the blood and the fat of the Pesaḥ victims were handled by the priests in accordance with the general procedure of sacrifice in the Temple.

From the Book of Jubilees we learn that in the second century B.C. the

Pesaḥ was becoming a less solemn occasion; the meal was now accompanied by wine, and the great crowds of pilgrims made necessary a sharper definition of the hour of the Pesaḥ sacrifice. By the time of Philo this trend had reached completion. Political events had led to the final abandonment of the military census at the Pesaḥ; the Pesaḥ sacrifice was still performed only in the Temple, but the bounds of the Temple were extended to include the city, and the meal was eaten in the houses of the city—though still by households. The solemn waving of the Sheaf was now held by the Pharisees on the second day of the Passover week, instead of the day after the Passover week—this is indicated already by the LXX of Lev. 23. Sectarians, on the other hand, who regarded the 'morrow after the Sabbath' as Sunday and who used (like the writer of the Book of Jubilees) to wave the barley Sheaf on the first Sunday after the Passover week, now performed the ceremony on the Sunday within the Passover week. By the time of Jesus the Passover entailed considerable preparation. The character of the household unit by which the Pesaḥ was performed had changed. The household might now include also women and boys above the age of twelve, or it might be extended to include friends outside the family circle; sectarians—and the early Christians—were inclined to adopt the latter practice. Josephus informs us that the Sheaf which was solemnly waved in the Temple on the second day of the Passover week was now treated like the firstfruits offering of grain. Finally, the Mishnah describes the minutiae of the Passover ceremonial in the last decades of the Temple. For all its complexity and its modification to suit changed social conditions, we can still detect in it motifs which had characterized this New Year spring festival from ancient times.

SELECT BIBLIOGRAPHY

AALEN, S., *Die Begriffe 'Licht' und 'Finsternis' im Alten Testament, im Spätjudentum und im Rabbinismus* (Skrifter utgitt av Det Norske Videnskaps-Akademie i Oslo. Hist.-fil. Klasse, No. 1), 1951.

ABEL, F.-M., *Géographie de la Palestine*, ii, 1938.

ACKROYD, P. R., 'Criteria for the Maccabean Dating of Old Testament Literature', *VT* iii, 1953, 113.

ADLER, S., 'Der Versöhnungstag in der Bibel, sein Ursprung und seine Bedeutung', *ZAW* iii, 1883, 178.

AESCOLY, A. Z., *Sepher haFalashim* (in Hebrew), 1943.

ALBECK, CH., *Das Buch der Jubiläen und die Halachah* (Beilage zum Jahresbericht der Hochschule für die Wissenschaft des Judentums in Berlin), 1930.

ALBRIGHT, W. F., 'The Nebuchadnezzar and Neriglissar Chronicles', *BASOR*, No. 143, Oct. 1956, 28.

—— 'The High Place in Ancient Palestine', in *Volume du Congrès Strasbourg 1956* (Supplements to *VT*, vol. iv), 1957, 242.

ALFÖLDI, A., *A Festival of Isis in Rome under the Christian Emperors of the IVth Century* (Dissertationes Pannonicae, ser. 2, fasc. 7), 1937.

ALLEGRO, J. M., 'A Newly Discovered Fragment of a Commentary on Psalm XXXVII from Qumran', *PEQ* lxxxvi, 1954, 69.

ALLIOT, M., 'Cultes d'Horus à Edfou au temps des Ptolémées', *RHR* cxxxvii, 1950, 59.

ALT, A., 'Zelte und Hütten', *Alttestamentliche Studien Friedrich Nötscher . . . gewidmet*, ed. H. Junker and J. Botterweck, 1950, 16.

—— 'Zu *hitʿammēr*', *VT* ii, 1952, 153.

—— *Kleine Schriften zur Geschichte des Volkes Israel*, 1953.

ANKORI, Z., 'Some Aspects of Karaite–Rabbanite Relations in Byzantium on the Eve of the First Crusade', *PAAJR* xxv, 1956, 157.

—— *Karaites in Byzantium*, 1959.

ANTOINE, P., art. 'Garizim', *Dict. Bib. Suppl.* iii, 1938.

ARBESMANN, R., 'Fasting and Prophecy in Pagan and Christian Antiquity', *Traditio*, vii, 1949–51, 1.

ARNOLD, W. R., 'The Passover Papyrus from Elephantine', *JBL* xxxi, 1912, 1.

AUERBACH, E., 'Die Feste im alten Israel', *VT* viii, 1958, 1.

AUTRUN, C., 'Sothis-Sirius et le monde préhellénique', in *Mélanges Maspero*, i, 1934–8, 529.

AUVRAY, P., art. 'Josué', *Dict. Bib. Suppl.* iv, 1941–9.

BACHER, W., *Die älteste Terminologie der jüdischen Schriftauslegung. Ein Wörterbuch der bibelexegetischen Kunstsprache der Tannaiten*, 1899.

BAETHGEN, F. W. A., *Beiträge zur semitischen Religionsgeschichte, . . . Der Gott Israel's und die Götter der Heiden*, 1888.

BALDENSPERGER, P. J., 'Religion of the Fellahîn of Palestine (Answers to Questions)', *PEFQS*, 1893, 307.

BAMMEL, F., *Das heilige Mahl im Glauben der Völker. Eine religionsphänomenologische Untersuchung*, 1950.

BAR-DEROMA, H., 'The River of Egypt (Naḥal Mizraim)', *PEQ* xcii, 1960, 37.

BARTHÉLEMY, D., 'Notes en marge sur les manuscrits de Qumran', *RB* lix, 1952, 187.

BARTHÉLEMY, D., and MILIK, J. T., *Qumran Cave I* (*Discoveries in the Judaean Desert*, vol. i), 1955.

BASSET, R., 'Recherches sur la religion des Berbères', *RHR* lxi, 1910, 291.

BATTEN, L. W., *A Critical and Exegetical Commentary on the Books of Ezra and Nehemiah* (I.C.C.), 1913.

VON BAUDISSIN, W. W. F., *Die Geschichte des alttestamentlichen Priesterthums*, 1889.

—— *Adonis und Esmun. Eine Untersuchung zur Geschichte des Glaubens an Auferstehungsgötter und an Heilgötter*, 1911.

BAUER, H., and LEANDER, P., *Historische Grammatik der hebräischen Sprache des Alten Testamentes*, 1922.

BAUER, J. B., 'Drei Tage', *Biblica*, xxxix, 1958, 354.

BAUMGARTEN, J. M., 'On the Testimony of Women in 1QSa', *JBL* lxxvi, 1957, 266.

—— 'The Beginning of the Day in the Calendar of Jubilees', *JBL* lxxvii, 1958, 355; lxxviii, 1959, 157.

BAYER, E., *Das dritte Buch Esdras und sein Verhältnis zu den Büchern Esra–Nehemia* (Biblische Studien, Bd. 16, Heft i), 1911.

BEA, A., 'De origine vocis פור . . .', *Biblica*, xxi, 1940, 198.

BEER, G., 'Miscellen', *ZAW* xxxi, 1911, 152.

—— *Pesachim* (*Ostern*). *Text, Übersetzung und Erklärung*, 1912.

BEGRICH, J., *Die Chronologie der Könige von Israel und Juda und die Quellen des Rahmens der Königsbücher*, 1929.

BELKIN, S., *Philo and the Oral Law. The Philonic Interpretation of Biblical Law in Relation to the Palestinian Halakah*, 1940.

BEN-MORDECAI, C. A., 'Notes on Chapter 33 of Exodus', *JQR* xxxi, 1940–1, 407.

BENTZEN, A., 'Bemerkungen über neuere Entwicklungen in der Pentateuchfrage', *Archiv Orientální*, xix, 1951, 226.

—— *Introduction to the Old Testament*, 1952.

BENZINGER, I., *Die Bücher der Chronik*, 1901.

—— art. 'Passover and Feast of Unleavened Bread', *EB* iii, 1902.

—— *Hebräische Archäologie*, 1907.

—— art. 'Viehzucht bei den Hebräern', *Realencyklopädie für protestantische Theologie und Kirche*, 1908.

BÉRARD, V., *Les Phéniciens et l'Odyssée*, 1927.

BERNHARDT, K.-H., *Das Problem der altorientalischen Königsideologie im Alten Testament, unter besonderer Berücksichtigung der Geschichte der Psalmenexegese dargestellt und kritisch gewürdigt* (Supplements to *VT*, vol. viii), 1961.

BERTHOLET, A., *Die Stellung der Israeliten und der Juden zu den Fremden*, 1896.

—— *Das Buch Deuteronomium, erklärt*, 1899.

—— *Die Bücher Esra und Nehemia, erklärt*, 1902.

BEWER, J. A., *Der Text des Buches Ezra. Beiträge zu seiner Wiederherstellung* (Forschungen zur Religion und Literatur des Alten und Neuen Testaments, N.F., Heft 14), 1922.

—— 'Notes on the Book of Ezekiel', *JBL* lxxii, 1953, 158.

BIČ, M., 'Bet'el — le sanctuaire du roi', *Archiv Orientální* (Hrozný Festschrift), xvii/1, 1949, 46.

BIRKELAND, H., 'Drei Bemerkungen zu den Elephantine-Papyri 1–3 (ed. Sachau)', *Acta Orientalia*, xii, 1934, 81.

BIROT, P., and DRESCH, J., *La Méditerranée et le Moyen Orient*, vols. i–ii, 1953–6.

BLINZLER, J., *Der Prozess Jesu. Das jüdische und das römische Gerichtsverfahren gegen Jesus Christus auf Grund der ältesten Zeugnisse . . .*, 1957.

BLUNT, A., *A Pilgrimage to Nejd . . .*, 1881.

BONNER, C., *The Homily on the Passion by Melito Bishop of Sardis . . .* (Studies and Documents, vol. 12), 1940.

BORGEN, P., '"At the age of twenty" in 1QSa', *Revue de Qumran*, x, 1961, 267.
BOTTÉRO, J., *Archives royales de Mari*, vii. *Textes économiques et administratifs*, 1957.
BOTTERWECK, G. J., 'Der Sabbat im Alten Testamente', *Theologische Quartalschrift*, cxxxiv, 1954, 134, 448.
BOWMAN, J., 'Is the Samaritan Calendar the Old Zadokite One?', *PEQ* xci, 1959, 23.
BRAUN, F.-M., 'L'Arrière-fond judaïque du quatrième évangile et la communauté de l'alliance', *RB* lxii, 1955, 5.
BREASTED, J. H., *History of Egypt*, 1950.
BROCKELMANN, C., *Grundriss der vergleichenden Grammatik der semitischen Sprachen*, 1907–13.
BROWNLEE, W. H., 'Light on the Manual of Discipline (DSD) from the Book of Jubilees', *BASOR*, No. 123, Oct. 1951, 30.
BRUNET, A.-M., 'Le Chroniste et ses sources', *RB* lx, 1953, 481; lxi, 1954, 349.
BÜCHLER, A., *Die Priester und der Cultus im letzten Jahrzehnt des Jerusalemischen Tempels*, 1895.
—— 'Zur Geschichte der Tempelmusik und der Tempelpsalmen', *ZAW* xix, 1899, 96, 329; xx, 1900, 97.
—— *Das Synedrion in Jerusalem und das grosse Beth-din in der Quaderkammer des Jerusalemischen Tempels*, 1902.
—— 'L'Enterrement des criminels d'après le Talmud et le Midrasch', *REJ* xlvi, 1903, 74.
—— *Der galiläische 'Am-ha'Areṣ des zweiten Jahrhunderts. Beiträge zur innern Geschichte des palästinischen Judentums in den ersten zwei Jahrhunderten*, 1906.
—— *Types of Jewish-Palestinian Piety from 70 B.C.E. to 70 C.E. The Ancient Pious Men*, 1922.
—— 'Studies in the Book of Jubilees', *REJ* lxxxii, 1926, 253.
—— 'Traces des idées et des coutumes hellénistiques dans le livre des Jubilés', *REJ* lxxxix, 1930, 321.
—— *Studies in Jewish History* (ed. I. Brodie and J. Rabbinowitz), 1956.
BUDDE, K., 'Das Deuteronomium und die Reform Josias. Ein Vortragsentwurf', *ZAW* xliv, 1926, 177.
BURCHARD, C., *Bibliographie zu den Handschriften vom Toten Meer*, 1957.
BURCKHARDT, J. L., *Travels in Syria and the Holy Land*, 1822.
—— *Travels in Arabia* . . ., 1829.
—— *Notes on the Bedouins and Wahábys* . . ., 1830.
VAN BUREN, E. D., 'Ear of Corn', in *Miscellanea Orientalia dedicata Antonio Deimel* . . . (Analecta Orientalia, No. 12), 1935, 327.
BURKILL, T. A., 'The Competence of the Sanhedrin', *Vigiliae Christianae*, x, 1956, 80.
—— 'The Last Supper', *Numen*, iii, 1956, 161.
BURNEY, C. F., *Notes on the Hebrew Text of the Books of Kings*, 1903.
BURROWS, M., *The Dead Sea Scrolls of St. Mark's Monastery*, i, 1950; ii, 1951.

CANAAN, T., 'Mohammedan Saints and Sanctuaries in Palestine', *JPOS* iv, 1924, 1; v, 1925, 163; vi, 1926, 1, 117; vii, 1927, 1.
CARMIGNAC, J., 'Les Citations de l'Ancien Testament dans "La Guerre des fils de lumière contre les fils de ténèbres"', *RB* lxiii, 1956, 234.
CARRINGTON, P., *The Primitive Christian Calendar. A Study in the Making of the Marcan Gospel* . . ., 1952.
CAUSSE, A., *Du groupe ethnique à la communauté religieuse. Le Problème sociologique de la religion d'Israël* (Études d'histoire et de philosophie religieuses, fasc. 33), 1937.
CAZELLES, H., art. 'Le Nouvel An en Israël', *Dict. Bib. Suppl.* vi, 1957–60.

CAZELLES, H., 'La Mission d'Esdras', *VT* iv, 1954, 113.
ČERNY, L., *The Day of Yahweh and Some Relevant Problems*, 1948.
CHAPMAN, A. T., and STREANE, A. W., *The Book of Leviticus*, 1914.
CHARLES, H., *Tribus moutonnières du Moyen-Euphrate*, 1939.
CHARLES, R. H., *The Ethiopic Version of the Hebrew Book of Jubilees*, 1895.
—— 'The Book of Jubilees', in *The Apocrypha and Pseudepigrapha of the Old Testament*, ed. R. H. Charles, 1913, ii. 1.
—— *The Book of Jubilees*, 1917.
CHAVEL, C. B., 'The Releasing of a Prisoner on the Eve of Passover in Ancient Jerusalem', *JBL* lx, 1941, 273.
CHRISTIAN, V., 'Zur Herkunft des Purim-Festes', *Alttestamentliche Studien Friedrich Nötscher . . . gewidmet*, 1950, 33.
CHWOLSON, D., *Die Ssabier und der Ssabismus*, 1856.
—— *Das letzte Passamahl Christi und der Tag seines Todes . . .* (Mémoires de l'Académie impériale des sciences de Saint-Pétersbourg, tome 41, no. 1), 1892.
CIRLOT, F. L., *The Early Eucharist*, 1939.
CLERMONT-GANNEAU, C., *Recueil d'archéologie orientale*, i, 1888.
COLSON, F. H., and WHITAKER, G. H., *Philo* (Loeb Classical Library), 1929–41.
COOK, S. A., '1 Esdras', in R. H. Charles, *The Apocrypha and Pseudepigrapha of the Old Testament*, 1913, i. 1.
—— 'The Significance of the Elephantine Papyri for the History of Hebrew Religion', *AJT* xix, 1915, 346.
—— *The Religion of Ancient Palestine in the Light of Archaeology*, 1930.
COOKE, G. A., *A Text-book of North-Semitic Inscriptions*, 1903.
—— *The Book of Joshua*, 1918.
—— *A Critical and Exegetical Commentary on the Book of Ezekiel* (I.C.C.), 1936.
COUROYER, B., 'L'Origine égyptienne du mot "Pâque"', *RB* lxii, 1955, 481.
COWLEY, A. E., *Aramaic Papyri of the Fifth Century B.C.*, 1923.
CRAWLEY, A. E., *The Mystic Rose. A Study of Primitive Marriage*, 1932.
CRÉTEN, J., 'La Pâque des Samaritains', *RB* xxxi, 1922, 434.
CROSS, F. M., and FREEDMAN, D. N., *Early Hebrew Orthography. A Study of the Epigraphic Evidence . . .*, 1952.
—— 'A New Qumran Biblical Fragment Related to the Original Hebrew Underlying the Septuagint', *BASOR*, No. 132, Dec. 1953, 15.
CROWFOOT, G. M., and BALDENSPERGER, L., *From Cedar to Hyssop. A Study in the Folklore of Plants in Palestine*, 1932.
CRUSIUS, O., 'Über das Phantastische im Mimus', *Neue Jahrbücher für das klassische Altertum*, xxv, 1910, 81.
CULLMANN, O., *The State in the New Testament*, 1957.
CUMONT, F., 'Les Mystères de Samothrace et l'année caniculaire', *RHR* cxxvii, 1944, 55.
CURTISS, S. I., *Primitive Semitic Religion Today . . .*, 1902.

DALMAN, G. H., *Palästinischer Diwan . . .*, 1901.
—— *Arbeit und Sitte in Palästina*, 1928–39.
—— *Jerusalem und sein Gelände*, 1930.
DANBY, H., *The Mishnah . . .*, 1933.
DAUBE, D., *The New Testament and Rabbinic Judaism*, 1956.
DAVID, M., '*Hitʿāmēr* (Deut. xxi 14; xxiv 7)', *VT* i, 1951, 219.
DELAPORTE, L., *Les Hittites*, 1936.
DELATTE, L., 'Recherches sur quelques fêtes mobiles du calendrier romain', *Antiquité classique*, v, 1936, 381; vi, 1937, 93.
DERENBOURG, J., *Essai sur l'histoire et la géographie de la Palestine d'après les Thalmuds et les autres sources rabbiniques*, 1867.

DHORME, É., *L'Évolution religieuse d'Israël*, 1937.
—— *Les Religions de Babylonie et d'Assyrie*, 1945– .
VAN DIJK, J., 'La Fête du nouvel an dans un texte de Šulgi', *Bibliotheca orientalis*, xi, 1954, 83.
DILLMANN, A., *Die Bücher Exodus und Leviticus*, 1880.
—— *Die Bücher Numeri, Deuteronomium und Josua*, 1886.
DODD, C. H., *The Interpretation of the Fourth Gospel*, 1953.
DONIACH, N. S., *Purim or the Feast of Esther*, 1933.
DOUGHTY, C. M., *Travels in Arabia Deserta*, 1926.
DOUTTÉ, E., *Magie et religion dans l'Afrique du Nord*, 1909.
DRIOTON, É., and VANDIER, J., *Les Peuples de l'orient méditerranéen, II. L'Égypte* (Clio. Introduction aux études historiques, vol. i, pt. 2), 1952.
—— 'La Date de l'Exode', *Revue d'histoire et de philosophie religieuses*, xxxv, 1955, 36.
DRIVER, G. R., 'Studies in the Vocabulary of the Old Testament. V', *JTS* xxxiv, 1933, 33.
—— 'Linguistic and Textual Problems: Isaiah xl–lxvi', *JTS* xxxvi, 1935, 396.
—— 'Ezekiel: Linguistic and Textual Problems', *Biblica*, xxxv, 1954, 145, 299.
—— 'Three Technical Terms in the Pentateuch', *JSS* i, 1956, 97.
—— *Aramaic Documents of the Fifth Century B.C.*, 1957.
DRIVER, S. R., *A Critical and Exegetical Commentary on Deuteronomy* (I.C.C.), 1895.
—— *The Book of Exodus*, 1911.
—— *An Introduction to the Literature of the Old Testament*, 1913.
—— *Notes on the Hebrew Text and the Topography of the Books of Samuel*, 1913.
DUMERMUTH, F., 'Zur deuteronomischen Kulttheologie und ihren Voraussetzungen', *ZAW* lxx, 1958, 59.
DUPONT-SOMMER, A., 'Sur la fête de la Pâque dans les documents araméens d'Eléphantine', *REJ*, N.S. vii (cvii), 1946–7, 39.
—— 'Sabbat et Parascève à Éléphantine d'après des ostraca araméens inédits', in *Mémoires présentés par divers savants à l'Académie des Inscriptions et Belles-Lettres*, 1950.
DUS, J., 'Die Analyse zweier Ladeerzählungen des Josuabuches', *ZAW* lxxii, 1960, 107.
DUSSAUD, R., *Les Religions des Hittites et des Hourrites* (Les Anciennes Religions orientales, vol. ii.), 1945.
—— *La Pénétration des arabes en Syrie avant l'Islam*, 1955.
—— and MACLER, F., *Voyage archéologique au Safa et dans le Djebel Ed-Druz*, 1901.

EERDMANS, B. D., 'Das Mazzoth-Fest', in *Orientalische Studien Theodor Nöldeke zum siebzigsten Geburtstag gewidmet . . .*, 1906, ii. 671.
—— *Alttestamentliche Studien*, 1908–12.
—— 'Passover and the Days of Unleavened Bread', *Expositor*, viii, 1909, 448.
EHRLICH, A. B., *Randglossen zur hebräischen Bibel . . .*, 1908–14.
EHRLICH, E. L., *Die Kultsymbolik im Alten Testament und im nachbiblischen Judentum*, 1959.
EISSFELDT, O., *Erstlinge und Zehnten im Alten Testament: ein Beitrag zur Geschichte des israelitisch-jüdischen Kultus*, 1917.
—— *Einleitung in das Alte Testament*, 1956.
ELHORST, H. J., 'Die deuteronomischen Jahresfeste', *ZAW* xlii, 1924, 136.
EMERTON, J. A., *Peshitta of the Wisdom of Solomon*, 1959.
ENGNELL, I., *Studies in Divine Kingship in the Ancient Near East*, 1943.
—— '*Pæsaḥ-Maṣṣōt* and the Problem of "Patternism"', *Orientalia Suecana*, i, 1952, 39.
ERMAN, A., *Die Religion der Ägypter*, 1934.
—— and RANKE, H., *Aegypten und aegyptisches Leben im Altertum*, 1923.

EWALD, H., *The Antiquities of Israel*, tr. Solly, 1876.

FAIRMAN, H. W., 'Worship and Festivals in an Egyptian Temple', *BJRL* xxxvii, 1954–5, 165.
—— 'The Kingship Rituals of Egypt', in *Myth, Ritual, and Kingship . . .*, ed. S. H. Hooke, 1958, 74.
FALKENSTEIN, A., 'akiti-Fest und akiti-Festhaus', in *Festschrift Johannes Friedrich . . . gewidmet*, 1959, 147.
FARNELL, L. R., *The Cults of the Greek States*, 1896–1909.
FICHTNER, J., 'Der AT-Text der Sapientia Salomonis', *ZAW* lvii, 1939, 155.
FINESINGER, S. B., 'Musical Instruments in O.T.', *HUCA* iii, 1926, 21.
FINKELSTEIN, L., 'The Book of Jubilees and the Rabbinic Halaka', *HTR* xvi, 1923, 39.
—— 'Some Examples of the Maccabean Halaka', *JBL* xlix, 1930, 20.
—— 'The Oldest Midrash: Pre-Rabbinic Ideals and Teachings in the Passover Haggadah', *HTR* xxxi, 1938, 291.
—— 'Pre-Maccabean Documents in the Passover Haggadah', *HTR* xxxv, 1942, 291; xxxvi, 1943, 1.
FOHRER, G., *Die Hauptprobleme des Buches Ezechiel* (Beihefte zur *ZAW*, No. 72), 1952.
FOWLER, W. WARDE, *The Roman Festivals of the Period of the Republic. An Introduction to the Study of the Religion of the Romans*, 1899.
DE FRAINE, J., *L'Aspect religieux de la royauté israélite. L'Institution monarchique dans l'Ancien Testament et dans les textes mésopotamiens* (Analecta biblica, No. 3), 1954.
FRANKFORT, H., 'State Festivals in Egypt and Mesopotamia', *Journal of the Warburg and Courtauld Institutes*, xv, 1952, 1.
FRAZER, J. G., *Folklore in the Old Testament*, 1918.
—— *The Golden Bough. Adonis Attis Osiris*, 1936.
—— *The Golden Bough. The Dying God*, 1936.
—— *The Golden Bough. Magic Art*, 1936.
FRÜCHTEL, L., 'Griechische Fragmente zu Philons Quaestiones in Genesin et in Exodum', *ZAW* lv, 1937, 108.
FURLANI, G., *La Religione degli Hittiti*, 1936.

GADD, C. J., *Ideas of Divine Rule in the Ancient East*, 1948.
—— 'The Harran Inscriptions of Nabonidus', *Anatolian Studies*, viii, 1958, 35.
GANDZ, S., 'The Calendar of ancient Israel', in *Homenaje a Millás-Vallicrosa*, 1954–6, i. 623.
GARBELL, I., 'The Dances of Maidens in Ramallah on Palm Sunday' (in Hebrew), *Edoth*, ii, 1946–7, 111.
GARDINER, A. H., and DAVIES, N. G., *The Tomb of Amenemhēt*, 1915.
GASTER, M., *The Samaritans: their History, Doctrines and Literature*, 1925.
GASTER, T. H., 'Ezekiel and the Mysteries', *JBL* lx, 1941, 289.
—— *Thespis. Ritual, Myth and Drama in the Ancient Near East*, 1950.
—— *Festivals of the Jewish Year*, 1953.
—— *Passover. Its History and Traditions*, 1958.
GAUDEFROY-DEMOMBYNES, M., *Le Pèlerinage à la Mekke* (Annales du Musée Guimet, Bibliothèque d'études, tome 33), 1923.
—— *Muslim Institutions*, tr. MacGregor, 1950.
GAUTHIER, H., *Fêtes du dieu Min* (Recherches d'archéologie, de philologie et d'histoire, tome 2), 1931.
GEIGER, A., 'Sadducäer und Pharisäer', *Jüdische Zeitschrift für Wissenschaft und Leben*, ii, 1863.

VAN GENNEP, A., *Les Rites de passage. Étude systématique des rites*, 1909.

GEORGE, A., 'Fautes contre Yahweh dans les livres de Samuel', *RB* liii, 1946, 161.

GEORGE, J. F. L., *Die älteren Jüdischen Feste, mit einer Kritik der Gesetzgebung des Pentateuch*, 1835.

GERSCHEL, L., 'Saliens de Mars et Saliens de Quirinus', *RHR* cxxxviii, 1950, 145.

GESE, H., *Der Verfassungsentwurf des Ezechiel* (*Kap. 40–48*) *traditionsgeschichtlich untersucht* (Beiträge zur historischen Theologie, Band 25), 1957.

GINZBERG, L., *The Legends of the Jews*, tr. Radin and Szold, 1946–7.

GLASSON, T. F., 'The "Passover", a Misnomer: The Meaning of the Verb *Pasach*', *JTS*, N.S., x, 1959, 79.

GOGUEL, M., *La Vie de Jésus*, 1932.

GOLDBERG, P. S., *Karaite Liturgy and its Relation to Synagogue Worship*, 1957.

GOODENOUGH, E. R., 'Philo's Exposition of the Law', *HTR* xxvi, 1933, 109.

—— *An Introduction to Philo Judaeus*, 1940.

—— *Jewish Symbols in the Greco-Roman Period*, v–vi, 'Fish, Bread and Wine', 1956.

GORDIS, R., 'The Heptad as an Element of Biblical and Rabbinic Style', *JBL* lxii, 1943, 17.

GORDON, C. H., *Ugaritic Literature—A Comprehensive Translation of the Poetic and Prose Texts*, 1949.

—— 'Šamši-Adad's Military Texts from Mari', *Archiv Orientální*, xviii, 1950, 199.

—— 'Sabbatical Cycle or Seasonal Pattern?', *Orientalia*, xxiii, 1953, 79.

—— *Ugaritic Manual* (Analecta Orientalia, No. 35), 1955.

VAN GOUDOEVER, J., *Biblical Calendars*, 1959.

GRAETZ, H., 'Das Korbfest der Erstlinge bei Philo', *Monatsschrift für Geschichte und Wissenschaft des Judenthums*, xxvi, 1877, 433.

—— *Geschichte der Juden von den ältesten Zeiten bis auf die Gegenwart*, ed. M. Brann, iii, 1905–6.

GRANQVIST, H. N., *Marriage Conditions in a Palestinian Village* (Commentationes Humanarum Litterarum, tome iii, No. 8, 1931; tome vi, No. 8, 1935), 1931–5.

—— *Birth and Childhood among the Arabs. Studies in a Muhammadan Village in Palestine*, 1947.

GRAY, G. B., *A Critical and Exegetical Commentary on Numbers* (I.C.C.), 1903.

—— 'The Misuse of the Term "Lamb" in the E.V.', *Expositor*, xxii, 1921, 241.

—— *Sacrifice in the Old Testament: its Theory and Practice*, 1925.

—— 'Passover and Unleavened Bread: the Laws of J, E, and D', *JTS* xxxvii, 1936, 241.

GRAY, J., 'Cultic Affinities between Israel and Ras Shamra', *ZAW* lxii, 1950, 207.

—— *The Legacy of Canaan. The Ras Shamra Texts and their Relevance to the Old Testament. . . .* (Supplements to *VT*, vol. v), 1957.

GREENUP, A. W., 'Fasts and Fasting', in *Essays in Honour of the Very Rev. Dr. J. H. Hertz*, ed. I. Epstein, E. Levine, and C. Roth, 1942, 203.

GRELOT, P., 'Études sur le "Papyrus Pascal" d'Éléphantine', *VT* iv, 1954, 349.

—— 'Le Papyrus pascal d'Éléphantine et le problème du Pentateuque', *VT* v, 1955, 250.

—— 'La dernière étape de la rédaction sacerdotale', *VT* vi, 1956, 174.

GRESSMANN, H., *Musik und Musikinstrumente im Alten Testament. Eine religionsgeschichtliche Studie*, 1903.

—— *Mose und seine Zeit. Ein Kommentar zu den Mose-Sagen . . .*, 1913.

—— *Die Schriften des Alten Testaments. Die Anfänge Israels*, i/2, 1922.

—— *Tod und Auferstehung des Osiris nach Festbräuchen und Umzügen . . .*, 1923.

—— 'Josia und das Deuteronomium', *ZAW* xlii, 1924, 321.

GRINTZ, J. M., *Sefer Yehudith* (in Hebrew), 1957.

—— 'Hebrew as the Spoken and Written Language in the Last Days of the Second Temple', *JBL* lxxix, 1960, 32.

GRÜNEISEN, C., *Der Ahnenkultus und die Urreligion Israels*, 1900.
GUILDING, A., *The Fourth Gospel and Jewish Worship. A Study of the Relation of St. John's Gospel to the Ancient Jewish Lectionary*, 1960.
GURNEY, O. R., *The Hittites*, 1952.
—— 'Hittite Kingship', in *Myth, Ritual, and Kingship* . . ., ed. S. H. Hooke, 1958, 105.
GUTESMAN, S., 'Sur le calendrier en usage chez les Israélites au Ve siècle avant notre ère', *REJ* liii, 1907, 194.
GUTHE, H., 'Passahfest nach Dtn 16', in *Abhandlungen zur semitischen Religionskunde und Sprachwissenschaft Wolf Wilhelm Grafen von Baudissin . . . überreicht* . . . (Beihefte zur *ZAW*, No. 33), ed. W. Frankenberg and F. Küchler, 1918, 217.
—— 'Zum Passah der jüdischen Religionsgemeinde', *Theologische Studien und Kritiken*, xcvi–xcvii, 1925, 144.

HAAG, H., 'Ursprung und Sinn der alttestamentlichen Paschafeier', *Luzerner Theologische Studien*, i, 1954, 17.
—— art. 'Sabbat', *Bibel-Lexikon*, 1956.
—— art. 'Pâque', *Dict. Bib. Suppl.* vi, 1957–60.
HALDAR, A., *The Notion of the Desert in Sumero-Accadian and West-Semitic Religions* (Uppsala Universitets Årsskrift, 1950, No. 3), 1950.
HALKIN, A. S., 'Samaritan Polemics against the Jews', *PAAJR* vii, 1935–6, 13.
HÄNEL, J., 'Recht des Opferschlachtens in der chronistischen Literatur', *ZAW* lv, 1937, 46.
HANOVER, S., *Das Festgesetz der Samaritaner nach Ibrâhîm ibn Ja'ḳûb*, 1904.
HARRISON, J. E., *Prolegomena to the Study of Greek Religion*, 1922.
—— *Themis. A Study of the Social Origins of Greek Religion*, 1927.
HAUPT, P., 'Babylonian Elements in the Levitic Ritual', *JBL* xix, 1900, 55.
HEAWOOD, P. J., 'The Time of the Last Supper', *JQR* xlii, 1951–2, 37.
HEINEMANN, I., *Philons griechische und jüdische Bildung. Kulturvergleichende Untersuchungen zu Philons Darstellung der jüdischen Gesetze*, 1932.
HELCK, W., 'Die Herkunft des abydenischen Osirisrituals', *Archiv Orientální*, xx, 1952, 72.
—— 'Bemerkungen zum Ritual des dramatischen Ramesseumspapyrus', *Orientalia*, xxiii, 1954, 383.
HEMPEL, J., 'Eine Vorfrage zum Erstgeburtsopfer', *ZAW* liv, 1936, 311.
HENNINGER, J., 'Les Fêtes de printemps chez les Arabes et leurs implications historiques', *Revista do Museu Paulista*, N.S., iv, 1950, 389.
—— 'Was bedeutet die rituelle Teilung eines Tieres in zwei Hälften?', *Biblica*, xxxiv, 1953, 344.
—— 'Ist der sogenannte Nilus-Bericht eine brauchbare religionsgeschichtliche Quelle?', *Anthropos*, l, 1955, 81.
—— 'Zum Verbot des Knochenzerbrechens bei den Semiten', in *Studi orientalistici in onore di Giorgio Levi della Vida*, i, 1956, 448.
HIGGINS, A. J. B., *The Lord's Supper in the New Testament* (Studies in Biblical Theology, No. 6), 1952.
HILGENFELD, A., *Der Paschastreit der alten Kirche nach seiner Bedeutung für die Kirchengeschichte*, 1860.
HOENIG, S. B., *The Great Sanhedrin. A Study of the Origin, Development, Composition and Functions of the Bet Din ha-Gadol during the Second Jewish Commonwealth*, 1953.
HOFFMANN, G., 'Kleinigkeiten', *ZAW* ii, 1882, 175.
HOLLIS, F. J., 'The Sun-cult and the Temple at Jerusalem', in S. H. Hooke, *Myth and Ritual* . . ., 1933, 87.

HOLMES, S., 'Wisdom of Solomon', in R. H. Charles, *Apocrypha and Pseudepigrapha of the Old Testament*, 1913, i. 518.
HOLZINGER, H., *Exodus*, 1900.
HOMMEL, F., *Die altisraelitische Überlieferung in inschriftlicher Beleuchtung. Ein Einspruch gegen die Aufstellung der modernen Pentateuchkritik*, 1897.
HOMOLLE, TH., 'Inscriptions de Delphes: règlements de la phratrie des ΛΑΒΥΑΔΑΙ', *Bulletin de Correspondance hellénique*, xix, 1895, 5.
HONEYMAN, A. M., 'Hebrew סַף, "Basin, Goblet"', *JTS* xxxvii, 1936, 56.
HOOKE, S. H., *The Origins of Early Semitic Ritual*, 1938.
—— 'The Theory and Practice of Substitution', *VT* ii, 1952, 2.
—— *Babylonian and Assyrian Religion*, 1953.
—— *The Siege Perilous. Essays in Biblical Anthropology and Kindred Subjects*, 1956.
VAN HOONACKER, A., *Une Communauté Judéo-Araméenne à Éléphantine, en Égypte, aux VIe et Ve siècles av. J.-C.*, 1915.
VAN HOORN, G., *Choes and Anthesteria*, 1951.
HORN, S. H., and WOOD, L. H., 'The Fifth-Century Jewish Calendar at Elephantine', *JNES* xiii, 1954, 1.
HORST, F., 'Die Kultusreform des Königs Josia', *ZDMG* lxxvii, 1923, 220.
—— *Das Privilegrecht Jahves. Rechtsgeschichtliche Untersuchungen zum Deuteronomium* (Forschungen zur Religion und Literatur des Alten und Neuen Testaments, N.F., Heft 28), 1930.
HOSKYNS, E. C., *The Fourth Gospel*, ed. F. N. Davey, 1947.
HROZNÝ, B., *Das Getreide im alten Babylonien. Ein Beitrag zur Kultur- und Wirtschaftsgeschichte des alten Orients* (Sitzungsberichte der kais. Akademie der Wissenschaften in Wien, Phil.-hist. Klasse, 173/i), 1913.
HULST, A. R., 'Der Name "Israel" im Deuteronomium', *Oudtestamentische studiën*, ix, 1951, 65.
HUMBERT, P., *La Terouʿa. Analyse d'un rite biblique* (Université de Neuchâtel. Recueil de travaux publiés par la Faculté des Lettres. Fasc. 23), 1946.

IRWIN, W. A., 'Ezekiel Research since 1943', *VT* iii, 1953, 54.

JACOB, G., *Studien in arabischen Dichtern. 3. Das Leben der vorislamischen Beduinen*, 1895.
JACOBSOHN, H., *Die dogmatische Stellung des Königs in der Theologie der alten Ägypter* (Ägyptologische Forschungen, Heft 8), 1939.
JAMES, E. O., *Origins of Sacrifice. A study in comparative religion*, 1933.
JASTROW, M., 'On ממחרת השבת', *AJSL* xxx, 1913–14, 94.
JAUBERT, A., 'Le Calendrier des Jubilés et de la Secte de Qumrân: ses origines bibliques', *VT* iii, 1953, 250.
—— *La Date de la Cène*, 1957.
—— 'Le Calendrier des Jubilés et les jours liturgiques de la semaine', *VT* vii, 1957, 35.
—— 'Jésus et le calendrier de Qumrân', *New Testament Studies*, vii, 1960, 1.
JAUSSEN, J. A., *Coutumes des Arabes au pays de Moab*, 1908.
—— *Mission archéologique en Arabie* (Publications de la Société Française de Fouilles archéologiques, No. 2), 1909.
—— *Coutumes palestiniennes. 1. Naplouse et son district*, 1927.
JEAN, C. F., *Archives royales de Mari. ii. Lettres diverses*, 1950.
JEREMIAS, J., *Die Passahfeier der Samaritaner und ihre Bedeutung für das Verständnis der alttestamentlichen Passahüberlieferung* (Beihefte zur *ZAW*, No. 59), 1932.
—— art. '*Πάσχα*', *Theologisches Wörterbuch zum Neuen Testament*, ed. G. Friedrich, v, 1954.
—— *Eucharistic Words of Jesus*, tr. Ehrhardt, 1955.
JOHNSON, A. R., *Sacral Kingship in Ancient Israel*, 1955.

Joüon, P., *Grammaire de l'hébreu biblique*, 1923.
Junge, E., *Der Wiederaufbau des Heerwesens des Reiches Juda unter Josia* (Beiträge zur Wissenschaft vom Alten und Neuen Testament. Folge 4, Heft 23), 1937.
Juster, J., *Les Juifs dans l'empire romain. Leur condition juridique, économique et sociale*, 1914.

Kaminka, A., 'Hillel's Life and Work', *JQR* xxx, 1939–40, 107.
Kamphausen, A. H. H., *Das Verhältnis des Menschenopfers zur israelitischen Religion*, 1896.
Kapelrud, A. S., *Baal in the Ras Shamra Texts*, 1952.
Kappelmacher, A., 'Zur Tragödie der hellenistischen Zeit', *Wiener Studien. Zeitschrift für klassische Philologie*, xliv, 1924–5, 69.
Kees, H., *Der Opfertanz des ägyptischen Königs*, 1912.
—— *Ägypten*, 1933.
—— *Der Götterglaube im alten Ägypten* (Mitteilungen der Vorderasiatisch-Ägyptischen Gesellschaft, Band 45), 1941.
Kennedy, A. R. S., art, 'Bread', *EB* i, 1899.
Kilpatrick, G. D., *The Trial of Jesus*, 1953.
Klein, H., 'Das Klima Palästinas auf Grund der alten hebräischen Quellen', *ZDPV* xxxvii, 1914, 217, 297.
Klein, S., 'Palästinisches im Jubiläenbuch', *ZDPV* lvii, 1934, 7.
Knox, W. L., 'John 13:1–30', *HTR* xliii, 1950, 161.
Knudtzon, J. A., *Die El-Amarna-Tafeln* (Vorderasiatische Bibliothek, Stück 2), 1915.
Kohler, K., 'Verbot des Knochenzerbrechens', *Archiv für Religionswissenschaft*, xiii, 1910, 153.
—— 'The Sabbath and Festivals in Pre-exilic and Exilic Times', *JAOS* xxxvii, 1917, 209.
Kraeling, E. G., *The Brooklyn Museum Aramaic Papyri*, 1953.
Kraus, H. J., 'Gilgal — ein Beitrag zur Kultusgeschichte Israels', *VT* i, 1951, 181.
—— *Gottesdienst in Israel. Studien zur Geschichte des Laubhüttenfestes*, 1954.
—— 'Zur Geschichte des Passah-Massot-Festes im Alten Testament', *Evangelische Theologie*, xviii, 1958, 47.
Krauss, S., 'Double inhumation chez les Juifs', *REJ* xcvii, 1934, 1.
von Kremer, A., *Studien zur vergleichenden Culturgeschichte, vorzüglich nach arabischen Quellen* (Sitzungsberichte der phil.-hist. Classe der kaiserlichen Akademie der Wissenschaften, Wien, Band 120/iii, viii), 1890.
Kuenen, A., *The Religion of Israel to the Fall of the Jewish State*, tr. May, 1875.
Kugler, F. X., *Von Moses bis Paulus. Forschungen zur Geschichte Israels, nach biblischen und profangeschichtlichen, insbesondere neuen keilinschriftlichen Quellen*, 1922.
Kuiper, K., 'Le Poète juif Ezéchiel', *REJ* xlvi, 1903, 48, 161.
—— 'Ad Ezechielem Poetam Judaeum curae secundae', *Rivista di Storia antica*, viii, 1904, 62.
Kupper, J. R., 'Le Recensement dans les textes de Mari', in A. Parrot, *Studia Mariana*, 1950, 99.
—— *Les Nomades en Mésopotamie au temps des rois de Mari* (Bibliothèque de la Faculté de Philosophie et Lettres de l'Université de Liège, fasc. 142), 1957.
Kutsch, E., 'Die Wurzel עצר im Hebräischen', *VT* ii, 1952, 57.
—— art. 'Feste und Feiern. II. In Israel', *Die Religion in Geschichte und Gegenwart* (3rd ed.), ed. K. Galling, &c., ii, 1958.
—— 'Erwägungen zur Geschichte der Passafeier und des Massotfestes', *Zeitschrift für Theologie und Kirche*, lv, 1958, 1.
—— 'Der Kalender des Jubiläenbuches und das Alte und das Neue Testament', *VT* xi, 1961, 39.

LABAT, R., *Le Caractère religieux de la royauté assyro-babylonienne* (Études d'Assyriologie, tome 2), 1939.

LAGRANGE, M.-J., *Études sur les religions sémitiques*, 1905.

LAMBDIN, T. O., 'Egyptian Loan Words in the Old Testament', *JAOS* lxxiii, 1953, 145.

LAMMENS, H., *L'Arabie occidentale avant l'hégire*, 1928.

VON LANDBERG, C., *Arabica*, v, 1898.

LANDESDORFER, S., *Studien zum biblischen Versöhnungstag* (Alttestamentliche Abhandlungen, x), 1924.

LANDSBERGER, B., *Der kultische Kalender der Babylonier und Assyrer* (Leipziger semitische Studien, Band 6, Heft 1/2), 1915.

LANE, E. W., *An Account of the Manners and Customs of the Modern Egyptians* (Dent, 1936).

LANGDON, S., *Babylonian Menologies and the Semitic Calendars*, 1935.

DE LANGHE, R., *Les Textes de Ras Shamra-Ugarit et leurs rapports avec le milieu biblique de l'Ancien Testament*, 1945.

—— 'Myth, Ritual, and Kingship in the Ras Shamra Tablets', in *Myth, Ritual, and Kingship* . . ., ed. S. H. Hooke, 1958, 122.

LARGEMENT, R., art. 'Nouvel An dans la religion suméro-akkadienne', *Dict. Bib. Suppl.* vi, 1957–60.

—— 'L'Arbre de vie dans la religion sumérienne', in *Akten des XXIV. Internationalen Orientalisten-Kongresses, München 1957*, ed. H. Franke, 1959, 188.

LAUTERBACH, J. Z., art. 'Philo', *JE* x, 1925.

LEACH, E. R., A possible method of intercalation for the calendar of the Book of Jubilees', *VT* vii, 1957, 392.

LEES, G. R., *Village Life in Palestine*, 1905.

LESLAU, W., *Falasha Anthology* (Yale Judaica Series, vol. 6), 1951.

—— *Coutumes et Croyances des Falachas* (*Juifs d'Abyssinie*) (Travaux et Mémoires de l'Institut d'Ethnologie, lxi), 1957.

LESZYNSKY, R., *Die Sadduzäer*, 1912.

LEVIAS, C., 'On the Etymology of the Term Ševâ', *American Journal of Philology*, xvi, 1895, 28.

LEWY, J., 'Ein Vortrag über das Ritual des Pesach-Abends', *Jahresbericht des jüdisch-theologischen Seminars . . . Breslau*, 1904, 13.

—— 'Old Assyrian *puru'um* and *pūrum*', *Revue Hittite et Asianique*, v, 1938–40, 117.

—— 'The Assyrian Calendar', *Archiv Orientální*, xi, 1939, 35.

—— 'The Feast of the 14th Day of Adar', *HUCA* xiv, 1939, 127.

—— and H., 'The Origin of the Week and the Oldest West Asiatic Calendar', *HUCA* xvii, 1942–3, 1.

LICHTENSTEIN, H., 'Die Fastenrolle. Eine Untersuchung zur jüdisch-hellenistischen Geschichte', *HUCA* viii–ix, 1931–2, 257.

LIDZBARSKI, M., *Ephemeris für semitische Epigraphik*, 1902–15.

LIETZMANN, H., 'Jüdische Passahsitten und der *ἀφικόμενος*', *ZNW* xxv, 1926, 1.

—— *Der Prozess Jesu*, Sitzungsberichte der preussischen Akademie der Wissenschaften, Phil.-hist. Klasse, 1931, 313.

LIGHTFOOT, R. H., *St. John's Gospel. A Commentary*, 1956.

LITTMANN, E., 'Das Buch der Jubiläen', in E. Kautzsch, *Die Apokryphen und Pseudepigraphen des Alten Testaments*, 1900, ii. 31.

LODS, A., *Israel, from its Beginnings to the Middle of the Eighth Century*, tr. Hooke, 1932.

LOHSE, B., *Das Passafest der Quartadecimaner* (Beiträge zur Förderung christlicher Theologie. Reihe 2, Band 54), 1953.

LOHSE, E., artt. '*Πεντηκοστή*', '*Σάββατον*', *Theologisches Wörterbuch zum Neuen Testament*, ed. G. Friedrich, vi, 1959; vii, 1960.

LÖW, I., *Die Flora der Juden*, 1924–8.
LOWY, S., 'The Motivation of Fasting in Talmudic Literature', *JJS* ix, 1958, 19.
LUCAS, A., *Ancient Egyptian Materials and Industries*, 1948.

MAAG, V., 'Erwägungen zur deuteronomischen Kultzentralisation', *VT* vi, 1956, 10.
MCCASLAND, S. V., 'Soldiers on Service', *JBL* lxii, 1943, 59.
MCCOWN, C. C., 'The Density of Population in Ancient Palestine', *JBL* lxvi, 1947, 425.
MCKENZIE, J. L., 'The "People of the Land" in the Old Testament', in *Akten des XXIV. Internationalen Orientalisten-Kongresses, München 1957*, ed. H. Franke, 1959, 206.
MCNEILE, A. H., *The Book of Exodus*, 1917.
MALAMAT, A., 'The Last Wars of the Kingdom of Judah', *JNES* ix, 1950, 218.
MALTER, H., art. 'Purim', *JE* x, 1925.
MANN, J., 'Tract by an Early Karaite Settler in Jerusalem', *JQR* xii, 1922, 257.
—— *The Bible as read and preached in the Old Synagogue*, i, 1940.
MANSON, T. W., 'The Cleansing of the Temple', *BJRL* xxxiii, 1950–1, 271.
MANTEL, H., *Studies in the History of the Sanhedrin* (Harvard Semitic Series, 17), 1961.
MARCUS, R., *Philo. Supplement, i, ii: Quaestiones et Solutiones in Genesin et Exodum* (Loeb Classical Library), 1953.
MARMORSTEIN, A., 'Comparisons between Greek and Jewish Customs and Popular Usages', in *Occident and Orient* (Gaster Anniversary Volume), ed. B. Schindler, 1936, 409.
MARMORSTEIN, E., 'The Origins of Agricultural Feudalism in the Holy Land', *PEQ* lxxxv, 1953, 111.
MARTI, K., *Geschichte der israelitischen Religion*, 1903.
MASSON, O., 'A propos d'un rituel hittite pour la lustration d'une armée . . .', *RHR* cxxxvii, 1950, 5.
MAY, H. G., 'The Relation of the Passover to the Festival of Unleavened Cakes', *JBL* lv, 1936, 65.
—— 'Some Aspects of Solar Worship at Jerusalem', *ZAW* lv, 1937, 269.
MEEK, T. J., *Hebrew Origins*, 1950.
MEISSNER, B., *Babylonien und Assyrien*, 1920–5.
MENDENHALL, G. E., 'Puppy and Lettuce in Northwest-Semitic Covenant Making', *BASOR*, No. 133, Feb. 1954, 26.
—— 'The Census Lists of Numbers 1 and 26', *JBL* lxxvii, 1958, 52.
MERCER, S. A. B., *Études sur les origines de la religion de l'Égypte*, 1929.
MERKEL, J., 'Die Begnadigung am Passahfeste', *ZNW* vi, 1905, 293.
MESSEL, N., 'Die Komposition von Lev. 16', *ZAW* xxvii, 1907, 1.
MEYER, E., *Die Israeliten und ihre Nachbarstämme. Alttestamentliche Untersuchungen*, 1906.
—— *Der Papyrusfund von Elephantine. Dokumente einer jüdischen Gemeinde aus der Perserzeit . . .*, 1912.
MEYER, R., 'Levitische Emanzipationsbestrebungen in nachexilischer Zeit', *OLZ* xli, 1938, 721.
—— art. 'Σαδδουκαῖος', *Theologisches Wörterbuch zum Neuen Testament*, ed. G. Friedrich, vii, 1960.
MILIK, J. T., 'Le Travail d'édition des manuscrits du Désert de Juda', in *Volume du Congrès Strasbourg 1956* (Supplements to *VT*, vol. iv), 1957, 17.
—— *Ten Years of Discovery in the Wilderness of Judaea*, tr. Strugnell, 1959.
MOMMSEN, A., *Feste der Stadt Athen im Altertum . . .*, 1898.

MONTGOMERY, J. A., *The Samaritans, the Earliest Jewish Sect. Their History, Theology and Literature*, 1907.
—— and GEHMAN, H. S., *A Critical and Exegetical Commentary on the Books of Kings* (I.C.C.), 1951.
MOORE, G. F., *Judaism in the First Centuries of the Christian Era. The Age of the Tannaim*, 1927–30.
MORALDI, L., *Espiazione sacrificale e riti espiatori nell' ambiente biblico e nell' Antico Testamento* (Analecta biblica, vol. 5), 1956.
—— 'Terminologia cultuale israelitica', in *Scritti in onore di Giuseppe Furlani*, i (*Rivista degli Studi Orientali*, xxxii), 1957, 321.
MORET, A., *Du caractère religieux de la royauté pharaonique*, 1902.
—— 'Du sacrifice en Égypte', *RHR* lvii, 1908, 81.
—— *Mystères égyptiens*, 1913.
—— *Rois et dieux d'Égypte*, 1923.
MORGENSTERN, J., 'The Bones of the Paschal Lamb', *JAOS* xxxvi, 1917, 146.
—— 'The Origin of *Maṣṣoth* and the *Maṣṣoth*-Festival', *AJT* xxi, 1917, 275.
—— 'The Etymological History of the Three Hebrew Synonyms for "to Dance", *ḤGG*, *ḤLL* and *KRR* . . .', *JAOS* xxxvi, 1917, 321.
—— 'Two Ancient Israelite Agricultural Festivals', *JQR* viii, 1917–18, 31.
—— 'Supplementary Studies in the Calendars of Ancient Israel', *HUCA* x, 1935, 1.
—— 'A Chapter in the History of the High-Priesthood', *AJSL* lv, 1938, 1, 183, 360.
—— 'The Despoiling of the Egyptians', *JBL* lxviii, 1949, 1.
—— 'The Calendar of the Book of Jubilees, its Origin and its Character', *VT* v, 1955, 34.
MOSCATI, S., *The Semites in Ancient History*, 1959.
MOULTON, W. J., 'Über die Überlieferung und den textkritischen Werth des dritten Esrabuchs', *ZAW* xix, 1899, 209; xx, 1900, 1.
MOWINCKEL, S., *Psalmenstudien*, ii, 'Das Thronbesteigungsfest Jahwäs und der Ursprung der Eschatologie' (Skrifter utgit av Videnskapsselskapet i Kristiana, 1921. Historisk-filosofisk Klasse, 2. Bind), 1922.
—— 'Die vermeintliche "Passahlegende", Ex. 1–15, in Bezug auf die Frage: Literarkritik und Traditionskritik', *Studia Theologica*, v, 1952, 66.
—— 'General Oriental and Specific Israelite Elements in the Israelite Conception of the Sacral Kingdom', in *La Regalità sacra* (VIII Congresso internazionale di storia delle Religioni, 1955), 1959, 289.
MÜLLER, J., *Kritischer Versuch über den Ursprung und die geschichtliche Entwicklung des Pesach- und Mazzothfestes*, 1883.
MUSIL, A., *Arabia Petraea*, 1907–8.
—— *The Manners and Customs of the Rwala Bedouins* (Oriental Explorations and Studies, No. 6), 1928.

NEMOY, L., *Karaite Anthology* . . . (Yale Judaica Series, vol. 7), 1952.
NICOLSKY, N. M., 'Pascha im Kulte der jerusalemischen Tempels', *ZAW* xlv, 1927, 171, 241.
NIELSEN, E., 'Ass and Ox in the Old Testament', in *Studia Orientalia Ioanni Pedersen . . . dicata*, 1953, 263.
NIESE, B., 'Zur Chronologie des Josephus', *Hermes*, xxviii, 1893, 197.
NILSSON, N. M. P., *Griechische Feste von religiöser Bedeutung, mit Ausschluss der attischen*, 1906.
—— *Cults, Myths, Oracles, and Politics in Ancient Greece* (Skrifter utgivna av Svenska Institutet i Athen), 1951.
NÖLDEKE, TH., 'Baethgen's Beiträge zur semitischen Religionsgeschichte . . .', *ZDMG* xlii, 1888, 470.
—— *Neue Beiträge zur semitischen Sprachwissenschaft*, 1910.

NORTH, C. R., 'The Religious Aspect of the Hebrew Kingship', *ZAW* l, 1932, 1.
—— 'Pentateuchal Criticism', in H. H. Rowley, *The Old Testament and Modern Study* . . ., 1951, 48.
NORTH, R., *Sociology of the Biblical Jubilee* (Analecta biblica, vol. 4), 1954.
—— 'The Derivation of Sabbath', *Biblica*, xxxvi, 1955, 182.
—— 'The Qumran "Sadducees"', *CBQ* xvii, 1955, 164.
NOTH, M., *Das Buch Josua*, 1938.
—— *Die Gesetze im Pentateuch. Ihre Voraussetzungen und ihr Sinn*, 1940.
—— *Überlieferungsgeschichtliche Studien*, i, 'Die sammelnden und bearbeitenden Geschichtswerke im Alten Testament' (Schriften der Königsberger Gelehrten Gesellschaft, Geisteswissenschaftliche Klasse, xviii/2), 1943.
—— 'Das alttestamentliche Bundschliessen im Lichte eines Mari-Textes', in *Mélanges Isidore Lévy*, 1955, 433.
—— *The History of Israel*, tr. Ackroyd, 1960.
NÖTSCHER, F., 'Zur Auferstehung nach drei Tagen', *Biblica*, xxxv, 1954, 313.
NYSTROM, S., *Beduinentum und Jahwismus. Eine soziologischreligionsgeschichtliche Untersuchung zum Alten Testament*, 1946.

O'CALLAGHAN, R., 'The Great Phoenician Portal Inscription from Karatepe', *Orientalia*, xviii, 1949, 173.
OESTERLEY, W. O. E., *The Sacred Dance. A Study in Comparative Folklore*, 1923.
—— 'Early Hebrew Festival Rituals', in S. H. Hooke, *Myth and Ritual* . . ., 1933, 111.
—— *Sacrifices in Ancient Israel. Their Origin, Purposes and Development*, 1937.
OESTREICHER, T., *Das Deuteronomische Grundgesetz* (Beiträge zur Förderung christlicher Theologie, Band 27, Heft 4), 1923.
OGG, G., *The Chronology of the Public Ministry of Jesus*, 1940.
—— *The Pseudo-Cyprianic De Pascha Computus* . . ., 1955.
ORLINSKY, H. M., '*Ha-roqdim* for *ha-reqim* in II Samuel 6^{20}', *JBL* lxv, 1946, 25.
OTTEN, H., 'Ein Text zum Neujahrsfest aus Boğazköy', *OLZ* li, 1956, 101.

PALLIS, S. A., *The Babylonian Akîtu Festival* (K. Dansk Videnskabernes Selskab. Hist.-fil. Meddelelser, Bd. 12, No. 1), 1926.
PARKER, R. A., *The Calendars of Ancient Egypt* (Studies in Ancient Oriental Civilization, No. 26), 1950.
PATAI, R., 'Dancing of Maidens on the Day of Atonement' (in Hebrew), *Edoth*, i, 1945, 55; ii, 1946–7, 186.
—— 'Hebrew Installation Rites. A Contribution to the Study of Ancient Near Eastern–African Culture Contact', *HUCA* xx, 1947, 143.
PATON, L. B., *A Critical and Exegetical Commentary on the Book of Esther* (I.C.C.), 1908.
PEDERSEN, J., *Der Eid bei den Semiten in seinem Verhältnis zu verwandten Erscheinungen sowie die Stellung des Eides in Islam*, 1914.
—— 'Passahfest und Passahlegende', *ZAW* lii, 1934, 161.
—— 'Canaanite and Israelite Cultus', *Acta Orientalia*, xviii, 1940, 1.
—— *Israel. Its Life and Culture*, 1959.
PERRUCHON, J. D., and GOTTHEIL, R., art. 'Falashas', *JE* v, 1925.
PETERMANN, J. H., *Reisen im Orient*, 1860–1.
PETUCHOWSKI, J. J., '"Do This in Remembrance of Me" (1 Cor. 11:24)', *JBL* lxxvi, 1957, 293.
PFEIFFER, R. H., *Introduction to the Old Testament*, 1952.
PIEROTTI, E., *Customs and Traditions of Palestine illustrating the Manners of the Ancient Hebrews*, tr. Bonney, 1864.
VAN DER PLOEG, J., 'Mélanges. 1. Le Sens de *gibbor ḥail*', *Vivre et Penser*, i, 1941, 120.
—— 'Les Chefs du peuple d'Israël et leurs titres', *RB* lvii, 1950, 40.

VAN DER PLOEG, J., 'The Meals of the Essenes', *JSS* ii, 1957, 163.
POZNANSKI, S., 'Philon dans l'ancienne littérature judéo-arabe', *REJ* l, 1905, 10.
PRITCHETT, K., 'Months in Dorian Calendars', *American Journal of Archaeology*, l, 1946, 358.
PROCKSCH, O., *Jesaia. Kapitel 1–39 . . .*, 1930.
—— 'Fürst und Priester bei Hesekiel', *ZAW* lviii, 1940–1, 99.
PURINTON, C. E., 'Translation Greek in the Wisdom of Solomon', *JBL* xlvii, 1928, 276.

RABBINOWITZ, J., *Mishnah Megillah*, 1931.
RABIN, C., *Qumran Studies* (Scripta Judaica, vol. ii), 1957.
—— *The Zadokite Documents*, 1958.
VON RAD, G., *Das Geschichtsbild des chronistischen Werkes* (Beiträge zur Wissenschaft vom Alten und Neuen Testament. Folge 4, Heft 3), 1930.
—— 'Herkunft und Absicht des Deuteronomiums', *ThLZ*, 1947, 151.
—— 'The Origin of the Concept of the Day of Yahweh', *JSS* iv, 1959, 97.
REYMOND, P., *L'Eau, sa vie, et sa signification dans l'Ancien Testament* (Supplements to *VT*, vol. vi), 1958.
RHODOKANAKIS, N., *Katabanische Texte zur Bodenwirtschaft* (Akademie der Wissenschaften in Wien, Phil.-hist. Klasse, Sitzungsberichte. Band 194), 1919.
RICHARDSON, C. C., 'The Quartodecimans and the Synoptic Chronology', *HTR* xxxiii, 1940, 177.
RIEDEL, W., 'Miscellen', *ZAW* xx, 1900, 315.
RIESENFELD, H., *Jésus transfiguré: l'arrière-plan du récit évangélique de la transfiguration de Notre-Seigneur* (Acta Seminarii Neotestamentici Upsaliensis, vol. xvi), 1947.
RITTER, B., *Philo und die Halacha. Eine vergleichende Studie unter steter Berücksichtigung des Josephus*, 1879.
ROBERTSON, E., 'Notes and Extracts from the Semitic Manuscripts in the John Rylands Library. vi. The Astronomical Tables and Calendar of the Samaritans', *BJRL* xxiii, 1939, 458.
ROHDE, E., *Psyche*, tr. Hillis, 1925.
RÖNSCH, H., *Das Buch der Jubiläen oder die kleine Genesis . . .*, 1874.
ROST, L., *Die Vorstufen von Kirche und Synagoge im Alten Testament. Eine wortgeschichtliche Untersuchung* (Beiträge zur Wissenschaft vom Alten und Neuen Testament. Folge 4, Heft 24), 1938.
—— 'Weidewechsel und altisraelitischer Festkalender', *ZDPV* lxvi, 1943, 205.
—— 'Erwägungen zum israelitischen Brandopfer', in *Von Ugarit nach Qumran. Beiträge zur alttestamentlichen und altorientalischen Forschung Otto Eissfeldt . . . dargebracht . . .* (Beihefte zur *ZAW*, No. 77), 1958, 177.
ROTHSTEIN, J. W., and HÄNEL, J., *Kommentar zum I. Buch der Chronik*, 1927.
ROWLEY, H. H., *The Relevance of Apocalyptic. A Study of Jewish and Christian Apocalypses from Daniel to the Revelation*, 1944.
—— 'Criteria for the Dating of Jubilees', *JQR* xxxvi, 1945–6, 183.
—— *From Joseph to Joshua. Biblical Traditions in the Light of Archaeology*, 1950.
—— (ed.), *The Old Testament and Modern Study. A Generation of Discovery and Research*, 1951.
—— *The Servant of the Lord, and Other Essays on the Old Testament*, 1952.
—— 'The Book of Ezekiel in Modern Study', *BJRL* xxxvi, 1953–4, 146.
—— 'Sanballat and the Samaritan Temple', *BJRL* xxxviii, 1955–6, 166.
—— 'Elijah on Mount Carmel', *BJRL* xliii, 1960, 190.
ROWTON, M. B., 'The Problem of the Exodus', *PEQ* lxxxv, 1953, 46.
RUDOLPH, W., 'Der Aufbau von Ex. 19–34', in P. Volz, F. Stummer, and J. Hempel, *Werden und Wesen des Alten Testaments*, 1936, 41.

RUDOLPH, W., *Esra und Nehemia*, 1949.
—— 'Problems of the Books of Chronicles', *VT* iv, 1954, 401.
—— *Chronikbücher*, 1955.
RYCKMANS, G., *Les Religions arabes préislamiques* (Bibliothèque du *Muséon*, vol. 26), 1951.

SACHAU, C. E., *The Chronology of Ancient Nations. An English Version of the Arabic Text of the Athâr-ul-Bâkiya of Albîrûnî*, 1879.
—— *Aramäische Papyrus und Ostraka aus einer jüdischen Militär-Kolonie zu Elephantine*, 1911.
SAFI, M., 'Mariage au Nord du Liban', *Anthropos*, xi–xii, 1917–18, 134.
ŠANDA, A., *Die Bücher der Könige*, 1911–12.
SAYCE, A. H., 'Aramaic Ostracon from Elephantine', *PSBA* xxxiii, 1911, 183.
SCHAEFER, R., *Passah-Mazzoth-Fest nach seinem Ursprunge, seiner Bedeutung und seiner innerpentateuchischen Entwicklung im Zusammenhange mit der israelitischen Kultusgeschichte*, 1900.
SCHÄFER, H., *Die Mysterien des Osiris in Abydos unter König Sesostris III*, 1904.
SCHECHTER, S., *Documents of Jewish Sectaries*, 1910.
SCHIAPARELLI, G., *Astronomy in the Old Testament*, 1905.
SCHMOEKEL, H., *Heilige Hochzeit und Hoheslied* (Abhandlungen für die Kunde des Morgenlandes, No. 32), 1956.
SCHOENFELD, E. D., *Die Halbinsel des Sinai in ihrer Bedeutung nach Erdkunde und Geschichte*, 1907.
SCHOTT, S., 'The Feasts of Thebes', in H. H. Nelson and U. Hölscher, *Work in Western Thebes 1931–33* (Oriental Institute Communications, No. 18), 1934, 63.
—— *Altägyptische Festdaten* . . . (Akademie der Wissenschaften und der Literatur in Mainz. Abhandlungen der geistes- und sozialwissenschaftlichen Klasse, 1950, No. 10), 1950.
SCHRANK, W., *Babylonische Sühnriten besonders mit Rücksicht auf Priester und Büsser untersucht*, 1908.
SCHULTZ, H., *Old Testament Theology*, tr. Paterson, 1892.
SCHÜRER, E., *Geschichte des jüdischen Volkes im Zeitalter Jesu Christi*, 1898–1901.
SCHÜRMANN, H., *Der Paschamahlbericht Lk. 22 (7–14) 15–18*, 1953.
—— *Der Einsetzungsbericht Lk. 22 19–20*, 1955.
—— *Der Abendmahlsbericht Lk. 22 7–38* . . ., 1957.
SCHWALLY, F., *Idioticon des christlich palästinischen Aramaeisch*, 1893.
SEGAL, J. B., 'Intercalation and the Hebrew Calendar', *VT* vii, 1957, 250.
—— 'The Hebrew Festivals and the Calendar', *JSS* vi, 1961, 74.
SEGAL, M. H., 'On the Problems of the Cave Scrolls' (in Hebrew), *Eretz Israel*, i, 1951, 39.
—— *Mebho' haMiqra'* (in Hebrew), 1955.
—— *Massoreth uBhiqqoreth* (in Hebrew), 1957.
—— 'The Book of Deuteronomy', *JQR* xlviii, 1957–8, 315.
SHALEM, N., 'La Stabilité du climat en Palestine', *RB* lviii, 1951, 54.
SIDERSKY, D., 'Le Comput des Juifs d'Égypte au temps des Achéménides', *REJ* lxxxii, 1926, 59.
SIERKSMA, F., 'Quelques remarques sur la circoncision en Israel', *Oudtestamentische studiën*, ix, 1951, 136.
SILVESTRE DE SACY, A. I., *Chrestomathie arabe* . . ., 1826–7.
—— 'Correspondance des Samaritains de Naplouse pendant les années 1808 et suiv.', *Notices et extraits des manuscrits de la bibliothèque du Roi* . . ., xii, 1831, 1.
SIMONS, J., *Jerusalem in the Old Testament. Researches and Theories* (Studia Francisci Scholten memoriae dicata, vol. 1 . . .), 1952.

SIMPSON, M. W. HILTON, 'Some Notes on the Folklore of the Algerian Hills and Desert', *Folklore*, xxxiii, 1922, 170.

SKEHAN, P. W., 'The Date of the Last Supper', *CBQ* xx, 1958, 192.

SKINNER, J., *The Book of the Prophet Isaiah, chapters i–xxxix*, 1915.

SMITH, G. A., *The Book of Deuteronomy*, 1918.

SMITH, P. GARDNER, *The Christ of the Gospels. A Study of the Gospel Records in the Light of Critical Research*, 1938.

SMITH, S., *Early History of Assyria to 1000 B.C.*, 1928.

—— art. 'Calendar (Babylonian and Assyrian)', *Enc. Br.*, 1958.

—— 'The Practice of Kingship in Early Semitic Kingdoms', in *Myth, Ritual, and Kingship* . . ., ed. S. H. Hooke, 1958, 22.

SMITH, W. R., *Lectures on the Religion of the Semites. The Fundamental Institutions*, ed. S. A. Cook, 1927.

SNAITH, N. H., *The Jewish New Year Festival. Its Origins and Development*, 1947.

—— 'The Historical Books', in H. H. Rowley, *The Old Testament and Modern Study* . . ., 1951, 84.

—— 'Sacrifices in the Old Testament', *VT* vii, 1957, 308.

VON SODEN, W., 'Das altbabylonische Briefarchiv von Mari', *Welt des Orients*, i, 1948, 187.

—— 'Gibt es ein Zeugnis dafür, dass die Babylonier an die Wiederauferstehung Marduks geglaubt haben?', *ZA*, N.F. xvii (li), 1955, 130.

SOMMER, F., and EHELOLF, H., *Das hethitische Ritual des Papanikri von Komana*, 1924.

SONNEN, J., 'Landwirtschaftliches vom See Genesareth', *Biblica*, viii, 1927, 65, 188, 320.

SPARKS, H. F. D., 'The Partiality of Luke for "Three" . . .', *JTS* xxxvii, 1936, 141.

SPEISER, E. A., 'Census and Ritual Expiation in Mari and Israel', *BASOR*, No. 149, Feb. 1958, 17.

SPIRO, A., 'Samaritans, Tobiads and Judahites in Pseudo-Philo', *PAAJR* xx, 1951, 279.

STADE, B., 'Nachwort der Herausgebers zu . . . Riedel's 5. Miscelle: פסח', *ZAW* xx, 1900, 335.

STAMM, J. J., 'Eine Erwägung zu Hos 6:1–2', *ZAW* lvii, 1939, 266.

—— *Erlösen und Vergeben im Alten Testament*, 1940.

STEIN, S., 'The Influence of Symposia Literature on the Literary Form of the Pesaḥ Haggadah', *JJS* viii, 1957, 13.

STEUERNAGEL, D. C., 'Zum Passa-Maṣṣothfest', *ZAW* xxxi, 1911, 310.

STEVENSON, W. B., 'Hebrew ʿOlah and Zebach Sacrifices', in *Festschrift für Alfred Bertholet*, 1950, 488.

STRACK, H. L., *Bücher Genesis, Exodus, Leviticus und Numeri*, 1894.

—— and BILLERBECK, P., *Kommentar zum Neuen Testament aus Talmud und Midrasch*, 1922–8.

STROBEL, A., 'Der Termin des Todes Jesu', *ZNW* li, 1960, 69.

STUMME, H., 'Gedanken über libysch-phönizische Anklänge', *ZA* xxvii, 1912, 121.

SUKENIK, E. L., and KUTSCHER, E. Y., 'Passover Ostracon from Elephantine' (in Hebrew), *Kedem*, i, 1942, 53.

SZYSZMAN, S., 'A propos du Karaïsme et dès Textes de la Mer Morte', *VT* ii, 1952, 343.

TADMOR, H., 'The Campaigns of Sargon II of Assur', *Journal of Cuneiform Studies*, xii, 1958, 22.

TALMON, S., 'The Calendar Reckoning of the Sect from the Judaean Desert', *Scripta Hierosolymitana*, iv, 1958, 162.

—— 'Divergences in Calendar-Reckoning in Ephraim and Judah', *VT* viii, 1958, 48.

TESTUZ, M., *Les Idées religieuses du Livre des Jubilés*, 1960.
THACKERAY, H. ST. J., and MARCUS, R., *Josephus* (Loeb Classical Library), 1926–43.
THIELE, E. R., *The Mysterious Numbers of the Hebrew Kings. A Reconstruction of the Chronology of the Kingdoms of Israel and Judah*, 1951.
—— 'New Evidence on the Chronology of the Last Kings of Judah', *BASOR*, No. 143, Oct. 1956, 22.
THOMPSON, R. C., *Semitic Magic: its Origins and Development*, 1908.
—— *Dictionary of Assyrian Botany*, 1949.
THOMSON, J. E. H., 'The Samaritan Passover', *PEFQS*, 1902, 82.
—— *The Samaritans: their Testimony to the Religion of Israel*, 1919.
THUREAU-DANGIN, F., *Rituels accadiens*, 1921.
TORREY, C. C., *Ezra Studies*, 1910.
—— 'The Date of the Crucifixion According to the Fourth Gospel', *JBL* l, 1931, 227.
—— 'The Letters prefixed to Second Maccabees', *JAOS* lx, 1940, 119.
—— *The Apocryphal Literature. A Brief Introduction*, 1945.
—— 'In the Fourth Gospel the Last Supper was the Paschal Meal', *JQR* xlii, 1951–2, 237.
TOUSSAINT, C., *Les Origines de la religion d'Israël*, 1931.
TOY, C. H., 'The Meaning of פֶּסַח', *JBL* xvi, 1897, 178.
TRENCSÉNYI-WALDAPFEL, I., 'Une Tragédie grecque à sujet biblique', *Acta Orientalia Academiae Scientiarum Hungaricae*, ii, 1952, 143.
TRITTON, A. S., 'Notes on Religion in Early Arabia', *Muséon*, lxxii, 1959, 191.
TRUMBULL, H. C., *The Blood Covenant. A Primitive Rite and its Bearings on Scripture*, 1885.
—— *The Threshold Covenant; or, the Beginning of Religious Rites*, 1896.
TULAND, C. G., 'Hanani–Hananiah', *JBL* lxxvii, 1958, 157.
TUR-SINAI, H., *HaLashon wehaSepher* (in Hebrew), i, iii, 1954–5.

ULLENDORFF, E., 'Hebraic-Jewish Elements in Abyssinian (Monophysite) Christianity', *JSS* i, 1956, 216.
UNGNAD, A., *Aramäische Papyrus aus Elephantine*, 1911.

VAJDA, G., 'Jeûne musulman et jeûne juif', *HUCA* xii–xiii, 1937–8, 367.
VAN-LENNEP, H. J., *Bible Lands*, 1875.
DE VAUX, R., art. 'Israël', *Dict. Bib. Suppl.* iv, 1941–9.
—— 'Les Patriarches hébreux et les découvertes modernes. VII', *RB* lvi, 1949, 5.
—— 'Fouilles de Kh. Qumrân', *RB* lxiii, 1956, 533.
—— *Les Institutions de l'Ancien Testament*, i, ii, 1958–60.
—— 'Les Manuscrits de Qumrân et l'archéologie', *RB* lxvi, 1959, 87.
—— *L'Archéologie et les manuscrits de la Mer Morte*, 1961.
VINCENT, A., *La Religion des Judéo-Araméens d'Éléphantine*, 1937.
VINCENT, L.-H., *Études bibliques. Canaan d'après l'exploration récente*, 1907.
—— and STEVE, A.-M., *Jérusalem de l'Ancien Testament. Recherches d'archéologie et d'histoire*, 1954–6.
VOGT, E., 'Antiquum kalendarium sacerdotale', *Biblica*, xxxvi, 1955, 403.
—— 'Kalenderfragmente aus Qumran', *Biblica*, xxxix, 1958, 72.
—— 'Hat šabbāt im A.T. den Sinn von "Woche"?', *Biblica*, xl, 1959, 1008.
VÖLTER, D., *Passah und Mazzoth und ihr aegyptisches Urbild*, 1912.
VRIEZEN, TH. C., 'The Term *Hizza*: Lustration and Consecration', *Oudtestamentische studiën*, vii, 1950, 201.

WADE, G. W., *The Book of the Prophet Isaiah*, 1929.
VAN DER WAERDEN, B. L., 'Babylonian Astronomy. III. The Earliest Astronomical Computations', *JNES* x, 1951, 20.

WALDE, B., *Esdrasbücher der Septuaginta* (Biblische Studien, No. 18), 1913.
WALTHER, J. A., 'The Chronology of Passion Week', *JBL* lxxvii, 1958, 116.
WEBSTER, H., *Rest Days*, 1916.
WEILL, R., 'Notes sur l'histoire primitive des grandes religions égyptiennes', *Bulletin de l'Institut français d'Archéologie orientale*, 1948, 59.
WEIR, C. J. MULLO, *A Lexicon of Accadian Prayers in the Rituals of Expiation*, 1934.
WEIS, P. R., 'Ibn Ezra, the Karaites and the Halakah' (in Hebrew), *Melilah*, i, 1944, 35.
—— 'Abu'l-Hasan al-Suri's Discourse on the Calendar in the Kitab Al-Tabbakh, Rylands Samaritan Codex IX', *BJRL* xxx, 1946–7, 144.
WEISER, A., *Einleitung in das Alte Testament*, 1939.
WELCH, A. C., *The Code of Deuteronomy. A New Theory of its Origin*, 1924.
—— 'On the Method of celebrating Passover', *ZAW* xlv, 1927, 24.
—— *The Work of the Chronicler. Its Purpose and its Date*, 1939.
WELLHAUSEN, J., *Prolegomena to the History of Israel*, tr. Black and Menzies, 1885.
—— *Skizzen und Vorarbeiten*, iv, 1889.
—— *Reste arabischen Heidentums*, 1897.
WENDEL, A., *Das Opfer in der altisraelitischen Religion*, 1927.
WENDLAND, P., art. 'Aristobulus of Paneas', *JE* ii, 1925.
WENSINCK, A. J., *Some Semitic Rites of Mourning and Religion. Studies on their Origin and Mutual Relation* (Verhandelingen der Koninklijke Akademie van Wetenschappen te Amsterdam. Afdeeling Letterkunde, N.R., Deel xviii), 1917.
—— *Arabic New-Year and the Feast of Tabernacles* (Verhandelingen der Koninklijke Akademie van Wetenschappen te Amsterdam. Afdeeling Letterkunde, N.R., Deel xxv. no. 2), 1925.
WERNER, E., '"Hosanna" in the Gospels', *JBL* lxv, 1946, 97.
WESTERMARCK, E. A., 'The Principles of Fasting', *Folklore*, xviii, 1907, 391.
—— *Ritual and Belief in Morocco*, 1926.
WHYTE, R. O., 'Phytogeographic Zones of Palestine', *Geographical Review*, xl, 1950, 600.
WIDENGREN, G., *Sakrales Königtum im Alten Testament und im Judentum*, 1955.
—— 'King and Covenant', *JSS* ii, 1957, 1.
WIEDEMANN, A., 'Notes on Some Egyptian Monuments', *PSBA* xxxvi, 1914, 199.
—— *Das alte Ägypten*, 1920.
WIESENBERG, E., 'The Jubilee of Jubilees', *Revue de Qumran*, ix, 1961, 1.
WILDEBOER, G., *Das Buch Esther erklärt*, 1898.
WINNETT, F. V., *The Mosaic Tradition* (Near and Middle East Series, No. 1), 1949.
—— *Safaitic Inscriptions from Jordan*, 1957.
WINTER, P., 'Marginal Notes on the Trial of Jesus', *ZNW* l, 1959, 14, 221.
—— *On the Trial of Jesus* (Studia Judaica. Forschungen zur Wissenschaft des Judentums, 1), 1961.
WISEMAN, D. J., *Chronicles of Chaldaean Kings, 626–556 B.C., in the British Museum*, 1956.
WITZEL, M., *Tammuz-Liturgien und Verwandtes* (Analecta Orientalia, No. 10), 1935.
WORDEN, T., 'The Literary Influence of the Ugaritic Fertility Myth on the Old Testament', *VT* iii, 1953, 273.
WRESCHNER, L., *Samaritanische Traditionen, mitgeteilt und nach ihrer geschichtlichen Entwickelung untersucht*, 1888.
WÜNSCHE, A., *Neue Beiträge zur Erläuterung der Evangelien aus Talmud und Midrasch*, 1878.
WÜRTHWEIN, E., *Der ʿamm haʾarez im Alten Testament* (Beiträge zur Wissenschaft vom Alten und Neuen Testament. Folge 4, Heft 17), 1936.

YADIN, Y., 'The Reorganization of the Army of Judah under Josiah' (in Hebrew), *Yediʿoth* (*Bulletin of the Jewish Palestine Exploration Society*), xv, 1949–50, 86.
—— *Hazor in Galilee*, 1958.
—— *The Scroll of the War of the Sons of Light against the Sons of Darkness*, tr. B. and C. Rabin, 1962.
YAHUDA, A. S., *The Language of the Pentateuch in its Relation to Egyptian*, 1933.

ZEITLIN, S., *Megillat Taanit as a source for Jewish chronology* . . ., 1922.
—— 'The Date of the Crucifixion According to the Fourth Gospel', *JBL* li, 1932, 263.
—— 'The Book of Jubilees, Its Character and Its Significance', *JQR* xxx, 1939–40, 1.
—— 'The Crucifixion of Jesus Re-examined', *JQR* xxxi, 1940–1, 327; xxxii, 1941–2, 175, 279.
—— 'The Political Synedrion and the Religious Sanhedrin', *JQR* xxxvi, 1945–6, 109.
—— 'Criteria for the Dating of Jubilees', *JQR* xxxvi, 1945–6, 187.
—— 'The Apocrypha', *JQR* xxxvii, 1946–7, 219.
—— 'Jewish Apocryphal Literature', *JQR* xl, 1949–50, 223.
—— 'The Last Supper as an Ordinary Meal in the Fourth Gospel', *JQR* xlii, 1951–2, 251.
—— 'The Titles High Priest and the Nasi of the Sanhedrin', *JQR* xlviii, 1957–8, 1.
—— 'The Beginning of the Day in the Calendar of Jubilees', *JBL* lxxviii, 1959, 153.
ZIMMELS, H. J., 'Nachtalmudische Fasttage', in *Jewish Studies in Memory of George A. Kohut*, ed. S. W. Baron and A. Marx, 1935, 599.
ZIMMERN, H., *Beiträge zur Kenntnis der babylonischen Religion*, 1896.
—— 'Religion und Sprache', in E. Schrader, *Die Keilinschriften und das Alte Testament* . . ., 1903.
—— *Zum Babylonischen Neujahrsfest*. Zweiter Beitrag (Berichte über die Verhandlungen der Sächsischen Gesellschaft der Wissenschaften zu Leipzig. Phil.-hist. Klasse. Band 70, Heft 5), 1918.
—— *Das babylonische Neujahrsfest* (Der Alte Orient, Band 25, Heft 3), 1926.
ZUCKER, M., 'The Part of Saadyah Gaon in the Polemics on "the Morrow after the Sabbath"' (in Hebrew), *PAAJR* xx, 1951, p. א׳.

GENERAL INDEX

Abib, 55, 111, 180, 193, 207.
age of participants at Pesaḥ, 22–23, 34, 135–6, 233–4, 237, 240, 241, 266, 269.
almsgiving, 34, 37, 243–4.
anthropomorphism, 22, 74, 231.
apotropaic significance of Pesaḥ, 23, 106, 171, 187, 233.
ʿAqedah, 236.
Aristobulus of Paneas, 29 n.
ʿaṣarah, see *ʿaṣereth*.
ʿaṣarta, 38, 212. See also *ʿaṣereth*.
ʿaṣereth, 63, 76 n., 208–9, 211–13, 268.
Atonement, Day of (Yom haKippurim), 40, 138, 145, 152, 153, 156, 162, 211, 234, 247–8, 251.

Bethel, 5, 133, 218.
bitter herbs, 22, 24 n., 31, 54, 58, 169–70, 207, 231, 259, 263, 268.
blood, sacrificial, 13, 15, 17, 19, 20–23, 29, 32, 52–53, 220, 226–8, 230, 259. *See also* blood-smearing, ritual.
—-smearing, ritual, 6, 20–21, 23–25, 31, 46–47, 48–49, 52–53, 57, 74–75, 76, 92, 105, 106, 157–65, 185, 192, 207–8, 211, 232, 240, 253, 260, 267, 268.
Boethusians, *see* Sadducees.
'Book of the Law', 14, 216 n.
booths, 152–3, 179.
burnt offerings (*ʿolah*), 4–5, 7, 13–16, 17, 18 n., 45–46, 91 n., 201–2, 204, 227–8, 263. *See also* continual burnt offering.

calendar, 40–41, 116–17, 126–7, 143, 194, 195, 207, 236, 239, 254, 258. *See also* Jubilees calendar, Qumran 'calendar'.
—, festal, 43, 76, 192, 194.
Canaan, 2, 3, 4, 193, 194, 198, 202–3, 208, 237–8, 267.
census, 136–8, 164, 215–16, 233–4, 237, 258, 266, 269. *See also* age of participants at the Pesaḥ.
centralization of Israelite cult, 5–6, 75, 91, 209, 213, 217–19, 224–5, 253, 268.
Christians, early, 237, 241–7, 269. *See also* New Testament.
Chronicler, 2, 5, 11, 12–19, 77, 78, 184, 189, 212, 217–18, 225–30, 232, 267–8.
circumcision, 3, 24 n., 53, 58, 135, 237, 266.
cleanness, ritual, 3, 8–9, 10, 12, 13, 15, 16–19, 21, 26, 30, 32–33, 36, 37 n., 39, 138–42, 171–3, 192, 199–200, 207, 224, 226, 228–30, 234, 244, 261–2, 268.
continual burnt offering (*Tamid*), 40, 146, 202, 227, 262.
Convocation, Holy, 63, 64, 178. *See also* Passover week, observances in.
courses, priestly, 12, 40–42, 247–9, 250.
Creation, 27, 29, 149.

D Source (Deuteronomist), 3, 6, 43–44, 55–57, 59–64, 66–67, 69, 72–73, 75–76, 145, 157, 161 n., 202–13, 219, 223, 224, 227, 232–4, 240, 246, 268.
dancing, ritual, 95–96, 98–99, 150, 266.
Deuteronomist, *see* D Source.
drink, fermented, 9, 10, 224.

E Source, 47, 50–51, 55, 61–64, 67, 72.
Elephantine, 1, 8–10, 221–4, 225.
equinox, 26–27, 29, 31, 38, 127, 132, 266.
Essenes, 37.
exodus, ritual, 151–3, 169, 173–4, 179, 187, 210–11, 214, 256, 267, 268.
Exodus from Egypt, date of, 187–8, 267.
— — —, legend of, 20–22, 23–24, 27, 42, 46–55, 72, 137, 183, 266.
Ezekiel, 1, 2, 6–8, 219–21, 224, 268.
Ezekielos, 1, 23–25, 233 n.

Falashas, 223, 255–6.
family unit, 24 n., 26, 31, 35, 38–39, 51–52, 75, 134–5, 140, 164–5, 207, 227, 234, 240, 241, 246, 256, 259, 266, 269.
fasting, 145–6, 255, 259, 266.
fat, sacrificial, 13, 15, 22, 32, 166–7, 226–7, 230, 232, 268.
fedu sacrifice, 105, 162–5.
fidyah, see *fedu*.
firstborn, slaughter of Egyptian, 20, 46, 47–49, 51, 72, 183–4, 187–8.
— dedication, 66–69, 164–5, 182–4, 187, 267. *See also* Passover, theories on origins of.
firstfruits, 28, 30, 38, 109, 180–1, 194–5, 257, 265, 266, 269.
firstlings, slaughter of Egyptian, 20–21, 46–50.
— dedication, 24–25, 66–69, 103– 5, 181–3, 266, 267. *See also* Passover, theories on origins of.

gifts, exchange of, 148–9, 239, 260, 266–7.

H Source (Holiness Code), 69–70, 72, 222.

LONDON ORIENTAL SERIES

1. W. S. ALLEN, *Phonetics in Ancient India.*
2. J. B. SEGAL, *The Diacritical Point and the Accents in Syriac.*
3. MARY BOYCE, *The Manichaean Hymn-Cycles in Parthian.*
4. E. G. PULLEYBLANK, *The Background of the Rebellion of An Lu-Shan.*
5. KENNETH BALLHATCHET, *Social Policy and Social Change in Western India, 1817–1830.*
6. D. L. SNELLGROVE, *The Hevajra Tantra*, 2 vols.
7. JOHN BROUGH, *The Gāndhārī Dharmapada.*
8. C. J. F. DOWSETT, *The History of the Caucasian Albanians by Movsēs Dasxurançi.*
9. D. N. MACKENZIE, *Kurdish Dialect Studies—I.*
10. D. N. MACKENZIE, *Kurdish Dialect Studies—II.*
11. C. D. COWAN, *Nineteenth Century Malaya.*
12. J. B. SEGAL, *The Hebrew Passover from the Earliest Times to A.D. 70.*
13. F. R. PALMER, *The Morphology of the Tigre Noun.*
14. R. WILLIAMS, *Jaina Yoga—A Survey of the Mediaeval Śrāvakācāras.*

PRINTED IN GREAT BRITAIN
AT THE UNIVERSITY PRESS, OXFORD
BY VIVIAN RIDLER
PRINTER TO THE UNIVERSITY